NTAL AND

18 0612198 9

THE MAKING AND UNMAKING OF EMPIRES

THE MAKING AND UNMAKING OF EMPIRES

Britain, India, and America
c.1750–1783

P. J. MARSHALL

OXFORD
UNIVERSITY PRESS

OXFORD
UNIVERSITY PRESS

Great Clarendon Street, Oxford OX2 6DP

Oxford University Press is a department of the University of Oxford.
If furthers the University's objective of excellence in research, scholarship,
and education by publishing worldwide in

Oxford New York

Auckland Cape Town Dar es Salaam Hong Kong Karachi Kuala Lumpur
Madrid Melbourne Mexico City Nairobi New Delhi Shanghai Taipei Toronto

With offices in

Argentina Austria Brazil Chile Czech Republic France Greece
Guatemala Hungary Italy Japan South Korea Poland Portugal
Singapore Switzerland Thailand Turkey Ukraine Vietnam

Published in the United States
by Oxford University Press Inc., New York

British Library Cataloguing in Publication Data

Data available

Library of Congress Cataloging in Publication Data

Data available

ISBN 0-19-927895-4

Typeset by Kolam Information Services Pvt. Ltd, Pondicherry, India
Printed in Great Britain on acid-free paper by
Biddles Ltd.
King's Lynn, Norfolk

Preface

ONE of the two main themes of this book—the history of Britain and India in the later eighteenth century—has been my concern ever since I first began historical research. My obligations to teachers, to pupils, to colleagues, including many in India, and to those who have commented in all sorts of ways on my work, although deeply felt, are therefore far too numerous to list here. I am, however, only too conscious that without the stimulus of contact with fresher minds over many years understanding atrophies and what once passed for 'knowledge' becomes stale and out of date. I hope that Rajat Datta, Chris Bayly, and Robert Travers may at least dimly recognise some of the stimulus to think again about British India that they have so abundantly provided. My interest in Britain and late colonial America is more recent and here the debts are more easily attributable. They begin with the unfailingly congenial members of a University of London undergraduate 'special subject' class on the American Revolution which I taught for a number of years, latterly, much to my advantage, with Stephen Conway. My first research in American archives in 1993–4 was supported by an Emeritus Fellowship awarded by the Leverhulme Trust and by a Fletcher Jones Fellowship at the Huntington Library. I am deeply grateful for the generosity of both these institutions and additionally to the Huntington Library for the magnificent services it extends to its readers. In the United States I have also benefited greatly from skills and kindness lavished on visitors by the staff of the William L. Clements Library at the University of Michigan, the Houghton Library at Harvard and the Massachusetts Historical Society. While I was working in Cambridge and Boston I enjoyed the warm hospitality of the Warren Center at Harvard.

In Britain I have a lifetime of obligations to libraries and record offices and to their staffs. I would, however, like to record an especial sense of debt to the Institute of Historical Research of the University of London, which houses superb collections and generates most pleasurable scholarly exchanges.

Full drafts of this book have been read by Huw Bowen and Stephen Conway. Sections of it at various stages have passed under the sharp and expert eyes of Daniel Baugh, Lige Gould, and Jack Pole and (among innumerable other kindnesses) of Andrew Porter. I am hugely indebted to all of them for the labour that they have undertaken and for the acuteness of their comments.

At the Oxford University Press both Ruth Parr and Anne Gelling have gone far beyond any reasonable call of duty in their support for this book, which owes much to Katie Ryde's exact copy-editing.

Many of the ideas in this book were first put forward in the addresses I was privileged to give as President of the Royal Historical Society and which were published in its *Transactions* from 1998 to 2001. Some of the material in Chapter 3 will appear in *Britain and America Go to War*, edited by Stephen Conway and Julie Flavell. I am grateful to the University of Florida Press for permission to include it here.

In quotations from original material capitalization has been modernised, but contemporary spelling and punctuation have generally been reproduced. The place of publication for published works is London, unless indicated otherwise.

P. J. M.
Braughing, June 2004

Contents

Maps

Abbreviations

The following abbreviations have been used for collections of manuscripts and records:

BL	British Library
HL	Huntington Library
HSP	Historical Society of Pennsylvania
HUHL	Harvard University, Houghton Library
MHS	Massachusetts Historical Society
OIOC	Oriental and India Office Collections, British Library
PRO	Public Record Office, The National Archives
WLCL	William L. Clements Library, University of Michigan

Introduction

THIS book brings together what it is conventional to keep apart, that is the loss of a British territorial empire in much of North America and the creation of a new territorial empire in eastern India.

There is a firmly established historiographical tradition that sees these developments as largely unrelated to one another and as belonging to distinct phases of British imperialism. The loss of the thirteen American colonies is said to have brought to an end a first British empire based on the Atlantic Ocean, whose origins can be traced back at least to the early seventeenth century, while the second, whose centre was to be in the Indian Ocean, was launched by the first waves of Indian conquests made by the East India Company and was to span the eastern world in the nineteenth century.[1] Such demarcations are reinforced by the entirely reasonable tendency of historians of the Atlantic or of Asia to stick to their own capacious territories and not to develop foolhardy worldwide ambitions.

Crucial developments in the death throes of the old American empire and the birth of the new Indian one occurred, however, at much the same time during the thirty years or so from about 1750 to 1783 that this book covers. The British position both in India and in North America was profoundly affected by the conflicts commonly called the Seven Years War that lasted from 1754 to 1763. In 1765 the British East India Company secured what was to be the base for its new empire, the grant of the Bengal *diwani*; in the same year the weakness of Britain's imperial position in North America was unmistakably exposed by the scale of colonial resistance to the Stamp Act. Fifteen years or so later, Britain was engaged in a war in North America to crush the revolt of large sections of the population supported by powerful French intervention; in India, East India Company and royal forces were locked in conflict with a formidable coalition of Indian powers also to be

---

[1] A most distinguished exception, which argues a case for overlapping first and second British empires, is the work of Vincent T. Harlow, *The Founding of the Second British Empire 1763–1793*, 2 vols. (1952–64). The cliché 'magisterial' can properly be applied to Harlow's volumes. Their main theme about first and second empires seems, however, to be vulnerable, see below, n. 6.

supported by French intervention. The wars ended very differently; while the British were forced to accept American independence, they held their Indian territory. The future territorial configuration of Britain's empire was thus becoming clear.

Any attempt to find a common explanation of these opposite outcomes must accept that they arose out of different conditions in parts of the world that were largely separate from one another. Recent global or 'Eurasian' approaches to eighteenth-century history suggest, however, some similarities between developments in different hemispheres.[2] By the mid-eighteenth century increased agricultural output, more intensive manufacturing with pre-industrial technologies and a greater volume of commercial exchange had been occurring over a long period in much of Europe, together with its appendages in America, as well as in large parts of Asia. The capabilities of both European and Asian states were being enhanced from the higher levels of revenue they derived from this economic growth. Professionalized state armies deploying similar firearms were common to both Europe and Asia. Historians have felt able to apply the concept of 'military-fiscal' states, that is states that maintained large armed forces through effective taxation and borrowing systems, to Asia as well as to Europe.

State development in the eighteenth-century world was, however, uncertain and uneven.[3] Some recently consolidated empires, notably in western and south Asia, were actually breaking up. The authority of apparently more compact and unified European states was still limited by the privileges of particular regions, localities, interests or orders. The effective exercise of power locally or through central institutions required the acquiescence and cooperation of elites. Eighteenth-century Britain was no exception. A relatively stable pattern of relations between the state and landed and commercial groups had evolved in England and Lowland Scotland, but the situation was more fluid when the British state extended its reach further afield.

In both America and India the fate of empire depended to a large extent on the responses of elites. The British found themselves very short of people of substance who were prepared to uphold their version of empire in the thirteen colonies, while many Indians of wealth and authority appear to have acquiesced in the establishment of East India Company rule in Bengal.

---

[2] C. A. Bayly, *The Birth of the Modern World 1780–1914* (2004), pt. 1; Victor Lieberman in *Strange Parallels: Southeast Asia in Global Context, c.800–1830*, I, *Integration on the Mainland* (Cambridge, 2003) has made illuminating studies of parallels between Europe and Asia; see also essays in Frank Perlin, *'The Invisible City': Monetary, Administrative and Popular Infrastructures in Asia and Europe 1500–1900* (Aldershot, 1993) and in A. G. Hopkins, ed., *Globalization in World History* (New York, 2002).

[3] Bayly, *Birth of Modern World*, pp. 29–36.

At first sight there seems to be no real basis for comparison between, say, George Washington, who turned against the British empire, and Muhammad Reza Khan, who served the East India Company throughout the later part of his life. The differences between the expectations and strategies of Americans and Indians within a British imperial framework may not, however, have been as dissimilar as is commonly supposed. The imperial regimes in America and in India cannot simply be characterized as rule over a free people with constitutional rights, on the one hand, and despotic sway over those who had no such rights, on the other. British regimes in both America and India were open to processes of 'negotiation' with their subjects through which local elites could seek to further their interests, if of course through different channels. Both colonial Americans and Indians had criteria of good governance by which they assessed their rulers. The question of why one set of elites was largely alienated while many from the other could be incorporated seems therefore to be an important one.

While comparisons seem to be valid, it is still the case that the making and unmaking of empires in India and America must primarily be explained in relation to the conditions that were particular to these very diverse entities. As Edmund Burke once put it, the 'natives of *Hindostan* and those of *Virginia*' could not be 'ordered in the same manner' and the '*cutchery* court' in Bengal and the 'grand Jury of *Salem*' were very different institutions.[4] There were, furthermore, great differences between South Carolina and New Hampshire or between the Madras and the Bengal presidencies. Generalizations about global trends can therefore be no substitute for studying the fortunes of empire in their varied Indian and North American contexts. This book will attempt to do that.

The British presence in both parts of the world did, however, link together eastern India and North America. By the 1760s the British were presuming to order both the natives of Hindostan and those of Virginia. However much they may have tried to adapt to local conditions, those British invested with authority at home or in the colonies inevitably applied some common assumptions and objectives throughout the world. This book is primarily about those assumptions and objectives. It is thus intended to be a contribution to British imperial history. It is written in the belief that understanding the British imperial experience in what were crucial decades in the evolution of the British empire requires an understanding of both America and India. Valuable as is the recent creation of a field of study called the history of the 'British Atlantic', an entity which includes Ireland, West Africa, eastern Canada and the West Indies, as well as the thirteen colonies, British imperial

---

[4] See below, p. 204

history in this period needs a still wider canvas. Conversely, enlightening as it is to see the early East India Company as primarily an Indian power, the British in India were also the agents of a worldwide British enterprise.

I

While trying to bring together geographical areas that are usually kept apart, this book also separates themes that are now often brought together. It begins with scene-setting chapters called 'Worldwide Expansion' and 'State and Empire'. Commerce, migration and the diffusion of British culture are thus treated as 'expansion', separately from 'empire', defined as imperial rule. Many historians would with good reason question the validity of such separations.[5] Some argue that rule, that is the coercion of one people by another, does not simply depend on the exercise of formal authority over them. International trade or the diffusion of culture between peoples who are not equally endowed with resources are not likely to be processes of equal exchange. The stronger will be able to impose on the weaker. For cases where there is a very marked degree of inequality, historians have developed the concept of 'informal' empires, that is the domination of one people over another without actual rule. Naval power, economic muscle and cultural self-confidence are often supposed to have given Britain a considerable informal empire in the nineteenth century.

It is, however, the contention of this book that in the eighteenth-century British Atlantic world the processes of British expansion were to a considerable extent separate from the exercise of overt coercion. Expansion certainly involved the coercion of numerous people. Hundreds of thousands of Africans were forcibly shipped across the Atlantic to provide enslaved labour to sustain commercial growth. The scale of transatlantic migration from Europe fuelled pressures for the forcible dispossession of Native Americans from land wanted for settlement. British cultural norms were propagated in Gaelic Scotland and Ireland at the expense of indigenous ones. Commerce, migration and the spread of British values were, however, processes in which the great majority of the white population of British America saw themselves as enthusiastic partners, not as forced victims. In India the situation was less clear-cut. The East India Company was always a potential political power as well as a commercial body, but at least until the 1750s the growth of the East India Company's trade took place largely in partnership with Indian com-

---

[5] Most recent exponents of 'Atlantic history' would do so; see, e.g. editors' Introduction to David Armitage and Michael J. Braddick, eds., *The British Atlantic World* (2002).

mercial elites and involved relatively limited usurpation of the authority of Indian rulers.

British Americans clearly seem to have made a distinction between expansion and rule. They might be enthusiastic producers for the British market and consumers of British goods and to have been increasingly willing to have their outlook shaped by cultural influences from Britain, but they were not willing to submit to an imperial authority that denied them what they regarded as the full rights of Britons. During the 1760s more and more Americans came to fear that this was what Britain intended for them and their fears drove them to resistance. Resistance generally aimed at preserving the connections of transatlantic expansion, while defeating unacceptable intrusions of political authority.

The reality behind the fears of British Americans was that successive British governments, at least from 1763 and the ending of the Seven Years War, were showing an increasing determination to exert an effective sovereign authority over British possessions overseas, over Ireland and the West Indies, as well as over the thirteen colonies of North America and the territorial rights being acquired by the East India Company, which are the subject of this book.[6] In trying to extend British sovereignty, governments were, albeit usually unwittingly or with little if any sense of overall purpose, embarking on the creation of a territorial empire of rule of a kind new to Britain's experience. By 1783 Britain had lost such imperial authority as it had previously been able to exert over the thirteen colonies, had suffered a severe but temporary check in Ireland and had been able to consolidate its hold over some Indian provinces and to preserve its stake in the West Indies. Territorial empire had survived and was quickly to resume its growth.

Whether empire was lost, as in America, or sustained, as in India, of course depended on local conditions. Historians of India have recently written illuminatingly about 'the indigenous processes that made empire possible'.[7] The literature on conditions in North America that rendered impossible the kind of empire that the British wanted has always been abundant. This book will try to take full account of such writing. Yet if the British could not determine outcomes, they were still neither the hapless victims—in North

---

[6] Harlow's *Founding of the Second British Empire* also sees the 1760s as a crucial period. In Harlow's view, new imperial strategies were being devised. 'Territorial jurisdiction' was to be avoided in favour of bases and trading posts which would give Britain access to new trading areas without rule, especially in eastern Asia and the Pacific. Territorial expansion in India was 'exceptional' (I. 4–5). New opportunities for 'trade without dominion' were certainly welcomed, but Harlow's emphasis on it seems seriously to distort British priorities, which were to maintain and render more effective territorial dominion in America for as long as possible, in India, in the West Indies, with which Harlow does not deal, and in Ireland.

[7] C. A. Bayly, *Imperial Meridian: The British Empire and the World 1780–1830* (1989), p. 13.

America—nor the unsuspecting beneficiaries—in India—of forces of change that they could not control, even if they had comprehended them. Their ambitions often acted as a catalyst for developments. As a recent verdict, very much in line with other current assessments of the American Revolution, has put it, 'The transformation of Britain's mainland colonies between 1680 and 1770 did not cause or necessitate the Revolution . . . It hinged on colonists' reactions to major changes that British politicians and administrators hoped to impose on the empire.'[8] Similarly, while the evolution of eighteenth-century Indian polities and the interactions of ambitious Britons and Indians in Bengal and on the Coromandel coast created the circumstances in which the East India Company could grasp political power, the kind of territorial empire that was to be established in Bengal and later exported to other parts of India reflected metropolitan British ideals and the intervention of the metropolitan British state as well as Indian modes of governance.

This book will therefore give much attention to British ambitions for empire. These reflected concerns for national security and for Britain's standing in the world as well as assumptions about the proper ordering of government. There was a strong element of fear in them and very little overt enthusiasm for the task of ruling. Without proper regulation, the meteoric growth of British America, that might turn it into a rival rather than a subordinate, or the corruption and luxury supposedly being generated by the new empire in India could bring Britain to perdition.

Although they had roots that went back much earlier,[9] new British concepts of territorial empire manifested themselves in the aftermath of the Seven Years War. In the early eighteenth century British opinion had gloried in an 'empire of the seas', defined by the 1730s as 'Protestant, commercial, maritime and free'.[10] That implied domination for Britain's worldwide trade supported by naval supremacy and by colonies of free, Protestant British citizens enjoying the rights of Englishmen abroad. In theory at least, the conquest of territory and the subjection of alien peoples had no part in any British empire. Those were the ambitions of would-be world-conquering 'universal monarchies', supposedly once of Spain and now of France, not of a free people.

    [8] Jon Butler, *Becoming America: The Revolution before 1776* (Cambridge, Mass., 2000), p. 229. For a similar recent verdict, see Fred Anderson, *Crucible of War: The Seven Years' War and the Fate of Empire in British North America, 1754–1766* (New York, 2000), p. 743: 'Thus the answer to the question, By what means could the British have created a durable empire after the Seven Years' War? is simply this: by refusing to exercise any new control, any new power, over the colonies.' Butler's conclusion is the more striking in that the theme of his book (unlike that of Anderson or what will be argued in this book) is that what he calls 'the modernisation' of America was making the colonies more and more distant from Britain well before the Revolution.
    [9] e.g. in the reforming policies of the board of trade in the 1740s and 1750s, see below, pp. 76–8.
    [10] David Armitage, *The Ideological Origins of the British Empire* (Cambridge, 2000), p. 173.

Commitment to the ideal of a free commercial empire of the seas was rarely to be disavowed, but by the 1760s it was coming to be seen as inadequate to the present state of the British empire and to Britain's new needs and aspirations. Victory in the Seven Years War and successful intervention in the affairs of Indian provinces meant that the British now ruled great extents of territory with subject populations of Native Americans, French Canadians, and above all of Indians. None of these were Protestant, British, or free, according to British notions of freedom. New systems of authoritarian government had to be devised for them. In the case of Bengal in particular, men who had seized power there believed that the future security of British interests required the assertion of an absolute sovereignty over the province to be protected by a large army.[11] This view came to be shared in Britain. Sovereignty over the Company's possessions was eventually to be claimed by parliament.

Something too, it was widely assumed, had to be done about the existing colonies of free British people in the Americas. Although North Americans and white West Indians remained strongly committed to the ideal of an empire of freedom, that is to empire as a partnership between equal peoples, to the British, the Seven Years War had exposed the limits to such an empire. It was supposed that many of the colonies had failed to make adequate contributions to the war effort and that they were trading extensively outside the imperial system. Reforms were introduced that were based on the assumptions of the British parliament's full sovereignty over the colonies, including the right to tax.

New assertions of imperial authority in America and India (and in some degree over Ireland as well) grew above all out of concerns for national security. From the 1740s Britain was only too aware of the immense power of France, not only in Europe but throughout the world. As Bob Harris, whose work has highlighted the anxieties and sense of insecurity of the mid-eighteenth-century British regime, has recently put it, the 'survival of an independent, free, Protestant, and prosperous Britain' often seemed to be in question.[12] The Seven Years War brought great victories, but a new sense of insecurity in its aftermath. It was presumed that France, now openly allied with Spain, would seek an opportunity for revenge. This did indeed happen. Both France and Spain joined in the War of American Independence on the side of the rebellious colonies. By the end of that war Britain was fighting against a European coalition with no continental ally and had faced threats of invasion.

[11] See below, pp. 154–5.
[12] Bob Harris, *Politics and the Nation: Britain in the Mid-Eighteenth Century* (Oxford, 2002), p. 6; see also, ibid. pp. 333–4.

In the prolonged series of cold and hot wars from the 1740s it was conventional wisdom that Britain was able to confront more populous enemies by the strength of her commercial and financial resources, which enabled the British state to raise large sums in taxation and to borrow extensively at sustainable rates of interest. Long distance trades, above all those with the West Indies, North America, and Asia were taken to be an essential part of these resources. Every effort must be made to protect them and to ensure that they made the fullest possible contribution.

Effective defence and commercial regulation throughout Britain's overseas possessions were thought to depend on the effective exercise of authority over them. The source of that authority must reside in Britain and could only be the British parliament. Assertions of parliamentary sovereignty over the colonies and the increasingly active role in colonial matters assumed by parliament in the 1760s were very much in accordance with contemporary doctrines of parliamentary sovereignty and with parliament's increasing confidence in its ability to regulate domestic affairs.[13] The involvement of parliament endowed imperial reform with ideological as well as with practical purposes. A territorial empire subject to parliament could be no danger to the virtue of a free people at home. Obedience to British parliamentary authority was also deemed to be entirely compatible with the political arrangements appropriate to Britain's subjects overseas. Parliament would safeguard their interests and such rights and privileges as they were entitled to. It would prevent colonial government from lapsing either into ungovernable settler oligarchies or even democracies in the Americas, or into uncontrolled Company despotisms in India.

War and preparations for war play a central part in this book, which begins with the transformation that the Seven Years War brought about in Britain's position in America and India and ends with Britain holding her own and thus guaranteeing an imperial future in the West Indies, Canada, Gibraltar, and India, while conceding defeat in the thirteen colonies. Yet if sometimes diverted or interrupted by war, the forces of 'expansion' described in the first chapter continued to operate. Ambitions for an empire of the seas were still very much alive. At the end of the period British trade and British migrants were poised to recover their access to the old thirteen colonies. British merchants were to lay even more intensive siege to the markets of Spanish America and Brazil. British ships in ever greater numbers were to scour the Pacific, looking for largely illusory commercial opportunities. With the destruction of other European navies in the 1790s and the rise of Britain's manufacturing industries, talk of an 'informal empire' becomes realistic.

---

[13] See below, pp. 78–9.

Territorial empire of rule might therefore seem to have been an aberration, which Britain's national leadership would gladly abandon once a huge segment of it had defected. Few, however, had envisaged any alternative to enforcing effective rule over the old and new possessions in America or the new ones in India. Defeat did not materially alter the determination to retain those parts of the empire that had been successfully defended in the American war. Britain was indeed to fight another great war to protect her territorial empire, this time in the West Indies, in the 1790s. There could be no doubt of Britain's 'persistence' in empire.[14]

II

'Britain' is of course a concept that requires definition. In studies of wars and attempts to regulate empires, 'Britain' is likely to become a shorthand term for ministers, officials, and their advisers at home and for generals, admirals, and governors overseas. In an age in which parliament was asserting its authority over imperial matters, MPs who took an interest in such things were also likely to be heavily involved. This book is not surprisingly much concerned with the thoughts and doings of this kind of elite leadership and draws heavily on their official and private papers and on the reports of parliamentary debates.[15] It is therefore in part a study of 'the official mind' of eighteenth-century imperialism, extended to include men overseas as well as at home.

The concept of an 'official mind' was coined for the attitudes of ministers and officials in the later nineteenth century by Ronald Robinson and John Gallagher in their classic *Africa and the Victorians: The Official Mind of Imperialism.*[16] Britain's leadership in the later eighteenth century had some similarities with its counterpart a hundred years later. They too 'had special notions of the national interest, and of supremacy and security in the world'. For them the national interest was defined as the survival of the order established by the Glorious Revolution of 1688, which must be defended from foreign enemies bent on its destruction and from subversion from within. By the 1750s a predominant interpretation of the legacy of the Glorious Revolution had emerged that laid particular stress on the

---

[14] Eliga H. Gould, *The Persistence of Empire: British Political Culture in the Age of the American Revolution* (Chapel Hill, NC, 2000).

[15] Use of these for the American crisis has been greatly facilitated by the six vols. of *Proceedings and Debates of the British Parliament respecting North America, 1754–1783* (Millwood, NY, 1982–6), eds., R. C. Simmons and P. D. G. Thomas.

[16] (1961, 2nd edn. 1981).

sovereignty of parliament. As Chapter 5 in particular shows, this interpretation merits very close attention from historians. It was to have a profound influence on attitudes to empire.

The official mind for Robinson and Gallagher prided itself on its detachment from the pressure of interests at home and from 'reality' overseas.[17] The eighteenth-century official mind was less likely to be detached. Commanders and governors overseas had their own interests to pursue and generally tried to win support at home for them. Ministers and officials at home were, like their Victorian successors, detached by distance and in most cases by ignorance from developments overseas. It was more difficult, however, for them to distance themselves from domestic interests and pressure groups. Since national power depended on the mobilization of wealth, economic issues were central to the management of empire. In the crudest outline, the Navigation Acts provided the principles which governments followed. But within those broad and often ambiguous guidelines ministers had to resolve numerous conflicting claims of particular interests and lobbies. A case can be made that by the 1760s a handful of politicians were applying sophisticated concepts of political economy to determine the national interest.[18] Some were self-interested in a way that would have outraged the Victorians, a blatant example being Charles Townshend, who tried to combine a career in imperial governance with making a fortune out of the speculative lures of the eighteenth-century empire that attracted many others, West Indian and North American land and East India stock and patronage. In 1772 leading ministers yielded to a powerful syndicate of speculators in sanctioning a huge land grant in the American west.[19] Most of those who concerned themselves with empire were likely, however, neither to be doctrinaire theorists nor especially on the make. They did not have overarching designs for the future development of the empire nor rigid commitments to what historians came to call 'mercantilism'. They probably applied certain crude rules of thumb, such as the prime importance of manufacturing and of encouraging British shipping, tempering them by political calculations. Some lobbies commanded more votes in the house of commons than others and some imperial issues had resonances with a wider public that could not be ignored. As recent work has stressed, even in the 1750s, once seen as a high plateau of oligarchic stability, members of the small, landed elite who filled the great offices of state still had to take account of wider opinion 'out of doors'.[20]

---

[17] Ibid., 2nd edn., pp. 20–1.
[18] Nancy F. Koehn, *The Power of Commerce: Economy and Governance in the First British Empire* (Ithaca, NY, 1994).
[19] See below, p. 324.
[20] Harris, *Politics and the Nation*, p. 63.

The influence of this wider public, at least until the rise of popular anti-slavery movements in the later eighteenth century, was conspicuously absent from older versions of imperial history. Recent work, based on the study of pamphlets and the London and the provincial press, has charted popular involvement in the period of this book with the fortunes of war overseas, with the repeal of the Stamp Act and with the debate about armed coercion of the American colonies in 1775.[21] Questions of empire have been shown to have been a major theme of English poetry.[22] Even when issues did not become topics for organized petitions or press campaigns, ministers must have had clear intimations as to what a wider public thought about such matters as the need to make the American colonies pay for their own defence after 1763 or to bring the East India Company to book in the early 1770s.

This book can make no claim to systematic research into public attitudes, beyond dipping into the London press for certain years, but it has been informed by the work of others in trying to relate policy-making and the views of a wider public. In the present state of knowledge, it is likely that on high-profile imperial issues 'British' policy emerged not only from the calculations of the official mind but from debates that in some degree involved the enfranchised 'political nation' in counties and boroughs, 'middling' opinion in London and the English provincial cities and professional, mercantile and landed groups in Scotland and Ireland. How far such debates had relevance to a yet wider audience is unclear, but Britain's involvement overseas could intrude in many ways into ordinary lives. In 1742 the vicar of Braughing, a rural parish in land-locked Hertfordshire, collected £1. 9s. 0d. from his parishioners in response to a royal and episcopal call for donations 'for the Propagation of the Gospel in the West Indys'. When the call came again ten years later, Braughing subscribed just over £2.[23]

[21] For pamphlets, see Gould, *Persistence of Empire*; for the metropolitan and especially for the provincial press, see Kathleen Wilson, *The Sense of the People: Politics, Culture and Imperialism in England 1715–1785* (Cambridge, 1995) and essays in Wilson, *The Island Race: Englishness, Empire and Gender in the Eighteenth Century* (2003); for the 1750s, see Harris, *Politics and the Nation*, ch. 3, 'Britain and France and the Empire of the Seas' and ' "American Idols": Empire, War and the Middling Ranks in Mid-Eighteenth-Century Britain', *Past and Present*, CL (1996), 112–41; for the American crisis, the work of James E. Bradley is of the utmost importance, see especially, *Popular Politics and the American Revolution in England: Petitions, the Crown and Public Opinion* (Macon, Ga, 1986).
[22] See the work of Karen O'Brien, e.g. 'Poetry against Empire: Milton to Shelley', *Proceedings of the British Academy*, CXVII (2001), *Lectures*, 269–96.
[23] Hertfordshire County Record Office, Braughing Vicars' Memorandum Book, D/P, 23, 3/1, pp. 37, 41.

III

This book shows how 'the British' in the wide sense just outlined, engaged with their interests overseas over three tumultuous decades. Chapters analysing the forces of expansion in British society and the imperial ambitions and capacities of the British state are followed by two chapters on the Seven Years War: one on the war around the Atlantic and one on the war in India. They conclude that war had created problems and opportunities that British opinion increasingly came to believe required new or reformed imperial systems. These would unequivocally assert metropolitan authority and establish acceptable structures of local government to ensure both that British territories were effectively defended and that the wealth of the empire was properly husbanded through a system of trade regulation. Two chapters that follow (5 and 6) examine in greater depth the debate about imperial objectives following the war, both in the established American colonies and in the new British dominions, of which the Indian provinces were the greatest additions of wealth and population. The story of the simultaneous making and unmaking of empire is then told in pairs of chapters, dealing first with India and then with North America. They explain how in India, in spite of failures in Madras and Bombay, an imperial structure consonant with British preoccupations emerged over seemingly alien new subjects in Bengal. Bengal was the base from which British domination was to spread across the subcontinent in the nineteenth century. The North American chapters try to show how imperial reform was frustrated and rule of any kind eventually proved to be impossible over people for the most part self-consciously English. A new round of wars confirmed these outcomes which were embodied in the peace of 1783. That is the theme of the concluding chapter.

I

British Worldwide Expansion

For reasons that the Introduction tried to explain, the first two chapters of this book, which attempt to set the scene for the years from 1750 to 1783, deal separately with 'expansion' and 'empire'. What is here called British expansion overseas, such activities as trade, the migration of peoples or the diffusion of British cultural influences, had effectively begun towards the end of the sixteenth century. By the eighteenth century significant elements of British society were involved in oceanic expansion in one form or another. From early in the seventeenth century the English, later the British, state began trying to assert its authority over British people settled overseas or over territory seized from other Europeans, beginning with Jamaica in 1655. Tentative and fitful efforts at exerting state power overseas came to be seen as having created an 'empire' of rule over land and people. By the middle of the eighteenth century contemporaries were in no doubt that Britain possessed a worldwide empire of great extent, although expansion, notably trade with the colonies of other European powers or with independent African or Asian polities, had spread beyond the bounds of empire. Expansion and empire, private enterprise and state action, were closely linked and mutually dependent. In most cases, however, expansion had preceded empire.

By the middle of the eighteenth century, British overseas trade had undergone a radical shift from being almost exclusively centred on Europe in the mid-seventeenth century to embracing much of the world a hundred years later. By 1772–4 more than half of British manufactured exports went to markets outside Europe and more than half of what Britain imported came from such sources. Not only were British merchants handling a huge volume of trade to and from Britain itself, but they were also engaging in complex patterns of global commerce, for instance between one part of the Americas and another, between West Africa and the Americas or around the Indian Ocean and the South China Sea. There was a continuing flow of migrants, either going abroad as permanent emigrants seeking to make their homes in a new land or as what are often called 'sojourners', that is people who went overseas for what they hoped would be a limited period. Cultural expansion is a more nebulous and certainly a far less quantifiable concept than commercial expansion or emigration, but there can be no doubt that metropolitan British ideals, beliefs and tastes were being exported. Many historians see an increasing degree of 'Anglicization', that is willingness among communities of British origin to conform to metropolitan values, in British America from mid-century. In the northern colonies Protestant Christian denominations, the great majority of which had originated in Britain, were consolidating their hold on the white population.[1] Some British churches and missionary societies were beginning, if as yet still on a limited scale, to engage with the christianizing of Native Americans and Africans in the new world. British books were being shipped out in ever larger quantities. British clothing, furniture or porcelain were setting standards of taste among colonial elites and wider sections of the population throughout the British world.

The dynamism that drove eighteenth-century British expansion came from a variety of sources. Assumptions about an overwhelmingly dominant England, bent on subjugating Scotland and Ireland as well as peoples overseas, or even about an all-conquering London, grasping the world in its tentacles, should be treated with caution. Other Europeans and no doubt indigenous peoples who encountered the British were inclined to lump them together as 'English'. In reality, British expansion involved all parts of the British Isles and the Scottish and Irish elements in it were becoming particularly prominent in the later eighteenth century. For all the immense power of London, which attracted merchants and money from all over Britain, and which set standards of taste and of conspicuous consumption for polite behaviour everywhere else, English outports that dealt with the overseas world, most obviously Bristol and Liverpool, asserted their own commercial interests. Scots developed their own trading networks and Scottish migrants took with them their own patterns of Christian worship, including those of their established Presbyterian church, as well as the distinctive intellectual culture fostered in their schools and colleges. Scotland was, moreover, by no means a single entity. Edinburgh, the west of Scotland dominated by Glasgow and the north-east with Aberdeen prominent all carved out their own stakes overseas.[2] The gentry of the Highlands competed avidly for office overseas and to provide soldiers from a population heavily involved in emigration. Ireland faced legal discrimination in its access to colonial trades at mid-century, but Ulster and the south-west in particular had developed strong transatlantic

---

[1] Jon Butler, *Awash in a Sea of Faith: Christianizing the American People* (Cambridge, Mass., 1990), especially ch. 4.
[2] Ned C. Landsman, *Scotland and its First American Colony, 1683–1765* (Princeton, 1985), p. 207.

connections. Irish migrants crossed the Atlantic in large numbers and Irish merchants operated in many American ports.[3]

By the middle of the eighteenth century much of the dynamism behind 'British' expansion was coming not directly from the British Isles, but from what historians are fond of calling the 'periphery', that is from colonial populations in North America and the West Indies and even from the small British communities residing in West African or Indian ports. Planters and farmers throughout the British Caribbean and in the mainland colonies were bringing more and more land under cultivation and seeking to extend the boundaries of British territorial control, while there were active local merchant communities in all the British American towns from Bridgetown, Barbados, to Halifax, Nova Scotia or St John's, Newfoundland. British creole societies had cultural ambitions of their own, even if they usually chose to express these in British terms. On the West African coast or in Indian port cities, small resident communities of British merchants pursued their own interests as well as those of their employers at home.

Certain general features were evident in all forms of British expansion overseas in the period of this book. The overall trend of most indicators that have any validity, such as the growth of British population overseas or the flows of trade, are clearly upwards. Cultural expansion escapes quantification, but an annual average shipment of 1,137 hundred weights of British books to the thirteen colonies of North America in the years 1764–74, compared with 345 hundred weights for the years 1739–48 is a very crude indication of growth.[4] If the overall trend was clearly upwards, growth was, however, erratic. Commercial expansion was not an even process in all parts of the British world. Some trades were more buoyant than others and all could be affected by periodic recessions. Migrants left the British Isles in spurts, rather than in a steadily increasing flow.

Another common feature of the period was an increasing degree of integration, especially around the Atlantic, where the British Isles, North America, the Caribbean, and West Africa were being tied ever closer together. Although the eighteenth century was not an especially significant period for the technological development of shipping, the number of vessels crossing the oceans greatly increased. People, goods, news and ideas thus all travelled from place to place with ever greater facility. Economic historians have stressed the 'growing interdependence' of the elements that were constituting a single

---

[3] Thomas M. Truxes, *Irish–American Trade, 1660–1783* (Cambridge, 1988).

[4] S. D. Smith, 'The Market for Manufactures in the Thirteen Continental Colonies, 1698–1776', *Economic History Review*, 2nd ser., LI (1998), 681.

Atlantic trading area.[5] Culturally the British Atlantic was also becoming one world.[6]

I

By the middle of the eighteenth century commerce between Britain and the world beyond Europe was being driven to ever higher levels by the capacity of Britain and those parts of Europe that were supplied by Britain to consume more and more commodities from the Americas and from Asia. Increasing imports stimulated British exports. The rising British demand for their produce gave greater purchasing power to the white populations in British America. This enabled them to buy more and more goods made in Britain.

Sugar, almost exclusively produced in the British West Indies, was the most valuable British import of any kind by the 1750s. In the 1720s annual per capita consumption of sugar in England and Wales has been estimated at 12 lb.; by the 1770s it had nearly doubled to 23 lb.[7] Between 1750 and 1775 the consumption of sugar quadrupled in Ireland.[8] Since the later seventeenth century Indian cotton cloth had become a staple item of dress and furnishing for most of the British population. Calicoes and muslins, imported by the East India Company, were also re-exported in large quantities to Europe, America and West Africa. India was becoming a major source of raw silk for British silk weavers. By mid-century tea from China, again imported by the East India Company, was being widely consumed in Britain. Imports exceeded one million lb. in 1721 and, although high duties were limiting official sales and encouraging smuggling from Europe, they rose to well over three million lb. in the 1750s.[9] Among other imported items from across the Atlantic for domestic consumption were dye stuffs, certain kinds of timber and naval stores, pig and bar iron and raw cotton.

Tobacco from the Chesapeake colonies of Virginia and Maryland was the most important colonial commodity the bulk of which was re-exported from Britain to continental European markets. Up to 85 per cent of what arrived in Britain in a year was transhipped. The volume of exports from the Chesapeake grew rapidly if erratically from the 1740s. Rice was established as a new

---

[5] Kenneth Morgan, *Bristol and the Atlantic Trade in the Eighteenth Century* (Cambridge, 1993), p. 9.

[6] Ian K. Steele, *The English Atlantic, 1675–1740: An Exploration of Communication and Community* (New York, 1986).

[7] Carole Shammas, *The Pre-industrial Consumer in England and America* (Oxford, 1990), p. 82.

[8] Truxes, *Irish–American Trade*, p. 50.

[9] K. N. Chaudhuri, *The Trading World of Asia and the English East India Company 1660–1760* (Cambridge, 1978), pp. 538–9.

crop in South Carolina early in the eighteenth century. It spread rapidly, exports doubling in the 1760s. Most Carolina rice was re-exported from Britain to northern Europe, but a considerable proportion went directly to southern European markets. This was part of a growing trade in foodstuffs from the British colonies in North America, which was legally permitted to go directly to Spain, Portugal and the Mediterranean or to the Spanish and Portuguese islands in the Atlantic. Exports to southern Europe supplemented the very large trade in provisions and timber from the mainland colonies with the British West Indies and with other European colonies around the Caribbean.

The reverse flow from Britain to the Americas consisted for the most part of manufactured goods. The strong upwards trend in British exports to America around the middle of the eighteenth century is very clear. English exports to the thirteen colonies were worth an annual average of a little under £1 million in 1750–1; they had reached about £2,500,000 in 1772–3.[10] By the time of the Revolution colonial Americans are thought to have been spending about 30 per cent of their income on imports. These included much West Indian sugar and molasses for rum, Indian cotton cloth and Chinese tea, but the great bulk of what they spent was on British goods.[11] Textiles, principally woollen cloth and linens, made up about a half of colonial imports from Britain. Metal goods were also very prominent, while the annual average of a million pieces of earthenware sent to North America in the years 1749–55 had risen to an average of one million-and-a-half for the years 1764–74.[12] The colonial American taste for British luxury goods had become discerning and demanding. By the 1760s Axminster, Milton, Persian, Scotch, Turkey, Weston and Wilton carpets were all being advertised in New York.[13] Population growth in the West Indies was largely confined to slaves who consumed relatively few foreign imports. But in addition to the demands of the local white population, a considerable portion of the British exports that went to the West Indies was re-routed illegally into Spanish America, above all via Jamaica.

While the overall trend in Atlantic trade was clearly upwards, there were periodic checks to growth. War was an obvious hazard. Shipping was then exposed to the depredations of French and Spanish warships and privateers, West Indian islands might be attacked and the frontiers of mainland colonies

[10] Table in Jacob M. Price, 'The Imperial Economy 1700–1776' in P. J. Marshall, ed., *Oxford History of British Empire*, II, *The Eighteenth Century* (Oxford, 1998), p. 101.

[11] Shammas, *Pre-industrial Consumer*, p. 292.

[12] Smith, 'Market for Manufactures', p. 681.

[13] T. H. Breen, ' "Baubles of Britain": The American and Consumer Revolutions of the Eighteenth Century', *Past and Present*, CXIX (1988), 80; see also his 'An Empire of Goods: The Anglicization of Colonial America, 1690–1776', *Journal of British Studies*, XXV (1986), 467–99.

raided by the French or the Spanish and the Indians who allied with them. War brought its compensations in heavy military spending that stimulated the mainland American economies during the Seven Years War, but recession on both sides of the Atlantic followed the ending of the war. Politics intruded in the 1760s when the North American colonies tried to enforce non-importation boycotts of British goods. A sharp credit crisis in Britain in 1772, triggered by the failure of Scottish banks, had damaging effects throughout the colonies as British credit was called in. Renewed non-importation and a ban on exports was followed by the War of American Independence, which eventually spread to the West Indies and to India, severely dislocating the whole Atlantic economy and diverting funds in India from trade to war.

The regional distribution of growth in British Atlantic trade was also uneven. In the Caribbean output increased steadily from the 1740s while rising consumption meant that prices for sugar in Britain remained generally buoyant.[14] The area under sugar cane grew with the additional islands that were acquired in 1763 and were quickly settled and developed by British planters, but the major increase in output came from Jamaica, which pulled well ahead of the smaller and longer settled Barbados and the Leeward Islands. By 1774 the aggregate value of Jamaica's plantations has been put at over £20 million,[15] making it the richest of all British overseas possessions. On the mainland, the most spectacular growth was in the south, above all in South Carolina, with its new crops of rice and later of indigo. Before the Revolution, population, boosted by massive imports of slaves, was growing more rapidly in the lower South than anywhere else on the mainland. A high proportion of the very richest men in late colonial North America were South Carolina planters.[16] The outlook for tobacco, the long established staple crop of the Chesapeake colonies, was less assured than that for sugar or rice. Output increased as tobacco spread further and further inland, but there were periods of glut and low prices in the early 1760s and again in the 1770s. By the outbreak of the Revolution the Chesapeake planters were far more heavily in debt than any other section of the colonial population. Yet they had succeeded in diversifying into the large-scale production of grain and meat to take advantage of the provision trade to southern Europe and the

[14] Richard Pares, 'The London Sugar Market 1740–1769', *Economic History Review*, 2nd ser., IX (1958), 254–70; Richard B. Sheridan, *Sugar and Slavery: An Economic History of the British West Indies 1623–1775* (Barbados, 1974), pp. 439–43.

[15] T. G. Burnard, ' "Prodigious Riches": The Wealth of Jamaica before the American Revolution', *Economic History Review*, 2nd ser., LXIV (2001), 512.

[16] Joyce Chaplin, *An Anxious Pursuit: Agricultural Innovation and Modernity in the Lower South, 1730–1815* (Chapel Hill, NC, 1993), p. 8; Russell R. Menard, 'Slavery, Economic Growth, and Revolutionary Ideology in the South Carolina Lowcountry' in Ronald Hoffman et al., eds., *The Economy of Early America: The Revolutionary Period, 1763–1790* (Charlottesville, Va., 1988), pp. 268–71.

West Indies. Professor Price, the great master of the history of the Chesapeake economy, considers the extent of the planters' indebtedness to have been 'quite reasonable, given the[ir] increasing wealth and income'.[17]

The economy of the middle colonies, especially of Pennsylvania, which was able to absorb waves of new migrants and settle them on productive land, was growing very rapidly. Large consignments of agricultural produce were being shipped to southern Europe and the West Indies. A considerable iron industry was also developing. Philadelphia was the most populous British city in the new world. The merchants of Philadelphia were major distributors of imported British manufactures. This was a buoyant but notoriously uncertain trade in which busts quickly succeeded booms, as British merchants flooded the American market with goods on enticingly easy credit terms.[18] The New England colonies with less accessible new land and only limited immigration were less expansive than the middle colonies to the south of them, but there too 'modest but durable economic growth' has been detected by mid-century.[19]

The elements of this expansive Atlantic commercial world were closely tied together by the mid-eighteenth century. In very crude terms there might appear to have been a division of function between Britain and the colonies: those who lived in the colonies being primarily engaged in the various forms of agriculture whose produce made up the bulk of colonial exports, while British merchants financed their operations, supplied them with new infusions of labour, above all with cargoes of slaves, organized the shipping of their crops and their sale in Europe and dispatched manufactured goods to them. Contrasting the colonial farmer with the British merchant does at least serve to emphasise a most important feature of the Atlantic economy, the dominant role of Britain as a source of finance through credit. West Indian planters paid for their slaves by bills of exchange on Britain drawn on long dates. They received goods on credit from their British factors who handled the sale of their sugar. Tobacco planters on the Chesapeake similarly obtained goods on credit either from the British merchants who sold their crops on commission or increasingly from British factors and storekeepers actually resident in Virginia or Maryland. The great flows of British manufactured

---

[17] Jacob M. Price, *Capital and Credit in British Overseas Trade: The View from the Chesapeake 1700–76* (Cambridge, Mass., 1980), p. 19. The uncertainties of tobacco are stressed in J. A. Ernst, 'The Chesapeake Colonies' in Hoffman et al., eds. *Economy of Early America*, pp. 196–243; T. H. Breen, *Tobacco Culture: The Mentality of the Great Tidewater Planters on the Eve of the Revolution* (Princeton, 1986).

[18] Thomas M. Doerflinger, *A Vigorous Spirit of Enterprise: Merchants and Economic Development in Revolutionary Philadelphia* (Chapel Hill, NC, 1986), pp. 95–6; Morgan, *Bristol and Atlantic Trade*, pp. 112–13.

[19] Gloria L. Main and Jackson T. Main, 'The Red Queen in New England', *William and Mary Quarterly*, 3rd ser., LVI (1999), 125.

goods that passed through Philadelphia, Boston, and other ports in the middle and northern colonies depended on credit. British merchants gave their American correspondents up to twelve months to pay who in turn extended credit to the retailers or travelling traders who disposed of the goods.[20]

If Britain was the main, although by no means the only, source of the credit that financed the expansion of the Atlantic economy, any simple division between colonial producers and British merchants breaks down at many other points. The colonial and metropolitan strands in the British commercial world were not easily separable. There were vigorous local merchant communities in colonial ports, while many people resident in Britain had an interest in American land and agriculture. The roles of planter and merchant, creole or Briton, seem to have been especially interchangeable in the West Indies. Would-be new planters were constantly coming from Britain to try their luck in the islands, as successful planters returned to Britain to live off the income of their West Indian estates. Many of those who acted as sugar merchants in Britain had been planters in the islands, while a number of British West India merchants acquired interests in Caribbean estates.[21] The ownership of land in the mainland colonies, including the plantation belt from Georgia to Maryland, was much more clearly in 'American' hands, that is in the hands of people likely to have been long resident in the colonies, than was the case in the West Indies. Nor was it so common for owners of land in North America to move to Britain as absentees. American landed families did, however, resemble West Indian planters in that they often sought wealth through commercial activities as well as through the direct exploitation of the land. They could be both merchants and planters.[22]

The acquisition of American land was a common pursuit both of those who lived in the North American colonies and of many in Britain. British interest built up in the 1740s, was greatly stimulated by the Seven Years War and reached fever pitch after the ending of the war, when it became clear that much land within the existing colonies, hitherto regarded as hazardous because of French or Indian incursions, was now ripe for development and that huge new areas were waiting to be settled in territory just incorporated into the British empire in Florida and Nova Scotia. Army officers who had served in America and officials in British government departments that dealt

---

[20] Jacob M. Price, 'Credit in the Slave Trade and Plantation Economies' in Barbara L. Solow, ed., *Slavery and the Rise of the Atlantic System* (Cambridge, 1991), pp. 293–339; Price, *Capital and Credit*; Doerflinger, *Vigorous Spirit of Enterprise*, pp. 86–8.

[21] Sheridan, *Sugar and Slavery*, p. 299; Kenneth Morgan, 'Bristol West India Merchants in the Eighteenth Century', *Transactions of the Royal Historical Society*, 6th ser., III (1993), 190–5.

[22] H. V. Bowen, *Elites, Enterprise and the Making of the British Overseas Empire, 1688–1775* (Houndmills, 1996), pp. 134–40.

with the colonies were well to the fore, but a very wide range of leading British political and mercantile families joined in the hunt.[23] In retrospect it seemed to the American loyalist George Chalmers that: 'Every man, who had credit with the ministers at home, or influence over the governors of the colonies, ran for the prize of American territory. And many land-owners in Great Britain, of no small importance, neglected the possessions of their fathers, for a portion of wilderness beyond the Atlantic.'[24] Americans were involved in many of the schemes being launched in Britain. In theory, they gave their British partners the benefit of their local expertise in return for British political influence and British money. The results were entirely disproportionate to the enthusiasm generated. Most of the land grants awarded in Britain were never taken up and most of those that were pros-ecuted with any seriousness lost money. Yet the lists of names enrolled for grants clearly indicate that a large section of the British upper classes were tempted by the prospect of becoming new-world landowners.

Oceanic commerce was also a common concern of those who lived on both sides of the Atlantic. By the middle of the eighteenth century Atlantic trade had long ceased to be the exclusive monopoly of merchants based in Britain. All colonial ports had their resident merchants. Inter-colonial trade, such as that between the West Indies and the continental colonies was largely in their hands. The role of colonial merchants in trade with Britain seems to have varied from region to region and according to commodity. The bulk of West Indian sugar was probably sent on consignment to British merchants in British-owned ships and on the eve of the Revolution the largest part of tobacco exports was being directly purchased in Virginia or Maryland by English and Scottish factors residing there, who then shipped it to Britain.[25] In South Carolina, by contrast, rice was obtained from the planters by local merchants based in Charleston, who sold it for their British correspondents to ship across the Atlantic.[26] Philadelphia merchants handled the inflow of British manufactured goods into their port and owned a considerable pro-portion of the ships in which the goods were carried,[27] as did merchants from New England ports. Only in Canada after the British conquest were local merchants unable to hold their own for what were obviously special reasons. The French merchant community, already crippled by the misfortunes of war

[23] Bernard Bailyn, *Voyagers to the West: A Passage in the Peopling of America on the Eve of the Revolution* (New York, 1986), p. 357.
[24] *An Estimate of the Comparative Strengths of Great-Britain during the Present and Four Preceding Reigns*, new edn. (1794), p. 123.
[25] Price, 'Imperial Economy' in Marshall, ed., *Oxford History*, II, p. 95.
[26] Kenneth Morgan, 'Organization of the Colonial American Rice Trade', *William and Mary Quarterly*, 3rd ser., LII (1995), 441.
[27] Doerflinger, *Vigorous Spirit of Enterprise*.

and the inability of the French crown to pay its debts,[28] generally gave way to British houses based in London or Scotland or to New Englanders. In any trade, whatever the prevailing arrangements, there were likely to be close relations of mutual dependence between British and colonial merchants. Many British merchants lived for long periods in Philadelphia, New York, Boston or Charleston, while Americans spent time in Bristol, Liverpool, or London.[29] Commercial ties were cemented by marriage and the education of American children in Britain was often entrusted to a British merchant with whom their father had dealings.

British merchants on the coast of West Africa or in Asian ports lived and worked under conditions that were obviously different from those in British colonies in America. The sea-borne trade of West Africa was, however, part of an Atlantic economy and shared some characteristics with other Atlantic trades. British ships, overwhelmingly from London or Bristol, which was dominant in mid-century, or from Liverpool, by then beginning to overtake Bristol, together with a few North American ships, went to a wide range of destinations from Angola in the south to Senegal in the north. Some of the ports at which they called, notably on the Gold Coast, contained permanent British forts or factories maintained by a nationally supported Company of Merchants Trading to Africa. The Company's employees together with a handful of British or mixed-race merchants lived all the year round at such places. They became involved with local African society and, as was common with the British in India, they tended to acquire what they called African 'country wives'.[30] At Bance Island off Sierra Leone a group of private merchants maintained a permanent settlement under their own control, complete with its own golf course.[31] In other areas, like the Bight of Biafra in modern Nigeria, where many of the largest shipments of slaves were being made by the mid-eighteenth century, British traders operated in African ports without any settlements of their own. Business was done from the ships. Even where there was a British fort, the ultimate authority remained with African rulers and trade was conducted under conditions that they laid down. Bance Island maintained some inland trading posts,[32] but otherwise Europeans rarely left the coast. They received their slaves or other commodities from African merchants or from the agents of rulers. British traders paid for their

---

[28] J. F. Bosher, *The Canada Merchants 1713–1763* (Oxford, 1987).

[29] Kenneth Morgan, 'Business Networks in the British Export Trade to North America 1750–1800' in John J. McCusker and Kenneth Morgan, eds., *The Early Modern Atlantic Economy* (Cambridge, 2000), p. 46.

[30] Margaret Priestley, *West African Trade and Coast Society: A Family Study* (1969).

[31] David Hancock, *Citizens of the World: London Merchants and the Integration of the British Atlantic Community 1735–85* (Cambridge, 1995), pp. 172–82.

[32] Ibid. p. 203.

cargoes of slaves with a wide variety of European manufactured goods, textiles, metals, alcohol, or firearms, or with Indian cowry shells and cotton cloth. Credit was as important in West Africa as it was in other parts of the Atlantic world. Goods were advanced to African merchants for considerable periods to enable them to make purchases of slaves. African merchants of good reputation were evidently regarded as a sound commercial risk, but additional security was often required in the shape of 'pawns', that is people, sometimes apparently his own relatives, whom the merchant left with his European client on the understanding that if he failed in his bargain to produce slaves, the pawns would be shipped to America instead.[33]

In West Africa British merchants were operating in a region whose sea-borne trade, if not the rest of its economy,[34] was an integral part of a European-dominated Atlantic system. In Asia the British were participants in economies that had some significant links with Europe and the Atlantic but which were largely separate from them. Flows of American silver had done much to create silver-based currencies in parts of India and in China, while Indian cotton cloth was being worn all over western Europe, West Africa, and the Americas and tea was being consumed throughout the English-speaking world. In other respects, however, the Asian ports at which the British traded in the mid-eighteenth century were primarily serving relatively integrated domestic economies that covered much of the territory once ruled by the Mughal emperors or that was still being ruled by the emperors of China. A common currency system, albeit with many local variations, operated throughout what had been Mughal India; even basic food grains were traded over long distances and bankers transferred funds by bill of exchange from one commercial centre to another throughout the subcontinent. The European East India Companies transacted a large volume of sea-borne trade between India and Europe and carried away much tea from Canton, the only Chinese port to which they had access. Trade with Europe was, however, only a part, and in the case of China probably only a small part, of a large volume of trade by sea and overland with other parts of Asia, the great bulk of it still in the hands of Asian merchants and carried in Asian ships.

In practical terms the British role in eighteenth-century Asian trade differed in two fundamental respects from the pattern of British trade in the Atlantic. Britain imported Asian commodities, but it was not the principal source of manufactured goods for its Asian trading partners: Asians

---

[33] Paul E. Lovejoy and David Richardson, 'Trust, Pawnship and Atlantic History: The Institutional Foundations of the Old Calabar Slave Trade', *American Historical Review*, CIV (1999), 333–55.

[34] The limited significance of sea-borne trade for the region as a whole is strongly argued by David Eltis, e.g. 'Precolonial Western Africa and the Atlantic Economy' in Solow, ed., *Slavery and the Rise of the Atlantic System*, pp. 97–119.

manufactured for themselves and, in the case of textiles, for much of the rest of the world. Britain also had a less dominant role in the source of credit. The East India Company advanced the bullion that it imported to its Indian suppliers, but there were vigorous indigenous banking systems in India and China. British private merchants relied to a very large extent on money borrowed from Indian sources.

By the middle of the eighteenth century company monopolies, apart from that operated in the Canadian north by the Hudson's Bay Company, had been broken all over the British Atlantic, including West Africa. In Asia, however, the East India Company's monopoly was still intact in theory, even if not always in practice. Only its ships were permitted to sail past the Cape of Good Hope and British settlements in Asia were under its authority. The chief settlements were in what had become effectively British-governed enclaves on the Indian coast, at Calcutta, Madras, and Bombay. Their European inhabitants could only be numbered in hundreds, but they had attracted large, if fluctuating, populations of Indian merchants—some extremely wealthy—artisans, and labourers. Calcutta is thought to have had 120,000 people living in it by the 1750s.[35] In size it, Madras, and Bombay dwarfed any British town in the Americas. The Company's presidency settlements had subordinate factories along the neighbouring coast and in the case of Calcutta far inland up the great rivers of eastern India. The Company also maintained posts on the Persian Gulf and the Red Sea and on the west coast of Sumatra. In China the Company's agents were permitted a seasonal residence at Canton.

The Company's ships from London brought out a limited range of woollen textiles and metals for sale in Asia together with large consignments of silver bullion. The ships chiefly took back cotton cloth and raw silk from India together with Chinese tea. Since the ventures of the Portuguese in the sixteenth century, Europeans had also been interested in participating in trade round the Indian Ocean and the China Seas. Well before the eighteenth century the English East India Company had largely withdrawn from this so-called 'country' trade, leaving it to private British merchants, that is to the Company's own servants, and to other British people residing in India. They owned Indian-built and Indian-crewed ships on which they carried their own goods and those of Indian merchants on freight to a variety of destinations from the Red Sea to China. This was a potentially lucrative business, making great fortunes early in the eighteenth century, comparable to those of the most successful West Indian planters, for men like Elihu Yale, only a small

---

[35] P. J. Marshall, *East Indian Fortunes: The British in Bengal in the Eighteenth Century* (Oxford, 1976), p. 24.

part of whose great wealth went to the college that bears his name, or Thomas ('Diamond') Pitt.

II

The movement of people was an essential part of the commercial expansion that was well under way round the Atlantic by the middle of the eighteenth century. New supplies of labour or new hands to bring land into cultivation were a necessity for parts of British America; the shipping of people to meet these needs was an important source of profit for some British merchants.

Indigenous sources of labour had long been eliminated throughout the plantation belt from the Chesapeake to the Caribbean. Only in Virginia and Maryland was an established imported labour force reproducing itself. Elsewhere, the working population had constantly to be replenished, while the expansion of cultivation throughout the plantation areas of the mainland colonies, in Jamaica and in the new West Indian possessions acquired in 1763 required large new imports of labour. By the eighteenth century the vast majority of those brought to work on the plantations were coming as slaves from Africa.

Although the British supplied slaves to other Europeans on a large scale, the growing needs of the British plantation economy was the engine that drove the British slave trade to its greatest extent in the period before the American Revolution. 364,800 slaves are thought to have been carried to America in British ships in the 1760s, the highest ten-year total in the history of British slaving.[36] Imports on this scale ensured that the population of all the Caribbean colonies, with the partial exception of Barbados, had vast black majorities. By 1768 Jamaica had 167,000 blacks to 18,000 whites.[37] In 1750 there were more blacks living in the West Indies than on the American mainland. By the outbreak of the Revolution, however, the balance was shifting and there were now more blacks in the continental colonies than in the islands.[38] South Carolina had a black majority of Caribbean proportions and Georgia was acquiring one. In the thirteen colonies as a whole some 21 per cent of the population was African in origin by 1770. This increasing Africanization had come about through large imports into the lower south and a rising rate of natural increase on the Chesapeake, reaching about 3 per

---

[36] Table in David Richardson, 'The British Empire and the Atlantic Slave Trade, 1660–1807' in Marshall, ed., *Oxford History*, II, p. 442.

[37] R. B. Sheridan, *The Development of the Plantations to 1750* (Barbados, 1970), p. 41.

[38] Philip Morgan, 'The Black Experience in the British Empire, 1680–1810' in Marshall, ed., *Oxford History*, II, p. 466.

cent a year in Virginia.[39] Slavery was spreading northwards into the towns of the middle colonies and of New England.

Although Africans quickly adjusted to skilled employment, there was still a demand for white labour in the plantation colonies. The servant trade from Britain, which had run at very high levels in the seventeenth century, remained significant, if on a much smaller scale, in the following century. In return for a passage across the Atlantic, mostly young single males from the British Isles continued to sell a period of their future labour, usually four years, to merchants or ships' captains in Britain, who would then sell the indenture to an American employer. Even the West Indies imported some white servants. Advertisements in the British press in the 1750s urged 'carpenters, wheelwrights, millwrights, bricklayers, blacksmiths, masons, and coopers' to apply for passages to Jamaica or Antigua.[40] The demand for servants from Britain was at its highest in Virginia, Maryland and Pennsylvania. Particularly desired were people with skills in building and construction as well as labour for the rapidly developing iron industry in Maryland, Pennsylvania, and New Jersey.[41] In spite of objections expressed in public debate, Virginia, Maryland, and Pennsylvania were willing to absorb most of the 50,000 or so British convicts sentenced transported to America between 1718 and 1750 and therefore available as servants under the provisions of an act of the British parliament of 1718.[42] Non-convict servants, especially in the exceptionally well documented years from 1773 to 1776, seem to have been predominantly southern English, shipped out from the wide hinterland of the port of London. Although they are likely to 'have experienced unemployment and pressing or threatening poverty', they may not have been 'sunk in absolute destitution'. The characteristic indentured servant of the 1770s is thought to have been 'an impecunious young artisan or craftsman who has probably served an apprenticeship or otherwise learnt something of a trade, found employment irregular or non-existent, and, without prospects, still unmarried and without other family encumbrances, is heading out to the colonies alone'.[43] Similar conclusions are being suggested for the servants shipped out from Irish ports. Unlike those who left in the years of economic crisis of the 1720s, those going from mid-century may also have had some

[39] Philip Morgan, *Slave Counterpoint: Black Culture in the Eighteenth-Century Chesapeake and Lowcountry* (Chapel Hill, NC, 1998), p. 81.

[40] *Public Advertiser*, 31 July 1755.

[41] Bailyn, *Voyagers to the West*, pp. 245–70.

[42] A. Roger Ekirch, *Bound for America: The Transportation of British Convicts to the Colonies, 1718–1775* (Oxford, 1987), p. 27.

[43] Bailyn, *Voyagers to the West*, pp. 197, 202. The case that the level of impoverishment among servants may in general have been greater than Bailyn found for the 1770s is put in James Horn, 'British Diaspora: Emigration from Britain, 1680–1815' in Marshall, ed., *Oxford History*, II, pp. 35–6.

skills and may have been going to America in hopes of improvement rather than as an act of desperation.[44]

Great tracts of land in the North American colonies outside the areas suitable for intensive cultivation by the main plantation crops, tobacco, rice or indigo, could be turned to profit by settling people to raise food crops or animals. Grants of uncultivated land, which were in most colonies nominally at the disposal of the crown, could be obtained on occasions in Britain or more commonly from the colonial governors. In Pennsylvania the Penn family disposed of the land. Enterprising men with a modicum of influence sought grants and were constantly on the look-out for people to settle on the land in order to realise an income from it. After the ending of the Seven Years War, the availability of new land dramatically increased, setting off a scramble for grants and for potential purchasers or tenants. Seasoned Americans, already farming in areas like New England where new land was in short supply, were probably the best prospect for opening up new grants, but land speculators were also very interested in bringing in immigrants from the British Isles or from western Europe. Unlike the servants recruited to work on the plantations and the iron works or in towns, those who came to cultivate the land usually paid for their own passages, rather than selling their labour in advance, and came in family parties, not as single males.

Families willing to settle on new land in America in this period tended to come from the north of England, from Scotland, from Ulster, and from the German Rhineland. They were drawn to venture to the new world by personal contact with people who had already gone there, by initiatives taken by some local notable who was able to persuade others to join with him, by captains of ships or merchants who hoped to profit by the passage money, and by those who acted as the recruiting agents for land speculators. In the case of the 110,000 Germans, nearly all of whom passed through the port of Philadelphia and who came in the largest numbers in the period 1749–55, there was a higher degree of commercial organization. They were brought down the Rhine and passed on to English ports by Dutch merchants, who often advanced them the amount of their passage to be repaid in America.[45]

Some pioneering schemes for bringing large parties of Scots to Georgia and North Carolina were launched in the 1730s, but the main movements from Scotland to America took place after 1763. By 1772–3 it seemed to one worried observer that a 'spirit of emigration' had spread throughout the

---

[44] L. M. Cullen, 'The Irish Diaspora in the Seventeenth and Eighteenth Centuries' in Nicholas Canny, ed., *Europeans on the Move: Studies on European Migration 1500–1800* (Oxford, 1994), pp. 143–7.
[45] Marianne S. Wokeck, *Trade in Strangers: The Beginnings of Mass Migration to North America* (University Park, Pa., 1999).

Highlands and Islands and was affecting Lowland Scotland as well. Not only 'the lower class of people but the better sort of farmers and mechanicks' were involved. People were thought to be going to America because of harvest failures, higher rent demands, and unemployment caused by the decline of manufacturing, but also in hopes of improving themselves, hopes fostered by the propaganda of 'emissaries' from the colonies.[46] Contemporaries were struck by the scale of Highland emigration, which may have amounted to 15,000 to 20,000 people between 1763 and 1775. Historians stress that most migrants from Highland or Lowland Scotland are again unlikely to have been fleeing from abject poverty, since they possessed the means to pay for their own passages and sometimes took money with them. Yet even those who lived above any poverty line were experiencing upheavals in a period of increasing commercialization in the Highlands, marked by the eroding of old systems of collective land tenure and by steep increases in rent.[47]

There was also a marked upsurge of emigration of family parties among the Scots-Irish, that is among the Protestants of Ulster, in the years between the ending of the Seven Years War and the outbreak of the Revolution. In 1763 a visitor to Dublin from Philadelphia reported 'a vast jealousy of America here on account of the vast numbers that go to America from the North of Ireland, which they say will in the end rob them of their best Protestants and manufacturers'.[48] Ulster emigration accelerated in the early 1770s. To the lord lieutenant in Dublin this was attributable to the excessive rents being extracted by Ulster landlords and to the oppressive way in which they administered justice.[49] Recent research accepts the stimulus provided by economic dislocation, including a sharp recession in the linen industry, but yet again stresses that those who left Ulster were generally people with some skills who paid for their passages and hoped to improve themselves.[50]

A distinction between servants, that is individuals mostly going under indentures to labour or follow crafts in the new world, and families going in search of land to cultivate and generally paying their own way is no doubt a crude and inexact one. It certainly omits those who went neither as artisans or labourers nor to seek land which they themselves would cultivate. Such people were likely to have been men of education, of some substance and

---

[46] T. Miller to Suffolk, 25 April 1774, PRO, SP 54/45, ff. 683–4.

[47] Andrew Mackillop, 'Highland Estate Change and Tenant Emigration' in T. M. Devine and. R. Young, eds., *Eighteenth-Century Scotland: New Perspectives*, (East Linton, 1999), pp. 237–58; T. C. Smout, N. C. Landsman, T. M. Devine, 'Scottish Emigration in the Seventeenth and Eighteenth Centuries' in Canny, ed., *Europeans on the Move*, pp. 100–11.

[48] W. Smith to R. Peters, 18 Oct. 1763, HSP, William Smith MSS, II.

[49] Townshend to Rochford, 21 March 1771, PRO, SP 63/435, f. 185; J. F. Erskine to Lees, 10 April 1772, ibid. ff. 276–8.

[50] Wokeck, *Trade in Strangers*, p. 214; Cullen, 'Irish Diaspora' in Canny, ed., *Europeans on the Move*, pp. 143–9.

of high ambition, who went abroad in the hopes of becoming planters, of acting as factors or agents for merchants in Britain or of setting up their own commercial businesses, filling public offices, practising professions, such as law or medicine, or becoming ministers of religion, college teachers, or private tutors. Unlike nearly all the servants and the farming families, such people did not confine their interests to North America. They went in some numbers to the Caribbean and some sought service with the East India Company in Asia. Whereas most of the indentured servants or the would-be farmers and their families were probably planning on living out their lives in America, commercial and professional people usually regarded themselves as 'sojourners', who would eventually return to Britain having acquired the means to live at home in a manner that they regarded as appropriate to their aspirations. The numbers of such people leaving Britain in the mid-eighteenth century are very hard to estimate; they surely cannot have amounted to more than a few hundred in any year. There are, however, clear indications that interest in opportunities abroad was rising among the socially aspiring in Britain and that more and more ambitious people were willing to pursue careers overseas.

To win public office overseas in the mid-eighteenth century one needed to be ambitious indeed and to have a powerful patron. The number of civil offices in the colonies open to British aspirants was not in fact very great. Ninety-two North American and West Indian offices were listed in 1747 as being in the gift of the secretary of state in Britain. Most office holders in colonies were in fact appointed locally by the governor and increasingly by the assemblies. Colonial posts have been estimated at no more than 3 to 4 per cent of all British public appointments in the 1760s, rising to 6 per cent with the new colonies created after the Seven Years War.[51] Governorships were the most prestigious and valuable offices. Although they could go to men with roots in colonial society or to distinguished soldiers or naval officers, they were likely to be the reward for British political influence. The major West Indian governorships, Jamaica, the Leeward Islands, or Barbados, were regarded as the most lucrative. Henry Grenville, governor of Barbados in the early 1750s, estimated his appointment as worth some £4,000 a year and hoped to build up a fortune of about £30,000 out of his service.[52] Mainland governorships, of which Virginia was the most coveted, were generally worth less, but they were still objects of eager competition, as were the so-called patent offices, posts like secretary to the colony, naval officer or receivers, and

[51] Jacob M. Price, 'Who Cared about the Colonies? The Impact of the Thirteen Colonies on British Society and Politics, circa 1714–1775' in Bernard Bailyn and Philip D. Morgan, eds., *Strangers Within the Realm: Cultural Margins of the First British Empire* (Chapel Hill, NC, 1991), p. 397.
[52] Letters to G. Grenville, 27 Sept. 1751, 30 Sept. 1752, HL, STG, Box 25 (33), (49).

surveyors of revenue, which were awarded for life and often held in absentia while being discharged by deputies.[53] The Seven Years War created new colonial governments with new hierarchies of offices in the West Indies, the Floridas, and Canada, but the competition for them seems to have been even fiercer than before. Army officers who had served in America and hoped to stay there in civil offices were particularly interested in them.[54] Many went to Scots. This was not a new development. The duke of Newcastle as secretary of state had been giving American appointments to influential Scottish families since the 1720s in return for their support in Scottish politics.[55] With the Scottish earl of Bute as the king's chief minister in 1763, Scots were now very well placed indeed; four of the new governorships went to them.[56]

During the eighteenth century professional positions in the mainland colonies, ministers of religion, teachers, lawyers or doctors, were increasingly being filled by home-grown recruits. On the eve of the Revolution a lawyer in Massachusetts was likely to have been a graduate of either Yale or Harvard who had served his apprenticeship in the colony,[57] and only 10 per cent of those practising medicine in the province had come from overseas.[58] Lawyers in the south were nearly all colonial-born, even if many had studied for a time in the London Inns of Court. The clergy of most religious denominations were also likely to be Americans. There were, however, exceptions. Anglicans could only be ordained in Britain and many of the colonial clergy were still being drawn from England or from the Scottish Episcopal church. Presbyterian clergy were also coming to America from Scotland or from Ulster. Recent immigrants in holy orders, both Anglican and Presbyterian, were very prominent in the wave of new colonial colleges that were springing up in the mid-eighteenth century. People from Britain with ambitions to practise their professions overseas had a much more open field in the West Indies. An English training was a requisite for practising the law in the Jamaican courts. Many graduates from the Scottish medical schools went to the islands, often

---

[53] P. S. Haffenden, 'Colonial Appointments and Patronage under the Duke of Newcastle, 1724–39', *English Historical Review*, LXXVIII (1963), 417–35; J. H. Parry, 'The Patent Offices in the British West Indies', ibid. LXIX (1954), 200–25.

[54] See Col. J. Robertson's letter to Loudoun describing his ambitions for 'a little government' among other things, 28 Jan. 1763, HL, LO 6330.

[55] James A. Henretta, '*Salutary Neglect': Colonial Administration under the Duke of Newcastle* (Princeton, 1972), pp. 131–3.

[56] Douglas Hamilton, 'Patronage and Profit: Scottish Networks in the British West Indies c. 1763–1807', Aberdeen University Ph.D. thesis, 1999, p. 209.

[57] Charles R. McKirdy, 'Massachusetts Lawyers on the Eve of the American Revolution: The State of the Profession' in *Law in Colonial Massachusetts: Publications of the Colonial Society of Massachusetts*, LXII (1984), 316.

[58] Eric H. Christianson, 'The Medical Practitioners of Massachusetts, 1630–1800: Patterns of Change and Continuity' in *Medicine in Colonial Massachusetts 1620–1820*, ibid. LVII (1980), 56.

in hopes of eventually becoming planters.[59] The East India Company also offered outlets for people with medical qualifications. During the 1760s its establishment of surgeons in Bengal for the white civilian population rose to 40 with 28 more attached to the army.[60]

Ambitious individuals who lacked either the political influence realistically to aspire to public office overseas or professional qualifications that they could exploit in colonial societies could still try to make their fortunes in trade or in plantation agriculture. Although West Indian sugar plantations were highly capitalized undertakings, the mid-eighteenth-century Caribbean still attracted numerous ambitious, if usually impecunious, hopefuls who went to the islands as factors for British merchants, as doctors or as managers, clerks or overseers in established plantations, hoping eventually to become planters in their own right. Jamaica probably attracted some 50,000 white immigrants in the first half of the eighteenth century.[61] In spite of horrendous mortality rates, as a pamphlet put it, it was possible even for a person who arrived as an indentured servant 'by frugality and good behaviour' to acquire between ten or twenty slaves 'in a few years', although land was likely to be hard to get.[62] Shortage of land was considerably relieved by the islands added to the British empire in 1763. Scots were particularly prominent in settling these new Ceded Islands. 'The principal planters' in Tobago were said to be 'the younger sons of gentlemen of good families in Scotland, who have undertaken their settlements upon borrowed money'.[63] Many young Scots also went to the Chesapeake colonies. There they seem for the most part to have remained in trade, acting as the factors of the Glasgow tobacco houses before perhaps setting up businesses on their own, rather than acquiring large holdings of land and entering planter society. On the eve of the Revolution the Scottish community in Virginia and Maryland was an isolated and vulnerable one.[64] The northern ports, such as Philadelphia, attracted 'a steady influx of geographically and socially mobile English merchants', often young men who lacked the means to establish their own businesses at home.[65]

---

[59] Hamilton, 'Patronage and Profit', Ph.D. thesis, p. 120.

[60] D. G. Crawford, *History of the Indian Medical Service 1610–1913*, 2 vols. (1914), I. 201–2.

[61] Trevor Burnard, 'European Migration to Jamaica 1655–1780', *William and Mary Quarterly*, 3rd ser., LIII (1996), 777.

[62] *The Reasons for Keeping Guadeloupe at a Peace preferable to Canada explained in Five Letters* (1761), p. 35.

[63] Macartney to Germain, 12 Oct. 1777, cited E. M. Johnston, 'Grenada, 1775–79' in P. Roebuck, ed., *Macartney of Lisanoure 1737–1806: Essays in Biography* (Belfast, 1983), p. 100. For the Scots in the West Indies, see Hamilton, 'Patronage and Profit', Ph.D. thesis.

[64] Alan L. Karras, *Sojourners in the Sun: Scottish Migrants in Jamaica and the Chesapeake 1740–1800* (Ithaca, NY, 1993); T. M. Devine, *The Tobacco Lords: A Study of the Tobacco Merchants of Glasgow and their Trading Activities, c.1740–1790* (Edinburgh, 1975), p. 84.

[65] Doerflinger, *Vigorous Spirit of Enterprise*, p. 160.

British people willing to pursue mercantile careers could also try their luck in India. In the 1770s the majority of the East India Company's servants were to be engaged in administrative tasks in the territory recently brought under the Company's control; up to then, however, the Company's service was essentially a commercial one. The servants of the Company managed their employer's trade and had every opportunity to trade on their own by sea from the Indian ports where they were stationed. A number of 'free merchants' also lived in India as traders. Asian trade was a precarious business for foreign merchants, but spectacular profits could be made, especially by the Company's servants who asserted privileges over any competitors. This meant that entry into the service as a young 'writer' was a desirable appointment only to be obtained by those who had substantial influence with the Company's directors. The great spoils that were made from successful war and political intervention in the affairs of Indian states put an even higher premium on appointments and opened the Company to much political influence from the 1760s, but even in the 1720s the value attached to appointments in India meant that they were being used in political bargains, initially for Scotland.[66]

Africans were by far the largest group of migrants coming into eighteenth-century British America. Some 900,000 were carried across the Atlantic on British ships between 1750 and the outbreak of the American Revolution, at least a quarter of whom may have been passed on to foreign colonies.[67] This was a forced migration whose volume was no doubt determined by British slave traders' estimates of the numbers that they could sell in America and by the capacity of African merchants and rulers to supply slaves. Evidence that slave prices were generally rising from about 1750 suggests that demand may have been running ahead of supply, in spite of the great expansion in the volume of the trade. European migration to America was on an altogether smaller scale. By comparison with the seventeenth or the nineteenth centuries, the level of British migration to the Americas in the eighteenth century was at a relatively low level. An estimate for emigration from the British Isles to the thirteen colonies of North America for the years 1750 to 1775 gives a rough total of 143,000—some 45,000 from England and Wales, 29,000 from Scotland and 69,000 from Ireland.[68] In general, this seems to have been migration prompted by expectations rather than by desperation or by the compulsion likely to have been produced by strong demographic pressure on resources. Presumably only the 50,000 convicts were forced migrants in the

---

[66] G. K. McGilvary, 'East India Patronage and the Political Management of Scotland, 1720–1774', Open University Ph.D. thesis, 1989.

[67] See table in Richardson, 'Atlantic Slave Trade' in Marshall, ed., *Oxford History*, II. p, 442.

[68] Table in Horn, 'British Diaspora' in ibid. p. 32.

African sense, although some indentured servants may have seen very little alternative to selling their labour in the new world.

By the mid-eighteenth century British emigration throughout the empire was becoming British in the fullest sense.[69] The great majority of the servants exported to the new world in the seventeenth century had come from England. English servants were still crossing the Atlantic up to the American Revolution, but numerous Irish servants were also being shipped out and the majority of the families in search of land were coming from Lowland and Highland Scotland or from Ulster. The ambitious fortune seekers were also drawn from all parts of the British Isles. Scots were prominent as new West Indian planters, Chesapeake merchants, colonial governors, doctors and clerics, and they were beginning to establish a firm foothold in the East India Company's civil service and especially in its rapidly expanding military service. Imperial opportunities were crucial in Scotland for renewing 'the economic strength and resources of the old elite'. They saved 'non-inheriting younger sons' and 'their families from poverty and extinction'.[70] Irish Protestants were also competing effectively. The extent of the involvement in empire of one Irish Protestant family may be indicative of the way in which new prospects overseas were opening up for those trying to make their way in British society from its fringes. The great Edmund Burke, his brother Richard and his kinsman William cooperated very closely in trying to make their careers in Britain and in the British empire. Edmund hoped to become colonial agent for the West Indian Ceded Islands, was appointed agent for New York, but declined the post of head of a commission of supervisors to go to Bengal. Richard became collector of customs in Grenada and tried to buy land in St Vincent. William held a number of offices in the conquered West Indian island of Guadeloupe before it was restored to France under the 1763 peace. He hoped to be governor of Grenada, later became the London agent of the raja of Tanjore in south India and was eventually to spend most of the rest of his life in India as paymaster to the royal troops there. Richard and William, but probably not Edmund, had speculative interests in the stock of the East India Company which went disastrously wrong. Even Edmund's son, another Richard, inherited a tract of land on Prince Edward Island in Canada.[71]

---

[69] This theme is strongly brought out in Bowen, *Elites and Enterprise*, ch. 7, 'The End of the English Empire'.

[70] T. M. Devine, *Scotland's Empire 1600–1815* (2003), pp. 348–9.

[71] These transactions can be followed in Thomas W. Copeland, et al., eds., *The Correspondence of Edmund Burke*, 10 vols. (Cambridge, 1958–70).

III

The increasing diversity of immigration into British territories overseas by the mid-eighteenth century, huge numbers of Africans to the West Indies and North America, over 100,000 Germans to North America, and Scots and Irish everywhere, might suggest a dilution rather than an expansion of British values and cultural influences throughout the world, especially if these are interpreted as being essentially English ones. Ethnic diversity was not, however, fully reflected in cultural diversity overseas. Nearly all the Africans and many of at least the first generation of German and Catholic Irish or Highland Scottish migrants must of course have remained largely outside any conventional pale of 'Britishness'. On the other hand, powerful forces were tending towards a greater degree of integration among the peoples of the British Isles and among large sections of those already settled in the colonies. Integration was being brought about both by the increasing ambitions and capacity to act overseas of the British state, the subject of the following chapter, and by the way in which what were metropolitan values were being adopted as a common standard, even if subjected to local interpretation, throughout the British Isles, the West Indies, and the North American colonies and among the British in India. Some distinctively Scottish features reproduced themselves overseas: a speaker in 1754 in the General Assembly of the Church of Scotland, for instance, called American Presbyterians 'a part of ourselves having adopted the same standard of doctrine, worship and government with this church'.[72] Even so, the increasing adherence to metropolitan norms can be crudely characterized as 'Anglicization', that is as accepting English norms.

In March 1754 Robert Craigie, on his promotion to the Scottish court of session, assured lord Hardwicke, the lord chancellor in London, that he would do his best to follow in 'your Lordship's steps at however great distance to deliver this country [Scotland] from the arbitrary power of the great and the barbarity of our Highlands. Blessings which I think we have now a fair prospect I am perswaded and for which his Majesty and your lordship have blessings from this country to the latest posterity.'[73] Such sentiments were representative of a considerable body of opinion, well entrenched within the administration of Scotland but probably even including some Jacobites (even if they could hardly conceive of 'blessings' received from a Hanoverian king), which believed that the union of 1707 had not assimilated Scotland closely

---

[72] G. W. Pilcher, ed., *The Reverend Samuel Davies Abroad: The Diary of a Journey to England and Scotland, 1753–55* (Urbana, IL., 1967), p. 92.
[73] Letter of 13 March 1754, BL, Add MS 35448, f. 75.

enough to England and that the future lay in further assimilation. This would liberate Scotland from its past. Craigie's views illustrate the recent dictum that 'The North British periphery . . . tended to assert its right to be reformed and anglicized more often than the freedom to be spared the intervention of central government.'[74] Some British ministers, notably Hardwicke, were very willing to forward this work of producing a closer union based on the wider dissemination of English principles. Assimilation was to include language as well as law. In the Highlands the 'Irish' language should be forcibly suppressed as 'the stronghold of ignorance and rebellion'.[75] Through the study of polite English *belles-lettres* and rhetoric aspiring young Scots were to be taught a 'pure' English that avoided Scotticisms.[76]

Scottish opinion of this sort strongly supported the British government's measures to 'pacify' the Highlands after the '45 rebellion, disarming, abolishing the judicial powers of clan chiefs and redistributing confiscated estates. Private bodies, such as the Church of Scotland's Society for the Promotion of Christian Knowledge, which supported ten missionary ministers and 170 charity schools by 1765,[77] were also active in the work of assimilating the Highlands to the Lowlands and therefore to Britain. Whatever the practical effect of these bold measures, which proved difficult to apply, the Highlands gradually ceased to trouble British ministers as an area of disaffection. Encouraged by the massive recruitment into the British army and by accounts of stability and order, ministers were so convinced that a French landing during the Seven Years War would not set off a rebellion that they refused to countenance any pre-emptive seizure of chiefs of supposedly uncertain loyalty.[78] By 1773 they were urging that further measures to discourage Popery in the Highlands were no longer necessary.[79] The War of American Independence was to show that not only had Highlanders long since ceased to be a fifth column in Britain itself but that they had become a strong force for loyalism to the British crown in North America. Many recent Highland immigrants to America were to fight for the king in the war and then to take themselves to Canada rather than live in the new republic. 'Nowhere in Scotland was the link with the imperial project stronger than in Gaeldom'.[80]

[74] Colin Kidd, 'North Britishness and the Nature of Eighteenth-Century British Patriotisms', *Historical Journal*, XXXIX (1996), 365.
[75] 'Memorandum for my Lord Advocate Concerning the Highlands of Scotland' by Mr Webster [1755], BL, Add MS 35891, f. 47.
[76] Robert Crawford, *Devolving English Literature* (Oxford, 1992).
[77] Dr Walker's Report on the Highlands, May 1765, PRO, SP 54/45, ff. 605–7.
[78] Holdernesse to Lord G. Beauclerk, 1 Nov. 1759, ibid. f. 327.
[79] Suffolk to Cathcart, 7 June 1773, ibid. SP 54/46, f. 210.
[80] Devine, *Scotland's Empire*, p. 339.

Some 400,000 Protestants constituted about one-quarter of the mid-eighteenth century population of Ireland. The rest were Catholics. Irish Protestants were divided between adherents to the established Church of Ireland and Dissenters, of whom Prebyterians were by far the most numerous. They were also divided between a relatively small elite, perhaps some 5,000, overwhelmingly Church of Ireland, and a mass of poor, who 'like the generality of Catholics . . . constitute a hiden Ireland'.[81] In the early eighteenth century the Protestant elite who dominated the Irish parliament and filled those public offices not secured by Englishmen from England seem generally to have regarded themselves as English living in Ireland. A union with England seemed to be an attractive prospect for them. By mid-century resentment both at what seemed to be British governments' insistence that Ireland was a subordinate of England rather than a sister kingdom and at the evident unwillingness of the English upper classes to accept them as fellow English was producing a degree of alienation. To some historians, this alienation led the Protestant elite to envisage themselves as the embodiment of an 'Irish nation'.[82] Others emphasize 'the astonishing range of circumlocutions' to which Irish Protestants resorted in order to avoid the use of the term 'Irish', which was 'so long associated with Catholicism, disloyalty and cultural inferiority'.[83] Yet even if men might not be sure that 'they wanted to be *called* "Irish" . . . they increasingly felt that this was what they were, one way or another'.[84] Self-confessedly Irish or not, what is not in doubt is that the Protestant elite could combine an unswerving commitment to their English inheritance with a prickly defence of the historic rights of their Irish institutions, their parliament, their courts and their corporations. Although Dublin with its viceregal court was a major centre of artistic patronage, especially for architects, in essentials it followed English taste and that of London in particular. Its literary talent gravitated to England and reprinting English books was the major part of the business of its forty-six booksellers in 1760.[85]

Most Catholic landowners who had been able to maintain their position together with other Catholics of substance were willing formally to pledge

[81] Toby Barnard, *A New Anatomy of Ireland: The Irish Protestants, 1649–1770* (New Haven, 2003), pp. 14–20.

[82] Thomas Bartlett, *The Fall and Rise of the Irish Nation: The Catholic Question in Ireland, 1690–1830* (Dublin, 1992), pp. 34–7 and ' "This Famous Island set in a Virginian Sea": Ireland in the British Empire, 1690–1801' in Marshall, ed., *Oxford History*, II, pp. 259–62.

[83] S. J. Connolly, *Religion, Law and Power: The Making of Protestant Ireland 1660–1760* (Oxford, 1992), p. 120. Jacqueline Hill makes a similar point about the reluctance of Irish Patriots in mid-century to use the term 'Irish' (*From Patriots to Unionists: Dublin Civic Politics and Irish Protestant Patriotism, 1660–1840* (Oxford, 1997), p. 104).

[84] R. F. Foster, *Modern Ireland: 1600–1972* (1988), p. 178.

[85] Connolly, *Religion, Law, and Power*, p. 72.

loyalty to the house of Hanover during the Seven Years War.[86] They did so again in the War of the American Revolution. Some Catholic lords and gentlemen even offered to raise Catholic troops for the crown. Although Irish Protestant suspicions made acceptance of such offers a matter of great delicacy, the lord lieutenant thought that professions of loyalty should give the king and his British ministers 'the same satisfaction they have given me'.[87]

The disposition of the great mass of Catholics was from the British point of view quite another matter. Even Irish Catholics in London could be thought of 'as a body of reserve' for the French should they invade.[88] Lords lieutenant repeatedly wrote of the poverty and the ignorance (equated with their religious beliefs) of the Irish Catholics, of endemic disorder in great parts of the country and of the threat of rebellion in the event of a foreign invasion. The duke of Bedford warned in 1758 that if the French landed in the 'Popish and disaffected counties' they could 'transfer the seat of war from the their own coasts, into . . . the wild parts of Munster and Connaught'. At any time he thought that peace depended on military force.[89] 'In the westernmost parts of Cork and Kerry', according to lord Townshend writing in 1770, 'there are remains of the old Popish clans, who keep up a constant correspondence with France and Spain, for smuggling, for recruits and for our deserters. They are a very lawless people, mostly armed, frequently forming themselves into bandittis, defying law and magistrates and committing the greatest outrages.'[90] Studies of Irish-language material do indeed suggest unremitting hostility to English and Protestant domination and the tenacity of Jacobite loyalties, even during the War of the American Revolution.[91] Policies of active assimilation, practised, it was believed, with some success in the Highlands of Scotland, seemed to be wholly impractical with the much greater problem of the Irish Catholic masses. Opinion was split as to whether the Irish language should be discouraged as far as possible or used as a vehicle through which to try to inculcate Protestantism and civility. Doubts about the ultimate loyalty of the mass of poor Irish Catholics did not, however, inhibit increasing recruitment of them into the British army.

In Scotland Presbyterians constituted an established church and, at least as institutionalized in the General Assembly, were reliable allies of the British state. In Ireland Presbyterians were Dissenters, deeply mistrusted by the Anglican Church of Ireland, and viewed with increasing misgivings by secular

---

[86] David Dickson, *New Foundations: Ireland 1660–1800*, 2nd edn. (Dublin, 2000), p. 103.
[87] Halifax to Egremont, – Feb. 1762, PRO, SP 63/421, ff. 75–7.
[88] *Public Advertiser*, 2 Sept. 1755.
[89] Letter to Pitt, 29 Aug. 1758, Public Record Office, PRO, 30/8/19, ff. 46–7.
[90] Letter to Weymouth, 16 Oct. 1770, PRO, SP 63/432, f. 83.
[91] Vincent Morley, *Irish Opinion and the American Revolution, 1760–1783* (Cambridge, 2002).

authority, to whom they offered a 'dour incivility'.[92] In 1759 the duke of Bedford as lord lieutenant blamed riots in Dublin on 'the new light Presbyterians, or Twadlers. Their tenets both here, and (I am sorry to say it) in the North of Ireland, are totally republican and averse to English government.' They were as great a danger as the Papists.[93] Pitt replied from London that 'Presbyterian Dissenters' must be regarded as 'a very valuable branch of the Reformation' and as 'zealous supporters of the glorious Revolution under King William and of the present happy establishment'. They should be armed and encouraged to defend themselves.[94] Lords lieutenant were to find such injunctions increasingly unrealistic. Presbyterians were involved in the 'Hearts of Oak' or 'Oakboy' disturbances in seven counties of Ulster during 1763. From 1770 Ulster was again in a seriously disordered state. The lord lieutenant believed that the province must be disarmed and deployed troops there in 1772.[95] In revolutionary America most Ulster Presbyterians did not prove to be well disposed to the crown.

The white population of the British West Indies was very closely tied to Britain. Their dependence on British finance for their capital-intensive agriculture, on a protected British market for the sale of their chief crop, sugar, and on British armed force for the ultimate security of under 45,000 whites living in 1748 in the midst of a black slave population of nearly 260,000[96] gave them little option but to cherish these ties. They made a virtue, however, out of necessity. Although some could feel a genuine pride in what they had created in the islands,[97] they saw themselves as a British community living in temporary exile, whose roots were in the British Isles, not in the Caribbean. Up to the mid-eighteenth century the whites who went to the West Indies had been overwhelmingly English. Thereafter the number of Scots greatly increased, particularly in Jamaica and in the settlement of the Ceded Islands after 1763. These new acquisitions also brought a French element under British rule, especially in Grenada.[98] The French constituted a resident creole population, but the English and the Scots, with the partial exception of those

[92] S. J. Connolly, 'Ulster Presbyterians: Religion, Culture and Politics, 1660–1850' in H. Tyler Blethen and Curtis W. Wood, eds., *Ulster and North America: Transatlantic Perspectives on the Scotch–Irish* (Tuscaloosa, Ala., 1997), pp. 30–1.

[93] Letter to Pitt, 25 Dec. 1759, PRO, SP 63/416, f. 260.

[94] Letter of 5 Jan. 1760, ibid. 63/417, ff. 152–3.

[95] Townshend to Rochford, 11 March 1772, PRO, SP 63/435, f. 128.

[96] Richard B. Sheridan, 'The Formation of Caribbean Planter Society, 1689–1748' in Marshall, ed., *Oxford History*, II, p. 400.

[97] This was particularly marked in Barbados, see Jack P. Greene, 'Changing Identity in the British West Indies in the Early Modern Era: Barbados as a Case Study' in Greene, *Imperatives, Behaviors and Identities: Essays in Early American Cultural History* (Charlottesville, Va., 1992), pp. 13–67.

[98] British policy towards them is examined more fully below, pp. 187–8.

in Barbados, were 'reluctant creoles'.[99] They were a 'sojourning' community with a heavy male predominance, aiming to return home and to establish their families there rather than in the West Indies. Wherever possible, white children were sent home for schooling, thus reinforcing their identification with Britain. The number of West Indians who had been educated at the leading public schools or at British universities was much larger than the number of North Americans.[100] The sending home of children gave little scope for the development of schools and colleges in the islands. Visitors frequently complained of the lack of these or of other civic or cultural institutions. Such as there were reflected English dominance. Even if by default, the Church of England had a virtual monopoly of formal religious observance: there was no Presbyterian church for the numerous Scots before the nineteenth century.[101]

Close identification with Britain and the dominance of English values did not, however, preclude a sensitivity as acute as anywhere else in the British world to any supposed infringement of the rights of Englishmen living overseas and to what were taken to be the established constitutional privileges of the islands. The Jamaica assembly was particularly militant. Planters were inclined to regard their governors as 'animals come over here only to suck our blood'.[102] The assembly's defiance of the governor had drawn on it the censure of the house of commons in 1757.[103] In the 1760s it was to embark on a new dispute in which the governor believed that it was trying to claim 'the same powers and privileges as are enjoyed by the British house of commons', while the council was trying to imitate the house of lords.[104]

New patterns of immigration during the eighteenth century were producing increasing ethnic diversity in the thirteen British colonies of North America. New England and the white population of tidewater Virginia and Maryland remained predominantly English by extraction, but the middle colonies had received large inflows of Scottish, Irish and German migrants who were spilling into the interior backcountry of the colonies to the south as

[99] See Michael Craton, 'Reluctant Creoles: The Planters' World in the British West Indies' in Bailyn and Morgan, eds., *Strangers within the Realm*, pp. 314–62.

[100] Andrew Jackson O'Shaughnessy, *An Empire Divided: The American Revolution and the British Caribbean* (Philadelphia, 2000), pp. 19–27.

[101] Hamilton, 'Patronage and Profit', Ph.D. thesis, p. 64.

[102] S. Taylor to C. Arcedekne, 2 May 1767 in Betty Woods, ed., 'The Letters of Simon Taylor of Jamaica to Challenor Arcedekne, 1765–1775', *Travel, Trade and Power in the Atlantic 1765–1784: Camden Miscellany*, XXXV (2002), 44.

[103] See below, pp. 79–80.

[104] W. Lyttelton to Board of Trade, 13, 24 Oct. 1762, PRO, CO 137/32, ff. 209. 212. This dispute is analysed by Jack P. Greene in 'The Jamaica Privilege Controversy, 1764–66: An Episode in the Process of Constitutional Definition in the Early Modern British Empire', *Journal of Imperial and Commonwealth History*, XXII (1994), 16–53.

far down as South Carolina and Georgia. New non-English settlers were also entering the southern colonies by sea. As a result, New York had become a rough point of division: to the north, people of English origin predominated; to the south, they were in a minority.

Ethnic diversity further stimulated a religious diversity that was already deeply rooted in North America. Both the older denominations, the Church of England, the Congregationalists, the Quakers, and the Dutch Reformed, and newer ones, Presbyterians, Baptists, Lutherans, and the German Reformed, were able to strengthen their hold on the population of the colonies. Denominational expansion was, however, competitive. Powerfully aided from Britain, especially by the Society for the Propagation of the Gospel, who raised large sums of money and sent out numerous missionaries, the Anglican church in America expanded far beyond its original base in Virginia and Maryland and even began to make inroads into New England. By 1750 the number of Anglican congregations in North America had risen from some seventy-five at the beginning of the century to more than three hundred.[105] Other denominations saw themselves as under threat and acted accordingly. The bishop of London urged caution on American Anglicans in 1758 since 'The Dissenters in America are so closely connected with those in England', who were likely to raise their grievances in parliament.[106] Presbyterians, stimulated by a flow of ministers and college teachers from Scotland and from Ulster, organized themselves into presbyteries and synods to become a powerful force in the middle colonies, resisting supposed Anglican pretensions in New York in particular. New England Congregational divines, such as Jonathan Mayhew in his *Observations on the Charter and the Conduct of the Society for the Propagation of the Gospel in Foreign Parts* of 1763, sounded strident warnings about the expansion of episcopacy into America.

Denominational rivalry, above all conflict between Dissent and the Church of England, was to inject suspicion and bitterness into Anglo-American relations in the 1760s and 1770s. With the outbreak of the Revolution, militant Anglicans in Britain were to interpret sympathy with the colonial cause as part of a Dissenting plot against the Church.[107] In mid-century, however, rivalries were contained to some degree by a rhetoric of a common Protestantism in battle against Popery. The purpose of the Society for the Propagation of the Gospel, as stated by government ministers, was to counter the vigilance of 'Popish emissaries', who were constantly seeking to subvert

---

[105] Patricia V. Bonomi, *Under the Cope of Heaven: Religion, Society and Politics in Colonial America* (New York, 1986), p. 61.

[106] T. Secker to W. Johnson, 27 Sept. 1758, Lambeth Palace Library, MS 1123, no. 121.

[107] See below, p. 170.

Britain's subjects in America,[108] not to win over fellow Protestants to the Church of England. The Seven Years War, in which the Popish peril to British America seemed for a time only too real, was fought under this banner. Americans of all denominations were invoked in the London press as 'our Protestant brethren', engaged, along with that somewhat unlikely Protestant hero, Frederick of Prussia, in the common worldwide struggle against a cruel and oppressive Popery.[109] This was the spirit in which Americans fought the war. The Anglican William Smith appealed in 1756 in a fast sermon for the people of Pennsylvania to resist the French as '*Britons and Protestants*'.[110] The Presbyterian Samuel Davies gave thanks in 1761 for the life of George II whose forces had brought about 'the reduction of that mongrel race of *French* and *Indian* savages, who would have been the eternal enemies of humanity, peace, religion and *Britons*'. The late king had been 'the guardian of Christians in general . . . the defence of the dissenter as well as the conformist'.[111] When lord Loudoun, commander-in-chief of the British army in America,.visited Boston in 1757, on the same Sunday he attended an Anglican chapel and a Congregational meeting house, while inviting a Presbyterian to say grace at dinner.[112] Loudoun—a firm Presbyterian in Scotland but easily slipping into Anglicanism when in England—himself embodied the fraying of denominational boundaries in the Protestant cause.[113]

Many British Anglicans recognized that the Church in America could never be more than a minority outside the southern colonies in which it was established and that it must therefore coexist peacefully with Dissent rather than seeking further privileges. 'Christians of various denominations' had lived in British America from its 'very first establishment', according to the Anglican John Brown, preaching in 1763. The 'contending religious interests are nearly equal' and there was therefore no alternative to uniting 'on principles of religious freedom'.[114] Successive British ministries seem to have endorsed this view. They were not prepared to alienate powerful American Dissenting interests, which had direct access to them through their British allies,[115] by overtly favouring Anglicans, above all on the issue

[108] Printed letter from Newcastle to T. Herring, 30 Aug. 1751, Lambeth Palace Library, MS 1123, no. 53.

[109] Letter of 'A Briton', *London Chronicle*, 27–9 Oct. 1757.

[110] *Discourses on Several Public Occasions During the War in America* (1759), p. 76.

[111] *Sermon . . . On the death of his Late Majesty King George II* (Boston [1761]), pp. 21–2.

[112] E. Atkin to W. Lyttelton, 25 Jan. 1757, WLCL, Lyttelton MSS. For a cautious assessment of the role of religion in the Seven Years War, see Bob Harris, *Politics and the Nation: Britain in the Mid-Eighteenth Century* (Oxford, 2002), pp. 136–8. The importance of anti-Popery in North America seems, however, to be irrefutable.

[113] Information kindly supplied by Professor Allan I. Macinness and Dr Andrew Mackillop.

[114] *On Religious Liberty: A Sermon Preached at St Paul's* . . . (1763), pp. iii–iv.

[115] Alison G. Olson, 'The Eighteenth-Century Empire: The London Dissenters' Lobbies and the American Colonies', *Journal of American Studies*, XXVI (1992), 41–58.

of a colonial bishopric.[116] Thus militant anti-Popery and religious freedom
for all Protestants provided for the time being at least one of the strands in a
common sense of Britishness binding the thirteen colonies to Britain.

Recent scholarship has identified many other strands binding the elites of
the thirteen colonies more closely to Britain by the middle of the eighteenth
century.[117] British models of refinement were becoming both more accessible
and more attractive to North Americans. More and more people were
crossing the Atlantic in both ways, especially Americans coming to Britain
on business, for education, and as tourists for pleasure,[118] and more and more
British goods and British books were spreading ideas of British taste and right
British conduct for emulation in the colonies. From the mid-eighteenth
century, British booksellers became increasingly interested in exporting to
the colonies, shipping ever larger quantities across the Atlantic. They dominated the market for novels, *belles-letttres*, and learned books, leaving the
supply of cheap publications, such as almanacs or devotional texts, to local
enterprise.[119] Most of the readers of these imported books lived in the ports
from Boston to Charleston and on the great plantations of the south. There
they built town houses or country mansions in approved English styles, filled
them with either imported furniture or with the work of colonial craftsmen
following English patterns and cultivated polite ways of living instilled by
imported 'courtesy books'.[120] Polite living also involved polite learning and
striving for acceptance into a cosmopolitan world of science and letters whose
focal point inevitably for the colonies was London. Prized accolades were
those such as the verdict in 1760 of governor Bernard of Massachusetts on
Boston, that it was 'perhaps the most polished and scientific town in America.
I shall find there a good public library, many very conversible men, tolerable
musick and other amusements.' In general, however, Bernard believed that
there was too little 'liberal' and too much 'illiberal' learning in America.[121]

British influences were spreading beyond the elite through the capacity of
British goods carried by peddlers and chapmen to penetrate even the most

---

[116] See below, p. 171.

[117] For a recent counter to this trend, arguing that the colonies were becoming distinctively
'American', see Jon Butler, *Becoming America: The Revolution before 1776* (Cambridge, Mass., 2001).

[118] Julie M. Flavell, ' "The School for Modesty and Humility": Colonial American Youth in
London and their Parents, 1755–1775', *Historical Journal*, XLII (1999), 377–403.

[119] James Raven, 'The Importation of Books in the Eighteenth Century' in Hugh Amory and
David D. Hall, eds., *A History of the Book in America*, I, *The Colonial Book in the Atlantic World*
(Cambridge, 2000), pp. 183–98; Stephen Boiten, 'The Anglo-American Book Trade Before 1776' in
William L. Joyce, David D. Hall, Richard D. Brown and John B. Hench, eds., *Printing and Society
in Early America* (Worcester, Mass., 1983), pp. 48–82.

[120] Richard L. Bushman, *The Refinement of America: Persons, Houses, Cities* (New York, 1992) is
conspicuous in a large body of literature on such topics.

[121] To Barrington, 19 April 1760 and to Bishop of Bristol, 7 Jan. 1760, HUHL, Sparks MSS 4/1.

remote colonial markets from mid-century, creating in T. H. Breen's phrase, 'an empire of goods'.[122] Deliberate efforts were also made to diffuse British-ness through education. From the 1740s there was a spurt of new colleges and academies to cope with the greatly increasing population of the middle colonies. The dominant teachers in the new institutions tended to be recruited from Britain, above all from Scotland. The new colleges were concerned with imparting polite learning but often with a distinctly Scottish emphasis,[123] for instance, on English *belles-lettres*. William Smith, brought up an Episcopalian at Aberdeen, explained the purposes of the English school in the new college at Philadelphia. Pennsylvania 'being made up of so great a mixture of the people, from almost all corners of the world, necessarily speaking a variety of languages and dialects, the true pronunciation of our own language might soon be lost'. To prevent this, 'the pupils are taught the mother-tongue grammatically, together with a correct and just pronunci-ation'. They would study 'Spectators, Ramblers &c. for the improvement of style and knowledge of life'.[124] Smith was also active in an attempt to assimilate the Germans of Pennsylvania to British ways through education. Money was raised in Britain following an appeal launched in 1754 for schools to spread the use of English among the Germans. Smith described this as a project for 'incorporat[ing] and mingl[ing] them in equal privileges with the sons of freedom'. The archbishop of Canterbury agreed that it was a design 'as great and as necessary to be put into execution as any that was ever laid before the British nation'.[125]

Political discourse in the thirteen colonies was almost without exception British political discourse. There was a strong demand for British political writings, from the classics of the seventeenth-century Whig tradition to Blackstone's *Commentaries*. Loyalty to the Hanoverian monarchy and to the British constitution was unquestioned. Nevertheless, understandings of the British constitution were by no means uniform. 'Country' or 'court' positions could, for instance, be taken up on it. Events were to show that Americans could interpret the constitution in ways that would not be acceptable to dominant opinion in Britain.[126] Conflicts of interpretation between officials in London and opinion in the colonies were already surfacing in the late 1740s as the assemblies of New York and New Jersey seemed to be claiming unwarrantable powers over the government of their

[122] *Journal of British Studies*, XXV. 467–99.

[123] Douglas Sloan, *The Scottish Enlightenment and the American College Ideal* (New York, 1971).

[124] 'An Account of the College and Academy of Philadelphia', *Discourses*, pp. 218, 220–1, 225.

[125] Cited P. J. Marshall, 'Who Cared about the Thirteen Colonies? Some Evidence from Philanthropy', *Journal of Imperial and Commonwealth History*, XXVII (1999), 56.

[126] This theme is developed in Chap. 5.

colonies.[127] Like self-consciously British communities in Ireland or the West Indies, Americans were totally committed to what they believed to be their rights as British subjects under the British constitution as they understood it and saw the privileges of their representative bodies, the colonial assemblies, as an essential part of those rights.

The small British merchant communities on the West African coast in the first half of the eighteenth century inevitably made some concessions to the societies among which they lived in matters such as cohabitation with indigenous women. In return, African merchants with long experience of Europeans often learnt their languages, or at least 'pidgin' versions of them, lived partially in a European way and sometimes sent their children to school in Europe.[128]

The East India Company's servants in Indian ports tended to remain self-consciously British, maintaining Anglican churches and courts using English law in their larger settlements. Their ultimate objective was always to return home and to take their places in British society. Cohabitation with Indian women was, however, very common.

Large numbers of Indians lived within the major British settlements. Few of them are likely to have had any close dealings with Europeans or to have been assimilated in any degree to British ways. Whereas some Africans became Christians in the slave trading posts, virtually no Indian of social consequence was converted at this time. Even so, while keeping their cultural distance from Europeans, a number of them built up close business relations with the East India Company and with individual British merchants. They evidently learnt something of how British institutions worked. They seem to have been perceptive observers of rivalries within the East India Company's councils, which they understood how to exploit. They made use of the local British courts and some even pursued their claims against Europeans through courts in Britain. The right of a non-Christian to resort to the court of chancery was unequivocally established in 1744 as the result of a case brought by the great Indian merchant, Omichund, against his defaulting British partner.[129] This small cadre of Indians in Calcutta, Madras, and Bombay who were closely entwined with the British were shortly to play a very important role in the creation of a British empire in India.

---

[127] See below, p. 77.

[128] Robin Law and Kristin Mann, 'West Africa and the Atlantic Community: The Case of the Slave Coast', *William and Mary Quarterly*, 3rd ser., LVI (1999), 307–34.

[129] P. J. Marshall, ed., *The Writings and Speeches of Edmund Burke, VII, India: The Hastings Trial 1789–1794* (Oxford, 2000), p. 164.

IV

There are abundant indications of the dynamic nature of mid-eighteenth-century British expansion, in a wide sense, including commerce, migration and the diffusion of culture, in the Atlantic and in a narrower commercial sense in India. What connections can be drawn between these powerful currents of expansion and the making and unmaking of empire which is the theme of this book? At first sight, it would seem reasonable to suggest that in different environments they both made and unmade empires. It can plausibly be argued that in North America the rigidities of an existing empire were to be torn apart by the forces of expansion which imperial authority vainly tried to control, while in India commercial expansion brought about the crises with Indian political authority from which a new empire was to emerge. What follows will test these hypotheses.

Some connections between expansion and the overthrow of imperial authority in the thirteen colonies seem clear. Commercial expansion had produced relatively broad-based local economies in the North American colonies, capable of supporting the political ambitions of their peoples if they chose to unite and throw off British rule. The expansion of population had in the same way produced a human platform for a sustainable independence. By contrast the much narrower base of the West Indian economy and of civil society in the islands virtually precluded its white population from a break with Britain. Paradoxically, British cultural expansion, which can reasonably be presumed to have cemented links between Britain and the colonies, may also have helped to lay the groundwork for independence. The Anglicization of ethnically diverse peoples from separate colonies gave them a sense of unity, albeit a British one, on which a common American identity could later be built.[130] Expansion also influenced new British policies towards the colonies. Awareness of the remarkable growth of the mainland colonies left informed British opinion in no doubt of their immense value to the mother country and created apprehensions that unregulated growth would ultimately prove disastrous.[131] Political control must therefore be maintained and, if need be, made more effective. Dire consequences were to follow from attempts to do that.

If expansion made independence possible, it is, however, more difficult to argue that it provoked the crisis in relations with Britain out of which independence was born. The opposite may even have been the case. Many

---

[130] Breen, 'An Empire of Goods', p. 497.
[131] See below, pp. 273–4.

contemporaries thought that expansion was cementing the empire rather than undermining it. They believed that it was bringing the peoples of the British Atlantic into ever closer and more mutually profitable relations to one another. Such optimism was well founded, even if it underestimated the strains that rapid growth in so many respects was placing on transatlantic relationships.

The virtues of an expanding commerce in creating national grandeur and human felicity were widely extolled in Britain and in the colonies.[132] Commerce was believed to be a civilizing influence as well as a source of power. Ambitious merchants saw themselves as 'improvers', leading the advance 'from barbarism towards civility'.[133] Conventional wisdom was embodied in such sentiments as: 'The power attained either by policy, or arms, is but of short continuance, in comparison to what is acquired by trade. If we reflect on the reason of the thing, it will appear, that commerce is founded on industry and cherished by freedom.'[134] The freedom generated by commerce was assumed to be the distinguishing feature of Britain's relations with her colonies by comparison with the oppressive empires of the other European powers. Colonial American poets as well as British ones 'embraced the opportunity to view themselves as agents of a heroic enterprise linked to a global scheme of commerce'.[135]

On both sides of the Atlantic there were dissenting voices expressing alarm at what seemed to be the likely effects of the unrestrained growth of commerce. In Britain a shift in opinion has been detected from around the 1760s from panegyrics on merchants towards a concern for the excesses of 'upstart wealth'.[136] John Brown, a popular Anglican preacher, wrote a much reprinted jeremiad against 'effeminacy' and 'luxury' in 1757, the black year of the Seven Years War, which he called *An Estimate of the Manners and Principles of the Times*. He inveighed against 'the ruling maxim of this age and nation, that if our trade and wealth are but increased, we are powerful, happy and secure'. Moderate commerce was very desirable, but Britain now had 'an exorbitant degree of trade and wealth', which had sapped her military spirit.[137] Colonial American concerns about commercial excess seem to have surfaced at much

---

[132] For British views, see Jack P. Greene, 'Empire and Identity from the Glorious Revolution to the American Revolution' in Marshall, ed., *Oxford History*, II, pp. 215–17; Linda Colley, *Britons: Forging the Nation 1707–1837* (New Haven, 1992), pp. 56–66.

[133] Hancock, *Citizens of the World*, p. 16.

[134] John Harris, ed., *Navigantium atque Itinerantium Bibliotecha. Or a Complete Collection of Voyages and Travels*, 2 vols. (1764), I. vii.

[135] David S. Shields, *Oracles of Empire: Poetry, Politics and Commerce in British America 1690–1750* (Chicago, 1990), p. 25.

[136] James Raven, *Judging New Wealth: Popular Publishing and Responses to Commerce in England, 1750–1800* (Oxford, 1992), pp. 4–7.

[137] 6th edn. (1757), pp. 150–1, 181.

the same time, that is in the aftermath of the Seven Years War. The huge
volume of imported manufactured goods and the extent of colonial debts to
British creditors aroused particular anxieties. Virtue was being undermined by
luxury. These anxieties were to find a powerful outlet in the non-importation
campaigns of the 1760s and 1770s, when Americans displayed their civic
virtue by rejecting imported British luxuries.[138] Frugality and mistrust
of individual acquisitiveness emerged as important strands in republican
ideology.

Nevertheless, pride in the improvements being brought about by an
expanding commerce seems to have been the predominant note on both
sides of the Atlantic. Few seriously contemplated disengaging from it; for all
the aspirations of Spartan republicans, the American Revolution was certainly
not a rejection of commerce as such. To some historians it has, however,
seemed to be in part at least a revolution that aimed to take control of the
tidal wave of commercial expansion that since the 1740s had seemed to be
putting the colonies increasingly at the mercy of domineering British interests. Self-rule was needed to protect America from exploitation.

Even if the growth of the Atlantic economy had brought increased wealth
and opportunities for consumption to the white population of North America
as a whole, as earlier sections of this chapter tried to indicate, growth had not
been an even process: some had benefited more from it than others and many
had suffered in periods of recession, such as those that had followed the end of
the Seven Years War or the failure of the British banks in 1772. Those who felt
themselves to be losers might well be inclined to blame what seemed to them
to be the increasing domination of 'English capital and English decisions'
over colonial economies.[139] British capital in the form of credit was indeed
dominant in the colonial export trades, but as events were to show after
independence, British credit was the indispensable basis for the continuing
development of the economy of North America. The Revolution did not
bring the hegemony of British credit to an end, even if the British could no
longer seek to regulate the economy of the new republic, as they had done
in the past through the Navigation Acts with numerous later modifications
and through legislation on such matters as the production of metal goods or
the issue of colonial paper currency. The effect of such regulations on
the development of the thirteen colonies has been a staple of debate for
generations of historians. The current consensus of scholarly opinion seems

---

[138] T. H. Breen, ' "Baubles of Britain" ', *Past and Present*, CXIX. 73–104 and 'Narratives of
Commercial Life: Consumption, Ideology and Community on the Eve of the American Revolution', *William and Mary Quarterly*, 3rd ser., L (1993), 471–501.

[139] Marc Egnal and Joseph A. Ernst, 'An Economic Interpretation of the American Revolution',
William and Mary Quarterly, 3rd ser., XXIX (1972), 3.

overwhelmingly to be that, partly due to laxity of enforcement, the terms of the colonies' economic subordination did not have a significantly adverse effect on their development.[140] At least until the 1760s, most Americans seem to have accepted that their close connection with Britain in an Atlantic economy increasingly based on mutual interdependence was essential for their prosperity. They were joined with Britain in a common enterprise for improvement and civility. Any burdens imposed on them by British legislation, so long as it was administered with some flexibility and understanding of colonial needs, was a necessary price.

A recent assessment of the Revolution describes 'the demographic explosion', of which immigration was a major part, as 'the most basic and the most liberating force working on American society in the latter half of the eighteenth century'. 'The population outran the society's political institutions . . . The growth and movement of people strained and broke apart households, churches and neighborhoods.'[141] The challenge posed for the somewhat fragile institutions of imperial control over the North American colonies by the rapid growth of a population that was becoming both ethnically and religiously diverse and increasingly mobile in the search for land and employment is obvious. In the years before the Revolution challenges to local authority became overt and violent in the backcountries of North and South Carolina, on the Pennsylvania frontier, in rural New York, and in lands disputed between New York and the New England colonies. Port towns were also prone to disorder. Alarmists might believe that demographic change was making North America ungovernable. In reality this was only likely to be the case if imperial authority lost the acquiescence of the colonial elites.[142] For all the pressures from below to which they were periodically subjected by assertions of popular grievances, colonial elites were still generally able to continue to exercise effective control of an expanding population through the institutions of local government and through their dominance of the assemblies. Even in Pennsylvania and New York, the two colonies probably receiving the largest numbers of ethnically diverse new immigrants and with the most rapid spread of settlements into new areas, a narrow political 'oligarchy' was able to dominate the assemblies into the 1770s.[143] During the Revolution, as has recently been pointed out, 'those colonies which received

---

[140] e.g. the verdict in John J. McCusker and Russell R. Menard, *The Economy of British America, 1607–1789* (Chapel Hill, NC, 1985), p. 354.

[141] Gordon S. Wood, *The Radicalism of the American Revolution* (New York, 1991), pp. 128–9.

[142] This argument is developed in the essays by Jack P. Greene in *Negotiated Authorities: Essays in Colonial Political and Constitutional History* (Charlottesville, Va., 1994).

[143] Alan Tully, *Forming American Politics: Ideals, Interests and Institutions in Colonial New York and Pennsylvania* (Baltimore, 1994), ch. 9.

migrants at the highest rate were those least likely' to rebel.[144] The challenge to the empire was at first to come not from an ungovernable people but from the disaffection of the elites.

There were objections to transported convicts, but otherwise colonial opinion seems to have been confident about absorbing new elements into the population, be they Scottish, Irish, or German, so long as they were Protestants. Africans were another matter. During this period, the mainland colonies never experienced slave resistance in any way approaching the great rising of 1760 under 'Captain Tacky' in Jamaica, when ninety whites were killed. White North Americans were generally 'complacent about the prospect of collective slave violence', even though there were periodic outbreaks of 'near hysterical' fear about it.[145] Ideals of patriarchy, involving 'protection, guardianship, and reciprocal obligation' eased consciences over the enslaving of Africans.[146] In the lower South planters came to pride themselves on their humanity towards their slaves.[147] Nevertheless, the increasing Africanization of American society was viewed with misgiving. For some it was one of the excesses of commerce. The Virginia radical Arthur Lee felt so strong a dislike of slavery and of Africans that he dreaded returning from England, 'the land of liberty and independence', to a dependent and corrupt America.[148] As the African population began to reproduce itself, dependence on the British slave trade declined. Even so an increasingly vocal movement against the slave trade came into being. Northern colonies and even Virginia and Maryland tried either to prohibit slave imports or to restrict them by heavy duties. Imports continued, however, at a high rate in South Carolina and Georgia. The institution of slavery was being challenged by Pennsylvania Quakers in the 1750s, while sections of British opinion were also beginning to turn against slavery[149] and to harbour derogatory views about the Americans in general for indulging in it. In 1766 William Warburton, bishop of Gloucester, branded Americans as 'sincere worshippers of mammon' for claiming a right of property over human beings.[150] Yet, whatever the reservations it may have been arousing, slavery was still undergoing a dynamic expansion in North America right up to the outbreak of the Revolution, which left it still dominant in its southern heartlands.

---

[144] Alison Games, 'Migration' in David Armitage and Michael J. Braddick, eds., *The British Atlantic World, 1500–1800* (2002), p. 47.

[145] Morgan, *Slave Counterpoint*, pp. 385–6.   [146] Ibid. pp. 258–9.

[147] Chaplin, *An Anxious Pursuit*, pp. 55–65.

[148] Letter to R. H. Lee, 20 March 1765, Lee Family Papers, University of Virginia microfilm, 1714.

[149] See below, p. 195.

[150] Cited in David Brion Davis, *The Problem of Slavery in Western Culture* (Ithaca, NY, 1966), p. 380.

The increasing diffusion of British cultural influences among the colonial populations might at first sight be supposed to have helped to strengthen the bonds of empire. So it no doubt did, but the enthusiasm for empire which it stimulated in North America was likely to be for an empire as American rather than British opinion conceived it. Anglicization did not necessarily imply unquestioning acceptance of metropolitan authority. On constitutional issues, in particular, there was no single definition of what was British or English. People living in the colonies developed their own interpretations. For them, Englishness and the subordination of free white men to any authority to which they had not consented were incompatible. Consent was defined more literally than in contemporary Britain. Thus colonial autonomies were defended in terms of the constitutional rights of Englishmen. The English constitution provided an ideal standard against which the incursions of governors, ministers or even ultimately of parliament itself could be measured and condemned. The modern English could be shown to have degenerated through luxury and the corruption of political life from the virtue of their ancestors. The Virginia gentry, for instance, were inclined to believe that they embodied the true qualities of the independence and public spirit of the English gentry of yore, qualities lost in the present generation at home.[151] In short, increasing identification with British values instilled loyalty to Britain, but it was a strictly conditional loyalty to a Britain appropriate to colonial peoples' own imagining. The potential for disillusion with what was thought to be an actual Britain clearly existed, but it required new British political initiatives in the 1760s to produce a deep sense of alienation.

Expansive impulses emanating both from different parts of the British Isles and from within the colonies were generating new wealth, resettling large numbers of people across the ocean and extending the influence of British ideas around the Atlantic at an accelerated pace from the 1740s. Three decades of rapid expansion made it possible for Americans to contemplate independence as a possibility by 1776. It does not, however, necessarily follow from that proposition that expansion had unleashed forces within the North American colonies that were driving them towards a break with Britain. Rapid change had been unsettling and left discontents and casualties in its wake. Most of those casualties were probably the inarticulate and powerless, such as transported convicts, enslaved Africans or displaced Native Americans, who, except on occasions like the Pontiac rising of 1763–5 or in the

---

[151] Michal J. Rozbicki, *The Complete Colonial Gentleman: Cultural Legitimacy in Plantation America* (Charlottesville, Va., 1998).

periodic disorders in the port towns, could not protest effectively.[152] Some of the relatively rich and powerful, such as hard-pressed Virginia tobacco planters, also felt themselves damaged by change. But the majority of the elites and a great range of other members of white society in North America had prospered from expansion and had high expectations of greater prosperity yet within an imperial framework.

Nor is there much to suggest that developments since the 1740s were driving Britons and Americans apart. Expansion was probably, in fact, producing closer integration between colonies and metropole. More and more people were crossing the Atlantic, as migrants from Britain seeking new lives in America, as merchants and their agents transacting an ever increasing volume of trade, as American students sent for education to Britain or as British soldiers and sailors in the forces of the crown. Americans and Britons were sharing common tastes and were reading the same books and much the same news in their respective newspapers.

Closer integration had a potential for conflict. The British presence in the colonies was becoming more intrusive. The growing number of British and notably of Scottish commercial factors, especially on the Chesapeake, aroused resentment. British speculators' interest in American land might be regarded as unfair and unwelcome competition. For Franklin, grants to exploit American resources made to British investors deprived Americans 'of the advantage God and nature seem to have intended us'.[153] Americans resented the designs of British placemen on colonial offices and were somewhat equivocal about the presence of large numbers of British regular troops on the continent in peacetime.

Exasperated Americans often felt that closer British involvement in the colonies was doing nothing to dispel what they regarded as the abysmal ignorance about them in Britain. Indeed, the tales of ill-disposed sojourners in America were thought to reinforce derogatory stereotypes about the people of the colonies as, in Franklin's words, a *'mixed rabble of Scotch, Irish and foreign vagabonds, descendants of convicts'*.[154] 'There was not a cobbler in the kingdom', wrote a visiting Virginian in 1766, 'but considered the Americans as indentured servants or convicts.'[155] Events were to show that Americans' anxieties as to how they were envisaged in Britain were well founded. Wide

---

[152] For the turbulence of the dispossessed see Marcus Rediker and Peter Linebaugh, *The Many-Headed Hydra: Sailors, Slaves, Commoners and the Hidden History of the Revolutionary Atlantic* (2000).

[153] To P. Collinson, 30 April 1764, Leonard. W. Labaree, et al., eds., *Papers of Benjamin Franklin* (New Haven, 1959–), XI. 182.

[154] Cited in Greene, 'Empire and Identity' in Marshall, ed., *Oxford History*, II, p. 225; See also Rozbicki, *Complete Colonial Gentleman*, pp. 81–101.

[155] E. Jenings to R. Beverley, 2 April 1766, Virginia Historical Society, MS J 4105a 1.

sections of British opinion seemed to regard American resistance from the mid-1760s, not as the justified rejection of oppression by fellow Britons, but as the disobedience of recalcitrant subjects.

For all the possibilities of friction and misunderstanding, expansion since the 1740s was helping to consolidate those who lived on both sides of the Atlantic into something like a single British community or perhaps more precisely into a series of closely linked British communities that spanned the Atlantic. There were communities based on those who had left particular parts of the British Isles and those who had stayed behind, on commerce, or on religious denominations who supported one another's interests. The work of Alison Gilbert Olson has revealed powerful networks of transatlantic interest groups functioning effectively in mid-century.[156] Families on both sides of the Atlantic were brought together by Anglo–American marriages. Good feeling towards the people of the colonies is suggested by the willingness of people in Britain to subscribe large sums of money for American philanthropic causes: the founding of Georgia, the work of the Society for the Propagation of the Gospel in Foreign Parts, missions to Native Americans, schools for Africans, schools for Germans, the rebuilding of Charleston after the great fire of 1740, and at least fourteen appeals by colonial colleges.[157]

On balance, therefore, expansion seems to have drawn the people of the North American colonies closer to Britain rather than alienating them. To explain the unmaking of empire we therefore need to look beyond the teeming world of private enterprise and the circulation of goods, people and ideas and look also at the world of imperial politics and the role of the British state.

Seen only as an instrument for the civil government of an empire, it is easy to underestimate the British state with its fragmented bureaucracy at home and its often ineffectual governors overseas. In the conduct of war, the British state was, however, much more formidable. The scale of the war that the British waged on the American continent from 1754 to 1760 and of the territorial gains made in 1763 had a profound effect on both sides of the Atlantic. One of their consequences was to stimulate successive British governments to introduce measures to reform the imperial connection and to enforce what they regarded as an acceptable pattern of empire. These measures set off the Anglo-American crisis. The role of the British state overseas will therefore be the theme of the next chapter.

---

[156] *Making the Empire Work: London and American Interest Groups 1690–1790* (Cambridge Mass., 1992).

[157] Marshall, 'Evidence from Philanthropy', *Journal of Imperial and Commonwealth History,* XXVII, 53–67.

V

Questions about the connections between expansion and political change are relevant to India as well as to America, even though the outcome was entirely different there. In the 1760s and 1770s, while an empire in America was disintegrating, an empire was being consolidated in eastern India. Did this new empire grow out of earlier pressures of British expansion, in the case of India almost exclusively commercial pressures?

The existence of some connection seems self-evident. Empire first came into being in parts of India—the south-east or Coromandel coast, Bengal and the port of Surat on the west coast—where British commerce, both that of the East India Company and that of private British merchants, was already well established. Trade and politics in eighteenth-century India were very closely linked. The East India Company had never been a wholly peaceable trading body. It maintained naval and military forces that could be used to weaken competitors or to extract commercial gains from local rulers where opportunities to do so existed. Successful European trade depended on a favourable political environment in which Indian rulers maintained order, limited their demands on foreign merchants and granted them privileges to establish autonomous settlements and move their goods freely. From the rulers' point of view, foreign merchants were generally welcome for the wealth that they generated, but claims of excessive immunities and privileges were likely to be resented.

The relationship between Indian states and British merchants was thus potentially an unstable one at the best of times and a case can certainly be made that it was becoming dangerously unstable by the middle of the eighteenth century. On the Coromandel coast and at Surat the British complained with some justification that rulers could no longer maintain order and that economic life was being disrupted to the detriment of their trade. In 1744 the British at Madras, their main settlement on the Coromandel coast, deplored 'the present distracted state of the country which has been so miserably harrass'd for many years past'.[158] In Bengal strong rulers generally maintained control, but the British believed that they were becoming increasingly rapacious in their demands on all merchants, including themselves.[159] At a time

---

[158] To Directors, 5 Sept. 1744, *Records of Fort St George: Despatches to England 1743–1746* (Madras, 1931), p. 20. For an authoritative verdict on conditions, see S. Arasaratnam, *Merchants, Companies and Commerce on the Coromandel Coast, 1650–1740* (New Delhi, 1986), pp. 164–212.

[159] P. J. Marshall, *New Cambridge History of India*, II, *Bengal: The British Bridgehead; Eastern India 1740–1818* (Cambridge, 1987), pp. 71–2; for a more sceptical view of the difficulties in Bengal, see Sushil Chaudhury, *From Prosperity to Decline: Eighteenth Century Bengal* (New Delhi, 1995).

when the Company's Indian trade was relatively stagnant and private merchants were also complaining about bad times,[160] the case for trying to bring
about a more favourable commercial environment through political intervention seemed to be an attractive one. It was made the more attractive by the
prospect of enormous gains for individuals out of political adventures. Indian
rulers could be expected to pay hugely for British military support.

For their part, the rulers of Bengal, its nawabs, were particularly concerned
at the growth of the British stake in their province. Calcutta had attracted a
large Indian population, including many wealthy merchants who lived under
British authority, out of the reach of the nawab, now effectively provincial
ruler. Neither the Indians of Calcutta nor the British themselves contributed
significantly to the nawabs' taxation. The British appeared to be fortifying
Calcutta and to be openly defying the nawabs' government. There was a clear
case for curbing their pretensions.

Chapter 4 shows how the unstable situations created by British commercial
expansion degenerated into conflicts from which the British emerged victorious with striking political gains that greatly enhanced their commercial stake
in India and made fortunes for individuals. In Surat a naval expedition from
Bombay took over the administration of the port from the Mughal governor
in 1759.[161] On the Coromandel coast the British allied with a contender for
authority over the newly-created province of the Carnatic, supporting him
against his Indian rivals and against the French and in return extracting grants
of weaving villages and territory that would pay revenue to the Company. By
the end of a long series of wars, the British-backed claimant to the Carnatic
had become nawab under the Company's protection and was paying heavily
for that protection. In Bengal the nawab was finally provoked into trying to
impose a proper subordination on the British and then into attacking and
taking Calcutta in 1756. An expedition from Madras under Robert Clive
recovered the city. He then conspired with the Indian enemies of the nawab
to bring him down and replace him. The replacement quickly proved to be a
British puppet. He was himself displaced and other changes ensured that an
indigenous government in any way independent of the British would not be

---

[160] Figures for the value of Company's shipments are given by K. N. Chaudhuri, *Trading World
of Asia*, table on p. 510. For indications of decline or stagnation in private trade, see Marshall, *East
Indian Fortunes*, pp. 90–7.

[161] For the increasing British stake in Surat, see Ashin Das Gupta, *Indian Merchants and the
Decline of Surat c.1700–1750* (Weisbaden, 1979), ch. 5. For differing interpretations of events there,
see the articles of Michelgugliemo Torri, 'Trapped inside the Colonial Order: Hindu Bankers of
Surat and their Business World During the Second Half of the Eighteenth Century', *Modern Asian
Studies*, XXV (1991), 367–401 and 'Mughal Nobles, Indian Merchants and the Beginning of British
Conquest in Western India: The Case of Surat, 1756–1759', ibid. XXXII (1998), 257–316; Lakshmi
Subramanian, *Indigenous Capital and Imperial Expansion; Bombay, Surat and the West Coast* (Delhi,
1996).

able to survive. Effective authority was transferred to the East India Company in 1765. The foundations of territorial empire had been laid.

An interpretation that explains the creation of empire in India in terms of expansive British commercial ambitions that succeeded in breaking through the constraints imposed by Indian political authority and in creating a new order sympathetic to British interests clearly has much to commend it. Yet, as later sections of this book will try to show, it is an incomplete interpretation of the great changes that took place in India at this time. The eventual outcome involved much more sweeping changes than might have been anticipated from the successful political intervention of an armed trading concern. In Java and Ceylon the Dutch had used political power to subordinate indigenous regimes for commercial and fiscal purposes, not to create an empire of direct Dutch rule. By the 1780s British people were drawing sharp contrasts between their own 'empire' in Asia and the commercial concerns of the Dutch.[162] Yet deeper British political involvement in one of its major Indian spheres, the Madras presidency, had at first followed the Dutch pattern. Outright territorial gains were limited, while a client ruler granted commercial privileges and was required to make large payments in return for protection. In Bengal, however, an entirely different kind of regime was being created by the 1770s. This was a regime claiming an absolute sovereignty for Britain over a directly administered province and with a huge revenue from taxation at its disposal and a great army at its command. Commerce was becoming a secondary objective.

The differing courses followed by the British at Madras and Bengal will be analysed in detail in later parts of this book.[163] A brief explanation would be that in Bengal the British inherited a centralized indigenous state with a structure through which they could impose their direct authority with relative ease. They had neither the need nor the inclination to preserve Bengal's Indian rulers. Relations between the Company and the Bengal nawabs had been consistently bitter, culminating in the sack of Calcutta in 1756. It was a British commonplace to argue that the Company must either be sovereign in Bengal or exist at the mercy of a brutal and unpredictable tyrant. In the south there was no comparable state structure and so the Company had no real alternative to working through the nawab of the Carnatic who was endeavouring to extend his authority over largely unincorporated local powers. In spite of much mistrust on both sides, a working relationship existed between the nawab and the Madras servants. Yet if the circumstances were propitious for a direct British take-over in Bengal, there was also an ideological

---

[162] P. J. Marshall, 'The British State Overseas, 1750–1850' in Bob Moore and Henk Van Nierop, eds., *Colonial Empires Compared: Britain and the Netherlands, 1750–1850* (Aldershot, 2003), p. 171.
[163] See below, pp. 146–51 and Chap. 8.

dimension to this take-over. The regime in Bengal embodied ideals of empire, based on an unfettered sovereignty, that were current throughout the British world. In Bengal the British were able to give free rein to such ideals.

Aspirations to empire in India came initially from British people already there rather than from Britain itself. The Company's senior servants saw India as a theatre in which Britain's national grandeur was being established by their efforts and where they were turning the Company's territories, beginning with those in Bengal, into an integral part of the British empire. In time the British state became involved in the new empire. Comparison with the Dutch is again instructive. The forces of the Dutch state were not deployed on a large scale in Asia until 1784. The Republic made no claim to the territorial rights acquired by the Dutch Company and that Company was in no significant way accountable to the state, certainly not to the States General. The British state behaved very differently. Royal regiments and warships played a decisive role in wars in India from 1748. Even though issues of sovereignty were not formally resolved, the Company's new possessions quickly came to be regarded as a national asset and how the Company conducted itself became a matter for parliamentary inquiry and regulation. Dutch Asian possessions remained the private fief of the Company; British Indian possessions were incorporated into the British empire.

Thus in India as well as in North America, the British state, through its capacity to wage war and through the concepts of empire that it sought to impose throughout the world, had a major role in the making and unmaking of empire. The next chapter will be concerned with the capacities of that state to operate overseas.

2
State and Empire

THE previous chapter was concerned with British worldwide 'expansion', defined as activities overseas by private individuals or groups. It dealt with trade, the movement of people and the diffusion of culture. It traced a pattern of accelerating expansion around the Atlantic, beginning in the 1740s and continuing with some fluctuations until the outbreak of the American Revolution. A narrower definition of 'expansion', largely confining it to trade, can also be applied to the British presence in India in this period.

The chapter ended with an attempt to assess the relationship between expansion and the unmaking and making of empires. In the thirteen colonies the framework of British imperial authority was put under stress by the need to adjust to rapid change, and conditions were coming about that would eventually make independence feasible, but the immediate effect of expansion seems generally to have been to consolidate links across the Atlantic and to weld self-consciously British communities closer together. These links were only to be ruptured by rebellion and war after several years of attempts by British governments to reform and strengthen the imperial framework. Increasing intervention by the British state to remake empire was to end by destroying it.

In India, on the other hand, the last chapter argued that a plausible connection can be drawn between commercial expansion and political change. It suggested that the uneasy coexistence between the needs and ambitions of a vigorous British commerce and those of the rulers of some of the successor states to the Mughals was breaking down in mid-century. It was becoming increasingly tempting for both sides to try to impose a new pattern of relations. The new pattern was to be determined by the power of the British and in Bengal was to take the form of an empire of rule over territory over which the East India Company claimed sovereign authority. Commercial expansion may have provided the incentive for political intervention in the name of the Company, largely by its agents. The British state, however, increasingly intervened in sustaining and trying to regulate the new empire.

Since the state had a major role in the story of both the unmaking of empire in North America and the making of empire in Asia, this chapter will be concerned with the imperial ambitions and the capacities of the eighteenth-century British state. War from the 1750s to the early 1760s did much to bring about change in both North America and India. War in the 1770s and early 1780s ended in British defeat in America but British survival in India. This chapter will therefore begin with an assessment of the military capacity of the British state.

I

Historians have for long assumed, as contemporaries were inclined to do, that the eighteenth-century British state, subject to parliament and accountable to the law, was a weak one by comparison with authoritarian continental states. This is now contested. In some areas at least, the eighteenth-century British state seems to have been a formidable one by contemporary standards. Recent historiography has above all focused on its highly developed capacity to make war. In the second half of the eighteenth century the British began to deploy more and more of their military and naval resources throughout the world in defence of their own colonies and to conquer those of their enemies. It was primarily through its capacity to wage successful war and the subsequent policies that it devised to defend its gains that the British state shaped the evolution of empire.

What can be regarded as imperial claims on Britain's military resources always had to compete with other claims usually deemed to be more urgent. worldwide commitments never displaced domestic and European ones. At times during both the Seven Years War and the War of American Independence Britain seemed to be in dire danger of invasion; home defence was therefore the first claim on its armed forces. In the Seven Years War Britain maintained an army in Germany, raided the coast of France, intervened in Portugal, and tried unsuccessfully to defend Minorca. During the American War continental commitments were limited to the defence of Gibraltar and Minorca.

Although commitments to home defence, to Europe and to the control of the European seas remained of the utmost importance in both wars, the scale of British deployments outside Europe reached unprecedented levels. In the major campaigns of the Seven Years War more than 20,000 British regulars served in North America. In 1778 at the height of British attempts to subdue the colonies, over 50,000 men were again committed in North America.[1]

---

[1] Piers Mackesy, *The War for America 1775–1783* (1964), pp. 524–5.

These deployments of troops were supported by naval squadrons. In both wars significant detachments of troops and warships were also sent to India and to the West Indies, which became the major overseas theatre of war after 1760 and again after 1778; nearly half the navy was posted there in the last year of the American War.

New overseas theatres were thus a significant element in the escalating demands that the two wars made on British manpower and on British public finance. Approximate estimates indicate that the number of men under arms in each year of war rose from nearly 113,000 for the Austrian Succession War of 1739 to 1748 to 167,000 for the Seven Years War and 190,000 for the American War. Another calculation suggests that one in nine or ten of all British males of military age may have been involved in some sort of military service in the Seven Years War and one in seven or eight in the American War, whereas the ratio for the Austrian Succession War had been one in sixteen. The annual average cost of war grew spectacularly: from about £8,750,000 during the Austrian Succession War to over £18 million in the Seven Years War and over £20 million in the American War.[2] From the 1760s the military and naval costs of empire born by the British state in peacetime also rose sharply with the augmentation of the garrisons kept permanently in the West Indies and North America.

Any attempt to determine the precise proportion of the British state's pouring out of men and money in war and peacetime defence that can be attributed to Britain's imperial ambitions runs into intractable difficulties for this period, as for any other. The price of empire cannot be precisely quantified because imperial commitments cannot be strictly defined. It is, for instance, hardly possible to separate the imperial element of expenditure on a navy predominantly stationed in the Western Approaches of the English Channel, where it could both protect the British Isles from invasion, inhibit French transoceanic trade and cut off enemy squadrons intended for operations against British oceanic trade or colonies.[3] Whatever the proportion of money and men that can, however, be attributed to worldwide objectives in the eighteenth century, in most circumstances, this required the raising of additional resources. With the exception of phases of the War of American Independence, war outside Europe did not involve a major diversion of resources away from home defence or continental commitments, as many

[2] Figures taken from John Brewer, *The Sinews of Power: War, Money and the English State* (1989), p. 30. The estimates of the involvement of males of military age are those of Stephen Conway in *The British Isles and the War of American Independence* (Oxford, 2000), pp. 28–9.

[3] N. A. M. Rodger, 'Sea-Power and Empire, 1688–1793' in P. J. Marshall, ed., *The Oxford History of the British Empire*, II, *The Eighteenth Century*, (Oxford, 1998), pp. 174–9.

contemporaries hoped might be the case. It was an additional burden on Britain's finances and manpower.

II

As the rough estimates given above clearly indicate, although British govern-ments were able to involve an increasing proportion of the population of the British Isles in military activity during wars, they found it easier to raise money than to raise men. Increasing the size of the army was particularly difficult: it was roughly the same size during the Seven Years War that it had been in the War of the Spanish Succession at the beginning of the century.[4] Figures for the regular army alone are misleading, since they do not include men raised for home defence through the militia. Yet even allowing for up to 40,000 militia, rising perhaps to 60,000 in the last years of the American War,[5] military planners never felt that they had adequate numbers of British troops available for the commitments that they faced. The army was under pressure not to drain too many men from what were judged to be vital civil occupations and in any case the pay and conditions that it offered did not make it an effective competitor with other employments, except in times of trade recession or unless expensive additional bounties were paid to lure in recruits. Powers for limited periods could be taken by act of parliament to conscript the able-bodied unemployed or paupers. These powers were rigor-ously applied in Scotland during the Seven Years War, but seem to have been sparingly used in England.[6] Official policy was in any case generally unen-thusiastic about coercive measures. The dilemma facing the army was cogently expressed by the long-serving secretary at war, lord Barrington, at the height of the Seven Years War in 1759. He felt that about 150,000 'British subjects in red coats' were needed for the army, the marines and the militia, but feared that 'we have not the means of keeping up so large a body of men by volunteers; and I never think of compulsive methods, being of opinion that they do more harm than good in this country.'[7] At the height of the American War in 1780, the army was short of its establishment by 27,000 men.[8]

---

[4] Brewer, *Sinews of Power*, p. 30.   [5] Conway, *British Isles*, p. 28.
[6] For impressment in the Seven Years War, see Stephen Brumwell, *Redcoats: The British Soldier and War in the Americas, 1755–1763* (Cambridge, 2002), pp. 63–6.
[7] To Newcastle, [Nov. 1759], Tony Hayter, ed., *An Eighteenth-Century Secretary at War: The Papers of William, Viscount Barrington* (1988), p. 53.
[8] Mackesy, *War for America*, p. 368.

The navy also had serious manning problems, especially at the beginning of wars. Yet it was generally more successful than the army at meeting its commitments. The manning situation for the navy in the Seven Years War has been called 'one of protracted difficulty rather than of failure'.[9] By the end of the American War the navy was able to recruit in excess of its establishment.[10] It seems to have enjoyed rather more competitive advantages with comparable civilian employments than the army and had a much more developed system of coercive powers to impress men.[11] In general, however, the authority that the eighteenth-century British state could exert over resources of native British manpower for both the army and the navy was a limited one. Manpower was therefore sought from many non-British sources.

In 1762 a British expedition was sent from Madras in southern India to take the rich Spanish settlement of Manila in the Philippines. It was a wildly heterogeneous body. The main striking force was a regular regiment of the British army. The supporting troops were small contingents of the royal and East India Company's artillery, some of the Company's European infantry, most of whom were French and German deserters from the defeated French army in India, a contingent of 'Cofferys' or African slave soldiers recruited by the Company, a large body of scarcely trained Indian sepoys in the Company's service and a small party of 'irregulars' in the service of an Indian prince, the nawab of Arcot.[12] The commander of the force observed that 'such banditti were never assembled since the time of Spartacus' and that 'sepoys, caffrees, lascars [Indian artillerymen], French and German deserters are but a precious tribe to build honour upon'.[13] The composition of the Manila force may have been an extreme example, but it was indicative of problems facing British commanders all over the world. British troops were likely to be in very short supply and men of all sorts had to be raised to supplement them.

British governments sought new sources of recruits, initially from sections of the population of the British Isles traditionally regarded as disloyal to the Hanoverian state. In 1757 the army in North America was reinforced by two Highland regiments raised in quick time. Even though it was supposed, improbably given the age of the majority of them, that most of the men

---

[9] N. A. M. Rodger, *The Wooden World: An Anatomy of the Georgian Navy* (1986), p. 152.

[10] Conway, *British Isles*, p. 18.

[11] Rodger, *Wooden World*, pp. 145–251. Cf. the interpretation in Stephen F. Gradish, *The Manning of the British Navy during the Seven Years' War* (1980).

[12] Return in N. P. Cushner, ed., *Documents Illustrating the British Conquest of Manila, 1762–1763* (1971), p. 57.

[13] W. Draper to Egremont, 27 July 1762, PRO, CO 77/20, f. 145.

'had been in the rebellion' of 1745,[14] this success led to a rapid expansion of Highland recruitment, repeated in the American War.[15] By then Irish Catholics, long regarded as a fifth column ready to aid any invader, were also being recruited in large numbers. It is clear that Catholics were being unofficially recruited during the Seven Years War. After 1771 they were openly accepted and a major recruiting drive for Irish Catholics took place at the beginning of the American War.[16]

British manpower could be supplemented from sources outside Britain and its interests in Europe were to a large degree sustained by European troops in British pay, during the Seven Years War in large part by the army of the king of Prussia. European troops could also be used in British colonies. Early in the Seven Years War the British government turned to the foreign Protestant communities in North America, such as the Pennsylvania Germans, as a source of soldiers. An act was passed in 1756 authorizing the commissioning of experienced officers from continental European countries who would be sent to America to recruit their fellow countrymen there. They were also instructed to recruit Germans, Swiss, and other Protestants on the continent of Europe. These 'foreign Protestants' were the nucleus of the four battalions of the Royal American Regiment. For its mid-eighteenth-century wars, the East India Company also turned to foreign Protestant recruits. In the War of American Independence the British hired large contingents of Hessian and other German troops to fight in the American colonies in their own units under their own officers. Just under 30,000 Germans were sent to North America during the war.[17] Hanoverian troops were sent to India.

Militias drawn from the free white population had existed in the North American and West Indian colonies from the beginnings of settlement. Since Cromwell's Western Design of 1656, the colonies had been regarded as a potential source of manpower for offensive operations against foreign colonial possessions. In 1740 a specially recruited American regiment of some 3,500 men was included in an expedition to attack the Spanish in the Caribbean. In 1742 it was estimated that there were nearly a quarter of a million potential 'fighting men' in the colonies. In the West Indies and the southern mainland colonies, where most of the labour force was black, few whites were available for military service outside the militias needed to guard against slave revolt, but in the northern colonies there was supposedly an abundance of

---

[14] Breadalbane to Hardwicke, 4 July 1759, BL, Add MS 35450, f. 262. A return for Montgomery's Highlanders in America on 18 September 1757, stated that the great majority were aged under thirty (HL, LO, 6695).

[15] Andrew Mackillop, *'More Fruitful than the Soil': Army, Empire and the Scottish Highlands, 1715–1815* (East Linton, 2001); Brumwell, *Redcoats*, ch. 8.

[16] See below, p. 340.

[17] Mackesy, *War for America*, p. 62fn.

potential soldiers, 60,000, it was thought, in Massachusetts alone.[18] New England troops won great renown for themselves in 1745 by capturing the French fortress at Louisbourg that dominated the Gulf of St Lawrence.

At the beginning of the Seven Years War the British assumption seems to have been that colonial American forces would be able to sustain most of the war effort against the French in North America and that such British regiments as needed to be sent across the Atlantic could have their numbers made up to strength by large drafts of American recruits. The deployment of British regulars in North America proved, however, to be much greater than anyone had envisaged at the beginning of the war. While the recruitment of Americans for the regulars was consistently disappointing, great numbers of American troops were put into the field in provincial regiments under their own commanders. From late in 1757 the colonies were asked to recruit as many men as possible and were promised large grants of British funds in part recompense. Some 20,000 provincial troops were mobilized in 1758.[19] Even before the ending of the war, the momentous decision had been taken to maintain a permanent garrison of regular British troops in America. This did not, however, mean that provincial American troops would not be required in any future war; they would, for instance, have been mobilized had the Falkland Islands crisis led to war with Spain in 1771.[20] In the War of American Independence American forces were now of course the enemies of the crown, but the British supplemented their own and German manpower with loyalist Americans. They were recruited into British regiments and separate provincial corps were raised. From 1778, when British regiments were transferred to the West Indies, Britain became increasingly dependent on using 'Americans to fight Americans', especially in the attempts to reestablish royal authority in the south.[21] Some 19,000 men may have served in American loyalist formations,[22] a figure close to the number of provincial soldiers who fought for the empire in the peak years of the Seven Years War.

People of African origin were drawn into the defence of the empire. Planter opinion in the West Indies noisily opposed any arming of blacks, but they were overruled on occasions. The Jamaica maroons, free communities who were the descendants of past generations of escaped slaves, were regarded as

---

[18] R. Dinwiddie to P. Ferry, Sept. 1743, Public Record Office, PRO 30/8/95, f. 9.

[19] Return in HL, LO 5772.

[20] Gage to Hillsborough, 2 April 1771, C. E. Carter, ed., *The Correspondence of General Thomas Gage with the Secretaries of State and with the War Office and the Treasury 1763–1775*, 2 vols. (New Haven, 1931–3), I. 295.

[21] K. G. Davies, Introduction to *Documents of the American Revolution 1770–1783*, 21 vols. (Shannon, 1972–81), XXI. 1–2. See also Paul H. Smith, *Loyalists and Redcoats: A Study in British Revolutionary Policy* (Chapel Hill, NC, 1964).

[22] Stephen Conway, *The War of American Independence 1775–1783* (Oxford, 1995), p. 46.

an essential force against slave risings. Authority was given to raise a regiment of 'free negroes' in Jamaica in 1762 for the attack on Spanish Cuba.[23] The labour of African slaves had long been regarded as indispensable support for white troops in the Caribbean. They too were sent to Cuba. Great numbers were again used as military labour in the American War, when units of free blacks and free coloured people were armed to defend Jamaica and a slave force was raised for St Lucia.[24] It was never official British policy to incite slave revolts in the southern colonies during the War of the American Revolution. Huge numbers of slaves were, however, attracted to the British army, in part by somewhat ambiguous promises of protection. Most of those who offered themselves were used as labourers or in non-combatant work, but some were armed, for instance, by lord Dunmore, governor of Virginia in 1775[25] and for the defence of Savannah in 1779. A black Carolina Corps was later raised to fight for the crown in South Carolina.[26] '[B]lack seamen, slave and free . . . were evidently quite common in the Navy'.[27] Warships in the West Indies, which suffered severe losses of sailors from disease, recruited slaves to make up some of the deficiencies.[28] As the Manila expedition of 1762 showed, the East India Company recruited a number of slave soldiers, known as 'cofferys', presumably obtained from Madagascar or from the East African mainland.

With good reason, contemporaries deemed the support of Native Americans to be essential for successful warfare in North America. Lord Halifax, then regarded as the leading British expert on the colonies, was reported to have said in the house of lords in 1755 that 'an alliance with any one of the wild nations of North America, would be of more service to us, than an alliance with the powerful empire of Russia'. He went on to complain of the failure to take 'proper measures for securing [Indian] allies in North America'.[29] His speech reflected the dismay in Britain at the success of the French in winning the Indian support that had led to the defeat in 1755 of general Braddock and the subsequent devastation of much of Pennsylvania in particular by Indian raids. Heavy spending on presents, a degree of diplomatic finesse, including the giving up of some contentious claims to Indian land, and concrete evidence that the British and Americans were likely to win the

---

[23] Egremont to Lyttelton, Jan. 1762, PRO, CO 137/61, ff. 50–6.
[24] Andrew Jackson O'Shaughnessy, *An Empire Divided: The American Revolution and the British Caribbean* (Philadelphia, 2000), pp. 175–81.
[25] See below, p. 343.
[26] Sylvia Frey, *Water from the Rock: Black Resistance in a Revolutionary Age* (Princeton, 1991), p. 190.
[27] Rodger, *Wooden World*, p. 159.   [28] O'Shaughnessy, *Empire Divided*, pp. 179–80.
[29] 10 Dec. 1755, R. C. Simmons and P. D. G. Thomas, eds., *Proceedings and Debates of the British Parliaments Respecting North America 1754–1783*, 6 vols. (Millwood, NY, 1982–6), I. 115.

war brought about a realignment of Indians to the British cause for the final invasion of Canada. Within a very short period from the ending of hostilities with the French, heavy-handed British policies again drove many Indians into disaffection, leading to the disaster of Pontiac's rising of 1763–5.[30] The War of the American Revolution forced Indians to make hard choices. Many of the communities were badly split about how to respond to it. Neutrality was an attractive course and the Americans were able to recruit support on a considerable scale, but the majority of those native peoples who actively participated in the war fought for the crown. The pro-British, or more properly anti-American, Indian alliances of the war have been described as 'the largest, most unified native American effort the continent would ever see'.[31]

Such British forces as existed in India in the middle of the eighteenth century were the small numbers of Europeans or Indian Christians employed by the East India Company to guard its settlements. During the wars against France in mid-century the Company tried to augment its forces by shipping out increased numbers of recruits from Britain. As its needs inevitably conflicted with those of the regular army, large-scale recruitment proved difficult and the Company had to ask the government for detachments of royal troops to be sent to India instead.[32] In addition, it began seriously to recruit Indian sepoys. Soldiers were abundantly available in eighteenth-century India. Europeans, it was said, 'could have as many as they chuse to pay'.[33] Large elements of the rural population were accustomed to bearing arms as a subsidiary occupation to cultivating the land and there was no shortage of clan chiefs, local notables or other entrepreneurs who contracted to provide soldiers for the rulers of the successor states to the Mughal empire. Such men were willing to deal with the British and the French as well. In the south the British could draw on the Telugu followers of local *nayaka* leaders; from Bengal they had access to the militarized peasants of parts of Bihar and Awadh in northern India.[34] By the end of the Seven Years War the Company

---

[30] This theme is authoritatively treated in Fred Anderson, *The Crucible of War: The Seven Years' War and the Fate of Empire in British North America, 1754–1766* (New York, 2000); see also Ian K. Steele, *Warpaths: Invasions of North America* (Oxford, 1994) and the very influential account in Richard White, *The Middle Ground: Indians, Empires and Republics in the Great Lakes Region, 1650–1815* (Cambridge, 1991).

[31] Gregory Dowd, *A Spirited Resistance: The North American Indian Struggle for Unity, 1745–1815* (Baltimore, 1982), pp. 46, 49, 59–61. For the Indian role in the war, see Colin G. Calloway, *The American Revolution in Indian Country: Crisis and Diversity in Native American Communities* (Cambridge, 1995).

[32] See below, pp. 139–40.   [33] G. Pocock to Holdernesse, 13 March 1758, HL, HM, 1000.

[34] Dirk H. A Kolff, *Naukar, Rajput and Sepoy: The Ethnohistory of the Military Labour Market in Hindustan, 1450–1850* (Cambridge, 1990); Stewart Gordon, 'Zones of Military Entrepreneurship in India, 1500–1700' in Gordon, ed., *Marathas, Marauders and State Formation in Eighteenth-Century*

was ceasing to treat sepoys as auxiliaries under their own commanders, but was drilling and arming them to the same level as its European troops and organizing them into battalions under British officers. While problems over recruitment and an appalling rate of mortality meant that the Company could rarely attain the target figures of at least 2,000 Europeans at each of its main Presidencies, the sepoy forces rose dramatically to over 20,000 by 1770 and to double that number by 1780. From the 1740s Royal Navy ships in Indian waters began to use lascars or Indian seamen to fill some of the gaps left by the heavy mortality among the British crews

The army and the navy were of course the instruments through which imperial conquests were made and colonial territories were defended from external threat or internal subversion. The imperial role of the British armed forces, however, went far beyond the strictly military. Through enrolment in the forces of the crown, large numbers of British people travelled to the empire and British military needs were likely to have been the part of the imperial presence with which societies overseas became most closely involved.[35]

The increased deployment of British forces overseas from mid-century meant that soldiers and sailors were probably the largest categories of British people with direct experience of the colonies. Many never came home. The British army was an important channel for emigration, especially to the North American colonies. This was officially recognized in the policy of land grants to officers and soldiers at the end of the Seven Years War. Highland soldiers in particular seem often to have enlisted with settlement in the colonies in mind. 'Scottish gentlemen of much consideration' in South Carolina welcomed the presence of a Highland regiment in the colony during the Seven Years War, anticipating that many of the soldiers would 'become settlers here'.[36] Regiments raised expressly to go to America recruited extremely well, although Highlanders seemed otherwise to be reluctant to serve abroad.[37] Men from other regiments discharged at the end of the Seven Years War often elected to stay in the colonies.[38] By contrast with North America, India and the West Indies with their dire mortality rates were postings

India (Delhi, 1994), pp. 182–208; H. H. Dodwell, *Sepoy Recruitment in the Old Madras Army* (Calcutta, 1922); Seema Alavi, *The Sepoys and the Company: Tradition and Transition in Northern India, 1770–1830* (Delhi, 1995), ch. 1.

[35] The importance of an 'expanding imperial garrison state' in the British empire from the mid-eighteenth century is well brought out in C. A. Bayly, 'The British and Indigenous Peoples, 1760–1860: Power, Perception and Identity' in Martin Daunton and Rick Halpern, eds., *Empire and Others: British Encounters with Indigenous Peoples 1600–1850* (1999), pp. 19–41.

[36] W. Lyttelton to Loudoun, 10 Dec. 1757, HL, LO 4987.

[37] Auchinleck to Loudoun, 12 March 1757, HL, LO 3029; Mackillop, '*More Fruitful than the Soil*', pp. 183–4.

[38] Brumwell, *Redcoats*, pp. 297–8.

generally dreaded by rank and file soldiers. Nevertheless, those who enlisted in the East India Company's European forces were likely to have been making a deliberate choice to go to India and once there, always supposing that they survived, they tended to sign on and spend the rest of their lives in India. So too did the surviving men from the royal regiments, who often transferred to the Company's service when their own unit left India.

The eighteenth-century British army may have had perennial problems in recruiting soldiers, but there was an over-supply of those who wished to be officers in it. From the 1750s the growth of empire enabled many more aspiring officers to fulfil their ambitions. The Seven Years War produced a large expansion in a long stable officer corps. Appointments in imperial garrisons helped to limit the inevitable post-war cutback to half pay of otherwise superfluous officers.[39] One of the reasons for maintaining a large force in peacetime in North America and the West Indies after 1763 was specifically to keep more officers on the active list.[40] Regular troops were withdrawn from India after the end of the Seven Years War, but, far from being reduced, the East India Company's own army, especially its sepoy regiments, grew rapidly. This created a new demand for officers. By 1772 the Company's officer corps in India was about 1,560 strong, more than half the number of regular British army officers at that time.[41] Regular officers were encouraged to transfer to the Company, but most of the increase was accounted for by the recruitment of very young men straight into the Company's army as cadets. Cadetships were the main channel through which families with genteel ambitions got their offspring to India.

The posting of Royal Naval ships or regular troops to a colony offered welcome opportunities for profit for the local community. Soldiers and sailors required food and drink. Stores might be needed for the ships to refit. As troops moved inland in North America, they demanded accommodation, boats or carts and draught animals. The march of troops in India was accompanied by moving bazaars and trains of mobile *banjara* traders who supplied the sepoys. The mode of payment, specie or bills certain to be honoured on the British treasury or other government departments, greatly enhanced the value of dealing with the forces of the crown. It is perhaps

[39] J. A. Houlding, *Fit for Service: The Training of the British Army 1715–95* (Oxford, 1981), pp. 110–11.

[40] John A. Bullion, ' "The Ten Thousand in America": More Light on the Decision on the American Army, 1762–1763', *William and Mary Quarterly*, 3rd ser., XLIII (1986), 646–57 and ' "Security and Economy": The Bute Administration's Plans for the American Army and Revenue', ibid. 3rd ser., XLV (1988), 499–509; John Shy, *Toward Lexington: The Role of the British Army in the Coming of the American Revolution* (Princeton, 1965), pp. 68–83.

[41] P. J. Marshall, 'Empire and Opportunity in Britain, 1763–75', *Transactions of the Royal Historical Society*, 6th ser., V (1995), 125.

hardly surprising that British officers should have complained so frequently about exorbitant over-charging. From the colonial point of view, much was at stake. Calculations of British government spending in the North American colonies, mostly on the army and navy, show that it went a long way to offset their persistent trade deficits with Britain.[42]

Military necessities brought huge numbers of people overseas into the orbit of the British empire. Colonial American and Indian soldiers, Native American auxiliaries, contractors, artificers, and labourers of all sorts were all involved. Solid rewards were offered. At a crucial point in the Seven Years War the British government assumed responsibility for the supply of the provincial regiments in North America and made recompense to the colonial governments for a considerable part of their cost. In return for their support of the British in war, Native Americans received arms, equipment, clothing, and food for their families at a cost that 'always dismayed the British'.[43] The East India Company had a justified reputation for not only paying better but for being a more reliable paymaster for its Indian sepoys than any Indian ruler was likely to be.

Those who gave military service to the empire could also be bound emotionally to it. For all their often bruising encounters with the British regular army during the Seven Years War, ordinary American provincial soldiers still seem to have taken a due pride in their achievement as partners in a great imperial victory.[44] The north Indian sepoys in the East India Company's service were able with British patronage to create a high-caste identity for themselves.[45] The Mohawk Joseph Brant was only the most notable Native American who took up arms for the empire to be honoured by the British. He was given a commission as captain, awarded a pension and accorded flattering receptions on two visits to London.

The integration into the empire that British military necessities offered to local populations was, however, an imperfect one. The great bulk of the colonial American soldiers who served the empire were unwilling to serve directly in the British army, dreading the discipline of British martial law and refusing to serve under regular officers, nor were the colonies willing to permit impressment into the navy. Colonial officers, on the other hand, were more than willing to be integrated, but were usually rebuffed. The British army needed new supplies of soldiers but it was extremely reluctant to accept additional officers. In part, there was inevitably a strong element of job protection involved: competition to get off the half-pay list onto the active

---

[42] Julian Gwyn, 'British Government Spending and the North American Colonies 1740–1775', *Journal of Imperial and Commonwealth History*, VIII (1980), 74–84.

[43] White, *Middle Ground*, pp. 404–5.   [44] Anderson, *Crucible of War*, pp. 411–14.

[45] Alavi, *Sepoys and the Company*, pp. 49–55, 75–94.

one was bitter enough without admitting new competitors. In part, there was an undoubted professional pride that made men believe that only those trained in the British service or, at a stretch, in continental European armies, were fit for command.

It was, however, difficult to get new soldiers without having to accept some new officers as well. New sources of recruits often depended on the influence of local notables over their followers. The Welsh were said to be 'extremely national and partial to their neighbours' so that they would only enlist under their own countrymen.[46] New Highland regiments were raised by lairds who were capable of enlisting men from their own or neighbouring estates. It was notorious that American soldiers would only sign up in large numbers under American officers whom they knew and trusted. In India the bulk of the Mughal army had been raised by military tenure holders or *mansabdars*, who depended on *jemadars* or local recruiters. Of these military contractors for the British, only the Highland gentry were fully integrated into the British army as regular officers. Few Americans were given regular commissions from the crown. They were, for instance, singularly unsuccessful in obtaining royal commissions in the Royal American Regiment, specifically raised to fight in America in the Seven Years War.[47] Most Americans had to be content with provincial commissions. The Mughal military elite had no place in the new British order. Both they and the *jemadars* quickly gave way to the East India Company's British officers, who themselves suffered discrimination. A clear line was drawn between British regular officers, on the one hand, and East India Company's officers and American provincial officers, on the other. They received their commissions from the Company or from the colonial governors, not from the king. When they served with regular officers, the latter enjoyed seniority over them. Honours and rewards after successful campaigns tended to go to the royal officers. George Washington was only the most famous of the provincial officers who greatly resented such discrimination. He did not see why he and his colleagues in the Virginia provincial regiments, 'because we are Americans . . . shou'd be deprived of the benefits common to British subjects'. They were 'defending part of the domains of Great Britain' and they therefore felt themselves entitled to the king's commission and to its privileges such as receiving half pay on being disbanded.[48]

---

[46] North to George III, 3 Jan. 1778, J. Fortescue, ed., *The Correspondence of King George III 1760–1783*, 6 vols. (1927–8), IV. 2.

[47] See the ethnic origins attributed to officers for part of the 1st Battalion and for the 2nd Battalion of the regiment in 1757, HL, LO 1345, 6639.

[48] Remonstrance, [16 April] 1757, J. C. Fitzpatrick, ed., *The Writings of George Washington*, II, 1757–69 (Washington, DC, 1931), 26–7.

Taking the king's or the East India Company's shilling to fight for him or for it probably associated more diverse people more directly with Britain than any other kind of imperial link in this period. For most, it is unlikely to have been a close or lasting association, or to have left much in the way of a legacy of loyalty to the empire. Men had served because it was in their interest to do so. Nevertheless the worldwide military reach of the eighteenth-century British state was still remarkable.

III

Britain was able to employ Germans, colonial and Native Americans, and Indian sepoys to fight its wars because of the capacity of the British state and of the East India Company in India to pay them. The powers of the British state to tax in Britain could make up for its difficulties in mobilizing British labour for military purposes.

Recent writing has demonstrated the effectiveness of the British system of taxation on which an impressive structure of public borrowing could be built.[49] Paradoxical as it may seem, it is clear that the British people, who prided themselves on their rights to call to account state authority and to consent to their government, were more heavily taxed than other European peoples, who allegedly could do neither of these things. The most productive taxes in this period were indirect ones on consumption, rather than direct taxes graded according to income. Although items that could be regarded as necessities for the poor, including most of what constituted their basic food, were largely exempt, a wide belt of 'middling' people, who might be presumed to be politically aware, paid quite heavily through customs duties on such imported items as sugar, tea, wine, or tobacco, and above all through excises on home-produced goods, including salt, beer, candles, or leather. Although the excise was a traditionally contentious form of taxation, it has been suggested that the political involvement of much of the population may in fact have facilitated the collection of such taxes, since they were levied with the consent of parliament and therefore had a popular legitimacy not accorded to the taxes of most European regimes.[50]

The level of tax revenue nearly doubled from £6,400,000 at the end of the War of the Austrian Succession in 1748 to £12 million late in the American

---

[49] Brewer, *Sinews of Power*; Patrick O'Brien, 'The Political Economy of British Taxation, 1660–1815', *Economic History Review*, 2nd ser., XLI (1988), 1–32 and 'Inseparable Connections: Trade, Economy, Fiscal State, and the Expansion of Empire 1688–1815' in Marshall, ed., *Oxford History*, II, pp. 63–74.

[50] Brewer, *Sinews of Power*, p. 132.

War.[51] The amount collected in taxes rose steeply on the outbreak of each war but remained generally at its wartime level once the war was over. This was because most of the increases in spending to fund the war effort were met by borrowing, not by taxation. These loans added to the long-term national debt, which rose from £74 million in 1756 to £245 million by 1783. Interest payments became the largest item of peacetime public expenditure that had to be met by taxation.[52]

The British government had a capacity to borrow very large sums at relatively low rates of interest that no other government could match. Central to the success of government borrowing by the mid-eighteenth century was a relatively small group of rich men dubbed 'the moneyed interest' by contemporaries. In 1757, at the height of the Seven Years War, they were described as 'a number of people of worth and honour, most of them proprietors in the large companies, men of knowledge and ability'. An analysis of the principal lenders of that year shows that big sums were allocated to five principal investors, representing Dutch and Jewish interests among others, with large blocks going to the directors of the Bank of England, the South Sea Company, the East India Company, and the insurance companies and lesser amounts to a range of bankers, government contractors, and other businessmen.[53] Such men were the intermediaries between the government and an extensive body of smaller investors in the national debt. They played an essential role in the British state's capacity to fund the deployment of naval and military power throughout the world.

The achievement of the British state over a long period both in raising the level of taxation ('by a factor of eighteen in real terms' between 1688 and 1815')[54] and in shouldering an ever larger national debt without, it would seem, imposing serious distortions on the growth of the British economy as a whole[55] looks so impressive that it is easy to underestimate the sense of despondency faced by ministers trying to raise yet more taxes or to float new loans during wars, especially in their later stages. The level of debt at the end of a war and of the taxation that would be needed to service that debt induced deep gloom. This was particularly marked after 1763, when there was a sense of national crisis over the burden of debt and much recrimination about the cost of the war. Not only was the prodigality of war in Germany condemned in retrospect, but even the success of colonial campaigns did not seem necessarily to 'compensate to the nation for the waste of its people, by

---

[51] Ibid. p. 89.
[52] For the rise of the debt and the cost of servicing it, see figures in ibid. pp. 115, 117.
[53] L. S. Sutherland, 'The City of London and the Devonshire-Pitt Administration, 1756–7' in Aubrey Newman, ed., *Politics and Finance in the Eighteenth Century: Lucy Sutherland* (1984), p. 92.
[54] O'Brien, 'Inseparable Connections' in Marshall ed., *Oxford History*, II, p. 68.
[55] Ibid. p. 69.

carrying on a war in unhealthy climates' or for 'the excessive rate of interest at which money was to be borrowed'.[56] Politicians like George Grenville, who were committed to defending the terms of a peace that was derided for having limited Britain's colonial gains, had an obvious interest in making such points, but they appear to have reflected the views of a wider public. One of Grenville's correspondents agreed with him.

Had the enormous loads so wantonly imposed during the late wars been levied to answer any capitall nationall purpose they might more easily have been born with, but many think they were chiefly raised to carrie on undertakings for the most part useless to this nation and many of them hurtfull in their consequences.

Far from blaming the Peace of 1763 for gaining too little, he concluded that 'the advantages have been in no sense adequate to the risques and expence with which they were obtain'd'.[57] The least that could be expected after so expensive a war was that the apparent beneficiaries, the North American and West Indian colonies and the East India Company, should make some return to Britain for services rendered. There were definite limits to supposed imperial euphoria when the bills had to be paid.

While the British paid out subsidies to their allies for their European wars and to their colonial subjects to support wars in North America, in India the East India Company received subsidies from the Indian rulers who were nominally its allies, if in reality becoming its satellites. These subsidies meant that the expense of war in India, if still imposing a considerable burden on the state for the cost of the royal forces sent there,[58] was significantly reduced. After the Seven Years War the Company gained rights to levy territorial revenue, directly in Bengal and from grants of territory around Madras. The cost of its armies became the first charge on these revenues. Thus in theory empire in India, far from being a burden on the British taxpayer, would pay for itself and even provide a tribute to be transferred into British public funds. In practice, later wars in India were to wreck the Company's finances and to force the British treasury to advance funds to it.

IV

By the mid-eighteenth century the British state had developed formidable capacities to raise funds and to sustain an effective war effort, often over

---

[56] [William Knox], *The Present State of the Nation: Particularly with Respect to its Trade, Finances &c.* (1768), p. 6.

[57] Letter of G. Chalmers, 16 Oct. 1766, BL, Add MS 57826, f. 89.

[58] See below, p. 128.

immense distances. The excise department, which was charged with levying the biggest single contribution to the tax yield, has been described as 'one of the most proficient organs of government'.[59] Even if it was for a lost cause, the achievement of organizing the transport of a huge army to North America during the War of American Independence and of keeping it equipped and supplied across the Atlantic for a long period was a very remarkable one.[60]

Outside the departments dealing with finance or the armed forces, the machinery of the eighteenth-century British state looks less impressive to historians. Its role was a circumscribed one; 'much of the responsibility for *domestic* government' was 'devolved to the localities' instead of being directly administered by the agencies of the central government.[61]

There was inevitably a very high degree of devolution in the government of the colonies as well. Much territory was not under any form of direct state management. This was the case with the domains of the chartered companies, the Hudson's Bay Company in northern Canada, the forts of the Company of Merchants Trading to Africa on the West African coast, and above all the settlements and later the provinces of the East India Company. In North America the British government did not exercise direct control over the two corporate colonies, Connecticut and Rhode Island, or over the surviving proprietary ones, Maryland and Pennsylvania. Although authority in the rest of the colonies of the West Indies or North America emanated from the crown-appointed governors, local elites managed their own affairs to a very large degree. Officials in London could not effectively supervise governors at a great distance and governors had to take account of local interests and opinions, which were given institutional representation as the elected lower houses of the colonial legislatures, generally known as the assemblies. In the northern colonies in particular, the assemblies were elected by a very wide franchise of white males. Control over finance gave the assembly a large measure of control over the governor and his executive.

That responsibilities should be devolved on chartered companies or to men of substance within individual colonies and that they should enjoy a considerable degree of autonomy was regarded as entirely appropriate by all shades of British opinion. Eighteenth-century Britain took a pride in the commercial vigour that was thought to flow from the local liberties appropriate to communities of free British people living overseas. Nevertheless, colonies were expected to submit to a degree of supervision and regulation to ensure

---

[59] Brewer, *Sinews of Power*, p. 102.

[60] David Syrett, *Shipping and the American War, 1775–83: A Study of British Transport Organisation* (1970).

[61] David Eastwood, *Government and Community in the English Provinces, 1700–1870* (Houndmills, 1997), p. 18.

that they fulfilled national purposes, by contributing to Britain's economic well-being, above all by obeying the code of regulations known as the Laws of Trade or the Navigation Acts, and—an increasing preoccupation after the Seven Years War—by contributing to their own defence. It was held that colonial law-making and colonial courts should be supervised from London to ensure the due administration of justice throughout the empire. The overseas companies were required to conduct their trade within parameters of the national interest laid down in their charters as well as in the Navigation Acts.

A number of government bodies had responsibility for attempting to supervise the colonies. The ultimate source of authority under the crown was the privy council, acting as the committee of council for plantation affairs. It received advice from government departments and issued orders to them. Until 1768, when a colonial or American secretary was appointed, the minister most involved in colonial business was the secretary of state for the southern department. For much of the period the southern secretary made major appointments in the colonies and was responsible for correspondence with the governors. He directed military operations in the colonies during wars. Southern secretaries had wide colonial responsibilities but usually had little time to attend to them, since they had a great mass of other business on their hands, not least the conduct of British foreign policy with southern Europe. The department that specialized in colonial matters was the board of trade. It scrutinized colonial laws, made inquiries, issued reports, and drafted recommendations and instructions for others to sign and execute. The board was regarded as the repository of governmental expertise on colonies and for a period, from 1752 to 1761, it actually made appointments and issued orders on its own responsibility. The colonial customs service, an essential agency for enforcing commercial regulations, was the responsibility of the treasury. Naval matters relating to the colonies were dealt with by the admiralty. The East India Company had its own staff of clerks, secretaries, and accountants, working to the orders of the Company's directors at its London headquarters. Governors and councils were responsible to the directors for running the Company's trade and administering its settlements in Asia. On questions of relations with foreign European powers in Asia and of military operations there in wartime the Company, usually through a secret committee of its directors, kept in close contact with ministers of the crown.

These complex administrative structures had defects of which many contemporaries were well aware. Responsibility was divided between different bodies. Although any concept of colonial 'policy' was alien to the mid-eighteenth century, it was clear that, with so many departments involved, coherence of approach to the colonies was very difficult. Division of responsibility also slowed down the transaction of business, which moved ponderously at the best of times, even when only one office was involved. After battling with the secretary of state's office, the privy council office and the board of ordnance for what he regarded as an urgent supply of cannon for South Carolina in time of war in 1759, the colony's agent wrote despairingly that: 'Business at the public offices is very lamely transacted and the grand object seems to be rather how to avoid, or get rid of it instead of entering into the real merits.'[62] Engagement in the effective exercise of their duties was patchy among office holders. Even members of the board of trade or its clerks who had served for very long periods and had become deeply learned about colonial regulations and precedents rarely had first-hand knowledge of the colonies. Senior politicians lacked such knowledge altogether. Lord Halifax, president of the board of trade from 1748 until 1761, and widely thought to be the leading expert on colonial issues in British politics, was dismissed by a North American governor as one

who deals out American facts upon very slight foundations, without the necessary enquiry; and was he not join'd in the ministry by men more ignorant than himself, he would soon be found out. His weight in parliament is very little; and nothing keeps him high in administration, but the opinion that he has knowledge in American affairs, and is diligent in the management of them, the first arises from the superlative ignorance of his fellow ministers, and the latter from a deal of bustle and stir about things of little consequence, made without judgement, without any plan or system and without understanding enough to form one. From this sketch you will easily account for the unsteadiness of the government with regard to their affairs here.[63]

Contemporaries were divided about how well the administrative system worked in practice. At the beginning of the period, activists in the board of trade in particular believed that the colonies were being permitted gradually to slip out of effective control. Governors were losing power to the assemblies. Commercial regulations were being flouted, defence was being neglected and the law was being administered partially and even corruptly. Reform was in their view becoming inescapably necessary. Many historians have echoed their opinion. Others, both at the time and since, have taken a different view of the administrative structures of the eighteenth-century British empire. They should not, it is argued, be judged solely as the means by which metropolitan authority was imposed on distant colonies, but should be seen rather as a channel for a two-way 'negotiation', whereby London tried to

[62] J. Wright to W. Lyttelton, 31 March 1759, WLCL, Lyttelton MSS.
[63] R. H. Morris to R. Peters, 6 April 1757, HSP, Peters Papers, IV. p. 86.

assert a degree of control over what in practice had long been autonomous polities overseas, but accepted that control could only be obtained in return for recognizing colonial privileges and making concessions.[64] Thus in practical terms the working of the imperial bureaucracy was not just a simple system of command by which colonies received their orders; it was also a channel through which they could make their desires known and try to shape decisions affecting them by lobbying government departments in London. The board of trade and the privy council in mid-century were likely to be responsive to such lobbying, especially when it was channelled through London pressure groups allied with interests in America or the West Indies. The empire thus functioned not so much as a system of command and obedience but by 'voluntary compliance by the Americans . . . based on the expectation of responsive restraint on the part of the British'.[65]

While accepting that a degree of negotiation in the working of empire was entirely appropriate and that the colonies should be able to express their concerns and be assured of consideration, some of those in London most actively concerned with colonial affairs were coming to believe by mid-century that there was too much negotiation and too little obedience. This view was strongly held by a new generation in the board of trade. Together with the board of customs, it collected evidence indicating that imperial commercial regulations, the essential sinews of empire, were being widely evaded.[66] Under lord Halifax's presidency after 1748 a number of proposals for strengthening imperial authority in the colonies were floated by the board of trade. Most of these had originated earlier in the century. The governors' powers were to be strengthened by giving their instructions from London the force of law in the colonies and by creating a corps of officials overseas who would be able to give reliable support to the governor because their salaries did not depend on votes of the assemblies. Attempts were made to create a stronger executive in Nova Scotia, which with intensive new settlement and the building of a major base was to be the pivot for the defence of the northern colonies. Other schemes were formulated for

---

[64] Jack P. Greene, 'Negotiated Authorities: The Problem of Governance in the Extended Polities of the Early Modern Atlantic World' in Greene, ed., *Negotiated Authorities: Essays in Colonial Political and Constitutional History* (Charlottesville, Va., 1994), pp. 1–24; id., 'Transatlantic Colonization and the Redefinition of Empire in the Early Modern Era: The British American Experience' in Christine Daniels and Michael V. Kennedy, eds., *Negotiated Empires: Centers and Peripheries in the Americas, 1500–1820* (New York, 2002), pp. 267–82.

[65] Alison Gilbert Olson, *Making the Empire Work: London and American Interest Groups 1690–1790* (Cambridge, Mass., 1992), p. 134.

[66] Thomas C. Barrow, 'The Background to the Grenville Program, 1757–1763', *William and Mary Quarterly*, 3rd ser., XXII (1965), 93–104.

improving colonial defence and for the better management of Indian affairs by closer coordination between the colonies under British supervision.[67]

Examples were to be made of colonies regarded as particularly delinquent in defying the authority of their governors. On the mainland, New Jersey and New York were singled out for especial displeasure. The case of New Jersey was considered at a 'grand meeting of all the ministry' with the board of trade in 1749. The board reported that outbreaks of rioting and disorder had reduced the province to 'a state of entire disobedience to all authority and law attended with circumstances that manifested a disposition to revolt from their dependence upon the crown of Great Britain'. The governor must be given a salary outside the control of the assembly and troops should be sent to New Jersey. Incorporation of the province into New York might be considered. In June 1750 the board of trade returned to the charge. The rioters were described as 'the dregs of the people, and many of them Irish'. The population of the province as a whole were 'in a particular manner averse to kingly government'. No action was in fact taken against New Jersey. In 1751 the privy council did no more than order the governor to indicate the king's displeasure to the assembly and promise them an inquiry into any grievances they might have.[68]

Nor was effective action taken against New York, although it too was subjected to the close attentions of the board of trade. In 1751 the board reported on the 'melancholy state of the affairs of this distracted province', in which 'the legal prerogatives of the crown (which alone can keep this or any province dependent on the mother country)' had been wrested from the governor, 'the province in time of war left exposed', its Indian allies, 'the Six Nations, disgusted' and 'the whole support of government for above two years entirely omitted'. All this had been done 'merely in resentment from personal quarrels'. The board of trade's remedy was for the New York assembly to be induced to vote 'a general perpetual revenue act', adequate for the cost of governing and defending the colony. Successive governors were instructed to obtain such an act, which successive assemblies refused to vote. With the outbreak of the Seven Years War, the board of trade reluctantly agreed with the governor that it would be impolitic to engage in further contests with the assembly over the issue.[69]

---

[67] Jack P. Greene, ' "A Posture of Hostility": A Reconsideration of Some Aspects of the Origins of the American Revolution', *Proceedings of the American Antiquarian Society*, LXXXVII (1978), 27–68; James A. Henretta, *'Salutary Neglect': Colonial Administration under the Duke of Newcastle* (Princeton, 1972), chs. 6, 7.

[68] William A. Whitehead, ed., *Documents Relating to the Colonial History of the State of New Jersey*, VII, *1746–51* (Newark, NJ, 1883), pp. 301, 312–14, 466–528, 632–4.

[69] E. B. O'Callaghan, ed., *Documents Relative to the Colonial History of the State of New-York*, 15 vols. (Albany, NY, 1856–87), VI. 635–8, 790, 948, 1022–3, VII. 32–3, 39–40.

Although colonial matters were said in 1750 to 'engage the whole thoughts of men in power',[70] the board of trade, even with the enhanced powers won for it by Halifax, clearly lacked the political muscle to enlist support for strong measures in the higher reaches of government. Halifax's last bid to win effective power for himself was to assert a claim in 1757 to become a secretary of state specifically for overseas interests, combining Asia and America or 'the East and West Indies'.[71] His bid failed, apparently thwarted by Pitt. No third or colonial secretary was to be appointed until 1768 (and then without any Asian responsibilities). By 1757 Halifax and other would-be colonial reformers were increasingly turning their minds to another strategy for enforcing the supremacy of Britain over the colonies. Parliament was directly to assert metropolitan authority.

In the 1760s the extent of parliament's authority over the colonies came to be questioned, above all in North America. In reply British spokesmen felt it necessary to vindicate parliament's claims, usually by unequivocal statements of its sovereignty over the whole empire.[72] In the first half of the century there was little debate. Parliament's powers over the colonies were not being publicly questioned and few in Britain seem to have felt any doubt about them or any need to justify them. Two speakers in a commons debate about the Molasses Bill in 1733 insisted that there could be no doubt that the British parliament had the right to tax the colonies.[73] For reasons which seem to have owed more to the desire of administrations to keep contentious colonial issues out of parliament than to any doubt about the propriety of doing so, little legislation was, however, passed directly affecting the colonies except on matters of commercial regulation with which parliament had of course long been concerned.[74] Direct parliamentary taxation was not attempted.

In the 1750s the volume of colonial legislation coming before the British parliament began to increase. In part, this reflected a change of generation in Britain's political leadership and the rise of men who were less fearful of bringing controversy about colonies into parliament.[75] Increasing resort to

[70] G. Clinton to C. Colden, n.d., 'Letters and Papers of Cadwallader Colden, IV', *Collections of the New York Historical Society for the Year 1920* (New York, 1921), p. 201.

[71] Calcraft to Loudoun, 8 July 1757, HL, LO, 3913; Hardwicke to Anson, 18 June 1757, BL, Add MS 15956, f. 37. Pitt's violent opposition to such a post is made clear in a letter to Bute; Romney Sedgwick, 'Letters from William Pitt to Lord Bute: 1755–1758' in Richard Pares and A. J. P. Taylor, eds., *Essays Presented to Sir Lewis Namier* (1956), p. 125.

[72] See below, pp. 168–8.

[73] Sir W. Yonge and T. Winnington, 8 March 1733, L. F. Stock, ed., *Proceedings and Debates of the British Parliaments Respecting North America*, 5 vols. (Washington, DC, 1924–41), IV. 190, 191.

[74] Alison Gilbert Olson, *Anglo-American Politics: The Relationship between Parties in England and Colonial America, 1660–1775* (Oxford, 1973), pp. 118–20; Henretta, *Salutary Neglect*, pp. 92–9; Ian K. Steele, 'The British Parliament and the Atlantic Colonies to 1760: New Approaches to Enduring Questions', *Parliamentary History*, XIV (1995), 30–46.

[75] Olson, *Anglo American Politics*, pp. 144–8.

parliament seems also to reflect a major development in the nature of the British state. Over a very wide area of domestic administration parliament was becoming 'a more important part of the machinery of government' during the eighteenth century.[76] The control of the agents of the executive government over local government in Britain was increasingly giving way to parliamentary control.[77] In practice, this control was largely exercised in response to local initiatives. Domestic legislation was rarely sponsored by ministers. The eighteenth-century parliament has been described as 'resembling nothing so much as a gigantic rubber stamp, confirming local and private enterprise, but rarely undertaking initiatives of its own'.[78]

Parliament's involvement in colonial matters followed a roughly similar pattern. It too became increasingly open to private initiatives, notably from the agents of the North American and West Indian colonies, the merchants trading to both areas, the West Indian planters resident in Britain, and the directors of the East India Company. In this sense parliament became a forum for negotiated colonial government. The coercive element in parliamentary intervention on colonial questions seems, however, to have been more marked than it was in British domestic affairs. By the mid-eighteenth century traditional Whiggish inhibitions that the mass of MPs may have felt about subjecting colonies to the prerogative of the crown through the edicts of the privy council or the powers of the royal governors was giving way to a willingness to use parliamentary authority to reinforce a royal power that was ultimately accountable to parliament and therefore could be no threat to the liberties of the subject.

The willingness of parliament to engage with colonial issues in support of the crown was clearly demonstrated by proceedings taken against Jamaica, a third delinquent colony of the late 1740s and early 1750s. The Jamaican assembly was notoriously fractious. In 1748 the governor wrote of a 'rebel faction' who threatened the security of the island.[79] There was dissatisfaction in Britain at the failure to develop the island's potential: much land remained uncultivated, the white population was small and could not on its own defend the island and sugar output was relatively low, thus keeping prices high in Britain. The board of trade pressed for remedies and the house of commons took a hand, ordering an inquiry.[80] On the basis of a report from

---

[76] Joanna Innes, 'The Domestic Face of the Military-Fiscal State: Government and Society in Eighteenth-Century Britain' in Lawrence Stone, ed., *An Imperial State at War: Britain from 1689 to 1815* (1994), p. 98.

[77] Eastwood, *Government and Community*, pp. 18–19.

[78] Paul Langford, *Public Life and the Propertied Englishman* (1991), p. 166.

[79] C. Knowles to Anson, 6 Nov. 1748, BL, Add MS 15956, f. 157.

[80] Holdernesse to Board of Trade, 28 March 1752, PRO, CO 137/25, ff. 219–20.

the governor endorsed by the board of trade in 1753,[81] the commons resolved that the legislature in Jamaica had failed adequately to populate the island with whites.[82] A member of the board of trade then introduced a bill 'for the better peopling of the Island of Jamaica with white inhabitants', declaring the colony's own legislation for this purpose 'ineffectual' and empowering the governor to dispose of land under certain conditions.[83] The bill was not proceeded with, but a crisis in the perennial wrangling between governor and assembly again brought Jamaica before the commons. In October 1753 the assembly had passed resolutions insisting on its right to appoint officers to raise and apply money voted for the government of the colony and it had rejected the inclusion of clauses suspending the operation of Jamaican acts until they were approved in London. Such clauses would be 'a very great alteration of the known and established constitution of this island'. The assembly's resolutions were referred to the house of commons, which resolved on 23 May 1757 that these claims were 'illegal . . . and derogatory to the rights of the crown and people of *Great Britain*'.[84] The implications of these resolutions were sweeping: the constitution of Jamaica could be defined by resolution of the house of commons and the proper enforcement of royal prerogative powers in the colonies was the concern of 'the people of Great Britain'. In practice, however, the resolutions did nothing to strengthen the hand of the governor and seems to have done little to moderate the opposition of the assembly.

If parliamentary intervention over Jamaica had not been effective, it was a clear portent of parliament's deeper involvement in colonial matters in future. During the Seven Years War British statutes were used to settle specific issues in North America, such as the recruiting of servants into the British army, the commissioning of foreign officers or the subjecting of provincial troops to the British Mutiny Act. Many people in Britain came to believe, however, that the war was raising much wider questions about the effectiveness of metropolitan authority over the colonies, especially in North America, and that these could only be settled by parliament. Thomas Penn, proprietor of Pennsylvania, believed that 'the colonys cannot be made so useful to their country without the interposition of parliament'.[85] 'What the king of his

---

[81] Report of 22 Feb. 1753, PRO, CO 138/19, pp. 388–452.

[82] Stock, ed., *Proceedings and Debates*, V. 543.

[83] Sheila Lambert, ed., *House of Commons Sessional Papers of the Eighteenth Century*, 145 vols. (Wilmington, Del., 1975), IX. 573–91.

[84] *Journals of the House of Commons*, XXVII (1754–7), 910–11; Jack P. Greene, 'The Jamaica Privilege Controversy, 1764–66: An Episode in the Process of Constitutional Definition in the Early Modern British Empire', *Journal of Imperial and Commonwealth History*, XXII (1994), 21.

[85] To R. H. Morris, 26 Oct. 1755, HSP, Penn Letter Books, IV, p. 168.

mere prerogative cannot effect with the aid of parliament he may', James Abercromby, agent for Virginia, told Pitt. A 'military plan' and a 'military fund' depended on parliament.[86] Major legislation directly affecting the colonies was not in fact to be attempted during the course of the war, but it was quickly to follow the peace.

V

The British state as a whole might have shown little inclination to intervene in detailed questions of colonial governance, but few doubted the importance of colonies and of their trade. The Walpole government had to some degree been pushed into a war with Spain in 1739 by what appeared to be a powerful popular response to opposition clamour about the need to vindicate Britain's national greatness which depended on her worldwide trade.[87] What began hopefully as a predatory war on Spain turned into a hard-fought struggle with France that lasted until 1748. During the course of the war opposition slogans about the importance of colonies and long-distance trade won acceptance right across the political spectrum. Trade with the colonies was coming to be seen as essential to the 'sinews of war' that enabled Britain to keep at bay a most formidable enemy, thought to be intent on 'universal monarchy', whose army had triumphed in the Netherlands and whose forces were capable of invading the British Isles and overthrowing the Hanoverian dynasty, even if they had failed to do so in conjunction with the Jacobite risings in 1745. British naval strength above all was thought to rest on the seamen trained in the oceanic trades, but public finance depended on them too. They generated important tax revenues through customs, as well as contributing much to the prosperity of the manufacturers and the wealth of the commercial communities who lent money to the government. A 'memo' of what in 1747 the elderly Scottish general, lord Stair, told Henry Pelham, the chief minister, summed up now widely-held beliefs. The French were set upon 'being masters of Europe' and 'ruining us', Stair was reported to have said. Even 'a small part of their land forces thrown amongst us, would endanger his Majesties crown, our religion and liberties'. Britain's fleet was her essential security. The key to maritime supremacy lay in North America. If Britain dominated the fisheries, the fur trade, and other trades 'from that part of the world', she would have an abundance of seamen, while the French would lack

[86] Letter of 25 Nov. 1756, Public Record Office, PRO 30/8/95, f. 202.
[87] For a carefully balanced assessment of the causes of the war, see Philip Woodfine, *Britannia's Glories: The Walpole Ministry and the 1739 War with Spain* (Woodbridge, 1998).

them. So 'we shall be a powerfull, rich, and flourishing people and can bid defyance to France'.[88]

When war with France threatened again over North America in 1755, there was no significant disagreement as to what was at stake. The opposition newspaper, The *Monitor*, tried to revive the 'patriot' cry of 1739 about ministerial neglect of colonial interests, which were the 'fountain and foundation of all our trade, wealth and maritime power'. If the French conquered British America, Britain would become 'a province to a nation of slaves'.[89] By 1755, however, ministers fully accepted such propositions. They needed no prompting to use force against France for the security of America,

upon which the prosperity of these dominions so much depends. 'Full one third of the whole export of the produce and the manufactures of the country is to our colonies, and in proportion as this diminishes and increases, the estates of landholders, and the business of the merchant, the manufacturer and the artificer must diminish or increase.'

From the American colonies

great part of the wealth we see, that credit which circulates, and those payments that are made at the bank, and the bankers in London, results; and they are so linked in with and dependent upon the American revenues and remittances, that if they are ruined and stopt, the whole system of public credit in this country will receive a fatal shock.[90]

Such statements by a secretary of state indicate that British official opinion was becoming fully aware of the growth and of the potential for further growth in worldwide trades, and above all in the colonial trades, described in the previous chapter. These immensely valuable overseas assets seemed to contemporaries to be very vulnerable. Fears were focused on the French. Dreams of the great wealth to be extracted by aggression against Spanish America were giving way to apprehension as to whether Britain's trade with the West Indies, North America, and India could be safeguarded from French incursions.

There seemed to be unmistakable evidence of French aggressive tendencies all over the world. In their diagnosis, British ministers were probably not mistaken, even if their belief in France's ambitions for 'universal monarchy' was a serious misunderstanding. Britain's fear of France was probably matched by France's fear of Britain. Deeply concerned about Britain's naval power and the resources that it derived from maritime trade, the French seem to have devised a strategy for trying to contain what they saw as Britain's ambitions for supremacy by constricting British trade and colonies all over the world.[91] In North America the French seemed to be especially threatening

[88] HL, LO 253.   [89] *Monitor*, 6 Dec. 1755.
[90] T. Robinson to Holdernesse, 29 Aug. 1755, BL, Egerton MS, 3432, ff. 293, 297–8.
[91] Daniel A. Baugh, 'Withdrawing from Europe: Anglo-French Maritime Geopolitics, 1750–1800', *International History Review*, XX (1998), 11–16.

in Nova Scotia and in the Ohio valley, where from 1749 French expeditions were trying to make good their claims to an area that was being penetrated by Indian traders and land speculators from the British colonies of Virginia and Pennsylvania. Skirmishes escalated to a conflict in July 1754 in which the French defeated a small party of Virginians under George Washington. It is likely that both sides exaggerated the sense of purpose and aggressive intent of the other. The French feared a concerted British drive to push their frontiers far to the west. To British ministers there seemed to be no doubt that the French were trying to force the British colonies into a narrow and ultimately indefensible coastal strip. For the duke of Newcastle what happened in 1754 confirmed his fears since 1748 and the ending of the last war.

The insults and encroachments of the French have alarm'd the inhabitants of our colonies to that degree that many of them have left their habitations, with crops upon their lands. All North America will be lost if these practices are tolerated: and no war can be worse for this country than the suffering such insults, as these. The truth is, the French claim almost all North America, except a liziere [lizere, a narrow border] to the sea, to which they could confine all our colonies, and from whence they may drive us whenever they please or as soon as there shall be declar'd war. But that is what we must not, we will not suffer.[92]

Ministers, Newcastle most of all, wished to avoid a general war with France that would involve both countries in Europe, but there could be no question of giving way to what was seen as a challenge to Britain's essential interests in America. Naval and military action must be taken.

British interests also appeared to be under threat in the West Indies. There the disputes were about the so-called 'neutral' islands, St Lucia, Dominica, St Vincent, and Tobago, which Britain and France had agreed to leave unsettled. There were frequent allegations after 1748 that the French were not keeping to this agreement and were making establishments on the islands. With the French having built up an already impressive lead over the British islands in the production of staple crops through their plantations in Martinique, Guadeloupe, and above all in Saint-Domingue (later Haiti), the prospect of even more land passing under French control aroused acute alarm. The governor of Barbados warned the board of trade that 'the effect of their increase of riches, power, and territory by their new acquisitions will soon be felt in the decay, if not the whole loss of that valuable trade the nation has hitherto carried on in the West Indies.'[93] Admiral Vernon prophesied in

---

[92] Letter to Albermarle, 5 Sept. 1754, BL, Add MS 32850, f. 218. The outbreak of fighting in North America is well covered in T. R. Clayton, 'The Duke of Newcastle, the Earl of Halifax and the American Origins of the Seven Years' War', *Historical Journal*, XXIV (1981), 571–603 and Anderson, *Crucible of War*, pts. 1, 2.

[93] Letter of H. Grenville, 7 Feb. 1748, WLCL, Shelburne MSS, 45, p. 45.

parliament that the French would shortly be in control of all the British sugar islands.[94] Diplomacy produced a renewed agreement to leave the islands unsettled. The British, however, believed that the French were dragging their feet and that only Tobago had actually been evacuated by 1754.[95]

The peace settlement of 1748 left unresolved tensions between Britain and France in India as well as in North America and the West Indies. The forces of the British and French East India Companies had fought one another on the Coromandel coast of south-eastern India during the War of the Austrian Succession. The peace had brought the restoration to the British of their main settlement at Madras, lost to the French in 1746, but it did not end the manoeuvring for gains through the Indian alliances in which both sides were engaged. In 1749 the British company's agents began to complain that the French under their governor, Joseph-François Dupleix, had intervened first in the succession to the nawabs of the coastal Carnatic province and then in that of the Deccan, the main successor state to Mughal rule in south India. Claimants backed by the French were rewarding them with territorial grants that threatened to cut off the British settlements from their trade inland. The French seemed to 'aim at nothing less than to exclude us from the trade of this coast, and by degrees from that of India'.[96] Admiral Boscawen, who had been sent to India with a royal squadron during the war, warned ministers that 'unless something is done to prevent it, the French will gain that profitable branch of trade from our nation'.[97] In the meanwhile, the British Company servants on the Coromandel coast retaliated by deploying troops in support of their own claimants and by taking territorial gains from the claimants in return.

As both companies became more deeply engaged in supporting their Indian allies, the British government was hesitantly drawn into dispatching its own forces to India. Ministers hoped for a peaceful settlement with the French, but were warned by the Company's directors that the French were building up a level of force in India that the Company on its own could not match. That could not be permitted. British governments could not accept 'a decisive superiority of force in the hands of the French in that part of the world'.[98] Lord Holdernesse, the minister who took the closest interest in India, described himself as 'too sensible of the consequences of our trade in India to suffer it to be diminished, much less lost'. He would do his utmost

---

[94] 16 Nov. 1749, Stock, ed., *Proceedings and Debates*, V. 369.
[95] For the Neutral Islands disputes, see Richard Pares, *War and Trade in the West Indies, 1739–1763* (Oxford, 1936), pp. 199–216.
[96] Letters from Ft. St David, 18 Oct., 2 Nov. 1749, 12 Feb. 1750, OIOC, H/93, pp. 41–54.
[97] Letter to Bedford, 29 May 1750, PRO, CO 77/18, f. 62.
[98] Holdernesse to Albermarle, 24 Jan. 1754, BL, Add MS 32848, f. 270.

'either to procure a safe peace in India or to fall upon the means of carrying on the war with honour and success'.[99] A squadron of warships and some regular troops were sent out in 1754 to support the Company. They were to avoid direct conflict with the French and in any case a local truce had been concluded by the time they reached the Coromandel coast. Both sides were, however, now well armed for the shift from war through Indian proxies to the formal outbreak of direct Anglo-French conflict in India that followed the open declaration of war between the two countries in 1756.

By then Britain had committed itself to defending its interests all over the world. When the fighting came to a formal end in 1763 what had begun as a defensive war had become a war of conquest. French and later Spanish possessions had been seized in North America, the Caribbean, on the coast of West Africa, in India, and even in the Philippines. This great worldwide war brought about many changes. Both British governments and the British people as a whole developed a new awareness of their colonial possessions and of their importance to Britain. Local colonial governments and bodies like the East India Company were drawn into much closer relations with metropolitan authority. The empire impinged much more directly on the lives of its peoples. More and more British soldiers and sailors had served throughout the empire and colonial Americans, Native Americans, Indian sepoys, and Africans had all been drawn into the empire's orbit to fight for it or to service its armed forces.

Given the strengths and weaknesses of the British state, it is not perhaps surprising that ministers should have found it easier to go to war in 1755 than to attempt the kind of reforms of civil government that Halifax and others were pressing on them. War, however, seemed to make reform inescapable. The territorial gains retained at the peace of 1763 transformed the British empire. New colonies raised new problems of government, while the war seemed to have made the case for reforming relations with the existing colonies one that could no longer be evaded. War had exposed the limitations of an imperial authority based on negotiation; those who thought seriously about the empire were coming to believe that it must be replaced by an authority also based on a degree of obedience.

[99] Holdernesse to R. Orme, 14 Oct. 1755, BL, Egerton MS, 3488, f. 96.

3

War and its Transformations: The Atlantic
1754–1763

B Y the winter of 1753–4 British ministers were steeling themselves to resist what they saw as systematic French aggression in North America and the Caribbean.[1] That French incursions must be checked was an issue on which there could be no compromise, but there was a profound desire to limit the scale of the apparently inevitable hostilities and above all to prevent a general war with France that would become a European war. British naval supremacy and the huge superiority that the British enjoyed in local manpower in North America would, it was hoped, bring the French to their senses and force them to conclude a settlement that would ensure the future security of the British colonies. Fighting in America must not be allowed to spread; in any conflict Spanish neutrality must be carefully preserved.

Hopes for a brief passage of arms confined to the French in North America were, however, to prove totally vain. War spread to Europe. What were intended to be limited operations on the colonial frontier, largely fought by Americans, escalated into a series of major campaigns in which British troops bore a large part. By the end of the war Britain was seeking security through the total elimination of the French in North America and was taking territory from the Spanish who had entered the war on the side of the French in 1762. French and Spanish possessions had also been seized in the West Indies and the French had been attacked on the West African coast. The scale of the war around the Atlantic, the degree of metropolitan involvement in colonial affairs brought about by the exigencies of war and the extent of Britain's territorial gains at the peace of 1763 were to transform the British Atlantic empire.

The course of the Seven Years War, above all the war in North America, is very well known. It has inspired some enduring classics of historical narrative, most notably Francis Parkman's *Montcalm and Wolfe* of 1884. The most

---

[1] See above, pp. 82–4.

Map 1. War in North America *c.*1750–83.

recent treatment, Fred Anderson's *The Crucible of War: The Seven Years' War and the Fate of Empire in British North America, 1754–1766*, published in 2000, is a worthy addition to the canon. For generations of British and American people the story of the war in America is a rich example of what they like to believe to be characteristic of their military history: the ability of a pacific people to reverse early defeats and to triumph over militarized aggressors by tenacity and by the emergence of an inspired leader.

Defeats came in abundance in the early years of the war. From 1753 British ministers were urging the colony of Virginia to force the French out of the Ohio valley. It was, however, the Virginians under Washington who were forced out. British regulars under general Braddock were sent to reinforce the colonial effort in a multi-pronged offensive in 1755. Braddock was catastrophically defeated on the Monongahela, a disaster which wholly overshadowed victories on the frontier of New York and in Nova Scotia. A new British commander, lord Loudoun, was dispatched to America with more regulars in 1756. He received further British reinforcements for a projected assault by sea on the great French base on the Gulf of the St Lawrence at Louisbourg in 1757. The operation had to be cancelled, but while British troops were massed for a sea-borne attack, the French struck south overland to take the British Fort William Henry. By 1758 direction of the war was perceived by the public, both in Britain and in America, to have passed wholly into the resolute hands of William Pitt, who alone, it was thought, had the vision and the capacity to bring about total victory, a view not entirely shared by recent historians.[2] Yet more troops and fresh commanders were sent from Britain. Louisbourg was taken by Jeffrey Amherst and the French were finally cleared off the Ohio, even though the overland attack into Canada up the Hudson valley failed at Ticonderoga. In 1759 the net was closing on New France: Quebec was captured by James Wolfe in the greatest epic of the war and the overland invasion was poised to take Montreal. That city duly surrendered with the rest of New France to Jeffrey Amherst in 1760. The North American war was over.

Britain had gone onto the offensive in the Caribbean in 1758 with an expedition sent to capture Martinique. It failed there but was able to seize Guadeloupe early in the following year. Troops from both Britain and North America were brought together to conquer Martinique in 1762 and then to expel the French from Grenada, Dominica, St Lucia, and St Vincent. When Spain entered the war a massive British expedition was fitted out against Havana in Cuba. The city surrendered in August 1762. In 1758 British expeditions took the French slave trading settlements around the Senegal River in West Africa.

I

War in the Caribbean was always the responsibility of British forces and was directed from London. The white populations of the islands were insufficient

---

[2] e.g. Richard Middleton, *The Bells of Victory: The Pitt–Newcastle Ministry and the Conduct of the Seven Years' War 1757–1762* (Cambridge, 1985), especially pp. 211–13; Marie Peters, 'The Myth of William Pitt, Earl of Chatham, Great Imperialist Part I: Pitt and Imperial Expansion 1738–1763', *Journal of Imperial and Commonwealth History,* XXI (1993), 43–6.

to provide a militia adequate for internal defence against their own slaves, let alone against an invasion by France or Spain. Although the apparent willingness of Jamaicans to provoke Spain by incursions on the Moskito Coast of Central America alarmed British ministers, the British West Indian colonies had no capacity on their own to mount expeditions against the main colonies of other powers. Indeed, they depended for their defence on forces from Britain. At the beginning of the hostilities that led to the Seven Years War the Jamaica council and assembly showed their sense of the island's vulnerability when they asked for the royal regiment stationed there to be brought up to strength and for another regiment to be sent.[3]

The situation was assumed to be very different in all the North American colonies from Virginia to the northward. The assumption was that abundant colonial manpower would enable the colonies to counter any French threat with only a limited commitment of resources from Britain. The initial response of British ministers to reports of French aggression was, as in previous wars, to rely on the forces of the colonies. In January 1754 the Virginian Edmund Jenings was told by lord Halifax that he understood the Virginia militia to number 13,000 and that 'such a force must be sufficient for every purpose of preventing French settlement'.[4] Thomas Penn, the proprietor of Pennsylvania, reported from London that 'it is supposed here that so great a number of Englishmen as are settled in North America, would not suffer a few French to settle in the king's dominions quietly'. The 'greatest people here' thought that 'the colonys should do something for themselves . . . and not let the whole lye on the mother country'.[5]

The use of colonial rather than British troops would of course save awkward requests to parliament to vote supplies for the defence of colonies that were 'well settled, and in a flourishing condition; and who enjoy their property with the same freedom and privileges as English men doe'. Requests of this nature would greatly alarm 'the landed gentlemen of this country'.[6] It was hoped too that the use of colonial troops would constitute a less overt escalation towards an open war with France than would the deployment of British regulars. This point was of particular concern to the duke of Newcastle. It was also widely believed that Americans were better suited to fight wars in America than British soldiers, an opinion that was to be reinforced by the initial failures of the British regulars.

[3] C. Knowles to T. Robinson, 18 Oct. 1755, PRO, CO 137/10, f. 218.
[4] Jenings to R. Dinwiddie, 25 Jan. 1754, Virginia Historical Society, MS J 4105a 1, pp. 27–8.
[5] To J. Hamilton, 29 Jan. 1754, HSP, Thomas Penn Letter Books, III, p. 289.
[6] H. Walpole to Newcastle, 14 June 1754, cited in J. A. Henretta, *'Salutary Neglect': Colonial Administration under the Duke of Newcastle* (Princeton, 1972), pp. 329–30.

'I have often heard' Newcastle wrote, 'from very intelligent persons that the operations in those countries would be best perform'd by troops of the country; who are best used to, and acquainted with, the nature of the service . . . Americans must fight Americans; and the regular troops must not be puff'd up . . . The Indians must be engag'd, if possible; and Americans must do our business'.[7]

American soldiers were also commonly, if usually incorrectly, assumed to be 'militia', as opposed to the 'mercenary' British standing army. There was therefore a strong ideological disposition in their favour in certain quarters. 'Our American countrymen' were said to have provided a glowing example for 'a British militia'.[8] An MP contrasted the New Englanders with 'our British mercenary soldiers'; the Americans were the type of citizen soldiers who had fought at 'Cressy, Nevil's Cross and Poitiers'.[9]

However strong the initial disposition might have been to devolve responsibility for resisting the French in North America onto the colonies themselves, indications reaching Britain quickly suggested that effective resistance required centralized British control over the colonial war effort and the deployment of British troops. What had begun as operations largely to be left to local colonial initiatives became step by step a British national concern in which the American role was ultimately deemed to be an entirely subordinate one.[10]

Virginia had at first been expected to make the main effort to clear the Ohio, but its governor complained that its militia could not be compelled to go beyond the colony's borders, that the house of burgesses would not sanction major military expenditure and that virtually no support was forthcoming from other colonies directly involved. The failure of the dominant Quaker group in Pennsylvania to commit resources to the colony's defence or of Maryland to make any significant contribution of any kind were held to be particularly culpable. Only the New England colonies seemed to be showing an inclination to engage seriously with the French. Halifax lamented 'the absurd and false œconomy, the ill-tim'd deficiency of spirit and the lethargic insensibility of the colonies'. Were other colonial militias in the same condition as that of Virginia, '5000 French might safely march from east to west in the heart of his Majesty's American dominions'.[11] The news of Washington's defeat at Fort Necessity was the 'intelligence that alarmed every body here

---

[7] To Holdernesse, 26 Aug. 1755, BL, Add MS 32858, ff. 289, 292.

[8] *Public Advertiser*, 10 Nov. 1755.

[9] Speech of Robert Vyner, 16 Dec. 1754, R. C Simmons and P. D. G. Thomas, eds., *Proceedings and Debates of the British Parliaments Respecting North America, 1754–1783*, 6 vols. (Millwood, NY, 1982–6), I. 31.

[10] Growing British control over the war in North America is analysed in D. Graham, 'British Intervention in Defence of the American Colonies, 1748–56', London University Ph.D. thesis, 1969.

[11] Letter to R. Dinwiddie, 6 July 1754, University of Virginia, McGregor MS 2693.

and convinced them of the absolute necessity of sending assistance from hence'.[12]

The scale of the initial British involvement in the war in America and the form that it would take emerged from confused manoeuvring within the government. The board of trade under Halifax's direction resurrected plans for coordinating the defence of the colonies that had been canvassed in the past. The management of Indian affairs was to be placed under British commissioners and a British commander-in-chief was to be empowered to levy quotas of troops and money from the colonies for joint operations.[13] Two Indian superintendents took up their appointments in 1755 and 1756, while ministers agreed to appoint Edward Braddock as commander-in-chief in America. He was to be sent out with two regular British regiments who would compel the French to retreat from the Ohio and then from other incursions if they still proved obdurate. Newcastle hoped by limited operations to avoid '*éclat*' and thus not to give the French a pretext for over-reacting in ways that would lead to all-out war.[14] Under the influence of the duke of Cumberland, captain-general of the army, a more ambitious and belligerent plan was, however, devised. The French would be attacked on four fronts, two more royal regiments would be raised in America and Braddock, as commander-in-chief was given extensive powers. The colonies were to contribute to a common defence fund at his disposal and to raise recruits for him. He could compel them to provide quarters and transport for his troops.[15] At the insistence of the duke of Cumberland, but in the face of protests from the agent for Massachusetts, a clause was inserted into the Mutiny Act subjecting colonial troops to British military law when they served with the forces of the crown.[16]

The outcome of the 1755 campaign was a less than triumphant vindication of the case for British direction of the war or for the superior fighting qualities of British troops. Braddock's regulars were routed, while the New England provincials won what could be represented as a great victory at Lake George. As a 'letter from Boston' in the London press put it, 'the despised militia of New England have all the glory. The regulars from England have ever treated them with great contempt, but not greater than we always had for them'.[17] The opposition *Monitor* insisted that the colonies should be defended by

---

[12] T. Penn to J. Hamilton, 17 Nov. 1754, HSP, Penn–Hamilton Correspondence, p. 32.
[13] Plan of 9 Aug. 1754, PRO, CO 5/6, ff. 121–2; Memorial to the King, 9 Aug. 1754, BL, Egerton MS 3490, ff. 173–84.
[14] Letter to Albermarle, 10 Oct. 1754, BL, Add MS 32851, f. 51.
[15] Braddock's instructions [25 Nov. 1754], PRO, CO 5/6, f. 7.
[16] S. Waldo to W. Pepperell, 13 Jan. 1755, MHS, Miscellaneous Bound MSS.
[17] *Public Advertiser*, 5 Nov. 1755.

their own 'brave and rough inhabitants' rather than by British 'mercenaries'.[18] Nevertheless, the duke of Newcastle, who thought differently, reported that 'those who govern absolutely in army affairs and military operations', still believed that regulars must be the main British force in America.[19] He was clearly referring to Cumberland, who regarded *'provincials'* as 'execrable troops',[20] and perhaps to Halifax, who had come to believe that 'the greatest part' of any British force must 'consist of regular troops. For whatever opinions may be entertain'd of the resolution and spirit of the New Englanders, they are at best undisciplined and therefore unequal to the attack of regular troops and fortified places.'[21] Following what was judged to be a poor performance by the New England troops in 1756, Thomas Penn feared 'that the great dependence will be on officers and men from hence, and that those of the country will be but little employ'd. The New England army are called here disorderly bad troops, they having gone home in vast numbers.'[22]

In 1756 a new commander-in-chief, more senior British officers and additional regiments of regulars were ordered to America. A new Royal American regiment was to be recruited in the colonies, especially from German speakers and other foreign Protestants, under British and continental European officers. Lord Loudoun, the new commander-in-chief, did his utmost to use the powers vested in his office in order to impose effective British control over the war effort. He intended that the provincial regiments should serve not as a separate force under their own officers but as part of a single army under his command. The colonies had done nothing to implement the orders conveyed to them that they must contribute to a common fund under the commander-in-chief. The requirement to do so was repeated in Loudoun's instructions. If quarters for troops or boats and horses for transporting the army and its supplies were unreasonably withheld, Loudoun was willing to requisition them and to threaten to take quarters by force. Parliament had passed an act authorizing British regiments to recruit servants in America and strenuous efforts were made to recruit for the royal regiments in the face of protests by employers that their labour force was being lured away. Loudoun was warned that the colonies had been guilty of illegal trade to supply the enemy and he was empowered to take all possible measures to suppress that trade. To achieve that and other purposes, Loudoun was to

---

[18] *Monitor*, 13 Sept. 1755.

[19] To Hartington, 30 Aug. 1755, BL, Add MS 32858, f. 352.

[20] To Loudoun, 22 Oct. 1756, Stanley Pargellis, ed., *Military Affairs in North America, 1748–1765: Selected Documents from the Cumberland Papers in Windsor Castle* (New York, 1936), p. 251.

[21] 'Remarks on Affairs in North America', HL, LO 722.

[22] To R. Peters, 11 Dec. 1756, HSP, Thomas Penn Letter Books, V. p. 51.

require the governors to impose periodic embargoes on the movement of ships out of colonial ports.

All these powers proved to be contentious and were resisted in varying degrees. Provincial troops openly refused to merge with the royal forces, since their officers would lose rank and they would be subjected to ferocious British military discipline. The common fund remained a nullity and Loudoun had to cajole individual colonies into making contributions of men and money. He complained that colonies were inclined to ask for details of the campaigns on which their troops would be employed and to try to attach conditions on their use. Loudoun felt it necessary to tell the New England colonies that 'the confining your men to any particular service appears to me to be a prepos- terous measure. Our affairs are not in such situation as to make it reasonable for any colony to be influenced by its particular interest.'[23] Provincial troops only served for limited periods and often left their posts as soon as the term had been completed. Quarters for the regular troops were withheld in Albany, Philadelphia, and Boston. Recruiting parties for the royal regiments were beaten up by mobs and arrested by local magistrates. Governors came under great pressure, to which they seemed easily to yield, to lift the embargoes ordered by the commander-in-chief. Once one colony broke ranks, others quickly followed.

Ill-feeling between the commander-in-chief and sections of colonial opin- ion reached the point where to some Americans Loudoun may have seemed to pose 'at least as grave a threat to their liberties as the French and the Indians—and one much closer at hand'.[24] There were fears that the powers being exerted by the commander-in-chief were part of a systematic British policy for remodelling constitutional relations with the colonies and for asserting metropolitan authority over them. The agent for Massachusetts believed that:

. . . it was intended by some persons of consequence that the colonies shou'd be govern'd like Ireland, keeping up a body of standing forces, with a military chest there; to which one of them, who was bred a lawyer, added an abridgement of their legislative powers, so as to put them on the same foot that Ireland stands by Poynings' law.[25]

Reforms imposed by statute of the British parliament were frequently men- tioned as imminent. In January 1754 Halifax warned a Virginian that one of the consequences of a failure of the colonies to defend themselves would

[23] To New England Commissioners, 29 Jan. 1757, 'Fitch Papers: Correspondence and Docu- ments during Thomas Fitch's Government of the Colony of Connecticut', *Connecticut Historical Society Collections*, XVII (1918), 279.

[24] Fred Anderson, *Crucible of War: The Seven Years' War and the Fate of Empire in British North America, 1754–1766* (New York, 2000), p. 167.

[25] W. Bollan to J. Willard, 5 March 1755, MHS, Miscellaneous Bound MSS.

be an act of parliament 'to oblige the plantations to support as well as to raise forces'.[26] He specifically proposed in April 1754 that colonial revenues should be consolidated by parliament into a fund to be appropriated for uses determined in Britain.[27] It was widely assumed in Britain that any agreements that emerged from the congress of the colonies at Albany could only be made effective by an act of parliament.[28] The government quickly lost interest in the Albany proposals, but Halifax still spoke in the house of lords in March 1755 about a union to be imposed by act of parliament.[29] Thomas Penn believed in January 1757 that 'some dutys or taxes will in a short time be laid on the colonys by act of parliament'.[30] In the event, however, the power of statute was only used for limited colonial purposes during the war. Moreover, all the indications are that, whatever individual ministers might wish, British governments as a whole were no more willing to try to enforce radical reforms on the colonies during the war than they had been before it.

Ministers' unwillingness to force issues was strongly demonstrated by their refusal to take advantage of a golden opportunity for using parliament's authority to remedy what were seen as the glaring abuses of Pennsylvania. The dominant Quaker group in the assembly was held to be deliberately leaving their colony defenceless in the face of the French and Indian onslaught in order to satisfy their own scruples and their aversion to the Penn family. Petitions against the assembly's failure to sanction the effective defence of the province were transmitted to Britain. Their arrival coincided with an outbreak of popular hostility against Quakers in London for their apparent refusal to obey the king's proclamation for a day of prayer and fasting for the war. The *Monitor* saw their behaviour as 'a specimen of that spirit, which has lately reduced Pennsilvania to the brink of destruction'.[31] Quakers were pilloried in the press and the windows of their shops and houses were broken. The leading London Quaker, John Fothergill, warned his American correspondents that Quakers were now as much disliked as they had ever been since the Restoration and that 'men high and low of all parties . . . seem not intent upon any thing more than how to manifest this dislike in the most signal manner'.[32] In January 1756 it was reported that ministers were considering a bill to disqualify Quakers from sitting in the

---

[26] E. Jenings to R. Dinwiddie, 25 Jan. 1754, Virginia Historical Society, MS J 4105a 1.

[27] 'Proposals for Forts in North America', 30 April 1754, PRO, CO 5/6, ff. 103–4.

[28] Alison Gilbert Olson, 'The British Government and Colonial Union, 1754', *William and Mary Quarterly*, 3rd ser., XVII (1960), 30–1.

[29] See reports by T. Penn to R. Peters, 26 March 1755, HSP, Thomas Penn Letter Books, IV, p. 79; E. Jenings to C. Carter [April 1755], Virginia Historical Society, MS J 4105a 1, pp. 124–5.

[30] To R. Peters, 8 Jan. 1757, HSP, Thomas Penn Letter Books, V, p. 61.

[31] *Monitor*, 14 Feb. 1756.

[32] To J. Pemberton, 16–19 March 1756, HSP, Etting Collection, XXIX, p. 10.

Pennsylvania assembly. A clause to that effect was proposed to be included in a bill to permit the recruiting of foreign officers. In the face of lobbying by the London Quakers, however, ministers drew back and accepted a temporary voluntary withdrawal from the assembly by the Pennsylvania Quakers instead. Thomas Penn reported that 'Quakers are a body of people much respected here' and that some ministers, notably lord Granville, president of the council, and lord Halifax, were 'unwilling to make them enemies by a permanent disqualification'.[33] Wary of resorting to parliamentary authority, ministers left it to the commanders-in-chief to try to extract men and money and the services necessary to support the army by cajoling or threatening the governors and the colonial assemblies.

With Pitt in full control of the war effort from the late summer of 1757, clear signals began to come from London that the exertion of metropolitan authority was to be moderated. Commanders-in-chief were no longer required to try to impose their will on reluctant Americans. With the failure of the campaign to take Louisbourg, Pitt was determined to recall Loudoun. Among his other shortcomings, Loudoun was warned that Pitt disapproved of 'your preference of military to civil power' and of his 'exerting too much authority over the people of the country, [and] not treating the provincial troops so well as they deserved'.[34] Another correspondent warned him that 'if any American folks will upon this occasion clamour against your lordship concerning acts of military power &c. they will be listened to'.[35] Pitt signalled his intentions for a new relationship with the colonies, based more on cooperation and less on coercion, by a series of measures. The northern colonies were to be encouraged to raise at least 20,000 troops for a new attempt on Canada. They were promised in return that 'strong recommendations shall be made to parliament . . . to grant a proper compensation for such expences'.[36] Parliamentary reimbursement for a large part of colonial military expenditure was duly granted and was to be repeated annually for the rest of the war. It proved to be a very powerful inducement for active cooperation.

Pitt also wished to see more use made of provincial officers. The principle that officers with the king's commission took precedence over all officers commissioned by colonial governors was stated in 1754. A limited concession gave senior provincial officers, including generals, rank above captains but below all more senior officers in the regulars. This was much resented.

[33] To R. H. Morris, 13 March 1756, HSP, Thomas Penn Letter Books, IV, p. 245.
[34] J. Calcraft to Loudoun, 29 Dec. 1757, HL, LO 5140.
[35] Cotterell to Loudoun, 28 Dec. 1757, HL, LO 5130.
[36] Pitt to Governors, 30 Dec. 1757, G. S. Kimball, ed., *Correspondence of William Pitt, when Secretary of State, with Colonial Governors and Military and Naval Commissioners in North America*, 2 vols. (New York, 1906), I. 136–43.

Samuel Waldo, who had taken troops to Louisbourg in 1745 and was a great Massachusetts landowner, believed that, while Cumberland 'had no manner of inclination to promote American officers', Pitt was sympathetic to them.[37] So he proved to be. To give 'due encouragement to officers serving in our provincial corps', George II granted provincial majors, colonels, and generals rank after the equivalent British ranks.[38]

With Pitt there was clearly a return to a belief in the potential of American manpower together with an acceptance that this manpower could only be effectively used if American susceptibilities were observed. Assemblies could not be coerced and American soldiers served best under their own officers, who must be treated with proper respect. Admiral Warren had made this point on the Louisbourg expedition in 1745. New England soldiers would only serve, he wrote, under 'a gentleman in whom they have confidence' and, in addition, as they had

the highest notions of the rights of Englishmen and indeed are almost levellers, they must know when, where, how and what service they are going on and be treated in a manner that few military bred gentlemen would condescend to, but if they do the work in which they are engaged, every other ceremony should in my opinion be winked at.[39]

Pitt seems to have been taught these lessons by two colonial governors, Charles Hardy of New York, who was in London, and Thomas Pownall, who wrote frequently to him from Massachusetts.

Whether any deeper sense of the nature of the colonies' relations with Britain lay behind Pitt's strategies for making the best of the resources of America to win the war is hard to fathom in so enigmatic a man, so given to making oracular pronouncements. His unpredictable responses to American developments after the war compound the problem.[40] Dr Marie Peters, whose valuable work generally stresses the limited nature of Pitt's thought about empire, suggests that he fully shared the American perception of themselves as 'emigrated Englishmen' enjoying the rights of Englishmen.[41] In February 1766 he spoke of the 'loyal, free and Protestant Americans'.[42] Ten years later he was to speak of 'the genuine descendants of a valiant and pious ancestry, driven to those desarts by the narrow maxims of a superstitious

[37] To T. Flucker, 14 May 1757, MHS, Henry Knox MSS 50.
[38] Warrant, 13 Dec. 1757, HL, AB 8.
[39] To Newcastle, 18 June 1745, HUHL, Sparks MSS 10/1.
[40] See below, pp. 298, 304–5.
[41] 'The Myth of William Pitt, Earl of Chatham, Great Imperialist Part II: Chatham and Imperial Reorganization 1763–78', *Journal of Imperial and Commonwealth History*, XXII (1994), 395; see also the treatment of American issues in her *The Elder Pitt* (1998).
[42] Speech of 5 Dec. 1766, Simmons and Thomas, eds., *Proceedings and Debates*, II. 161.

tyranny'.[43] Such people were to be cherished as valuable members of a free Protestant empire. He had the same view of the Irish Protestants. Ulster Presbyterians 'were a zealous, brave and flourishing people'; their military potential too should be fully exploited.[44] Americans were not of course to be treated as equal partners in empire; Pitt had a high view of imperial authority on such matters as economic regulation. Their assemblies were, however, genuine representative bodies, even for matters of taxation, and, as Englishmen, Americans should not be made the victims of undue exertions of military power by men like Loudoun. Americans may have seriously misunderstood Pitt to the point in later years of investing totally unrealistic hopes in him, but during the war the New Englanders had real grounds for holding him in 'so much honor and affection' as almost to 'idolize' him.[45]

Relations between the colonies and British commanders-in-chief eased somewhat after Pitt began to impose his control over American policy. Amherst, commander-in-chief from 1758, dismayed those officers who had admired Loudoun. He is 'an amiable man', one of them wrote, 'but vainly fancys that he can govern these provinces by yielding and the arts of complyance'. When a New York notable threatened to prosecute an officer 'for pressing a slay for the publick service . . . the general in place of punishing the fellow, bowed and flatter'd and advised him'. He evidently had not learnt that in America 'fear' was 'a more effectual motive for action than flattery'.[46] Although privately he might share many of his brother officers' prejudices, Amherst was evidently well aware that Pitt expected him to cultivate smooth relations with colonial authorities and did not wish to hear protests from America about the army's high-handedness. He was 'a great dancer' and while in winter quarters beguiled New York society with 'plays, routs and assemblies almost every day'.[47]

With the recall of Loudoun, the political role of the commanders-in-chief in America largely went into abeyance, but the role of the British army in the conduct of the war continued to grow. All shades of British opinion appear to have been committed to the view that victory could only be won by a huge deployment of British regulars. In the summer and autumn of 1756 Braddock's defeat and the devastating Indian raids that followed it were taken up by the opposition in Britain as part of their criticism of the conduct of the war. The loss of Minorca was the main accusation against the government,

---

[43] Speech of 20 Jan. 1755, ibid. V. 276.
[44] To Bedford, 21 Nov. 1759, PRO, SP 63/416, ff. 159–60; see also letter to Bedford, 5 Jan. 1760, PRO, SP 63/417, f. 152.
[45] E. Stiles to B. Franklin, 30 Dec. 1761, Leonard W. Labaree et al., eds., *The Papers of Benjamin Franklin* (New Haven, 1959–), IX. 403.
[46] J. Robertson to Loudoun, 3 Feb. 1759, HL, LO 6039.
[47] J. Abercromby to Loudoun, 4 Feb. 1759, HL, LO 6041.

but America frequently featured in the addresses to the crown or instructions to MPs from counties and boroughs. The addresses repeated the language used by Pitt in December 1755 when he had castigated the ministry for sending only 'two miserable battalions' to America.[48] The commons was repeatedly asked to inquire into why the colonies had been left 'defenceless'. The Norfolk grand jury, for instance, expressed its 'most anxious fears for the neglected and deplorable condition of our fellow-subjects in America' and significantly called for a militia at home, so that the 'regular forces' could be sent overseas.[49] As Thomas Penn put it, 'People of all sorts, the opposition most loudly, declare the colonys must be supported'.[50] Ministers felt that they must increase the British military commitment to America. Under the short-lived Pitt–Devonshire administration a large reinforcement of regulars was sent to America in the early months of 1757. When consulted by Newcastle in 1754, Pitt had spoken of the need both to send British troops and to arm large numbers of Americans, since 'it was not to be done by troops from Europe'.[51] Now he seems to have been personally committed to sending the maximum number of regiments to America even, it was said, at the risk of weakening home defence. It was supposed that he would rather 'this island [be] left bare' than that America should be 'without a very considerable reinforcement'.[52] Regulars for America had evidently become part of the programme of what had been the opposition as well as of the duke of Cumberland. Even those who regarded themselves as friends of the colonies were coming to see them not as allies capable of defending themselves, but as dependants who had the right to be defended by Britain. The implications of this change of view for the future of British relations with the colonies were ominous.

Pitt's return to power was followed during 1758 by the first military successes in North America since 1755. Provincial troops had major roles in some of the campaigns. John Bradstreet's force that took Fort Frontenac in 1758 was almost entirely provincial. Provincials were the major part of the force that made the long slog to the Ohio at Fort Duquesne under John Forbes and they were well represented at the taking of Fort Niagara. Yet from the point of view of the British press and public the heroes were the regulars. Their successes were blazoned across the newspapers through the reprinting

[48] 5 Dec. 1755, Simmons and Thomas, eds., *Proceedings and Debates*, I. 110.
[49] *Public Advertiser*, 9 Sept. 1756. For the addresses, see Kathleen Wilson, *The Sense of the People: Politics, Culture and Imperialism in England, 1715–1785* (Cambridge, 1995), pp. 178–85; L. S. Sutherland, 'The City of London and the Devonshire–Pitt Administration, 1756–7' in Aubrey Newman, ed., *Politics and Finance in the Eighteenth Century: Lucy Sutherland* (1984), pp. 72–6.
[50] T. Penn to R. Peters, 13 Dec. 1755, HSP, Thomas Penn Letter Books, IV, p. 190.
[51] Newcastle to Hardwicke, 2 Oct. 1754, BL, Add MS 35414, f. 198.
[52] Cathcart to Loudoun, 4 Feb. 1757, HL, LO 2858.

of the dispatches of the victorious British generals in the *London Gazette*. The spectacular victories by sea-borne attack, Louisbourg in 1758 and Quebec in 1759, had been won by the navy and by the redcoats. The British army at last redeemed itself and put an end to suspicions that it could not fight in America.

The taking of Louisbourg in 1758 was the turning point for the reputation of the regulars. The victory was ecstatically celebrated by illuminations, firing salutes and feasting throughout Britain and Ireland. The captured French colours were paraded by the guards from Kensington to St Paul's.[53] The *Monitor*, which had deplored the use of 'mercenaries' in America in the past, drew the conclusion that America, not 'the plains of Germany' was the proper sphere for the British army.[54] The Highlanders began their long career as popular British military heroes. A letter published in the press told how they swam ashore and routed the French with their broad swords.[55] The French were said to fear them as the 'English savages'. Amherst was told that engravings of him were 'hung up at every ale house in London'.[56] The fall of Quebec the following year produced 'the greatest illuminations . . . throughout the city and suburbs that were ever known',[57] as well as the apotheosis of general Wolfe as a British military hero killed in battle. The victory at Quebec was the focus for a day of national thanksgiving 'for the signal success to our arms both sea and land' to be observed by churches throughout the British Isles that was proclaimed for 29 November 1759. Thirty-six sermons delivered for the occasion were subsequently published.[58] British admirals and generals became household names, while provincial generals, with the possible exception of Sir William Johnson, remained unknown.

As their personal correspondence shows, most British officers remained unimpressed by the American contribution to the war even in the years of victory. Their complaints to ministers tended, however, to be less strident and recriminations about what was happening in America increasingly gave way to more optimistic stories in the London press. A letter from New York of 17 March 1758, for instance, stated that 'A most noble spirit at present prevails over the whole continent.'[59] Massachusetts was reported to have made 'an effort for the common cause, a greater than which could not have been

---

[53] *London Chronicle*, 5–7 Sept. 1758.

[54] *Monitor*, 26 Aug. 1758.

[55] 'Letter from a Man of War returned from Louisbourg', 18 Sept. 1758, *London Chronicle*, 23–6 Sept. 1758.

[56] Letter of Col. West, 10 Feb. 1759, PRO, WO 34/77, f. 8.

[57] *Gentleman's Magazine*, XXIX (1759), 495; see also H. V. Bowen, 'British Conceptions of Global Empire, 1756–83', *Journal of Imperial and Commonwealth History*, XXVI (1998), 1–2.

[58] R. C. Simmons, *British Imprints Relating to North America, 1621 to 1760: An Annotated Checklist* (1996), p. xviii.

[59] *London Chronicle*, 25–7 April 1758.

made'.[60] Reports that parliamentary intervention was being contemplated to impose unity or reform on the colonies dried up.

Well before the end of the war, however, the question of trading with the enemy began to exert a very damaging effect on British opinion about the colonies. From the outbreak of the war governors and naval officers had reported that the French West Indies and Canada were regularly supplied by ships from the British North American colonies. Stories to this effect appeared in the London press.[61] The issue was brought to a head in 1759 by a report from the board of trade which focused on the huge number of British colonial ships, 150 at a time, going from North America to a port of convenience in Spanish Hispaniola (now the Dominican Republic), called Monte Christi. From there their bullion or supplies went straight to the French Hispaniola ports. The American ships then loaded up with French produce. Rhode Island was particularly implicated. According to the board, it and Connecticut 'assume to themselves an absolute government, independent not only of the crown, but of the legislature of the mother country'.[62] All this was more than Pitt could tolerate and he sent a circular to all the governors ordering them to put a stop forthwith to 'this dangerous and ignominious trade'.[63] Shortly afterwards, Amherst was given evidence that judges in New York were conspiring to silence those who had information about trade with the enemy.[64] Francis Bernard, governor of Massachusetts, opined that such trade would never be suppressed 'till Rhode Island is reduced to the subjection of the British empire; of which it is at present no more a part than the Bahama Islands were when they were inhabited by the buccaneers'.[65] In 1762 Amherst returned to the charge with yet more evidence of 'a most iniquitous proceeding in an illicit trade, by which the enemy has been furnished with provisions and stores from many parts of the continent'.[66] Dramatic evidence of how damaging these repeated allegations were to the standing of the colonies in British political circles was provided by an encounter in 1763 between James Jay, agent for King's College, New York, and lord Granville, president of the council. Jay was asking for the council's permission to launch an authorized charitable collection on behalf of the college. Granville told him that 'the people in New York were a set of traitors and deserved to be hang'd instead of being assist'd'. They were traitors because they had traded

[60] Letter from Boston, 8 May 1758, ibid. 5–8 Aug. 1758.

[61] e.g. *London Chronicle*, 28–30 March 1758.

[62] James Munro and W. L. Grant, eds., *Acts of the Privy Council of England, Colonial Series*, 6 vols. (1908–12), IV. 444–5.

[63] 23 Aug. 1760, Kimball, ed., *Correspondence of William Pitt*, II. 320.

[64] See material in PRO, CO 5/60, ff. 52–3, 60, 170.

[65] To J. Pownall, 9 May 1761, PRO, CO 5/891, f. 32.

[66] To Egremont, 12 May 1762, PRO, CO 5/62, f. 4.

with the enemy. Jay found that these 'horrid imputations of treason and disloyalty' were widely believed by 'numbers of every rank and description'.[67]

War put strains on relations between metropolitan authority and local communities in the Caribbean as well as on the North American mainland. With the prospect of raids and invasions, the unleashing of French privateers and the dangers to shipping to and from Britain, wars were always a period of acute anxiety for the British Caribbean, even if the Seven Years War was the least damaging for them of all the great eighteenth-century wars.[68] In the events that concerned them so greatly, the small white populations of the islands, unlike the North Americans, had, however, only a limited role. They expected to be protected by the squadrons of the Royal Navy and by garrisons of British regulars, while the offensive operations that led after 1759 to the capture of French islands and finally to the seizure of Havana were mounted by troops and ships that came to the Caribbean from Britain or from North America after the final victory over New France in 1760.

Nevertheless, British ministers and local navy and army commanders expected the island whites to make some contribution to their own defence and to support the forces of the crown. White males had to serve in the militia. Only in Barbados was the militia thought to be an effective force. Elsewhere, regular British troops were deemed essential for security. The island governments maintained barracks and fortifications for them at their own expense and paid extra allowances to the officers and men. Slaves were allocated to support the garrisons and the expeditionary forces. These expenditures were a major charge on colonial budgets.[69] Self-interest seemed generally to incline the West Indian colonies to contribute to the imperial war effort. In 1758, for instance, 'several gentlemen of Jamaica resident in London' personally guaranteed that barracks would be built and extra allowances paid to the additional regiment requested for the island.[70] Local political interests were, however, thought by jaundiced British observers to be just as likely to obstruct national purposes as they were in North America. A British naval officer wrote in 1756 that the Jamaica assembly would rather see 'the forts in ashes than complete them'.[71] The British commander of the Havana expedition of 1762 was infuriated by the Jamaica assembly's 'delay'

[67] Cited P. J. Marshall, 'Who Cared about the Thirteen Colonies? Some Evidence from Philanthropy', *Journal of Imperial and Commonwealth History*, XXVI (1999), 59–60.
[68] The classic account is Richard Pares, *War and Trade in the West Indies 1739–1763* (Oxford, 1936).
[69] Andrew Jackson O'Shaughnessy, *An Empire Divided: The American Revolution and the British Caribbean* (Philadelphia, 2000), pp. 43–54.
[70] Privy Council proceedings, 24 Feb. 1758, PRO, CO 137/30, f. 147.
[71] G. Townshend to J. Clevland, 17 Nov. 1756, BL, Egerton MS 3490, f. 97.

and 'obstruction' in providing the slaves that he required.[72] At the end of the war the governor believed that the island was no more secure than it had been at the beginning; 'the militia in a wretched state and the forts indefensible'.[73] By then he was embarked on a struggle with the assembly as bitter as any in North America. After the war, conflict was to paralyse the government of Jamaica as the assembly refused to vote supply, including the allowances that it was committed to pay to the royal troops that defended the island. The British treasury was left to foot the bill.[74]

II

Few historians have doubted the importance of the Seven Years War for the history of the eighteenth-century Atlantic empire. Most of them have seen it as a crucial stage in the march of the people of the thirteen colonies towards independence. The war had brought the realities of what the British now seemed to intend by empire too close to them for comfort. They might, albeit with reluctance and under protest, accept an intrusive imperial presence under the threat of French and Indian attack, but they would not accept it when those dangers had been exorcized and it seemed that British interference in their affairs was being perpetuated and even being reinforced. Valuable studies have examined in detail the conflicts generated by the increased wartime imperial presence in the colonies, above all by the large British military presence. Such conflicts have been seen as the precursor of conflict in the era of the Revolution. This was the theme of Alan Rogers's *Empire and Liberty: American Resistance to British Authority 1755–1763*[75] and, as its title implies, of Douglas Edward Leach's *Roots of Conflict: British Armed Forces and Colonial Americans, 1677–1763*.[76] Leach recounts the long history of ill-feeling between regular British troops and colonial soldiers. He sees these as coming to a head during the Seven Years War and as thus sowing the 'living seeds of revolution and separation'.[77]

There was certainly no shortage of conflicts between the British military and the colonial population during the war and it is easy to detect future resonances in some of them. The struggle between lord Loudoun and the town of Boston over the quartering of troops for the winter of 1757–8 was

[72] Albermarle to W. Lyttelton, 18 May 1762, David Syrett, ed., *The Siege and Capture of Havana, 1762* (1970), pp. 122–3.

[73] W. Lyttelton to G. Grenville, 11 Jan. 1763, HL, STG, Box 22 (64).

[74] Jack P. Greene, 'The Jamaica Privilege Controversy, 1764–66: An Episode in the Process of Constitutional Definition in the Early Modern British Empire', *The Journal of Imperial and Commonwealth History*, XXII (1994), 16–54.

[75] Berkeley (1974).   [76] Chapel Hill, NC (1986).   [77] Ibid. p. 166.

such a one. Loudoun believed that the colonies were bound to provide quarters by the British act of parliament. The Massachusetts legislature insisted that an act of their own was needed for troops to be quartered in Boston. Loudoun saw this as an 'attempt to take away the king's undoubted prerogative and the rights of the mother country; they attempt to take away an act of the British parliament', and he urged the governor, Thomas Pownall, to stand firm.[78] Pownall replied that 'in a free government' governors must '*lead*' their people; they could not '*drive*' them, and that there were suspicions that 'I am in league with the army . . . to subvert the present constitution to a military government, and to putt the whole service of this country under the command of the regulars under military discipline &c. and the articles of warr'.[79] Loudoun indignantly rejected any such imputation: 'I have ever been equally for supporting the prerogative of the crown and the liberty of the people to the bounds that the constitution has allotted them'.[80] Even so, the council and assembly prided themselves that by passing their own quartering act they had both removed the need for 'military government' and had asserted 'the natural rights of English born subjects'.[81]

The dispute over quartering was only an episode in a wider pattern of conflict between Massachusetts and the British army and royal authority. The resentment that Massachusetts soldiers felt against their treatment by the regulars has been abundantly documented.[82] Recruiting for the royal regiments in Massachusetts was a hazardous business. 'The whole country is against the regulars', an officer reported from Marblehead.[83] Sailors could not be pressed for the navy in any Massachusetts port. Even someone so well disposed to the imperial war effort as Thomas Hutchinson, future governor and loyalist, felt bound to tell Loudoun that there was a 'universal complaint of the weight of taxes and of the entire cession of trade' produced by the embargoes, which were destroying the cod, whale, and timber trades.[84] Attempts by the customs service to suppress illegal trade were resisted in the courts and by mob action.

Yet for all its apparent fractiousness, no colony committed itself more wholeheartedly to the war than Massachusetts: it put nearly 10,000 men into the field in 1758.[85] At the end of the war it was estimated that £206,250 of the

---

[78] To Pownall, 6 Dec. 1757, HL, LO 4955.
[79] Letters of 15 and 19 Dec. 1757, HL, LO 5014, 5041.
[80] Letter to Pownall, 26 Dec. 1757, Public Record Office, PRO 30/8/95, f. 372.
[81] Resolutions of 16 Dec. 1757, 6 Jan. 1758, PRO, CO 5/18, ff. 322, 324.
[82] Fred Anderson, *A People's Army: Massachusetts Soldiers and Society in the Seven Years' War* (Chapel Hill, NC, 1984).
[83] G. Cottman to J. Forbes, 13 Dec. 1757, HL, LO 5003.
[84] Letter of 23 April 1757, HL, LO 3437.
[85] T. Pownall to Pitt, 30 Sept. 1758, PRO, CO 5/18, f. 499.

£461,268 spent by the province on the war remained as a debt on which interest at 6 per cent was being paid, while the province's economy had 'suffered extreamly' from 'so great a part of its working people being taken off' to fight.[86] Massachusetts, as well as contributing nearly one third of all the money raised for the war in America, kept something like one in seven of its adult male population under arms for most of the war.[87] It is hardly surprising, if ironic in view of his role in the future, that the province's new governor, Francis Bernard, should have described the people of Massachusetts on his arrival in 1760 as 'better disposed to observe their compact with the crown than any other on the continent that I know'.[88] Bernard also wrote to Pitt about 'the distinguishing loyalty and public spirit of this people'.[89]

Massachusetts' loyalty to the monarchy and to the British empire was incontrovertible. 'We love, esteem and reverence our mother country, and adore our king', wrote the radical James Otis in 1764.[90] Pitt was the colony's idol; popular British generals became heroes in Massachusetts as well as in Britain. The house of representatives voted money for a monument to lord Howe, killed at Ticonderoga in 1758, 'fighting in the cause of the colonies'.[91] The taking of Quebec was a great deliverance, appropriately celebrated. The case of Massachusetts was, if in an extreme form, the case of all the colonies, which collectively had made a considerable contribution. In 1758 16,307 provincial soldiers took the field out of the 20,000 voted. These men 'behaved as well as could be expected from raw and undisciplined men' in the view of the British commander-in-chief.[92] Again required to raise over 20,000 men for the campaigns of 1759 and 1760, the colonies succeeded in putting into the field 80 per cent of them in the first year and 75 per cent in the next.[93] The colonies as a whole paid out over £2.5 million during the war of which they received reimbursement from Britain for about £1 million.[94]

Resentment at British high-handedness was by no means confined to Massachusetts but neither was commitment to the war and to an empire that in American eyes had triumphed mightily in a righteous cause over its

---

[86] A. Oliver to J. Mauduit, 16 June 1763, MHS, Mauduit–Oliver MSS.

[87] William Pencak, 'Warfare and Political Change in Mid-Eighteenth-Century Massachusetts', *Journal of Imperial and Commonwealth History*, VIII (1980), 52.

[88] To board of trade, 18 Aug. 1760, PRO, CO 5/891, f. 3. He later set out in detail the extent of the province's contribution to the war in a letter to the board of trade, 1 Aug. 1764, PRO, CO, 323/19, f. 14.

[89] Letter of 6 April 1760, HUHL, Sparks MSS 4/1.

[90] 'The Rights of the British Colonies Asserted and Proved' in Bernard Bailyn, ed., *Pamphlets of the American Revolution*, I, *1750–1765* (Cambridge, Mass.), p. 458.

[91] *Journals of the House of Representatives of Massachusetts, 1758–9* (Boston, 1963), p. 238.

[92] Abercromby's 'Note on Provincial Troops', 1758, HL, AB 846.

[93] *Crucible of War*, pp. 805–6.

[94] Jack P. Greene, 'The Seven Years' War and the American Revolution: The Causal Relationship Reconsidered', *Journal of Imperial and Commonwealth History*, VIII (1980), 98.

Popish and absolutist foes. For all its hardships for them, the Seven Years War had been in John Shy's words 'a time of triumph' for the colonies as a whole, 'educative and euphoric in effect'.[95] As Jack P. Greene has put it, 'on balance the war seems to have been for the colonists a highly positive experience'. It had 'intensified the pride of the colonists in their attachment to Britain'. It had also 'heightened their expectations for a larger—and more equivalent—role within the Empire, a role that would finally raise them out of a dependent status to one in which they were more nearly on a par with Britons at home'.[96] Fred Anderson strongly endorses this view. He too sees the war as giving Americans, not intimations of separation, but a deeper involvement with the British empire. For them, it was, however, an empire 'of trade partnership and military alliance, superintended by a protector-king'.[97] Francis Bernard's choice of the term 'compact' to describe Massachusetts' relations with the crown is not what one would expect from his later reputation as a 'prerogative man', but it was a perceptive summary of the colonial view of their relationship with Britain during and after the war. The colonies envisaged empire as based on implied compact. As his Majesty's loyal subjects, they had faithfully fulfilled their part in the alliance with Britain against the common enemy. In return they expected recognition of what they had achieved and respect for what they saw as their rights as Englishmen. As a pamphleteer put it, Americans felt that Britain was not 'indebted to itself alone for victories and that therefore the colonies should have no reason to complain that they have been lavish of their blood and treasure in the late war only to bind the shackles of slavery on themselves and their children'.[98] Francis Bernard again took on the improbable role as spokesman for colonial views. The colonies' 'rights', he wrote in 1763, having been 'effectually vindicated by a successful war and firmly secured by an honorable peace', 'British America' now 'wanted nothing more than to be well known to the mother country'.[99]

III

'British America' was indeed much better known in Britain at the end of the war than it had been at the beginning, but it was not necessarily known in

[95] *Toward Lexington: The Role of the British Army in the Coming of the American Revolution* (Princeton, 1965), p. 143.

[96] Greene, 'Seven Years' War and American Revolution', 97, 99.

[97] *Crucible of War*, p. 743.

[98] Oxenbridge Thacher, 'The Sentiments of a British American' (1764) in Bailyn, ed., *Pamphlets*, I. 490.

[99] To C. Townshend, 18 May 1763, HUHL, Sparks MSS, 4/3, p. 60

ways that would have pleased British Americans. Much of the abundant news and information about the colonies that had reached Britain during the war had tended to reinforce notions of empire very different from those envisioned by the Americans. It made the imperial relationship seem not to be a partnership of more or less equals, but one in which Britain had exerted itself mightily, while the colonies had failed to play an adequate part.

The promoters of *The American Magazine, or Monthly Chronicle for the British Colonies* had announced when launching their new venture in October 1757 that the war had

rendered this country, at length, the object of a very general attention, and it seems now become as much the mode, among those who seek to be useful or conspicuous in the state, to seek an acquaintance with the affairs of these colonies, their constitutions, interests or commerce, as it had been before to look upon such matters as things of inferior or secondary consideration.

As a major theatre of war, North America of course took a prominent place in the calculations of those directing the war. Although the overwhelming impression from the press is that much more accessible news from the battlefields of Europe took up far more space, American news was constantly put before the politically-concerned public. Detailed reports of battles from the dispatches of British commanders, published first in the *London Gazette*, together with columns of information, usually in the form of letters, appeared in the newspapers. The war stimulated the publication of numerous pamphlets and books on American topics in Britain.[100] To the already vibrant transatlantic channels of communication by letter or word of mouth that passed between merchants and their customers, between migrants and those who stayed at home or between fellow members of religious denominations had been added the exposure to America of large numbers of British soldiers and sailors. The great celebrations at the fall of Louisbourg and Quebec showed that America for a wide British public had become a conspicuous stage for national valour and glory.

Many British people must have acquired a new awareness of America, of its wealth and importance to Britain and of the stirring deeds performed there by the forces of the crown in the later years of the war. Opinions about Americans themselves and their contribution to the war were, however, more equivocal. From 1759 Benjamin Franklin began to express what was to be a lasting concern for him about the quality of the information on America being disseminated in the British press and its effects on British public opinion. He wished to refute letters in the press 'tending to render the

---

[100] Simmons, *British Imprints*, pp. 217–53.

colonies despicable and even odious to the mother country'. New Englanders in particular were not 'levellers' (a view very tenaciously held by many British army officers, as their correspondence abundantly shows) or religious fanatics who hated the Church of England. Nor were they bad soldiers. They were a universally literate people, who spoke English as the English themselves did and read the latest books from London.[101]

Franklin had every reason for concern about the views of the colonies that were being disseminated to the British political elite during the war. The dispatches of the governors to the southern secretary of state or to the board of trade were the main channel of official information transmitted to Britain. During the war they were supplemented by the correspondence of the commanders-in-chief and other senior military and naval officers. Neither the majority of governors nor the commanders-in-chief tended to describe the American contribution to the war in favourable terms.

In the early years of the war, nearly all governors enthusiastically pointed out the failings of other colonies. Several of them complained of the way in which their own people obstructed their best efforts to prosecute the war. Most governors were also keen to expose fundamental defects in the constitutions of British America as a whole and to press for sweeping reforms that would strengthen imperial authority, particularly by bringing parliament into play.

With good reason, the governors of the New England colonies generally commended their own peoples' response to the war. Thomas Fitch of Connecticut assured the secretary of state that 'No one exerted itself in this part of his Majesty's service beyond the colony of Connecticut.'[102] Governor Stephen Hopkins called the people of Rhode Island 'dutiful children' of George II.[103] New England governors were, however, free in their comments on other colonies. William Shirley of Massachusetts detailed the failings of Virginia, Pennsylvania, South Carolina, and Maryland and considered that those of New York and New Jersey were too notorious to need retelling. All this, he felt, not only made it essential that a 'parliamentary union' be imposed on America, but that Britain should levy 'suitable assessments' of taxation in the colonies.[104] Lieutenant governor James DeLancey of New York believed that his province was doing all that could be expected of it, but he blamed 'the backwardness of some of the colonies to fall into measures of common utility'

---

[101] Letter to *London Chronicle*, 9 May 1759, Labaree et al. eds., *Papers of Benjamin Franklin*, VIII. 340–56.
[102] To Holdernesse, 17 Nov. 1757, PRO, CO 5/18, f. 249.
[103] To T. Robinson, 14 Nov. 1755, PRO, CO 5/17, f. 155.
[104] To T. Robinson, 4 Feb. 1755, C. H. Lincoln, ed., *Correspondence of William Shirley, Governor of Massachusetts and Military Commander in America, 1731–1760*, 2 vols. (New York, 1912), II. 123–4.

and he was particularly censorious of those, no doubt the New England colonies, who were supplying the French at Louisbourg. He too felt that parliamentary intervention was the only option left.[105] Robert Dinwiddie of Virginia, who had been most strident in raising the alarm about French incursions on the Ohio and had taken wholly unsuccessful measures to eject them, tried to pin the blame both on the inertia of other colonies and on the resistance of the Virginia house of burgesses. The burgesses were 'extremely obstinate and self-opinionated, and at the same time infatuated, to be so unactive and indolent, when the enemy is so near our frontiers'.[106] Other southern colonies would not support the efforts being made by Virginia. Dinwiddie too had heard that the French were being supplied by British American merchants and he too believed that the authority of parliament was needed to raise funds for the war in the colonies.[107]

The two proprietary colonies, Maryland and Pennsylvania, were regarded as pariahs, both by their own governors and those of the other colonies. After the first years of the war, Pennsylvania appeared to mend its ways and to make significant contributions; Maryland never did. When the fighting began, Dinwiddie lamented that Pennsylvania, the most populous colony and directly threatened by the French and the Indians would do nothing for its own defence.[108] The governor of Pennsylvania, Robert Hunter Morris, considered that the problem went far beyond the Quaker pacifism, which attracted so much odium. He interpreted the opposition of the majority in the assembly to the proprietors as putting 'their own ambitions before every consideration of public safety'. The assembly, moreover, was 'annually chosen by a people, a great part if not a majority of whom, are foreigners, unattached to our English government'.[109] Ministers were bombarded with warnings about the defenceless state of the province; the French could march to the sea virtually unhindered. Governor Denny joined the chorus calling for parliamentary taxation with a militia act passed by the British parliament as well.[110]

The disillusionment of the British commanders-in-chief and other senior officers with what they found in America, the inadequacies of the support offered by the provinces and the poor quality of American soldiers, has attracted a considerable body of writing. The misunderstandings that arose

[105] To T. Robinson, 19 March 1755, PRO, CO 5/15, f. 248.
[106] To T. Robinson, 23 Sept. 1754, R. A. Brock, ed., *The Official Records of Robert Dinwiddie, Lieutenant-Governor of the Colony of Virginia, 1751–1758*, 2 vols. (Richmond, Va., 1883–4), I. 324.
[107] Letters to board of trade, 23 Sept. 1754, to T. Robinson, 20 Jan. 1755, ibid. I. 329, 473.
[108] To T. Robinson, 16 Nov. 1754, ibid. I. 405.
[109] To T. Robinson, 9 April 1755, PRO, CO 5/15, f. 257.
[110] To W. Pitt, 9 April 1757, PRO, CO 5/18, f. 37.

from fundamentally different military cultures in the British army and the colonial forces have been sensitively explored.[111]

Edward Braddock left his superiors in Britain in no doubt as to what he thought about arrangements for prosecuting the war in America. 'It would be endless, sir', he told the secretary of state, 'to particularize the numberless instances of the want of publick and private faith, and of the most absolute disregard of all truth, which I have met with in the carrying on of his Majesty's service in the continent.'[112] Lord Loudoun was pleased to say that he had 'contracted no ill will against any set of men in his Majesty's American dominions; but have the happiness to contract friendships with men I have met with who have both parts and judgement' that they applied to 'the common cause of the whole'.[113] His strictures on the colonies during his command in 1756 and 1757 were, however, as bleak as Braddock's, if much more circumstantial and carefully considered. In a letter of August 1757 he reviewed the contributions of the colonies. The governors of Massachusetts, New York, and even Connecticut, though it was 'a strange government', were all able to ensure that their provinces did their duty. South Carolina was probably doing its limited best. Georgia, North Carolina, and New Hampshire were too poor to do anything significant. The rest were all delinquent in various ways. Virginia had not fulfilled its quota, Pennsylvania had only produced half of what was required. The unspeakable Maryland was trying to keep its small contingent out of the hands of the king's general, there was 'no government' in New Jersey. To make matters worse, New Jersey, Maryland, and Pennsylvania were all 'under refractory Quaker influence'. Finally, the people of Rhode Island had turned out their governor for supporting the war effort and were 'a lawless set of smugglers who continually supply the enemy with what provisions they want'.[114] He expressed concerns that went far beyond the military failings of the colonies. He feared that America had become ungovernable.

In all the backcountry, where we have been all the summer, the common language of the people is, that they full as lieve be under the French as the English government; and this they never fail to say, when any thing gives them the least uneasiness or displeasure.

The next I have from very good authority likewise; that it is very common, for the people in the lower and more uninhabited country, to say, they would be glad to see

---

[111] Anderson, *A People's Army*. See also Leach, *Roots of Conflict* and material in Pargellis, ed., *Military Affairs*.
[112] To T. Robinson, 5 June 1755, PRO, CO 5/46, f. 21.
[113] To T. Pownall, 18 Jan. 1758, HL, LO 5418.
[114] To Holdernesse, 16 Aug. 1757, PRO, CO 5/46, ff. 288–9.

any man, that durst offer to put an English act of parliament in force in this country.[115]

He warned the duke of Cumberland that the governors were '*cyphers*' and that 'till you find a fund, independent of the province, to pay the governors, and new model the government, you can do nothing with the provinces'. Reforms must be pushed through now, while there was a military force to command obedience.[116]

Jeffrey Amherst, commander-in-chief in the last years of the war, was more circumspect in his comments. He had no regard for the provincial forces. 'The disregard of orders, and studying of their own ease, rather than the good of the service, has been too often just grounds for complaint against some of the provincial officers and all their men.'[117] The best that he could say of them was that 'they are excellent ax men, [and] the work could not be carry'd on without them'.[118] With a generosity unusual for a king's officer, in his dispatch on the capture of Montreal in 1760 he commended 'the zeal and bravery which has always been exerted by the officers and soldiers of the regular and provincial troops, as also by his Majesty's faithful Indian allies'.[119] Unlike his predecessors Amherst seems not to have been inclined to give his opinion gratuitously on the state of the colonies. When he was specifically asked for his views, he suggested that it was desirable to 'put the several provinces upon the same footing, yet to keep them separate'. To this end, Pennsylvania, Maryland, Connecticut, and Rhode Island should be converted into royal colonies.[120]

For most British political figures official dispatches were likely to have been only one source of information about America and were not necessarily the most important one. The American colonies were a part of the British political world, if a peripheral part of it. Most major British politicians therefore had contacts of some sort in the colonies, relatives, protégés, or connections of families whose influence they wished to cultivate. For their part, governors, senior army officers, and ambitious colonial notables all cultivated British patrons. Without strong support from home, such men were vulnerable to their rivals and to swings of the British political wheel. To ensure their support, patrons had to be kept informed of developments in America by a stream of private letters. Those on the other side of the Atlantic got their friends in Britain to pay court to the great man, to pass on

[115] To Halifax, 26 Dec. 1756, HL, LO 2416.
[116] Letter of 22 Nov. 1756, Pargellis, ed., *Military Affairs*, p. 273.
[117] Cited Anderson, *Crucible of War*, p. 372.
[118] To W. Pitt, 22 Oct. 1759, PRO, CO 5/56, f. 140.
[119] To W. Pitt, 8 Sept. 1760, *London Gazette*, 6 Oct. 1760.
[120] To Egremont, 12 April 1763, PRO, CO 5/63, f. 26.

information to him, and to report on his disposition towards them. Major politicians were also lobbied in Britain by the supporters of colonial interests. Agents appointed by the colonies, merchant groups who traded with a particular colony or the leaders of British religious denominations acting on behalf of their colleagues in America all sent memoranda to ministers or sought audiences with them.[121]

A great deal of information about the colonies must have been fed into British political circles through such private channels. It is hard to generalize about what was passed through such a diverse body of contacts, but much of it was not likely to have been reassuring. Colonial officials and army officers seem to have written of the colonies in their private letters in much the same terms as they used for their official dispatches. Colonial interests in London competed for British troops or warships by stressing their vulnerability, as the West Indian agents did. South Carolina and Georgia may have had good cause for so doing, but even Virginia and Maryland were represented by their London merchants as being 'entirely defenceless both by sea and by land'.[122]

Pennsylvania was almost certainly the province whose affairs intruded themselves most into the British political world. It seems to have attracted a far fuller coverage in the British press than any other colony and Pennsylvanians were particularly active in cultivating British politicians. Bitter rivalries were fought out in public and by personal communications in London as well as in the colony. Thomas Penn, the proprietor, sought British political allies to protect his interests. He assiduously cultivated what he called 'the greatest people here'.[123] In a single letter in February 1756 he described meetings with Granville, Henry Fox, Newcastle, and Halifax.[124] Considerable as his 'weight and interest' were thought to be from his 'connections and acquaintance',[125] other Pennsylvania voices also clamoured to be heard in Britain. Essentially sympathetic to the proprietors' point of view, those who despaired of the failure of the majority in the assembly to sanction defensive measures on the outbreak of war launched a vigorous campaign in Britain.[126] The crown was petitioned to intervene and the addresses on the 'defenceless state of the province of *Pensylvania*' were laid before the commons.[127]

---

[121] Alison Gilbert Olson, *Making the Empire Work: London and American Interest Groups* (Cambridge, Mass., 1992), pp. 136–40, describes the operations of London pressure groups on behalf of the colonies during the war.

[122] Petition of 1 Jan. 1757, PRO, CO 5/18, f. 2.

[123] To R. H. Morris, 27 Jan 1756, HSP, Thomas Penn Letter Books, IV, p. 219.

[124] To W. Allen, 17 Feb. 1756, ibid. IV, p. 238.

[125] R. H. Morris to R. Peters, 6 April 1757, HSP, Peters Papers, IV, p. 86.

[126] For an analysis of the conflicts in Pennsylvania which stresses the willingness of the Quakers to defend the province if not on the proprietors' terms, see Alan Tully, *Forming American Politics: Ideals, Interests and Institutions in Colonial New York and Pennsylvania* (Baltimore, 1994), pp. 149–59.

[127] Simmons and Thomas, eds., *Proceedings and Debates*, I. 140–1.

Inflammatory pamphlets, William Smith's *Brief State of the Province of Pennsylvania* and *Brief View of the Conduct of Pennsylvania*, appeared together with numerous newspaper paragraphs, warning of the dire dangers facing the colony. 'How long must this province groan under the government of a set of enthusiasts, who will not suffer us to put forth our strength, even when the sword is at our throats?'[128] Such diatribes did not go uncontested. Through its agents the assembly also used the British press to counter 'scandalous and groundless reflexions' on it,[129] while the Quakers, the objects of particular vituperation, resorted to more discreet lobbying. They could not match Thomas Penn in the range of their contacts, but notables like the great merchant John Hanbury, Dr John Fothergill, and the scientist Peter Collinson waited on 'all who are immediately concerned in public affairs'.[130] The appearance in London in 1757 of the already renowned Benjamin Franklin on a mission to represent the assembly against the proprietors added yet another competing voice. Thomas Penn warned all who would listen to him against Franklin. He comforted himself that 'great people' would not be interested in Franklin's 'electrical experiments',[131] but Franklin was thought to have 'acquired the confidence and esteem of many persons in high station and by his clear and solid reasoning has in some degree recover'd a favourable ear'.[132] Only in the later years of the war were rival factions in Pennsylvania able to present something like a united front to project the province in an optimistic light in the British press. In 1758 'the people' were said to be showing 'a great spirit . . . to defend their country'.[133]

Hard as the cacophony emanating from Pennsylvania must have been for British politicians to decipher, its overall drift was clear. A valuable colony was in disarray. This was the message being received in the early years of the war from all over North America, through private as well as official channels. French encroachments were presumed to threaten the very existence of empire in North America and the colonial response, with the possible exceptions of the New England colonies, was proving to be wholly inadequate. Even New England seemed to have fallen from grace in the 1756 campaign when volleys of complaints about the behaviour of its troops reached Britain. 'We begin, here, to know the *New England* men' wrote the

---

[128] 'Letter from Philadelphia' in *Public Advertiser*, 19 Jan. 1756.
[129] 'Letter from a Gentleman in Philadelphia', ibid. 12 July 1755.
[130] J. Fothergill to J. Pemberton, 16–19 March 1757, HSP, Etting Collection, XXIX, no. 10.
[131] To R. Peters, 14 May 1757, MHS, Thomas Penn Letters.
[132] J. Fothergill to J. Pemberton, 9 April 1759, HSP, Etting Collection, XXIX, no. 40. For his own account of the difficulties he faced from 'The little knowledge of (and indeed inclination to know) American affairs, among most of those concerned in the administration' and from 'the scandalous and malicious falshoods' circulated by the proprietors, see his letter to E. Graeme, 9 Dec. 1757, Labaree et al., eds., *Papers of Benjamin Franklin*, VII. 289–90.
[133] *Lloyd's Evening Post*, 31 July-2 Aug. 1758.

already hostile Cumberland in December 1756 with evident satisfaction, 'and we have had so many disappointments from them, that the *cry* here, at least among the knowing sensible people, is no longer in their favour.'[134]

The case for imperial intervention to take control of the war and for maintaining that control in the later years of the war, even when a generally satisfactory colonial contribution was forthcoming, seemed irrefutable. When the war on the American continent was over, virtually no one in Britain seems to have questioned the proposition that the British regulars and the British commander-in-chief must remain to defend the colonies and the new conquests in peacetime. Much was to follow from that decision.

How far down the social scale adverse opinions about Americans had penetrated is hard to assess. A wide public had, however, been fed with stories of stirring victories, won at great expenditure of men and money, by British forces. For all their wealth, Americans had not apparently done much to defend themselves. They had been saved by Britain. Gratitude and a willingness to contribute to relieving Britain's burdens after the war were the least that could be expected.

IV

In the last years of fighting in North America, from 1758 to 1760, during the ascendancy of Pitt, the American view of empire as a partnership between more or less equal communities enjoying the rights of Englishmen seemed to prevail in Britain too. Imperial authority continued to be 'negotiated'.[135] Schemes for reform, by giving the governors more independence from the assemblies, by creating a union for defence with a common fund and by asserting the power of parliament to regulate colonial affairs and raise taxes in America for imperial purposes had apparently been abandoned.

Yet if Pitt and his main ally in the coalition, the duke of Newcastle, may have accepted something like the American vision of empire as a partnership of equals, there were clear limits to the equality of the colonies with Britain that even Pitt was prepared to concede. Like virtually everybody else in Britain, he believed that the colonies must submit to having their overseas trade regulated by Britain and he seems to have regarded American troops as auxiliaries rather than partners with the forces of the crown. Pitt strongly supported the stationing of a large force of regulars in America after the war

---

[134] To Loudoun, 2 Dec. 1756, Pargellis, ed., *Military Affairs*, p. 255.
[135] See above, pp. 75–6.

and would have increased their number.[136] Even if Pitt and Newcastle determined policy for a time, there were still important people in British politics who did not accept anything like the American vision of empire. For Halifax and the board of trade before the war, there had been too much negotiation and too little obedience in the colonial relationship with Britain.[137] The lessons of the war, above all of its early years, seemed to make reforms even more urgent and various proposals had been canvassed. The case for parliament as the only effective instrument of reform was frequently stated. The dominant opinion seems, however, to have been that contentious issues should be avoided so long as the colonies were required to contribute to the war effort. Reform of the constitution of Pennsylvania by statute to limit Quaker influence was, for instance, defeated.[138] In 1757 Halifax had resigned and the ascendancy of Pitt thereafter ensured that nothing significant would be attempted.

Those who were dissatisfied with the degree of autonomy exercised by the colonies seemed, however, to be biding their time. One notable American observer, Benjamin Franklin, remained uneasy. In March 1759 he reported that 'ministers and great men' believed that the colonies 'have too many and too great privileges'. He had heard that the privy council and the board of trade were planning measures to give royal instructions the force of law in the colonies. Indeed, lord Granville had told him that 'the king in council is the LEGISLATOR OF THE COLONIES' and that their instructions 'ought to be OBEYED'. Franklin believed that politicians were divided between supporters of the prerogative, such as Granville, Hardwicke, and Halifax, and 'friends of liberty' like Pitt and Charles Pratt, later lord Camden. He also detected 'a good deal of prejudice' against the colonies in the house of commons.[139] Some of these anxieties were not without foundation. In 1760 in supporting a strong board of trade report against what it saw as encroachments by the Pennsylvania assembly, the attorney and solicitor general urged that the state of the province be referred to parliament.[140] Thought was being given to what might happen after the war. Governor Bernard of Massachusetts was producing memoranda in 1761 on the assumption that 'a revisal and settlement of the political state of N[orth] America' would soon 'have a place in the British councils'.[141]

---

[136] 4 March 1763, Simmons and Thomas, eds., *Proceedings and Debates*, I. 440–1.
[137] See above, pp. 76–7.   [138] See above, pp. 94–5.
[139] To I. Norris, 19 March 1759, Labaree et al. eds., *Papers of Benjamin Franklin*, VIII. 293–5.
[140] T. Penn to R. Peters, 9 June 1760, HSP, Thomas Penn Letter Books, VI. p. 258.
[141] To Barrington, 15 Dec. 1761, E. Channing and A. C. Coolidge, eds., *The Bernard–Barrington Correspondence and Illustrative Matter, 1760–70* (Cambridge, Mass., 1912), pp. 43–4.

The case for reform seemed to rest on the huge volume of adverse reports relayed to Britain by the governors and by the officers in the army and the navy. Even in the last years of the war, trading with the enemy seemed to be endemic in the colonies. In reality the American response, especially in the later years of the war, had often been creditable. An empire that worked by negotiation rather than command had proved itself in the massive deployment of provincial troops and the laying out of provincial money. Such a case had not, however, been effectively made in British political circles or to a wider public. America had spoken in Britain too often with discordant voices, as exemplified in the public feuding of the Pennsylvania factions, while the great victories had been hymned as exclusively British ones. As John M. Murrin wrote with perception many years ago, there were two phases to the war: the years of failure and Anglo-American disunity up to 1757 and the years of cooperation and victory thereafter.[142] British perceptions of the colonies remained for the most part rooted in the years of failure.

V

The overall effect of the Seven Years War had been to give a powerful stimulus to the forces of expansion in the British Atlantic described in the first chapter of this book. Far from experiencing serious disruption, British overseas trade as a whole maintained its pre-war levels in the early years of the war and increased greatly in the later years. In part these gains reflected the damage that Britain was able to inflict on France, by incorporating the highly productive sugar island of Guadeloupe into the British system, by seriously damaging exports from the remaining French Caribbean possessions, and by ruining the French slave trade. The main increase in British exports during the war has, however, long been seen as the direct result of very heavy British government spending on its forces overseas and in subsidies paid to its allies.[143] Much of this went to Britain's European allies, but the North Americans and the West Indians received large payments for supplying and equipping the troops and warships of the crown and the North Americans received a kind of subsidy in the parliamentary grants reimbursing them for part of what they spent on their provincial troops. For the years 1756 to 1763 British government spending in North America has been calculated at just

---

[142] John M. Murrin, 'The French and Indian War, the American Revolution, and the Counterfactual Hypothesis: Reflections on Lawrence Henry Gipson and John Shy', *Reviews in American History*, I (1973), 307–16.

[143] T. S. Ashton, *Economic Fluctuations in England 1700–1800* (Oxford, 1959), pp. 60–1.

under £8 million.[144] Together with the expenditures of the provincial governments, largely made by the issue of paper money, British payments offered
valuable compensation for the damage inflicted by heavy taxes and labour
shortages on those colonies most engaged in the war effort, notably Massachusetts and Connecticut, or for the ravaged frontier areas of New England,
New York, Virginia, and above all Pennsylvania, which had suffered so severely
after Braddock's defeat. By 1760 it was being said of Pennsylvania that 'The war
which at first was look'd upon as the greatest misfortune that could happen to
this country, has really been productive of the greatest blessing to it. Numbers
have got rich by it; and all enjoy plenty and peace.' Goods worth £800,000
were said to have been imported into the province in a year. Philadelphia was
booming and the proprietor could expect high prices for land.[145]

The West Indian colonies also profited from government spending.
Although British planters faced unwelcome competition in the home market
from sugar captured off French ships and from Guadeloupe sugar after 1759,
no British island was lost and British naval supremacy curbed the menace of
the Martinique privateers, while ensuring that the sugar fleets reached Britain
with relatively few losses.[146] Prices on the London market rose, while the
disruption of French exports opened possibilities for new markets for British
sugar in Europe.

The Seven Years War gave an enormous impetus to British territorial
expansion around the Atlantic. Vast extents of territory were acquired in
North America, valuable islands were annexed in the Caribbean, and a new
colony of Senegambia was created in West Africa. Gains on this scale were rarely
envisaged before the war. Ambitions for further territory in the West Indies and
for an additional colony in Africa arose directly from success in war.[147] In North
America, however, pressures to extend colonial frontiers were of long standing.
Would-be settlers and traders were pushing westward long before the outbreak
of the fighting. Powerful groups in many of the colonies were committed to
expansion.[148] Those in Virginia and Pennsylvania who were seeking land and
Indian trade beyond the Alleghenies had a major role in precipitating the war, as
they came into conflict with the French in the Ohio valley and provoked French
counter measures. Success in war released vast areas for new settlement and set

---

[144] Julian Gwyn, 'British Government Spending and the North American Colonies 1740–1775',
Journal of Imperial and Commonwealth History, VIII (1980), 77.

[145] Letters of T. Graeme and T. Barton to T. Penn, HSP, Penn Official Correspondence, IX,
pp. 136, 148.

[146] For the effects of the war, see Pares, *War and Trade*; Richard B. Sheridan, *Sugar and Slavery:
An Economic History of the British West Indies, 1623–1775* (Barbados, 1974), pp. 448–52.

[147] For the West Indies, see Pares, *War and Trade*, pp. 182–5, 219–26; for West Africa, see James L.
A. Webb, 'The Mid-Eighteenth Century Gum Arabic Trade and the British Conquest of Saint-
Louis du Sénégal, 1758', *Journal of Imperial and Commonwealth History*, XXV (1997), 37–58.

[148] Marc Egnal, *A Mighty Empire: The Origins of the American Revolution* (Ithaca, NY, 1988), pt. 1.

off a gigantic scramble for land. Americans, the British army in America, where 'an allmost universal desire amongst the officers and soldiers here to have grants of land to settle on this continent' was anticipated,[149] and would-be British investors all took part.[150] The availability of great quantities of North American land for new settlement was in turn to set off waves of new migration from Britain and parts of western Europe, as labour and potential farmers to rent the new lands were brought across the Atlantic.[151]

The Seven Years War did much to bring about closer integration between Britain and its Atlantic colonies. Although they might interpret one another's roles very differently, Britons and Americans saw themselves as participants in a highly successful imperial war effort. War had created a demand for news and information about America, which had become more readily available in Britain. It had stimulated trade, a large part of it financed by government spending. It created an awareness in British people of opportunities for employment, for acquiring land, and for aspiring to public office in the colonies. Ex-soldiers were encouraged to settle and new migrants joined them after the war. Closer integration had a potential for tension, for instance, between British creditors and colonial debtors or between British and American competitors for land grants or for offices. The pressure in colonial societies to acquire new land to the westward was eventually to lead to conflict with new British policies. The immediate prospect in 1763, however, was of an abundance of new land for all. Expansion stimulated by war seems in this respect, as in others, to have brought the elements of a British world into closer relations with one another for the advantage of most of them.

Different concepts of empire were, however, eventually to drive Britons and Americans apart. The Seven Years War actively fostered these differing concepts. It encouraged Americans' confidence in their role as Britain's allies and partners, while it convinced a wide British public of the importance of the colonies for Britain and of the need for ensuring that a proper subordination to British authority was maintained.

War had involved the British state more closely with the colonies and the imperial presence had been strengthened in certain specific ways. The great military commitment would not be revoked. The number of British troops permanently stationed in the colonies in peacetime was greatly increased. A British commander-in-chief would remain. Indian relations had become an imperial concern, managed not by the colonies but by British-appointed superintendents and by the British army in the vast territories over which the French had claimed authority. Imperial authority intervened to prevent new alienations

---

[149] Amherst to Egremont, 27 Jan. 1763, PRO, CO, 5/63, f. 3.
[150] See above, pp. 20–1.   [151] See above, pp. 27–8.

of Indian land. An instruction to governors in 1761 required them to refer all applications for land involving Indian interests to London.[152] Indian trade was to be closely regulated and only to be conducted at military posts. The customs service had always been an imperial one, but during the war the Royal Navy had been drawn into enforcing operations against illegal trade.

Collectively these increases in the imperial presence in America did very little to shift the balance of power away from effective local autonomy or to lay any sort of foundation for coercion of the colonies. Nevertheless, increased imperial involvement in certain sensitive areas, such as access to land or the enforcement of commercial regulations, increased the possibility of conflicts between colonial interests and metropolitan authority. The larger military presence could also be a source of conflict. Disputes over quartering the king's troops were to raise constitutional issues after the war as they had done when Loudoun tried to enforce what he saw as the army's rights.

Limited as had been the immediate enhancements of imperial power brought about by the war, opinion on both sides of the Atlantic recognised that they were only the first instalment of change. There was much unfinished business. New colonial governments had to be created in the conquests kept by the peace. Measures had to be devised for dealing with the great acquisition of unsettled western lands. New French subjects had to be incorporated into the empire. Few believed that the existing colonies would be exempt from the process of imperial reorganisation that must follow the war. Colonial opinion viewed that prospect with some apprehension. In June 1762 the Massachusetts council and assembly briefed their agent in London with arguments about 'the natural rights of the colonists', which were to be used to counter any British attempts to nullify the colony's charter by use of the royal prerogative.[153] Even if, in focusing on the power of prerogative rather than on the power of parliament, Massachusetts failed to anticipate the main source of future danger, it and other colonies concerned to preserve their autonomies had real grounds for apprehension.

[152] J. M. Sosin, *Whitehall and the Wilderness: The Middle-West in British Colonial Policy, 1760–1775* (Lincoln, Nebr., 1961), pp. 42–8.
[153] Instructions to J. Mauduit, 14 June and A. Oliver to Mauduit, 15 June 1762, 'Jasper Mauduit: Agent for the Province of Massachusetts Bay, 1762–1765', *Massachusetts Historical Society Collections*, LXXIV (1918), 39–53.

4
War and its Transformations: India 1754–1765

EUROPEANS, that is the British and the French with a brief and disastrous intervention by the Dutch, were engaged in a complex series of armed conflicts in India, stretching over some twenty years from 1746 to 1764. There were passages of arms at points on the west coast. Intensive warfare took place on the southeast or Coromandel coast, reaching far inland into the Deccan and northwards up the coast of what is now Andhra Pradesh. Further east, war along the Hughli river in Bengal spread into the neighbouring province of Bihar and beyond into the territory of the wazir of Awadh. European involvement took many forms. British and French troops, always with large Indian contingents under command and often supported by warships, fought one another directly, attacking and taking one another's settlements. Europeans fought as the auxiliaries of Indian allies in the Deccan and on the Coromandel coast. They also waged war on their own against Indian enemies in the Carnatic, Bengal, and Bihar. Nearly two decades of war in its different forms left the British in a position of supremacy over much of eastern India.

So complex a pattern of warfare defies simple analysis. In part, the wars were an extension to India and to the Asian seas of the global rivalry of Britain and France. The British and French East India Companies, supported by the forces of their respective states, fought to protect their own trade and to destroy that of their rivals. Although the stakes were thought to be lower, the Asian trades contributing less to metropolitan economies than the North American or West Indian ones, war in Asia had the same objective as war in the Atlantic, the protection and promotion of the commercial wealth that was believed to contribute crucially to national prosperity and therefore to national power.

The global rivalries of Britain and France were, however, only one strand in a series of Indian wars, which were also local conflicts in which the British and French were drawn into Indian rivalries. In certain coastal regions, the British and French companies had become part of an Indian political world by the mid-eighteenth century. As participants in this world, Europeans took part in

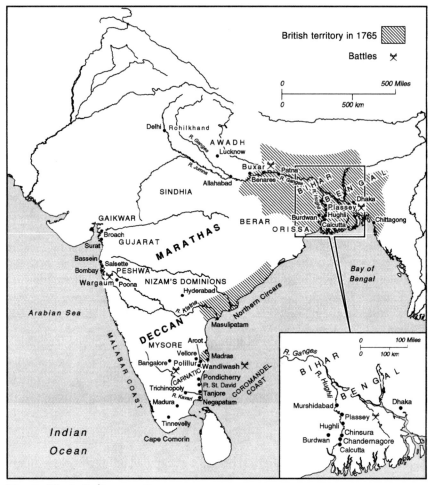

Map 2. War in India *c*.1750–83.

wars for their own reasons, either seeking advantages for the companies or personal gains for individuals. Their participation did not necessarily have any direct connection with the calculations of their metropolitan states or even of those who directed the affairs of the companies at home. In involving themselves in Indian wars Europeans undoubtedly tried to manipulate Indian participants for their own purposes, but they often ended up being themselves manipulated for Indian purposes. There were marked similarities between developments in India and in North America. The indigenous societies of the Ohio valley and the Coromandel coast were very different from one another, but in the 1750s the interplay of diverse British and French local interests, be they those of traders and land speculators in North America or of ambitious servants of the companies in India, and those of rival Native American and Indian groups was generating conflict in both areas. The duke of Newcastle, not usually regarded by historians as well informed about the non-European world, was aware that Europeans were not the only actors overseas. He thought that the apparent success of the French in North America and in India gave reason 'to fear, that the *Indians* in both are not our friends', which with good reason he found 'a very melancholy consideration'.[1]

For western historians of past generations, the Indian context of the Anglo-French wars of the eighteenth century was readily explicable. The Indian political system was in irredeemable decline. Central Mughal imperial authority had collapsed leaving in its ruins a series of unstable successor states, racked by internal rivalries and a prey to predatory raiders, such as the Marathas or the Afghans, who plundered and laid waste vast swathes of territory. Europeans were forced to take their swords in their hands if their trade and their settlements were to survive in this anarchic world. Recent scholarship has substantially revised such simplicities. The failure of a central Mughal political order is of course beyond question, but in large parts of India relatively strong successor states were emerging, in some cases controlled by former Mughal governors, in others by leaders of those who had rebelled against the Mughals, notably the Marathas. These new rulers were capable of maintaining stable regimes and of sustaining flourishing economies. Eighteenth-century India had not relapsed into anarchy. Decline and disruption in some areas was matched by growth and prosperity in others.[2]

Changing conditions in eighteenth-century India are, however, still an important explanation for the increasingly belligerent role coming to be played by Europeans in parts of the subcontinent, even if the changes were more complex than was commonly assumed in the past. In the first place, the creation of a new order of stable successor states was an uneven process. Such states were slow to emerge in the south-east of the peninsula, which was subject to upheavals in mid-century as claimants to Mughal authority in the eastern Deccan and the coastal Carnatic struggled to establish their regimes and to resist Maratha incursions. In a fluid situation Europeans had both incentives and opportunities for intervention. Secondly, even where a strong

---

[1] To Hardwicke, 21 Oct. 1754, BL, Add MS 35414, ff. 203-4.
[2] For introductions to eighteenth-century Indian history, see the material collected in P. J. Marshall, ed., *The Eighteenth Century in Indian History: Evolution or Revolution?* (New Delhi, 2003) and Seema Alavi, ed., *The Eighteenth Century in India* (New Delhi, 2003).

successor state had emerged, as in Bengal, Europeans had possibilities for involvement in its political life that would not have existed in an earlier Mughal order.

The Mughal ideal of governance was that the taxable resources of a province should be allocated to members of an imperial nobility who received their salaries and maintained bodies of troops for the service of the empire from what they raised in taxation, primarily from the 'revenue' levied from the produce of the land. During the eighteenth century, government in the successor states is said to have become increasingly 'commercialised'.[3] This meant that taxation was now directly managed by the state through contracts with moneyed men who rented or 'farmed' areas for a sum to be rendered to the government in cash. Cash was needed, above all, by the new rulers of successor states to pay for their increasingly professionalized armed forces of mercenaries, who were replacing the cavalry contingents of the Mughal aristocracy. In this new order, merchants and bankers willing to undertake the revenue contracts, or at least to advance the money due to the state from the contractors, and professional army officers able to command mercenary troops were much in demand. Both the British and the French companies could provide such people. The companies were served by men who were often at the same time both bold financiers, apparently able to command large sums on credit from Indian investors, and commanders of considerable forces drilled and armed to levels that few indigenous armies could at first match.

An Indian contender for power might be tempted to strike bargains for such services. In return for the use of their potent infantry and artillery, the Europeans were likely to ensure that they were remunerated for their services by claiming the right to collect taxation from large blocks of territory. This would enable them to pay their troops, to recompense the companies that employed them and to make personal fortunes for themselves. In times of commercial difficulty, the profits to be made from fighting wars and managing taxes might offer a better return than the profits of trade, both for the companies and for individuals. In south India, French and English competed in offering their armies in return for grants of taxable territory from rival Indian contestants. In Bengal, the British were quickly able to establish a monopoly of such arrangements.

If it was becoming increasingly likely by mid-century that Europeans in India would be drawn into military adventures for reasons that had little if any connection to anything that was happening in Europe or America, local

---

[3] D. A. Washbrook, 'Progress and Problems: South Asian Economic and Social History, 1720–1860', *Modern Asian Studies*, XXII (1988), 57–96 is a helpful exposition.

conflicts could be transformed into something of much greater potential consequence when they became part of a global war. The forces of the states were then deployed as well as those of the companies. These greatly enhanced the power of the British and French in India, enabling them to inflict decisive defeats on their European and Indian enemies. In 1756, for example, the British company's garrison at Calcutta was easily overwhelmed by the troops of the ruler of Bengal. The following year, however, the warships of the Royal Navy, sent out to fight the French in the Indian Ocean, brought an army up the Hughli to recover the city and then went on to destroy the French settlement at Chandernagore. In 1761 Pondicherry, the main settlement of French India, was blockaded by the Royal Navy at sea, while the assault from the land was led by two royal regiments.

The wars in India were fought, like the wars in North America, by a system of alliances, involving national and local European forces together with their indigenous supporters. Forces of the British crown were dispatched to India, beginning with a naval squadron in 1744, followed by a large force of troops and ships sent out in 1747 and by a new expedition in 1754, which was reinforced at intervals by additional squadrons and regiments during the course of the Seven Years War. The three East India Company presidencies, Bengal, Madras, and Bombay, like the thirteen colonies of North America, raised separate armies of their own. These consisted of both European and Indian troops. They bore the brunt of the initial fighting and fought alongside royal forces in all subsequent campaigns. The Company depended very largely for the money which sustained its forces and for some additional manpower, particularly cavalry, on the Indian powers with whom it was allied.

I

Major European wars were most unwelcome developments for the East India Company's directors in London. The Seven Years War was no exception. The Company's trade was badly disrupted at times and it was required to spend very heavily on making war. Yet the Company emerged from the war as a successful upholder of Britain's national interest in close alliance with the British state.

In war the Company's trade was vulnerable both at sea and on land. In the early eighteenth century, French warships and privateers had taken a heavy toll of the Company's shipping. During the Seven Years War, its losses were lighter. Three of its ships were taken by the French at sea and one had to be burnt to prevent its falling into French hands at Benkulen in Sumatra. The wars of the mid-eighteenth century, however, posed new threats to the Company's trade on land. Wars on land disrupted the procurement of the Company's export cargoes, though in the event, the value of the Company's sales of Indian goods was perhaps less badly affected than might have been expected. Madras exports were, however, disrupted in 1754–6 and were at a very low ebb in 1759, when Fort St David had been captured and Madras itself was under siege. Bengal exports collapsed in 1757, after the loss of Calcutta. In bad years the value of sales could be some 20 or 25 per cent below those in expansive times in the early 1750s.[4]

To sustain a war in India, the Company had to spend heavily in Britain on military stores and on recruiting and transporting extra soldiers. Over £75,000 was spent on 'procuring soldiers' by payments to contractors between 1753 and 1763.[5] Even so, by 1757, because of the demands for recruits for the forces of the crown, it became impossible for the Company to raise the numbers of men that it needed. Two royal regiments, for which the Company had to pay the recruiting costs, were instead specifically raised for service in India. To meet these increased costs, the Company had to reduce the dividend which it paid to its shareholders by 2 per cent from 1756, saving some £63,000 a year.[6]

During the war the price of the Company's stock fell from a peace-time level of just under £200 to hover around £120 to £150. War also adversely affected the Company's capacity to borrow money at interest for short periods. It had to raise the rate on its bonds in the credit crisis of 1762–3 and, presumably because it was regarded as a bad risk, in certain years it was unable to borrow from the Bank of England or other institutional lenders and had to resort to loans from its own directors.[7]

Laurence Sulivan, the dominant director in the later stages of the war, later wrote a highly coloured version for his son of how the Company with him at the helm had been able to survive its difficulties.

From 1757 to 1763 my power at the India House was absolute, for this plain reason the vessel was sinking and no man had courage or (to my son I say ability) to take the helm. Bengal and Fort St David taken. Madras besieged. The Company bankrupt at home in credit, not more than 5000 £ could be borrowed in their name from man or men. In this dreadfull hour my fame and fortune (perhaps my personal safety) were hazarded to save them. I concealed their danger, comforted the proprietors . . . and having secured their tottering internal state boldly attempted and successfully

---

[4] K. N. Chaudhuri, *The Trading World of Asia and the English East India Company 1660–1760* (Cambridge, 1978), p. 510, see also figure on p. 82.

[5] Company's Ledgers, OIOC, L/AG/1/1/19, pp. 237–40, L/AG/1/1/20, pp. 93–6.

[6] Chaudhuri, *Trading World of Asia*, p. 451.

[7] Information on the Company's stock and bonds and other aspects of its finances in war has been kindly provided by Dr Huw Bowen.

prevailed upon that glorious minister Mr Pitt to send out instantaneously fleets and troops to India which saved the Company.[8]

The Company did indeed turn to the crown for military support, albeit long before Sulivan assumed control of its affairs or Pitt took over direction of the national war effort. It did so on the grounds that the East India trade, like the American trades, was a matter of high national importance and that it was beyond the capacity of the Company alone to sustain a war with a major European power. It could not match the flow of men and supplies alleged to be going to India from France. In reality, the French company had no clear superiority over the British in the manpower at its disposal, nor did the French state commit significant numbers of men to India until the outbreak of the Seven Years War. Nevertheless, it was an article of faith with the directors of the British company that the French state was fully committed to the cause of the French company in India; the British state should follow suit.

In 1747 the secret committee of the directors warned ministers that, having taken Madras, the French would 'utterly destroy' British trade if the forces of the crown did not intervene.[9] In 1753 the secretary of state was warned that large French forces were being sent eastwards and that the Company, whose trade was 'the trade of the English nation . . . and is so far a national concern', could only effectively respond with government assistance.[10] In memoranda in August and September 1756 the Company made the most elaborate statement of its claims to public support. It repeated that its trade was a 'national' one and spelt out the implications of that. What the state received from the Company in duties was four times more than what its shareholders were paid in dividends. Were the French to disrupt the Indian trade, the public revenue would be damaged, the 'navigation of the kingdom would be greatly diminished', the vital imports of saltpetre on which Britain depended for its gunpowder would be endangered and 'a general distress upon public credit will succeed'.[11]

Ministers seem to have needed little persuading of their obligation to the Company or of the opportunities that war in India might give them to damage French trade. It was accepted that it was 'beyond the strength of the India Company *alone* to carry on the war', even if 'the extent of the assistance the nation can and will afford to give' the Company might be uncertain.[12] In the allocation of resources, India seems always to have had a considerably lower priority than either North America or the West Indies,

---

[8] To S. Sulivan, 27 Feb. 1778, Bodleian Library, MS Eng. hist. c. 472, f. 4.
[9] Secret Committee to Newcastle, 24 April 1747, PRO, CO 77/18, ff. 32–4.
[10] Directors to Holdernesse, 14 Sept. 1753, PRO, CO 77/19, f. 101.
[11] Secret Committee to H. Fox, 18 Aug., 20 Sept. 1756, OIOC, H/94, pp. 20–2, 29–31.
[12] Holdernesse to R. Orme, 14 Oct. 1755, BL, Egerton MS 3488, ff. 96–7.

but a returned Company servant with contacts with ministers advised his colleagues still in India that 'If the Company is not better supported, it is owing more to their own indolence, and want of proper representations to the ministry, than any want of good inclination towards them in the latter.'[13]

The planning and control of operations in India from London, approximately six months' sailing time away from the scene of action, was an undertaking of great difficulty. The secret committee of the Company's directors told Pitt that men in London could only be 'very inadequate judges' of what was to be done in India. 'Latitude' must therefore be given to the servants abroad, including the right to disregard 'positive instructions from hence' if need be.[14] Ministers, who hardly knew anything about India, showed little inclination to try to impose their views on how the war should be fought.[15] They seem to have accepted that attempts to direct strategy by orders from London to a royal commander-in-chief on the spot, as in North America, would be quite impractical. They generally left it to the directors' secret committee to draft the outlines of instructions to be given to admirals or senior army officers departing for India. Apart from being given very general statements of objectives, these officers were usually told to ascertain from the Company's governors and councils when they got to India what services 'may be most conducive to the interest' of the Company and to form operational plans jointly with them.[16] Eyre Coote, commander-in-chief of the royal land forces in India for a time, explained to a house of commons committee in 1767 that he was ordered to act for 'the good service of his Majesty and the Company. I understood we were sent out to assist the Company and to cooperate with them. What the governor and council recommended I followed', so long as they did not 'interfere with military operations' in detail.[17]

If ministers seem to have recognized that there was no practical alternative to virtually putting the forces of the crown at the disposal of the Company in India, their acceptance that war in India was a national concern in which the forces of the state must be involved inevitably meant that they would try to exercise some degree of control, at least over its scope and objectives. In

---

[13] H. Speke to R. Orme, 26 Jan. 1759, OIOC, Orme MS, OV 293, f. 66.

[14] Letter of 13 Jan. 1757, Public Record Office, PRO 30/8/99, f. 97.

[15] The obvious exception was the enthusiastic support given by lord Holdernesse for a plan to contest the French hold on the Deccan by sending royal troops to the west coast, where they would ally with the Marathas. Henry Fox, who disapproved of the plan, dated 6 Dec. 1754 (see OIOC, H/94, pp. 80–3), attributed it to Holdernesse, who replied that, although it had not originated with him he thought it neither 'a strange nor a chimerical undertaking' and gave it his full support (letters to Fox of 30 and 31 March 1755, BL, Egerton MS, 3432, ff. 113–15).

[16] e.g. instructions to admiral Watson, 2 March 1754, OIOC, H/93, pp. 160–8.

[17] Coote's evidence, 3 April 1767, OIOC, MS Eur. D. 1018/1, p. 9.

particular, the Company could not be allowed unlimited freedom in its dealings with other European powers. India was becoming a part of the overall pattern of Britain's European diplomacy. In 1753 the British and French companies at home engaged in protracted negotiations to try to settle disputes on the Coromandel coast. Ministers kept a close watch. The duke of Newcastle explained their point of view. The negotiations were 'purely between company and company; tho' the East India Company would (as became them) do nothing without his Majesty's permission'. When the directors of the Company were inclined to accept a proposed Anglo–French neutrality east of the Cape of Good Hope, the government firmly vetoed it.[18]

In the later stages of the war British governments began to devise strategies of their own to widen the war in Asia beyond India. On one possible objective, the taking and destruction of the French settlements on the Indian Ocean islands of Mauritius and Bourbon (Réunion), there was no disagreement between Company and government. The elimination of bases from which the French could mount operations against the British in India was an old objective of the Company. In 1761 plans to attack Mauritius were simultaneously being devised by royal and Company officers at Madras[19] and by ministers in London, prompted by Pitt. Neither set of plans came to fruition. At the end of 1761 a new project was, however, taken up by the government. This involved an attack on the Spanish settlement at Manila in the Philippines. Royal forces already in India would be committed, but the Company was expected to participate fully by providing its troops and shipping. The directors had grave reservations about what was proposed. They were anxious that the defence of their Indian settlements should not be weakened by the diversion of forces from them, they did not want to pay for the expedition and they most emphatically did not wish to see a separate British colony established in the area of their monopoly. They insisted that any conquest from the Spanish must therefore be handed over to the Company. Yet they were in a sense hoisted on the petard of their own rhetoric about the national importance of Asian trade. They evidently felt that they had to accept their role as allies of the state in the pursuit of 'a great national object' that would 'greatly extend the commercial interest of this kingdom'.[20] Albeit with a reluctance that provoked the local royal commander to complain that its servants saw 'themselves as quite unconnected with the general

---

[18] To J. Yorke, 26 June 1753, PRO, CO 77/19, f. 51.

[19] For the characteristically acrimonious way in which this was done, see admiral Cornish's letter to Anson, 24 June 1761, PRO, Adm. 1/162, ff. 138–9.

[20] Secret Committee to Egremont, 14 Jan. 1762, N. P. Cushner, ed., *Documents Illustrating the British Conquest of Manila 1762–1763* (1971), pp. 15–17.

plan of the war',[21] the Company played its part in the expedition that succeeded in conquering Manila.

With the ending of the war, India was treated no differently from any other part of the world; instead of leaving the negotiations about India to the British and French companies on their own, the government handled them itself. This was, however, what the Company wanted (there was 'nothing they dreaded more than being left to a seperate and future negotiation' with the French company),[22] close consultation was maintained with the directors and most of what they hoped for was embodied in the final treaty.[23]

In retrospect, the Seven Years War can be seen as a significant stage in the incorporation of the East India Company into the British state and therefore of its closer integration as an agency of the British empire. The working of the alliance between state and Company seems to have given reasonable satisfaction to both sides. In the aftermath of the war the unfitness for a quasi-imperial role of an organization in which ultimate power rested in a large body of shareholders, prone to factionalism and to the pursuit of sectional interests and able to change the executive direction of the Company at annual elections, was to become only too apparent. During the war, however, the shareholders were apparently content to leave the control of military operations to the directors.[24] Relations between the directors, largely acting through a small secret committee, and ministers seem to have been generally harmonious.[25] There was only one major upheaval in the direction of the Company. This was a bitterly contested election for directors in 1758, the outcome of which consolidated the hold on the Company of Laurence Sulivan, who was to prove to be a dynamic leader.[26]

During the war the Company obtained military and naval assistance, which was calculated to have cost the crown £4.5 million between 1756 and 1760.[27] This suggests that, although India was a relatively minor theatre of war, it was by no means a cheap one. British government spending on North

---

[21] W. Draper to Egremont, 27 July 1762, PRO, CO 77/20, f. 143.

[22] 'Sentiments of the Secret Committee of the East India Company', 4 Sept. 1762, Public Record Office, PRO 30/8/99, f. 146.

[23] L. S. Sutherland, 'The East India Company and the Peace of Paris', *English Historical Review*, LXII (1947), 179–90.

[24] Evidence of Robert James, 13 April 1767, OIOC, D. 1018/2, pp. 4–5.

[25] The lack of material on the direction of the war is a surprising lacuna in the rich archive of the Company in OIOC. Neither minutes nor collected correspondence of the secret committee appear to survive. The material in PRO, Adm. 1/3912 clearly indicates, however, how close cooperation was between the admiralty and the secret committee or the Company's secretary acting on its behalf in exchanging intelligence, arranging convoys for outgoing and incoming ships or protecting the crew of the Company's ships from press gangs.

[26] L. S. Sutherland, *The East India Company in Eighteenth-Century Politics* (Oxford, 1952); for the election of 1758, see pp. 69–73.

[27] Account in [Alexander Dalrymple], *The Rights of the East India Company* (1773), p. 16.

America, including reimbursements to colonies, amounted to nearly £8 million.[28] The main charge which the Company bore for the support of the royal troops was a commitment from 1754 to make their pay up to the level that the Company paid its own Europeans.[29] It also paid the recruiting charges for two regiments specially raised for India in 1758 and 1759.[30] In return it received £20,000 a year for the rest of the war as a grant from parliament in compensation for the withdrawal of another regiment in 1757.[31] In India the Company spent very heavily on the costs of war, putting them at over £8.5 million, well over half of which it recovered from subsidies paid by its Indian allies or from the revenue which it collected from the territory ceded by them.[32] A formidable war machine emerged from this spending. In 1761, the last year of fighting against the French, the Company had over 2,000 of its own Europeans and nearly 23,000 Indian sepoys under arms in its two main armies, those of Bengal and Madras.[33] It had thrown up war leaders who had caught the public imagination and become national heroes, above all Pitt's 'heaven-born general', Robert Clive. In India, wrote the *Annual Register* for 1758, 'the English East India Company . . . with an handful of men in a short campaign' in Bengal had won more 'solid profit' than had been gained by 'all the great powers engaged in the present bloody wars in Europe, in which such torrents of blood are spilled and so many millions of treasure are wasted'.[34] All in all, the Company had made a contribution comparable to one of the most heavily committed American colonies and could pride itself on having been a worthy ally of the British state.

II

Seen from London, the management of the war in India might seem to have been relatively straightforward. Government and Company cooperated without undue difficulty in delivering the resources that had enabled Britain's aims of protecting a trade of national importance to be achieved with éclat in

[28] Julian Gwyn, 'British Government Spending and the North American Colonies, 1740–1775', *Journal of Imperial and Commonwealth History*, VIII (1980), 77.

[29] Directors to Ft. St George, 2 March 1754, *Records of Fort St George: Public Despatches from England 1753–1754* (Madras, 1963), p. 56.

[30] J. West to J. Payne, 30 Jan. 1758, S. Martin to P. Godfrey, 30 May 1759, OIOC, E/1/41, nos. 11, 190.

[31] *Journals of the House of Commons*, XXVII (1754–7), 894.

[32] *Rights of East India Company*, p. 17; for what appears to be a year-by-year breakdown of this total, see WLCL, Townshend MSS, 8/3/91.

[33] G. J. Bryant, 'The East India Company and its Army, 1600–1778', London University Ph.D. thesis, 1975, p. 330.

[34] *Annual Register*, I (1758), 33.

a minor theatre of war. For all the victories ultimately won, the conduct of the war in India itself had, in reality, been fraught and complex. There had been very little singleness of purpose. Conflicts were endemic: between soldiers and civilians, between royal officers and Company personnel, and between the different Indian presidencies. Private objectives had intruded at many places. If in the end British commercial interests had been successfully defended, which was the ostensible purpose of the wars, much else had also been achieved that was neither envisaged nor desired in London. War had transformed the British presence in India into a territorial empire.

In part, the conflicts generated by the war arose from institutional rivalries, similar to those which caused so much ill-feeling in North America. Royal officers anywhere in the world had an exalted sense of their own worth. Those in India had feelings of disdain for the Company's officers as strong as most of those in America felt for provincial ones. William Draper, one-time Fellow of King's College, Cambridge, and later brigadier in India, complained that 'as most of the Companys officers are people of a very low education they are seldom fit for the stations of field officers either from behaviour or know-ledge'. They should not therefore be promoted to take command over royal officers.[35] Nor did royal officers usually take kindly to being placed under the authority of the Company's civil governments. George Pigot, governor of Madras, who had to wade through screeds of what he regarded as 'ungentle-manly' polemics from colonels and admirals, wrote wearily of 'the frequent altercations we are obliged to be engaged in with the king's officers, or abandon every thing to their rule, to obtain which is, in truth, the cause of all these struggles on their part, although the constant plea, when other arguments fail, is the honour of his Majesty's service'.[36] After the storming of Calcutta and Pondicherry the forces of the crown and of the Company faced one another in almost armed confrontation as they wrangled about which was to take possession of the conquests. The governors and councils in the Company's presidencies tenaciously upheld their civilian authority, based on the Company's charters, over all military pretensions, whether from their own officers or those of the crown.[37] Although the Madras council put their own defence at risk in detaching a powerful force to recover Calcutta in 1756,

[35] To C. Townshend, 27 July 1762, Cushner, ed., *Conquest of Manila*, p. 35.
[36] To Secret Committee, 3 Nov. 1760, OIOC, H/96, p. 103. There is a full exposition of the controversies involving the deployment of the first royal regiment on the Coromandel coast in John Roach, 'The 39th Regiment of Foot and the East India Company, 1754–1757', *Bulletin of the John Rylands Library*, XLI (1958), 102–38.
[37] This theme is well treated in Bryant, 'East India Company's Army', Ph.D. thesis, see especially pp. 98–100.

coordination of the war effort of three presidencies generally proved no easier than getting North American colonies to act together.

In any part of the eighteenth-century British world institutional conflicts in wartime were likely to be exacerbated by conflicts of personal interest. In North America the spoils of war were limited to land grants, openings for Indian trade or opportunities for lucrative trading with the enemy. In India the spoils of war were potentially enormous. Indian rulers made huge distributions of 'presents' to their British allies and to the armies that fought for them. Those made by Mir Jafar, who became nawab of Bengal after the victory at Plassey in 1757, acquired a special notoriety since they were investigated and fully listed by a committee of the house of commons as amounting to £1,238,575. Clive confessed to personally receiving some £170,000, in addition to his share in collective donations. Other individual senior civil servants and army officers received very large sums too. Over and above those payments, fifty lakhs of rupees, more than £500,000, was handed over to be divided between the army and the navy collectively. Large distributions were also made when new nawabs succeeded to the Bengal throne under British auspices in 1760 and 1765.[38] British soldiers who fought in the cause of Muhammad Ali Khan, the nawab of Arcot, received rewards from him far beyond their pay. His 'generosity' is said to have been so 'conspicuous . . . that there is not an officer but has gained very handsomely since they have been abroad'.[39] The nawab of Arcot's gifts were less publicized than those made by the nawabs of Bengal, but had the great disadvantage of usually being made in the form of bonds for which cash payments, if they could ever be obtained, were likely to be in the distant future.[40] War in India was also likely to be lucrative because it took place not in a frontier wilderness, but in densely populated countries where rich towns could be ransomed or plundered; hence the bitter rivalry between the crown forces and the Company about who was to have the disposal of Calcutta and Pondicherry after their capture. At Pondicherry the navy and the regular army officers had agreed to share 100,000 pagodas (£40,000) between them, when the Company stepped in to organize its own distribution.[41] £150,000 was shared out in prize money for the navy and supporting troops after the taking of the Maratha base at Gheriah in 1756.[42] Manila was ransomed for 4 million dollars

[38] P. J. Marshall, *East Indian Fortunes: The British in Bengal in the Eighteenth Century* (Oxford, 1976), pp. 164-74.
[39] Ft. St David to Directors, 6 Aug. 1751, OIOC, H/93, p. 18.
[40] J. D. Gurney, 'The Debts of the Nawab of Arcot, 1763-1776', Oxford University D.Phil. thesis, 1968, pp. 37-8.
[41] S. Cornish to J. Clevland, 31 July 1762, PRO, Adm. 1/162/2, f. 21.
[42] 1st Report, Select Committee, 1772, *Reports from Committees of the House of Commons*, 12 vols. (1803-6), III. 146.

in 1762, half payable by a bill of exchange on the Spanish government, which was never to be honoured. Inevitably, there were prolonged disputes between the Company's agents and the royal officers about the distribution of what was collected at Manila.

Raising money in India for war on any large scale involved extracting grants of revenue from Indian allies and enforcing the payments from these grants. Europeans who took part in such operations collected money for themselves as well as for the Company. Clive reported in 1765 that he had 'vouchers' proving that all the Bengal Company servants posted outside Calcutta 'have obliged the zemindars of the country to make them presents'.[43] He secured for himself an income of £27,000 a year from the Bengal revenues from what was called his *jagir* grant. Soldiers from Madras took payments from the local chieftains or poligars whom they 'pacified'. In the name of the nawab of Arcot, wrote the exuberantly opinionated Draper, 'they murder and rob and pillage the whole country to the great scandal of our nation'.[44]

Articulate men who fought in India, Company servants as well as royal officers, spoke and wrote about honour and about the duty that they owed to the king, their country, and to 'the honourable Company', as readily as did men fighting anywhere else in the world. They believed that those less formally articulate than themselves, sailors and soldiers, both Indian and British, shared their sentiments. Draper wrote, for instance, that his own regiment of 'British conquerors', in whose memory he was later to erect a cenotaph with Latin verses on the downs near Bristol, had lost 800 men, had not received the prize money due to them, and that other 'circumstances added to the heat of the country have put them somewhat out of temper. Yet', he added, 'they have gone upon every service recommended to them with the greatest spirit and chearfully' and were embarking for Manila 'with such joy that I cannot but look upon it as an omen of my good success'.[45] While eloquently testifying to their own sense of honour and their own zeal for the service, few could resist the temptation to impugn the motives of others or fail lovingly to relate episodes in which the public interest had been scandalously set aside for private gain by other people. 'I find the principle most people in India go upon is, every man for himself only', wrote George Scott, a royal officer.[46] Allegations about the power of private interest were often only too well founded.

---

[43] To R. Palk, 14 July 1765, OIOC, MS Eur. G. 37/35, f. 42.

[44] To C. Townshend, 2 Nov. 1762, Cushner, ed., *Conquest of Manila*, p. 148.

[45] To C. Townshend, 27 Nov. 1762, ibid. p. 35; to Egremont, 27 July 1762, PRO, CO 77/20, f. 145. For the cenotaph, see *Asiatic Annual Register*, I (1799), 207.

[46] To [C. Townshend], 30 Nov. 1761, PRO, WO 1/319, p. 263.

Men serving far from home in intense discomfort and with the ever present threat of disease as well as of death or mutilation in action were not likely to disregard opportunities for making money for themselves. On occasions private interest seems to have driven out all other considerations as money was crudely extorted from Indians or the Company was systematically defrauded. Most men on most occasions, however, tried to strike a balance, at least to their own satisfaction, between public duty and private interest.

Both British and Indian soldiers were mercenaries fighting for pay and plunder. If they were not paid or felt themselves cheated of their reasonable expectations, which for the British included generous allowances, usually called 'batta', for taking the field at all, they would mutiny or desert. As the French commander, Lally, lost access to supplies of ready money in the last stages of the Carnatic war, his army disintegrated, many of them eventually enlisting with the British. The British were only too aware that their army might do the same in similar circumstances. George Pigot dreaded 'the consequences of an unpaid army'.[47] Small-scale mutinies were endemic. The bulk of the Bengal army was paralysed by mutinies of both Europeans and sepoys in 1764, when they believed that largesse distributed by the nawab of Bengal was not coming their way. Yet Draper's euphoria about his regiment was surely not entirely misplaced. So long as they got what they regarded as their due, both British and Indian soldiers would give more than could have been expected of them on any rational grounds, presumably because they were impelled by pride and self-regard as well as by self-interest. So it was with many men who held senior positions. The Company's civil servants and its army officers aspired to gentility. Gentility of course required money, since only by the possession of money could an independent status in Britain be sustained. The most ambitious, Clive above all, aspired to 'power' and 'grandeur',[48] which required a great deal of money. Yet most men wished to square the circle: they wanted an honourable name and recognition of distinguished service as well as money. They wished to avoid the taint conventionally attached to 'nabobs', as men who had acquired great wealth in India by dubious means. They devised rules for themselves, which may or may not have convinced others, by which a good reputation and the accumulation of wealth could be reconciled.[49] Clive could without conscious hypocrisy assure his friends before 'that great Being who is the searcher of all hearts', that he had 'a mind superior to all corruption'.[50]

---

[47] To Steevens, 27 Aug. 1760, OIOC, H/96, p. 266.

[48] To J. Pybus, 27 Feb. 1762, John Malcolm, *The Life of Robert, Lord Clive*, 3 vols. (1836), II, 195.

[49] See the valuable comments on 'conventional official morality' in Sutherland, *East India Company*, pp. 53–4.

[50] To J. Carnac, 6 May 1765, National Library of Wales, Clive MS 218, pp. 10–11.

Although put under intense strain, cults of service and honour together with a concern for a good reputation at home seem to have been strong enough to prevent the British presence in India from degenerating into bands of plunderers pursuing their own interests to the exclusion of all other considerations. A degree of control was exerted from home and hierarchies of authority were more or less maintained within the Company's civil and military service, if with much difficulty. For all the discord between them, the forces of the crown and those of the Company still combined to fight together successfully on many occasions. National purposes were achieved in the defeat of the French and of those Indian powers that had challenged the British, even if a multitude of private purposes were also achieved along the way. 'There is no part of the world' than India, wrote the Company's own historian, Robert Orme, without undue exaggeration, 'in which British arms have, of late years, acquired more honour.'[51] Edmund Burke, who had very different views of the British in India, still believed that British officers there had 'shewed as much military skill and bravery as any men'.[52] Nevertheless, if public purposes were more or less sustained, private interest was always present. Wars and conquests can rarely be attributed exclusively to it, but the pursuit of private gain made Europeans even more belligerent and aggressive in exploiting Indian opportunities than might otherwise have been the case.

The Company's rationale for taking up arms had been to protect its trade from what had seemed to be persistent French attempts to curtail it or even to eliminate it altogether from the Coromandel coast. Government support had been enlisted in the cause of trade protection. The French had been defeated by 1761 and thereafter British trade on the coast was to expand markedly. The Company's great settlement at Calcutta had been overrun by the nawab of Bengal in 1756, but it had quickly been recovered by force and the Company's trade in Bengal had been restored on highly advantageous terms. Thus professed national purposes had indeed been achieved. Much else had, however, been achieved that was not a professed national or even a Company purpose. In Bengal the nawabs ruled at the Company's pleasure after 1757 and it had begun to assert control over territory, first of all over a district close to Calcutta, later, in 1760, over three more districts and after 1765 over the whole province. On the Coromandel coast the nawab, Muhammad Ali Khan, owed his throne to the British, whose arms had coerced a number of smaller polities over which he claimed suzerainty and compelled them to pay tribute to him.

[51] Cited in P. J. Marshall, 'Britain and the World in the Eighteenth Century: III, Britain and India', *Transactions of the Royal Historical Society*, 6th ser., X (2000), 11.
[52] P. J. Marshall, ed., *The Writings and Speeches of Edmund Burke*, VI, *India: The Launching of the Hastings Impeachment 1786–1788* (Oxford, 1991), p. 339.

He owed huge financial obligations to the Company for past services and had been forced in 1763 to make a substantial cession of territory near Madras, called the Company's *jagir*. Muhammad Ali was, in short, the Company's dependant, even if he was a resourceful one well able to manipulate his protectors. French influence had been eliminated from the Deccan. Although British influence had not replaced it, the Company was in the process of detaching coastal territory once consigned to the French, called the Northern Circars, and annexing it for itself. On the west coast, the British had assumed control over the port of Surat. Thus by 1763 wars in protection of trade had ended by creating the basis for a territorial empire. The grant in 1765 of the *diwani*, direct administrative responsibility for the whole province of Bengal, removed any lingering doubts about what had been achieved.

This transformation from trade to the domination of territory took most British opinion at home by surprise. The Company's orders to its servants, both at Madras and in Bengal, had invariably been to stand on the defensive and to limit the Company's political and military involvements to the minimum that would protect its commercial interests. Robert James, the very experienced secretary to the East India Company, explained to a committee of the house of commons in 1767 that military commitments in India 'grew insensibly from one trouble to another. We could form no judgement of their progress.' The Company had not sought territorial dominion. 'We dont want conquest and power. It is commercial interest only we look for.'[53]

The 'conquest and power' that so surprised men in Britain had arisen from the nature of the mid-eighteenth wars, in which British and Indian interests were inextricably intertwined. In making war on one another, the French and the British needed Indian manpower to supplement their own limited forces. Above all, they needed Indian revenues to sustain wars whose costs would otherwise drive trading companies out of business in a very short time.

In the course of any war, Europeans inevitably penetrated Indian state structures. This penetration was not only driven by the needs of the companies but by their servants' search for private profit from war and from the handling of revenue. The levying of an effective revenue was usually thought to require European intervention: Indian renters of lands were appointed who were directly responsible to the companies, supervised by their agents and supported by detachments of their troops. Thus European involvement in Indian states inevitably brought Indians into close relations with the companies and their servants. Rulers who owed their thrones to European armies, commandants of sepoys, renters, bankers, and revenue administrators were all drawn into the orbit of the Europeans. Together with the merchants,

---

[53] Evidence on 13 April 1767, OIOC, MS Eur. D. 1018/2, pp. 5, 37.

who had long dealt with the companies and the European private traders, and the 'dubashes' (the term used in the south) or the 'banians' (the term current in Bengal), who acted as personal business agents for individual Europeans, these men formed a network of Indians whose fortunes had been linked to those of the British or the French.

With the ending of the wars there was little prospect that British penetration of Indian states would be checked or that the connections formed between Europeans and sections of the elites in those states would be dissolved. The opposite was in fact to happen. Both on the Coromandel coast and spectacularly in Bengal, penetration was to be consolidated into domination and many more Indians were to be drawn into the British orbit and to forge ties of common interest with them.

III

British trade had been attracted to the south-east coasts of India during the seventeenth century by opportunities for obtaining cotton textiles, initially largely shipped to the Indonesian archipelago, where the East India Company used them to purchase pepper and spices, and later exported them to London for resale in Europe, America, or on the African coast. This trade was transacted at a cluster of ports to the south, of which Madras, the seat of the Company's government, and Fort St David, were the most important, and to the north around Masulipatam in the former sultanate of Golconda. By the mid-eighteenth century the southern trade was dominant; Madras had become a major port, attracting large Indian merchant communities as well as its European residents.

Mughal rule came late to the south-east and quickly fragmented. At the end of the seventeenth century the armies of Aurangzeb overthrew the Bijapur and Golconda sultanates. Imperial officials were left to assert their authority over the territory of the sultanates and over Hindu princes and chiefs further south who had been autonomous since the dissolution of the kingdom of Vijayanagar in the sixteenth century. By the early eighteenth century two centres of ex-Mughal power were emerging, that of the nizam of the Deccan, based on Hyderabad, and that of his nominal subordinate, the *faujdar*, or nawab, of Arcot. In face of formidable difficulties, the nawabs of Arcot were carving out a separate jurisdiction for themselves, coming to be known as the *subah* or province of the Carnatic. Within the area that they claimed for their province they were opposed by local powers, such as the wealthy and effectively independent state of Tanjore (Thanjavur), by autonomous 'poligars' (*paleakaran*), who paid tribute to the Mughal emperor through the nawabs, and by the holders of grants of rights over fortresses or revenue collection. The nawabs were also threatened from outside by the Marathas and the expansionist ambitions of the neighbouring kingdom of Mysore. To make matters worse, the clans with claims to the office of nawab were bitterly divided among themselves. Contestants for power were willing to turn to Europeans for support.

By the 1740s both French and British on the Coromandel coast were seeking to establish contacts with leading participants in the unstable politics of the Carnatic and to extract concessions from them. The spread of the Anglo-French worldwide war to Asia after 1744 gave a new urgency to such manoeuvres. In 1746, in retaliation for crippling losses inflicted by British warships on French trade, a French expedition took Madras. The then nawab of Arcot objected to so flagrant a breach of the peace in his territory, but the French routed the troops that he sent to evict them from Madras and began to give their support to a rival family to that of the nawab. The nawab therefore turned to the British, sending troops to act with them. By the time that the Anglo-French war came to an end in 1748, Indians had been left in no doubt as to the effectiveness of even small European armies, while certain ambitious Europeans had become aware that they might be able to determine who would rule in the Carnatic and to derive great advantages thereby.

The French governor, Dupleix, put the matter to the test in 1749. Rather than disbanding the army that had been built up to fight the British, he let it out for hire to contestants not only for Arcot, but for the Deccan as well, where a violent succession dispute had broken out on the death of the nizam in 1748. Dupleix's Indian clients were required to pay for the use of French troops and to endow the French company with grants of land that would enable it to maintain its army and to finance its trade in future from Indian revenue rather than from shipments of bullion from Europe or from the profits of Asian trade. In 1749 French troops enabled their ally Chanda Sahib to win the Arcot throne by defeating and killing the incumbent nawab. At the same time the French also backed a claimant to be nizam of the Deccan. A French army moved inland in 1751 to enable their ally to make good his claim. These moves were an extremely bold and ambitious development of tactics in which Europeans had already experimented. Although Dupleix seems to have had none of the designs sometimes attributed to him for a great French territorial empire, his interventions threatened to put French trade in southern India into a very advantageous position.[54]

---

[54] The standard treatment of Dupleix's aims remains that in Alfred Martineau, *Dupleix et l'Inde française*, 4 vols. (Paris, 1928), vol. III; for recent assessments, see Catherine Manning, *Fortunes à Faire: The French in Asian Trade, 1719–48* (Aldershot, 1996), pp. 208–18; Philippe Haudrère, *La Compagnie française des Indes au xviii* siècle (1719–95)*, 4 vols. (Paris, 1989), III. 979–1012.

The price paid for these coups brought about by French troops soon became apparent to the British. The French in the Carnatic were rewarded with a tract of territory around Pondicherry, including an area threatening to cut off the British settlement at Fort St David from its hinterland. The nizam whom the French supported gave them grants on the coast of the Deccan which included British settlements.

The British Company servants had themselves been dabbling in Carnatic politics and were in the process of adding to their territory around Madras, but they interpreted Dupleix's strategy as aiming at 'nothing less than to exclude us from the trade of the coast and by degrees from that of India'.[55] The theme that the French were contriving 'the ruin of your settlements' was elaborated in subsequent dispatches to London. It convinced both the Company directors, who agreed that Dupleix's success would make it 'impossible for us to carry on our trade or even to preserve a footing upon the coast of Choromandel',[56] and ultimately the British government, who committed forces to support the Company in 1754.

The British Company servants decided to take immediate counter-action by supporting alternative candidates for the two disputed thrones. Their rival to the French in the Deccan was quickly eliminated, but the British found an alternative nawab of Arcot who was to be sustained by them until his death in 1795. This was Muhammad Ali Khan, Walajah, son of the nawab who had been killed in 1749 by Chanda Sahib with the aid of the French. The long alliance between Muhammad Ali and the East India Company was by no means the unequal one that it is often assumed to have been. Neither side could do without the other. It is certainly true that Muhammad Ali depended on British arms both for acquiring his throne and for keeping it and that he had to pay the British enormous sums for their services. On the other hand, he was able to use British protection for his own purposes to incorporate the territory to which he laid claim, but had little prospect of subjugating with his own unaided resources, and welding it into a more or less unitary state based on a 'tradition of kingship which was authentically Islamic'. He achieved 'the delicate task of creating a Muslim dynastic tradition within the debilitating embrace of his English sponsors'.[57] Whether they were aware of his objectives, the British had no real alternative to furthering such ambitions unless

---

[55] Ft. St David to Directors, 12 Feb. 1750, OIOC, H/93, p. 54.

[56] Directors to Ft. St George, 24 Jan. 1753, *Records of Fort St George: Public Despatches from England 1751–2* (Madras, 1958), pp. 34–5.

[57] Susan Bayly, *Saints, Goddesses and Kings: Muslims and Christians in South Indian Society 1700–1900* (Cambridge, 1989), pp. 157, 171. There is an excellent account of the creation of the Carnatic state by the nawab and the British in Bayly's book, ch. 4. See also David Ludden, *Peasant History in South India* (Princeton, 1985), ch. 3; Jim Phillips, 'A Successor to the Moguls: The Nawab of the Carnatic and the East India Company, 1763–1785', *International History Review*, VII (1985), 364–89.

they were prepared to try to create their own state in south India, a task clearly beyond them in the mid-eighteenth century.

The British were neither willing nor able to create a state of their own in the Carnatic, but war forced them into a deep involvement in the state that Muhammad Ali Khan was creating. From 1749 they felt bound to give him military assistance on a steadily increasing scale, even if they at first acted as his nominal auxiliaries, carefully avoiding any direct action against the French. Effective military intervention meant dispersing the Company's forces inland. The power of any nawab of the Carnatic depended in the first instance on control of two major centres, Trichinopoly (Tiruchchirappali) in the south and Arcot, the nawabs' nominal capital, inland from Madras. Since Muhammad Ali Khan was already in control of Trichinopoly, early British efforts concentrated on helping him beat off French-supported efforts to dislodge him. In 1751 Robert Clive gained his first military success by seizing Arcot and repelling attacks on it. British support was thus beginning to give Muhammad Ali Khan some credibility as nawab. His credibility was greatly boosted by a serious defeat inflicted on the French and by the capture and murder of his rival Chanda Sahib in 1752.

By then the East India Company was beginning to count the cost of the war. The deployment of troops to support Muhammad Ali Khan meant that the Company had to develop forces, consisting of infantry and field artillery, not merely capable of defending its coastal settlements but of operating far inland. Dupleix was able to persuade the French company to dispatch him some 400 to 500 recruits a year from France, ostensibly for protection against the aggressive British.[58] The British Company committed itself to sending Madras 'such a force from time to time as we may make no doubt will enable you to act upon the defensive at least'.[59] The directors, however, found recruits both expensive and difficult to raise, especially when war in Europe became likely and the needs of the regular army took priority. The Company was, for instance, forbidden to recruit in Ireland,[60] and was obliged to accept men under 5 feet 2 inches, the minimum height for the royal army.[61] As was the case in North America, the Company turned to 'foreign Protestants' to supplement British manpower, recruiting Swiss and Germans. Only 1,258 recruits were, however, sent from Britain to the Coromandel coast from 1750 to 1753.[62] For its part, the Madras presidency was able to persuade a number of the royal troops sent out to India in 1747 to sign on into its own army, to

[58] Martineau, *Dupleix*, III. 4.
[59] Directors to Ft. St George, 23 Aug. 1751, *Despatches from England, 1751–2*, p. 17.
[60] R. Rigby to Directors, 1 Jan. 1760, OIOC, E/1/43, no. 1.
[61] Ligonier to C. Townshend, 2 Feb. 1762, PRO, WO 1/319, p. 301.
[62] Henry Dodwell, *Dupleix and Clive: The Beginning of Empire* (1922), p. 82.

commandeer recruits going to other presidencies and to purchase Madagascar slaves, known as 'cofferys', who were thought to make fine soldiers. By 1751 Madras had assembled 900 men, but feared that a large French reinforcement was on the way.[63]

Inadequate supplies of its own European soldiers forced the Company to solicit the dispatch of royal regiments, however obnoxious it found their officers. By 1757 the directors reported that all their recruiting efforts had proved ineffectual and so they had been forced to accept a royal battalion especially for Indian service, 'draughted out of the new raised regiments'. Another one was sent out in 1759.[64] Even with these reinforcements, the Company increasingly had to rely on Indian soldiers. The British tried to enlist as allies not only the troops of the nawab, but those of the raja of Tanjore, of Mysore and of the Marathas. They had, however, little regard for the fighting qualities of what they called 'Moors' armies; 'any European nation, resolved to war on them, with a tolerable force may overrun their whole country'.[65] Indian troops must be brought under their own direct control. Madras apparently recruited its first Indian soldiers on the Malabar coast and by 1752 the Company had an establishment of 1,300 of its own sepoys, armed with muskets, under Indian commanders, sometimes with European sergeants attached.[66]

This expansion of the Madras army was enormously expensive. At the outset the nawab had been told that he must pay for the troops whenever they moved out of the coastal garrisons and took the field. In July 1750 he gave the Company a 'mortgage bond' on the revenue of Trichinopoly.[67] By 1752, however, he was already heavily in arrears and had paid 'but trifling sums' towards liquidating his debt.[68] It was clear that he would only be able to make significant payments if he was sufficiently in control of large tracts of territory to collect revenue effectively from them. This would require further deployment of the Company's troops to support the nawab's collectors and to coerce the major revenue payers. Although payment for these troops inevitably added to the sums owing by the nawab, such a strategy began to be followed from 1752. The British complained, however, that little of the money which

---

[63] Ft. St David to Directors, 6 Aug. 1751, OIOC, H/93, pp. 14–15.

[64] Directors to Ft. St George, 23 Dec. 1757, *Records of Fort St George: Public Despatches from England, 1757–8* (Madras, 1952), p. 33.

[65] Ft. St David to Directors, 6 Aug. 1751, OIOC, H/93, p. 15.

[66] There is much material on the early Madras army in W. J. Wilson, *A History of the Madras Army*, 5 vols. (Madras, 1882–9), vol. I. On sepoys, see H. H. Dodwell, *Sepoy Recruitment in the Old Madras Army* (Calcutta, 1922).

[67] Ft. St David to Directors, 6 Aug. 1751, OIOC, H/93, p. 14.

[68] *Records of Fort St George. Diary and Consultation Book: Military Department, 1752* (Madras, 1910), p. 9.

their forces enabled the nawab to collect actually reached them; it was 'immediately dissipated' by those around him for their own purposes.[69]

The Company therefore tried to guarantee a flow of revenue by assuming direct control itself over the administration of certain districts. Leases were taken for them from the nawab. This was a tactic already extensively used by the French. Dupleix got all revenues of the Carnatic nominally allocated to him in person on behalf of the French monarchy, appointing his Indian deputies in areas under French control, while his lieutenant in the Deccan, Bussy, obtained huge grants there. The British grants in the Carnatic were less extensive. By 1755, when Muhammad Ali Khan owed nearly 2 million pagodas (about £800,000), five districts were under Company administration, but the revenue yielded was inadequate to defray even the peace-time costs of the army. A request to the nawab that he transfer the whole of his revenue to the Company and live as their pensioner at Madras was refused both then and in 1757, when it was repeated.[70] Unwilling to seize his revenues from him by open force, the Company felt that it had no alternative to taking bonds from the nawab and committing itself to yet more extensive campaigns to raise revenue on his behalf. The most ambitious of these campaigns took British influence in 1755 south from Trichinopoly down to Cape Comorin, into the lands of the autonomous *nayakas* of Madura and Tinnevelly, from whom the nawabs of Arcot had been trying to extract tribute. The Company decided to depose the nawab's brother from the management of Madura and to replace him with a renter of their own, supported by their troops. From the Company's point of view, however, the amount realised from the revenue rarely defrayed the cost of the military operations required to make the collections. The southern districts were eventually entrusted in 1759 to the remarkable Yusaf Khan, commandant of the British sepoys, the Nostromo of the Madras council, 'the bravest man . . . amongst the sons of Mahomed in India' that Robert Orme ever knew, but one who was to show the same ambiguity as Nostromo about his ultimate loyalties.[71]

Once they had been able to blunt the immediate threat that they saw in Dupleix's new tactics, the Company's servants at Madras were only too aware that further military operations would achieve little except to add to the obligations which the nawab owed to them and which he showed no sign of paying off. Since the nawab seemed to be incapable of overcoming 'his present difficulties', 'the whole burthen of the war is likely to lye on the

---

[69] R. Orme to J. Payne, 28 July 1757, OIOC, Orme MS, OV 28, f. 99.

[70] Madras Select Committee, 3 Aug. 1755, 29 Aug. 1757, OIOC, P/C/48, unpaginated; P/C/51, pp. 743–4.

[71] R. Orme to J. Payne, n.d., OIOC, Orme MS, OV. 28, f. 24. For Yusaf Khan, see S. C. Hill, *Yusuf Khan: The Rebel Commandant* (1914) and Bayly, *Saints, Goddesses and Kings*, ch. 5.

Company, the heavy charges of which are already insupportable'.[72] If at all possible, they wanted peace with the French, so that they could stabilize the debt to them by the nawab and then try systematically to reduce it. So long as Dupleix remained in India, they believed that they had no realistic hopes of peace. Dupleix was, however, recalled in 1754 and a provisional peace was eventually agreed between the companies in India. The Madras council explained that the cost of the war without prompt payments by Muhammad Ali Khan was 'too heavy for a trading society' to bear and that the French were not only in control of the Deccan but had detached Mysore and the Marathas from the nawab. Maratha cavalry raids would ravage the Carnatic and make revenue collection impossible. Peace was therefore essential to enable the nawab's debt to be paid off.[73] Once they were assured of a truce, the British went ahead with more expeditions to enforce Muhammad Ali Khan's authority over his tributaries. Madras was therefore unable to retrench its military expenses. By February 1756 it had nearly 2,400 Europeans and 7,000 sepoys in its pay.[74]

Whether peace would have survived in India if matters had been left to the Company servants in Pondicherry and Madras is uncertain but unlikely. War in Europe in 1756 was to spread to India and settle the issue. The British and the French governments sent warships and royal troops to India in a competitive cycle, aimed at preventing their enemy from attaining supremacy rather than at winning supremacy for their own side. The long interval before the arrival of the major French reinforcement, warships and two royal regiments under the comte de Lally, enabled the Madras council to detach Clive and ships of the Royal Navy in an expedition to recover Calcutta. By the summer of 1758 the French were able to undertake the siege of Madras. The British had to pull in virtually all their scattered troops to defend the presidency with the inevitable consequences that the nawab's 'authority in the country' collapsed and so did the flow of cash to the Company.[75] Madras, however, was successfully defended and with the arrival of two royal regiments the British went onto the offensive. Lally was decisively defeated at Wandiwash in 1760, driven into Pondicherry and forced to surrender in February 1761.

Victory over the French left the British Company free to try once and for all to put its finances into order. There could be no return to a small pre-war garrison army nor, unlike in America, was the government willing to allow

[72] *Records of Fort St George. Diary and Consultation Book: Military Department, 1753* (Madras, 1910), p. 94.
[73] To Directors, 12 Jan. 1755, OIOC, H/93, pp. 261–2.
[74] Account of 28 Feb. 1756, OIOC, H/94, p. 98.
[75] Ft. St George to Directors, 26 June 1758, OIOC, H/95, p. 205.

the royal regiments to stay in India after the signing of the peace, although the directors wanted both warships and troops to remain.[76] For the last stages of the war the Madras army had been restructured to consist of two battalions of European infantry and seven battalions of sepoys with distinctive uniforms and a much larger element of European officers in command of them.[77] A post-war military establishment for Madras of 2,600 Europeans and 4,000 sepoys was ordered from London.[78] With heavy on-going military expenses, it was more than ever necessary to guarantee the nawab's contributions.

A settlement was made with Muhammad Ali in 1760 in which the Company gave up all the leases that it had held from him, placing the whole Carnatic under his direct management, except for the areas around Madras, ceded outright at the beginning of the war. In return, he guaranteed to pay a stipulated sum each year until the debts, put in 1762 at 26 lakhs of pagodas (rather more than £1 million) were paid off. The reason given for this apparent step away from an extensive British territorial empire in south India was that the Company had neither the knowledge nor the experience needed to manage large revenues.[79] Since whether the nawab would be able to pay his instalments with any regularity now depended on the amounts that he could borrow and since many prominent Europeans were engaged in lending him money at very high rates of interest,[80] it is not difficult to conclude that there may have been private motives for returning the revenue of the Carnatic to his management. Whatever the reason, the Company had renounced any policy of direct management of the revenues of the Carnatic of the kind that it was pursuing in Bengal. Indeed, when the nawab was induced by George Pigot to transfer a valuable *jagir* of 330 square miles and 221 villages near Madras to the Company with a revenue said to be worth £160,000, that too was handed over to him as the Company's revenue farmer.[81]

Intervention in the Carnatic to extend the nawab's authority over potential revenue payers continued remorselessly, however. Even the raja of Tanjore was threatened and in 1762 was made to conclude a settlement for the arrears that the nawab claimed from him. The Company's most prized Indian collaborator, Yusaf Khan, astonished them by rebelling in 1762. This was seen as a test of 'that reputation which the Company's arms have justly

---

[76] 'Mr Rous Queries' [1763], PRO, CO 77/20, f. 123. The secret committee was fearful of the intentions of the Dutch and wanted naval protection against them, see their letter to Halifax, 16 Jan. 1764, OIOC, H/97, pp. 9–16.

[77] Wilson, *Madras Army*, I. 122–3, 142–9.

[78] 9th Report, Secret Committee, 1773, *Reports from Committees*, IV. 599.

[79] *Records of Fort St George. Diary and Consultation Book, 1760* (Madras, 1953), pp. 197–210.

[80] Gurney, 'Nawab's Debts', D.Phil. thesis.

[81] For the history of the *jagir*, see Eugene F. Irschick, *Dialogue and History: Constructing South India, 1795–1896* (Berkeley, 1994), pp. 19–29.

acquired' and his fort at Madura was reduced after a long and costly siege.[82] The great fort of Vellore, which had defied the nawab for long under its governor or *killedar* surrendered in December 1761. The northern poligars had been 'entirely subdued' by 1765, when the Madras council congratulated itself that there was now 'peace and quietness from the River Kistna to Cape Comorin',[83] a peace, which if it ever really existed, was to be shattered two years later by a costly and indecisive war against Mysore, which did little either for the finances of the Carnatic or for the Company's military reputation.

What had emerged in the Carnatic by 1763 was certainly not a British colonial state; unlike in Bengal, direct British control over territory and revenue was limited. The Carnatic was rather a successor state to the Mughals, created by Muhammad Ali Khan under British protection. British interests, both those of the Company and those of private individuals, intermeshed with Indian interests at many points. The British had been able to use the resources of the Carnatic to finance the war effort that had defeated the French, even if much of what the nawab owed them had yet to be paid off. Not only had their commercial interests been protected, but the political influence which they had gained over the Carnatic under Muhammad Ali Khan enabled their trade and that of private British merchants to grow into a dominant position after the war at the expense of the trade of their European competitors and that of Indian merchants who were not associated with them.[84]

Muhammad Ali Khan's rule of course depended on British arms. He maintained large forces of his own, but the British believed that they were of no military value. Much of his revenue was formally committed to the British and he was being subjected to a multitude of unofficial British claims on his resources as well. It seemed to be symbolic of his dependence that he ceased to live at Arcot, but moved into a new palace at Madras. On occasions he openly expressed his fears that the British would depose him and take over his country.[85]

Yet in return for a degree of dependence, the nawab had been able to vanquish his rivals for the throne and his right to it had been guaranteed in 1763 in Europe by the terms of the Anglo-French peace. Moreover, thanks to British military campaigns, his rule extended, if by no means uniformly, over

---

[82] Ft. St George to Directors, 3 Sept. 1763, OIOC, E/4/300.

[83] Ft. St George to Directors, 8 Aug. 1765, OIOC, H/98, p. 140.

[84] This is the theme of much writing by S. Arasaratnam, notably *Maritime Commerce and English Power (Southeast India 1750–1800)* (Aldershot, 1996).

[85] J. D. Gurney, 'Fresh Light on the Character of the Nawab of Arcot' in Anne Whiteman, J. S. Bromley, P. G. M. Dickson, eds., *Statesmen, Scholars and Merchants: Essays in Eighteenth-century History presented to Dame Lucy Sutherland* (Oxford, 1973), p. 231.

territory where previous nawabs could rarely enforce their claims. Dependence could also be mitigated by the exercise of influence over those on whom he depended. Muhammad Ali Khan was lavish in gifts and promises of gifts to Company servants. George Pigot was reputed to have gone home with a large pension. The loans which the nawab raised to keep the Company at bay paid very high rates of interest and often included an element of *inam*, or present, in them. To become the nawab's creditor was thus in many cases to receive a favour from him. Many of the most important Company servants invested in the nawab's loans and were therefore obligated to him. He began cultivating influence beyond the Company's service, with the royal officers who came to India, with directors and ministers in London and, he hoped, even with George III with whom he began to correspond in 1760. He was later to dispatch agents to represent him in London.

The pattern of dependence mitigated by influence, set by the nawab and the governors and council of Madras, was to be reproduced at lower levels by other Europeans and their Indian clients. Over a long period the Company had built up a network of Indian merchants who dealt with it, above all providing it with the textiles that it exported, and who also dealt with the British private traders. The size and wealth of the Indian merchant community living in Madras had been the envy of the French, who had tried to attract its members to Pondicherry and even to force them to go there when Madras was taken in 1746. Nearly all of them had, however, refused to move and, much to the pleasure of the British, had flocked back to Madras when it was recovered in 1748, while insisting that the British must provide Madras with a proper garrison in future.[86] The size of the Company and private orders for textiles, the regularity with which they paid their advances, usually in imported bullion, and the investment opportunities that they offered to Indians who acquired property in the flourishing city of Madras cemented the bonds between Indian merchants and the British. In return, Indian merchants provided short-term credit to the Company and especially to private traders. By the mid-eighteenth century Indo-British mercantile 'interdependence had reached its peak'.[87]

Individual Europeans of any standing were likely to be closely linked to another group of Indians, the Madras 'dubashes', literally men of two languages, or interpreters, who served as the personal agents of their white

---

[86] To Directors, 30 Aug., 2 Nov. 1749, *Records of Fort St George: Despatches to England 1746–51* (Madras, 1932), pp. 109, 142.

[87] S. Arasaratnam, 'Trade and Political Dominion in South India, 1750–1790: Changing British–Indian Relationships', *Modern Asian Studies*, XIII (1979), 22–3. Relations between Indian merchants and the British are examined in Prasannan Parthasarathi, *The Transition to a Colonial Economy: Weavers, Merchants and Kings in South Asia, 1720–1800* (Cambridge, 2001), pp. 135–40.

employers. These were men not usually drawn from merchant castes but from rural groups with a tradition of service to earlier regimes, who might not otherwise have had dealings with Europeans. They managed their masters' accounts, raised loans and arranged business for them. As the British increasingly took on a political role, the dubashes seized the opportunities that this presented for tax farming or managing offices under the Company.[88] A military officer engaged in enforcing the nawab's revenue demands in the south believed that only the expertise of 'some of the most creditable of the Company's dubashes', could prevent the Company from being cheated.[89] Dubashes of course made money for themselves as well as for the Company or their European employers. The dubashes of prominent Europeans became rich and powerful men in their own right, the founders of what were to be distinguished Madras families, patrons of temples and learning.

To censorious contemporaries and to most later commentators, the 'double government' in the Carnatic of the nawab and the Company, with its lack of clear definitions and its blurring of British claims to sovereignty that were being so clearly established in Bengal, was deplorable. The interdependence of British and Indians seemed to encourage the corruption embodied in 'the Nabob of Arcot's debts', the vast fabric of usury that Edmund Burke was later to excoriate. In these debts and in other matters the nawab and the Madras servants seemed to be colluding for their own advantage with no regard either for the good government of the Carnatic or for Company interests. Until corruption was rooted out, it was assumed that empire would not be secure in south India.

The Madras presidency was long to enjoy a dubious reputation and to be racked by periodic scandals, but the interdependence of Indians and British may have been a firmer foundation for eventual empire than was commonly supposed. Bold as were the ambitions of Dupleix and Bussy, the French had sunk no roots in south India and their paper dominions collapsed with military defeat. Indians fled from Pondicherry in the later years of the war.[90] The British survived the loss of Madras in 1746 and built enduring alliances with the merchants of the coast and the soldiers, bankers and administrators who committed themselves to their cause. Corruption, that is the pursuit of their own interest by both sides of the alliance, may have been the cement that held it together.

[88] Arasaratnam, 'Trade and Political Dominion', pp. 23–6; Susan Neild-Basu, 'The Dubashes of Madras', *Modern Asian Studies*, XVIII (1984), 1–31.

[89] J. Caillaud to R. Orme, [1755], OIOC, Orme MS, OV 293, f. 33.

[90] Arasaratnam, *Maritime Commerce and English Power*, pp. 4–5.

IV

While the Carnatic state that emerged from the war was in a real sense a British creation, in Bengal the British had been dealing since early in the eighteenth century with a strong successor state already in being. The nawabs of Bengal had to fight to prevent incursions along their western boundaries in Bihar and Orissa, but their control over the interior of the provinces was rarely openly contested, once a ruler had survived the virtually inevitable crisis at his succession.

Control over revenue resources was the crucial issue. Whereas the raising of much of the revenue in the Carnatic required the coercion of recalcitrant tributaries by force, in Bengal the nawabs received the greater part of theirs in regular payments from what amounted to revenue contractors under the supervision of state officials. Early in the eighteenth century most of the Mughal grants of revenue in Bengal had been revoked and extensive blocks of revenue-paying land had been put into the charge of a group of large *zamindars* who paid in cash to the nawabs. The office of *zamindar* in Bengal became a form of hereditary property and the major *zamindars* became local potentates with police and judicial powers enforced by armed retainers. Nevertheless, they were subject to much closer supervision from the nawabs' officials than was the case with the poligars of the south and armed rebellion against the nawabs by *zamindars* outside Bihar was rare. '[A]ttentisme rather than rebelliousness' has been said to have 'characterized the zamindars of Bengal'.[91]

The revenue of the Carnatic was notionally supposed to be worth 3 million pagodas (approximately £1.2 million) a year to the nawab, a sum which he had little hope of getting anywhere near to attaining until the 1770s.[92] Just before Plassey, the nawab of Bengal was believed to be able to raise Rs. 15 million (about £1.7 million) out of an assessment of Rs. 16.6 million.[93] This disparity reflected the wealth of Bengal as well as the greater effectiveness of its rulers' system for realising the revenue. Irrigated rice production was the basic source of eastern India's taxable wealth. By contrast with the Carnatic where high levels of rice production were achieved only in the deltas of the great rivers, such as the Kaveri (the source of Tanjore's prosperity) or the

---

[91] John R. McLane, *Land and Local Kingship in Eighteenth-Century Bengal* (Cambridge, 1993), p. 27. For a fuller account of the Bengal revenue system, see below, Chap. 8.

[92] Phillips, 'A Successor to the Moguls', p. 371. See also estimates in 4th Report, Secret Committee, 1782, *Reports from Committees*, VII. 685–6.

[93] Rajat Datta, *Society, Economy and the Market: Commercialization in Rural Bengal, c.1760–1800* (New Delhi, 2000), pp. 333–8.

Kistna, virtually the whole of lower Bengal was a rice producing delta. These lands were highly assessed for revenue and provided abundant surpluses of grain for export. A huge trade in agricultural produce was greatly facilitated by the ease of transport by water throughout the province. Bengal's grain surpluses fed other parts of India. The British believed that by eliminating the French settlement in Bengal in 1757, they could cut off the food supply of Pondicherry and Mauritius. By the mid-eighteenth century Bengal also had a commanding position in Indian textile production. It was the major source of silk and its cotton cloth dominated India's exports by sea to the Middle East and to Europe and overland to Central Asia. Most of the saltpetre on which European gunpowder production depended came from Bengal.

For the British, both the Company and private traders, but also for the Dutch and the French, Bengal had become the centrepiece of Asian trade. Although tea shipments from China were growing in importance, some 60 per cent of all the East India Company's exports from Asia were still coming from Bengal at the mid-eighteenth century.[94] Europeans had established their major trading settlements in Bengal, that is, British Calcutta, French Chandernagore and Dutch Chinsura, along the river Hughli, then the most easily navigable arm of the Ganges delta. To gain access to particular kinds of textiles or other products the Europeans had also spread inland in a way that was never attempted in the south, where they stayed on the coast. There were trading stations as far west along the Ganges as Patna in Bihar and to the east in modern Bangladesh, above all at Dacca (Dhaka), source of some of the highest quality cottons.

The size of the European stake in Bengal's economic life before 1757 has become matter for controversy. The proposition that European purchases were much greater than those of Asian merchants has been questioned.[95] What is not in question, however, is that European and particularly British penetration of the economy was very significant and on a much greater scale than in the south. Calcutta was a larger city even than Madras and the British were involved in provincial centres far from the coast. Many Indians therefore did business with them. Merchants who took the Company's *dadni*, or cash payments in advance, to provide it with silk or cotton cloth lived in Calcutta or in the main textile-producing districts. Some of the most ambitious of these merchants not only executed large contracts for goods for the Company but also dabbled in the politics of the nawabs' court, managing trades which had become government monopolies.[96] The Company and individual British

---

[94] Chaudhuri, *Trading World of Asia*, p. 510.

[95] Sushil Chaudhury, *From Prosperity to Decline: Eighteenth Century Bengal* (New Delhi, 1995).

[96] Kumkum Chatterjee, *Merchants, Politics and Society in Early Modern India: Bihar: 1733–1820* (Leiden, 1996).

people provided additional business for the highly developed banking networks of Bengal, the largest of which was the house of Jagat Seth, banker to the nawabs. The rough equivalent of the Madras dubashes were the Calcutta 'banians'. They too entered the service of individual Europeans, running their households, keeping their personal accounts, lending them money and acting as their business agents.

Bengal was thus potentially a very attractive target for foreign intervention. A relatively centralized structure of authority was in place, operated by a skilled bureaucracy mostly drawn from Bengali Hindus accustomed to working with what was to them an alien Mughal regime. Large revenues were being generated. Agriculture and manufacturing were highly developed. Finally, there were important groups within Bengal who were already associating with Europeans to their own advantage and might not be averse to deeper European involvement.

Europeans, notably the British, already had a privileged stake in Bengal. Their Calcutta settlement was for all practical purposes beyond the nawabs' jurisdiction. British trade passed through the province custom-free under a grant from the Mughal emperor of 1717. The merchants and artisans who worked for the Company even outside Calcutta were largely under its authority rather than that of the nawabs' government. Any attempt to enlarge these privileges, for instance by adding to the Company's revenues through the kind of piecemeal territorial acquisitions being made on the Coromandel coast in the 1740s would, however, fall foul of the nawab. In the war of 1744 to 1748 the French had been able to disregard the nawab of the Carnatic's prohibition on hostilities within his territory and had attacked Madras. Both they and the British thought it advisable, by contrast, to observe a neutrality on the Ganges, as required by the nawab of Bengal. Europeans knew that their settlements were vulnerable to the nawabs' troops. That this was so was fully demonstrated in 1756 when the army of the nawab Siraj-ud-daula took Calcutta.

The storming of Calcutta in 1756 set off a chain of events that ended in a British army winning the battle of Plassey and in the murder of Siraj-ud-daula by his rivals in June 1757. What was to follow was not the acquisition of limited territorial gains, while sustaining an ally as nawab, as happened in the south, but the rapid dismantling of the nawabs' power and its almost total usurpation by the British. This had been achieved by 1765.

The overthrow of the nawabs' regime began with the arrival in the Hughli in December 1756 of the British forces from Madras under admiral Charles Watson and colonel Robert Clive. Siraj-ud-daula was forced to relinquish the British settlements and to sign a treaty restoring the Company's privileges. Shortly afterwards the British eliminated French Chandernagore and began clandestine negotiations with Siraj-ud-daula's enemies. The outcome of this plotting was that much of Siraj-ud-daula's army refused to fight for him at the battle of Plassey in June 1757. The British won the battle and the leading conspirator, Mir Jafar, became the new nawab. He was obliged to pledge himself to make vast payments as indemnities and rewards to the victors, amounting, as Clive put it, to 'three million sterling',[97] and to concede territory around Calcutta to the Company. These pledges, together with the cost of the Company's army, for which he was expected to pay as it moved inland to establish his power and drive out incursions, left Mir Jafar, like Muhammad Ali Khan, with an immense debt. As they had done in the south, the British insisted on the mortgaging of territorial revenue to pay off the debt. In 1760 they took outright possession of three rich districts as part of a settlement with a new nawab, Mir Kasim, whom they chose to replace Mir Jafar. Mir Kasim's position was quickly undermined, chiefly by the unbridled expansion of private British trade into the interior of Bengal. In 1763 Mir Kasim resorted to arms to resist this invasion of his authority. He was driven out of Bengal, but allied with powers in northern India in a determined attempt to curb the British. The alliance was defeated at the battle of Buxar in 1764, after which the British formally sealed their total domination of Bengal by accepting the grant of the *diwani* at the hands of the emperor in the following year.

This brief outline suggests similarities as well as differences from what happened in the south. The most obvious difference was the unwillingness of the British to make the accommodations with an indigenous regime that would have enabled it to survive for any length of time. The sack of Calcutta in 1756 had left bitter memories. The British were determined never again to be dependent on Indian goodwill. Ruthlessness in dealing with the nawabs was also clearly driven by a belief that the great wealth of Bengal was readily accessible to Europeans. The nawabs were thought to have accumulated a huge state treasure ripe for plunder. It was supposed that Bengal's revenue resources, to which the British, as in the south, needed access to sustain their army could easily be tapped. In Bengal there were also commercial rewards to be won for the Company and above all for individuals on a scale that dwarfed those in the south. In 1761 Laurence Sulivan told Clive that territorial dominion in the south would have no commercial benefits, whereas in Bengal he considered that the Company had 'a solid, extensive, and valuable commerce' and had already acquired 'provinces abounding in manufactures and tillage whose revenues are great and encreasing'.[98] Subjected to even greater

---

[97] To Richard Clive, 19 Aug. 1757, G. W. Forrest, *The Life of Lord Clive*, 2 vols. (1918), II. 36.
[98] Letter of 27 July 1761, ibid. II. 190

pressures than he faced, it is hardly surprising that Bengal's nawabs, notably Siraj-ud-daula and Mir Kasim, lacked the suppleness of Muhammad Ali Khan in seeking influence over the British rather than confronting them. They chose confrontation with a formidable military power.

The new British Bengal army was built on the Madras Europeans and sepoys and the elements of the king's troops that had been sent to recover Calcutta in 1756. Few of those that survived ever went back to Madras. Immediately after Plassey, the Bengal council set out the need for very substantial additions to its forces. A great new Fort William was to be built at Calcutta and this would need a 'respectable garrison' of 2,000 Europeans.[99] At the same time it was also becoming clear that the Bengal army could not simply be regarded as a garrison force for Calcutta. Clive was not content to leave the defence of Bengal and its internal order to the troops of the nawab, for which he had the utmost contempt. The Company thus had rapidly to build up a Bengal army with the same capacity as the Madras army for conducting operations far inland to defend the province at its boundaries. Large numbers of European recruits only came in 1763–4 when, with the ending of the European war and therefore of competition at home from the British army, 1,511 were sent.[100] In the meanwhile, Bengal sepoy battalions began to be raised. Few of the Bengal sepoys came from the province of Bengal: even in lower Bengal, where most of the new regiments were recruited, there appear to have been abundant migrants from Bihar or north India willing to take up military employment. A British officer later recalled:

There is seldom occasion to seek for means of recruiting sepoys, such a concourse of lusty young fellows present themselves daily on our parades for employment, many of them Ragepoots: when there is scarcity of men, the best method is to send trusty jemmatdars or havildars into their own country, with smart new turban, glaring sword, laced coat and some money; for as in England, fair speeches and tinsel coats attract many followers: they should always be instructed too to get in with the wenches, for love brings many more; at other times enquiries should be made about their families; and if there be found several sons, nephews or brothers, in them, a clever fellow should be detached on purpose, who may enlist them all: for whole families are to be preferred whenever you can procure them. I wish we could keep sepoys as easily as we can get them amongst us; but recruiting is too frequent; the rogues desert in shoals on changing of quarters . . . [T]he army is often,

---

[99] To Directors, 14 July 1757, H. N. Sinha, ed., *Fort William–India House Correspondence*, II, *1757–1759* (Delhi, 1957), p. 228.
[100] 9th Report, Secret Committee, *Reports from Committees*, IV. 636.

however, a resource for an unfortunate farmer or tradesman; they remain with us for a few months, save money, and return again to the relief of their unhappy families.[101]

One of the battalions was specifically raised at Patna in Bihar, largely from men from Bojpur, a district long famous for soldiers.[102] By 1764 the Bengal army still had only about 1,000 Europeans of all arms fit for duty, but it had raised eighteen battalions of sepoys, some 13,000 men.[103]

In January 1758 Clive began the deployment of the Company's army throughout the province when he took British troops into Bihar to stabilize the new regime there. In 1759 and 1760 the Mughal crown prince, later the emperor Shah Alam, appeared in Bihar inciting rebellion among the *zamindars*. On both occasions the Company's forces drove him out and chastised those who had rebelled.

The cost of such operations was added to the enormous debt, scheduled to be paid off over three years, which Mir Jafar had already incurred both to the Company and to individuals in repayment for the Plassey coup. In November 1758 Clive and his colleagues warned the directors that 'a large addition of territory' would be needed to fund the army in the future.[104] By then they had already established the Company's claims to some of the most valuable districts in lower Bengal. The nawab had assigned the revenue from these districts over to the Company and the *zamindars* entered into obligations to it. The Company assumed the right to send in its own Indian collectors and later appointed Europeans to supervise them. With the appointment of its own collectors, the Company began to attract into its service some of the highly skilled professional revenue administrators who had served the nawabs. The chief collector of the 1758 assignments was the Brahmin Nandakumar, known from his close association with Clive at that time as 'the Black Colonel'. His career was to have a trajectory not unlike that of Yusaf Khan in the south. He too was eventually to turn against the British, although much less overtly, and he too was to be hanged by them. The Company kept its assignments until 1760, when a crisis in its finances forced it to look for a more radical solution. This was to compel the nawab to cede territory to them outright. When Mir Jafar demurred, he was replaced by a nawab who would make the cessions. What the Company took in 1760 were three districts, one of which, Burdwan, had the highest revenue return in Bengal, yielding some £650,00 a year.[105] In these newly acquired districts European

---

[101] Ibid. IV. 550. The source of these remarkable comments is not identified.

[102] For the early Bengal sepoys, see Arthur Broome, *A History of the Rise and Progress of the Bengal Army* (1850), pp. 93, 194, 356–7.

[103] To Directors, 27 Sept. 1764, C. S. Srinivasachari, ed., *Fort William–India House Correspondence*, IV, *1764–1766* (Delhi, 1962), pp. 258–9.

[104] To Directors, 10 Nov. 1758, Sinha, ed., *Fort William–India House Correspondence*, II. 327.

[105] 3rd Report, Secret Committee, 1773, *Reports from Committees*, IV. 60–1.

Company servants directly involved themselves in the administration of the revenue to a much greater extent than seems to have been the case in the south. In Burdwan, Europeans actually undertook revenue farms for their own profit.[106] In another district, Chittagong, the banian of the senior Company servant there acquired a huge landed estate.[107] A trend was being set for exploiting the revenues of Bengal both for official and for British and Indian private purposes.

The cessions of 1760 did not, however, set a limit on the Company's demands on the nawabs. Military costs continued to spiral upwards. In 1763–4 the Company in Bengal was involved in costly wars that were much more bitterly contested than the one-sided encounters of the 1750s. In 1763 the Company fought against an army created by the nawab Mir Kasim with 'artillery mounted in the English manner' and with sepoys 'armed, cloath'd and accouter'd like our own . . . and posted in a very advantageous manner'.[108] At the closely-fought battle of Buxar in 1764, the British artillery was outnumbered by the guns of the nawab of Awadh.[109] The financial cost of victory was very high for the Company. Military charges for the year 1764–5 escalated to £873,186, far exceeding what was being received from the newly-acquired districts.[110] The council felt that 'this encrease of expence' must be met by 'further assignment out of the revenues of the country'.[111] 'Further assignment' came in the following year when Clive negotiated the transfer of all the remaining revenues of Bengal to the Company in the grant of the *diwani* in 1765 by the Mughal emperor at Allahabad in August 1765.

With the grant of the *diwani*, the Company acquired direct responsibility for the administration of Bengal. By then it had also assumed the obligation through its army both to defend Bengal and to maintain internal order, formally the concerns of the nawab as *nazim*. By then too the Company and individual British people with their Indian coadjutors had also greatly extended their privileged stake in Bengal's economy. The Company claimed a monopoly over trading in saltpetre for itself in 1758. Its servants did the same for opium. The Dutch quickly began to complain that their access to weavers was being restricted. The nawabs objected strongly to a massive extension of private British trade into commodities like salt, previously under state

---

[106] McLane, *Land and Local Kingship*, p. 189.

[107] For the activities in Chittagong of Gokal Ghosal, banian of Harry Verelst, see A. M. Serajuddin, *The Revenue Administration of the East India Company in Chittagong, 1761–85* (Chittagong, 1971), ch. 6.

[108] T. Adams to Egremont, 5 Oct. 1763, OIOC, H/97, p. 105.

[109] C. E. A. W. Oldham, 'The Battle of Buxar', *Journal of the Bihar and Orissa Research Society*, XII (1926), 1–38.

[110] 3rd Report, Secret Committee, 1773, *Reports from Committees*, IV. 60.

[111] To Directors, 27 Sept. 1764, Srinivasachari, ed., *Fort William–India House Correspondence*, IV. 259.

control, and to the way in which British private traders used their privileged position to refuse customs payments and to eliminate competition from Indian merchants. These were the issues which drove Mir Kasim to war in 1763.[112]

The nawabs of Bengal had been swept aside by the British drive to maximize revenue resources for their new army and commercial gain for the Company and for individuals. The apparent abundance of Bengal's resources together with their accessibility meant that the assault would be particularly ruthless. The British assault on the nawabs of Bengal was, however, also driven by what amounted to a political programme different from that in the south: the Company must have absolute control over its own affairs; it would no longer permit the nawabs to claim jurisdiction over any of its operations. This turned out to be an open-ended programme whose ultimate conclusion was that the Company felt impelled to exclude the nawabs from virtually every aspect of the government of Bengal.

There had been isolated talk of military action against the nawabs to force further concessions from them well before Plassey. Robert Orme, for instance, complained that the nawab Alivardi Khan was becoming so rapacious in his exactions that it would be worth the Company's while to try to 'swinge the old dog'.[113] Orme claimed responsibility for the terms in which the Madras council appealed to admiral Watson to go up to the Hughli with his warships in 1756. Not only must 'exemplary reparation' be obtained, but the British must be re-established 'even on better terms than they have hitherto obtained'.[114] Clive saw his task as not being confined to 'the retaking of Calcutta only'. He would ensure that 'the Company's estate in these parts will be settled in a better and more lasting condition than ever'.[115] The lesson that he and his contemporaries seem to have drawn from the debacle of the loss of Calcutta was that the British position in Bengal had never been a secure one. Previous nawabs had been able to withhold what the British claimed to be due to them under the Mughal grants of 1717 and to threaten them from time to time. Siraj-ud-daula had actually carried out his threats.

Security for the future would come, in the first place, from possession of an overwhelming force, hence the building of the great new fort at Calcutta and the demand for the reinforcement of 2,000 European soldiers. Security also required the possession of rights that were not in any sense conditional on Indian authority. After he had been driven out of Calcutta, Siraj-ud-daula was forced to sign a treaty confirming the Company's right to trade without

---

[112] The growth of private trade is described in Marshall, *East Indian Fortunes*, ch. 5.
[113] Cited in S. C. Hill, ed., *Bengal in 1756–1757*, 3 vols. (1905), I, p. xxxiii.
[114] Ibid. 199–201.   [115] Ibid. 222–3.

paying customs and to fortify Calcutta.[116] Mir Jafar was compelled to cede a valuable slice of territory south of Calcutta outright to the Company. The Company, in the view of its leading Bengal servants, was now not only 'to look upon themselves as a trading company, but as a military company also, possessed of a considerable landed property'.[117] In 1759 Clive wrote speculatively to Pitt about a further great territorial 'dominion' or 'sovereignty' in Bengal.[118] In the following year the Company's 'landed property' was greatly augmented by the three districts ceded by Mir Kasim. Mir Kasim's war in 1763 convinced Clive that any kind of co-existence between the authority of the Company and the authority of the nawab was now impractical. 'We shall eternally find enemies in the very nabobs whom we support who either from ambition or from fear will be perpetually contriving schemes for our destruction'. It would probably be necessary to 'take the whole for the Company'. Only then would the government of Bengal acquire 'consistence and stability'.[119] That was accomplished at Allahabad in August 1765 with the grant of the *diwani*. The Company's servants felt that there had been no alternative to 'advance as we have done and grasp at the sole power'.[120]

The legal basis of what the Company had acquired in Bengal rested on conditional grants of trading privileges, revenue rights or the office of *diwan* from the nawabs of Bengal or from the Mughal emperors. All these implied duties to higher authorities in the exercise of the rights conceded. Refusing, however, to accept any subordination to Indian authority, the Company servants treated their grants as conveying absolute rights to the Company. 'The experience of years has convinced us that a division of power is impossible . . . All must belong either to the Company or the nabob.' The acquisition of the *diwani* settled the matter: all belonged to the Company. 'You are now become the sovereigns of a rich and potent kingdome', the directors were told.[121] The sovereign dominion which the Company's servants claimed to be exercising in Bengal seems to have been accepted as a *fait accompli* in Britain. What was in contention was whether sovereignty was vested in the East India Company or in the British state.[122]

---

[116] C. U. Aitchison, ed., *A Collection of Treaties, Engagements and Sanads Relating to India and Neighbouring Countries*, revised edn., 14 vols. (Calcutta, 1891–1930), II. 197.

[117] To Directors, 31 Dec. 1758, Sinha, ed., *Fort William–Indian House Correspondence*, II. 391.

[118] Forrest, *The Life of Clive*, II. 176.

[119] To J. Walsh, 4 Jan. 1765, OIOC, MS Eur. D. 546/III–VII, ff. 102–3.

[120] To Directors, 31 Jan. 1766, Srinivasachari, ed., *Fort William–India House Correspondence*, IV. 380.

[121] 30 Sept. 1765, Amba Prasad, ed., *Fort William–India House Correspondence*, XIV, *Secret and Select Committee 1752–1781* (Delhi, 1985), pp. 174, 177.

[122] Huw V. Bowen, 'A Question of Sovereignty? The Bengal Land Revenue Issue, 1765–67', *Journal of Imperial and Commonwealth History*, XVI (1988), 158–9.

Yet if Bengal had indeed become a British dominion, it was still a dominion built on Indian foundations and offering rich pickings for Indian participation, even if the nawabs had been relegated to insignificance. Clive did not believe that British people should be actively involved in the collection of the revenues under the grant of the *diwani*. The company was to work through a great Muslim nobleman, Muhammad Reza Khan, but others from 'the principal families in Bengal' must be involved with him.[123] The expertise of the skilled revenue administrators who had served the nawabs remained indispensable. The great bulk of the revenue would still be paid by a group of large *zamindars*. What they paid could still only be turned into cash through the services of Indian bankers and the Jagat Seths seemed set to become bankers to the East India Company.[124] Wherever Europeans were directly involved in the government of Bengal, their banians became involved too, much to their profit. In the absence of adequate supplies of European soldiers the Bengal army was overwhelmingly a sepoy army, even if the Indian officers were relegated to subordinate roles.

The directors of the Company had generally viewed with misgivings the developments that had transformed its role into a territorial power in India. They fully accepted, however, that there could be no going back. The Company could no longer exist without large armies and large armies required extensive territorial revenues. These had now been secured from Bengal and they must on no account be relinquished. Without the territories that had just been acquired, the secret committee of the directors wrote in a memorandum on the terms of the 1763 peace settlement, the Company 'must sink under the expences it has already incurred and must continue to incur in order to support its ancient possessions in their present state . . . These territories in short are the only advantages of successful war which we wish to preserve.' Without a guaranteed territorial revenue the 'ruin of the Company will ensue'.[125]

Awareness in a wider public of the rise of territorial empire in India is hard to assess. India received relatively limited coverage by comparison with North America in the British press during the war.[126] Dispatches describing actions in India only appeared in the *London Gazette* and thereafter in the rest of the British press when senior royal officers who corresponded directly with

---

[123] Malcolm, *Life of Clive*, II. 353.

[124] For the early working of the *diwani*, see Abdul Majed Khan, *The Transition in Bengal 1756–1775: A Study of Saiyid Muhammad Reza Khan* (Cambridge, 1969), ch. 6.

[125] 'Sentiments of the Secret Committee', 4 Sept. 1762, Public Record Office, PRO, 30/8/99, ff. 145–6.

[126] For the limited amount of material that appeared in the British press reporting the loss of Calcutta in 1756 and subsequent events, see Hill, *Bengal 1756–57*, III. 69–95, 101–16.

British ministers were involved.[127] The *Annual Register* for 1761 believed that the war in India had been 'marked by as many striking events, uncommon circumstances, and singular reverses of fortune', but that not enough was known 'to treat of them in the manner in the least suitable to their dignity and importance'.[128] That great victories had been won nevertheless became common knowledge. Clive's success at Plassey was commemorated by one of four huge pictures of national triumphs by Francis Hayman displayed in the Vauxhall Gardens.[129]

Those congratulatory addresses to the king on the peace of 1763 that mentioned India tended to exult in the prospects of commercial 'superiority' there by contrast with the 'enlargement of empire' in North America.[130] An occasional address, however, explicitly praised a peace that had 'greatly widened our dominions in the East'.[131] When the Society of Arts struck a medal to commemorate Clive's victory at Plassey, it featured a cornucopia symbolizing riches, a rudder 'for the augmentation of our navigation and commercial privilege' and 'the globe for our territorial acquisitions'.[132] Following the news of the granting of the *diwani*, the British public was to hear more and more about 'our territorial acquisitions' in India.

---

[127] Plassey and 'Wondivash' were duly reported by Watson and Pocock and Coote respectively (*London Gazette*, 11–14 Feb. 1758, 20–3 Sept. 1760).

[128] *Annual Register*, IV (1761), 57.

[129] Brian Allen, *Francis Hayman* (New Haven, 1987), pp. 68–9.

[130] e.g. address of Lord Provost and Council of Edinburgh, *London Gazette*, 17–21 May 1763.

[131] Address of Northumberland, ibid. 24–8 May 1763.

[132] Malcolm, *Life of Clive*, II. 283–4fn.

5
Ideas of Empire 1763–1776: The 'Old' Empire

'EMPIRE' was defined at the beginning of this book as the exercise of authority over territory and peoples. Authority over the British empire at any time in its history flowed from the allegiance that its peoples owed to the king, whose subjects they were. In 1763, at the end of a worldwide war, the extent of territory and number of people subject to the king had increased very greatly. This increase in scale together with a legacy of problems from the existing empire stimulated intense debate about the nature and future organization of the British empire.

The king of England has been described as the ruler of 'a composite monarchy with both contiguous and overseas components'.[1] He was king of Scotland and of Ireland. Scotland was united with England by what was known as the 'incorporating' union of 1707, although Scotland preserved certain autonomies, notably a separate legal system and a separate established church. Ireland was a kingdom in its own right with its own parliament, over which the British parliament claimed supremacy, and its own administration, subject to a contested degree of supervision by British ministers. The Channel Islands had been dominions of the dukes of Normandy which had passed to the English monarchy. They preserved separate institutions of their own. In the Mediterranean, Gibraltar and Minorca had been ceded to Britain by Spain.

Across the Atlantic, the crown had made grants, based on the right of assumed prior discovery or occupation, to individuals or to corporations to take possession of territories from Hudson Bay and Newfoundland down the eastern seaboard of North America into the Caribbean. Most of these grants had lapsed or been revoked by 1763, placing the territories under the direct authority of the crown, but four colonies enjoying grants of delegated authority survived on the North American mainland. Other colonies, beginning with Jamaica in 1655, had been added to the king's dominions by direct state conquest. Cessions by France and Spain after the Seven Years War

[1] H. G. Koenigsberger, 'Composite States, Representative Institutions and the American Revolution', *Historical Research*, LXII (1989), 143.

greatly extended the crown's possessions in North America and in the Caribbean. A new colony had also been added by recent conquest on the West African coast. Other British settlements there were administered by a Company of Merchants Trading to Africa. On the Indian coast the crown had long ago transferred Bombay to the East India Company, which had acquired other port enclaves by grants from Indian rulers. Military intervention had recently given the Company a preponderance on the south-east coast and in Bengal, where within two years of the ending of the Seven Years War preponderance was to be converted into *de facto* rule over the whole province. The Company also had settlements in Sumatra and in the Persian Gulf as well as trading access to the Chinese port of Canton.

Royal authority over this heterogeneous collection of possessions was exercised in a very uneven manner. The four 'private' colonies in North America and the territories administered by companies in the Canadian north, on the West African coast and in Asia were not under direct royal rule. In Ireland and in the old established North American and West Indian colonies local representative institutions competed for power with the royal viceroy or royal governors. The strength of the royal executives in America varied from colony to colony, but historians have come to characterise the exercise of British authority as government by negotiation with local interests rather than by fiat from Whitehall. There was much uncertainty about the nature of the new authority that the East India Company had acquired in India and no easy conclusions were in prospect to questions that were beginning to be raised about the right of the British state to these new acquisitions.

The extent of parliament's authority over the overseas dominions of the crown was another area of uncertainty. Parliament had been ordering their commerce for many years. In 1720 it had proclaimed its legislative sovereignty over Ireland, although in practice the exercise of this authority was circumscribed. It was not to make a similar declaration of sovereignty over the American colonies until 1766 and its active involvement in their affairs was also circumscribed, although becoming less so by mid-century. The trading companies depended for their charters on parliamentary enactments, but were not as yet generally subjected to close parliamentary supervision over the conduct of their affairs.

Contemporaries had been referring to this miscellaneous collection of possessions, or at least to the European and American parts of them, as 'the British empire' since late in the seventeenth century.[2] 'Empire' was, however,

---

[2] What follows is heavily indebted to David Armitage, *The Ideological Origins of the British Empire* (Cambridge, 2000). The pioneering work of Richard Koebner, *Empire* (Cambridge, 1961) is still of value.

a term with diverse and shifting meanings. By the middle of the eighteenth century what has been called the 'institutional heterogeneity' of the British possessions around the Atlantic was being overlaid by the vigorous propagation of an ideology intended to unite the British Isles and people of British origin in North America and the West Indies within a framework of empire.[3] This framework was commonly called an 'empire of the seas' to distinguish it from the 'universal monarchies', based on territorial conquest, established in the ancient world and aspired to more recently, so British people alleged, by Spain or by France. Britain's empire of the seas was endowed with certain qualities. These have been neatly summed up in the mantra that the empire was 'Protestant, commercial, maritime and free'.[4] In other words, it was an empire made up of Protestant communities of British origin, enjoying the specifically English rights to representative government and to the security of person and property guaranteed by the common law. It was built on transoceanic commerce carried in British ships and safeguarded by British naval power.

This ideology of empire has been described as essentially an oppositional one, that is, one devised by those advocating the interests of British communities overseas and given the support of the political opponents of the Walpole administration in Britain.[5] Whatever its origins may have been, the proposition that the British empire was Protestant, commercial, maritime, and free was rarely contradicted in mainstream eighteenth-century political discourse. It was a slogan that encapsulated for contemporaries the dynamic expansion of trade and the diffusion of British culture and ideals described in the first chapter.

The difficulties in giving concrete form to an empire that might embody such ideological aspirations were very apparent. At no time had the population of any version of a British empire been exclusively Protestant or solely British in origin. The majority of the Irish population was not of course Protestant. There were considerable communities of Protestants in British North America, such as the Huguenots, the Dutch, or the Germans, who were not of British origin. Neither Protestant nor British were those who lived under British rule in Gibraltar and Minorca, the bulk of the inhabitants of the Asian and African trading settlements or nearly all the African slaves who made up the vast majority of the West Indian population and who were spreading so rapidly in North America. The conquests of 1763 made the empire even more religiously and ethnically polyglot by bringing within it French in Quebec and the West Indies, creolized Africans in Senegal, American Indians in the lands between the mountains and the Mississippi, and

---

[3] Armitage, *Ideological Origins*, p. 171.   [4] Ibid. p. 173.   [5] Ibid. p. 8.

millions of Indians within the East India Company's new possessions. An empire that was still undoubtedly maritime and commercial was also becoming more extensively territorial. In India the rationale of empire was coming to be a tribute collected in taxation from the population as much as the profits of commerce. Before the Seven Years War only limited garrisons of British troops had been maintained overseas. Now more British troops were stationed overseas than at home. After 1763 the garrisons in the western world were considerably strengthened and the East India Company began to maintain a large standing army. In short, it was not only ill-disposed foreigners who were coming to see the British empire as beginning to resemble an aspiring universal monarchy.

The most immediately contentious problem in sustaining an older ideology of empire in new conditions was how to reconcile the exercise of authority over the empire with the aspiration that it be free. This was not a new problem. Free British people throughout the empire were forced to submit to commercial regulation and discrimination and they were subject to the exercise of extensive royal prerogative powers, even if in most colonies their effectiveness was considerably weakened. The Seven Years War had compounded the problem of how to reconcile freedom with the exercise of an imperial authority that had tried to direct a common war effort. Victory left these problems unresolved and added new ones. British ministers feared that France and Spain would seek an opportunity for revenge in the near future. All parts of the empire were in their view in danger and all must be ready to contribute to the common defence, more effectively, they hoped, than they had done during the late war. Britain finished the war with a greatly enhanced national debt and with high levels of taxation to service the debt and to pay for the increased peacetime army and navy; many in Britain looked to her dependencies for contributions to ease her burdens.

I

Enthusiasm for a more close-knit empire was being expressed throughout the British world. From early in the eighteenth century 'the notion of the British Empire' had for many colonial Americans become 'a symbol of the new possibilities to which they looked forward'.[6] Victory in war increased their expectations. In 1765 the elected governor of Rhode Island, perhaps the most loosely attached of all British possessions, called 'the empire of Great Britain'

---

[6] Koebner, *Empire*, p. 89. American expectations of empire are analysed in chs. 3 and 4 of that book.

an 'imperial state', which needed an authority to regulate and to order 'the proper interest and fit government of the whole commonwealth'.[7] A tract attributed to James Otis, the Boston radical, advocated a 'thorough beneficial union of these colonies to the realm, or mother country, so that all the parts of the empire may be compacted and consolidated'.[8] Benjamin Franklin had long been an advocate of imperial union. As late as 1773 he urged on the Massachusetts house of representatives the advantages of a 'strict union': Britain would get additional military resources and commercial profit; the colonies would receive 'protection' and 'a common umpire in our disputes'.[9]

Calls for closer imperial integration from Britain itself were largely articulated by the few politicians who specialized in colonial matters, by officials in departments like the board of trade and by self-confessed experts who attached themselves to politicians, rather than from the main body of political opinion. Much of what was advocated consisted of nostrums current since early in the eighteenth century.[10] There was a strong emphasis on the need for closer commercial regulation. The remarkable recent growth of the colonial populations and of the colonial economies seemed to make this a particularly urgent matter. Questions of the defence of the empire and of possible contributions from the colonies to the cost of their own defence or to relieve Britain's financial exigencies were also discussed. All such schemes supposed closer ties between Britain and its colonies.

Malachy Postlethwayt included a plea for 'the wisdom of the nation to determine upon such a union in government and constitution in every part of it's dominions as may tend to strengthen the whole British empire' in his treatise on *Britain's Commercial Interests Explained and Improved* of 1757.[11] Thomas Whately, then secretary to the treasury, urged in a pamphlet published in 1765 that to develop the colonies and 'to cement and perfect the necessary connection between them and the mother country, should . . . be the principal object of a British minister's care'.[12] Thomas Pownall, former

---

[7] Stephen Hopkins, 'The Rights of Colonies Examined' in Bernard Bailyn, ed., *Pamphlets of the American Revolution. 1750–1776*, I (Cambridge, Mass, 1965), pp. 512, 519.

[8] *Considerations on Behalf of the Colonies*, 2nd edn. (1766), p. 40, cited in Peter N. Miller, *Defining the Common Good: Empire, Religion and Philosophy in Eighteenth-Century Britain* (Cambridge, 1994), p. 231 fn.

[9] 7 July 1773, Leonard W. Labaree et al., eds., *The Papers of Benjamin Franklin* (New Haven, 1959–), XX. 282–3.

[10] R. T. Cornish, 'A Vision of Empire: The Development of British Opinion Regarding the American Colonial Empire, 1730–70', London University Ph.D. thesis, 1987.

[11] 2 vols., I. 469.

[12] *The Regulations Lately Made Concerning the Colonies, and the Taxes Imposed upon them, Considered* (1765), p. 4. On Whately, see I. R. Christie, 'A Vision of Empire: Thomas Whately and *The Regulations Lately Made Concerning the Colonies*', *English Historical Review*, CXIII (1998), 300–20.

governor of Massachusetts, agreed that oceanic commerce must now be the dominant concern of British governments and that therefore 'our possessions in the Atlantic and in America' should be regarded as 'united into a one empire, in a one center, where the seat of government is'.[13] George Grenville, especially after he left office in 1765, seems to have been the major politician with the strongest commitment to the unity of Britain and its overseas territories. He was strongly opposed to any 'different mode of obedience between the subjects within this kingdom and those without it'.[14] He thought that 'all the subjects of the kingdom [ought to] contribute to the public burthens for their own defence, according to their abilities and situation'.[15]

For some in Britain hopes for closer imperial integration went beyond the American and West Indian colonies to include Ireland and even India. By the 1760s Ireland was increasingly being seen in Britain as 'our principal colony' rather than as a sister kingdom.[16] An Irish pamphleteer noted and resented 'illiberal expressions' in the British parliament, such as that 'Ireland was no more than a colony; that it might be taxed without its consent; that it was a dependent country'.[17] Ireland already made a major contribution to the common defence. As an Irish MP put it, 'Ireland is not only a nursery but a college of soldiers for England; from whence they relieve their garrisons by entire regiments, and replenish their army by perpetual drafting'.[18] An English act of parliament of 1699 stipulated that 12,000 British troops should be maintained in Ireland, paid for by the Irish revenues and available to serve overseas. In war the number could be increased; it was 24,000 in 1761.[19] This was a model that some thought might be appropriately adopted elsewhere in the empire.[20] In theory the troops on the Irish establishment were recruited in England or Scotland; in practice the regiments recruited extensively in Ireland so that Irish-born soldiers made up 27.5 per cent of the British

---

[13] *The Administration of the Colonies*, 2nd edn. (1765), pp. 9–10.

[14] To W. Knox, 11 Sept. 1768, *Historical Manuscripts Commission: Various MSS*, VI, Knox MSS (1909), p. 99.

[15] To Pownall, 17 July 1768, W. J. Smith, ed., *The Grenville Papers*, 4 vols. (1853), IV. 318.

[16] C. Yorke, 15 Feb. 1765, R. C Simmons and P. D. G. Thomas, eds., *Proceedings and Debates of the British Parliament respecting North America*, 6 vols. (Millwood, NY, 1982–6), II. 27.

[17] *A Letter to the Right Honourable J[ohn] P[onsonby], S[peake]r of the H[ous]e of C[ommon]s in Ireland* (1767), p. 23.

[18] [Hercules Langrishe], *Considerations on the Dependencies of Great Britain with Observations on a Pamphlet Intitled The Present State of the Nation* (1769), p. 44.

[19] A. J. Guy, 'The Irish Military Establishment 1660–1776' in Thomas Bartlett and Keith Jeffery, eds., *A Military History of Ireland* (Cambridge, 1996), p. 216; Eoin Magennis, *The Irish Political System 1740–1765* (Dublin, 2000), pp. 51–4.

[20] Yorke, 15 Feb. 1766, Simmons and Thomas, eds., *Proceedings and Debates*, II. 26, 27.

force in North America in 1757.[21] In 1766 the British government was reported to be considering ways of increasing Ireland's contribution to the common cause.[22] An 'augmentation' of the peacetime army establishment to over 15,000 was pushed through the Irish parliament in 1769, one of the fruits of the deeper British involvement in the government of Ireland brought about by the appointment of a permanently resident lord lieutenant. In 1768 William Knox, under secretary with colonial responsibilities and a prolific publisher, set out proposals for levying cash contributions from the American colonies, Ireland, and the East India Company. He took the unusual line of urging that in return for her contributions Ireland should be recognized as a partner in empire, united with Britain in 'interest and connection with the colonies'. In his view the new possessions of the East India Company had become 'British colonies', whose population were bound like those in other parts of the empire 'to contribute to the burdens of the state'.[23] From 1766 persistent efforts were indeed being made to tap the wealth of India for British state purposes.[24]

If the principle was widely accepted that all parts of the empire should be brought more closely together, how this might be done became an intensely contentious matter. Much British theorizing about the possible mechanics of imperial reorganization emerged after 1763, most of it focusing on the 'old', pre-1763, colonies in the West Indies and North America.

By 1763 it had become received wisdom that schemes for closer union of the colonies across the Atlantic, such as that discussed at Albany in 1754, were now off the British agenda. A strengthening of links between the colonies, as opposed to links between individual colonies and Britain, would be danger-ous. Large colonial blocks would sink their rivalries, become economically self-sufficient and aspire to independence. Britain must therefore preserve the 'happy division' among them, in Whately's words.[25] Where coordination between the colonies was needed it should be entrusted to officials appointed by and directly accountable to the crown: a commander-in-chief in America, Indian superintendents and customs boards.

Reform of the constitution of individual colonies was, however, very much on British agendas. Francis Bernard, governor of Massachusetts, who bom-barded ministers with his views, told his correspondents that all the systems

---

[21] Stephen Brumwell, *Redcoats: The British Soldier and War in the Americas 1755–1763* (Cambridge, 2002), p. 318.

[22] M. J. Powell, *Britain and Ireland in the Eighteenth-Century Crisis of Empire* (2003), p. 90.

[23] *The Present State of the Nation; Particularly with Respect to its Trade, Finances &c.* (1768), pp. 78, 85. Knox later declared that he had hoped to give the Irish 'the same views as Great Britain in continuing the colonies dependent' (*Extra Official State Papers*, 2 vols. (1789), II. 30).

[24] See the following chapter.   [25] *The Regulations Lately Made*, p. 18.

of government in North America were deficient since none of them was based 'upon a true English constitutional bottom'.[26] Bernard was one of many who advocated, as a start, revision of the charters of the proprietary colonies and above all of what he called 'the two republicks', Rhode Island and Connecticut. What he had in mind for all the colonies was the strengthening of the separation between the executive and the legislature in order to create an independent executive, equivalent to the British privy council. Councils in the colonies should become more like the house of lords, their members being tied to the crown by 'honour and posts of profit'. This would provide an 'equilibrium', allowing a due influence for the royal governor instead of domination of the executive by the assemblies, or the 'democratical' element, that was so characteristic of colonial governments.[27]

These and many similar suggestions remained paper projects. Even charter revision was deemed a hazardous business and was only to be attempted in 1774 in the case of Massachusetts. New constitutions for the colonies conquered in the war did, however, create opportunities to try to apply principles similar to those enunciated by Bernard. Thinking in official British circles was that colonial societies were entitled to elect representative bodies, wherever this was practicable. In the view of the board of trade, this was 'essential to the liberties of the subject'. The elected element should not, however, be allowed to dominate colonial governments. The board used as its model for new governments the constitutions of the two most recent royal colonies, Georgia and Nova Scotia, where conscious attempts had been made to reproduce British conditions of a balanced constitution with a strong executive. Their examples would be found 'in every respect most advantageous to the state in general and the most eligible to those who live under it'. The board of trade also recommended that, wherever possible 'the laws of England' should operate in the colonies, 'under which laws we humbly apprehend the subject will live more secure and happy and the state be much better governed than under the imperfect regulations of an American assembly'.[28]

Few in the colonies were likely to quarrel with such views in principle. Most colonies, except for those with charters, which were inclined to believe that they already possessed all its benefits to the full, wished for the security for their rights which they believed that full adoption of the British constitution

---

[26] To Barrington, 15 Dec. 1761, E. Channing and A. C. Coolidge, eds., *The Barrington–Bernard Correspondence and Illustrative Matter, 1760–1770*, (Cambridge, Mass., 1912), p. 44. Bernard's views are analysed in Koebner, *Empire*, pp. 130–49.

[27] To Halifax, 9 Nov. 1764, PRO, CO 5/755, ff. 135–9.

[28] Report on the constitution of Grenada, WLCL, Shelburne MSS 49:20; see also 'Hints Relative to the Division and Government of the Conquered and Newly Acquired Countries in America', PRO, CO 323/16, ff. 97–8; John Pownall's 'General Propositions', WLCL, Shelburne MSS, 48:46.

would confer on them. Richard Henry Lee, for instance, contrasted the 'happily poised English constitution' with the formidable prerogative powers of the crown in Virginia over the appointment of councillors, the tenure of judges, and the sittings of the assembly.[29] It was soon to become apparent, however, that interpretations of the British constitution to which colonial opinion aspired were not necessarily the same as those which British officials wished to prescribe for them.

Concern for the good of colonial subjects was no doubt genuine, but the advantages of the state, as the board of trade put it, were clearly the predominant motive behind schemes to redress the constitutional balance and to reverse the trend to 'democracy' in the colonies. An executive supported by a council independent of the assembly would be able to put into effect instructions from Britain. These instructions would continue to emanate largely from the crown through what was sometimes envisaged as a reformed bureaucracy at home.[30] There was, however, almost complete unanimity that major issues affecting the empire should now be settled by parliament and that it was the duty of colonial governments to carry out the wishes of parliament.

The doctrine that parliament was the sovereign body for the whole British empire had become the overwhelming orthodoxy in British thought.[31] There might be reservations about the wisdom of exercising parliament's sovereign power in all cases, but the principle was rarely contested. This was not a new doctrine in the 1760s, although there had been no pressing need to state it unequivocally in the past.[32] The evident failure of the executive agencies of government to exercise effective control over the colonies, both immediately before and during the war, provided a new urgency for turning to parliament now. Would-be reformers also believed that issues always deemed to be beyond the scope of royal authority on its own, such as taxation or charter revision, could no longer be evaded.

To involve parliament more closely in colonial affairs was entirely consistent with its increasingly intrusive role in domestic matters.[33] The 1760s have been called 'a watershed in the recognition of parliamentary supremacy' in Britain.[34] It seemed axiomatic to British opinion that colonial concerns which

---

[29] To A. Lee, 20 Dec. 1766, Lee Family Papers, University of Virginia, microfilm 1714.

[30] e.g. Pownall, *Administration*, pp. 12–24.

[31] H. T. Dickinson, 'Britain's Imperial Sovereignty: The Ideological Case against the American Colonies' in Dickinson, ed., *Britain and the American Revolution* (1998), pp. 64–96.

[32] Precedents of 'Matters Relative to His Majesty's Plantations in which the House of Commons have Interposed' are listed in BL, Add MS 35909.

[33] See above, p. 78

[34] Paul Langford, *Public Life and the Propertied Englishman* (Oxford, 1991), p. 149.

were now of such national importance should take up more of parliament's time and be subject to its regulation.

Were parliament's authority to be openly questioned the consequences would be very serious. Grenville laid down what was at stake in 1764. Speaking of proposals for taxing the American colonies, he stated that 'Britain has an inherent right to lay inland duties there. The very sovereignty of this kingdom depends on it.'[35] In the years ahead few in Britain were to dissent from that proposition. British political opinion had a highly developed doctrine of parliamentary sovereignty, most famously enunciated by William Blackstone in his *Commentaries*. Parliament, he wrote, was 'the place where that absolute despotic power, which must in all governments reside some-where, is entrusted by the constitution of these kingdoms'.[36] What applied to the kingdoms applied to the whole empire. Indeed an empire without a sovereign power in it was deemed not to be an empire at all. For lord Hillsborough, the first of the new American secretaries, 'the supremacy and legislative authority of parliament' was 'a principle essential to the existence of the empire'.[37] Charles Yorke, son of the great Whig lord chancellor, lord Hardwicke, described 'the universality of the legislative power' as 'the vital of your whole empire'.[38] When Edmund Burke first came into parliament in December 1765, he found it 'in possession of an unlimited legislative power over the colonies. I could not open the Statute-Book without seeing the actual exercise of it, more or less in all cases whatsoever'.[39] He believed that sovereignty must include the right to tax, even if, as he personally hoped, it would never be used. 'If Great Britain were stripped of this right, every principle of unity and subordination in the empire was gone for ever.'[40]

The Irish parliament or the legislatures of the North American and West Indian colonies could not therefore be permitted to claim powers that were independent of the British parliament. Were they to do so, this would be to create an *imperium in imperio*, an empire within an empire, dismissed even by James Otis as 'the greatest of all political solecisms'.[41] They would cease to be part of a British empire and become at best Britain's allies. A divided sovereignty was a recipe for weakness. It was the characteristic of the failed

---

[35] 9 March 1764, Simmons and Thomas, eds., *Proceedings and Debates*, I. 492.

[36] *Commentaries on the Laws of England* (1765–9), Bk. I, ch. 2.

[37] W. Johnson to W. Pitkin, 3 Jan. 1769, 'The Trumbull Papers, I', *Massachusetts Historical Society Collections*, 5th ser., IX (1885), 307.

[38] 3 Feb. 1766, Simmons and Thomas, eds., *Proceedings and Debates*, II. 146.

[39] 'Letter to the Sheriffs of Bristol', W. M. Elofson and J. A. Woods, eds., *The Writings and Speeches of Edmund Burke*, III, *Party, Parliament and the American War 1774–1780* (Oxford, 1996), p. 314.

[40] 'Observations on a Late State of the Nation', Paul Langford, ed., *The Writings and Speeches of Edmund Burke*, II, *Party, Parliament, and the American Crisis 1766–1774* (Oxford, 1981), p. 196.

[41] 'Vindication of the British Colonies' in Bailyn, ed., *Pamphlets*, I. 563.

or failing states of eighteenth-century Europe, Poland, or the Dutch Republic. 'Sub-division of power', Charles Yorke reportedly said, had 'brought Holland to destruction', but Britain was 'governed by one plan of uniform power'.[42]

There was no alternative to parliamentary sovereignty. To locate sovereignty over the empire in the crown alone was to seek to reverse all that had been achieved at least since the Revolution of 1689. Parliament willingly helped to enforce the royal prerogatives over the colonies, but to accept claims made on behalf of the colonies that while they owed allegiance to the crown they were not obliged to obey parliament in all things would be, in Grenville's words, 'the highest species of treason against the constitution and sovereign authority of this kingdom'.[43] This to him was 'Tory doctrine'[44] and its outcome would be that the colonies 'are to be considered as independent communities in alliance with us and only governed by the same prince as Hanover is'.[45] This entirely unacceptable analogy from the British point of view was indeed one that North Americans would eventually be willing to apply to their own constitutional position.[46]

It became increasingly clear, however, that, while professing loyalty to the crown, those who spoke for the North American colonies in the 1760s were insisting on the ultimate sovereignty of the people as a whole over the legislature and on the existence of certain fundamentals and inalienable rights of the subject that parliament could not transgress. These were impeccable Whig doctrines with which few in British public life were willing to take direct issue. Their application to practical politics was another matter. The divergence between British and American views was encapsulated in an exchange between the Virginian radical, Arthur Lee, and lord Hillsborough in 1768. Asked for his opinion of John Dickinson's *Letters from a Farmer in Pennsylvania*, which Hillsborough privately regarded as 'extremely wild',[47] his lordship suavely remarked 'that he was greatly pleased and informed by them, but he wished Mr Dickinson had accommodated his reasoning to the necessity of a supreme power.' 'I observed that Mr Locke had executed that with great perspicuity', Lee replied.[48] Had Hillsborough thought that sally worth an answer, he would no doubt have said that Lockean ideas of power

---

[42] 3 Feb. 1766, Simmons and Thomas, eds., *Proceedings and Debates*, II. 137. Yorke probably derived his derogatory view of the Dutch, widely shared in Britain, from his brother Joseph, veteran ambassador at The Hague and stern critic of the Republic.

[43] To W. Knox, 15 July 1768, *HMC, Various*, VI. 97.

[44] To Whately, 15 Nov. 1769, HL, ST 7, vol. 2.

[45] To S. Hood, 30 Oct. 1768, ibid.

[46] e.g. Franklin's marginalia on Allan Ramsay's *Thoughts on the Origin and Nature of Government* [1769], Labaree et al. eds., *Papers of Benjamin Franklin*, XVI. 317.

[47] Franklin to W. Franklin, 13 March 1768, ibid. XV. 75.

[48] To R. Lee, 27 Dec. 1768, Lee family papers, University of Virginia microfilm 1714.

originating from the people were theoretically admirable, but were the people to invoke their sovereignty against the legitimate acts of a properly constituted legislature, government would be totally subverted. The right of resistance of course existed, but by the mid-eighteenth century its use was deemed 'virtually unthinkable'.[49] As Grenville put it, government is 'a trust delegated by the society to the person or persons so appointed'. In the British case this was to the king and parliament. They embodied the consent of 'the whole community . . . so long as the form of government subsists'.[50]

Propositions about inalienable rights suffered from the same defect. Their theoretical existence was not in doubt. Natural law and natural rights featured prominently in Blackstone's *Commentaries*. Grenville, who has properly been described as 'a thoroughly conventional Whig',[51] thought that Locke had written 'an excellent work . . . to defend the natural rights of man'.[52] But natural rights could not be asserted against the legitimate acts of the legislature without dire consequences. Charles Yorke admired the Americans' 'genuine language of liberty. He approved it in many instances; he would accept it. But when it is said the legislative power of this country is against natural rights and too great to be trusted with it, it becomes indeed of a serious and dangerous nature', or, according to another report, he found that this was 'a language destructive of all government'.[53] Lord Lyttelton explained to the house of lords that governments arose from contracts by the people, by which they handed over 'power over their persons, liberties and estates, for the safety of the whole'. If this power was challenged 'there is an end of all government'.[54]

An increasingly authoritarian interpretation of Whig principles, stressing the sovereignty of parliament, did not, however, mean that the main body of the British political elite was beginning to espouse Tory principles, whatever Americans may have believed. It was certainly the case that men like Bute or Mansfield, who have been seen as occupying the political right in the hiatus between the Toryism of the first two Georges and the Tories of the early nineteenth century, were likely to take a very hard line against colonial claims.[55] So too would country gentlemen who maintained a Tory tradition into the reign of George III.[56] Nevertheless, colonial policy after the war was

---

[49] Langford, *Propertied Englishman*, p. 154.   [50] To Knox, 27 June 1768, HL, ST 7, vol. 2.
[51] Paul Langford, 'Old Whigs, Old Tories and the American Revolution', *Journal of Imperial and Commonwealth History*, VIII (1980), 109.
[52] To Knox 15 July 1768, HL, ST 7, vol. 2.
[53] 3 Feb. 1766, Simmons and Thomas, eds., *Proceedings and Debates*, II. 139, 147.
[54] 3 Feb 1766, ibid. II. 126.
[55] See the analysis in James J. Sack, *From Jacobite to Conservative: Reaction and Orthodoxy in Britain, c.1760–1832* (Cambridge, 1993), especially pp. 74–80.
[56] Langford, 'Old Whigs, Old Tories', 121–8.

shaped by men who were still self-confessedly Whigs, albeit in the 'court Whig' tradition,[57] and increasingly of a younger vintage and with rather weaker ideological convictions than the court Whigs of the generation of Walpole, Henry Pelham, Newcastle, and Hardwicke.

Attitudes to religion were seen as the main test for any weakening of Whig convictions. Some Americans were especially concerned about what seemed to them to be the waning of the 'old Whiggish spirit' of religious freedom, which had frustrated attempts in the past to bind the 'spiritual shackles' of privileges for the Church of England onto the colonies.[58] It was widely feared that militant Anglicanism was gaining the ascendancy in British governing circles to the advantage of resurgent Anglicanism in the colonies. By 1775, when a great public debate about war or peace in America was under way, religion had certainly become a prominent issue. British Dissenters were commonly lumped together with their colonial brethren in the government press and in many Anglican sermons as enemies to the established order in church and state. Such accusations had long been the polemical stock in trade of American Anglicans. Dissenters were, they warned, determined to constrict the colonial Church, 'joyning and making interest with even the enemies of Christianity itself to undermine her, and if possible to raze her even to the foundations'.[59] 'Itinerant Presbyterian, Baptist, and Independent preachers' not only spread hatred of episcopacy but disseminated 'fatal republican notions and principles', which assumed that parliament had no more authority in the colonies than 'the Turk or Pope'.[60] Identification of colonial Americans with militant Dissent and with the 'Oliverian' and 'Levelling' excesses of the seventeenth century seems to have been commonplace in Britain long before the Revolution. Franklin felt it necessary to try to dispel such beliefs in the press in 1759. American Dissenters 'are become less rigid and scrupulous'. They showed 'goodwill' to other Christians and there was nothing like a ' "levelling spirit" ' in the colonies.[61]

If many British people came after 1775 to see the American Revolution as a conflict in which assaults on the Church at home and abroad were an integral part of a challenge to ordered government throughout the empire, there is little to suggest that those who were shaping colonial policy before the Revolution shared that view. Support for the Church in the colonies certainly seems to have been a nostrum of members of the board of trade who had been

[57] Reed Browning, *Political and Constitutional Ideas of the Court Whigs* (Baton Rouge, La., 1982).

[58] W. Allen to T. Penn, 12 Nov. 1766, HSP, Thomas Penn Papers, 176, pp. 70–2.

[59] W. Johnson to T. Secker 20 March 1759, Lambeth Palace MS 1123, no. 133.

[60] Rev. Charles Woodmason, cited J. C. D. Clark, *The Language of Liberty 1660–1832: Political Discourse and Social Dynamics in the Anglo-American World* (Cambridge, 1994), p. 215.

[61] To *London Chronicle*, 9 May 1759, Labaree et al., eds., *Papers of Benjamin Franklin*, VIII. 341.

pressing for reform since the 1740s. They insisted on an Anglican establishment in the new colonies. One was enacted in Nova Scotia in 1758 and orders
to do the same were issued to the governors of the Floridas, Grenada, and
Quebec after 1763.[62] Lord Halifax, the leading board of trade reformer, was
said to be 'very earnest for bishops in America', by far the most contentious
issue of support for the church.[63] This was, however, a measure which was
repeatedly blocked by ministers, not only in the 1750s by those like the duke
of Newcastle and Henry Pelham who might be supposed to have been
upholders of old Whig traditions of alliance with Dissent, but also by their
successors in the 1760s. If the doctrine of parliamentary sovereignty was, as
has been suggested, a 'quintessentially Anglican' one,[64] ministers evidently
felt that their commitment to that doctrine did not oblige them to support
the Church in America in ways that might produce damaging political
consequences. Archbishop Secker doubted whether even Halifax had 'zeal
enough to undertake what will certainly meet with opposition'.[65] Ministers
evidently saw no need to disrupt the Protestant pluralism so powerfully
invoked in fighting the Seven Years War.[66] The archbishop of Canterbury
made a last appeal in 1767, but was said to have been told that the government would give no support to the appointment of a bishop because they
wanted 'to sustain the connection between the colonies . . . and not break off
any one'. The archbishop lamented that 'political considerations should take
the place of religious ones' but saw no redress.[67]

The apparent willingness of British ministers to consider religion in the
colonies from a 'political' point of view seems to be consistent with their
approach to constitutional principles. They were not prepared to disavow
propositions either that government derived its authority from the consent of
the governed or about the duty of the state to uphold the Church, but there
are clear indications that their political strategies, both at home and for the
colonies were being influenced by other considerations, primarily by those of
raison d'état or of a concept of public utility, based, as Peter Miller has
helpfully put it, on 'the common good'. The highest common good for
them was the survival of Britain as a great power in a dangerous world, an

---

[62] Peter M. Doll, *Revolution, Religion, and National Identity: Imperial Anglicanism in British
North America, 1745–1795* (Cranbury, NJ, 2000), pp. 47–54; L. W. Labaree, ed., *Royal Instructions to
British Colonial Governors 1670–1760*, 2 vols. (New York, 1935), II. 497.

[63] Doll, *Revolution*, p. 185.

[64] Clark, *Language of Liberty*, p. 5.

[65] To J. Duché, 16 Sept. 1763, W. S. Perry, ed., *Historical Collections Relating to the American
Colonial Church*, II, *Pennsylvania* (Hartford, Conn., 1871), p. 390.

[66] See above, p. 41.

[67] N. Rogers to T. Hutchinson, 2 July 1768, MHS, Hutchinson Transcripts, XXV. 267; see the
treatment of the colonial episcopacy question in Doll, *Revolution*, ch. 5.

objective which required the exercise of effective authority through a sovereign parliament over the empire and its resources.[68] If that also required leaving colonial Dissenters undisturbed or, as we shall see, tolerating the religious life of Catholics, not to mention Hindus and Muslims, that was the necessary price of empire.

Arguments based on concepts of a sovereignty that could enforce the common good appeared most overtly in debates on the sanctity of charters. On both sides of the Atlantic charters were revered as guarantees of historic rights. This was the soundest of Whig doctrines. Yet when lord North's government brought in a bill in 1774 to revise the charter of Massachusetts without a judicial process, a government supporter laid it down that 'the supreme legislature' must have power to act when it found chartered rights 'inconvenient for public utility'.[69] According to North, a chartered privilege could not be allowed to 'subsist longer than was found beneficial to the public'.[70] Amendment of the charter was 'necessary for the preservation of the state', said Jeremiah Dyson, a constitutional authority of high standing. 'Private rights', he asked, 'Can that be a subject of consideration for the legislature, who are now considering at large, for the British empire at large?'[71]

II

Insistence on the sovereignty of parliament raised questions about the nature of representation in that parliament and thus ultimately about the relations between the king's subjects in the colonies and those that lived in Britain. The view of the majority of politically articulate North Americans, white West Indians, and Irish Protestants was that they were represented in their own legislatures, not in the British parliament, and that they enjoyed in full equality all the rights of their fellow British subjects. British opinion generally held that all the peoples of the empire were in some sense represented in the British parliament, to which they were certainly subject, and that while British people living in the colonies were indeed entitled to the rights of British people at home, certain limitations on the enjoyment of those rights might be necessary.

On the eve of the Revolution, James Abercromby, agent for Virginia, made a careful examination of the status of the colonies that reflected the views

---

[68] *Common Good*, especially chs. 3, 4.
[69] W. Ellis, 22 April 1774, Simmons and Thomas, eds., *Proceedings and Debates*, IV. 263.
[70] 22 April 1774, ibid. IV. 260.   [71] 29 April 1774, ibid. IV. 316.

generally held by British officials. In no way, he thought, were British colonies to be regarded as separate 'states'. They were subject to the 'national sovereignty' of Britain in all things, above all in their economic subordination. But they were not mere local 'corporations' either, as was sometimes argued in Britain. They were 'provincial governments'. Extensive judicial and legislative powers were of necessity devolved on them. In addition, their inhabitants enjoyed the rights of 'citizens, and subjects of England'. Even so, Englishmen in the colonies had to forego those rights that could only be exercised in England. Prominent among these was the suffrage. Colonists could only vote for British MPs if they moved to Britain and acquired voting rights there or if special colonial constituencies were to be created, a solution that never attracted much support in Britain or in the colonies, although it was advocated by the imperial reformers, Whately, Pownall, and Knox. George Grenville thought colonial representation in the commons was entitled to 'the most serious and favourable consideration'.[72] Inability to vote did not, however, mean in Abercromby's view that the colonists were not represented in the British parliament. They enjoyed 'virtual representation' there.[73]

This was a proposition that George Grenville had enunciated in February 1765.[74] Whately explained the doctrine of virtual representation in his pamphlet. MPs represented not merely their immediate constituencies but the whole community.[75] Great accumulations of manufacturing and commercial wealth in new towns did not, for instance, enjoy their own parliamentary seats. There were, however, many in the commons to speak for their interests. So there were for the colonies: Americans who now lived in Britain, the British merchant interests who traded with them, and army and navy officers who had served overseas. If North Americans felt themselves to be at a disadvantage in the house of commons, it was sometime suggested that this was their own fault. Unlike the West Indians, they had failed to organize effective parliamentary lobbies. The American merchant, Christopher Kilby, 'did not know why they should not do as others do, and by dint of labour, address and money put some of their patriots and orators into parliament'.[76] However persuasive British opinion might find the case for the virtual representation of the colonies, the concept was firmly rejected in North America. As will be shown later in this chapter, their political culture was based on direct representation. They could not be represented by others. In

---

[72] To Pownall, 17 July 1768, Smith, ed., *Grenville Papers*, IV. 317.
[73] 'De Jure et Gubernatione Coloniarum', *c*.1774, in J. P. Greene, C. F. Mullett and E. C. Papenfuse, eds., *Magna Charta for America* (Philadelphia, 1986), pp. 174, 204, 211–12, 229–31.
[74] 6 Feb. 1765, Simmons and Thomas, eds., *Proceedings and Debates*, II. 9.
[75] *Regulations Lately Made*, p. 109. See the discussion in Miller, *Common Good*, pp. 248–52.
[76] To R. Morton, 27 Dec. 1765, BL, Add MS 35637, f. 318.

any case, they believed that the identity of interests between Britain and America was not sufficiently close to ensure that British MPs would not prefer the immediate interests of their own constituents or of metropolitan Britain to the detriment of those of the colonies.

British opinion that engaged seriously with the problems of the empire seemed to be offering white Protestants in America and the West Indies what purported to be inclusion in a wider British nation.[77] Whately believed that the colonies and Britain were a single 'nation'.[78] Lord Hillsborough told the agent for Connecticut that 'he was very sure his Majesty had equal affection for his American and his other subjects . . . and that I might be perfectly assured that he, and all his Majesty's ministers . . . considered us all as Britons having one common interest with them'.[79] For William Knox the people of the colonies were part of 'the community of Great Britain'.[80] Full equality between the peoples of the colonies and those of Britain would, however, raise insuperable problems. Maurice Morgann, adviser to lord Shelburne, pointed them out with unusual frankness in 1765. Full incorporation with Britain would mean that the colonies became 'so many counties' and were bound to pay all British taxes, but, on the other hand, it also implied that they could not be treated as separate entities for commercial purposes under the Navigation Acts. This would be acceptable to neither side. Ideas of a single transatlantic nation were therefore 'absurd and chimerical'. The colonies had to be classed as separate but subordinate 'dependencies'.[81] Reform proposals, for all their expression of generous sentiments about the benefits of a common Britishness, were ultimately intended to maintain colonial subordination.

To the British reformers, the empire after the Seven Years War would still, like the earlier ideal of the 'empire of the seas', be based on freedom, the freedom that was embodied in the British constitution. Their interpretation of the British constitution was, however, a somewhat restricted one, for all their lip service to traditional Whig doctrines. It reflected their concern not only for the exercise of effective control from London but for the maintenance of order at home as well as in the empire.

George III, endorsing in this respect as so often the conventional wisdom of many of his subjects, believed that 'all orders' of his people showed 'great licentiousness' and an unwillingness to pay 'due obedience to law', which was

---

[77] See Eliga H. Gould, *The Persistence of Empire: British Political Culture in the Age of the American Revolution* (Chapel Hill, NC, 2000), pp. 199–202.

[78] *The Regulations Lately Made*, p. 40.

[79] Johnson to W. Pitkin, 13 Feb. 1768, 'Trumbull Papers, I', *Mass. Hist Soc. Colls.*, ser. 5, IX. 261.

[80] *The Controversy between Great Britain and her Colonies Reviewed* (1769), p. 50.

[81] 'On the Right and Expediency of Taxing America', WLCL, Shelburne MSS, 85.

making them 'despised by all civilised nations'.[82] Disorder in America was part of a wider problem. Alarmist interpretations were immediately put on reports of riots in 1765 against the Stamp Act in Boston, Newport, Rhode Island, and New York. Grenville detected 'enthusiastic levelling principles' and he and lord Mansfield drew analogies with the Jacobite risings.[83] Grenville feared that a government that would not coerce the populace of Boston would not be bold enough to stand up to riots in London,[84] of which the disorder by the silk weavers in 1765 had been a frightening example. If the security of the north of Scotland now gave little concern, this was certainly not the case with Ireland, afflicted by 'whiteboy', 'oakboy', and 'steelboy' movements. Robert Nugent, a supporter of Grenville, spoke of an 'earth quake in North America', whose 'vibrations have been felt in Ireland'.[85] Lord Hardwicke was concerned in 1763 about the 'hearts of oak' disturbances in Ireland as well as the Devonshire cider riots.[86] The duke of Newcastle agreed with him that 'Ireland is not in more confusion, than, to a degree, England is at present.'[87]

Disorder anywhere in the empire must be met by willingness to use force. Inhibitions about the use of a standing army to maintain domestic order were declining.[88] From Boston in 1775 general John Burgoyne, reflected that 'the respect and control and subordination of government' depended on the belief that 'trained troops' would always prove invincible against an 'undisciplined rabble'.[89] Subversive doctrines must not be allowed to spread from one part of the empire to another. They must be firmly resisted wherever they appeared. North American arguments about taxation depending on representation would have repercussions in Britain. Subjects must be reminded that 'true liberty', in the words of a house of commons resolution of 8 December 1763, required a 'due veneration for the legislative authority of the kingdom and a perfect obedience to the law'.[90] This legislative authority did not in practice depend on the subject's consent beyond the original contract which set it up.

---

[82] To H. Conway, 20 Sept. 1766, J. Fortescue, ed., *Correspondence of King George III 1760–1783*, 6 vols. (1927–8), I. 394.

[83] 17 Dec. 1765, 3 Feb. 1766, Simmons and Thomas, eds., *Proceedings and Debates*, II. 150, 565.

[84] To Whately, 13 April 1768, HL, ST 7, vol. 2.

[85] 7 Feb. 1766, Simmons and Thomas, eds., *Proceedings and Debates*, II. 172.

[86] 1 Aug. 1763, BL, Add MS 35422, f. 299.

[87] 2 Aug. 1763, BL, Add MS 32950, ff. 17–18.

[88] Paul Langford, *A Polite and Commercial People: England 1727–1783* (Oxford, 1989), pp. 688–9.

[89] To Germain, 20 Aug. 1775, WLCL, Germain Sackville MSS, 3.

[90] *Journals of the House of Commons*, XXIX (1761–4), 698–9.

III

British Americans at the end of the Seven Years War were enthusiastically committed to the British empire. This commitment remained strong until well into the 1770s. In 1774 John Adams expounded to his wife Abigail the agonizing question that he and so many others who thought like him were now forced to confront after ten years of Anglo-American controversy: ' . . . whether the American colonies are to be considered as a distinct community? . . . Or whether they are to be considered as part of the whole British empire, the whole English nation, so far as to be bound in honour, conscience or interest by the general sense of the whole nation.'[91] In his 'Novanglus' letters of the following year Adams finally made his choice. He dismissed the concept of the British empire as having no standing in law, but being merely 'the language of news papers and political pamphlets'. The colonies were not 'part of the British empire' in any contemporary British sense; they were separate 'realms' of 'the king's dominions'.[92]

British Americans not only willingly accepted their membership of the British empire until almost the last moment, but they shared, at least on the surface, many of the objectives of imperial reformers in Britain: most of them wanted colonial constitutions to be modelled as closely as possible on the British constitution with the law of England as their law. They accepted that the British parliament had a supreme authority to regulate the affairs of the empire. The commercial subordination embodied in the Navigation Acts was rarely openly challenged. Both sides saw the British empire as an empire of freedom. Yet it became clear that there were stark differences between their interpretations of a free empire and of the British constitution that under-pinned it and the ideals for empire of the imperial activists in Britain as well as the beliefs of the main body of British political opinion. Differences in interpretations were, however, argued out within the framework of a com-mon acceptance of empire. What was at stake until 1775 for nearly all North Americans was not separation but 'the terms of the imperial relationship'.[93] White West Indians were also engaged in the debate about the definition of empire, but separation never became an issue for them.[94]

[91] L. H. Butterfield, ed., *Adams Family Correspondence*, I, *December 1761–May 1776* (Cambridge, Mass., 1963), p. 127.
[92] R. J. Taylor, ed., *The Papers of John Adams*, II, *December 1773–April 1775* (Cambridge, Mass., 1977), pp. 250, 314, 329.
[93] Fred Anderson, *Crucible of War: The Seven Years' War and the Fate of Empire in British North America 1754–1766* (New York, 2000), p. xxi.
[94] Their views are illuminatingly discussed in Andrew Jackson O'Shaughnessy, *An Empire Divided: The American Revolution and the British Caribbean* (Philadelphia, 2000), pt. II.

A colonial view of the nature of empire had been evolving since the later seventeenth century.[95] Its essential assumption was that the colonies were communities enjoying the same rights as English people at home. Such claims led to long-running struggles in most colonies to limit the prerogative powers of royal governors, to establish the rights of the colonial assemblies on the same footing as those of the house of commons and to assert the independence of the colonial judiciary on English principles. At the end of the Seven Years War there were persistent fears that prerogative powers were to be enforced; in particular that proposals to give the governors' instructions the force of law would be revived. Governors and assemblies were locked in often acrimonious disputes, notably in Jamaica about the privileges of the assembly and in New York about the tenure of judges.

Disputes between governors and assemblies were to continue until the outbreak of the Revolution, but they were increasingly overshadowed by conflicts with Britain about the extent of parliament's authority in the colonies. From 1764 acts of parliament became the main instrument for new colonial regulations, including highly contentious new taxes. In 1766 Thomas Hutchinson, lieutenant governor of Massachusetts, reflected that until the last two years it had been commonly assumed in the colonies that 'in all matters of privilege or rights the determination of the parliament must be decisive' and that it was 'high treason' to oppose an act of parliament. This was no longer the case. Parliament's powers were being openly questioned.[96] Questioning began with the recognition that a supreme authority for the whole empire was essential and that this could only be the British parliament. Parliament's powers should, however, be limited in their application. Taxation together with local legislation involving the domestic affairs, usually called the 'internal police', of the colonies should be left to colonial legislatures. Dickinson, for instance, in his *Farmer's Letters* of 1767 continued to accept that 'Great Britain had a legal right to make laws for preserving' the 'dependence' of the colonies, although this did not include the power to tax them.[97] Such attempts to limit the scope of parliament ran against the rock of British insistence on an indivisible parliamentary sovereignty. As this became apparent, colonial opinion shifted at varying speeds to the proposition that their legislatures had full equality with parliament, which could exercise no authority over them, except by their consent.[98] Landon Carter of Virginia

[95] For an authoritative account, see Jack P. Greene, *Peripheries and Center: Constitutional Development in the Extended Politics of the British Empire and the United States 1607–1788* (Athens, Ga., 1986).
[96] To T. Pownall, 8 March 1766, MHS, Hutchinson Transcripts, XXVI, p. 394.
[97] *Letters from a Farmer in Pennsylvania* (Philadelphia, 1768), p. 36.
[98] There is an abundant literature on these developments, see especially John P. Reid, *The Constitutional History of the American Revolution, II, The Authority to Tax* (Madison, 1987) and

had reached this conclusion as early as 1765.[99] Arthur Lee later wrote that he too had believed that parliament had no legislative authority over the colonies 'from the very beginning of the dispute'.[100] In 1768 Otis was reported to have described the commons as 'a parcel of button-makers, pin-makers, horse jockeys, gamesters, pensioners, pimps, and whore masters', in no way fit to make laws for the colonies.[101] When the young Benjamin Rush visited the commons chamber in 1768 he was far from awed. 'Here the usurping commons endeavored to rob the king of his supremacy over the colonies and divide it among themselves', he reflected. 'O! Cursed haunt of venality, bribery and corruption.'[102] In January 1773 the Massachusetts house of representatives told their governor that 'The power and authority of parliament [was] constitutionally confined within the limits of the realm and the nation collectively of which alone it is the representing and legislative assembly'. Colonies were 'distinct states from the mother country'.[103] Denials of all parliamentary authority were to follow in due course from the other thirteen colonies.

In refuting claims by the British parliament to exercise an absolute sovereignty over the whole empire, North Americans deployed ideas about the nature of representation, about the existence of fundamentals that circumscribed the power of the legislature and about the right of resistance that the majority in British politics found dangerously subversive. Although the claims of the British parliament forced Americans to articulate such beliefs with a new force and clarity, historians have shown that they were both rooted in seventeenth- and early eighteenth-century English ideals and in the actual practice of politics in the colonies.[104] Most British politicians made obeisance to Whig traditions of contract and rights, while strictly limiting their practical application to the necessities of stable government in the face of threats from within and without. Crude contrasts between an oligarchic British political system and an open colonial one are, however, over-simplifications. Britain's political leadership was subject to pressure from a lively press and an

E. S. Morgan, 'Colonial Ideas of Parliamentary Power, 1764–1766', *William and Mary Quarterly,* 2nd ser., V (1948), 311–41.

[99] Jack P. Greene, 'Introduction', *The Diary of Colonel Landon Carter of Sabine Hall, 1752–1776,* 2 vols. (Charlottesville, Va., 1965), I. 36–7.

[100] To S. Adams, 23 June 1772, R. H. Lee, ed., *Life of Arthur Lee LLD.,* 2 vols. (Boston, 1829), I. 219.

[101] Report of speech to General Assembly of Boston, June 1768, HUHL, Sparks MSS 10/2.

[102] To E. Hazard, 22 Oct. 1768, L. H. Butterfield, ed., *Letters of Benjamin Rush,* 2 vols. (Princeton, 1951), I. 68.

[103] Message of 26 Jan. 1773, *Journals of the House of Representatives of Massachusetts,* XLIX, 1772–1773 (Boston, 1980), p. 184.

[104] Bernard Bailyn's *Ideological Origins of the American Revolution* (Cambridge, Mass., 1967) is the classic treatment of this theme.

engaged public, at least within the 'middling orders' of society, while colonial politics were coming to be dominated by increasingly Anglicized oligarchies. Nevertheless, the colonial leadership was far more directly accountable to a widely enfranchised white male population than was the case in Britain. Thomas Hutchinson described the system of town meetings in the New England colonies, where the authority of the provincial houses of representatives, let alone that of a remote parliament in London, was frequently challenged. If a man who is a 'legislator in his own town thinks it hard to submit to laws which he does not like and which were made by a house of representatives . . . for one or two only of which he could give his vote', he was hardly likely to submit easily to the laws of a parliament for whose membership he had no vote.[105] John Adams expounded the New England view of representation in 1766.

It is in reality nothing more than this, the people chuse attornies to vote for them in the great council of the nation, reserving always the fundamentals of the government, reserving also a right to give their attornies instructions how to vote, and a right, at certain stated intervals of discarding an old attorney, and choosing a wiser and a better.[106]

Institutions that were particular to the New England colonies favoured popular participation there, but the political elites were held to account in other mainland colonies. Those in New York and Pennsylvania have been described as being 'accessible', 'open to community influence' and responsive to it.[107] In Virginia and Maryland, where the gentry generally exercised authority with the apparent deference of the rest of the white population, sensitivity to the wishes of the mass of small planters was the price of deference. A large body of voters could assert themselves at contested elections.[108]

Colonial American conceptions of an empire that was free thus had strong overtones of equality. Americans had always believed in equality between communities of the king's Protestant male subjects wherever they lived. Assertions of sovereignty by the British parliament in the 1760s were taken

[105] To R. Jackson, 19 Nov. 1767, F. Madden and D. Fieldhouse, eds., *Select Documents on the Constitutional History of the British Empire and Commonwealth, II, The Classical Period of the First British Empire, 1689–1783. The Foundations of a Colonial System of Government* (Westport, Conn., 1985), p. 505.

[106] Clarendon to Pym [27 Jan. 1766], R. J. Taylor, ed., *Papers of John Adams, I, September 1755– October 1773* (Cambridge, Mass., 1977), p. 168.

[107] Alan Tully, *Forming American Politics: Ideals, Interests and Institutions in Colonial New York and Pennsylvania* (Baltimore, 1994), p. 377.

[108] Trevor Burnard, *Creole Gentlemen: The Maryland Elite 1691–1776* (New York, 2002), pp. 195–6; J. G. Kolp, *Gentlemen and Freeholders: Electoral Politics and Political Commentary in Colonial Virginia* (Baltimore, 1998).

to imply that Americans were the subjects of the British people as well as of the British crown. As Franklin put it, 'Every man in England seems to consider himself as a piece of a sovereign over America . . . talks of OUR *subjects in the colonies*.'[109] Colonial opinion indignantly rejected such notions. If the colonies could be taxed by parliament, Samuel Adams wrote, they became 'tributary to the people of Great-Britain, instead of fellow subjects, co-equal in dignity and freedom'.[110] Colonial opinion was also moving towards a belief in equality between the units of the empire. Deference was due to England as the mother country or 'the nation' in common colonial parlance and to its parliament, so long as that parliament did not involve itself in colonial affairs in intrusive ways. But their confidence in the value of their contribution to the victories of the Seven Years War had given the colonies a strong sense of what was due to them within the empire. As they sought to restrict or to deny parliamentary sovereignty, North Americans edged their way to claiming equality of status between Britain and the individual colonies, or, much more rarely until the mid-1770s, between Britain and an entity called 'America', as, for instance, when William Samuel Johnson of Connecticut in a letter of 1766 altered the phrase 'Great Britain and her colonies' to 'Great Britain and America', referring to them as 'both countries'.[111] In rejecting the analogy to 'corporations' sometimes used by British pamphleteers, Otis insisted that the colonies were 'subordinate states' or 'dominions'.[112] The epithet 'subordinate' began to be dropped around 1770. For Jefferson in 1774 the colonies were 'the several states of British America' and the British empire consisted of 'Great Britain' and 'the several American states'.[113] Equality, for virtually all Americans, emphatically did not mean the ending of ties. It meant that subordination would be replaced by an alliance of virtual equals.

As with their concepts of rights or of representation, in invoking equality between the king's subjects and his different dominions within the empire, colonial Americans were using a language that they shared with those who were trying to manage the empire in London. Equality was certainly implied when men like Whately wrote of incorporating the people of the colonies in a single 'nation' with Britain.[114] But if the ideals seemed to be held in common on both sides of the Atlantic, there were crucial differences as to how these

---

[109] To Kames, 25 Feb. 1767, Labaree et al., eds., *Papers of Benjamin Franklin*, XIV. 65.

[110] T. Z. in *Boston Gazette*, 9 Jan. 1769, H. A. Cushing, ed., *Writings of Samuel Adams*, 4 vols. (New York, 1904–8), I. 288.

[111] To J. Dickinson, 24 May 1766, HUHL, bMS Am Sparks, 49:2.

[112] 'The Rights of the British Colonies Asserted and Proved' in Bailyn, ed., *Pamphlets*, I. 456, 468.

[113] J. P. Boyd, ed., *The Papers of Thomas Jefferson*, I, *1760–1776* (Princeton, 1950), pp. 117, 119, 127.

[114] *Regulations Lately Made*, p. 40.

ideals were to be applied. Those responsible for empire in Britain willingly accepted that the interests of all the king's subjects in all his dominions merited the fullest and most careful consideration, but they insisted that the empire could not survive as an alliance of equals under one crown. A due subordination must be maintained in the interest of the whole and that interest could only be determined by the British parliament. Those who refused to accept that sovereignty seemed to be aiming at the dissolution of the empire. The arguments about the nature of representationand the limits to the power of the legislature that they used in vindication of their refusal seemed to go much further and to threaten the dissolution of all government. Superficial similarities could not mask an unbridgeable chasm.

6
Ideas of Empire 1763–1776: The 'New' Empire

For the old-established colonies of North America and the West Indies contested definitions of what constituted an empire based on freedom put increasing strain on the fabric of the British empire after 1763 and were to tear it apart twelve years later. Over the same period Britain was trying to absorb into its empire peoples who were new to it and, unlike most of the North Americans or whites of the West Indies, were outside the pale of Britishness: French in Quebec, in Grenada and small numbers in some other ceded West Indian islands as well as in West Florida, a very few Spanish in East Florida, Native Americans all over the new continental acquisitions, Caribs in St Vincent, Africans in Senegambia, and the huge populations of provinces in southern and eastern India. Nevertheless, when the dust settled on a shattered American empire after 1783, most but not all of the king's new subjects were his subjects still. Their descendants were often to remain the subjects of his successors until modern times.

I

The British empire of the first half of the eighteenth century has been characterized as being Protestant, commercial, maritime, and free. New acquisitions after 1763 turned the empire into a territorial one, comparable in extent, contemporaries believed, to those of China and Russia. While it was still linked by maritime communications and by commercial enterprise, the great bulk of the new peoples were not Protestant; they were Catholic, if they were Christian at all. Nor had most of them benefited in the past from what the British regarded as a free system of government and it was usually assumed that they would find British freedom alien to them.

How peoples who were not Protestant nor thought to be accustomed to freedom should be treated was not a new issue in 1763. The Catholic population of Ireland was of course the classic case, but that of the Spanish in Minorca was frequently cited. The scale of the problem had, however, suddenly become vastly greater, especially when the population of Bengal was put into the balance. How far, for instance, should toleration or even state patronage be extended to Islam and to Hinduism, let alone to Popery? What would be the effect on Britain itself if British possessions were to be ruled despotically? Could British courts enforce indigenous legal systems that differed fundamentally from the laws of England? The alternatives facing British policy-makers were, put in very crude terms, either to try to assimilate the king's new subjects to British norms or to accept the existence of a new diversity within the empire by incorporating into it hitherto alien religions, laws, and modes of government.

There was probably an underlying disposition among the British elite towards assimilation. The generations in power in the 1760s and 1770s generally subscribed to views of human development according to patterns that had universal applicability. As an advanced 'commercial' society, Britain was a model of what other societies might hope to become. British people were fully aware of the admiration accorded to them by other Europeans. British political institutions, English law, British commercial vigour and manufacturing expertise, the inquiring spirit of British science, and the rationality of British Protestantism were seen as the pillars upon which Britain's eminence rested. Allowing for the adjustments needed for less developed societies, these were attributes that could be exported and indeed had been successfully exported. Adam Smith summed up received opinion when he wrote that 'There are no colonies in which the progress has been more rapid than that of the English in North America.' This was because the 'political institutions of the English colonies have been more favourable' to improvements and cultivation than those of Spain, Portugal, France, or the Dutch. The English allowed their colonies to flourish in freedom with 'perfect security' of person and property.[1] British Protestantism was certainly for export. In congratulating the king on the peace of 1763, the Convocation of Canterbury hoped that now 'the Gospel of Jesus Christ, in its native purity' would be spread among 'those who have hitherto, eiter been ignorant of it, or mixed it with dangerous error'. George III replied that he would do his best 'to extend our most holy religion throughout the vast dominions added to my crown'.[2]

There were, on the other hand, intellectual trends that might lead to different conclusions, such as a relativism which accepted that religion and civil institutions evolved in ways that were appropriate to a society at its particular stage of development. '[F]orms of government', Lord Lyttelton

---

[1] *An Inquiry into the Nature and Causes of the Wealth of Nations*, IV, ch. vii, pt. ii.
[2] *London Gazette*, 12–16 April 1763.

argued in the lords, 'must always be suited to the disposition of the governed and infinitely varied in different climates'. '[T]he mild constitution of this country' would, he felt, 'be rejected with contempt by the sons of despotism in Asia, and an excess of liberty happily spread over England would degenerate into an excess of licentiousness in Canada.'[3] A commitment to religious toleration as desirable in itself and a cult for admiring the values of supposedly simple people also conflicted with policies of assimilation.

Whatever their intellectual dispositions may have been, policy-makers rarely had much freedom to indulge them. Issues of assimilation or accommodation could turn out to be politically explosive, as the hostility aroused by attempts to incorporate new Catholic subjects into the empire were to show. They also raised acute problems of security. Over-zealous assimilation might provoke disaffection and even rebellion by peoples supposedly deeply attached to their own religion, laws and customs, such as the French Canadians, Native Americans, and above all the East India Company's new subjects. Pontiac's rising in 1763 against heavy-handed attempts to change the pattern of relations with Native American peoples and the resistance of the Caribs in St Vincent culminating in the war of 1772-3 showed that these were not unfounded fears.

The issues to be resolved in settling Britain's widely scattered and socially very diverse new possessions seemed to contemporaries to be very much the same, even if the solutions would vary from colony to colony. Questions of governance, law and religion were all crucial.

There was no doubt that representative government would be introduced in areas, such as the Floridas and most of the Ceded Islands, where new settlers of British origin would predominate. It was, however, to be representative government on an approved British model, not by the transfer of constitutional practices current in most existing British American colonies, where the executives were thought to be too weak and the assemblies too strong. In overwhelmingly French Quebec representative government was delayed and then shelved in 1774. Representative government was unthinkable for Native Americans or in the East India Company's provinces. In India the urgent questions of governance were how to transform indigenous institutions into an acceptable instrument of autocratic rule that was accountable to supervision from home, and the degree to which the Company's British servants should intervene in the business of administration.

The long-established legal doctrine throughout the British empire was that Christian peoples conquered by the British crown, such as the French in

---

[3] 17 June 1774, R. C. Simmons and P. D. G. Thomas, eds., *Proceedings and Debates of the British Parliament Respecting North America, 1754–1783*, 6 vols. (Millwood, NY, 1982–6), V. 231.

Canada and Grenada, kept their own laws until the king chose to introduce other laws. Infidel peoples, a category that presumably included the Native Americans and the Indians brought under Company rule, immediately forfeited their right to their own laws. By the 1760s, however, there was a strong tendency, conspicuously embodied in the dicta of lord Mansfield, to accept the validity of all different systems of laws and to allow them to continue within the British empire. The 'crown of England', Mansfield wrote, 'has always left to the conquered their own laws and usages'.[4] To impose new laws on the millions of Bengal, to give an extreme case, would be neither just, politic, nor practical. Yet there were also pressures for change. Were people of British origin, even if they were only a minority of the population, to be obliged to live under alien laws in what were now British colonies? Were what were deemed to be retrogressive systems to be preserved? The outright ownership of land and a free market in it were believed to be distinguishing features of the British empire and to be cardinal reasons for its astonishing prosperity. Should not the lands claimed collectively by communities of Native Americans or settled under French seigneurial tenure therefore be converted to individual ownership through the mechanism of a free market in land?

Religious diversity raised acute problems in Britain's new acquisitions. In colonies that had been established by other Europeans the future status of the Catholic church was an issue of the utmost urgency and delicacy. Assuming increasing British settlement in former French colonies, what was to be done to advance Protestantism, and, in particular, how far should the Church of England be privileged? What obligations did the British empire have to spread Christianity to its non-Christian subjects? In the case of the Indians of North America, a very strong sense of obligation was felt in Britain after 1763. Christianizing the East India Company's provinces, on the other hand, hardly seemed to be a realistic objective, but calls were already being made for Protestant missions to India. George III made regular annual payments of ten guineas to support the German Protestant missions in the East Indies.[5]

In the twelve years between the ending of the Seven Years War and the outbreak of the American Revolution, British attempts to lay down the constitutional, legal, and religious terms on which the new subjects would live in the empire veered between the alternatives of assimilation and efforts to accommodate the alien. Preferences may have been for assimilation, but practical necessities often meant that accommodations had to be reached.

[4] To G. Grenville, 24 Dec. 1764, W. J. Smith, ed., *Grenville Papers*, 4 vols. (1853), II. 477.
[5] G. M. Ditchfield, *George III: An Essay in Monarchy* (Houndmills, 2002), p. 88.

There were precedents, if hardly encouraging ones, for French populations to be brought into the empire by conquest. The so-called 'neutrals', or Acadians, of Nova Scotia had lived under British authority from the Peace of Utrecht until 1755. Many of them had then been expelled from their lands as irreconcilable enemies of the British empire who were to be scattered throughout the British North American colonies, where it was expected that they would be rigorously assimilated. Lord Halifax even recommended that their children be 'taken from them and educated in the Protestant religion, by which means they at least, however stubborn their parents might prove, would have become good and usefull servants'.[6] For all the savage hatred for the French Canadians felt by most colonial Americans and by some British soldiers, extirpation or forced assimilation were not deemed practical alternatives for the much greater number of French, thought to be about 75,000, who remained in Quebec at its surrender in 1760. Mass expropriation was also ruled out for those of the French planter community in Grenada who did not voluntarily sell their lands. In Canada Jeffrey Amherst quickly assumed the mantle of benevolent protector, a role to be commemorated in a huge picture for the Vauxhall Gardens by Francis Hayman. As his army moved up to Montreal in 1760, 'the country people', he wrote, fled into the woods, but he 'fetched them out, and put them quiet in their habitations, and they are vastly happy'.[7] He repeated the language of his instructions from home to the commanders who were occupying Louisiana and the Floridas. He had been told that it was 'essential to his Majesty's service' that the French population should remain in the conquered colonies.[8] Amherst therefore reminded British officers that the French were now the king's subjects and were entitled to 'the full benefit of that indulgent and benign government', which 'constitutes the peculiar happiness of all who are subject to the British empire'. They should not be subjected to 'harsh and provoking observations on their language, dress, manners, customs or country or by uncharitable reflections on the errors of that mistaken religion, which they unhappily profess'.[9] French Americans, in other words, were no longer to be seen as murderous fanatics, as savage as the Indians with whom they had allied in raiding British colonies, but as simple, hardworking folk, commendably obedient to their social superiors. General Murray, first British military governor of Quebec, called them 'a frugal, industrious and moral

[6] To W. Lyttelton, 13 Aug. 1756, WLCL, Lyttelton MSS.

[7] To J. Yorke, 8 Sept. 1760, N. J. O'Conor, *A Servant of the Crown in England and in North America, 1756–61* (New York, 1938), p. 148.

[8] Egremont to Amherst, 12 Dec. 1761, WLCL, Amherst MSS, 5, no. 114.

[9] Orders of 23 Aug. 1763, PRO, CO 323/17, f. 31.

race of men'.[10] Once the malign influences of the French royal officials and the religious orders had been removed, they could be expected to respond to the stimulus of British freedom and of the settlement of enterprising British settlers among them. They would thus become valuable citizens of empire. Highly unrealistic expectations were held as to their loyalty and willingness to fight for the empire at the beginning of the American Revolution. While they were becoming acclimatized to a new order of liberty, rationality and prosperity, toleration should be extended to their customs and their superstitions. To allow Popery to be practised within the empire was not to sup with the devil, even though the popular rhetoric of the Seven Years War had been strongly that of a war of religion, but was to extend reasonable indulgence to the beliefs of unsophisticated people, which were harmless and would eventually wither away.[11] A Catholic church subject to British royal authority would not be a danger. Assimilation was the British objective in the long run; there must, however, be accommodations in the immediate future.

The terms on which the new Atlantic colonies were to be established were laid down in the royal proclamation of 1763. This was strongly assimilationist in tone. For the 'security of the liberties and properties' of the inhabitants, as soon as 'the state and circumstances' of the individual colonies allowed, 'general assemblies' would be called. The assemblies would make local laws 'as near as may be agreeable to the laws of England' and in the meanwhile courts would be constituted to operate on the same principle, that is enforcing English law.[12] Under the terms of the peace, Catholics had been promised freedom of worship 'according to the rites of the Romish church, as far as the laws of Great Britain permit'.[13] No foreign ecclesiastical jurisdiction, above all that of the Papacy, was to be exercised in Canada. The first instructions to the governor ordered him to take steps to establish the Church of England with grants of land and schools, 'so that the . . . inhabitants may by degrees be induced to embrace the Protestant religion'.[14]

In Grenada, where there was an influx of British planters, but the French population had a 'vast superiority in point of number . . . tho' inferior in point of property',[15] a partial incorporation of the French into a British system of government was immediately attempted. The governor was permitted to set up an elected assembly for which propertied French Catholics

---

[10] To Shelburne, Aug. 1766, National Army Museum, MS 6806–41–4.

[11] Colin Haydon, *Anti-Catholicism in Eighteenth-Century England, c.1714–80: A Political and Social Study* (Manchester, 1993), pp. 168–9; see also P. M. Doll, *Revolution, Religion and National Identity: Imperial Anglicanism in British North America 1745–1795* (Cranbury, NJ, 2000), pp. 94–6.

[12] A. Shortt and A. G. Doughty, eds., *Documents Relating to the Constitutional History of Canada 1759–1791*, 2nd. edn., 2 vols. (Ottawa, 1918), I. 165.

[13] Ibid. I. 115.   [14] Ibid. I. 191–2.

[15] Petition of Protestant Inhabitants, 14 Feb. 1766, PRO, CO 101/1, f. 215.

were allowed to vote, provided that they swore allegiance to the British crown. Only those who were willing to take the test renouncing Popery would, however, be eligible for membership of the assembly or for office in the island.[16] In enfranchizing the French, the governor seems to have been concerned to try to keep them from deserting the island by granting them rights that would 'attach them to our constitution'. At this point he was optimistic that the French wished 'to become British as far as possible'.[17] His optimism was quickly dissipated. He complained that the French used their voting power to ally with 'the worst of the natural born British subjects' and to launch a campaign for full political rights.[18] He now believed that the French would not become 'truly English and Protestants' and therefore that the island would not be secure in the next war against France, unless 'the rising generation' were educated in Britain.[19] Governor Melvill was aware that the French were sending emissaries and petitions to London, but was confident that ministers would reject such advances. His confidence was misplaced. On the advice of the board of trade, reinforced by legal opinion that the tests debarring Catholics from office did not apply in the colonies, an order in council was issued on 7 September 1768 allocating a quota of seats in the assembly and on the council together with some judicial offices to Catholics, who had sworn allegiance but had not renounced their faith.[20] Ministers were evidently concerned not to give needless 'dissatisfaction' to the king's new subjects and indeed wished to 'gratify' them 'in every reasonable desire'.[21] The king's Protestant subjects in Grenada were, however, far from gratified. For them, '[T]he very existence of the constitution of Great Britain' and therefore of those of its colonies depended on 'the support of the Protestant religion, and the driving from the councils and offices of the nation, all enemies of that persuasion'.[22] They withheld taxes, producing a state of 'virtual paralysis' in the island's government for several years.[23] Their spirited resistance to Popery and to the prerogative power that had enforced concession to Catholics through an order in council won widespread sympathy in Britain and North America.

Attempts to incorporate the French into British institutions progressed much more slowly in Quebec, where Anglophone immigration had produced a vocal merchant community but no large-scale influx of new settlers.

---

[16] Ordinance of 10 Feb. 1766, ibid. ff. 228, 230.
[17] R. Melvill to board of trade, 7 Feb. 1765, ibid. ff. 296–7; to Hillsborough, 27 Dec. 1767, PRO, CO 101/12, f. 56.
[18] Melvill to board of trade, 31 Jan. 1768, ibid. f. 254.
[19] To Hillsborough, 27 Dec. 1767, ibid. f. 56.
[20] W. L. Grant and James Munro, eds., Acts of the Privy Council of England; Colonial Series, 6 vols. (1908–12), V. 8–9.
[21] Hillsborough to Melvill, 8 March 1768, PRO, CO 101/12, f. 44.
[22] Observations upon the Report made by the Board of Trade against the Grenada Laws (1770), p. 18.
[23] Andrew Jackson O'Shaughnessy, An Empire Divided: The American Revolution and the British Caribbean (Philadelphia, 2000), pp. 124–6.

Whatever might have been intended in 1763, accommodations with the huge French majority could not be avoided. The calling of an elected assembly was postponed. It was recognized that the survival of the Catholic church required more than merely allowing its adherents to worship without persecution. In 1766 the appointment of a Catholic bishop for Canada was sanctioned by the British government. Conversely, little was done to realise the declared objective of an established Church of England in the colony. Some of the most distinguished British lawyers, notably lord Mansfield and the crown law officers in 1766, expressed disquiet at replacing French civil law by English law. 'Wise conquerors', urged the law officers, 'proceed gently and indulge their conquer'd subjects in all local customs.'[24] Trends towards accommodation, at least for the immediate future, were embodied in the Quebec Act of 1774. The right 'to the free exercise of the religion of the Church of *Rome*' was confirmed and in addition the clergy were permitted to collect tithes for the maintenance of the church. For the '*Canadian* subjects', issues of 'property' and 'civil rights' would be settled according to 'the laws of *Canada*'. Since it was still 'inexpedient to call an assembly', the colony was to be administered by its governor with a nominated council, but without an elected body.[25] By 1774 opinion within British governments had long since concluded that a predominantly French colony could not be kept securely within the empire if the mass of its population felt that their religion and the legal basis of their society were under assault. Many North Americans and large sections of opinion in Britain were, however, outraged. To them what was happening in Quebec confirmed fears aroused by concessions to Catholics in Grenada. Popery and despotism were taking root in the British empire. Assailed in these terms in parliament and the press, ministers invoked arguments that went beyond statements about the need to ensure the security of Quebec and appealed, in the words of the solicitor-general, Alexander Wedderburn, to 'the principles of humanity, the principles of natural justice' that entitled a people to live in ways to which they were accustomed. To try to force on them institutions that were no doubt objectively superior to theirs would be to revert to the 'barbarity of former ages'.[26]

---

[24] Report of C. Yorke and W. De Grey, 14 Aug. 1766, Shortt and Doughty, eds., *Documents*, I. 255.

[25] 14 Geo. III, c. 83, secs. 5, 7, 12.

[26] 26 May 1774, Simmons and Thomas, eds., *Proceedings and Debates*, IV. 51. Valuable recent contributions to the extensive literature on early British rule in Quebec are Doll, *Revolution, Religion and National Identity*; Philip Lawson, *The Imperial Challenge: Quebec and Britain in the Age of the American Revolution* (Montreal and Kingston, 1990); Peter Marshall, 'British North America, 1760–1815' in P. J. Marshall, ed., *The Oxford History of the British Empire*, II, *The Eighteenth Century* (Oxford, 1998), pp. 372–93; P. D. G. Thomas, *Tea Party to Independence: The Third Phase of the American Revolution 1773–1776* (Oxford, 1991), ch. 6.

Relations with the Indians was the aspect of North American affairs in which the metropolitan government was most directly involved after 1763. It was also a topic in which a wider British public took a keen interest. British officials had long believed that, in their dealings with the Indian peoples beyond their boundaries, the American colonies pursued short-sighted and conflicting policies, driven by the desire to acquire Indian land and to maximize profits in unfair trade with them. The alienation of the Indians was a potential danger which seemed to have been fully realized in the early years of the Seven Years War, when so many of them allied with the French to take what seemed to be a terrible revenge on some of the British colonies. The British government's response was to bring Indian affairs under direct metropolitan management. '[T]he only effectual method of conducting Indian affairs', the board of trade explained in 1757, 'is to establish one general system under the sole direction of the crown and its officers.'[27] Superintendents were appointed for the northern and southern Indians, who corresponded directly with the board of trade in London. The superintendents were reinforced by the British army, who occupied most of the French posts in the west in the closing stages of the war and remained in them when the war was over. The army was to prevent colonial encroachments on Indian land and trade was to be conducted at its posts under regulations. In the south, the later phases of the Cherokee wars, begun by the governor of South Carolina with his provincial forces in 1759, had largely been waged by regular British troops and the peace that brought them to an end in 1761 was the work of British army officers.[28] By the Peace of Paris the lands claimed by the French between the Mississippi and the mountains were formally ceded to the British crown. Although their lands were now the dominions of the crown, Indians outside the colonies were not considered to be the king's subjects. They were declared in the royal proclamation of 1763 to 'live under our protection'.

Whatever their formal status, Indians were an object of concern to a wide British public. Material about them appearing in the British press after the war exceeded that on any other topic concerning the colonies.[29] The public's interest in them had been greatly stimulated by accounts of the war and in particular of the devastation wrought by the Indians on the frontier settlements, especially those of Pennsylvania and Virginia. The success of the French in winning Indian allies was commonly attributed to 'the indefatigable zeal' of the Catholic missions, above all of the Jesuits, which had enabled

[27] To Governor of South Carolina, 9 Nov. 1757, WLCL, Lyttelton MSS.

[28] John Oliphant, *Peace and War on the Anglo-Cherokee Frontier, 1756–63* (Houndmills, 2001).

[29] F. J. Hinkhouse, *Preliminaries of the American Revolution as seen in the British Press, 1763–1775* (New York, 1926), p. 38.

'the superstitious and diabolical spirit of Popery' to ensnare them.[30] A stable peace required that these malign influences be rooted out and replaced with wholesome Protestant ones. The Church of Scotland congratulated George III on a peace in 1763 which would bring 'the American nations' to 'the holy faith, which civilizes and refines the manners of men, at the same time that it improves and sanctifies their hearts'.[31] To achieve that would be more than a politic measure of self-interest; it was a response, pious Christians believed, incumbent on Britain in return for divine favour manifested in victory. This was the theme of many sermons. For the Anglican John Brown the British had become 'the instruments of heaven in spreading the Gospel through regions and climates yet unknown'.[32] Millenarian expectations seem to have been aroused from the conversion of the Indians. '[T]he children of God in England' were reported by Dennys De Berdt, a prominent London Dissenter and agent for Massachusetts, to be 'importunate for the spread and success of the gospel among the natives that the heathen may hear and know the joyful sound, and your western end of the earth become the willing subjects of that Divine Emanuel who is promised the ends of the earth for his possession'.[33] Considerable sums were subscribed for missions to Indians, both through the English Society for the Propagation of the Gospel and the Scottish Society for Propagating Christian Knowledge. Largely thanks to the indefatigable Mohegan convert, the Revd Samson Occom, who preached three hundred sermons throughout Britain, £12,000 was collected for Eleazar Wheelock's Indian school at Lebanon, Connecticut, in 1765–6.[34] The Scottish SPCK circulated an appeal for this project to 'all the ministers in Scotland', considering that 'the conversion and civilizing of the Indians merits the highest regard from all who wish well to the interests of the Mediator's kingdom, and the prosperity of the British colonies'.[35] Official patronage was to be extended to Anglican missions. The board of trade urged that the Society for the Propagation of the Gospel should be asked to supply four missionaries each to the jurisdictions of the two Indian superintendents.[36] Sir William Johnson, the renowned superintendent of the northern Indians, was an enthusiastic exponent of Anglican missionaries and a member of the Society.

[30] 'Letter from an Officer in North America', *London Chronicle*, 3–6 Feb. 1759.

[31] *London Gazette*, 31 May–4 June 1763.

[32] *On Religious Liberty: A Sermon Preached at St Paul's* (1763), p. 16.

[33] D. De Berdt to E. Wheelock, 24 Mar. 1759, 'Letters of Dennys De Berdt 1757–70', *Publications of the Colonial Society of Massachusetts*, XIII (1910–11), 413.

[34] William Kellaway, *The New England Company 1649–1776, Missionary Society to the American Indians* (1961), p. 191.

[35] *Recommendation of the Society in Scotland for Propagating Christian Knowledge, in favour of the Academy established by Mr Eleazar Wheelock* (Edinburgh, 1767), p. 4.

[36] Plan for the Future Management of Indian Affairs, 10 July 1764, E. B. O'Callaghan, ed., *Documents Relative to the Colonial History of the State of New-York*, 15 vols. (1856–87), VII. 637.

William Warburton, bishop of Gloucester, in a sermon preached in 1766, urged caution on the missionary enthusiasts. No lasting conversions of Indians could be expected until 'these barbarians' have been 'taught the *civil arts of life*'.[37] Plans for assimilating Indians to British norms were widely discussed. A project appeared in the press in 1763 for teaching them how 'to obtain and enjoy the advantages of civil society', making them 'obedient to law and introducing a proper subordination among them'.[38] An account in the *Annual Register* of the Indian war of 1763, conventionally called Pontiac's rising, while showing both insight into and sympathy for the Indians, concluded that the only way forward for them was 'gradually [to] assimilate to the English' as the result of 'kind and gentle treatment'.[39]

The aims of the British government were, however, much more limited. Positive attempts at assimilation for the moment were obviously impractical. To endeavour to keep the peace and avoid future Indian wars was all that could be attempted. The assumption was that the threat to the peace came from Americans settling on Indian lands and cheating them in trade. Hence the provisions for at least a temporary halt on land transfers and for a regulated trade. The army was to be the instrument for enforcing these provisions. In reality the army not only proved to be unable effectively to curb settlement or impose a new commercial order, but by its presence in the west, exacerbated by the heavy-handed policies of British commanders, it largely provoked the devastating new Indian war waged by Pontiac and his allies. To the Indians the British army evidently seemed to be a much more threatening presence than the French had ever been. It was an instrument of conquest. British officers set about imposing a more rigorous dependence. Indians were no longer to be conciliated by presents or to be treated as equals in treaty negotiations. A new dispensation was to be laid down for them, which they must accept or suffer the consequences. In 1763 it was apparently not so much the threat of losing land as issues of 'authority and submission' that drove the Indians to war. British garrisons were overrun or besieged and the frontier settlements were again devastated in a war that dragged on into 1765.[40]

When peace was restored, British agents, notably Sir William Johnson, tended to return to a policy of treating the Indians as allies to be negotiated with rather than as dependants to be commanded.[41] Land, however, now became a burning issue. Illegal settlement across the frontier resumed on a

---

[37] *The Works of the Right Reverend William Warburton, Bishop of Gloucester*, 7 vols. (1788), V. 328–9.

[38] 'Philo – Indicus', *Gentleman's Magazine*, XXXIV (1763), 125–7.

[39] *Annual Register*, VI (1763), 38.

[40] Gregory Evans Dowd, *War under Heaven: Pontiac, the Indian Nations, and the British Empire* (Baltimore, 2002), see especially p. 82.

[41] Richard White, *The Middle Ground: Indians, Empires and Republics in the Great Lakes Region, 1650–1815* (Cambridge, 1991), pp. 305–14. Cf. Dowd, *War under Heaven*, pp. 234–7.

large scale. Johnson engineered a huge alienation of land in 1768 which stimulated great speculative interests in western lands on both sides of the Atlantic. The British had shown that they could neither impose their will on the Indians nor on the British Americans who wished to trade with them or to acquire land. The army, the chosen instrument of control, was unable to perform the role allocated to it and was in any case withdrawn from the western posts in the early 1770s. In 1774 the governor of Virginia waged war for new lands against the Shawnees, unhindered by imperial authority.[42]

Missionary enthusiasm also achieved very little. The Society for the Propagation of the Gospel was unable to do what was expected of it. Johnson complained in 1767 that no Anglicans were ministering to the Six Nations, only a few Massachusetts 'Dissenters' of whom he deeply disapproved.[43] The only effective missionary endeavour among peoples newly brought within the British empire was one established in 1771 by Moravians, with British government approval, with the Inuit on the coast of Labrador.[44]

Yet in spite of the huge disparity between expectations and achievement— far from being able to assimilate the Indians to British ways, royal authority could not even keep the peace—a rhetoric of protection survived in British official circles and public debate. British opinion could not accept that 'the army itself was the problem'.[45] Frontier Americans' covetousness and violence were the problem. Franklin commended British soldiers who had protected mission Indians from a lynch mob in Pennsylvania in 1763. This served to 'impress the minds of the discerning with a still greater respect for our national government' and for 'the military'.[46] General Gage, the British commander-in-chief, wrote in 1768 of the necessity for 'framing new laws in the provinces, and inforcing obedience thereto, for the better securing the Indians in their persons and properties'.[47] The secretary of state agreed that everything possible should be done to instil 'ideas of the uprightness and equity of his majesty's intention towards' the Indians.[48] The British never

[42] British policy is analysed in Jack M. Sosin, *Whitehall and the Wilderness: The Middle-West in British Colonial Policy, 1760–1775* (Lincoln, Neb., 1961); for the Indian context, see White, *Middle Ground*.

[43] 'Review of the Trade and Affairs of the Indians in the Northern District of America', E. B. O'Callaghan, ed., *Documents Relative to the Colonial History of New-York*, 15 vols. (Albany, NY, 1856–87), VII. 969.

[44] J. C. S. Mason, *The Moravian Church and the Missionary Awakening in England, 1760–1800* (Woodbridge, 2001), pp. 28–41.

[45] Dowd, *War under Heaven*, p. 79.

[46] 'A Narrative of the Late Massacre in Lancaster County' [Jan. 1764], L. W. Labaree et al., eds., *The Papers of Benjamin Franklin* (New Haven, 1959–), XI. 69. Reprinted in *Gentleman's Magazine*, XXXIV (1765), 172–8.

[47] To Shelburne, 22 Jan. 1768, C. E. Carter, ed., *The Correspondence of General Thomas Gage with the Secretaries of State, with the War Office and the Treasury*, 2 vols. (New Haven, 1931–3), I. 157.

[48] Hillsborough to Gage, 14 May 1768, ibid. II. 67.

effectively discharged any responsibility that they may have felt for the Indians of the west and easily divested themselves of these responsibilities in 1783. A rhetoric of concern and protection was, however, to be transferred to other non-European peoples.

The so-called 'black' Caribs of St Vincent were such a people. As was the case with the Native Americans, British dealings with them ended in bloodshed which attracted much publicity. It was of great significance for the future that their affairs came to be discussed in parliament in a way that those of Native Americans never had been. The estimated 2,000 black Caribs were thought to be descendants of escaped slaves. They occupied a considerable area of St Vincent when it was incorporated into the British empire in 1763. The agents of the British treasury wished to sell as much land as possible on behalf of the crown to white planters, who regarded the Caribs as brutal savages incapable of living in peaceful coexistence with them and advocated their mass deportation to another island or to Africa. British officials at first used the language of gentle assimilation. It was 'by no means consistent with his Majesty's clemency nor indeed the common rights of mankind', for the Caribs to be 'extirpated'. They must be settled in 'a manner productive of their own happiness as well as the future improvement of the country'. The Caribs were to be taken under the king's protection as his 'loving subjects' and they would be resettled on lands 'convenient and sufficient' for their use which would be allocated to them. The rest of the land would be sold on behalf of the crown to European planters.[49]

Negotiations broke down, however. Surveys and road making were resisted and the Caribs finally declared themselves to be an independent people. Regular troops were deployed against them in September 1772. Ministers professed that this was a war for the security of the island against a people who would not accept British sovereignty and who maintained contacts with the French rather than a war for the Caribs' lands. 'It is the welfare and happiness of the deluded people, and not their extirpation that are the objects of the king's measures.'[50] After the Caribs were brought to terms which included the recognition of British sovereignty and, as the military commander put it, 'a great addition of excellent lands' to the crown,[51] the secretary of state still insisted that it was British policy to conciliate 'their affection by acts of benevolence and humanity and the introducing amongst them the arts and advantages of civil polity'.[52] Even so, the 'cruel outrage against humanity'

---

[49] W. Young's Memorial, 11 Aug. 1767, *Authentic Papers Relative to the Expedition Against the Charibs and the Sale of Lands in the Island of St Vincent* (1773), pp. 5–10.

[50] Dartmouth to W. Dalrymple, 9 Dec. 1772, PRO, CO 101/16, ff. 218–19.

[51] W. Dalrymple to Barrington, 22 Feb. 1773, PRO, WO 1/57, f. 15.

[52] Dartmouth to W. Leyborne, 10 June 1773, PRO, CO 101/17, f. 195.

committed against the Caribs[53] and the losses from disease among the troops were raised in the house of commons. Colonel Isaac Barré memorably likened the Caribs to the ancient Britons, fighting for their freedom against the Romans, and asked who the 'barbarians' were now.[54] Lord North argued in reply that the government had done its best to 'put the negroes upon the footing of happy, civilized subjects'.[55]

Some public interest was also being shown in the condition of African peoples in British colonies, whose status as slaves conventionally excluded them from being regarded as the king's subjects. Africans in the colonies had long been objects of limited missionary endeavours by the Church of England. The first effective propagation of Christianity in British slave communities seems, however, again to have been the achievement of the Moravians. Their mission in Antigua, founded in 1756, was claiming numerous conversions in the early 1770s. By then there was a growing consensus, at least in polite society, that slavery and the slave trade, however necessary for national prosperity, were morally indefensible. John Wesley unequivocally denounced both in his *Thoughts upon Slavery* of 1774.[56] Slavery in Britain itself was coming under attack. The campaign under the leadership of Granville Sharp culminated in lord Mansfield's judgement on the Somersett case in 1772, which made the forcible deportation from Britain of a slave illegal, even if it left the legal status of slavery in Britain undetermined. Plans for reform of slavery in the colonies and of the slave trade were also being devised, if without any official backing. William Knox, for instance, called for parliament to intervene. He considered it to be 'most reproachful to this country that there are more than five hundred thousand of its subjects for whom the legislature has never shewn the least regard'.[57] The ultimate objective in some proposals was even envisaged as the gradual dismantling of the whole system of slavery throughout the empire.[58]

The record of British governments in their dealings with the empire's new subjects around the Atlantic was one of almost unrelieved failure. The British could neither assimilate nor protect the Indian peoples of North America. Later observers did not believe that the black Caribs of St Vincent had become an industrious property-owning peasantry as a result of being

---

[53] T. Townshend, 9 Dec. 1772, W. Cobbett, ed., *Parliamentary History of England from the Norman Conquest in 1066 to the Year 1803*, 36 vols. (1806–20), XVII. 572.

[54] 15 Feb. 1773, BL, Egerton MS, 244, f. 139.   [55] 15 Feb. 1773, ibid. f. 132.

[56] Mason, *Moravian Church and Missionary Awakening*, pp. 106–13.

[57] *Three Tracts Respecting the Conversion and Instruction of the Free Indians with the Negro Slaves in the Colonies* (1768), p. 27.

[58] Christopher L. Brown, 'Empire Without Slaves: British Concepts of Emancipation in the Age of the American Revolution', *William and Mary Quarterly*, 3rd ser., LVI (1999), 273–306; see also Paul Thomas, 'Changing Attitudes in an Expanding Empire: The Anti-Slavery Movement, 1760–83', *Slavery and Abolition*, V (1984), 50–72.

chastised in 1772.[59] When the French invaded the island in 1779 the Caribs were solid in their support for them. A case can be made that even the Quebec Act, long regarded as a piece of far-sighted imperial statesmanship, in reality did little either to meet the needs of most French Canadians or to ensure the loyalty of the colony during the American Revolution.[60] The French of Quebec were not conspicuous in their loyalty to the empire during the war, even if they did not support the Americans. Attempts to integrate the French in Grenada certainly did not achieve that effect. At the outbreak of the American War, they were reported to be 'totally disaffected and . . . incapable of any sincere attachment to us'.[61] They appear to have welcomed the French reconquest of the island in 1779.

To detect a new climate of humanitarianism in responses to the problems posed by the incorporation of new subjects is probably to claim too much, although it is undeniable that concern for non-British peoples featured increasingly both in official rhetoric and in public debate. Yet whatever the outcome of the attempts and whatever may have been the motives for them, government, parliament and public had engaged with the problems posed by the inclusion within the empire of peoples who were neither Protestant nor free. This willingness to accept a degree of responsibility for French, native Americans and even, by as yet a small minority, for African slaves no doubt helped to break down inhibitions about bringing within an imperial framework Indians, people who were thought to be completely alien to all previous traditions of British imperial rule.

III

At the end of the Seven Years War the British East India Company had established itself as the dominant power over the south-east coast of the Indian peninsula and in the great provinces of Bengal and Bihar in eastern India. In the south, the Company's outright territorial possessions were on a limited scale until the last decade of the eighteenth century, although it exercised an increasingly assertive protectorate over the rulers of the Carnatic. In Bengal and Bihar the authority of Indian rulers was quickly demolished and replaced by the exercise of what the East India Company's servants regarded as sovereign British rule in the name of the Company, the acquisi-

---

[59] See, e.g., [T. Coke], *The Case of the Caribbs of St Vincent* [1787].

[60] Thomas, *Tea Party to Independence*, pp. 113–17.

[61] E. M. Johnston, 'Grenada 1775–79' in P. Roebuck, ed., *Macartney of Lisanoure 1737–1806: Essays in Biography* (Belfast, 1983), p. 121.

tion of the *diwani* in 1765 being the most conspicuous landmark in this process.

The rights and duties of the British state over these great new dominions raised complex and contentious questions that were gradually resolved in ways that will be described in the next chapter. Initial solutions were embodied in legislation of 1773 known as lord North's Regulating Act. The assumptions underlying this Act were that sovereignty was vested in the crown (although this was not made explicit), but that the Company would act as the sovereign power on the state's behalf, subject to a degree of regulation. Some of the Act's provisions sought to regulate in general terms the way in which Indian provinces should be governed. Thus by 1773 few could doubt that the Company's provinces were a part of the British empire and that the British state had taken on itself ultimate responsibility for their government.

Empire in India was the total antithesis of all ideals for a British empire that was characterized by freedom. It was a deeply rooted stereotype of nearly all European notions over many centuries about government in Asia that it was despotic. Empire in any part of Asia must involve despotic rule and therefore must ultimately be destructive of freedom in Europe itself. This was the lesson above all of Roman history. 'All the LATIN classics, whom we peruse from our infancy', wrote David Hume, ' . . . universally ascribe the ruin of their state to the arts and riches imported from the East'.[62] Adam Ferguson's *History of the Progress and Termination of the Roman Republic* was written to explain

the great revolution, by which the republican form of government was exchanged for despotism; and by which the Roman people from being joint sovereigns of a great empire, became, together with their own provinces, the subjects and often the prey, of a tyranny which was equally cruel to both.

A decline of 'national character' had brought about that revolution. The evils ensuing from an overgrown empire had done much to sap the character of the Roman people. The wealth derived from conquest brought 'a ruinous corruption' at home. Men who had learnt habits of 'arbitrary and uncontrouled command' abroad became tyrants in their own country.[63] In his *Essay on the History of Civil Society* of 1767 Ferguson had drawn lessons for his own time. 'Disciplined and mercenary' European armies could now conquer Asia almost at will. Conquered provinces would be ruled by military force. The 'perpetual enlargement of territory' would lead to despotism at home. The

---

[62] 'On Refinement in the Arts', T. H. Green and T. H. Grose, eds., *The Philosophical Works of David Hume*, 4 vols. (Darmstadt, 1964), III. 305.

[63] 3 vols. (1783), I. 3, 276–9.

conquered may appear to have 'lost their liberties; but from the history of mankind, to conquer or to be conquered, has appeared, in effect, the same'.[64] Beilby Porteus, later bishop of London, expressed similar misgivings in a sermon to the commons in 1767. 'There is not in all antiquity a single instance of any nation long preserving its liberty, with such an extent of territory, and such a degree of wealth, as we now enjoy. This is an alarming consideration!'[65]

The lessons for Britain seemed clear, yet they appeared to be being wantonly disregarded. Such perceptions were often sharpest to Americans. For Arthur Lee,

For the future, the story of lord Clive will be that of every military plunderer . . . It begins in blood and plunder, it ends in servility and dependence. The wealth would be insecure under the crimes by which it was acquired without ministerial influence and protection to cover them from enquiry of parliament or screen them from punishment. In a few years the two houses will be filled with Omrahs and Subedars, nurtured in the corruption and despotism of the East. What will be the consequence? We must fall as Greece and Rome have fallen.

Happily, he reflected, liberty 'will fix her favourite seat in the rising regions of America'.[66]

Americans were especially prone to see empire in India as evidence of the degeneration of Britain, but there were British people too who shared that view and wished to have no part in it. When the highly respected MP for Yorkshire, Sir George Savile, was voted onto a commons select committee on India in 1772, he refused to serve, 'being against the whole system of India affairs'. The Company's trade 'brought too great an increase of money, which would overturn the liberty of this country' and he thought that 'the territorial acquisitions' were 'public robberies'.[67] No doubt he spoke for many, particularly those of an older generation with older ideals of civic virtue. Horace Walpole, who developed a life-long detestation of empire in India was using the term 'nabob' as early as 1761 for the obnoxious parvenus whom that empire appeared to spawn. By 1773 he believed that England had become 'a sink of Indian wealth, filled by nabobs'.[68] Dr Samuel Johnson thought that

---

[64] D. Forbes, ed., *An Essay on the History of Civil Society* (Edinburgh, 1966), p. 272. See also J. G. A. Pocock, *Barbarism and Religion*, II, *Narratives of Civil Government* (Cambridge, 1999), pp. 346–52.

[65] *A Sermon Preached before the Honourable House of Commons* (1767), p. 25.

[66] To S. Adams, 3 Dec. 1773, R. H. Lee, ed., *The Life of Arthur Lee LLD.*, 2 vols. (Boston, 1829), I. 261.

[67] 16 April 1772, Cobbett, ed., *Parliamentary History*, XVII. 464.

[68] To Sir H. Mann, 3 March 1761, 13 July 1773, W. S. Lewis et al., eds., *Horace Walpole's Correspondence*, 48 vols. (Oxford, 1937–83), XXI. 484, XXIII. 499.

'discoveries' always ended in 'conquest and robbery' and thus the discovery of the sea route to India was for him 'disastrous to mankind'.[69]

Most active politicians, however, felt that they could not afford to wash their hands of empire in India and were being increasingly drawn into some involvement with it, albeit often with expressions of misgiving. Chatham, for instance, had encouraged state intervention in the affairs of the Company by his demand for money from it in 1767,[70] but he envisaged disaster if the crown were to seize the revenues of India independent of parliament. There would be 'an end of the shadow of liberty. English kings would become moguls; rich, splendid, weak; gold would be, fatally, substituted in the place of trade, industry, liberty, and virtue.'[71]

A wider public outside the political world was also acquiring an awareness of new imperial commitments in India and coming to accept them as inescapable. There was a great outpouring of books and pamphlets on the subject. Three hundred publications about India appeared in Britain between 1750 and 1785.[72] A few of these works had high literary ambitions, like Robert Orme's *History of the Military Transactions of the British Nation in Indostan*, whose first volume appeared in 1763; most served polemical purposes. The newspaper press came to be filled with material about India. An examination of London newspapers for the year 1772 concludes that India had become 'part of the daily newspaper diet' of those with access to the press.[73] By 1780 it was thought that:

We find many individuals also who are very considerably versed in Indian affairs from conversation, correspondence, reading and reflection: and in truth these matters have of late years become so much the subject of public attention that almost every one has gained a sufficient knowledge of the history, manners and politics of that country.[74]

By the early 1770s most politicians and much of the politically involved public seem to have accepted there could be no retreat from empire in India.[75] In seconding the motion of thanks for the king's speech at the

---

[69] G. B. Hill and L. F. Powell, eds., *Boswell's Life of Johnson*, 6 vols. (Oxford, 1934), I. 455fn.

[70] See below, pp. 208–10.

[71] To Shelburne, 17 July 1773, W. S. Taylor and J. H. Pringle, eds., *The Correspondence of William Pitt, Earl of Chatham*, 4 vols. (1838–40), IV. 284–5.

[72] Listed and assessed in Frank Van Aalst, 'The British View of India, 1750–85', University of Pennsylvania Ph.D. thesis, 1970.

[73] J. R. Osborn, 'India, Parliament and the Press under George III: A Study of English Attitudes Towards the East India Company and Empire in the Late Eighteenth and Early Nineteenth Centuries', Oxford University D.Phil. thesis, 1999, p. 95; see also J. P. Thomas, 'The British Empire and the Press, 1763–1774', Oxford University D.Phil. thesis, 1982.

[74] *Thoughts on Improving the Government of the British Territorial Possessions in the East Indies* (1780), pp. 49–50.

[75] Opinions about the value of empire in India at this time are perceptively analysed by M. E. Yapp, ' "The Brightest Jewel": The Origins of a Phrase' in Kenneth Ballhatchet and John Harrison, eds., *East India Company Studies: Papers Presented to Sir Cyril Philips* (Hong Kong, 1986), pp. 31–67.

beginning of the new parliamentary session in November 1772, an otherwise obscure MP, William Burrell, wished that it had 'never been in our power to use these words "our Indian empire" ' and that 'the wealth of Bengal had never been wrung from the hands of its innocent possessors'. Nevertheless, he recognized that it was now too late for such regrets.

When we recollect the riches brought from the East Indies, the duties and excises on the imports, and what will be the fatal consequence of the annihilation of them, let every creditor of the public think and tremble . . . [L]et every one recollect, how intimately his fortune and estate, his comfort, and if I may so call them, his innocent luxuries, are connected with this vast object of trade.[76]

A pamphleteer tried to quantify what was at stake. He believed that the 'consequences of dominion' in India, which he too regarded as a 'detestable tyranny', was an influx of £1,400,000 a year. Were this to be lost 'national bankruptcy' would follow. Even worse would be the 'loss of future credit, of trade and navigation, and consequently of naval power and defence'.[77] In addressing the commons, Clive characteristically put what was at stake much higher. 'INDIA yields at present a clear produce to the public and to individuals of between two and three millions sterling.'[78] In the opinion of another pamphleteer: 'We cannot now relinquish those possessions without endangering our future freedom and independency as a nation . . . [T]herefore whilst we continue to exist, we must follow the current which impells us.'[79] For yet another author, it would be

absolutely impossible to return back to our former situation with any hopes of profit, or indeed of security. We must preserve what we have acquired upon principles of self defence . . . That insatiate desire after wealth and power, which possesses every civilized nation, will not allow us to retreat; we must preserve our consequence or be trampled under foot.[80]

For Clive, the consequences of retreat would be French domination of India and that would give them 'the empire of the sea' and ultimately 'universal monarchy'.[81]

Not only was it accepted that the British parliament now had ultimate responsibility for the good government of the British provinces in India, but

[76] 26 Nov. 1772, Cobbett, ed., *Parliamentary History*, XVII. 523.
[77] *The Present State of the British Interest in India: with a Plan for Establishing a Regular System of Government in that Country* (1773), pp. 9–13; see also H. V. Bowen, *Revenue and Reform: The Indian Problem in British Politics 1757–1773* (Cambridge, 1991), pp. 22–3.
[78] *Lord Clive's Speech in the House of Commons, 30 March 1772* [1772], p. 46.
[79] *General Remarks on the System of Government in India* (1773), pp. 12, 58–9.
[80] *Observations on the Present State of the East India Company; and on the Measures to be Pursued for Assuring its Permanency and Augmenting its Commerce* (1771), pp. 5, 81.
[81] *Lord Clive's Speech*, p. 47.

there seems to have been increasing confidence in its capacity to discharge those responsibilities. India was remote and alien from Britain and therefore detailed decisions about its governance would have to be taken by the Company's servants on the spot. Nevertheless, MPs seem to have believed that they now knew enough at least to lay down principles, as in the clauses of the 1773 Regulating Act relating to the government of India. Their confidence was based on acceptance of certain stereotypes, long entrenched in European interpretations of India, but reinforced in the great flood of recent writing. The vast majority of the population of Bengal and the Carnatic was assumed to be Hindu. Hindus were supposedly a mild, weak, industrious people, deeply set in ways that had not varied in the slightest over the centuries. Their fate was to be ruled by others. In recent times they had been ruled by Muslim outsiders who had imposed a despotic regime on them with all its usual adverse effects of insecurity and consequent poverty. Conditions had deteriorated since the break-up of the Mughal empire and had become even worse since the British seized power.

The remedy was to establish a benevolent autocracy accountable to parliament which would be able to curb the excesses of Europeans and to protect the Company's provinces from Indian marauders. Representative institutions were inconceivable. Indians were totally unused to freedom. They could 'only be governed by *despotick power*', a pamphlet argued, 'and they will be *happily* governed, if that *despotic power* is constantly amenable to *impartial* justice'.[82] Lord North agreed. Indians did not want 'political freedom of which they have no idea but a quiet enjoyment of their property'.[83] The justice and the property rights which the Company's absolute government must enforce impartially were to be those to which Indians were accustomed. English law could not be introduced. 'As well might we transplant the full-grown oak to the banks of the Ganges, as dream that any part of a code, matured by the patient labours of successive judges and legislators in this island, can possibly coalesce with the customs of Bengal', wrote Harry Verelst, a reflective former governor. To attempt to do so would 'dissolve the ties of domestic life without substituting any government in their place', he added.[84] Thomas Pownall, late governor of Massachusetts, in a pamphlet on India saw the same dangers. If British justice was to '*derange the grounds of the old national customs, or the spirit of their civil morality or the orders and casts by which the people as a nation are divided . . . it will tear up all law by the roots*'.[85] These

[82] [Alexander Dalrymple], *Considerations on a Pamphlet entitled 'Thoughts on our Acquisitions in the East-Indies, particularly respecting Bengal'* (1772), pp. 21–2.
[83] 27 April 1773, BL, Egerton MS 247, f. 33.
[84] *A View of the Rise, Progress and Present State of the English Government in Bengal* (1772), pp. 134, 139.
[85] *The Right, Interest and Duty of Government as Concerned with the Affairs of the East India Company* (1773), p. 36.

views were reflected in the Regulating Act. The jurisdiction of the new royal court with its English law was to be confined to 'British subjects',[86] a term which was not yet taken to apply to the mass of the population, described in the act as 'inhabitants of India'. They were to be subject to the Company's new courts in which 'the laws of the Koran for Mahometans, and those of the Shaster with respect to Gentoos' were to be used. The provisions for these courts, drawn up by Warren Hastings and his council in Calcutta in 1772, had just been published in Britain and were referred to by the commons secret committee that was investigating the affairs of the East India Company in 1773.[87] One of Hastings's friends told him that 'you have anticipated the whole of their intended regulations'.[88] North commended them as being 'as far as I am able to judge . . . wisely adapted to the principles, notions, prejudices of that country'.[89] The separation between English law for Europeans in India, while the rest of the population was 'permitted to live according to their customs, free in all respects from constraint and oppression', was taken as a fundamental principle on which 'a mild and settled' British government was being built in India.[90]

Such rhetorical flourishes show that the language of benevolent rule, invoked for St Vincent, was being invoked for British India as well. Detestation of British crimes, perhaps most searingly expressed by John Wesley in his journal when he anticipated divine vengeance on a nation which had allowed 'devils incarnate' to commit 'such merciless cruelty' in India,[91] was giving way to expectations that reform would follow due punishment. '[L]et us endeavour', wrote Jonathan Shipley, the bishop of St Asaph, 'to wipe away the tears from the poor oppressed natives of India; and suffer them, if possible, to enjoy some taste of the legal security and civil liberty.'[92] Few thought that 'civil liberty' was even a remote possibility, but 'legal security' was presumed to be within Britain's power to confer. British government in India was as yet assumed to have a strictly limited role, providing protection and curbing abuses and thus enabling potentially rich provinces to recover under indigenous systems of government well fitted to their needs.

---

[86] 13 Geo. III, c. 63, sec. 14.

[87] 'Plan for the Administration of Justice', 15 Aug. 1772, *Reports from Committees of the House of Commons*, 12 vols. (1803–6), IV. 348–51; see also *Extract of a Letter from the Governor and Council at Fort William . . . transmitting . . . a Plan . . . for the Administration of Justice in Bengal* [1773].

[88] F. Sykes to Hastings, 8 Nov. 1773, Sophia Weitzman, *Warren Hastings and Philip Francis* (Manchester, 1929), p. 208.

[89] 27 April 1773, BL, Egerton MS 247, f. 34.

[90] John Campbell, *A Political Survey of Britain*, 2 vols. (1774), II. 615.

[91] Journals, 23 Feb., 13 Nov. 1776, *The Works of John Wesley*, 14 vols. (1872), IV. 68, 88–9.

[92] *A Sermon Preached before the Incorporated Society for the Propagation of the Gospel in Foreign Parts; . . . on Friday February 19, 1773* (1773), p. xxi.

The commons secret committee had, however, reported that even under the Mughals, 'the administration of justice was liable to great abuse and oppression' and that the courts in Bengal were 'the instruments of power rather than justice'.[93] It was assumed that Hastings's new courts would remedy those deficiencies and that the Company would collect a fixed revenue through taxation of the produce of the land without the corruption or oppression that were thought to be inseparable parts of the order which the British had inherited. Hastings's despatches very much encouraged such expectations. With beguiling if wholly misleading optimism, he stated his aim as being to 'establish fixed rates for the collections, to make the mode uniform in all parts of the province, and to provide for an equal administration of justice'.[94]

Autocracy, even if it could be portrayed as a benevolent autocracy, had thus been domesticated within the British empire. Fears about its corrupting effects on Britain were by no means wholly allayed. Nabobs continued to be hounded as agents of corruption at least until the 1790s. There seems, however, to have been a growing confidence that whatever might be the lessons of Greek and Roman history, British virtue need not be contaminated by the exercise of absolute power abroad. The British empire was thought to have arrived at 'that height of power and glory' to which Rome 'in all her grandeur did not equal'. It was, however, an empire founded upon the 'sound policy' of a people who enjoyed 'security of property and person', not, as Rome's had been, upon 'blood, plunder and rapine' or 'an ambition, that could not bear an equal in power'.[95] This was an early statement of what would become the standard argument used to still doubts about empire in Asia. A people secure in their freedom would not be corrupted, as the Romans had been, by exercising autocratic rule in Asia. Men of high principle would be chosen for service in India, who would be accountable to the law and subject to the unremitting vigilance of parliament for any deviation from rectitude.

There was also an increasing tendency to dismiss analogies with the ancient world as irrelevant.[96] The British empire was now something quite unlike any previous empire. This seems to have been the view of the greatest contemporary interpreter of ancient empires. For Gibbon, it would seem, modern empires, like that of the British, based on the commerce of a number of

[93] *Reports from Committees*, IV. 324–5.
[94] Governor and Council to Directors, 3 Nov. 1772, ibid., IV. 302.
[95] John Entick, *The Present State of the British Empire* . . . *in Europe, Asia, Africa and America*, 4 vols. (1775), I. 1.
[96] Peter N. Miller, *Defining the Common Good: Empire, Religion and Philosophy in Eighteenth-Century Britain* (Cambridge, 1994), p. 231fn.

sovereign states, had nothing in common with the Roman empire of conquest and universal monarchy.[97] The rise of empire in India, on which he was
well informed, suggesting, for instance, in a footnote to the *Decline and Fall*
that the site of Timur's last great victory in northern India 'must be situate'
near the site in 1774 of 'a British camp',[98] seems not to have perturbed him.
'Indian adventure' was one of the 'lucrative pursuits' that in retrospect he
lamented, if unconvincingly, that he had not embraced 'at the proper age'.[99]

Referring in 1769 to empire in the Atlantic, Edmund Burke pointed
out that the British empire was an 'object . . . wholly new in the
world . . . [N]othing in history is parallel to it'.[100] In 1773, in support of
his political connection's attack on state intervention in the Company, Burke
had expressed fears that 'the East-India Company, annexed as an appendage
to the British empire, rendered the whole an object of too vast a magnitude
for the capacity of any administration whatever to grasp' and that the
Company would be 'the destruction of the country'.[101] Within a few years
he was expounding maxims for governing a worldwide empire in the west
and the east. It was Britain's duty

in all soberness, to conform our government to the character and circumstances of
the several people who compose this mighty and strangely diversified mass. I never
was wild enough to conceive, that one method would serve for the whole; I could
never conceive that the natives of *Hindostan* and those of *Virginia* could be ordered
in the same manner; or that the *Cutchery* court and the grand jury of *Salem* could be
regulated on a similar plan. I was persuaded that government was a practical thing,
made for the happiness of mankind, and not to furnish out a spectacle of unity, to
gratify the schemes of visionary politicians.[102]

For Burke, an empire based on ideological propositions about Protestantism, commerce, maritime power and freedom had given way to an empire
based on the practical needs of the very diverse peoples who were now the
king's subjects.

Burke's shaft about 'visionary politicians' who envisaged the empire as a
'spectacle of unity' was aimed at his ministerial opponents. This was less than

---

[97] John Robertson, 'Gibbon's Roman Empire as a Universal Monarchy: The *Decline and Fall*
and the Imperial Idea in Early Modern Europe' in Rosamond McKitterick and Roland Quinault,
eds., *Edward Gibbon and Empire* (Oxford, 1997), pp. 249-50, 254; J. G. A. Pocock, *Barbarism and
Religion*, I, *The Enlightenment of Edward Gibbon 1737-1764* (Cambridge, 1999), pp. 106-14.
[98] Ch. LXV, fn. 26.
[99] *The Autobiography of Edward Gibbon* (Oxford, 1978), p. 163.
[100] 'Observations on a Late State of the Nation', Paul Langford, ed., *Speeches and Writings of
Edmund Burke*, II, *Party, Parliament and the American Crisis 1766-1774* (Oxford, 1981) p. 194.
[101] 5 April 1773, ibid. pp. 391-2.
[102] 'Letter to the Sheriffs of Bristol', Warren M. Elofson and John A. Woods, eds., *Speeches and
Writings of Edmund Burke*, III, *Party, Parliament and the American War 1774-1780* (Oxford, 1996),
pp. 316-17.

fair. Those who exercised power from George Grenville to lord North had shown themselves to be willing to vary patterns of rule to suit what they perceived to be varied needs. Strict upholders of imperial uniformity were to be found in a very different quarter, that is among the militant asserters of colonial rights in North America together with their British sympathisers. Their principle of uniformity was that of English liberty. James Otis's hopes for the 'British empire' were 'that that vast empire may be prospered and extended till all men shall become truly free and rejoice in that liberty [by] which God has made them free'.[103] In such an empire there could be no compromises with any deviation from the strict ideals of English liberty. Even the Scots were deeply suspect, especially to the Virginians. For William Lee 'the principles' of 'that accursed country' threatened the liberty of both England and America.[104] He envisaged a future for the colonies in which 'the lowest cow-herds in Scotland will be your task masters in every department, and for them you will be worse than hewers of wood and drawers of water'.[105] French Catholics of course had no part in such an empire. To London radicals, the British government was emulating James II in its concessions to the French Catholics in Grenada.[106] In the Declaration of Independence George III was accused through the Quebec Act of 'abolishing the free system of English laws in a neighbouring province, establishing therein an arbitrary government'. For Americans, dominion in India could not be part of a free British empire, nor could Indians be members of it. John Dickinson thanked God that 'we are not Sea Poys, nor Marattas, but *British subjects* who are born to liberty, who know its worth, and who prize it high'.[107] In the later stages of the war some Americans came to envisage Indians as allies against British tyranny. Haidar Ali of Mysore became a cult figure: Philadelphia merchants named a warship after him.

To many Americans and to British radicals the increasing diversity of patterns of governance, of laws and of religions within the British empire was a deeply disturbing development. It signified to them that a corrupt British elite had rejected the eternal truths of Protestant freedom and was cultivating despotism and Popery in their place. The threat to liberty in England and America was, they thought, only too clear.

Such fears were very far-fetched. Those entrusted with power over what was now a complex empire were probably assimilationist by instinct but felt

[103] To D. De Berdt, 8 Sept. 1766, Lee Family Papers, University of Virginia microfilm 1714.
[104] To F. Lee, 7 Sept. 1774, HUHL, bMS Am 811. 1 (25).
[105] To R. C. Nicholas, 6 March 1775, W. C. Ford, ed., *Letters of William Lee*, 3 vols. (New York, 1891), I. 142.
[106] O'Shaughnessy, *Empire Divided*, pp. 125–6.
[107] Cited in Arthur. M. Schlesinger, *The Colonial Merchants and the American Revolution 1763–1776* (New York, 1918), pp. 275–6.

themselves obliged to pursue pragmatic strategies to ensure the empire's survival. Toleration of religious diversity, including Popery, Islam, Hinduism, a plurality of laws and systems of autocratic government were the necessary price of an expanding empire. Maintaining an expanding empire was the price of Britain's national security.

Yet far fetched as the apprehensions of the radicals undoubtedly were, they were not entirely without some foundation. As the previous chapter tried to show, there was a deep ideological divide between mainstream British opinion and those who asserted the rights of colonial America. What was in contention was the interpretation of a common constitution and of the rights appropriate to Englishmen. As this divide became patently unbridgeable with the outbreak of fighting in 1775, the British government turned to ultra-loyal Scots, to Irish Catholics, to French Canadians, to Native Americans, and even to some Africans as allies against those who claimed to be their fellow Englishmen.[108] The ideal of empire built on communities enjoying British freedoms had certainly not been renounced. It was to survive 1783, to be restated for the new Canadian colonies and to be enshrined in the early British Commonwealth. Nevertheless, the British were showing that they were willing to absorb into an empire diverse peoples, assumed to be unfit or at least not yet ready to be treated as British. What they could not absorb were some two million fellow Britons claiming equality with them and apparently challenging their interpretations of what it meant to be British.

[108] See below, pp. 339–43.

7
The Making of Empire, I: India, New Imperial Structures 1765–1783

THE previous chapter dealt with British expectations and apprehensions about a new empire in India and with the discussion of the principles that contemporaries felt should be applied to rule in India. This chapter is concerned with the shaping of a new apparatus of rule for India, both at home and in India itself.

During the Seven Years War and in its aftermath, culminating in the Bengal *diwani* grant of 1765, the East India Company won extensive territorial rights from Indian rulers in south-east and in eastern India. Private British individuals or corporations had in the past often exercised dominion over land and people overseas. Some still did so as proprietors of North American colonies or as directors of the Hudson's Bay Company, and private colonizing ventures were to continue, as in Sierra Leone from 1787. The scale—contemporaries came to estimate the population of Bengal as at least twenty million—and the obvious national importance of the new acquisitions in India, however, quickly made the continued vesting of these acquisitions in a private body seem highly anomalous. The state clearly had a vital interest in them. Yet the East India Company was to remain as ruler of British India until into the second half of the nineteenth century. Lord North, as the king's minister in 1773, expressed a wish to take the Company's territories under the authority of the state, but he was deterred from trying to do so. Ten years later, Charles Fox introduced legislation to authorize what would have amounted to a state take-over. His bill and his government were defeated.

The Company survived as a territorial ruler, developing its own administrative systems at home and abroad, pursuing its own foreign policy in relations with other Asian powers and creating an army comparable in size to the forces of the crown. It thus acquired the attributes of an autonomous imperial power in its own right. Yet its autonomy was restricted in certain crucial respects. The British state acquired powers that enabled it to shape policy-making at home and to a lesser degree in India. In particular, the defence of British interests in Asia against European rivals passed under state direction. The Company thus developed as a subordinate instrument for carrying out imperial purposes rather than as an autonomous member of the British empire. The degree of effective subordination that the British state was able to impose on the East India Company was in marked contrast with its failure at the same time to impose effective subordination to imperial interests on the American colonies.

I

Whatever might be the terms of the grants made to them by Indian rulers, the Company's servants generally acted on the assumption that they enjoyed sovereign power over what they thought of as the Company's provinces. Their views were disseminated in Britain. In a pamphlet of 1764 Clive stated that the Company had 'absolute power' over Bengal and its subordinate provinces,[1] while Warren Hastings told the house of commons in 1767 that the nawabs of Bengal had exercised the powers of a sovereign and that 'we must now be considered as the masters and governing power of the country'.[2] Such propositions seem rarely to have been questioned by British opinion.

Defining the state's right to these new Indian territories and its role in their governance was to be a long and complex process. In 1757, the crown law officers, Charles Yorke and Charles Pratt (later lord Camden), had made a nice if unworkable distinction between property rights over territory granted by Indian rulers, which, they said, belonged to the Company, subject to the king's sovereignty over 'the settlements as English settlements and over the inhabitants as English subjects', and territory acquired by the crown's subjects by conquest, which was clearly vested in the crown.[3] This verdict did not resolve the question that became crucial after news reached Britain of the grant of the *diwani* of Bengal in 1765: did the revenues of Bengal, thought to be likely to yield a clear surplus of over £2 million, belong to the Company or, in a phrase now widely used, 'to the public'? Too much was at stake for claims not be made on behalf of the public. William Pitt, now earl of Chatham, as the king's chief minister in 1766 was determined to obtain a substantial share of the revenue for the state in order to resolve what he saw as Britain's dire postwar financial problems. India, he wrote, had become 'a transcendent

---

[1] *A Letter to the Proprietors of the East India Stock from Lord Clive* (1764), p. 37.
[2] Evidence, 31 March 1767, OIOC, D. 1018/1, pp. 34–5.
[3] Cited in Huw V. Bowen, 'A Question of Sovereignty? The Bengal Land Revenue Issue, 1765–67', *Journal of Imperial and Commonwealth History*, XVI (1988), 163. The article is an admirable discussion of the issues.

object' that 'possesses my heart and fixes my thoughts' and through the resources that he would gather from it he intended 'to fix the ease and pre-eminence of England for ages'.[4] George III fully shared these hopes. '[T]he real glory of this nation', he wrote, depended on the wealth of India, which offered 'the only safe method of extracting this country out of its lamentable situation owing to the load of debt it labours under'.[5]

Like virtually everybody else, however, Chatham recognized that simply to expropriate the Company was not an option. The British state did not have the means directly to assume the administration of Indian provinces and the anticipated surplus from India could only be transferred to Britain through a favourable balance of trade. On both counts, therefore, the Company must remain in being. Chatham's preferred course of action seems to have been to refer the issue of right to parliament and then, assuming that the decision went his way and the right was declared to lie with the state, to determine how much could be extracted from the Company, while leaving it sufficient for the defence and administration of its provinces and for a reasonable commercial profit.

Imposing the ministry's will on the East India Company was to prove no simple matter. Dealing with the Company was not unlike dealing with an American colony. It enjoyed chartered privileges and its equivalent of a colonial assembly, its general court of shareholders, was tenacious in the defence of those privileges. The Company proved to have more friends in parliament than the Americans did. Few doubted that the Company, whose charter since 1698 had depended on parliamentary enactments, must ultimately yield to the wishes of a sovereign parliament. Coercing a chartered body was, however, always a delicate matter. Perhaps paradoxically in view of his firm stand on the right to tax America, George Grenville urged that 'every man who wishes to preserve the publick faith and private property free from violation' should rally to support the Company against Chatham.[6] The sanctity of chartered rights was a cry to be raised repeatedly against those who trespassed upon the Company on other occasions. Moreover, welcome as was the prospect of relief, the vastness of the sums supposed to be involved in the new revenues to be derived from India caused disquiet. An executive with such resources at its disposal might pass out of parliamentary control. Grenville warned the commons that there might one day be a minister 'wicked and base enough' to advise the king to use the Indian revenues for

---

[4] To C. Townshend, 2 Jan. 1767, WLCL, Townshend MSS, 296/3/35.
[5] To Grafton, 9 Dec. 1766, J. Fortescue, ed., *Correspondence of King George III 1760–1783*, 6 vols. (1927–8), I. 423–4.
[6] To Richard Clive, 19 Dec. 1766, BL, Add MS 57826, f. 96.

his own purposes.[7] With the government split and the opposition supporting the Company, the Chatham ministry had to shift to a strategy of a negotiated settlement that would leave issues of right undecided. In 1767 the Company conceded that it would make an annual payment of £400,000 to the state, while retaining full control over its new territory and revenues.

Although the question of sovereignty had not been settled and was not definitively to be resolved until 1813, the predominant assumption quickly came to be that the Company's acquisitions did belong ultimately to the British state, although the Company should be left to manage them on the state's behalf. In 1768 William Knox referred to the Indian provinces as 'British colonies', whose inhabitants were 'British subjects'.[8] In the words of Thomas Pownall, an established theorist of the Atlantic empire, the crown had delegated its sovereign rights in India to the Company.[9] In debates in the commons in 1772 and 1773 the Company was variously described as 'trustees for the state',[10] 'the representatives of the state'[11] or 'farmers to the publick'.[12] In 1773 the house of commons resolved that all acquisitions of territory, whether by conquest or by treaty with a foreign power, belonged to the state.[13] Yet it still seemed no more practical than it had been in 1766 for the state to take over the direct management of its property and, for those who feared the great accession of influence to the crown that would come from Indian wealth and patronage, it was no more desirable. In 1772 lord Rockingham, leader of the main opposition group, professed to believe that 'the lucrative offices and appointments' controlled by the Company would 'at least equal' all the patronage at present at the crown's disposal 'in army—navy—and revenue, church &c.'[14] Such an accession of crown patronage would be a dire threat to the independence of parliament.

Whatever objections might be made against state intervention in the affairs of the Company, India was becoming too important to be left solely to the directors and shareholders. The national government felt compelled to assert its active interest in what was happening in India. For all the great prospects

[7] 14 April 1767, P. D. G. Thomas, ed., 'The Parliamentary Diaries of Nathaniel Ryder, 1764–7', *Camden Miscellany*, XXIII (1969), 339.

[8] *The Present State of the Nation: Particularly with Respect to its Trade, Finances &c.* (1768), pp. 40–1.

[9] *The Right, Interest and Duty of Government as Concerned in the Affairs of the East India Company* (1773), p. 30.

[10] J. Burgoyne, 13 April 1772, W. Cobbett, ed., *The Parliamentary History of England from the Norman Conquest in 1066 to the year 1803*, 36 vols. (1806–20), XVII. 457.

[11] Sir W. Meredith, 10 May 1773, BL, Egerton MS 246, f. 118.

[12] North, 9 March 1773, cited Bowen, 'A Question of Sovereignty?', 171.

[13] *Journals of the House of Commons*, XXXIV (1772–4), 308.

[14] To [C. Turner, 1772], cited in W. M. Elofson, *The Rockingham Connection and the Second Founding of the Whig Party* (Montreal and Kingston, 1996), p. 152.

of wealth, in the years after the acquisition of the *diwani*, the new empire seemed to be a precarious thing beset with dangers. It was rooted in an entirely alien population, about whose institutions and ways of life British people knew virtually nothing. Within the Company's new provinces, acquiescence in foreign rule could by no means be guaranteed. British arms had won spectacular victories, which gave the Company's servants an overweening confidence in their military prowess, but territorial empire was drawing the British into conflicts with other Indian powers whose metal they had yet to test. There was a worrying prospect that the Company might become involved in interminable wars of uncertain outcome and enormous cost against formidable enemies such as Mysore or the Marathas. There could be little doubt that the French would intervene in future conflicts with Indian powers and they were likely to launch attacks on their own account.

The apparent revival of French ambitions in Asia was of obvious concern to the national government. So too was the commercial viability of the Company, on which a significant slice of the public revenue, customs and duties on tea as well as the annual £400,000, depended. The fragility of eastern empire was exacerbated by the complex role that the East India Company had assumed in becoming a military power and the ruler of territory as well as remaining a trading corporation enjoying a monopoly. This fusing of functions seemed to offer great potential benefits for Britain. The taxation that the Company was able to levy from its new provinces should greatly augment its trading capital, leading, it was hoped, to a much increased flow of commodities as a tribute to Britain. But there were also dangers from the fusion of military and political power with commerce. Were the costs of governing and above all of defending an empire to exceed what could be extracted from it, the Company's trade would suffer and it would eventually face bankruptcy at home as its Indian deficits were passed back to Britain. The failure of so huge a financial and commercial body would, it was feared, have catastrophic effects on the national economy. Were the Company to get into serious financial difficulties, as it was soon to do, not only would it default on what it owed the state and demand state aid, but it would probably drag down the whole system of commercial credit in Britain with it.

By 1772 it became clear that the Company was indeed in deep financial trouble. The problems that brought on the crisis seemed to have been caused by chronic mismanagement in India exacerbated by irresponsible conduct by the directors at home. The Company could not sell the great stocks of Chinese tea which it had accumulated. The anticipated flow of wealth from the new territorial acquisitions, above all from Bengal, was not materializing and in bad years deficits in India caused by heavy spending on war were being transferred to Britain by bills of exchange drawn by its servants on the

Company in London. At the same time, dividends were still being paid at an unrealistically high level. In 1771 the directors learnt that in the next three years they would have to meet bills for over £1,500,000. The following year they had to petition for a loan of £1,400,000 from the state to stave off bankruptcy.

Even if vital national interests had not been at stake, the way in which Indian affairs were presented to the public gave rise to powerful pressures for parliamentary intervention on the grounds that Britain's national honour was at stake. Factional disputes that convulsed the East India Company, as men struggled for power over the Company, both in India itself and in Leadenhall Street, were fought out with full publicity in the press. Allegations and counter allegations were bandied about the way in which individuals had exploited power in India to the detriment both of the Company and of the population of its provinces. Both certainly appeared to have suffered grievously. Madras had been crippled by an unsuccessful war from 1767 to 1769 and Bengal was being devastated by famine, while returned nabobs flaunted their great fortunes. Sensibilities outraged by the reported treatment of the St Vincent Caribs or native North Americans, were aroused by stories of crimes against indigenous people seemingly on a colossal scale. After his return to Bengal in 1765 Robert Clive had denounced the corruption that he found in the service in scathing terms. When he came back to England, he faced a barrage of counter-accusations about how he had acquired his great wealth. There was much public clamour for punishment and for measures to prevent further abuses.

A select committee of the house of commons was set up in 1772 to investigate abuses in India. A secret committee followed in 1773 to probe into the way in which the Company conducted its affairs at home and in India. The case for parliamentary regulation both to stabilize the Company and to try to curb and punish abuses in India seemed irrefutable. Reform of the Company was the inevitable price of state financial aid that was the only way out of its financial difficulties and of its apparent failings at home and abroad. When resolutions condemning Clive were moved in the commons in May 1773, Lord North endorsed them. 'The publick', in his view, 'had a right to call to account all persons civil and military.' There needed to be 'some regulations aim'd I confess against sudden ways of making fortunes, with some other regulations, calculated if possible to bring offenders to justice'.[15] The Regulating Act which North introduced in 1773 included such provisions, chiefly the setting up of a royal court in Calcutta to try European offenders together with prohibitions on the practices assumed to have led to

---

[15] 10 May, 28 May 1773, BL, Egerton MSS 246, f. 170; 249, ff. 87–8.

the making of great fortunes: the taking of presents through corrupt dealings with Indians and the exploitation of political power in abusive private trading by Company servants.

Reforms of the Company's electoral practices, aimed at bringing stability to the direction of its affairs, were also included in the Act. Limits were put on the number of shareholders who could vote and the directors were given a four-year term of office rather than having to submit to annual re-election. The motives for such changes had some affinity with designs to strengthen the position of the governors and councils in American colonies. As the executive authority at home over British India, the directors were to become a more stable body, less subject to the pressures of the shareholders, regarded as irresponsible and likely to be dominated by partisan interests, such as those who hoped for quick profits from unsustainably high dividends or from a share of the wealth being made by servants in India. The Regulating Act also aimed to produce a stronger executive in India itself. At least in Bengal, the highest power would no longer be exercised by a council of men whom the accident of seniority had brought to the top of the Company's service. A governor general and supreme council, consisting of five men personally named in the Act, was established at Calcutta to govern British Bengal and it was given some supervisory powers over the other presidencies of Bombay and Madras.[16] Warren Hastings, already the Company's governor of Bengal since 1772 was confirmed as governor general. He was to fill the office for another twelve highly contentious years, beating off the determined opposition of the three new councillors sent out from Britain under the Act and leaving a lasting mark both on the way in which the Company administered Bengal and on how it conducted relations with other Indian powers.

In 1773 lord North spoke of 'such continual excesses, such frauds at home, oppressions abroad, that all the world may cry out, let it go to the crown'. That for him was the best solution and it was his 'open purpose' to bring it about 'directly or indirectly'. What was 'so ill administered by directors so incapable of governing it' must be 'better administered by the crown'.[17] Yet he had already committed the government to leaving 'the territorial possessions lately obtained in India' under the management of the Company for up to six more years.[18] A state take-over would have been in the highest degree politically hazardous and was administratively impractical: the existing

[16] The standard accounts of relations between the state and the Company, culminating in the Regulating Act are those in L. S. Sutherland, *The East India Company in Eighteenth-Century Politics* (Oxford, 1952), chs. viii, ix and H. V. Bowen, *Revenue and Reform: The Indian Problem in British Politics 1757–1773* (Cambridge, 1991), chs. 8–11.

[17] 28 May 1773, BL, Egerton MS 249, ff. 84–6.

[18] Bowen, *Revenue and Reform*, p. 162.

bureaucracy for managing colonial business was in no way fit to assume
governmental responsibilities for India. Reform of the Company not its
replacement by the state was therefore the principle of the Regulating Act.

Reforms included the provision that Company would have to submit to
regular inspection of its affairs in future. Its incoming dispatches were to be
sent to the secretary of state's office and to the treasury.[19] Lord North
concluded, however, that the main burden of supervision would be born by
parliament, which with its committees of inquiry and willingness to legislate
had assumed a role in the eastern empire at least as intrusive as that which it
was playing in America. North believed that 'We must look upon ourselves as
engaged in a business likely to hold out long. There must be a constant
inspection of the parliament over the conduct of the Company.'[20] George III
agreed with him. Only 'constant inspection from parliament' could save the
Company.[21]

II

In spite of the reforms enacted in the Regulating Act, the East India Company still seemed to be a body singularly ill-equipped to cope with the
responsibilities of empire with their attendant hazards. Indian policy continued to be made by the Company's directors, a body predominantly of
London businessmen, elected by and answerable to those who happened to
have invested in East India stock, often, it was assumed, for narrowly interested purposes. The internal politics of the Company might now be less
volatile, but the directors could still be overruled at the whim of the shareholders. Continuity of Indian policy could not therefore be guaranteed. The
orders of the directors were executed in India by the servants of the Company
chosen, apart from the new supreme council in Bengal, by the patronage of
the directors. In as far as the servants had any professional qualifications, they
were those of merchants buying and selling on the Company's behalf, not of
administrators of territorial domains. The Regulating Act had provisions to
deter abuses, but it seemed likely that many servants would still be set on
personal enrichment rather than committed to the prudent management of a
great national asset. It was assumed that the directors would have little
inclination to curb fortune-making by their own protégés, even if it was at
the Company's expense.

[19] 13 Geo. III, c. 63, sec. 9.   [20] 9 March 1773, BL, Egerton MS, 244, f. 296.
[21] To North, 11 June 1773, Fortescue, ed., *Correspondence of King George III*, II. 501.

A crisis in the Company's affairs in the early 1780s, very similar to that of 1772–3, suggested that the Regulating Act's reforms had achieved little. An exasperated George III lamented in 1781 that 'the whole conduct of the Company both at home and abroad must end in utter destruction if not greatly changed'.[22] The directors appeared to have lost control over the servants in India, who indulged in bitter faction fighting and involved the Company in expensive wars against Indian powers in some of which the British were spectacularly worsted. The costs of war crippled the finances of the Indian presidencies. Bills were again drawn on London for large amounts. The Company again had to seek state aid. New reforms through parliamentary intervention were again proposed. Edmund Burke, by now well embarked on his long involvement in Indian affairs, came to the conclusion that the Company by 1783 had become 'totally perverted from the purpose of its institution'. It was 'utterly incorrigible' and therefore must be deprived of all its power over India.[23] He incited Charles Fox to sponsor Indian legislation that would have done precisely that.

The Company was saved by the king's determination to destroy the Fox–North coalition government by effectively vetoing the bill in the house of lords and by the deep unpopularity of that government that kept its replacement, the administration of the younger Pitt, in office at the subsequent election in 1784. Fox had been endlessly portrayed as bent on appropriating the wealth and patronage of India for party political purposes. Thereafter, no British government was willing to risk a direct assault on the right of the Company to govern India and thus to expose itself to similar accusations.

The Company owed its escape to a great political upheaval for which Fox's bill was no more than the pretext and it survived as a territorial power because it seemed to be too dangerous to attempt directly to replace it. Yet for all the difficulties that it was encountering in the early 1780s, incentives to replace the Company were weakening. In the years after the Regulating Act it was developing capacities that were turning it into an acceptable mechanism for ruling an empire. At the same time, a pattern of relations with the state was evolving which enabled the national government to intervene effectively in the direction of Indian affairs without taking direct powers over them.

Company politics remained turbulent after the Regulating Act with the shareholders on occasions frustrating intentions of the directors which had the backing of the government. An attempt to force Warren Hastings to leave India was, for instance, countermanded by a huge majority among the

---

[22] To North, 5 Aug. 1781, ibid. V. 261.
[23] 'Speech on Fox's India Bill', P. J. Marshall, ed., *The Writings and Speeches of Edmund Burke*, V, *India: Madras and Bengal 1774–1785* (Oxford, 1981), p. 440.

shareholders in 1782.[24] The Company's leadership seems, however, to have been generally of a higher quality than it had been when it was pilloried during the crisis of 1772. Men with a genuine engagement with the effective government of India gained control. Laurence Sulivan, veteran of the Seven Years War, returned to the direction and became chairman again at the height of the American War.

Continuity in attempts to supervise the government of India from home was coming to be provided by the officials employed by the Company at its India House in Leadenhall Street as much as by the directors themselves. The directors did most of their work in committees served by a staff of secretaries and clerks, of a quality recognized to be at least on a par with those who were employed in the major government offices.[25] The system of committees and departments seems to have been extended relatively easily to embrace administrative and military matters as well as commerce. The committee of correspondence and the new office of the examiner of Indian correspondence greatly expanded the range of their activities, drafting the dispatches on diplomacy, war, revenue or civil administration which went out to India in the name of the directors.[26] In wartime, the chairman and his deputy were the essential members of a committee of secrecy which dealt with the government, as in the previous war. The Company had developed a system of record- and account-keeping which drew praise even from Burke. He commended 'a discipline and order which no state should be ashamed to copy. It is perhaps the best contrivance that ever has been thought of by the wit of men for the government of a remote, large disjointed empire.' The directors insisted on 'a minuteness and strictness of correspondence which no state has ever used with regard to its public ministers' abroad.'[27] The elaborate records kept by the Company left it unusually accountable to scrutiny by parliamentary inquiry.

It had been assumed in 1773 that regular parliamentary inquiries would ensure that the Company remained accountable to the public. Parliamentary involvement with India was in fact to be fitful until the crisis years of 1781 to 1783, when house of commons select and secret committees again subjected the Company to very close scrutiny as they had done in 1772–3. By then intervention by the government was taking effect largely through the development of an informal system of 'management' that was to be an enduring

[24] Sutherland, *East India Company*, pp. 389–90.   [25] Ibid. pp. 74–5.

[26] H. V. Bowen, ' "No Longer Mere Traders:" Continuities and Change in the Metropolitan Development of the East India Company, 1600–1834' in Bowen, Margarette Lincoln and Nigel Rigby, eds., *The Worlds of the East India Company* (Woodbridge, 2002), pp. 27–32.

[27] Opening of Impeachment, 15 Feb. 1788, P. J. Marshall, ed., *The Writings and Speeches of Edmund Burke*, VI, *India: The Launching of the Hastings Impeachment 1786–1788* (Oxford, 1991), p. 296.

feature of the Company's future relations with the state. The court of directors, now insulated to some degree from the pressures of the share-holders, was being subjected to an increasing degree of government 'man-agement'. Ministers were able to build up considerable followings among the voting shareholders so as to enable them to influence elections in favour of directors who would ally with government. During the 1770s management of the Company became a major preoccupation of the treasury, the government department which transacted other political business, with the aim, as the most assiduous treasury manager put it, of guiding the Company 'towards publick principle and a regular plan'.[28] Men on the supreme council in Bengal remained the servants of the Company, accountable to it, but they were well aware that they owed their appointments to ministers. They developed private channels of correspondence with members of the govern-ment in addition to their dispatches to the directors, to which ministers now officially had access.

Well before the passing of the Regulating Act, one issue above all others had compelled ministers to concern themselves with the Company's affairs and to try to influence its policies. That issue was the defence of the Company's stake in India from European enemies, in effect from France. During the Seven Years War the government had accepted the Company's pleas that its Asian trade was an object of prime national importance that required naval and military protection from the forces of the crown during European wars. The Company was largely dependent on the Royal Navy to counter any European enemy at sea, while the government preferred to send out royal regiments to India rather than permit unrestricted recruiting in Britain for the Company's own European troops. During the Seven Years War considerable forces had been dispatched to be used largely as the Company determined. At the end of the war, the terms of the peace in Asia had been negotiated by the British government as part of the overall settle-ment with France.

The warships and the royal troops were withdrawn after the peace in 1763, but ministers now clearly regarded the defence of India as a continuing national commitment. They were in no doubt that an attack on Britain's position in India was a part of French designs to reverse the result of the late war. The nature of the French threat was soon identified. Forces would be built up at Île de France (Mauritius) and Île de Bourbon (Réunion), bases about which intelligence was particularly hard to obtain. From the islands, troops would be held ready to move into Pondicherry, whose fortifications were being restored, or even to Chandernagore in Bengal, which the French

---

[28] Sutherland, *East India Company*, pp. 274–80; for quotation from John Robinson, see p. 280.

were bound to leave unfortified. Bombay was thought to be particularly vulnerable to direct attack. Any movement of French troops to India would, it was assumed, be undertaken in coordination with one or more of the Indian powers who might wish to see the overthrow of the British.[29] There were many reports of French contacts with Indian rulers. Assessments of the extent of the danger varied, but could be alarmist, as, for instance, when lord Sandwich, first lord of the admiralty, speculated in 1772 that had war broken out then, 'we should have lost the East Indies' before naval reinforcements could arrive.[30]

In the years of peace, relations between the government and the Company over the defence of India were more fraught than they had been in the Seven Years War, when ministers had largely responded to requests for aid from the secret committee of the directors by putting royal forces virtually at the Company's disposal. In 1768, however, when concern about the French strength at Mauritius became acute, ministers took the initiative. They turned the Company's arguments about the national importance of India against the Company itself. In neglecting the defence of India, the Company was failing the nation. The Bengal council was censured for apparently allowing the French to transgress the terms of the peace in their province.[31] The directors shared ministers' anxieties, but governments had no confidence in their capacity to respond effectively to any threat. They believed that the directors were withholding information from them and that their servants' mismanagement of relations with Indian rulers was exacerbating the danger. India was 'an object of the greatest national importance and . . . the servants of the Company, both at home and abroad, are too much taken up with partial and selfish schemes, to admit that liberal and enlarged consideration of Indian affairs which includes the good of the whole.'[32]

Support would no longer be unconditional. In return for naval or military assistance the Company must concede a role for representatives of the crown in India, not only in directing military dispositions but in diplomacy with European and Indian powers. This issue came to a head in the summer of

---

[29] For French strategies, see Sudipta Das, *Myths and Realities of French Imperialism in India 1763–83* (New York, 1992); S. P. Sen, *The French in India, 1763–1816*, 2nd edn. (New Delhi, 1971); B. E. Kennedy, 'Anglo-French Rivalry in India and the Eastern Seas 1763–93: A Study of Anglo-French Tensions and their Impact on the Consolidation of British Power in the Region', Australian National University, Ph.D. thesis, 1969.

[30] To North, 10 Sept. 1772, G. R. Barnes and J. H. Owen, eds., *The Private Papers of John, Earl of Sandwich, First Lord of the Admiralty 1771–1782*, 4 vols. (1932–8), I. 24. Nicholas Tracy, *Navies, Deterrence and American Independence: Britain and Seapower in the 1760s and 1770s* (Vancouver, 1988) is the fullest account of British counter-measures; see also H. W. Richmond, *The Navy in India, 1763–1783* (1931), chs. 1, 2.

[31] Shelburne to Directors, 27 Jan. 1768, OIOC, H/99, pp. 1–3.

[32] Secret Instructions to J. Lindsay, 13 Sept. 1769, OIOC, H/101, pp. 127–8.

1769, when after two Royal Navy frigates had been promised for India, some shareholders called for ships of the line and for two battalions of regular infantry.[33] The secretary of state, lord Weymouth, countered with a demand that the officer in command of the king's ships should have 'plenipotentiary' powers in dealing with Indian rulers. The Company refused to transfer control over Indian diplomacy from its servants to any agent of the crown. The outcome of a prolonged wrangle was to give the commander of the squadron no more than a share in determining policies that might involve the royal forces in war. He and his successor were, however, frozen out of any effective participation in shaping the company's diplomacy with Indian powers and the claims to plenipotentiary authority on behalf of the senior naval officer in India were dropped in 1773.[34]

A bold attempt to assert direct ministerial authority in India had been beaten off, but close government involvement in the defence of India was to grow. Ministers increasingly took their own decisions about India's naval defence, as well as reacting to the appeals of the directors. Four warships were dispatched in 1771 to remain in India until 1774, when they were replaced by a smaller force. With the intervention of the French in the War of the American Revolution, the squadron in Indian waters was greatly reinforced until the admiral had eighteen ships under his command in the last battle of the war in 1783.

The Company's military dependence on the forces of the crown in the event of a European war was also becoming clear. It was axiomatic that a strong body of white troops was the essential basis of the Company's security. At the lowest, the directors were prepared to accept that there should be three battalions of European infantry (over 2,000 men) and three companies of artillery at both Madras and Bengal with a smaller force at Bombay. Others like Clive put the needs of Bengal even higher.[35] European soldiers were, however, difficult and expensive to recruit and died in huge numbers when they got to India; 'casualties' were estimated at 18 per cent a year.[36] The target military establishments were therefore never attained. In 1776 the Company complained that it needed 2,700 men to bring its Europeans up to strength, but that only 700 recruits had been obtained that year.[37] The following year, the Bombay European force was said to be so diminished as soon to be 'nearly

---

[33] General Court Minutes, 27 July 1769, OIOC, B/257, p. 284.
[34] Rochford to Harland, 6 Nov. 1773, OIOC H/112, p. 3. For the negotiations in 1769, see Bowen, *Revenue and Reform*, pp. 76–83; Sutherland, *East India Company*, pp. 194–201.
[35] 9th Report, Secret Committee, 1773, *Reports from Committees of the House of Commons*, 12 vols. (1803–6), IV. 576–8.
[36] Directors to Weymouth, 28 April 1777, OIOC, H/84, p. 65.
[37] Secret Committee, 13 Nov. 1776, ibid. p. 55.

extinct'.[38] The hostility of the regular British army to competition for recruits from the Company compounded the problem. Proposals to facilitate the Company's recruiting in Britain and on the continent were introduced in the house of commons in 1770 and 1771, but were blocked by the war office and by senior army officers.[39] Unable to maintain a European force of its own at the level that it required, the Company felt that it had no alternative but to appeal for the dispatch of royal forces to India at times of danger. Warned about the increasing proficiency of the gunnery of Indian powers, the directors asked for three companies of the royal artillery to be sent to India in 1769.[40] That proposal and other requests for royal troops in the early 1770s were rejected. On the outbreak of the war with France in 1778, the East India Company was able to eliminate the French settlements in India with its own forces, aided by the Royal Navy. A royal battalion was, however, sent to India in 1779, the first of increasingly large contingents, as the Company's Madras army suffered disastrously at the hands of Haidar Ali of Mysore in 1780 and was threatened by French expeditions and later by the hostility of the Dutch. Four more royal battalions were sent in 1781. A cavalry regiment, two British and two Hanoverian infantry battalions followed them. 'The whole European force in India thus came to compare in size with the garrison of Jamaica. Ten thousand miles from home, these troops were the force that saved the Carnatic.'[41]

III

Although the forces of the crown were regarded as essential reinforcements in time of European war, the Company greatly augmented its own armies at its Indian presidencies. Unlike the militias or the temporarily-embodied provincial regiments of the American colonies, these were permanent standing armies. The Company was also developing an elaborate civil administration, especially in Bengal, where Europeans came to be actively involved in the governance of the province. This 'civil service'[42] constituted an imperial bureaucracy unparalleled anywhere else in the contemporary British empire.

---

[38] Secret Committee, 4 June 1777, ibid. p. 69.

[39] Huw V. Bowen, 'The East India Company and Military Recruitment in Britain, 1763–71', *Bulletin of the Institute of Historical Research*, LIX (1986), 78–90.

[40] Chair and deputy to Weymouth, 13 Dec. 1769, OIOC, H/101, p. 439.

[41] Piers Mackesy, *The War for America 1775–1783* (1964), p. 495; see list on pp. 500–1.

[42] According to the canonical *Hobson-Jobson*, the term 'civilian' 'came into use about 1750–1770' (Henry Yule and A. C. Burnell, *Hobson-Jobson: A Glossary of Colloquial Anglo-Indian Words and Phrases* . . . , new edn., William Crooke, ed. (1903), p. 222.

Between the ending of the Seven Years War and the spread of the War of the American Revolution to India, the Company's three presidency armies developed on roughly similar lines. The specially recruited European infantry and artillery were regarded as the essential nucleus for each. At any time their numbers were seriously below establishment, hence the need to call for the dispatch of royal regiments in an emergency. Indian soldiers were recruited abundantly from long-established sources of military manpower. The numbers of sepoys in each of the armies rose by 1770 to 28,000 in Bengal, 18,000 in Madras, and 6,000 in Bombay.[43] New armies required a new officer corps, headed by general officers with hierarchies of commissioned ranks under them, most of them commanding Indian sepoys. There were 735 officers holding the Company's commission in the Bengal army alone in 1772 out of a total of 1,560 in all three armies.[44]

The Company's armies had been outstandingly successful in the later stages of the Seven Years War and in the campaigns in northern India that had culminated in the battle of Buxar of 1764. Their record thereafter was more equivocal. The Bombay army was to be humiliated both by Mysore and by the Marathas. The Madras army was to have serious difficulties in coping with the forces of Mysore. A pamphleteer reflected in 1769 that 'an army of 3000 Europeans and 10,000 seapoys' had recently been repulsed by Haidar Ali of Mysore, 'a black adventurer at the head of his country troops'. Yet three years ago, he added, such an army would have been thought 'equal to the reduction of Indostan'.[45] In part, the declining effectiveness of the Company's troops was recognized to be due to the rapidity with which other Indian armies were adopting European techniques. Well drilled sepoys and artillery batteries became a part of the armies of ambitious Indian rulers. Certain deficiencies were, however, attributed to the Company's forces, such as the lack of effective cavalry to counter the raiding horsemen of the Marathas or Mysore or the failure to sustain logisitic support by supply trains over long distances. Reliance on sepoys caused some anxiety. It was conventional to rate them considerably lower than white troops, although Hector Munro, a royal officer who had commanded the Bengal forces, told the house of commons in 1767 that 'sepoys properly disciplined and led on and with Europeans are good soldiers and will do any thing.'[46] It was assumed that the loyalty of the sepoys ultimately depended on prompt and regular pay. It was axiomatic that

[43] G. J. Bryant, 'The East India Company and its Army 1600–1778', London University Ph.D. thesis, 1975, appendix 1.

[44] 9th Report, Secret Committee, 1773, *Reports from Committees*, IV. 592.

[45] *An Address to the Proprietors of India Stock, shewing, from the Political State of Indostan, the Necessity of Sending Commissioners* (1769), p. 9.

[46] Evidence of 3 April 1767, OIOC, D. 1018/1, p. 37.

this must be ensured, but that a proper balance of European forces was also necessary to curb the 'dangerous insolence and turbulent spirit' of the sepoys and keep them 'in awe and subjection'.[47]

Royal officers inevitably questioned the quality of the Company's officers. Such criticism reflected a good measure of social prejudice. The Company recruited a great many young men enlisted as cadets through the directors' patronage. The value attached to a cadetship in the Company's army was much lower than that of a writership in its civilian employment. Cadets therefore tended to come from families whose standing did not enable them to hope for anything better. The Company's military service was particularly attractive to the progeny of poor Scottish gentry.[48] Most cadets were probably more committed to getting to India and its supposed riches than to the professional niceties and the cult of honour deemed essential to a military career. There was, however, no lack of brave and resourceful Company officers. Like the sepoys, the officers served for pay and were tenacious in defence of what they regarded as the established rewards of the service. They too were capable of mutiny, as they demonstrated in 1766 when Clive enforced orders on the Bengal army for reducing the long established allowances, known as 'batta', intended to be compensation for expense in the field; 173 officers resigned their commissions rather than accept the reductions. Clive managed to maintain his authority over the Bengal army and to extract submissions from virtually all those who had defied him, but the Company officers remained a body with a strong sense of corporate rights and *ésprit de corps* in protecting them.[49]

The prospect that a mercenary Company standing army, not accountable to parliament at home, might take control of British India was a recurring nightmare for those mindful of Roman history. Army officers did indeed intervene in a sinister way to arrest and depose the governor of Madras, lord Pigot, in 1776. Burke believed that what was at stake then was 'whether the *military* was to mount over the *civil*'.[50] Official Company policy was, however, invariably to keep its army subject to its civil power. Supreme power over the military was lodged in the civilian governor and council at each of the presidencies.

To British military planners a separate Company's army, in their view of a lower standard than the royal army, was increasingly to seem an anomaly. Nevertheless, the Company had at its own expense made a huge addition to

[47] 9th Report, Secret Committee, 1773, *Reports from Committees*, IV. 578.
[48] Ronald M. Sunter, *Patronage and Politics in Scotland 1707–1832* (Edinburgh, 1986), p. 9.
[49] For the Company's officers, see Gerald Bryant, 'Officers of the East India Company's Army in the Days of Clive and Hastings', *Journal of Imperial and Commonwealth History*, VI (1978), 203–27.
[50] 22 May 1777, Marshall, ed., *Writings and Speeches of Edmund Burke*, V. 39.

Britain's armed forces. The Company's armies were generally capable, with some reinforcements of royal troops, of defending British interests in India and might, as the Manila expedition of 1762 showed, be used for wider national purposes outside India. These new Indian armies were a very significant contribution, as Edmund Burke put it, to 'the aggregate strength and dignity of the British empire'.[51]

The Company's military contribution became even larger in 1781, when it yielded to the demands of the government that it must pay in full for any royal troops sent out to India. In the previous war it had done no more than to make up the pay of royal troops to the level of their own Europeans and to pay some of their 'extraordinary' expenses. For lord North in 1778, 'Nothing is more reasonable than that the E: I: Company, which is richer than the public, should defray the expence of the king's troops serving in India.' He accepted, however, that the issue should be resolved in the new settlement for the renewal of the Company's charter by act of parliament.[52] In the course of protracted negotiations, the government tried to extract payments for warships as well as troops: £30,000 a year for a 74-gun ship and less for smaller ones. The final settlement in 1781 required the Company to pay two lakhs of rupees a year in India (more than £20,000) for every thousand soldiers and to provide the stores and victualling of the fleet, for which they would be partially reimbursed at home.[53] Lord North's government had extracted from the Company a concession far more valuable than anything that had been envisaged in the Stamp Act or in any other attempt to raise a revenue for defence in America. A principle had also been established that India must pay for British troops, that was to last until the end of the Raj and to provoke much bitter controversy in the years ahead.

The Company's civil services also grew spectacularly, especially in Bengal, where by the mid-eighteenth century there were some seventy-five to eighty servants with about fifty in Madras.[54] By 1770 there were 180, rising to 247 by 1774, serving in Bengal with 112 in Madras.[55] This expansion had taken place within the framework of the existing service. To transact their largely commercial affairs, the directors nominated young men as 'writers', who rose by seniority through a series of ranks. The most senior of those who survived became members of the governing council of the presidency and the most senior of all became the governor. There was thus a hierarchy of authority

---

[51] Speech, 31 May 1779, W. M. Elofson and J. A. Woods, eds., *The Writings and Speeches of Edmund Burke*, III, *Party, Parliament and the American War 1774–1780* (Oxford, 1996), p. 442.

[52] To Weymouth, [Aug. 1778], OIOC, H/141, pp. 333–4.

[53] 21 Geo. III, c. 65, secs. 17–19. Various preliminary drafts of these clauses and comments on them can be found in OIOC, A/2/10.

[54] OIOC, L/F/10/1; L/F/10/111.   [55] OIOC, l/F/10/2; L/F/10/112.

based on seniority, although the chain of command in the Company's settlements was often subverted by the vicious factional disputes to which European communities abroad were very prone. The Company's service was relatively free of what were regarded as abuses in the public offices at home or in the Atlantic colonies: posts were not obtained by purchase or held as a form of property for life and they were executed in person, not by deputy.

War and the territorial gains which followed from war produced a great expansion of the Company's civil service. More servants were of course needed as the Company decided that Europeans should be involved in entirely new responsibilities arising from territorial dominion. Some ten years after the acquisition of the Bengal *diwani* the Company's servants were supervising the assessment and collection of taxation and the administration of justice at a local level, were running a customs service and were organizing the marketing of salt, as well as being involved in the traditional commercial work of the Company's procurement of goods for export and the sale of its imports. The expansion of civil appointments was, however, more than a response to new needs. The directors were yielding to powerful pressures exerted to create extra patronage to meet the demands for supposedly lucrative positions, above all in Bengal. The chairman from 1769 to 1773 recalled that he 'been able to gratify a great many of the first people of the kingdom, and had received applications from more. The number of letters that I received . . . was equal to that of a prime minister. My house likewise was crowded with petitioners.'[56] Warren Hastings was later to complain of 'a system charged with expensive establishments and precluded by the multitude of dependants and the curse of patronage from reformation'.[57]

Men scrambled for posts in the Company's civil service because they believed that they would get rich. In Bengal the huge distributions of money that were made when one nawab was replaced by another came to an end in 1765. But there were still abundant openings for private profit from the new official positions as the British began to intervene in the administration of the province. Company servants could, for instance, make lucrative deals with Indian revenue managers or pocket commissions on the revenue that they handled. Political power notoriously enabled private trade to move from the sea inland and for large profits to be extracted from fixing prices and eliminating competition. Inland trade by Company servants remained highly profitable, until it was curbed by prohibitions and deteriorating economic

[56] Sir George Colebrooke, *Retrospection or Reminiscences Addressed to my Son*, 2 vols. (1898), I. 196.
[57] Cited in P. J. Marshall, *East Indian Fortunes: The British in Bengal in the Eighteenth Century* (Oxford, 1976), p. 181.

conditions in the 1770s.[58] In Madras Muhammad Ali Khan survived as an autonomous ally of the Company in control of revenues of his own from which he could promise to make large payments to Company servants who would serve his interests and on the security of which he borrowed from Europeans at very high rates. Opportunities from managing the Company's revenues were more limited than in Bengal, but rich pickings could be got in the newly-acquired Northern Circars. In Bombay, there were few opportunities for turning office to profit and the European community remained dependent on sea-borne trade for its prosperity.

The scramble for private profits exacerbated the tendency to factionalism in the Company's service, as groups of servants competed with one another to control offices from which fortunes could be made. In Madras public purposes were seriously distorted by private concerns for long periods, culminating in the overthrow by force in 1776 of a governor who appeared to be challenging the most powerful of the interest groups at Madras, the creditors of the nawab of Arcot.[59] A more even balance between public and private was maintained in Bengal after the powers of the nawabs had been circumscribed in 1765. By then, however, Clive believed that hierarchy and obedience to authority had been fatally undermined in the Bengal service by the ease with which even junior officials could enrich themselves. This produced 'a licentious and levelling spirit' contrary to 'proper ideas of subordination [and] duty to their superiors'.[60] He faced mutiny among the army officers and hostility from many of the civil servants, even though he forced what he regarded as the most notorious offenders to leave India. From 1774 to 1780 Bengal was to be split by a factional divide between those who supported the governor general, Warren Hastings, and those who aligned themselves with new councillors from Britain appointed to the supreme council under the Regulating Act.

Factional rivalries were never to be eliminated from the British services in India, but they became less damaging in the 1780s and 1790s when lord Cornwallis was able to separate private profit from most offices in Bengal and largely to insulate the service from the pressures of patronage from home in a way that the politically insecure Warrren Hastings could not afford to do. The end result was a relatively disciplined imperial bureaucracy. The Madras and Bombay services, it was commonly supposed, remained unregenerate for rather longer.

Yet well before Cornwallis, in Bengal in particular, an effective administrative service was beginning to be formed from among the throng of young

[58] Ibid. pp. 147-9.   [59] See below, pp. 236-7.
[60] Bengal Public Consultations, 12 Feb. 1766, OIOC, P 1/38, ff. 53-4.

and not-so-young men on the make shipped out to India at the behest of directors or of political figures with whom the directors wished to ingratiate themselves. The prestige attached to writerships meant that social aspirations and educational standards could be quite high. Cleverness could pay dividends in Bengal. Under Warren Hastings, in particular, it paid to acquire linguistic skills and knowledge of the religions, laws and history of India. Those who did so were likely to attract the governor's attention and to be suitably rewarded with lucrative offices. The abundant writings of the Company's servants of this period often reveal a taste for theorizing about such matters as social development or political economy. There was also something of a cult of honourable public service. Men in India were eager to compare their duties with those of 'office in England' and to find them equally responsible and far more testing and complex. Indian administration was said to be

> intricate, laborious, and manifold, in as much as it comprizes all the various duties of a minister;—of civil and criminal magistracy;—of investigator of the resources of provinces;—of receiver of revenue;—of comptroller of tax, duties, and customs;— and of treasurer, &c. &c. with all the most difficult management of finance.[61]

Those who performed such tasks were engaged in 'a pursuit of honour and profit'.[62]

The East India Company had responded to the challenge of a new empire by the creation of armies and civil administrations in its presidencies on an impressive scale. The integration of the Company's new Indian imperial structure into the British empire as a whole remained, however, imperfect, if in a different way from the imperfect integration of the North American colonies. Americans openly resisted closer integration, rejecting the authority of parliament and obstructing actions of imperial agencies, such as the customs administration, which were unacceptable to them. The shareholders of the Company had also contested parliamentary authority, usually ineffectually, as when they had been overruled by a determined government that had imposed the Regulating Act on them. Thereafter, the directors, subject to vigorous government management, generally followed policies acceptable to ministers. It was, however, becoming clear that the obstacles to effective metropolitan control over empire in India lay not in a refractory Company at home, but in the intractable practical problems that beset any exercise of authority from home over men in India, either by the Company or by the state. Such men might not openly defy, but they did not necessarily obey.

---

[61] *An Appeal from the Hasty to the Deliberative Judgment of the People of England* (1787), p. 38.
[62] Ibid. pp. 28–9.

In part, the obstacles to control from home were the notorious ones of distance and ignorance. On questions of revenue or judicial administration, some directors with Indian experience might have views but most did not, while politicians before Edmund Burke or Henry Dundas in the 1780s certainly did not. On the other hand, almost everybody had views on war and peace, but events in India often moved far too fast in unexpected ways for those in command in India to receive much guidance from home. Sailing times round the Cape meant that news took about six months to reach home and even an instant response to news from India would take another six months. Military operations could not be directed from London. Nor was it possible to dictate how the Company should conduct its relations with Indian powers. All that could be attempted was to lay down certain maxims. With limited exceptions, the directors insisted in the firmest possible terms that they were fully satisfied with the possessions that they had acquired up to 1765. They wanted no more conquests and no further wars. In 1767 these principles were reiterated to the Bengal select committee: you must never 'extend your possessions beyond their previous bounds . . . nor enter into any offensive war . . . We think we discern *too great an aptness to confederacies or alliances with the Indian powers.*'[63]

Yet in the period of fifteen years between the two European wars, the Company was only at peace in India for a short time in the early 1770s. It engaged in protracted and costly wars and in much interventionist diplomacy. Those at home who followed the unfolding of events in India with mounting exasperation often concluded that the apparently incurable belligerence of the Company's servants could only be explained by corrupt motives, carefully suppressed in the dispatches sent back to London. A naval officer serving in India warned ministers that the Company's servants at Madras made 'princely fortunes from the disputes, quarrels and misunderstandings amongst the princes and other great men in India'. He thought that every conflict in which the Company engaged could be explained in such terms. 'For whether to carry on a war or to make peace, large presents are the constant custom of India.'[64] Such suspicions could be amply justified. War and the making of alliances were likely to be a profitable business for the soldiers involved and for the civil authorities who sanctioned them. Yet material self-interest is an inadequate explanation for the role in Indian politics which men of the calibre and ambition of Clive or Warren Hastings envisaged for the Company. Like so many of their successors they saw themselves as statesmen guiding the destinies of an empire according to the

---

[63] 20 Nov. 1767, Amba Prasad, ed., *Fort William–India House Correspondence (Secret and Select Committee)*, XIV, *1752–81* (Delhi, 1985), pp. 15–16.
[64] R. Harland to Rochford, 15 Feb. 1772, PRO, CO 77/22, f. 229.

lights of their own judgement, in which they had supreme confidence. They were not prepared to regard directors' injunctions as binding on them on all occasions. Once opinion in Britain had accepted 'the Plassey revolution' and the huge extension of the Company's effective rule brought about in the grant of the Bengal *diwani*, Clive could be portrayed as a figure of 'moderation' (a favourite term with him), committed to no further territorial expansion beyond Bengal and to no exertion of influence except in support of the wazir of Awadh to whom the Company was bound by treaty. Hastings's ambitious diplomacy and military interventions aroused deep misgivings in Britain. He insisted, however, that he must have an ultimate discretion on matters of state necessity. 'But though I profess the doctrine of peace', Hastings wrote at the end of his Indian career, 'I by no means pretend to have followed it with so implicit a devotion as to make sacrifices to it.' There had been occasions on 'which I should have deemed it criminal not to have hazarded both the public safety and my own in a crisis of uncommon and adequate emergency, or in an occasion of dangerous example'.[65] Such sentiments were often to be repeated in the future.

The discretion that strong-willed and self-confident men claimed to be able to exercise in India for the national good was not to be effectively regulated from Britain for a long time to come. Governors of British India were indeed somewhat like Roman proconsuls with their own armies and their own civil administrations, subject to only limited control from home. This was a prospect that an earlier generation which took pride in a maritime empire of freedom would have viewed with dread. Burke continued to sound the alarm into the 1790s. If there was no prospect of the proconsul bringing his legions to overthrow established government at home, he could still bring his wealth and that of his supporters to corrupt parliament and, even more insidiously, bring ways of thinking that were utterly alien to those of 'a free country'.[66] By then, however, few felt alarmed. A despotic administration supported by a standing army, both of them subject in the first instance to a trading company, were now an acceptable form of imperial rule.

The East India Company system had proved its durability by 1783. Empire in America had been overwhelmed by internal revolt and French intervention. Empire in India had survived a series of wars against a formidable coalition of Indian powers in which the French had also tried to intervene.

---

[65] Warren Hastings, *Memoirs Relative to the State of India*, new edn. (1787), pp. 111–12.

[66] Speech of 14 Feb. 1791, P. J. Marshall, ed., *The Speeches and Writings of Edmund Burke*, VII, *India: The Hastings Trial 1789–1794* (Oxford, 2000), p. 102.

8

The Making of Empire, II: India, Madras, Bombay and Bengal 1765–1778

THE company's new imperial system took a roughly similar pattern at each of its three presidencies, Madras, Bombay, and Bengal. Each presidency had its own service organized on the same hierarchical principle with governors and councils exercising ultimate authority. Each had commercial functions, primarily providing commodities for export. Each now maintained a considerable army of Europeans and sepoys. The commitment to a large army meant a commitment to seek revenue resources, usually the taxing of land and people, with which to fund the army. Each presidency therefore administered territory: little more than the island and a string of port settlements in Bombay; recent acquisitions around Madras itself and to the north; and two great provinces, probably containing up to twenty million people, in Bengal.

Apparent similarities can, however, be highly misleading. They suggest that the British were able to impose their own pattern of rule throughout India. This was not the case. The strength or weakness of the British position in each of the Company's presidencies depended much less on their intentions or even on the empire-building proclivities of great men, such as Clive or Hastings, than on the Indian environments in which the presidencies were situated. Early empire was built on Indian foundations, which varied greatly.

Interpretations of eighteenth-century India now stress not political and economic failure uniformly throughout the subcontinent in the wake of the collapse of the Mughal empire, but rather an uneven pattern with areas of prosperity and stable successor states as well as areas of political fragmentation and economic disruption.[1] Bengal was an area of relative economic prosperity and political stability. There the Company was able to infiltrate and take over an effectively functioning post-Mughal state built on a highly productive agriculture, much manufacturing and a sophisticated commerce.

[1] See above, pp. 121–2.

The British were less fortunate in Bombay and Madras. Any attempt to expand inland from Bombay itself to acquire revenue yielding territory was blocked by the formidable military power of the Maratha peshwas. Bombay's subordinate trading factories along the Malabar coast were hemmed in by strong state formations, by Travancore and by Mysore under Haidar Ali. Only in Gujarat where the Company had settlements in ports still nominally under Mughal governors and the hinterland was contested by the peshwas and the founders of the Maratha Gaikwad dynasty, were prospects of empire-building at all inviting. The British at Madras were not the inheritors of an established successor state but were of necessity partners in making one, the Carnatic of Muhammad Ali Khan, nawab of Arcot. Their access to resources continued to depend, as it had done during the wars, on their ability both to enforce and extend his authority and to extract wealth from him.

Only in Bengal were the British able to create an extensive territorial dominion. The survival of empire thus depended on Bengal. Without the resources of Bengal, British territorial ambitions would probably have withered in Bombay and Madras and it seems likely that there the Company would have reverted to a largely commercial role.

Madras

In the aftermath of the Seven Years War, Madras was the point at which the British stake in India was most vulnerable. Political conditions in peninsular India were volatile and potentially threatening and it was a likely objective for any French intervention. The Company was yoked in an uneasy alliance with Muhammad Ali Khan, nawab of the Carnatic. This brought them into conflict both with those who resisted the nawab's authority from within and with Muhammad Ali's Indian rivals, Mysore, the nizam of Hyderabad, and the Marathas, all of whom had claims on the Carnatic. From 1767 to 1769 the Company fought an expensive and inconclusive war with Mysore and intermittently with the nizam. In 1780 they were to be exposed to a devastating fresh onslaught from Mysore, later backed by the French.

The Madras presidency had born the brunt of the fighting in the Seven Years war and had emerged triumphant with the surrender of Pondicherry in 1761. Attempts to build on victory after the war were, however, markedly unsuccessful. The inability of Madras to sustain its pretensions to be the dominant political force in south India was to be cruelly exposed by the war with Mysore from 1767 to 1769. The war arose from the Madras council's desire to consolidate their hold on the coastal territory belonging to the nizam of Hyderabad, called the Northern Circars. Under Clive's influence, these had been formally granted to the Company by the Mughal emperor in 1765 without the nizam's consent. Having moved troops into the Circars in the following year the Madras council sought to obtain the nizam's agreement as part of a treaty of alliance. That treaty also involved joint action against Haidar Ali of Mysore. The pretext for making war on Mysore was that Haidar was plotting to depose Muhammad Ali and either to incorporate the Carnatic into his own dominions or to replace the nawab. The Madras council argued that war against Mysore was highly desirable. Haidar's recent success in incorporating rich territory on the Malabar coast alarmed the British. His 'immense conquests and the riches and power he has already obtained added to the pride and ambition that have of late manifested themselves' made it imperative to try to reduce 'the Mysore government within its ancient and proper limits'.[2] The Hindu dynasty of Mysore, eclipsed by Haidar, was to be restored to full authority.

The war against Haidar proved to be a chastening experience for the Madras council as they found out how formidable Mysore had indeed become. It also shattered many illusions in Britain about British invincibility in India. The Madras troops had to contend with an army that was at its core said to be organized in a way that was 'totally European' with sepoy infantry, mobile artillery and European officers,[3] but also deployed a huge force of light cavalry, put at 40,000 men by a British officer.[4] Haidar himself was recognized to be a leader 'of genius and capacity'.[5] At full strength, the Madras army could defeat Haidar in set-piece battles, but smaller detachments were vulnerable to him and Haidar's raiding parties could break past the British armies, cut off their supplies and ravage the Carnatic, as they did in the autumn of 1767, when they created panic in Madras itself. In 1768 the British tried to carry the war into Mysore. The Bombay army was to attack Haidar's coastal possessions, while the Madras army laid siege to Bangalore, one of his main fortresses. At this point, if not earlier, territorial gains were entering into British calculations. The nizam agreed to cede the *diwani* of Mysore to the Company, whose troops would garrison it.[6] This would give Madras revenue resources comparable to those of Bengal and fulfil the ambitions of those Europeans who had lent money to the nawab and wanted more territory from which to service their loans. Territorial ambitions were, however, idle speculations. The British armies had to retreat from Mysore. As

[2] Madras to Directors, 22 Jan. 1767, OIOC, E/4/301, ff. 280–90.
[3] *An Address to the Proprietors of India Stock, shewing, from the Political State of Indostan, the Necessity of Sending Commissioners* (1769), p. 17.
[4] J. Smith to Council, 16 Sept. 1767, OIOC, H/99, p. 28.
[5] J. Smith to Directors, [9 Oct. 1768], OIOC, Orme MSS, OV, 64, p. 32.
[6] Madras to Directors, 1 March 1768, OIOC, E/4/302, ff. 121–2.

they did so, there were fears that the Marathas would come south and that their forces would combine with those of Mysore to attack the Carnatic. The Maratha threat did not materialize, but the Mysore cavalry were back in the Carnatic in the early months of 1769. The Madras council were advised by their commander-in-chief that with 'the reduced state of the troops, the distressed condition of the country together with inability to procure any certain resources of money', the Company had no alternative to making peace on any terms.[7] Peace was concluded on 3 April 1769. The Company gained nothing from it.

News of the failures in war caused dismay in Britain. In May 1769 fears that the Marathas and the French would join Mysore and that there might be a war involving Bengal as well sent India stock down by nearly twenty points in two days,[8] part of 'an alarming and unparalleled fall of India stock within these few weeks' that was said improbably to have wiped off £7 million 'of property in that stock'.[9] The government was asked to provide naval support. There were also urgent demands for retribution and reform in the Company's Indian administration. The governor of Madras was dismissed and plans were drawn up for special commissioners to go to India to inquire into abuses and remedy them. The vulnerability of empire in India had been unmistakably displayed.

Unsuccessful war emphasised the weakness of the Madras presidency's financial position. This was set out in the report of a parliamentary secret committee of 1782. Madras's resources were 'barely sufficient' to fund 'its current ordinary expences' and were wholly inadequate for a war.[10] The war of 1767–9 against Mysore reduced the Company's finances to a parlous state. During the war Madras had to beg for funds from Bengal, receiving £450,000 in bullion,[11] and to suspend sending cargoes to Britain. By the end of the war the Madras presidency had incurred an 'immense load of debt', its 'credit [was] reduced to the lowest ebb' and it would not have been able to pay for an army to take the field if it had been required to do so.[12]

Such revenues as were under Madras's direct control were not effectively managed. What were known as the *jagir* lands near Madras, granted by the nawab in 1763, were leased back to him. The Northern Circars, extracted from Hyderabad in 1766, was potentially a valuable resource. But the Company's control over the Circars was at first tenuous, and when they were

---

[7] Madras to Directors, 27 June 1769, OIOC, E/4/303, f. 159.

[8] *Gazetteer*, 17 May 1769.

[9] Letter of 'A Real Stockholder', *Public Advertiser*, 5 June 1769.

[10] 4th Report, Secret Committee, 1782, *Reports from Committees of the House of Commons*, 12 vols. (1803–6), VII. 641–74.

[11] 3rd Report, Secret Committee, 1773, ibid. IV. 62.

[12] Select Committee to Directors, 31 Jan. 1770, OIOC, H/102, p. 496.

brought under some form of direct administration, the revenue return was still low. Both the Indian revenue payers and the Company servants who collected from them seem to have kept large sums for themselves.[13]

Money therefore had to be obtained from the nawab.[14] Muhammad Ali had ended the war with a very large debt to the Company, whose military costs, amounting to more than £1 million, he had undertaken to defray. After the war he was also required to pay some £175,000 a year for the troops which the Company provided for the defence of the Carnatic.[15] The Madras council eventually decided that the nawab should be charged too with two-thirds of the costs of the 1767–9 Mysore war. With undischarged debts from the past, they calculated that he then owed them nearly £900,000.[16] What the nawab would be able to pay ultimately depended on his ability to realize his own revenues. These consisted of the taxation of lands that he directly administered and of tribute which he collected, nominally on behalf of the Mughal emperor, from 'poligars' and other autonomous chiefs, who took every opportunity to refuse payment. Whether tribute was paid often depended on whether force could be applied, usually by the Company's troops. In 1765 and 1767 expeditions were sent against the southern poligars. 'Pacification' was, however, by no means achieved. Were the Company to withdraw its troops, the Madras council believed that the nawab would lose control over the poligars and his rule would collapse.[17]

The biggest target of all for enhancing the nawab's resources was the Maratha ruler of the principality of Tanjore. He derived a very large revenue from rich deltaic lands, maintained a considerable army and pursued his own diplomatic strategies. In 1762 the Company had intervened to impose a settlement by which his tribute to the nawab was fixed. Payment of the tribute fell into arrears and this provided the nawab with a pretext for enlisting the Company's help in a conquest that could potentially transform his finances and therefore his ability to pay what he owed. The Company's army moved against Tanjore in 1771, but made a compromise settlement with the raja, obtained, it was presumed, by huge bribes from him, which left him in power. In 1773 another expedition was mounted and this time was pressed to a conclusion. Tanjore was conquered and placed under the nawab's rule. With the great addition to his revenues, the nawab should have been able to

---

[13] See letters 'Of the Northern Circars', OIOC, H/768.
[14] What follows is heavily indebted to J. D. Gurney, 'The Debts of the Nawab of Arcot, 1763–1776', Oxford University D.Phil. thesis, 1968; see also Jim Phillips, 'A Successor to the Moguls: The Nawab of the Carnatic and the East India Company, 1763–1785', *International History Review*, VII (1985), 364–89.
[15] Madras to Directors, 22 Jan. 1767, OIOC, E/4/301, f. 269.
[16] Madras to Directors, 31 Jan. 1770, OIOC, E/4/303, f. 271.
[17] To Directors, 16 Sept. 1769, ibid. f. 170.

stabilize his finances and pay off the Company. This did not happen and in 1776 intervention from London brought about a restoration of the raja. The campaigns against Tanjore had been extremely lucrative for the army and for the governor and council at Madras, who had been liberally bribed by both sides. But the nawab's finances were not put onto a stable footing by Tanjore's revenues and so his debts to the Company were not paid off.

The nawab's inability to put his finances in order in spite of the Tanjore windfall was an indication of how complex they had become. From the later stages of the war with the French, Muhammad Ali had taken to borrowing money from Europeans to provide him with the ready cash that the Company needed to pay its troops. These loans came to be secured on assignments of the nawab's revenues, which took up a large proportion of the resources of the Carnatic. In as far as they were aware of such arrangements, the directors in London disapproved of them and insisted that the Company rather than private individuals should have the first claim on the nawab's revenues. Such orders could not be enforced. The creditors kept their assignments and added greatly to them after the conquest of Tanjore. One of the nawab's European bankers, the notorious Paul Benfield, undertook to pay off the nawab's obligations to the Company in return for having all the revenue of Tanjore put under his control, but he was defeated by rivals at the nawab's court and unable to establish full control.[18]

The alternative to relying on the nawab and his bankers was for the Company to take over the management of the nawab's revenues for itself. This was a measure that the Madras council had contemplated during the Seven Years War and was to consider again during the Mysore War. It was only to be brought about in a desperate crisis of a new war in 1782. The council were in no doubt that the nawab was deliberately keeping the Company short of funds. To seize his revenues, would, however, be incompatible with the implied terms of the alliance between him and the Company. Muhammad Ali was not their dependant, as the nawabs of Bengal had become to the council at Calcutta. His autonomy had to be respected. During the 1760s the nawab's position vis-a-vis the Company was in fact becoming progressively stronger, making it more difficult to extract concessions from him. This strengthening of the nawab was a serious constraint on the effectiveness of British authority in Madras.

Recent scholarship has shown that Muhammad Ali was no mere puppet of the British. He was seeking to establish his own Islamic state in the manner of other post-Mughal provincial rulers.[19] He recognized that his alliance with

---

[18] Gurney, 'Arcot Debts', D.Phil. thesis, pp. 250–70.
[19] See above, p. 138.

the British was a necessary means to that end, but he was well aware of the dangers that such an alliance posed to him. He often told Europeans that he feared that the fate of the nawabs of Bengal would also be his fate. He developed a number of strategies to keep his allies at bay. He cultivated the support of important members of the Company's service in Madras, trying to enlist them in his cause by financial inducements—bribes, allowances or a stake in his loans. He also learnt to reach out beyond the British at Madras to the British at home. A stream of letters, drafted by a clique of European advisers who had been able to insinuate themselves into the nawab's service, went to the directors, to George III, and to British ministers. Exploiting the recognition accorded to him by name as ruler of the Carnatic in the 1763 Peace of Paris, the nawab proclaimed himself to be the independent ally of the British crown. Matters of common interest between him and Great Britain must therefore be dealt with as affairs between two sovereign states. They could not be left to be managed exclusively by the Company. This strategy won him some success. An emissary on his behalf managed to make contact with ministers in 1768. The naval officer sent out to India in 1769 with what were described as 'plenipotentiary' powers was told that the king was not willing to leave 'engagements which he has contracted with other crowned heads' solely in the hands of the Company's servants. He was therefore to deal directly with the nawab and to investigate his grievances.[20] Little came of these contacts, but new agents from the nawab arrived in London in 1775. Thereafter there was much activity in Britain on the nawab's behalf: pamphlets and paragraphs appeared in the press, ministers were lobbied, the king was addressed and there was talk of petitions to parliament. John Macpherson, the Scottish adventurer who was acting as the nawab's agent, bought himself into the house of commons in 1779, beginning the allegations that 'the nabob of Arcot' was corrupting British political life by building up a parliamentary following. All this activity was largely prompted by the agents' desire to extract money from the nawab for themselves (a generally fruitless exercise since he wisely declined to honour nearly all the bills drawn on him) and it is doubtful whether it produced any major change in British policy. Nevertheless, awareness of the extent of the contacts made on his behalf in Britain was a serious constraint on the degree of coercion that the Madras servants felt able to apply to the nawab. It had become dangerous to affront him. The nawab was not the only Indian prince to seek access to the London political world. The raja of Tanjore had an agent in London from 1778, committed to keeping his territory out of the nawab's hands. He was

---

[20] Lindsay's Instructions, 13 Sept. 1769, OIOC, H/101, pp. 109–11.

able to enlist Edmund Burke in the cause of Tanjore.[21] Too overt coercion of Tanjore was now also risky.

The effectiveness of the Company's government at Madras was also undermined by the strength of factions within the presidency. Groups competed to subvert official policy in their own interests. The creditors of the nawab of Arcot was the most powerful of these groups. Many Europeans at Madras were involved in the nawab's loans. '[T]he fortunes of the natives' and the money 'of officers who carry on no business, [and] of the Company's civil servants who had no means of employing it better' were all said to have been invested in the nawab's bonds.[22] The funds of this mass of investors reached the nawab through the activities of a small number of large speculators, such as Paul Benfield, who for a short time came close to being the nawab's sole banker. Such men needed access both to the nawab's court and to the Company's council, whose decisions they tried to influence. The nawab's creditors, for instance, were generally supporters of military campaigns that would bring more territory under the nawab's control and therefore more resources to repay them. That many senior Company servants, including members of the council and governors, were themselves holders of the nawab's bonds eased the exercise of influence by the creditors. In as far as their loans enabled the nawab to maintain his payments to the Company, they performed what might be regarded as a public service. On the other hand, they levied interest at an extortionate rate and their claims competed for the nawab's revenue with those of the Company.

In 1775 East India Company politics at home turned against the nawab and his creditors. Lord Pigot, hero of the Seven Years War, was sent out to restore the autonomy of the raja of Tanjore, conquered for the nawab in 1773. The creditors saw the restoration of the raja without what they regarded as adequate safeguards for their large assignments on his territory as a dire threat to their fortunes. Benfield and other leading creditors therefore supported a coup in 1776 to seize and depose Pigot. Army officers were involved in the plot; it was supposed that the savings of half of the Madras officer corps had been deposited with Benfield.[23] News of Pigot's arrest and subsequent death in captivity created a furore in Britain. Leading creditors therefore felt obliged to extend their ambitions beyond trying to manipulate the Madras

---

[21] For the representation of the nawab and the raja in Britain, see L. S. Sutherland, *The East India Company in Eighteenth-Century Politics* (Oxford, 1952), pp. 198, 303–4, 321–8, 380; P. J. Marshall, ed., *Writings and Speeches of Edmund Burke V, India: Madras and Bengal 1774–1785* (Oxford, 1981), pp. 6–10, 41–2.

[22] [W. Ross] to W. Burke, [February 1778], cited in ibid. p. 630.

[23] C. Russell to J. Du Pre, 18 Sept. 1776, OIOC, MS Eur. E. 276/1, no. 26.

government to seeking also to influence the Company and ministers at home. Benfield bought himself into parliament in 1780.

Not only had the Madras government apparently become the instrument of private interests, but it proved to be inept in its diplomatic relations with its Indian neighbours. During the 1770s conflict between the Marathas and Mysore took pressure off the British at Madras, who preserved an uneasy neutrality with both sides. The Madras council however, eventually succeeded in antagonizing both the nizam and Haidar Ali.[24] When Haidar Ali attacked the Carnatic again in 1780 with an army said to be of 80,000 men, the Company's defences were wholly inadequate. Mysore cavalry again swept across the Carnatic almost to Madras itself. The presidency was only to be saved by the dispatch of troops and money from Bengal and by the arrival of royal regiments and warships from Britain.

Bombay

The Bombay Presidency consisted of a string of settlements along the west coast of India and in the Persian Gulf. Bombay itself was of only limited commercial importance, by comparison with the great trading ports of Gujarat further north, but its population was growing rapidly as migrants moved away from periodically disordered conditions to the relative security of Company rule. The spread of European wars to Asia gave Bombay great strategic importance. It had a fine harbour and three dry docks, one completed in 1773 being capable of accommodating a 74-gun warship. Naval stores were kept there and the skill of the Indian labour force in the docks was greatly admired. As the commander of the British naval force in India wrote at the end of the American War, there was nowhere else in Asia where warships could be 'properly refitted, much less repaired'. Without Bombay 'no squadron or force could be kept up in this country'.[25]

The Company's governor and council at Bombay were responsible for ensuring the protection of the various subordinate settlements and of British trade in the western Indian Ocean and the Persian Gulf. This was deemed to require garrisons, a field force of infantry and artillery, on a similar pattern to if somewhat smaller than those at Madras and Bengal, and naval forces, called the Bombay Marine. In 1772 the Bombay Marine had five 'cruisers' with up to twenty guns and eight 'gallivats', large sailing row boats with six to eight

[24] B. Sheikh Ali, *British Relations with Haidar Ali 1760–82* (Mysore, 1963), pp. 174–225.

[25] Cited in Andrew Lambert, 'Strategy, Policy and Shipbuilding: The Bombay Dockyard, the Indian Navy and Imperial Security in Eastern Seas, 1784–1869' in H. V. Bowen, Magarette Lincoln and Nigel Rigby, eds., *The Worlds of the East India Company* (Woodbridge, 2002), p. 140.

small guns.[26] The purpose of the Bombay Marine was to counter what Europeans conceived as 'piracy', the ships of the Muscat Arabs, of sheikhs in the Persian Gulf, or of the Maratha chiefs called the Angrias. It also acted vigorously to promote the private trade of Europeans at Bombay. It was not a force intended for action against the ships of European navies.

Bombay had very little revenue from which to defray the costs of its army and navy. In 1768 the Bombay troops sent to aid Madras in its war against Haidar Ali were said to be deserting 'for want of pay'.[27] In 1771–2 revenue from customs, duties, and rents on the island just about paid for the costs of the presidency's civil government; the Marine, costing £80,000, and the army, costing £215,000, had to be financed by other means. This meant subventions from Bengal worth £234,000[28] and bills drawn on the Company in London. In 1773 the pay of the army in peacetime was seriously in arrears and the presidency needed nearly £100,000 to repay what it had borrowed on bond. In addition large sums were required to carry on Bombay's commercial operations.[29] Bombay could only be freed from its financial strangulation by the acquisition of territorial revenue of its own.

In 1768 the directors in London authorized efforts to obtain the neighbouring island of Salsette. This was an old objective. As early as 1737 the Bombay council had asked for 3,000 European soldiers in order to expel the Marathas from Salsette, which would provide both secure supplies of food and additional revenue.[30] Bassein, another former Portuguese settlement taken by the Marathas, was also envisaged, both in Bombay and in London, as a desirable acquisition. The first significant gains, however, came further north in Gujarat, where the Company already had establishments in major ports. Privileged trading status in Surat, the greatest of these ports, was turned into outright political power when an expeditionary force from Bombay took control in 1759.[31] An allocation of the port's revenues was included in the gains from this coup. Broach, another port in which the Company had a factory, was the next target. Troops and ships were sent against the Mughal governor in 1771 with the intention of 'obtaining a considerable and permanent revenue'. The attack was given up but the governor promised to make payments.[32] When these did not materialize, a new expedition stormed the town. The Broach revenues were to be shared with the Marathas, giving the Company some £40,000, if they could be realized.[33]

[26] H. W. Richmond, *The Navy in India, 1763–1783* (1931), p. 383.
[27] W. A. Price to Clive, 12 June 1768, OIOC, H/100, p. 22.
[28] 5th Report, Secret Committee, 1782, *Reports from Committees*, VII. 747–8.
[29] Bombay to Directors, 28 Oct. 1773, OIOC, E/4/466, ff. 72–3.
[30] W. S. Desai, *Bombay and the Marathas up to 1774* (Delhi, 1970), pp. 100–1.
[31] See above, p. 54.
[32] Bombay to Directors, 22 Dec. 1771, OIOC, E/4/465, pp. 41–2.
[33] Bombay to Directors, 2 Dec. 1772, ibid. p. 411.

By 1772 a dynastic crisis afflicting the Maratha peshwas seemed to be opening up the prospect of spectacular gains. In 1772 the peshwa Mahdav Rao died. The British had regarded him as a formidable figure. His young successor was immediately murdered and his uncle, Raghunath Rao, was proclaimed the next peshwa. He was opposed in the name of a yet unborn child. This seemed to be a very tempting opportunity for intervention. Bombay decided to put its support behind Raghunath Rao. The Bombay council do not seem to have taken very seriously the military capacity of the Marathas. They were confident that with British aid Raghunath Rao would be able to obtain 'full possession of the government of the Mharatta empire'.[34] The price that he would pay was to be more revenue from land around Surat and Broach, as well as the long desired Salsette and Bassein. The yield would be over £200,000 a year[35] and Bombay would thus cease to be 'a burthen to the presidency of Bengal'.[36] To enable Raghunath Rao to fulfil his promises the Company's army joined his in a leisurely campaign in Gujarat. Bombay servants seemed to be at last catching up with their colleagues in Madras and Bengal as putative builders of empire. The young Charles Malet, with a long diplomatic career ahead of him, clearly relished the role. He rejoiced in the 'entire confidence these people have in us and in our manners' and considered that 'at a time when we are taking so great a share in regulating the government of this side of India', he should be granted an allowance 'to support an appearance adequate to the dignity' of the Company.[37] The Bombay council was not, however, prepared to leave the acquisition of Salsette to chance or to Raghunath Rao's generosity. They took it by force in 1774, on the pretext that the Portuguese were poised to try to recover it.

The first phase of Bombay's empire building was, however, to be brought to an abrupt halt by intervention from an unexpected quarter, not the directors in London but the new supreme council in Calcutta, who objected to Bombay's involvement in a war against the policy of the Company and without their authority. Using their powers to overrule the other presidencies, the supreme council annulled Bombay's treaty with Raghunath Rao and sent an emissary of their own to negotiate a treaty with his rivals. Under the new treaty, Salsette was to be kept as were the revenues from Broach, but otherwise Bombay's hopes for 'the glory and advantage of being arbiters of the Mahratta empire' had been dashed.[38] Malet thought that 'extreme folly and unpolicy'

---

[34] Bombay to Directors, 1 Dec 1774, , OIOC, E/4/466, p. 455.
[35] Bombay to Directors, 16 Feb. 1775, ibid. p. 484.
[36] Bombay to Directors, 14 Sept. 1775, ibid. p. 629.
[37] To R. Gambier, 2 March, 1 May 1775, OIOC, MS Eur. F. 149/89, pp. 37, 85.
[38] Bombay to Directors, 21 March 1776, OIOC, E/4/466, p. 735.

had let slip the opportunity which control of Raghunath Rao 'gave us of reducing the Mahratta power to a total subjection on English councils'.[39]

Bombay was, however, to have another chance. The failure of the Marathas to implement their side of the settlement made in 1776, the apparent willingness of some of the leaders at Poona to seek a connection with the French and new political upheavals at the court of the peshwas opened the way for another attempt to advance Bombay's ambitions through Raghunath Rao. In April 1777 a French ship arrived at Chaul near Bombay. On it was Pallebot de St Lubin, an official French emissary to the Marathas. He was received at Poona to negotiate two treaties, about which Bombay was well informed. The French were aiming at an immediate grant of a commercial settlement and at a military alliance in the event of a new war.[40] These agreements were signed on 18 June 1777 and St Lubin returned to France in an unsuccessful attempt to get a French force dispatched immediately to act with the Marathas. Bombay made an urgent case, both to London and to Calcutta, for pre-emptive action. The news of the outbreak of war between France and Britain in 1778 seemed to make action imperative. Some 4,000 troops were assembled to take Raghunath Rao from Bombay to Poona, where it was hoped that he would be strongly supported. In return he would give the Company what he had promised in 1775, that is lands worth more than £200,000 in annual revenue. The Bombay council congratulated the directors on 'the prospect of retrieving those most valuable acquisitions' lost in the 1776 treaty and of 'restoring such a government at Poonah as will greatly contribute to the security of your possessions in Hindostan'.[41] Charles Malet exulted that 'The eyes of the whole Eastern world are fix'd on the execution of an atchievement, which will form the climax of national grandeur.'[42]

None of this was to be. The army moved too slowly and support at Poona for Raghunath Rao evaporated. At the top of the Ghats on their way to Poona the Bombay force was surrounded by overwhelming numbers of Marathas and forced to capitulate at Wargaum on 16 January 1779. It was allowed to return to Bombay on dictated terms which included the surrender of Raghunath Rao.

Bombay's bid for its own empire through establishing a dominant influence at Poona had finally failed. Thereafter British relations with the Marathas were to be directed from Bengal. Even before the defeat of January 1779, Warren Hastings had lost confidence in the Bombay presidency, who had

---

[39] To J. Hartley, 23 Aug. 1776, OIOC, MS Eur. F. 149/49, f. 21.

[40] Bombay to Directors, 30 Nov. 1777, OIOC, H/138, p. 97. For French strategies, see Sudipta Das, *Myths and Realities of French Imperialism in India, 1763–83* (New York, 1992), pp. 183–8; for St Lubin's instructions, see V. G. Hatalkar, trans. and ed., *French Records (Relating to the Marathas)*, 6 vols. (Bombay, 1978–83), II. 36–8.

[41] 29 Dec. 1778, OIOC, E/4/468, p. 95.

[42] To J. Carnac, 11 Dec. 1778, OIOC, MS Eur. F. 149/49, f. 78.

'either overrated their own abilities or wanted constancy to prosecute the design which they had formed'.[43] Also alarmed by the threat of a French alliance with the Marathas, he developed a counter strategy of his own. The raja of Berar, one of the great leaders who had established a domain owing only nominal dependence to the peshwa, was to be encouraged to make his own bid for power at Poona. Bengal's interest in what had previously been Bombay's sphere of influence was to be given concrete backing by the dispatch of a force of sepoys to march overland across northern India. On its arrival on the west coast, it was to act independently of the Bombay presidency. Hastings's Berar strategy produced no significant result, but it was a recognition that practical power in the Maratha world was now passing away from the peshwa at Poona to the new chieftains with what amounted to their own states. The future in fact lay not so much with Berar as with another one of them, that is, with Mahadaji Sindhia, whose territory and ambitions lay in northern India, where he encountered the British in Bengal. Through pressure from the incursions of the formidable Bengal army and diplomacy managed by Hastings, Sindhia was to be induced to bring the Marathas into a new pattern of relations with the British, directed from Calcutta not Bombay. By the end of the next round of wars, the Bombay presidency remained an impoverished backwater, deprived even of the revenues that it had acquired from Broach.[44]

Both in western India and in the south, ambitious schemes of empire building had ended in failure. Empire was, however, to be firmly established in Bengal and from Bengal it was eventually to spread throughout India.

Bengal

In 1761 Laurence Sulivan, then the dominant figure in the court of directors, had insisted on the priority that the Company must give to Bengal over all its other commitments in India. There the Company already had 'a solid, extensive, and valuable commerce' and had begun to acquire 'provinces abounding in manufactures, and tillage'. He believed that the value of the British stake in southern India was small in comparison to Bengal.[45] In 1769 the directors made exactly the same point. In the south the Company was

---

[43] To L. Sulivan, 18 Aug. 1778, G. R. Gleig, ed., *Memoirs of the Life of the Right Hon. Warren Hastings*, 3 vols. (1841), II. 197.

[44] Pamela Nightingale, *Trade and Empire in Western India 1784–1806* (Cambridge, 1970), pp. 14–16.

[45] To Clive, 27 July 1761, G. W. Forrest, *Life of Lord Clive*, 2 vols. (1918), II. 190.

over-extended militarily and revenue could only be collected from 'Rajahs and Poligars' by military force. Bengal was 'the great object of our attention and every thing must yield to that'.[46] The overwhelming importance of Bengal was becoming received wisdom. George III thought that any other Indian settlement could be sacrificed for Bengal, 'which is the capital of our commerce and revenues'.[47]

The Company's Bengal servants were in no doubt of their success by comparison with the dismal record of Madras and Bombay. As Warrren Hastings put it, they had incorporated into the British empire a country whose 'extent . . . and its possible resources, are equal to those of most states in Europe'.[48] They believed that they exercised full sovereignty over this new domain. In Bengal 'The rhetoric of an exclusive state sovereignty, in which the sovereign power tried to claim a supreme power over the persons, and more especially the property of its subjects was a feature of British Indian politics from the beginning.'[49] Warren Hastings was particularly committed to such propositions. In his view both the Mughal emperor and the nawab of Bengal had lost any capacity to exert effective authority and he had no patience with those who argued that it was expedient for the Company to perpetuate the fiction that they acted as agents for either of them. Nor were local autonomies to be regarded as any effective check on the Company. 'Every intermediate power is removed and the sovereignty of the country wholly and absolutely vested in the Company . . . [T]he sovereign authority of the Company is firmly rooted in every part of the provinces and in every branch of the state.' He further believed that the sovereign powers that the Company's servants exercised in Bengal emanated from 'the British nation', not from the Company in London. The matter had been definitively resolved for him by the 1773 Regulating Act, which had made him governor general 'under the auspices of my sovereign', George III. Hastings therefore felt himself to be 'bound to conduct the great and important affairs committed to my charge to the best of my abilities for his honour and the advantage of his people'.[50] He hoped eventually to see the Company openly displaced by the state in the government of British India.[51]

---

[46] To Madras, 17 March 1769, Ambar Prasad, ed., *Fort William–India House Correspondence: Secret and Select Committee*, XIV, *1752–81* (Delhi, 1985), p. 716.

[47] Undated essay, cited in G. M. Ditchfield, *George III: An Essay in Monarchy* (Houndmills, 2002), p. 117.

[48] To Directors, 11 Nov. 1773, Gleig, ed., *Memoirs of Hastings*, I. 368.

[49] R. T. Travers, 'Contested Notions of Sovereignty in Bengal under the British, 1765–1785', Cambridge University Ph.D. thesis, 2001, p. 17.

[50] These quotations are taken from my 'The Making of an Imperial Icon: The Case of Warren Hastings', *Journal of Imperial and Commonwealth History*, XXVII (1999), 3–4.

[51] Neil Sen, 'Warren Hastings and British Sovereign Authority in Bengal, 1774–80', ibid. XXV (1997), 59–81.

There was inevitably a wide gap between the new regime's claim to sovereign power over Bengal and its capacity effectively to exercise any such power. Conditions in Bengal by the middle of the eighteenth century were, however, more conducive to a successful British takeover than was the case in other parts of India. Bengal was indeed a rich province 'abounding in manufactures and tillage', as Sulivan had called it. Its wealth had not only given it a dominant position in the Company's commerce from early in the eighteenth century but also generated a large territorial revenue for the nawabs, its post-Mughal rulers.

During the first half of the eighteenth century the East India Company and private British merchants had built up a privileged position in certain sectors of Bengal's economy. They operated from a major port, Calcutta, and a string of inland settlements, or 'factories', linked to the coast by the great river system of eastern India. British settlements enjoyed virtual immunity from the nawabs' government. British trade travelled duty-free throughout the province. Indian weaving communities around the British settlements often worked for the Company under some degree of coercion. With the collapse of independent indigenous political authority in Bengal in the 1760s, both the scale of British trade and the privileges that it enjoyed expanded greatly. The sterling equivalent of the value of the East India Company's Bengal exports rose from some £400,000 per annum at the time of the *diwani* grant to well over £1 million by the late 1770s.[52] Textiles, that is cotton piece goods increasingly supplemented by raw silk, were the staples of the Company's export trade, but political power brought some diversification of the British stake in Bengal's economy. The production of opium was put under Company control, augmenting its revenue and providing private merchants with a valuable item of trade to China and South-east Asia. Salt was also brought under Company control for fiscal reasons. During the 1770s the first experiments were made by private British entrepreneurs to produce indigo and sugar for export.

The province's rulers drew on the wealth generated by Bengal's highly developed agriculture and manufacturing by taxes on the produce of the land and by duties on trade. In instalments after 1757 and spectacularly in 1765, the Company developed a new role as tax collector in addition to that of merchant. Its trade quickly came to be seen as little more than the means of transferring revenue surpluses as a 'tribute' to Britain. The collection of revenue required an effective state machinery, not only capable of assessing and accounting for what was due to it but of enforcing its will on the major

---

[52] P. J. Marshall, *The New Cambridge History of India*, II, 2, *Bengal: The British Bridgehead. Eastern India 1740–1828* (Cambridge, 1987), p. 104.

holders of revenue rights and of protecting its provinces from outside pred-
ators. The state apparatus which the British inherited from the nawabs of
Bengal was already a powerful one. Revenue was raised with regularity and
with relatively little resort to armed coercion. The equivalent of the turbulent
'Rajahs and Poligars of the south', from whom revenue could only be
extracted by a military expedition, that is the great *zamindars*, only indulged
in open defiance in Bihar and in some of the frontier districts of Bengal.
Under the nawabs Bengal had enjoyed immunity from invasion, apart from
Maratha raids from 1743 to 1751.

I

The structure of revenue rights which the East India Company inherited in
Bengal had been largely shaped from early in the eighteenth century by a
series of masterful nawabs, the increasingly autonomous Mughal governors of
the province. Few subordinate chieftains with long-standing claims to exercise authority over land and people had survived their attentions. They had
also succeeded in greatly reducing the number of *jagirs*, that is imperial grants
to noblemen in return for military and other service to the Mughal empire. In
place of an ancient nobility or of appointments from Delhi, the nawabs had
substituted their own revenue contractors. Some had held contracts for
several generations and had established hereditary quasi-property rights to
them; others were farmers of revenue appointed for limited terms.[53]

Some 60 per cent of what the province yielded passed through the hands of
fifteen major contractors or *zamindars*, a term meaning no more than
landholder and applied to many different types of people in different parts
of India. The dominance of a small number of large *zamindars* was the
distinctive feature of eighteenth-century Bengal's revenue system. The major
zamindari estates had been built up by the incorporation of a mass of smaller
revenue tenures. Through them revenue could be realized with a minimum of
direct government involvement. In origin large *zamindars* might be little
more than revenue contractors, assessing and collecting tax through a complex bureaucracy of under-collectors and accountants, but they had become
much more than that. They governed their localities, maintaining their own
armed forces, enforcing law and order and administering justice in their own
courts. Their local authority was usually reinforced by their role as patrons of
shrines and religious ceremonies.

[53] Notable among recent work on the revenue history of Bengal are Ratnalekha Ray, *Change in
Bengal Agrarian Society c.1760–1850* (Delhi, 1979) and Rajat Datta, *Society, Economy and the Market:
Commercialization in Rural Bengal, c.1760–1800* (Delhi, 2000).

A mass of small revenue tenures survived in areas that had not been incorporated into large *zamindaris*. These tenures constituted a 'property in the land', as an early British investigator put it, 'alienable and saleable much in the same manner as with us'.[54] Small independent *zamindars* were particularly prevalent in frontier areas, where land had been granted in return for military service, or in territory, as in south-east Bengal, where new land was being cleared and brought into cultivation. In Bihar, in particular, many of those possessing revenue rights were little more than peasants themselves. Whereas the large *zamindars* rendered their payments directly to the nawabs' treasury, collections from areas with a mass of small revenue payers had perforce to be made by officials of the state.

Such officials, who also manned the central treasury and revenue offices, were part of an administrative service that was an important legacy of the Mughals to the British. By the middle of the eighteenth century most of the Bengal revenue administrators were locally recruited Hindus. They had to be skilled in Persian, the language of Mughal administration, and in complex revenue accounts. They had too to be politically adept, carefully studying the shifting balance of power among the nawabs and their grandees at Murshidabad, capital of Bengal since the early eighteenth century. They were quickly to become equally skilled at navigating in the political waters of the British regime in its new capital at Calcutta. Much as the British tended to revile them as corrupt and self-seeking harpies, who siphoned off huge sums into their own pockets and prevented the British from getting any clear knowledge of Bengal's resources, they were indispensable in the early years of Company rule. They alone had the knowledge of what could be realistically extracted from different parts of Bengal and of the pressures that could be effectively applied to particular *zamindars* to make them pay. British Company servants acquired such knowledge slowly and with difficulty. Men like Nandakumar in the first stages of the Company's search for revenue,[55] Muhammad Reza Khan in the later 1760s,[56] or Ganga Govind Singh under Warren Hastings, especially in the early 1780s,[57] exercised as much power as any European.

Bengal's public finance, like that of contemporary Britain, was sustained by credit. A banking system that enabled *zamindars* and revenue farmers to borrow in advance of their collections and the government to receive what was due to it promptly in cash was another valuable legacy to the British. At

[54] J. Johnstone to Committee of New Lands, 24 June 1761, OIOC, P/98/10.
[55] See above, p. 152.
[56] For him, see Abdul Majed Khan, *The Transition in Bengal 1756–1775: A Study of Saiyid Muhammad Reza Khan* (Cambridge, 1969).
[57] For him, see P. J. Marshall, 'Indian Officials under the East India Company in Eighteenth-Century Bengal' in Marshall, *Trade and Conquest: Studies in the Rise of British Dominance in India* (Aldershot, 1993), no. V.

the centre of this system was the huge business of the Jagat Seths, often likened by British people to the Bank of England. Bankers' bills were the means by which money collected in country districts was made available where the state needed it to pay its troops or, in the Company's case, to finance its trade.

Bengal's wealth, easily tapped through its sophisticated revenue system, had long made it a supremely desirable object for conquest. So long as they were maintained, Bengal remittances of bullion to Delhi had been the main financial prop of the Mughal emperors. Bengal revenue quickly became the main prop of the British in India, providing most of the tribute in goods to London, financing much of the China trade and enabling the Madras and Bombay presidencies to fight their wars.

The Company initially had little difficulty in keeping up and even augmenting the levels of revenue extraction that they took over. The last of the nawabs had made vigorous efforts to increase their revenue to meet extra military costs in response to the incursions of the Marathas and to the threat posed by the Europeans. Assessments had risen and *zamindars* had been put under pressure to pay more or had been displaced by short-term contractors. How much had actually been realised is uncertain; in 1755 the nawab was reputed to have collected some £1,500,000. In administering the first grants of revenue after the battle of Plassey, those allocated to it in 1757 and in 1760, the Company used much the same tactics as the late nawabs. Increases were ordered and short-term contracting, or farming, was introduced in the lands around Calcutta, ceded in 1757, and in the great *zamindari* of Burdwan, ceded in 1760.[58] These new acquisitions yielded some £600,000 a year. In 1765 the Company obtained the *diwani* revenues for the whole of Bengal and Bihar. These were placed under the direct management of an experienced administrator, Muhammad Reza Khan, with a British resident at the nawab's capital as a check on him. The Khan was for a time spared direct British intervention, but he was left in no doubt that he must maximize the revenue yield. He chose to do so by imposing a new tax on all revenue payers, to which, it has been suggested, they submitted as a lesser evil than being subjected to intrusive British inquiries into their resources.[59] In the years 1766–9 the Company realized net annual revenues of some £1,750,000 from Bengal.[60]

---

[58] For Burdwan, see John R. McLane, *Land and Local Kingship in Eighteenth-Century Bengal* (Cambridge, 1993), pp. 185–90.

[59] Khan, *Transition*, pp. 107, 128.

[60] For these figures, see H. V. Bowen, *Revenue and Reform: The Indian Problem in British Politics* (Cambridge, 1991), p. 104. For revenue totals over a long period, see Datta, *Society, Economy and Market*, pp. 333–4.

Abundant as Bengal's revenue resources were by comparison with those available to the Company elsewhere in India, the British quickly became aware that there were limits to what could be collected, and that Bengal might not be able to bear the burdens that were being heaped on it. As Hastings wearily concluded at the end of his long governorship, 'It is true that the resources of Bengal are great; but they are not inexhaustible.'[61] The late 1760s and early 1770s were perceived as a time of crisis in British Bengal. 'The present state of the revenues, public and private commerce, manufactures and agriculture are such as to give room for the most serious apprehension', the then governor wrote.[62] Shortage of specie and a diminishing volume of trade were seen as evidence of a general decline. A devastating if localized famine was to follow.

The British were being made aware that the flow of revenue from Bengal could by no means be taken for granted. It depended on the ability of peasants or artisans, most of whom lived in precarious circumstances, to pay in cash up to a half of the value of what they produced. In good times most of them were likely to be in debt to the merchants who advanced them funds with which to cultivate their land or to purchase yarn to be woven into cloth. In times of dearth or famine, caused by extremes of drought or flood, when food prices escalated, they were reduced to indigence and could not pay their taxes. In the very bad drought years of 1769 to 1770, large numbers died in certain districts of western Bengal. If this was not the all-encompassing disaster for the whole province that it was long thought to have been, it still devastated highly productive parts of Bengal.[63] This was reflected in a marked decline in the amount of revenue collected in the years 1769 to 1771.[64]

While the famine in western Bengal in 1769–70 was a clear indication of the ceiling which mass poverty imposed on revenue extraction, contemporary British opinion believed that the Company was being cheated of a disproportionate amount of the revenue that was actually being collected. The Company had no informed knowledge of the extent of the revenue resources of Bengal. Ignorance was a constraint on effective revenue administration that was never overcome. Revenue was in theory assessed according to the quality of the land and the crops which were grown on it. Assessment on such principles, however, required survey and record-keeping operations that were beyond the resources of either the Mughal or the British regimes, except in isolated areas. By default therefore revenue assessment was generally based on what had traditionally been collected to which the agents of government tried to add extra cesses, while revenue payers tried to bargain for remissions.

---

[61] *Memoirs Relative to the State of India*, new edn. (1787), p. 32.
[62] H. Verelst, cited in Marshall, *Bengal: The British Bridgehead*, p. 116.
[63] Datta, *Society, Economy and Market*, pp. 260–4.   [64] Ibid. p. 257.

The coercive force of the regime was pitted against the powers of concealment and evasion of those who held revenue rights. Many British observers believed that the government was usually the loser in such contests, a large proportion of what was extracted from the mass of the population never finding its way into the coffers of the state. Very considerable sums were thought to be lost to the government in spurious grants for services or charity, while tenure holders, the officials of the *zamindars* and of the state all rewarded themselves at far beyond the levels that they were authorized to deduct from the revenue. By 1769 the Company's servants had come to believe that they were being kept in 'ignorance of the real produce and capacity of the country . . . by a set of men who first deceive us from interest and afterwards continue the deception from fear'.[65] This view was endorsed by the directors in London, who deplored the embezzlements and oppression of 'the numerous tribes of fougedars [*faujdars*], aumils [*amils*], sikdars [*sikdars*] &c. . . . which must amount to an enormous sum'.[66]

The sense of crisis was made more acute by the escalation of demands on Bengal's revenue. The presidency's own military charges were running at more than £1,000,000 a year. It was having to subsidize the other presidencies: Bombay was a permanent drain on Bengal and Madras had to be bailed out during its war with Mysore. Some £700,000 a year had to be found for Bengal's own cargoes for London and large sums had to be sent to Canton to pay for increased tea shipments. The accounts drawn up for parliament for the year 1770–1 showed that Bengal only balanced its income and expenditure by raising over £1,000,000 by bills of exchange on the directors in London for money borrowed from the European community in Bengal. Acceptance of bills on this scale brought the Company in London to the edge of bankruptcy. In addition, Bengal's local debt borrowed on bond stood at the equivalent of nearly £950,000 in October 1771.[67]

An increase in revenue was therefore a matter of urgency. Higher revenue for the Company and the alleviation of mass poverty seemed to British opinion to be perfectly compatible objectives. Those who illegally enriched themselves from the revenue both cheated the government and oppressed the poor taxpayers by their exactions. Were their frauds to be eliminated, the Company would of course gain greatly, but the peasant and the artisan would also be relieved from extortion. In areas where the Company had been

---

[65] Select Committee Proceedings, 16 Aug. 1769, OIOC, P/A/9, p. 470.

[66] To Bengal, 30 June 1769, N. K. Sinha, ed., *Fort William–India House Correspondence (Public Series)*, V, *1767–1769* (Delhi, 1949), p. 212.

[67] 3rd Report, Secret Committee, 1773, *Reports from Committees*, IV. 60.

directly involved in revenue administration there was said to be 'plenty, content, population [and] increase of revenue without increase of burden'.[68]

Exact knowledge of Bengal's revenue resources was believed to be the key to eliminating illegal exactions and therefore to bringing about prosperity, both for the Company and for the peasants. Knowledge was to be attained by two strategies: by the wider deployment of trustworthy Europeans in place of duplicitous Indian revenue officials and by submitting revenue rights to the test of the market, that is by putting them up to auction. What informed bidders were willing to pay for revenue rights was presumed to be an accurate indication of what they were really worth. During the next fifteen or so years the Company's government pursued the goal of a more complete knowledge of what Bengal could afford to pay by empowering Europeans and by experiments in revenue farming. Neither device had much success. Exact knowledge of Bengal's revenue resources remained elusive and attempts to push extraction to higher levels stalled. In the late 1770s the Company was receiving less from the territorial revenues of Bengal than it had collected between 1766 and 1768, and this was at a time when wars that involved all the presidencies of British India were creating another crisis in which Bengal's resources would be severely stretched to meet the demands being made upon them.

The first systematic involvement of Europeans in the *diwani* revenues acquired in 1765 took place in 1769 with the appointment of what were called supervisors, officials who were to inquire into the way in which revenue was assessed and collected in particular districts and to expose abuses and oppression. In 1770 the supervisors were given executive authority over the administration of revenue in their districts and Indian officials were dismissed. A European presence at local level was thereafter to be permanent, although its form and intensity varied. Warren Hastings was sceptical about the capacity of most European officials and believed that they were just as likely to defraud the Company and to oppress the population as their Indian counterparts. He considered that there was no adequate European substitute for an experienced *mutasaddi* or local revenue administrator and he tried to curb European influence.[69] European revenue administrators remained, however, as what were called collectors or in councils set up in 1774 to supervise large areas. Collectors and councils were also given judicial functions to supervise the Company's new courts. In the hope of stimulating prosperity by easing exactions on internal trade, Company customs posts were set up to replace those of the nawabs and the tolls of the *zamindar*s. For all the practical limits

---

[68] Select Committee Proceedings, 16 Aug. 1769, OIOC, P/A/9, p. 474.
[69] Marshall, 'Indian Officials', pp. 109–10.

on what it could achieve, the Company was endeavouring to extend the reach of its authority with an ambition not matched by the government of any other British colonial possession.

Even the largest of the Bengal *zamindar*s were having to submit to British interference in their affairs. The Company's servants tried to regulate the way in which the revenue was administered, to impose economies on the numbers of people employed within the *zamindari*, to abolish *zamindari* tolls and market dues, to demilitarize the *zamindari*s by dismissing armed retainers and demolishing forts and to enforce the power of the Company's courts over *zamindari* justice. British governors even sought to determine the succession in important *zamindari*s. In short, although the process was to be a very protracted one, *zamindar*s were gradually being turned from local potentates into contractors for the government's revenue.[70] By 1782 a British revenue expert was looking forward to the eventual dismemberment of the great *zamindari*s. They constituted alternative sources of authority to that of the Company. 'The safety of our possessions requires that no native shall hold too powerful or extensive an influence in any part and of all men the great zemindars are least fit to be trusted . . . The English influence cannot be too firmly established in every part of the country.'[71]

The central revenue administration was moved from Murshidabad to Calcutta in 1772 and put under direct British control. Muhammad Reza Khan who had run the system since 1765 was dismissed and no Indian was vested with formal authority in any way comparable to his. British account-ants and secretaries moved into the revenue offices.

Neither the empowering of Europeans nor the auctioning of revenue rights produced the desired effect of an enhanced revenue yield based on greater knowledge of the province's resources. Hastings was responsible for the main attempt to dispose of revenue rights by competitive bidding for five-year farms in 1772, often in fact leased to the *zamindar*s themselves but in some cases taken over by outside speculators. It was assumed that this process would reveal the real value of the lands. The 1772 settlement was commonly deemed to have been a failure, since many successful bidders defaulted on the revenue that they had committed themselves to raise. The Bengal council had to admit by 1774 that although the farmers had promised a higher assessment, there was no prospect that the amount actually realized would increase.[72]

---

[70] This is the theme, as applied to Bengal, of the later chapters of McLane, *Land and Local Kingship*. For early British intervention in the great *zamindari* of Dinajpur, see R. T. Travers, 'Contested Notions of Sovereignty', Ph.D. thesis.

[71] D. Anderson to C. Croftes, 1 May 1782, BL, Add MS 45440, f. 22.

[72] To Directors, 18 Oct. 1774, OIOC, E/4/33, pp. 153–5.

Faced with a largely inelastic territorial revenue whose yield could not be enhanced, Hastings had to augment his government's resources by other means. He was able to levy what amounted to an indirect tax on salt by enforcing a Company monopoly over its sale in Bengal from 1772 and over its production from 1780. The origins of the salt monopoly can be traced to grants made by the nawabs to privileged merchants. Individual Europeans created their own monopolies in the years after Plassey, culminating in a general monopoly for the benefit of the service as a whole. Hastings claimed this for the Company in 1772. The right to make salt was then farmed out on five-year leases. Under Hastings's new scheme of 1780, agents on behalf of the Company directly organized the production of the salt which was sold at auctions to Indian merchants. The profits of the salt monopoly fluctuated wildly at first, but after the 1780 reform began to raise some £600,000 of additional revenue.[73] The monopoly also constituted a further considerable extension of direct British intervention through the appointment of European salt agents in the areas where salt was manufactured.[74] Opium too was turned into a separate source of revenue for the Company by Hastings. Again a private monopoly was converted into a public one. Exclusive rights to produce opium to be disposed of on the Company's behalf were sold to individual contractors from 1773. By the 1780s, the Company's profits from selling its opium were some £50,000 a year.[75]

In years of general peace and of relatively high revenue yields in the mid-1770s Bengal's finances were sufficiently buoyant to finance exports of goods of over £1 million.[76] Good years were, however, to be followed by a further crisis with the outbreak of a new series of wars. Military charges rose to nearly £3 million. Large supplies had to be sent to the other presidencies, especially to the beleaguered Madras, which received over £1 million in 1783–4.[77] No money could be spared for exports, which were provided by borrowing money from the Company's own servants. Over £2 million was owed on bond by 1783 and current spending, including the pay of the army, was being met by issuing interest notes which sold at a heavy discount.[78] Bills were again drawn on London on a scale which threatened to create a new crisis in the Company's affairs. By February bills from Bengal for nearly £1,400,000 had

[73] Account in Sheila Lambert, ed., *House of Commons Sessional Papers of the Eighteenth Century*, 145 vols. (Wilmington, Del., 1975), LVII. 997.
[74] Balai Barui, *The Salt Industry of Bengal 1757–1800* (Calcutta, 1985).
[75] Account in Lambert, ed., *Sessional Papers*, LVII. 995.
[76] Invoice values of cargoes are given in the 9th Report, Select Committee, 1783, *Reports from Committees*, VI. 112.
[77] Account in Lambert, ed., *Sessional Papers*, LVII. 1009.
[78] Bengal's financial problems in the early 1780s were summarized in the Commons Select Committee Report of 12 Feb. 1784. See Lambert, ed., *Sessional Papers*, XL 161–243.

accumulated in London.[79] The situation would have been even worse if Warren Hastings had not resorted to levying resources from outside Bengal's borders.

II

Awadh was the Bengal Presidency's main external source for financial subventions. It became the model of a state reduced to profitable dependency that Madras vainly tried to achieve with Mysore or with the nizam or Bombay with the Maratha peshwas.

Awadh was a conglomeration of territory across the densely populated Ganges and Jumna valleys of northern India. It had been welded into a single entity by a dynasty claiming from 1748 the office of wazirs of the Mughal empire.[80] In 1764 the then wazir, Shuja-ud-daula, had allied with the Mughal emperor and the deposed nawab of Bengal, Mir Kasim, to oppose the East India Company in Bihar. The combined forces were defeated at the battle of Buxar and the Company's army subsequently occupied much of Awadh. In 1765 Shuja-ud-daula had relatively generous terms imposed on him by Clive. He was to be restored to nearly all his territory, to become an ally whom the Company was committed to defend and to pay an indemnity of some £500,000, the first of many transfers of funds from Awadh to Bengal.

From the British point of view, an alliance with a stable Awadh insulated Bengal from incursions from northern India down the river valleys by Marathas, Afghans, or others seeking to plunder its wealth. From the wazir's point of view, the alliance blocked his expansion further eastward but gave him security to expand in the west, which he did to good effect.

The early stages of the alliance were fraught with difficulties. Shuja-ud-daula embarked on an ambitious programme of modernizing his army, which alarmed some British observers. 'Leave him to himself', Clive was told, 'and he will work at our destruction *because* we prevent him from destroying others, we are the thorn that has already wounded him and yet remain within his side.'[81] Fears that he was about to fight a war of revenge against the Company, duly reported in the London press,[82] fuelled the panic about the war with Mysore that so badly affected the price of India stock in the summer of 1769. By then, however, Shuja-ud-daula had come to a new agreement with

---

[79] Bengal's financial problems in the early 1780s were summarized in the Commons Select Committee Report of 12 Feb. 1784. See Lambert, ed., *Sessional Papers*, XL. 133.

[80] What follows is heavily indebted to Richard B. Barnett, *North India between Empires: Awadh, the Mughals and the British 1720–1801* (Berkeley, 1980).

[81] R. Barker to Clive, 21 April 1768, OIOC, H/100, p. 16.

[82] e.g. *Public Advertiser*, 17 May 1769.

the Company to reduce and limit his armed forces. A further agreement of great importance followed in 1773, negotiated by Warren Hastings. The Company's troops would undertake the defence of Awadh and the wazir was to pay some £250,000 for each brigade of troops sent into his territory. Since one of the three brigades into which the Bengal army had been divided came to be stationed permanently in Awadh, a very considerable part of Bengal's huge military costs had been shifted onto the wazir. A further charge of £400,000 was added in 1774, when the Company's troops were used by the wazir to defeat the Afghan Rohillas and to add the territory of Rohilkhand to his dominions. More Company troops were later placed on the wazir's payroll. It has been estimated that British claims on Awadh's revenues under Shuja-ud-daula's successor, Asaf-ud-daula, had risen to about half of the wazir's total revenue by 1777.[83]

This seemed to be highly successful exploitation of a dependent ally. Yet actually realizing these huge claims and bringing them to Bengal's relief proved to be very difficult. As at times in the Carnatic, the Company insisted on being allocated territory from which it could enforce collections itself. Even so, arrears mounted rapidly. By the year 1779–80 the Company had accumulated claims amounting to a staggering £1,400,000.[84] These demands were largely unenforceable. The collection of revenue to meet them depended ultimately on the ability and willingness of the Awadh revenue administrators to realize huge sums and pass them on to the British. This they would not do. Money was deliberately not collected so as to prevent the Company from getting it.[85] The Company thus had no alternative but to reduce its demands and to write off much of what it claimed as debt. This it eventually did.

Awadh had made a very significant contribution to reducing the Company's defence costs (and had incidentally greatly enriched very many individual British people). Around £1 million, nearly all of it spent on troops in Awadh itself, was collected by the Company in the Hastings years.[86] Extraction at this rate could, not, however, be sustained and demands had to be scaled down.

During Hastings's governorship, Bengal's revenues were also augmented by payments from Benares, a territory from which the wazirs of Awadh received tribute, but which was taken from them by the Company. The transfer of tribute obligations took place in 1775 at the accession of Asaf-ud-daula. The rajas of Benares were bound thereafter to pay the Company £250,000 a year and were given assurances that their autonomy would be respected. Although he had not been instrumental in the acquisition of Benares, Hastings came to

[83] Barnett, *North India*, p. 127.   [84] Set out in ibid. p. 157.
[85] Ibid. pp. 151–4.   [86] Account in Lambert, ed., *Sessional Papers*, LVII. 1011.

see it as a resource to be exploited to relieve Bengal's financial necessities. He was convinced that the tribute was only a small proportion of the revenue that was being collected in Benares. The raja was required to contribute troops for the Company and in 1781 a fine of £500,000 was imposed on him. This demand was made by the governor general in person at Benares, an escapade that provoked armed resistance and a popular revolt. The revolt provided the pretext for a new and potentially more lucrative connection between Benares and the Company. A new raja with much more limited autonomy was bound to pay over £400,000 a year. By the 1780s Awadh and Benares were contributing approximately one-fifth of Bengal's total resources.

The directors of the Company in London recognized that the Bengal presidency had a vital interest in Awadh as a buffer ally and source of funds, but strictly prohibited diplomatic or military adventures further afield. They succeeded in deterring their Bengal servants from embarking on what they regarded as the most pernicious of all adventures, restoring the Mughal emperor to Delhi under the Company's protection. Their injunctions took little account, however, of Bengal's inevitable commitments to support other presidencies or of the strategic visions of its governors. In 1768 Harry Verelst, for instance, expounded a doctrine of the Company as 'umpires of Hindostan'; it would maintain an Indian balance of power by siding against any state that aspired to dominance.[87] Such views were firmly rejected in London. The Indian powers must be left to check one another. The Company must steer clear of all entanglements.[88]

Strict non-intervention was an unacceptable policy for Hastings. He insisted that territorial expansion was never part of his agenda, but he developed increasingly ambitious schemes to extend British influence far beyond the Company's boundaries. The influence that he sought to extend was that of the British crown as much as that of the East India Company. As governor general appointed by parliament in the Regulating Act, he felt it his duty to obtain for the king 'pledges of obedience and vassalage from the dependants of the British empire in India', who would be bound by 'ties of direct dependence and communication with the crown'. Such an arrangement would free them from 'the fluctuations in this unstable government'.[89] Hastings believed that the nawab of Arcot was already in such a relationship and he hoped to include the wazir of Awadh.[90] Nathaniel Middleton,

---

[87] e.g. his letter of 28 March 1768, Sinha, ed., *Fort William–India House Correspondence*, V. 398–406.
[88] To Madras, 13 May 1768, Prasad, ed., *Fort William–India House Correspondence*, XIV. pp. 711–12.
[89] To N. Middleton, 3 Nov. 1774, BL, Add MS 29135, f. 302.
[90] To North, 26 Feb. 1775, Gleig, ed., *Memoirs of Hastings*, I. 508–9.

Hastings's personal nominee as resident with the wazir, was told in 1774 to broach the subject with him, but nothing appears to have been achieved before Middleton was dismissed by the majority on the new supreme council who were hostile to Hastings. Hastings believed, however, that Shuja-ud-daula 'would have thought it an honour to be called the vizier of the king of England, and offered at one time to coin siccas [rupees] in his majesty's name'.[91]

Three years later Hastings returned to the project of binding Indian states into an alliance with the British crown. On this occasion he was looking for an alliance with another power whose territory was adjacent to Bengal, the Maratha leader Mudaji Bhonsle, ruler of Berar and most of Orissa. Friendly communication with a view to an alliance similar to that with Awadh had been going on for some time, when news of the French embassy to the peshwa in 1777 gave them a new urgency.[92] While encouraging Bombay's designs to make Raghunath Rao peshwa, Hastings decided also to back the rival claims of Mudaji of Berar to be titular sovereign of the Marathas. The Bengal government was to intervene decisively in Maratha affairs. Bombay was to be reinforced by a contingent from Bengal that would march across the continent to the west coast and an embassy would be sent to Berar. Under criticism by his colleagues for recklessly committing forces in remote adventures, Hastings defined his doctrine of the need to extend British influence beyond the Company's territorial boundaries. The French could not be allowed to gain an ascendancy at Poona; neither Bombay nor even Bengal would be safe if that were to happen. French influence must be replaced by British influence. Through an alliance with Berar Bengal's intervention would 'totally overthrow the present power of the Maratta state and give us a lasting ascendant in its operations'.[93] When goaded by his critics, he used language as grandiloquent as that used by supporters of Bombay's intervention in favour of Raghunath Rao.[94] He refused to accept that

. . . with such superior advantages as we possess over every power that can oppose us, we should act merely on the defensive; and abruptly stop the operations of a measure of such importance to the national interest, as that to which we have now so decidedly engaged, with the eyes of all *India* turned upon it. On the contrary, if it be really true that the British arms and influence have suffered so severe a check in the western world [at Saratoga], it is the more incumbent on those who are charged with

---

[91] To A. Elliot, 12 Jan. 1777, ibid. II. 137.   [92] See above, p. 240.

[93] Minute of 9 July 1778, 6th Report, Secret Committee, 1782, *Reports from Committees*, VIII. 497.

[94] See above p. 240.

the interests of *Great Britain* in the east to exert themselves for the retrieval of the national interest.[95]

The alliance with Berar was no more of a glorious triumph than the expedition to take Raghunath Rao from Bombay to Poona. Mudaji showed no inclination to commit himself to the British and in fact joined the great alliance against them that most of the other Maratha chiefs were forming with Haidar Ali and the nizam. The Berar troops had to be bought off by secret subsidies from raiding into Bengal. Far from being able to draw Indian states into alliances with the British crown to extend British influence throughout India, Hastings had to fight a desperate war on many fronts. Men and money had to be poured out to defend Madras and Bombay, while Hastings applied all his diplomatic and strategic skills to the task of breaking up the alliance against him. Ultimately he succeeded in bringing British India through years of war into a series of peace treaties which left its territory virtually intact. The price in terms of the drain on Bengal's resources was, however, very high indeed. Instead of providing welcome relief for Bengal's finances, foreign adventures beyond Awadh had imposed an unsustainable burden on them.

III

Men in India by the 1770s were increasingly using high-flown language about how they were furthering Britain's national interests through the creation of a new empire based on the uncontested exercise of sovereign power within the Company's provinces and the extension of a predominant British influence further afield. Used at Madras or Bombay, such language was hollow in the extreme. In Bengal under Warren Hastings it had some substance, although British ambitions tended to outrun the realizable resources of even a rich province, forcing Hastings to resort to expedients that were to be characteristic of the later Raj. Since the British could never extract as much from the territorial revenue of Bengal as they hoped, taxation on the produce of the land had to be supplemented by government monopolies, including one over salt, a basic commodity of mass consumption, evocative of the French *gabelle*. Resources also had to be raised from beyond Bengal's borders by exporting a high proportion of the Company's military costs onto its pliant allies, such as the wazir of Awadh, the origins of what was to be called the subsidiary system.

---

[95] Minute of 22 June 1778, 6th Report, Secret Committee, 1782, *Reports from Committees*, VIII. 485.

With such extraneous help, a hard-pressed Bengal had become the Atlas sustaining British interests in Asia.

For all the strains to which it was subjected, Bengal remained a secure base for empire. It was immune from outside attacks after 1765 and open internal resistance was on too limited a scale ever seriously to threaten Company rule.

Attack from without and resistance from within had combined in the early 1760s. In 1763–4 considerable sections of the Mughal nobility in Bengal and northern India joined forces under the leadership of the Mughal emperor and of Mir Kasim, recently deposed nawab of Bengal, in what has been called 'a last bid to expel the British and assert Mughal control over the great valley of the Ganga'. Some of the largest Bengal *zamindars* joined in as well. A 'popular element' has even been detected in this 'Mughal patriotic war'.[96] The Mughal army was, however, defeated by the British at Buxar in 1764 and in subsequent campaigns the aristocratic alliance disintegrated. The British thereafter faced no significant resistance from disaffected elites within Bengal. What can be interpreted as popular resistance, but was often dismissed by the British as mere banditry, was more persistent. It was associated with the migrations of armed mendicants, fakirs and *gossains*—plunderers to the British, collectors and distributors of charity by their own account—with incursions of hill peoples in the border districts, and with protests by peasants, usually led by their headmen, against what they saw as excessive revenue exactions. Widespread as rural disorder might be at certain times, it never interrupted the Company's commercial and revenue operations and never required the deployment of the might of the Company's regular army. 'Pacification' was the duty of specially recruited militias who enforced revenue collection.[97]

Most British contemporaries seem to have taken the stability of their regime in Bengal for granted. Disobedient and mutinous Europeans ('oblique hints' that the whites of Calcutta might follow the 'example of the Americans' were being thrown out in 1779)[98] often seemed to them a more pressing danger than a mass insurrection of their native subjects. Those who did question why the British enjoyed security in Bengal usually gave answers that reflected deeply held stereotypes about Indian society. Bengal was assumed to be an overwhelmingly Hindu province. Its Muslims were thought largely to consist of alien immigrants from north India or further afield;

[96] Rajat Kanta Ray, 'Colonial Penetration and the Initial Resistance of the Mughal Ruling Class, the English East India Company and the Struggle for Bengal 1756–1800', *Indian Historical Review*, XII (1985), 41.

[97] G. J. Bryant, 'Pacification in the Early British Raj, 1755–85', *Journal of Imperial and Commonwealth History*, XIV (1985), 3–19.

[98] Sir E. Impey to Weymouth, 25 March 1779, BL, Add MS 16259, f. 177.

awareness of the great indigenous Muslim populations of eastern Bengal seems to have grown slowly. Bengali Hindus were assumed to be a submissive, often, it was said, an effeminate people without martial spirit or anything that could be described as 'political' concerns. They had no sense of patriotism that could be invoked against foreigners. They could only relate to the small-scale communities of their castes or villages and to the wider sense of a common religion that sanctified every aspect of their way of life. They were deeply conservative and resistant to any sort of change. Their political spirit had been sapped by generations of Islamic despotism. All they now expected from their rulers was to be left alone. They had learnt to bear a great deal of oppression and could only be provoked to resist by interference with what they held to be sacred.

The British assumed that the replacing of one set of alien rulers by another would therefore initially be a matter of indifference to the mass of Bengal's population. They would accept any authority that did not attempt to disrupt their way of life without questioning its credentials. The British certainly did not intend to provoke them by undue innovation. In the two areas where the government came into contact with the mass of its subjects—the collection of revenue and the administration of justice—the Company intended to follow custom and in particular to enforce what they took to be Islamic and Hindu law. Whether it was possible for foreigners to apply alien systems of law and administration without unconscious innovation was a question that was rarely asked.

Thus it was presumed that if the East India Company did no more than govern in the manner of indigenous rulers it could gain the acquiescence of its new subjects. Conventional wisdom was that: 'To our government they have no attachment. They submit to its authority from a habit of submission founded on the despotism under which they have lived, but this disposition would equally lead them to submit to any other government.'[99] From the outset, however, some assumed that British rule would offer its subjects positive benefits beyond any that an Indian regime could confer. Even politically inert Hindus, assumed to be content with a frugal standard of living, were thought to be committed to the pursuit of material advantage. A British regime would create conditions where secure accumulation would become possible. Bad as things were thought to have been in the early years after the *diwani* that culminated in the 1770 famine, improvement was still thought to be within the capacity of the Company. The captious oppression of the nawab's agents, that took the form of extra cesses on taxes or the plundering of property without judicial process, would be replaced by a

---

[99] J. Bristow to P. Francis, 29 Feb. 1788, OIOC, MS Eur. G. 4, f. 348.

government of regularity that respected rights of private property. As early as 1769, a young Company servant wrote that with the appointment of Europeans to administer localities:

We have it in our power to perform the noblest task that can be allotted to men of honor and humanity, that of changing the condition of a people from a state of oppression to happiness, and the country from desolation to prosperity and that the scheme will in general have this effect is undoubted by the advantages English gentlemen have over natives of this country in education, principles and disposition.[100]

By the end of his administration, Hastings was sure that the potential of British rule for improvement had been abundantly fulfilled.

I am authorised by my own experience to assert, what every man who has resided long in Bengal and has had opportunities of visiting the countries beyond the Company's jurisdiction, is qualified to affirm, that the territorial possessions of the English in Bengal and Bahar, are not only better cultivated than the lands of any other state of Hindostan, but infinitely superior to what they were at the time the Company received the grant of the Dewanny, or for many years preceding that period.[101]

Such assertions about overall standards of living in British Bengal are speculative in the extreme. Optimistic assessments, like those of Hastings, were opposed by the pessimistic ones of many other Europeans. Historians tend to take their pick according to their dispositions, which almost invariably lead them to be pessimistic. Whatever the reality, the notion that the mass of the Bengal population felt bound to the Company by ties of gratitude for benefits received strains credulity. Nevertheless, considerable sections of the local elites may well have acquiesced in Company rule in return for very real material benefits. It is not difficult to identify potential 'collaborators' in the *argot* of imperial historiography, who stood to gain from the new order.

Those among Bengal's elites who did well out of the British have to be set against those who lost. The Mughal nobility played a prominent part in the manoeuvres that brought the Company to power in Bengal between 1757 and 1763. For a time, they had sought to integrate leading British figures into the Mughal order, awarding them Persian titles of honour. The Mughal imperial service had always been a cosmopolitan one and 'there was no reason why the English should not be found a place' in it.[102] The limitations of such a strategy quickly became apparent. Most of the old nobility seemed to be dispensable in the new British order. Clive was committed to Muhammad

---

[100] G. G. Ducarel to his mother, 15 Dec. 1769. I owe this reference to the kindness of Robert Travers.

[101] *Memoirs Relative to the State of India*, p. 131.

[102] Khan, *Transition in Bengal*, p. 12.

Reza Khan to run his revenue administration, but he mistrusted 'fat, expensive moormen' as revenue contractors. They should be replaced by frugal 'Jentoos'.[103] After Clive left India, the Khan fought a losing battle to keep the administration of Bengal to his ideal of Mughal principles and in the hands of men brought up in that tradition. The pensions and allowances paid by the nawabs were ruthlessly pruned. Aristocratic military employment largely disappeared. There was no place for Mughal *mansabdar* grant holders and their cavalry troopers in the professionalized Bengal army of north Indian peasant infantry under British officers. A nostalgic nobleman lamented that while Bengal had once maintained 'forty or fifty thousand horse', now 'service for troopers and cavalry there is none at all'.[104]

A group of privileged merchants and bankers, mostly Hindus, had been essential supporters of the nawabs' government, advancing it money in return for privileges, such as the management of its mints or the right to monopolies over certain trades.[105] These men could not usually adapt to the new British order. The fate of 'Omichund', merchant prince under the late nawabs, who was cheated by Clive out of the political profits which he had tried to grasp in 1757, was only the most spectacular example. Within a few years of the rise of British power, the great banking house of Jagat Seth was in irreversible decline. Most of the large Bengal *zamindars* survived the early years of Company rule, but they were beginning to lose their military and administrative powers, were having to accept more overt government interference and in some cases the management of their lands was put under the temporary control of revenue farmers. The future was not promising for them.

For many who aspired to wealth and preferment, however, the new regime had much to offer. Under certain constraints, Indian commercial enterprise flourished. Some Indian merchants came under pressure from the growth of privileged British trade, as the East India Company sought to extend its control over the production of textiles for export and enforced monopolies over salt and opium. Private British merchants also claimed political authority in expanding their trade and trying to eliminate Indian competition. The success of both official and private British trade, however, depended largely on Indian expertise and on Indian finance, while most of Bengal's commerce, above all a vast trade in food grains, remained beyond any effective British penetration. Some two hundred European civil servants might lay claim to what were nominally the most senior offices in a huge state apparatus, but

---

[103] To F. Sykes, 3 Aug. 1765, G. W. Forrest, *The Life of Lord Clive*, 2 vols. (1918), II. 282.

[104] Seid Gholam Hossein Khan, *The Seir Mutaqherin or Review of Modern Times*, 4 vols. (Calcutta, 1789; reprint, Calcutta, 1902–3), III. 203.

[105] Kumkum Chatterjee, *Merchants, Politics and Society in Early Modern India: Bihar 1733–1820* (Leiden, 1996).

they were not numerous enough nor were most of them skilled enough to exercise effective authority. That remained mostly in the hands of Indian revenue *diwan*s or law officers, a large share of the profits of office going to them as well. The notorious Ganga Govind Singh was believed to have become a millionaire in European terms through his management of the Bengal revenues under Hastings.[106] The lower ranks of a great bureaucracy engaged in the administration of revenue, justice, the customs or government monopolies remained exclusively Indian. Even in the army where European officers were thickest on the ground and obstacles to Indian preferment were most rigid, young Muslims of parts and ambition could still make a career. Dean Mahomet was later to write how as a youth in 1769 he had been so entranced by the sight of the British officers of the brigade at Patna in Bihar, that 'Nothing could exceed my ambition of leading a soldier's life'. He ingratiated himself with them, gained a European patron and was eventually appointed 'market master' to supply the sepoys.[107]

Under the Company, the revenue system was by far the largest source for the accumulation of wealth in Bengal. In the past the major *zamindar*s had been the greatest beneficiaries from it but in the early years of Company rule profitable involvement in the revenue became more widely diffused. The British were inclined to encourage subdivision of large holdings. As the great estates weakened, smaller tenure holders were able to assert their independence and deal directly with the government. At the same time a market in titles to land developed, thus enabling outside investors, especially those who had influence with the British, to acquire their own holdings. These became the landed patrimony of families resident in towns, above all of the urban elite of Calcutta. Highly profitable grants of land exempted from paying any revenue because they were nominally awarded for charity or for service rendered to the state multiplied. Indians who administered the collection and assessment of the revenue under British collectors or revenue councils not only made great fortunes from clandestine deductions of the revenue for their own benefit, but were very well placed to acquire their own landed estates. The overall effect of these trends was to enable a numerous gentry to gain access to revenue rights at the expense of a small group of great landed magnates.[108]

The greatest Indian entrepreneurs under the early Company rule were people known as the 'banians' of particular Europeans. This implied a relationship of servant and master. It was usually, however, a partnership in

---

[106] Marshall, 'Indian Officials under the East India Company', pp. 111-12.

[107] Michael H. Fisher, ed., *The Travels of Dean Mahomet: An Eighteenth-Century Journey through India* (Berkeley and Los Angeles, 1997), pp. 23, 38.

[108] For the proliferation of rights to revenue, see Ray, *Change in Bengal Agrarian Society*.

which the British 'master' contributed his influence while his banian provided the money and the local knowledge through which great fortunes were made either by trade or from the profits of office. The richest banians generally came from socially respectable families. They used their connections with prominent Europeans to further their personal trade, for instance, in salt acquired under the Company's monopoly, or to win lucrative revenue contracts which could become the basis of landed estates. Men like Nabakrishna (Nobkissen), associated with Clive among others, Krishna Kanta Nandy (Cantoo Baboo), banian of Hastings, or Gokal Ghosal, banian of Harry Verelst, accumulated huge fortunes with extensive property in Calcutta as well as landed estates throughout Bengal. Their descendants were to dominate Calcutta society in the nineteenth century.[109]

In the years after Plassey, Calcutta, long a rich settlement, was transformed into a great and opulent city. The spectacular buildings of European Calcutta attracted much contemporary notice, but the white town was only a small enclave in an Indian conurbation, whose richest inhabitants lived in the great houses to the north of the Company's settlement, while the poor lived in shacks and 'bustees' or in the villages inhabited by fishermen, weavers or market gardeners, that were being incorporated into the expanding city.

Calcutta was becoming a religious and cultural centre as the rich Hindus who lived there began to challenge the rural *zamindar*s as patrons of Brahmin pandits, festivals, and shrines. The very richest became chiefs of factions who competed for leadership over the caste Hindus of the city.[110] In Calcutta and far beyond, especially in areas with flourishing commerce, there was 'an immense proliferation of temple building' in the later eighteenth century.[111] Increasingly confident assertions of Hinduism in areas under Company control have sometimes been attributed to the replacement of Mughal Islamic persecution by British toleration or at least indifference. The Bengal nawabs had, however, generally shown no inclination to persecute. They, like the British, found it expedient to patronize Hindu festivals. A more mundane explanation therefore seems probable. The British order provided a framework within which new families were able to accumulate wealth and to mark their new status by appropriate displays of conspicuous piety. It is most unlikely that such families came to revere the Company as their patron, but

---

[109] For a brief account of the banians, see P. J. Marshall, 'Masters and Banians in Eighteenth-Century Calcutta' in B. B. Kling and M. N. Pearson, eds., *The Age of Partnership: Europeans in Asia before Dominion* (Honolulu, 1979), pp. 191–214.

[110] S. N. Mukherjee, 'Daladali in Calcutta in the Nineteenth Century' in Mukherjee, *Calcutta: Myths and History* (Calcutta, 1977), pp. 68–72.

[111] Hitesranjan Sanyal, 'Temple Building from the Fifteenth Century to the Nineteenth Century: A Study in Social Response to Technological Innovation' in B. De, ed., *Perspectives in Social Sciences* (Calcutta, 1977), p. 135.

they had no reason to wish to see the new order give way to an uncertain future.

IV

Eighteenth-century assumptions that Indians were a people without any sense of politics, whose mental horizons were limited to village or caste, whose conduct was motivated by self-interest and who could only be goaded into opposing their rulers by flagrant assaults on deeply engrained traditions, as in 1857, have enjoyed a remarkably long life in western historiography. Indians are presumed not to have engaged with politics until the emergence at the end of the nineteenth century of a nationalism largely inspired by concepts borrowed from the west. Nevertheless, even eighteenth-century Europeans recognized the existence of what they referred to as an Indian 'public opinion' that was well aware of political events. Warrren Hastings believed that 'This government subsists more by the influence of public opinion than by its real power or resources.'[112] He was not alone in believing that the British acted in 'the eyes of all India'.[113] Indian rulers certainly kept a very closely informed watch on their rivals, including the British. Intelligence and speculation about military and diplomatic moves circulated with great rapidity. There are indications that the appetite for news was quite widely diffused throughout Indian society,[114] and that informed Indians were not necessarily indifferent observers of the unfolding of events, but judged them, as has recently been argued, by 'popular ideas of political morality and good government', derived from 'an encompassing discourse of south Asian politics'.[115] In other words, some Indians were not only well informed about the doings of the British, but had certain expectations of them. They applied criteria of right conduct to them as they did to indigenous rulers. There are therefore grounds for caution about the implied contrast between the exercise of imperial authority in the western world over peoples who were only too-overtly political and the exercise of authority in India on despotic principles over an inert and submissive people, who wished only to be left alone or at the most to reap material benefits. That is not a convincing explanation for the

---

[112] To Shelburne, 13 Dec. 1782, Gleig, ed., *Memoirs of Hastings*, III. 23.
[113] See above, p. 255.
[114] C. A. Bayly, *Empire and Information: Intelligence Gathering and Social Communication in India 1780–1870* (Cambridge, 1996).
[115] C. A. Bayly, 'Patriotism and Political Ethics in Indian History' in Bayly, *Origins of Nationality in South Asia: Patriotism and Ethical Government in the Making of Modern India* (Delhi, 1998), p. 14. The early chapters of this book examine pre-colonial 'ideologies of good governance' and argue convincingly for the existence of 'patriotisms' applied at least to 'regional homelands' (ibid. p. vii).

making and unmaking of empires. Some 'natives' took a keen interest in the workings of the Company's government, were well informed about them, judged them and tried to influence them. Although no doubt in a very different sense, authority in India as well as in America required a degree of 'negotiation' between rulers and ruled.

Europeans accepted the existence of some kind of Indian public opinion when they repeated the commonly held maxim that British authority, sustained by very small numbers of whites, rested less on the exercise of overwhelming coercive power than on Indian beliefs in the superior qualities of the British, 'bravery, clemency and good faith', according to the future governor general, John Shore,[116] and in their virtual invincibility. Such beliefs must be carefully fostered. The defeats inflicted on the Madras and Bombay armies by Mysore and the Marathas had been very damaging. The Bengal army had avoided defeat, but there was increasing concern that even in Bengal Indian opinion was losing respect for the British and that British authority was therefore being endangered. Two episodes seemed to embody these concerns.

The first was a riot that took place in the European quarter of Calcutta on 29 January 1779. The presence in the city of the Shi'ite nobleman, Saadat Ali Khan, future wazir of Awadh, was said to be the pretext on which Muharram processions turned into attacks on Europeans. Bricks were thrown at the royal supreme court and at the Company's writers' building. Allegedly on the orders of Saadat Ali, an allegation that he firmly denied, Europeans on horseback or being carried in palanquins were ordered to dismount. Some were called 'kafir', beaten and had their palanquins broken up. William Hickey, who saw two drunken British sailors in the middle of the riot, characteristically found the episode hilarious, but most were thoroughly alarmed. There were many complaints of 'a very extraordinary degree of insolence and licentiousness' never seen before from the natives. A year later a petition to the British house of commons by the white inhabitants of Calcutta complained that 'a spirit of contempt for [the Company's] authority and for Europeans in general' was spreading, which must 'terminate in disaffection and resistance'. The 'late most daring tumult in Calcutta' was a dire warning and seemed to be part of a pattern of 'resistance to government in various parts of the province'.[117]

---

[116] 'Memoir on the Administration of Justice and the Collection of the Revenues' (1785), Lord Teignmouth, ed., *Memoir of the Life and Correspondence of John, Lord Teignmouth*, 2 vols. (1843), I. 487.

[117] For this episode, see the depositions forwarded by the supreme court, OIOC, Bengal Public Consultations, P/2/31, ff. 132; A. Spencer, ed., *The Memoirs of William Hickey*, 4 vols. (1913–25), II. 178–81; Petition of 4 Dec. 1780, *Journals of the House of Commons*, XXXVIII (1780–2), 97.

The other episode was altogether more serious. In August 1781 Warren Hastings arrived at Benares in person to call to account the raja, Chait Singh, for what Hastings regarded as flagrant disobedience. The confrontation ended in disaster for Hastings as the party of troops that he sent to arrest the raja was massacred and, in a situation of acute personal danger, he himself had to flee from the city. What developed into a considerable insurrection in Benares was crushed, but European observers were greatly alarmed at the speed with which news of the check to the British and of rumours that Hastings had been killed spread throughout eastern India and at reactions to such stories. Hastings believed that the 'the fate of the British empire in India' was embodied in him as 'the essence of the state itself; representation, title and the estimate of public opinion'. His death would, he considered, have been 'decisive of the national fate; every state around [the Company] would have started in arms against it; and every subject of its own dominion would, according to their several abilities have become its enemy'.[118] A member of the governor's party agreed that the loss of Hastings 'might have been fatal to the English dominion in this part of the world'. Only the speed with which the uprising was crushed had prevented a concerted attack by 'all the neighbouring powers'.[119] The revolt at Benares was matched by uprisings in districts in eastern Awadh, where British officers were enforcing revenue collections, and by zamindars in western Bihar. In Bengal itself it was reported by a French Muslim at the nawab's court at Murshidabad that 'all, all, all . . . think of rising on the English'.[120] The directors of the Company were warned of the danger of 'a general commotion from Rohilcund [Rohilk-hand] to the mouths of the Ganges which would terminate in the forfeiture of your revenue and possessions'.[121] Native acceptance of British dominance suddenly appeared to be fragile, hanging on the thread of a single life.

If the Calcutta Muharram riot of 1779 was hardly the equivalent of the Stamp Act riots in American ports in 1765, and the commotions following Chait Singh's defiance in 1781 in no way matched the overthrow of royal authority throughout the thirteen colonies in 1774 and 1775, they were still reminders that Bengal was not entirely docile. It was fortunate for the Company that it was able to face the challenge of the alliance of Indian princes with a belated French intervention without a serious internal

---

[118] 'A Narrative of the Insurrection in the Zemeedary of Benares', G. W. Forrest, ed., *Selections from the State Papers of the Governors General of India: Warren Hastings*, 2 vols. (Oxford, 1910), II. 160.
[119] D. Anderson to F. Anderson, 15 Oct. 1781, BL, Add MS 45440, f. 4.
[120] Haji Mustapha, cited by Rajat Kanta Ray, 'Indian Society and the Establishment of British Supremacy, 1765–1818' in P. J. Marshall, ed., *The Oxford History of the British Empire*, II, *The Eighteenth Century* (Oxford, 1998), p. 520.
[121] John Macpherson to Directors, 2 April 1783, OIOC, H/212, p. 824.

challenge in the territory that provided most of the resources with which it waged war throughout India. That this was so may have represented some element of choice by Bengal's elites, as well as lack of opportunity.

V

The subjects of a despotism, it was conventionally supposed, had no alternatives between either total submission or outright resistance to the will of their government. In reality, however, the subjects of the East India Company, as of its Mughal or post-Mughal predecessors, were not devoid of means of negotiating with their rulers and of trying to influence them. Under the British, Indians both used what might be regarded as 'traditional' strategies for trying to exert influence as well as developing new ones appropriate to the new order.

A good ruler in Indian traditions must be open to the complaints of his subjects. He must be accessible in order to do justice to those who sought redress from him. Even Mughal princes were not supposed to show 'any impatience at the screams and reproaches of the crowds that pressed upon them.'[122] British officials were inundated with petitions and all must have experienced the clamour of discontented peasants or artisans, when their sense of what was due to them had been violated in some way. At Benares Warren Hastings, more inclined, it would seem, to behave like a Mughal prince in northern India than in Bengal, held 'a large levee every day where persons attended with petitions',[123] and he described how on a journey 'From the confines of Buxar to Benares, I was followed and fatigued by the clamours of the discontented', who presented him with 'a multitude of petitions' which he duly minuted.[124] In Calcutta Indian notables, including the *vakils* or ambassadors of rulers and the agents of the great Bengal *zamindars*, had access to the governor's house at certain times. Other senior Company servants also seem to have held regular levees. An Indian who observed the British closely believed that whatever efforts Company officials made, 'the gates of communication and intercourse' were being shut up under the new regime, most of whose members 'constantly express an aversion to the society of Indians and a disdain against conversing with them' as well as a dislike of public appearances and 'extreme uneasiness, impatience and anger on seeing themselves surrounded by crowds' with their 'complaints and clamours'.

[122] *Seir Mutaqherin*, II. 200.
[123] Evidence of F. Fowke to Committee of Managers, BL, Add MS 24266, f. 249.
[124] To E. Wheler, 2 April 1784, cited in P. J. Marshall, ed., *The Writings and Speeches of Edmund Burke*, VII, *India: The Hastings Trial 1789–1794* (Oxford, 2000), p. 367.

They were too reluctant to show themselves in public, as good rulers should.[125] 'Keating Saheb . . . the first English lord', that is collector, of Birbhum in western Bengal, perhaps came closer to what was expected. A little Bengali boy remembered in old age how his mother had 'held me up in her arms to look at him when he passed with his sepoys and elephants'.[126]

If face-to-face access to British officials was restricted, some Indians were learning how to refine the technique of petitioning to make their points in new ways. Written petitions, translated into English, could be recorded on the Company's official proceedings, where they might catch the attention of senior Company servants and even perhaps of the directors in London. They could thus be used as a weapon to discredit local officials who were not complying with the wishes of the petitioner. Even apparently unsophisticated people, often, it was assumed, coached by professional Indian petition writers and even by designing Europeans, could resort to petitions. The grievances in the early 1770s of some Dhaka weavers, for instance, were eventually publicized in Britain by a parliamentary committee. In 1773 the weavers had 'travelled in multitudes' from Dhaka to Calcutta in order to enlist the authority of the Company's council against the Dhaka servants. No doubt, like a group of cotton merchants, also from Dhaka, they were confident that Warren Hastings, the governor, would welcome the incrimination of Richard Barwell, head of the Dhaka factory, who he was known to dislike. Sadly for them, when they reached Calcutta, they found that Hastings and Barwell had suddenly become friends. So they had to wait until Hastings had new enemies on the council who would be glad to take up their cause.[127] For an Indian to commit himself in public by a petition against official policy or against the actions of highly placed Company servants was an extremely risky proceeding, as the varied fortunes of the Dhaka weavers and cotton merchants showed. Nevertheless, Company servants could not be entirely sure that their subjects might not try to expose them to unwelcome publicity by launching petitions against them.

By the end of the eighteenth century the British in Bengal had developed a powerful rhetoric that not only was their government conducted according to law, but that both it and individual Europeans were accountable to law. It is scarcely conceivable that any Indian took such propositions seriously or regarded the Company's courts with their European judges as a potential device for bringing their rulers to justice. To attempt to bring the Company to book before its own courts would not only almost certainly be a complete

[125] *Seir Mutaqherin*, II. 154, 200.
[126] W. W. Hunter, *Annals of Rural Bengal* (1868), p. 422.
[127] The weavers' and merchants' grievances were taken up by Edmund Burke in 9th Report, Select Committee, 1783, Marshall, ed., *Writings and Speeches of Edmund Burke*, V. 259–70.

waste of time but would be inviting dire retribution. In the years after 1774, however, astute Indians began to become aware of a crucial divide in British justice. The royal supreme court at Calcutta was headed by judges who were showing themselves to be more than willing to challenge both official policy and the privileges of Europeans. Indian suitors made extensive use of the court. The chief justice, Sir Elijah Impey, openly avowed that the court's purpose was to act as a check on arbitrary acts by the Company and to give 'security to the persons and property of the natives' from the rapacity and violence of Europeans. He rejoiced that cases had been settled which awarded extensive damages against British defendants who had assaulted Indians, and that Indians now 'feel themselves entitled to the rights of humanity in common with the Europeans, the meanest of whom they before considered to be their lords and masters'.[128] Not surprisingly, the intrusive ambitions of the supreme court aroused intense white hostility. The Bengal council was determined to keep its administrative processes out of the jurisdiction of the supreme court. It fought an ultimately successful campaign in Britain to achieve this end. Europeans in Bengal also campaigned against the court. According to John Shore, the court had been the most important influence to 'the elevation of the natives and to the depression of the Europeans'.[129] It was introducing deeply subversive principles of equality before the law that would undermine the respect and awe for the British that was the foundation of their rule. European inhabitants petitioned the British parliament for the court's powers to be curbed. One consequence of the activities of the supreme court was to involve Indian groups in Calcutta in the internal politics of the British. The opponents of the court tried to enlist Indians to petition against its ambitions, which were represented as seeking to impose English law over Indians. The judges were, however, assured by other Indians that 'they were sensible of the benefit they had received from the court' and were willing to sign 'a counter petition'.[130]

Although the controversies aroused by the supreme court drew many Indians into public politics in Calcutta, the informal involvement of Indians in the politics of the British settlements was very old indeed. British and Indian merchants had formed alliances to further their own trade against that of their rivals. In the twenty years or so after Plassey, British-Indian political entanglements became particularly intricate and frenetic. The stakes were very high. As presumably had been the case at the court of the nawabs, Indians who aspired to great posts in the management of the revenue needed patrons to support their interests against their rivals. British people for their

---

[128] To G. Johnstone, n.d., BL, Add MS 16259, f. 195.
[129] Teignmouth, ed., *Life and Correspondence of Teignmouth*, I. 487.
[130] E. Impey to J. Dunning, 15 April 1779, BL, Add MS 16259, f. 215.

part needed the services of such men if the Company's revenue was to be effectively realized and if they were to be able to make substantial fortunes for themselves. Leading Company servants backed the main contenders for managing the *diwani* after 1765, Nandakumar and Muhammad Reza Khan, and were willing to organize support for them among the directors in London. Between 1772 and 1775 faction fighting in Calcutta became literally a matter of life and death. Those Indians who had allied themselves with Warren Hastings since his return to Bengal in 1772 faced challenges from their enemies, chiefly from Nandakumar, who threw in their lot with Hastings's opponents, the new councillors arrived from Britain in 1774. Temporarily worsted, Hastings's Indian dependants fought back and brought Nandakumar to his death at the hands of the supreme court on a charge of forgery.[131] Hastings's renewed ascendancy ultimately entailed the ascendancy of Ganga Govind Singh, but as soon as the governor-general left Bengal in 1785, Ganga Govind Singh's rivals staged a coup that forced him from office. Only a systematic onslaught on Indian influence in the higher reaches of the service under Cornwallis brought the rise and fall of linked British and Indian factions to an end.

The faction fighting of later eighteenth-century Calcutta was hardly an edifying spectacle. There are, however, indications that Indians competed for power under the new order not just for the wealth that it brought but to advance certain principles by which they believed that government should be conducted. Muhammad Reza Khan is the best documented case. He had clear ideals of what had constituted good governance under the Mughals and, in the words of his biographer, 'his constant aim . . . was to persuade his English masters to accept Mughal ideals and practices as their own'.[132] He was successful at least in persuading Philip Francis, Hastings's great enemy, to devise programmes for the future government of British Bengal derived from the expositions of best Mughal practice provided by the Khan.[133] Other Indians, such as Ali Ibrahim Khan,[134] were able to propagate their interpretations of Mughal ideals directly to Hastings. Hastings responded to a petition from a group of Muslims 'of credit and learning' in endowing a college, or *madrasa*, in Calcutta to teach law and 'such of the sciences as are taught in

---

[131] The tortuous Anglo-Indian politics of this episode are deftly analysed in L. S. Sutherland, 'New Evidence on the Nandakuma Trial', *English Historical Review*, LXXII (1957), 438–65.

[132] Khan, *Transition in Bengal*, p. 16.

[133] Ibid. pp. 347–8. The Khan's influence on Francis is further demonstrated by Robert Travers as part of a cogent argument that Indians were full participants in the nominally British debates about Bengal's future, based on different interpretations of its Mughal past, Travers, 'Contested Notions of Sovereignty', Ph.D. thesis.

[134] For him, see Bayly, *Empire and Information*, pp. 81–2.

Mahometan schools'.[135] Hastings was also the first patron of Hindu legal scholars, the pandits who produced the early codes or digests of Hindu law for use in the Company's courts. Pandits became the salaried employees of the Company and were supervised by Europeans who had strong views about the nature of law. Even so, they had much discretion in directing their patrons to texts and in interpreting them. They too tried to educate their masters.

The necessity for keeping Indians innocent of British politics was expounded by an experienced Company servant. We should 'never relinquish the exercise of a direct, and even, an arbitrary power, when necessary. Nor in any instance to make appeals to their reason, or, communicate to them, any of our proceedings or transactions, by way of information. In short, government should never be known to the natives, but by its orders and regulations.'[136] The implication was that if Indians became participants in the contentions and debates among their rulers they would lose their awe for the power that imposed its just but inscrutable will on them. The aspiration to keep Indians innocent of politics was, however, entirely unrealistic. Indians were not only well aware of the divisions among the British but were taking sides in them. This may well have been a source of strength for the regime, rather than the weakness that was commonly supposed. In no way could British authority be said to be accountable to an Indian public, but it was not completely remote from it. There were channels of communication that made the regime accessible to some of its subjects and open to their influence. Alternatives between total submission or outright resistance certainly existed.

VI

On the eve of the American Revolution, the commercial advantages to Britain of the North American colonies, with their huge market for British manufactures and their great export staples, easily outweighed those that had as yet been realized from empire in India. Yet viewed as a component of an empire intended to sustain Britain against European rivals presumed to be bent on revenge, India was fulfilling criteria by which the American colonies were manifestly proving themselves to be wanting.

The East India Company in London had been turned into a generally compliant partner in empire, yielding its autonomies in ways that no American colony was prepared to do and submitting to reforms that turned it into a reliable agency for imperial purposes. In India the Company maintained a

---

[135] Petition cited in Marshall, ed., *Writings and Speeches of Edmund Burke*, VII. 650.
[136] J. Bristow to P. Francis, 29 Feb. 1788, OIOC, MS Eur. G. 4, f. 349.

huge standing army at its own cost as well as paying for the forces of the crown when they were posted to India. It had developed local executives generally responsive to directions from home, even though their leading members might have minds of their own and strong inclinations to pursue their own policies. A professional administrative service was developing in each of the three presidencies. Above all, great sums were at the disposal of the Company's governments, collected from the population without any process of formal consent. There were of course no local standing armies in America, funds to pay for British troops were not forthcoming, the colonial executives were weak in the face of local opinion, imperial administrators were very thin on the ground and any funds that could be raised locally for defence or for the costs of government required the consent of recalcitrant local assemblies.

The contrast between India, where empire in the sense increasingly envisaged by British opinion was being successfully made, and America, where it was being unmade, was glaring. Indeed so glaring was the contrast that it lent itself and still lends itself to simple explanations. Contemporary Americans offered what to them was a compelling explanation. The intentions of British ministers were despotic. In India, the land of despotism, they could fulfil their wicked intentions; in the colonies, the land of freedom, they were resisted. As John Dickinson put it, 'We are not Sea Poys, nor Marattas, but *British subjects* who are born to liberty, who know its worth, and who prize it high.'[137] The assumption that eighteenth-century India was in sad decline produced by the ravages of despotism and therefore that its people had become easy victims for any determined conqueror from outside was to have a very long life in western historiography.

The proposition that empire-building in America was frustrated by the commitment of its peoples to freedom, while empire could be built in India on the authoritarian systems of government long existing there, is an explanation of the fall and rise of empires that needs much qualifying. This chapter has tried to show that the establishment of empire in India was far from the imposition of despotic rule over an inert people. In the first place, Indians had successfully resisted the attempts of the Madras and Bombay presidencies to enlarge their dominions. A potent territorial empire had indeed been created in Bengal, but it had been built on the success of the nawabs in fashioning a revenue system that gave the state access to a significant proportion of Bengal's wealth, on the expertise of a corps of administrators who had worked for the nawabs and on the willingness of north Indian peasants to serve in great numbers in the Company's army. In short, empire had been built not on

[137] Cited in Arthur M. Schlesinger, *The Colonial Merchants and the American Revolution 1763–1776* (New York, 1918), pp. 275–6.

Indian weakness but on the highly developed economy and administrative system of a particular region. The early development of the new regime was shaped by the aspirations of important sections of Indian society, commercial men who put their resources into nominally British trade, investors in revenue tenures or scholars who deigned to impart their learning to the foreigners. Whatever their positions in the hierarchy of offices, some Indians could still effectively influence the policies of the new regime.

Both in India and America the evolution of empire was shaped by its subjects, if in very different ways. The bleak contrast between an empire of freedom and an empire of despotism therefore needs to be modified. Empire in both America and India can also perhaps be seen as falling within the concept of 'negotiated empires', whose shape was determined as much by processes of negotiation between metropolitan authority and peripheral interests as by the unfettered exertion of imperial power.

9

The Unmaking of Empire, I: North America
1763–1768

THE terms of the peace that ended the Seven Years War had been fiercely assailed, but the British public as a whole seems to have derived much satisfaction from what had been won. Addresses to the king from all parts of the British Isles anticipated great future benefits in which North America featured prominently. A war that had been fought to protect colonies and trades that already enriched Britain had resulted in the prospect of even more lucrative opportunities. The magistrates and council of Glasgow, for instance, anticipated a greatly enlarged trade and commerce from 'the immense territories added to the British empire in North America'.[1] The mayor and common council of Bristol agreed that new territories ceded to Britain would not only give security to Britain's existing 'colonies and settlements', but would also 'greatly extend the trade and navigation of your majesty's commercial subjects'.[2] In his answer to an address from the City of London, the king promised that 'the improvement' of the 'vast countries . . . added to the British empire' would produce 'most solid, and lasting advantages to all my subjects'.[3] Individuals quickly showed that they had every intention of partaking in these advantages as they made claims for grants of land in North America or for rights to exploit the mineral resources of the new territories.

Yet from the outset, euphoria at the prospect of the prosperity that was to follow from territorial gains was tempered by a sense of potential future hazards. It was the tritest of maxims about the history of empires that over-expansion had invariably brought about decline and ultimate collapse. British expansion must be carefully regulated if Britain was not to follow the same path as Rome or Spain. The new American territories required settlement to make them fruitful. This could lead to a mass exodus from across the Atlantic of useful subjects, above all of British artisans and craftsmen employed in

---

[1] *London Gazette*, 5–9 April 1763.   [2] Ibid. 26–30 April 1763.
[3] Ibid. 17–21 May 1763.

manufacturing. Migration should therefore be regulated. So too should patterns of settlement. The growth of population in America was highly desirable, since it would enable new lands to be profitably cultivated and thus increase the already buoyant transatlantic market for British exports of manufactured goods. Yet it was commonly supposed that most of the benefits of population growth would be lost if settlement was permitted to spread too far from the coast and into the newly acquired lands in the west. There the new settlements would be out of the range of British exports and would consequently be obliged to manufacture for themselves. It was axiomatic that the development of colonial manufacturing in competition with British goods was an evil particularly to be discouraged. Finally, trade must continue to be regulated, as it had been for so long. The colonies must buy from Britain and send important commodities directly to Britain. Otherwise, the benefits of the expansion of empire would accrue to Britain's European commercial and military rivals rather than to Britain herself.

Charles Jenkinson, secretary to the treasury, summed up in 1765 the conventional view of the balance to be sought between expansion and regulation.

The increase of our colonies is certainly what we wish but they must increase in such a manner as will keep them usefull to the mother country; and any regulations that are essential to the last object, tho' they may in some small degree prevent the increase of the colonies, are founded on true policy and should be complied with . . . [A]nd as far as it is necessary for this purpose to restrain the commerce of our colonies, it is an evil to which I think they ought to submit for the good of the whole.[4]

Political authority must be maintained to enforce due regulation. In 1767 Charles Townshend, who unusually for an ambitious politician had concerned himself with American affairs over a long period, was reported to have said 'that if we once lose the superintendence of America, this nation is undone'.[5]

British euphoria over the fruits of victory was also tempered by immediate considerations that were strongly to influence the making of policy for North America, that is by fear that France and Spain would soon seek an opportunity to fight a war of revenge and by dismay at the effects on Britain of the great debt left by the last war.

In August 1763 Pitt vented his spleen against the peace that he had opposed by lamenting that France and Spain were now more closely united than ever before and by prophesying that there would be 'an immediate rupture'

[4] To R. Wolters, 18 Jan. 1765, N. S. Jucker, ed., *The Jenkinson Papers 1760–1766* (1949), p. 348.
[5] Germain to J. Irwin, 13 Feb. 1767, WLCL, Germain Sackville MSS, 3, no. 54.

between them and Britain 'in both the Indies'.[6] More realistic opinion recognized that neither France nor Spain were in any position immediately to seek to reverse the result of the war, but that it was undoubtedly their intention to build up their navies and to strike back when the time was ripe. Both powers believed that Britain could best be crippled by attacking her colonial possessions and thus depriving her of the great wealth that she was presumed to derive from the colonial trades.[7] In 1765 the duc de Choiseul, a minister fervently committed to cutting Britain down to size, felt that it would probably be necessary to wait until there was a revolution in the British colonies, a development that he regarded as ultimately inevitable.[8] Yet throughout the 1760s rumours were rife that French or Spanish forces were being massed in the West Indies to attack the British islands and the mainland colonies. Immediately after the peace it was reported that the French would have 23,000 men serving with their fleet and in the West Indies.[9] The Spanish were believed in 1764 to be creating a 'standing army' of 25,000 men 'at the back of New Mexico, Louisiana and Mississippi'.[10] The following year 10,000 regular Spanish troops were said to have arrived at Cuba.[11] There were similar reports of French reinforcements being massed on Mauritius for a descent on British India.

Maintaining Britain's naval superiority of the Seven Years War was the obvious counter to such threats. In addition, adequate land forces had to be available overseas to protect the colonies from sudden attack and to deter insurrection by the surviving French population or the Native Americans in areas newly incorporated into the empire. Few believed that this could be done on the pre-war basis of limited British garrisons with local forces being raised by the individual North American colonies as the need arose. There must be a considerable permanent British military presence. A strong navy and colonial garrisons would, however, require heavier expenditure than post-war governments with their obsession about the size of the national debt would willingly sanction.[12] The debt at the end of the war was

---

[6] Conversation reported in Newcastle to Devonshire, 11 Aug. 1763, BL, Add MS 32950, f. 70.

[7] For an authoritative assessment of international rivalries after the war, see H. M. Scott, *British Foreign Policy in the Age of the American Revolution* (Oxford, 1990), chs. 3 and 4.

[8] Frank Spencer, ed., *The Fourth Earl of Sandwich: Diplomatic Correspondence 1763–1765* (Manchester, 1961), p. 16.

[9] John L. Bullion, 'Securing the Peace: Lord Bute and the Plan for the Army, and the Origins of the American Revolution' in Karl W. Schweizer, ed., *Lord Bute: Essays in Re-interpretation* (Leicester, 1988), p. 21.

[10] P. Stephens to E. Sedgwick, 11 July 1764, J. Reddington, ed., *Calendar of Home Office Papers of the Reign of George III, 1760–1765* (1878), p. 425.

[11] W. Lyttelton to Halifax, 11 July 1765, PRO, CO 137/62, f. 49.

[12] For the problem of financing the navy, see N. A. M. Rodger, *The Insatiable Earl: A Life of John Montagu, Fourth Earl of Sandwich 1718–92* (1993), pp. 135–6.

commonly estimated at £148 million. Annual payments of £5 million were required to service it. The increased peacetime naval and military establishments added to the burden. Spending on defence (the necessary 'military guard') in 1764 was estimated to cost £1,500,000 more than it had done before the war. All this meant that taxes must remain at an unacceptably high level that would force up labour costs and render British exports uncompetitive. Economic decline leading to military weakness would be the inevitable result.[13] Hence it seemed imperative that the colonies, Ireland, and the East India Company should be required to contribute something to the cost of defending a worldwide empire. George Grenville was to tell American colonial agents in 1764 that 'beside the yearly interest of that debt, the nation had incurred a great annual expence in the maintaining of the several new conquests which had been made so much for the benefit of the Americans'. The cost of the army in the colonies had risen from £70,000 in 1748 to £350,000 and 'he thought that America ought to contribute towards it'.

For many reasons therefore, if the gains of the peace were to be turned to good account, there must be effective British intervention in the affairs of the colonies: the movement of people, the distribution of land, the development of colonial economies, above all the flows of trade, colonial defence and the cost of that defence were all now matters of urgent national concern. Effective intervention supposed structures of authority in the colonies that would be responsive to metropolitan requirements. In the case of territory taken from the French and the Spanish, new governments had of course to be created. Proposals for reform of the existing colonies had been canvassed both before and in the early years of the war. Nothing had come of them, but changes were again to be advocated with the ending of the war.

I

The story of how successive British governments sought to impose a degree of regulation on North America and of how their efforts encountered colonial resistance which set off a slide to armed conflict and revolution has been the subject of a vast corpus of historical writing to which many generations of historians have made their contributions. This and the following chapter will not attempt yet another comprehensive retelling of that story. They will, however, take narrative form in which the focus will be, on the British side, on attempts to embody in North America the ideas of empire discussed in

---

[13] [William Knox], *The Present State of the Nation: Particularly with Respect to its Trade, Finances &c.* (1768), pp. 18, 23–9, 32, 35.

Chapter 5 and on such indications as exist of wider public engagement with the colonial problem. On the American side the coverage will be highly selective, limited to an attempt to describe the alienation in certain key colonies of groups whose cooperation or at least acquiescence was essential for the effective working of imperial rule. The emphasis will thus be on the colonial elites. Such an approach flies in the face of current historiography that has demonstrated beyond question the depth of popular participation in the overthrow of the colonial order, at least from 1774, and in sustaining the revolutionary war effort thereafter. From the British point of view, however, the elites were the necessary partners in empire. '[E]lites', as a recent study has put it, 'everywhere in British America were firmly in control of important political processes' from early in the eighteenth century and they 'gathered more power to themselves as the century pogressed', right up until the outbreak of the Revolution.[14] It was through the influence of local elites, as events in the Seven Years War had clearly demonstrated, that men and money could be mobilized for imperial purposes. Provincial regiments under American officers recruited men in the colonies on a scale that the royal regiments could not possibly match. Taxes could only be raised through votes by the assemblies. The colonial merchants and planters were the indispensable intermediaries for tapping the American market and for directing the flow of commodities to Britain. After 1763, however, the great bulk of the colonial elites not only declined to play their part in the reordering of empire, but propagated doctrines that challenged the basis of imperial authority, obstructed British policy through the political institutions that they dominated, above all the assemblies, and on occasions may have connived in popular violence. The unmaking of the British empire in North America was thus in the first instance largely the achievement of the elites in the thirteen colonies. The revolution that was to remake America was something altogether different. These two chapters are concerned with the unmaking of empire, not with the fashioning of the new republic.

Few in British politics doubted that 'the due government of the colonies; which', in the words in 1763 of the then attorney-general, Charles Yorke, 'now formed so vast an empire in America' was high on the list of urgent problems facing any British government after the war.[15] Some individuals who prided themselves on their expertise in colonial matters, such as Francis Bernard, governor of Massachusetts, hoped to contribute to a thorough 'revisal and settlement of the political state of N[orth] America', when this came to be discussed 'in the British Councils'. In his view it was necessary 'to ascertain

---

[14] Trevor Burnard, *Creole Gentlemen: The Maryland Elite, 1691–1776* (New York, 2002), pp. 252, 254.
[15] Report of 'Conversation with Lord B[ute]', 9 Apr. 1763, BL, Add MS 32948, f. 93.

principles for connecting America with Great Britain with a true regard for both my countries'.[16]

He and those who thought like him were repeatedly to stress the need to define a constitution for the British empire. They were, however, to be disappointed. British governments were guided in their dealings with the colonies by certain generally accepted considerations, such as the need to maintain effective regulation of trade and to provide for an adequate defensive system, but they did not seek comprehensively to remodel relations with the colonies. Instead, a series of measures was introduced to deal with specific problems. There were obvious reasons for this piecemeal approach. As is notorious, there was little continuity in policy-making. British ministries in the 1760s succeeded one another in quick succession. In the crucial post-war period, the administration of lord Bute lasted less than a year before he gave way to George Grenville in April 1763. Grenville was to be replaced by the marquess of Rockingham in July 1765, who in turn was succeeded by William Pitt, soon to be earl of Chatham, in August 1766. Within a year Chatham was no longer an effective member of his administration. Within ministries, responsibility for colonial matters was divided between different departments, which enjoyed a high degree of autonomy, even in the administration of George Grenville, who was to be personally identified with some of the most important colonial measures of his administration.[17]

The way in which measures affecting America came to be enacted after the war has been thoroughly studied in a body of distinguished work.[18] Decisions about the future defence of America were taken even before the formal conclusion of peace. American manpower would still be used; requisitions were sent out for colonial troops to fight in the Indian war against Pontiac in 1763 and it was hoped that Americans could be recruited into under-strength British regiments if need be. A high degree of direct British involvement would however continue. A British commander-in-chief and a strong force of British regular troops had been sent to the colonies during the war. There seems never to have been any question that a commander-in-chief would remain and in February 1763, he was told that he would have under him

---

[16] To Barrington, 15 Dec. 1761, 27 Dec. 1764, E. Channing and A. C. Coolidge, eds., *The Bernard–Barrington Correspondence and Illustrative Matter* (Cambridge, Mass., 1912), pp. 43, 85.

[17] For departmental responsibilities, see above, p. 74. The lack of any integrated policy-making is stressed in the magisterial account of P. D. G. Thomas, *British Politics and the Stamp Act Crisis: The First Phase of the American Revolution, 1763–67* (Oxford, 1975), see especially ch. 2 and pp. 112–13.

[18] See especially, Thomas, *British Politics and the Stamp Act Crisis*; Lawrence Henry Gipson, *The British Empire before the American Revolution*, 15 vols. (New York, 1936–70), vols. X–XII; John Shy, *Toward Lexington: The Role of the British Army in the Coming of the American Revolution* (Princeton, 1965); and John L. Bullion, *A Great and Necessary Measure: George Grenville and the Genesis of the Stamp Act 1763–1765* (Columbia, Mo., 1982).

twenty British battalions of some ten thousand men to be stationed in North America and the West Indies. This was a measure decided by the war office with the active involvement of the king. It was approved by the cabinet and by the house of commons, when the army estimates for the year came before it. The motives behind the decision have been described as 'security' with 'economy'. The need for security seemed clear. As the king put it, 'If we don't take precaution whenever a new war breaks out we shall run great risk of losing the great advantages we are at this hour to be blessed with.'[19] The dangers were seen as the disaffection of the newly conquered French population of Canada or of the Indians, whose territory would need some form of policing, and the prospect of French or Spanish attacks from the West Indies or Louisiana. Whether possible disaffection among the British population of the colonies was also considered at the time is unclear; there was certainly discussion later in official circles of the potential role of the army in retaining 'the inhabitants of our antient provinces in a state of constitutional dependence upon Great Britain'.[20] Economy was to come from recovering part at least of the cost of the garrisons from the colonies themselves. This was made clear in the debate on the army estimates, although no specific means by which payment would be obtained was proposed.[21] That some form of tax to be paid by Americans would be voted by parliament was assumed to be inevitable. By the winter of 1763, Richard Jackson, an MP with close colonial connections, considered that 'A revenue to be raised for the support of British troops in America is not now to [be] argued against: it would answer no purpose to do so.'[22]

Before any revenue measure was introduced, what was to be the most comprehensive attempt to settle post-war American issues was enacted. This was the proclamation of 7 October 1763. It was the handiwork of the core of the London colonial bureaucracy, the secretary of state, the board of trade and their respective officials. Work on it began under the Bute ministry and it was finally approved by that of George Grenville. The proclamation was ostensibly concerned solely with the new territory acquired at the peace, that is with the French inhabited areas of Canada and western Florida, the huge expanse between the boundaries of the old British colonies and the Mississippi river, the great bulk of whose inhabitants were Indians, the former

---

[19] Cited in John L. Bullion, ' "Security and Economy": The Bute Administration's Plans for the American Army and Revenue, 1762–1763', *William and Mary Quarterly*, 3rd ser., XLV (1988), 502.

[20] 'Plans of Forts and Garrisons', PRO, CO 323/16, f. 85.

[21] See John L. Bullion, ' "The Ten Thousand in America": More Light on the Decision on the American Army, 1762–1763', *William and Mary Quarterly*, 3rd ser., XLIII (1986), 646–57; Bullion, ' "Security and Economy" '; Shy, *Toward Lexington*, pp. 69–83.

[22] To Franklin, 27 Dec. 1763, Leonard W. Labaree et al., eds., *The Papers of Benjamin Franklin* (New Haven, 1959–), X. 415.

Spanish colony of Florida and certain islands in the West Indies. What was laid down in the proclamation, however, throws much light on official thinking on colonial issues in general. New governments were to be created in areas where there was already or was expected to be significant British settlement. In their provisions for such governments British officials showed that no radical break with previous patterns of colonial constitutions was contemplated. To demonstrate the king's 'paternal care for the security of the liberties and properties' of his subjects, assemblies similar to those in the existing colonies would be called as soon as circumstances allowed.[23] 'Hints' submitted to lord Egremont, then the secretary of state, probably by Henry Ellis, a former governor of Georgia, urged that the model of the newest of the existing colonies, that is Georgia and Nova Scotia, should be adopted, as being 'freest from a Republican mixture and most conformable to the British constitution'.[24] Nothing was said in the proclamation about migration, but the board of trade in one of its reports urged that the new colonies should seek their populations not directly from Britain but from surplus people crowded into some of the older colonies and from new Protestant emigrants from continental Europe.[25] The author of 'Hints', strongly recommended that new settlement should be directed to coastal areas, especially to the new colonies and to Nova Scotia and Georgia, which alone of the existing colonies were allocated additional territory. There the population would be 'usefull to their mother country, instead of planting in the heart of America, out of the reach of government' and probably indulging in manufacturing.[26]

That was clearly an important consideration behind the most famous of sections of the proclamation, those that limited westward settlement, 'until our further pleasure be known', to a fixed line along the mountains that more or less constituted the existing limits of settlement. All land to the westward was to be reserved for the time being for the Indians 'as their hunting grounds'.[27] The imperatives of security were likely to have been an even more powerful consideration against unlimited settlement. The at least temporary curbing of western expansion was a confirmation of policies to conciliate Indians adopted in the later stages of the war. A government unsure of the disposition of the conquered French population and fearful of attacks from Britain's old enemies could not risk Indian disaffection which, it was assumed, would be the consequence of unregulated settlement in the west.[28]

---

[23] Text in A. Shortt and A. G. Doughty, eds., *Documents Relating to the Constitutional History of Canada 1759–1791*, 2nd edn., 2 vols. (Ottawa, 1918), I. 163–8.
[24] PRO, CO 323/16, f. 97.
[25] Report of 8 June 1763, Shortt and Doughty, eds., *Documents*, I. 137.
[26] PRO, CO, 323/16, ff. 95–6.　　　[27] Shortt and Doughty, eds., *Documents*, I. 166–7.
[28] For the proclamation, see the works cited in note 18 together with R. A. Humphreys, 'Lord Shelburne and the Proclamation of 1763', *English Historical Review*, XLIX (1934), 241–64.

Enforcing the proclamation line and regulating dealings between traders and Indians beyond it became a major commitment for British regulars who were already dispersed in forts throughout the west. Relations with the Indian peoples beyond the colonial frontiers were to remain the responsibility of superintendents appointed by the crown and corresponding directly with the board of trade in London.

The question of how the Grenville government intended to fulfil its promise that a revenue would be raised in the colonies to defray the costs of the peace-time garrison was initially merged with another urgent post-war problem: how to curb illegal trade and enforce the Navigation Acts effectively. Trade in contravention of the Navigation Acts was long thought to have been endemic in colonial America. There had been frequent complaints about it before the Seven Years War. During the war illicit colonial trade with the enemy had reached scandalous heights in British eyes. Smuggling was an almost obsessive concern of Grenville's. He believed that it damaged legal trade and cheated the public revenue of huge sums.[29] He told the house of commons that it was 'particularly desirable to prevent intercourse of America with foreign nations. And yet many colonies have such a trade. Such a trade has been opened by three or four colonies with France to the amount of £4 or 500,000 a year'.[30] Reducing smuggling at home and in the colonies was said to be 'a favourite object of the present administration and nothing will be omitted that can tend to accomplish it'.[31] Anti-smuggling measures for the colonies were embodied in a series of orders in council and acts of parliament, culminating in the variously named Sugar, Molasses, Plantations, or Revenue Act of 5 April 1764. In it the powers of the colonial custom service against smuggling were strengthened, including the use of naval ships, and the courts of admiralty that tried such cases were given what was to be a highly contentious new superior court at Halifax, Nova Scotia. To prove its legality, trade by sea between colonies was to be subjected to an elaborate new system of documentation. Finally, levels of duties were adjusted, generally to give a stronger advantage to goods shipped from Britain to American markets or to American exports to Britain.

At least one of the adjustments in the level of duties was aimed at raising a revenue 'for defraying the expenses of defending, protecting and securing' America. That was the duty to be levied at the reduced rate of 3d. per gallon on molasses brought into North America from foreign West Indian islands.

[29] Bullion, *Great and Necessary Measure*, p. 52.

[30] 9 March 1764, R. C. Simmons and P. D. G. Thomas, eds., *Proceedings and Debates of the British Parliaments Respecting North America, 1754–1783*, 6 vols. (Millwood, NY, 1982–6), I. 488.

[31] T. Whately to J. Temple, 8 June 1764, 'The Bowdoin and Temple Papers, I', *Massachusetts Historical Society Collections*, 6th ser., IX (1897), 19.

The original duty of 6*d*. a gallon, enacted in 1733, had been intended to give the British West Indies a virtual monopoly of supplying molasses to the huge North American rum industry. It had proved to be unenforceable, a large volume of cheaper foreign molasses reputedly evading the customs system. The government's inquiries led it to believe that 3*d*. was a rate that importers could realistically bear and would thus pay rather than resorting to smuggling. Grenville hoped that it might raise between £40,000 and £60,000, only a small proportion of what was required. Grenville therefore warned that 'some further tax will be necessary' and indicated what he had in mind. 'Stamp duties' seemed to be 'the least exceptionable'.[32]

Another piece of legislation directly affecting North America was introduced before the end of the 1764 session. This became the Currency Act. It was the initiative of the board of trade, who were concerned about the effects on imperial trade of the quantities of depreciating American paper currency that had been issued during the war. British merchants claimed that payment of their debts in such paper, particularly in the devalued currency of Virginia, was an unacceptable hardship. After much consultation with the those concerned, including the agents of the American colonies, further issues of paper money as legal tender by colonies whose currency had not been regulated by a previous act were forbidden. Charles Garth, agent for South Carolina, saw the bill as part of the board of trade's 'grand plan, to establish throughout North America one uniform system of government and policy', but took comfort that proposals to make it illegal to offer existing paper currency as legal tender had been beaten off.[33]

After a delay of some months to collect more information, and, at least ostensibly, to enable colonial opinion to be heard, the promised stamp duties were introduced on 6 February 1765. Nobody could doubt that this had become a highly charged issue. It was made even more so by a provision that offences against it could be tried without juries in admiralty courts. Colonial opinion believed that there was no precedent for parliament to levy a direct tax on the colonies as opposed to imposing duties on their trade. Grenville was well aware of American hostility and made an elaborate defence of the right of parliament to tax the whole empire. 'This law', he concluded, 'is founded on that great maxim, that protection is due from the governor, and support and obedience on the part of the governed.'[34] The bill was carried on its main division by 245 votes to 49.

[32] 9 March 1764, Simmons and Thomas, eds., *Proceedings and Debates*, I. 489.
[33] To South Carolina Committee of Correspondence, 21 Jan., 20 Dec. 1764, WLCL, Garth Letter Book, ff. 92, 143.
[34] 6 Feb. 1765, Simmons and Thomas, eds., *Proceedings and Debates*, II. 11.

The Stamp Act was followed later in the 1765 session by the American Mutiny or Quartering Act. This originated in the war office as a response to the concerns of the commander-in-chief in America about arrangements for billeting soldiers in the colonies. The original bill included a clause that soldiers might be billeted in private houses, a highly emotive issue for contemporaries. This was strongly opposed in many parts of the house of commons, with the American agents helping to drum up support against it. The bill was amended and new clauses were included which allowed for billeting in uninhabited buildings at the expense of the colony, a provision which was to cause serious trouble later.

The adjournment of parliament at the end of the 1765 session brought to a close two years in which the British presence in North America had been considerably strengthened. There was now a commander-in-chief to coordinate defence with an enlarged regular garrison at his disposal. His powers for making arrangements for 'the marching and quartering' of his troops had been enhanced. Indian policy remained under imperial direction. Metropolitan authority had taken control over the distribution of land outside colonial boundaries and had imposed limits on settlement. Additional regulations for colonial trade had been devised and the imperial customs service had been given greater powers to enforce commercial regulations, including a strengthened system of admiralty jurisdiction. Finally, by passing the Stamp Act the Westminster parliament had unequivocally ended any doubts, at least in its own mind, over its right to lay taxes and therefore to exercise an unlimited sovereignty over the colonies. The measures may have been introduced in a piecemeal manner by different government departments in response to a series of specific problems, but taken as a whole they amounted to a significant increase of imperial power and in American eyes precedents had been established for what might be unlimited further increases: in particular, it was feared that the colonies could be milked dry by escalating British taxes.

As Chapter 5 tried to establish, the great body of mainstream British political opinion did indeed believe in an unlimited parliamentary sovereignty over the colonies. They insisted, however, that this sovereignty was being used for strictly limited measures aimed at the common good of Britain and the colonies. Taxes went no further than to raise money to meet part of the costs of defence. Americans need not fear for the liberties to which they were justly entitled. Grenville went out of his way to profess his concern for the colonies and his good intentions towards them. Richard Jackson reported that Grenville had spoken 'of the colonies in general in terms of great kindness and regard and in particular assured the house there was no intention to abridge or alter any of the charters'.[35] He began his conversations with colonial agents by 'the kindest expressions of regard to the colonies'.[36] Thomas Whately, secretary to the treasury, was particularly effusive in his assurances to his American correspondents of the government's goodwill towards them. 'I always loved the colonies. I am, I always was curious about them, and very happy when I am employed in any business that relates to them . . . I know that those who are at present in administration are anxious for the prosperity of the colonies and highly sensible of their importance.'[37] He left it to his correspondents to judge whether there was any 'want of proper attention to the colonies. I am sure there is no want of regard to them.'[38]

Such professions probably did not cut much ice with Americans, who were inclined to believe that, whatever ministers said, they would in practice invariably put British interests first and usually even put those of the West Indies before the concerns of North America. Even if they were prepared to concede that ministers wished them well, Americans were in no doubt that good intentions were being vitiated by ignorance and a determination to force through damaging decisions, based on false premises about the colonies, above all on erroneous assumptions about their huge disposable wealth, at unprecedented speed and without proper consultation. The arrangements for transatlantic negotiation, which had been characteristic of the empire in the mid-eighteenth century, seemed to have been abrogated and to have been replaced by dictation from Whitehall, usually in the form of acts of a would-be sovereign parliament. Parliament, wrote Benjamin Franklin, had dealt with 'trade, duties, troops and fortifications in America. Our opinions or inclinations, if they had been known, would perhaps have weigh'd but little among you. We are in your hands as clay in the hands of the potter.'[39]

Ministers rejected such criticisms. They seem to have recognized that North America was not well represented in the commons, and so appeared to accept the convention that colonies should be given due warning and a proper length of time to respond to important pieces of legislation that affected them before they were enacted. Advanced warning was indeed given for by far the most contentious piece of legislation, the Stamp Act, almost a year before it was introduced, in Grenville's words 'to give Americans

[35] To T. Fitch, 9 Feb 1765, 'The Fitch Papers, II, Correspondence and Documents during Thomas Fitch's Governorship of the Colony of Connecticut, 1754–1766', *Collections of the Historical Society of Connecticut*, XVIII (1920), 317.
[36] J. Mauduit to Massachusetts Speaker 11 Feb. 1764, 'Jasper Mauduit: Agent in London for the Colony of Massachusetts Bay', *Massachusetts Historical Society Collections*, LXXIV (1918), 146fn.
[37] To J. Temple, 5 Nov. 1764, 'Bowdoin and Temple Papers, I', 38.
[38] To Temple [Feb. 1765], ibid. I. 51.
[39] To P. Collinson, 30 April 1764, Labaree et al, eds., *Papers of Benjamin Franklin*, XI. 181.

an opportunity of conveying information to this house, whose ears are always open to receive knowledge and to act on it'.[40] American interests were fully engaged in the preparation of the Currency and Quartering Acts and had a considerable influence on the final form taken by the legislation in both cases.

An American agent conceded that ministers were indeed prepared to hear them 'patiently, to listen attentively to the reasonings and to determin at least seemingly with coolness and upon principle upon the several measures which are resolved on'.[41] Even so, most Americans who had contact with ministers believed with good reason that whatever opinions they might hear, they were not to be deflected from their purposes. If they could obtain colonial endorsement for them, so much the better; but they would still proceed without it on what they regarded as essentials. Some agents, for instance, believed that Grenville had given them an opportunity to propose alternative means of raising money in place of the stamp duty. This was shown not to be the case. Grenville made it clear that the delay in introducing the duties was to give an opportunity 'for information not for opposition'.[42] The principle that the colonies would be required to contribute to their defence through paying stamp duties voted by parliament was not negotiable. Colonial pressure could secure amendments in the currency and the quartering bills but it could not defeat them. Behind their studied politeness and their willingness to listen, there seems to have been a new inflexibility on the part of ministers and officials and, as a recent study has put it, 'a shift in emphasis toward enforcing colonial obedience to laws, however unpopular, and away from working with interests either to prepare laws the colonists would comply with voluntarily or to wink at selective evasion'.[43] Underlying this inflexibility seems to have been a sense of urgency: defence against future Bourbon revenge, curbing British public expenditure and therefore reducing the debt and directing colonial trade back into its legal courses were all issues that could not be allowed to drift. Before and during the war, colonial reforms had been shelved by politicians unwilling to risk controversy and wary of bringing colonial issues before parliament.[44] There was now a political leadership that did not fear controversy and was only too willing to involve parliament. Urgency was reinforced by an overweening confidence in the rightness of what was being proposed. Even the conciliatory Whately

---

[40] 6 Feb. 1765, Simmons and Thomas, eds., *Proceedings and Debates*, II. 9.

[41] J. Ingersoll to T. Fitch, 6 March 1765, 'Fitch Papers, II', 336–7.

[42] Speech of 15 Feb. 1765, Simmons and Thomas, eds., *Proceedings and Debates*, II. 26. See the interpretation in Thomas, *British Politics and the Stamp Act Crisis*, pp. 72–8.

[43] Alison Gilbert Olson, *Making the Empire Work: London and American Interest Groups 1690–1790* (Cambridge, Mass., 1992), p. 143.

[44] See above, p. 78.

could not see how anyone could accept 'a proposition so untenable as that an acknowledged sovereign legislature cannot lay taxes'.[45]

Men convinced of the rightness of what they were doing and of the need to enforce solutions to problems of the highest importance as soon as possible were not likely to be tolerant of opposition. There were clear indications that in the new climate after the war dissent would be given short shrift. In December 1764 the privy council referred to the board of trade resolutions and addresses passed in the assemblies of New York and Massachusetts which had responded to the threat of a stamp tax by questioning the right of parliament to lay taxes on America. The privy council considered that such sentiments showed 'the most indecent disrespect to the legislature of Great Britain' and the board of trade urged that the matter be referred to parliament.[46] In March 1765 the privy council turned its attention to a long-running dispute between the governor and assembly of Jamaica. It resolved that if the assembly continued to refuse to vote supply that dispute would also be referred to parliament to enable it to 'take such measures for raising the usual supplies within the said island'. Put bluntly, Jamaica would be taxed by the British parliament if it would not tax itself.[47]

The authority of parliament had clearly become a central issue. If Americans opposed measures that had the sanction of parliament, they were not merely refusing to cooperate in the common purposes of empire but they were rebelling against its supreme constitutional authority. Grenville had stated as early as 9 March 1764 that 'the very sovereignty of this kingdom' was at stake in the question as to whether parliament could lay 'internal' taxes on America.[48] As Americans began to show how strongly they opposed parliamentary taxes, the passing of the Stamp Act became a matter of fundamental principle for Grenville and his colleagues, whatever the yield of the duties might prove to be. To 'establish the right of parliament' had become 'a great and necessary measure'.[49]

Few people in British politics appear to have disagreed with Grenville. Americans writing to their correspondents at home repeatedly stressed that no objections to the right of taxation would be tolerated. No 'man of consequence' could be expected to 'stand up in his place and avow an opinion that . . . acts of parliament . . . were not obligatory upon all his majesty's

[45] To J. Temple, 10 May 1765, 'Bowdoin and Temple Letters, I', 52

[46] W. L. Grant and J. Munro, eds., *Acts of the Privy Council of England: Colonial Series*, 6 vols. (1908–12), IV. 692.

[47] Ibid. IV. 708. For the dispute, see above p. 102 and Jack P. Greene, 'The Jamaica Privilege Controversy, 1764–66: An Episode in the Process of Constitutional Definition in the Early Modern British Empire', *Journal Of Imperial and Commonwealth History*, XXII (1994), 16–53.

[48] Simmons and Thomas, eds., *Proceedings and Debates*, I. 492.

[49] Bullion, *A Great and Necessary Measure*, p. 5.

subjects in all parts of his dominion'.[50] There was indeed very little parliamentary opposition to any of the measures affecting the colonies. The main part of the opposition to the Bute and the Grenville administrations consisted of a group now under the leadership of the marquess of Rockingham, which included the duke of Newcastle and considered itself to be the heirs of the Whig party of Walpole. Pitt and his followers constituted the other wing of the opposition. America does not seem to have been an issue on which the Rockingham group were strongly committed. There are indications that they had reservations about the increase of the army in America and the act revising colonial duties of 1764, but any doubts that the group's leading members may have had about the Stamp Act only became apparent in retrospect. On American questions the Rockinghams tended to wait for signs of the line that Pitt was going to take. These were usually hard to detect. He professed to be opposed to any 'measures of power, or force' against the colonies,[51] although he pressed for a larger army in America and stated that he found the proclamation better than nothing.[52] Whatever he may have thought about issues, he attended very few debates and vouchsafed no opinion about the Stamp Act.

MPs who did not belong to formal political groups seem in general to have supported Grenville on America. They appear to have accepted that his colonial measures were an essential part of his overall strategy of economy and revenue enhancement that were so necessary in the aftermath of a vastly expensive war. Moreover, parliament's sovereignty must be vindicated. It was reported that, except for a few individual members of the opposition groups or men with commercial interests in the colonies, 'there are scarce any people here, either within doors or without, but what approve the measures now taking with regard to America'.[53]

Americans in Britain commonly believed that public opinion in the widest sense was behind the government. To the ignorance of the colonies, of which American visitors had long complained, was being added, they thought, prejudices generated by reports of their failures in the last war and their ingratitude and over-assertiveness since. The Virginian Edward Jenings reflected in 1766 that Grenville had formed 'a scheme of corruption and rapacity which the generality of the nation approved of from self interest and jealousy of the colonies'.[54] Benjamin Franklin lamented that opposition to the Stamp Act had been fruitless. '[T]he tide was too strong against us. The

---

[50] J. Mauduit to Massachusetts Secretary, 7 April 1764. 'Jasper Mauduit', 147fn.
[51] Newcastle to Devonshire, 11 Aug. 1763, BL, Add MS 32950, f. 71.
[52] Newcastle to Devonshire, 16 Aug. 1763, BL, Add MS 32952, f. 7.
[53] J. Ingersoll to T. Fitch, 6 March 1765, 'Fitch Papers, II', 334.
[54] To R. Beverley, 2 April 1766, Jenings Letter Book, Virginia Historical Society, MS J 4105a 1.

nation was provok'd by American claims to independence, and all parties joined in resolveing by this act to settle the point.'[55] In as far as such assertions about public opinion had any foundation, they are likely to have been based on impressions gathered in London. Indications of opinion about the colonies further afield are hard to find. One source of some interest is the letters written in 1762 and 1763 by the agents in Britain of King's College, New York, and the Pennsylvania Academy, two colonial colleges trying to raise funds from donations. At one level, their mission suggests that there was much goodwill towards America in Britain. A great deal of money was raised: contributions were made by many people in different parts of England and Scotland and the court and all shades of political opinion from Bute to Pitt were generous. Tensions between the Church and Dissent about the denominational dispositions of the colleges were largely overcome and both contributed. Nevertheless, the agents, particularly William Smith for the Pennsylvania Academy, reported hostility to the colonies as well as benevolence. Pitt told Smith that he should apply for a parliamentary grant but Smith thought that inadvisable. '[W]e can expect nothing from that quarter, as a great majority of members think we do no[t] do enough for ourselves.'[56] Both he and the New York agent reported that the allegations that New York had traded extensively with the enemy during the war were very widely believed and were extremely damaging to the colonies.[57] Smith reported 'a strong prejudice that we stand in need of no help, have got all the benefits of a war that has plunged the mother country so deep in debt; that we will do nothing for ourselves and that learning will create independence.'[58] Although £300 was collected in Liverpool, Smith was given a particularly rough ride there, being told that 'our scheme was the beginning of independency, the worst of policy for the mother country; that we were able enough to build our colleges ourselves; that we had got all the advantages of the war, had born little of the burden, and were impudent beggars that would do nothing for ourselves'.[59] Such fragmentary and to some extent contradictory evidence is hard to interpret. Smith was, however, surely right when he wrote: 'It was once thought that we were too little an object for national notice here. Time and a fair trial have taught us better on this head.'[60] The war had ensured that the North American colonies were an object of notice to a great many British people. Historians' assumptions about the ignorance and indifference of

---

[55] To C. Thomson, 11 July 1765, Labaree et al., eds., *Papers of Benjamin Franklin*, XII. 207.
[56] To R. Peters, 11 March 1763, HSP, William Smith MSS, II.
[57] See above, pp. 100–1.
[58] To T. Penn, 23 July 1763, HSP, William Smith MSS, II.
[59] To T. Penn, 25 Aug. 1763, ibid.
[60] To R. Peters, 12 Feb. 1763, ibid.

British opinion may need revision. A wide public seem to have wished the colonies well, even to the extent of parting with considerable sums of money to them. But they wished them well on their own terms, that is as a prosperous but also as a dutiful part of the British empire. Legislation that aimed to enforce the colonies' obligations of which they seemed not to be sufficiently mindful was likely to be popular.[61]

Americans disliked the substance of much that was enacted. Little was said against the increased British garrison, as opposed to the attempts to raise taxation to pay for it. Not only did such attempts raise the great question of the right of taxation, but Americans felt no inclination to pay for an army mostly stationed in the newly conquered territories, which they regarded as British imperial interests rather than as any interest of theirs. They were indeed excluded from settling in a wide swath of these territories by the proclamation of 1763. This was, however, presumed to be a temporary prohibition that could in any case be subverted and so the proclamation attracted little criticism.[62] The Sugar Act of 1764, by contrast, was denounced, even by government officials like Francis Bernard, as imposing highly damaging restrictions and discriminations on American trade in a time of acute postwar economic depression. Britain's true interest, it was endlessly asserted, was to foster not to blight colonial prosperity, on which the ability of Americans to buy British goods depended. Stamp duties would be yet another clog on the colonial economy. The restriction on the money supply imposed by the Currency Act threatened to do yet more damage. On all such issues, Americans resented the lack of regard now apparently being shown to them by British opinion. The refusal of parliament to consider petitions against taxation was particularly exasperating. William Smith of New York asked what could be expected of Americans when they 'reflect upon the parliament's refusal to hear their representations—when they read abstracts of the speeches within doors and the ministerial pamphlets without, and find themselves tantalised and contemned, advantages taken of their silence heretofore and remonstrances forbidden in time to come'.[63] John Watts, also of New York, complained of the 'air of both severity and contempt' with which new measures were being promulgated.[64] Thomas Hutchinson,

---

[61] The fund raising for New York and Pennsylvania is examined in my 'Who Cared about the Thirteen Colonies? Some Evidence from Philanthropy', *Journal of Imperial and Commonwealth History*, XXVII (1999), 57–65.

[62] The point has been well made that while settlers could cross the proclamation line with relative impunity, large-scale speculators needed the security of title that the proclamation denied them (Woody Holton, *Forced Founders: Indians, Debtors, Slaves and the Making of the American Revolution in Virginia* (Chapel Hill, NC, 1999), pp. 7–8).

[63] To R. Monckton, 30 May 1765, 'Aspinwall Papers, II', *Massachusetts Historical Society Collections*, 4th ser., X (1871), 571.

[64] To Monckton, 1 June 1765, HUHL, Sparks MS 38, f. 30.

lieutenant governor of Massachusetts, wrote with gloomy foreboding that he was 'now convinced that the people thru' the continent are impressed with an opinion that they are no longer considered by the people of England as their fellow subjects and entitled to English liberties'.[65] Above all, many politically aware Americans were deeply concerned at the principle of an unlimited parliamentary sovereignty over the colonies which was finding so much support in Britain. They set to work to produce their own theories by which limitations could be placed on the powers of parliament over them.[66]

Much as they disliked what had been done, such Americans might have derived some comfort from what had not been attempted. No change had been made in existing colonial constitutions. The much denounced chartered privileges of Rhode Island and Connecticut remained intact. Nothing had been heard of the long-dreaded proposal that governors' instructions be given the force of law in the colonies. For Francis Bernard this was Grenville's great mistake. He had tried to impose new policies without ensuring that there was a structure of authority in place in the colonies capable of carrying them out. As Bernard put it, 'the business of the finances', that is taxation, 'took the lead'. But, as the debacle of trying to enforce the Stamp Act was to show, the colonial governments were 'weak and impotent to an amazing degree'. Although he feared that it was now too late, there must be a reform of colonial government before anything else was attempted.[67] Grenville might have replied that reforming colonial government would be a very long-term prospect of doubtful success and that the needs of defence, levying a contribution for it and enforcing the laws of trade could not wait that long. But it seems clear that he disagreed with Bernard and others who thought like him, not only on the practicality of constitutional reform but as to its propriety as well. The first step towards reform was usually assumed to be the strengthening of the executive by the creation of a colonial civil list not dependent on the assemblies. This had been a favourite nostrum of the board of trade and former members of the board, such as Charles Townshend and lord Halifax, continued to advocate it. Grenville, however, specifically rejected any proposal for paying a colonial civil list out of parliamentary taxes. Tactical reasons have been suggested for this,[68] but it seems likely that when Grenville assured American agents that he intended scrupulously to respect the chartered rights of the colonies, he was demonstrating his Whig credentials.[69]

---

[65] To unknown, 16 Aug. 1765, MHS, Hutchinson Transcripts, XXVI, p. 294.
[66] These are discussed in Chap. 5.
[67] To Barrington, 23 Nov. 1765, Channing and Coolidge, eds., *Bernard–Barrington Correspondence*, pp. 93–4.
[68] Bullion, *Great and Necessary Measure*, pp. 94, 148.   [69] See above, p. 169.

The extent of colonial opposition, which quickly passed from protests by the assemblies to disorder in the towns, took ministers by surprise, as it did most Americans living in London. Grenville had assumed that the stamp duty would enforce itself, in that those who failed to pay it would automatically put themselves outside the law, which he presumed that they could not afford to do. If he had any thoughts as to how American compliance could be ensured for executing his policies, he seems to have expected that the colonial elites would accept the rightness of what had been enacted and assert their authority to implement it. Their acceptance was to be bolstered by inducements. American rather than British stamp distributors were appointed. Grenville chose some of 'the most respectable people in their several provinces. They will find their account in it, both as a place of emolument and of influence, as the appointment of under distributors will be left to them'.[70] Some prominent Americans were indeed willing to take Grenville's bait. When he heard of the beginnings of disorder throughout the colonies, Whately could still hope that 'the most sensible men amongst them' would on reflection accept that 'the Stamp Act is not a grievance' and that 'The most leading and popular men amongst them are engaged by their offices or their interests to oppose the mob and will soon regain their authority.'[71]

Such hopes were based on serious misunderstandings. Even if some of them had acquiesced in disorder in the later months of 1765, the colonial elites would certainly do their utmost to reassert their authority after the riots. They would not, however, commit themselves to asserting imperial authority. For them British intervention, as embodied in the Stamp Act and other measures, meant that the mother country was not the distant and acquiescent partner in empire that they had fondly imagined after the war, but a rival to be resisted. The implications of a sovereign parliament's ability to lay taxes on America was that colonial assemblies and the provincial political leaderships that dominated them would eventually lose much of their power. They had already lost control over the defence of the colonies and relations with Indians beyond their borders. The full enforcement of the Navigation Acts would put new powers into the hands of a detested imperial customs service and enable it to disrupt the trade of important groups of merchants, notably in Boston, who depended on operating outside the system.[72] The extended powers of the admiralty courts were seen as a challenge to the colonial judiciaries.

Far from accepting the Stamp Act and rallying to imperial authority, the colonial elites took the lead in resisting the act and in the process exposed the

---

[70] Whately to J. Temple, 10 May 1765, 'Bowdoin and Temple Letters, I', 52.

[71] Whately to Grenville, 25 Oct. 1765, BL, Add MS 57817A, f. 47.

[72] John W. Tyler, *Smugglers and Patriots: Boston Merchants and the Advent of the American Revolution* (Boston, 1986), especially pp. 100–7.

powerlessness of imperial authority. Beginning with the Virginia house of burgesses in May 1765, the assemblies passed resolutions denying the right of parliament to tax them. Practical resistance followed. Violence and intimidation were widely used to render the Stamp Act unenforceable. By 1 November, the date when the act was supposed to take effect, it was clear that no stamps could be sold in the older mainland colonies. All the appointed distributors of stamps were forced to resign their offices. Customs officers were compelled to allow ships to come and go without having stamps on their papers. Colonial courts were either closed down or forced to operate without stamps on legal documents. Popular opposition to the Stamp Act was very widespread. In ports already suffering from an economic recession with high unemployment and with a tradition of popular political participation through disorder, violence could not be confined to targets immediately connected with the stamps.[73] In Boston the house of the lieutenant governor, Thomas Hutchinson, was destroyed 'with a savageness unknown in a civilised country'.[74] In New York rioters also attacked the property of the lieutenant governor and of a major in the British army and then threatened to storm the fort and overwhelm its small royal garrison. General Gage, the commander-in-chief, described what had happened in New York as an 'insurrection composed . . . of great numbers of sailors headed by captains of the privateers and other ships; the inhabitants of the towns joined by many who have come in from the neighboring country and provinces; the whole may amount to some thousands'.[75] He warned the British government that violent outbreaks could be expected elsewhere. Sons of Liberty throughout the colonies were binding themselves, he wrote, 'to oppose the Stamp Act, even to take the field, at the risk of their lives and fortunes'.[76] Bernard reported that 'the common people' of Massachusetts 'talk of revolting from Great Britain'.[77]

Relative stability was to be restored throughout North America in 1766, but there could be no doubt that the lesson of the disorders was that the capacity of local governments to carry out imperial purposes had been tested and found totally wanting. In the words of the classic account of Edmund and Helen Morgan 'regular government' had for a time been 'all but extinguished'.[78] Governors had been opposed by their assemblies and got very

[73] Gary B. Nash, *The Urban Crucible: Social Change, Political Consciousness and the Origins of the American Revolution* (Cambridge, Mass, 1979).

[74] F. Bernard to Board of Trade, 19 Oct. 1765, PRO, CO, 5/891, f. 333.

[75] To H. Conway, 4 Nov. 1765, C. E. Carter, ed., *The Correspondence of General Thomas Gage with the Secretaries of State and with the War Office and the Treasury, 1763–1775*, 2 vols. (New Haven, 1931–3), I. 71.

[76] To Conway, 22 Feb. 1766, ibid. I. 84.

[77] To Conway, 25 Jan. 1766, PRO, CO 5/755, f. 495.

[78] Edmund and Helen Morgan, *The Stamp Act Crisis: Prologue to Revolution*, 2nd edn. (New York, 1962), p. 255.

little support from their disaffected or intimidated councils. If a council had been willing to call out the militia, it was usually regarded as unsafe to do so, since the militia would side with the rioters. Bernard graphically described his helplessness in Massachusetts. He had become a 'meer nominal governor . . . In the case of a popular tumult I can't command ten men that can be depended upon.'[79] The Boston populace had been able to establish 'a formal democracy in this town'.[80] Gage reported that the New York magistrates were 'entirely under the influence of the people' and would do nothing to restore order.[81] He concluded that there seemed 'throughout the provinces to be a dissolution of all legal authority, that subordination is entirely destroyed, and that all coercive powers in government are annihalated'.[82] The only power on which the British government could rely was his own regulars. Most of them were posted in the newly conquered territories and they were too scattered to intervene effectively in the riots. Fresh troops from Britain would have to be sent and even then they would need legal authority to act in support of the civil power. The civil power in the colonies was likely to be too cowed to give him that authority.

Beleaguered governors, Bernard of Massachusetts or Cadwallader Colden of New York, encouraged ministers in Britain to believe that a limited application of force would be enough to turn the tide and prepare the way, so Bernard thought, for imposing the constitutional reforms that should have preceded the Stamp Act.[83] That was probably bad advice. In reality the choice facing ministers was either to sanction a large commitment of force to try to crush what would almost certainly have been a vigorous and prolonged resistance or to be willing to accept that attempts to consolidate empire had failed because they lacked any basis of effective American support on which to build.

Neither course was palatable. There were serious scruples about launching what would have amounted to large-scale military operations against fellow subjects in the colonies with the possibility of French and Spanish intervention. Nor was it acceptable to most British opinion to abandon what seemed entirely reasonable attempts to make Americans contribute to their own defence or to confine their overseas trade within the undoubtedly generous parameters of the Navigation Acts. Above all, to concede that the authority of a sovereign parliament could be defied by cliques of supposedly self-interested

---

[79] To R. Jackson, 24 Aug. 1765, HUHL, Sparks MSS 4/4, f. 19.

[80] To J. Pownall, 26 Nov. 1765, PRO, CO 5/891, f. 336.

[81] To Conway, 16 Jan. 1766, Carter, ed., *Correspondence of General Thomas Gage*, I. 82.

[82] To Conway, 22 Feb 1766, ibid. I. 84.

[83] Bernard to Conway, 25 Jan. 1766, HUHL, Sparks MSS 4/4, f. 195; Colden to Conway, 21 Feb. 1766, 'Colden Letter Books, II', *Collections of the New York Historical Society for the Year 1877* (New York, 1878), p. 99.

colonial politicians backed by disorderly rabbles in the American ports was deeply offensive, and seemed a dire precedent to men who were seriously worried about the prevalence of disorder at home. The prospect of ever closer integration of the colonies with Britain through commercial growth, the movement of people and the tightening grip of British cultural values on the colonies seemed to be an inadequate compensation for recognizing the failure to create a functioning rather than a nominal empire. If commercial and demographic expansion were indeed leading to closer integration between Britain and America, this was often thought to be extremely hazardous for Britain unless proper political controls were maintained.

Faced with desperately hard choices, British governments tried for the next ten years to avoid them. The predominant inclination was certainly not to launch large-scale military intervention. The strictly logical corollary of that would have been to abandon attempts at imperial consolidation. At least until 1774, imperial consolidation was in fact to be pursued with less intensity than had been shown by George Grenville. It was never, however, abandoned altogether. British governments continued to test what the colonies would accept and continued to encounter resistance.

II

The administration that had to make the choice between using force or withdrawing was no longer that of George Grenville. For reasons that had no connection with America, on 10 July 1765 Grenville was replaced as the king's chief minister by the marquess of Rockingham.[84]

As an opposition group, Rockingham and his supporters were in no way committed to Grenville's colonial policies. Whatever views of their own the new ministers may have had, as the story of colonial defiance of parliament's authority, of riot and disorder and of the failure of the Stamp Act to take effect began to unfold in Britain in the autumn and winter of 1765, it became clear that their response would have to take account, first of all, of widespread public outrage at reports of what was happening across the Atlantic and, secondly, of the serious economic consequences anticipated for Britain from the commotions in America.

Grenville, now in opposition, immediately saw the situation in the starkest terms. He interpreted the resolutions of the Virginia house of burgesses as

[84] For the Rockingham ministry, see Thomas, *Stamp Act Crisis*, chs. 8–13; Paul Langford, *The First Rockingham Administration, 1765–1766* (Oxford, 1973); John L. Bullion, 'British Ministers and American Resistance to the Stamp Act, October–December 1765', *William and Mary Quarterly*, 3rd ser., XLIX (1992), 89–107.

'declaring the parliament of Great Britain enemies of their country'.[85] In his view, if the colonies refused to be taxed by Britain they were asserting that they were 'independent of the mother country'.[86] As soon as parliament reassembled, in the debate on the king's speech on 17 December, he proclaimed that the colonies were as much in 'open rebellion' as the Jacobites had been in 1745.[87] There was also talk of 'rebellion' and of 'traitors' in the house of lords at the same time.[88] Such views were widely shared. Thomas Penn reported that 'people here' considered that the Americans had raised a 'rebellion . . . against the king, lords and commons'.[89] He and other sympathizers with the colonies were doing their best 'to moderate the anger that the bulk of the people here have shewn against the colonys for not paying obedience to the Stamp Act and for shewing their dislike of it in so disrespectful and outrageous a manner . . . The common cry is that the colonys want to throw off all dependence on the mother country.'[90]

The new ministry would not of course give any countenance to colonial disobedience. Rockingham himself told the agent for Massachusetts that the 'unlawful and violent proceedings' in the colonies were 'utterly inconsistent with all government'.[91] Some of his colleagues were inclined to firm action. Among these, it was rumoured, was the ministry's patron, the duke of Cumberland, 'butcher' of the Highlands, and commander-in-chief at the beginning of the Seven Years War, when he had expressed jaundiced opinions about the soldierly qualities of Americans.[92] There were rumours that he was contemplating dispatching a military force to compel obedience to the Stamp Act.[93] The practical problems of assembling and moving such a force in winter, however, ruled that out.[94] Cumberland died on 31 October 1765 and no attempt was to be made to reinforce the troops in America. All the Rockingham ministry did was to advise the governors to call on the existing forces there for help if need be.[95] None of them took up this offer. The crisis would not be resolved by force. Nevertheless, intense resentment against the Americans in parliament and outside it was a major constraint on any other solutions that the new government might wish to propose.

[85] To R. Nugent, 13 Aug. 1765, HL, ST 7, vol. 2.   [86] To Whately, 13 Aug. 1765, ibid.
[87] 17 Dec. 1765, Simmons and Thomas, eds., *Proceedings and Debates*, II. 59.
[88] Debate on 17 Dec. 1765, ibid. II. 57.
[89] To W. Allen, 15 Dec. 1765, HSP, Thomas Penn Letter Books, VIII, pp. 338–9.
[90] To B. Chew, 11 Jan. 1766, ibid. p. 341.
[91] W. Bollan to T. Hutchinson, 14 Oct. 1765, MHS, Hutchinson Transcripts, XXV, p. 35.
[92] See above, p. 92.
[93] Thomas Hutchinson, Jun. told his father that he had heard from Richard Jackson that 'if the Duke of Cumberland had not died instead of a repeal of the act there would have been a number of regiments in America' (letter of 2 July 1766, MHS, Hutchinson Transcripts, XXV, p. 89).
[94] Bullion, 'British Ministers and American Resistance', 95.
[95] Thomas, *British Politics and the Stamp Act Crisis*, p. 138.

The urgent need to reach a settlement with the colonies was soon being pressed on the government by merchant and manufacturing opinion. With the British economy badly affected by recession and with colonial markets still slack, the prospect of political disruption exacerbating problems further was very unwelcome. A 'standing committee' of merchants trading to America had come into existence by August 1765 and it was being regularly attended by three of the most prominent colonial agents.[96] Benjamin Franklin was one of those agents. He believed that the new government was generally well disposed to the colonies.[97] Ministers were certainly accessible to lobbying by commercial interests. As a great Yorkshire landowner, Rockingham took a keen interest in the problems of the county's textile manufacturers. His government also cultivated links with London business interests connected with America and with midland metalware manufacturers.[98] In October Rockingham assured William Bollan of Massachusetts that ministers were 'enclined to relieve the American trade in general in all points wherein it was improperly curbed and to put the whole upon the best foot for the common good of the kingdom and the colonies'.[99] What was to be offered would be a full inquiry into commercial regulations affecting the colonies, presumably including sections of the new Sugar Act. On 6 November Barlow Trecothick, a leading London American merchant, warned Rockingham that it was the Stamp Act itself that was likely to have the most dire economic consequences. Americans would, he believed, refuse to participate in any commercial transactions that involved the use of stamped paper. This would mean that British exports to the colonies would cease, that the West Indies would be starved of food and that British commercial houses would fail. Credit would dry up. There would be a slump in manufacturing and massive unemployment would follow.[100] News of American boycotts of British goods so long as the Stamp Act remained unrepealed reinforced Trecothick's message. Making the Stamp Act the key to any restoration of commercial prosperity, however, sharply raised the stakes for ministers. As Thomas Penn pointed out, had Americans only set forth 'the hardships of the Stamp Act, without denying the power of parliament, it would be repealed'.[101] That was not of course what Americans had done. They had challenged the power of

---

[96] C. Garth to South Carolina Committee of Correspondence, 20 Aug. 1765, WLCL, Garth Letter Book, f. 156.

[97] To W. Franklin, 26 July 1765 and to D. Hall, 20 Aug. 1765, Labaree, et al., eds., *Papers of Benjamin Franklin*, XII. 222, 241.

[98] John Money, *Experience and Identity: Birmingham and the West Midlands 1760–1800* (Manchester, 1977), pp. 164–5.

[99] Bollan to Hutchinson, 14 Oct. 1765, MHS, Hutchinson Transcripts, XXV, p. 35.

[100] His letter is summarized in Langford, *First Rockingham Administration*, p. 110.

[101] To W. Allen, 15 Dec. 1765, HSP, Thomas Penn Letter Books, VIII, p. 339.

parliament and, however impolitic the Stamp Act had now come to seem to them, for the government to ask parliament to withdraw unconditionally in the face of such a challenge was impossible. Franklin thought that the only way out for them might be a suspension for a year, after which the act could be quietly dropped without bringing 'the question of right to a decision'.[102] There was also much talk about modifying the Stamp Act in certain ways to make it less objectionable.

After much sounding of opinion and many internal debates within the government, a policy emerged in January 1766 which attempted to square the circle by conclusively deciding 'the question of right' in favour of parliament's sovereignty over the colonies, but at the same time dropping the Stamp Act altogether as an inexpedient measure that had seriously damaged the imperial economy.[103]

The question of right was to be established by introducing a series of resolutions that would be embodied in a Declaratory Act, modelled on the Irish act of 1720, declaring the sovereignty of the British parliament over the colonies. The attorney-general, Charles Yorke, who held very strong views about the subordination of the colonies, was entrusted with drafting the resolutions. He was evidently inclined to go beyond the terms of the Irish act, but more moderate views, notably those of Rockingham himself, prevailed and the final version laid down that parliament 'had, hath and of right ought to have, full power and authority to make laws and statutes of sufficient force and validity to bind the colonies and people of *America*, subjects to the crown of *Great Britain*, in all cases whatsoever'.[104]

The case for the repeal of the Stamp Act, rather than modification or suspension, neither of which, ministers evidently believed, would restore stability, was to be based on economic necessity, not on any denial of constitutional right. To prove the case, merchants and manufacturers, working closely with the American agents in a new committee, were given every encouragement by ministers to petition parliament and a number of them were summoned to give verbal evidence to the commons about the loss of trade, the likelihood that Americans would default on their very large debts and the unemployment that would follow with the threat of disorder in the manufacturing districts. These tactics were eminently successful and repeal was carried by a large majority on 21 February 1766.

If the outcome was eventually triumphant, the parliamentary campaign to secure the dual aims of the Declaratory Act and the repeal of the Stamp Act was fraught with difficulty. A vast majority of both houses endorsed the

[102] To W. Franklin, 9 Nov. 1765, Labaree et al., eds., *Papers of Benjamin Franklin*, XII. 362.
[103] For this decision, see Thomas, *British Politics and the Stamp Act Crisis*, ch. 10.
[104] 6 Geo. III, c. 12.

Declaratory Act and the principle of parliamentary sovereignty. There was, however, one very distinguished dissenter. Pitt broke his long silence on colonial matters on 14 January 1766 by proclaiming that the Stamp Act was not merely impolitic but unconstitutional. The colonies were not represented in the British parliament which had no right to lay an 'internal' tax on them. American resistance could therefore be justified. This was a point of view that found virtually no support in parliament. Much more serious for the government was the campaign against repeal led by Grenville. For him 'it was a shameful and pernicious measure . . . which is intended to give up for ever the fundamental rights of the kingdom and parliament of Great Britain'.[105] Unless at least a modified version of the Stamp Act was retained, the principles laid down in the Declaratory Act would mean nothing. Many people, including George III in private, probably agreed with him. Lord Bute and a number of men holding minor offices who were still associated with him certainly did and opposed the government, which risked defeat on several occasions in the house of lords. The king's publicly stated support for his ministers ultimately, however, carried the day in the lords, while the government achieved a large majority in the commons. It seems clear that repeal was supported by most MPs who had no party affiliations and that, whatever they may have felt about the iniquities of American resistance, they were convinced by the case, so zealously propagated by government, that conciliation of America would restore prosperity. Disorder at home as a result of unemployment was an even more immediately intimidating prospect than disorder in the colonies.[106]

Evidence about wider responses to the great debate about empire are, as usual, scanty and hard to assess. The extensive coverage of colonial affairs in press and parliament provoked by the Stamp Act was believed by Americans in London to have given the British public 'some little insight into the nature of America'. They now, for instance, knew that Virginia was not an island.[107] Be that as it may, the crisis seems to have given a sharper focus in Britain to a sense of a collective 'American', meaning North American, identity with a potential for antagonism with Britain. The North American colonies appeared to be developing a common interest, most obviously through the Stamp Act Congress and the close cooperation of their agents in Britain. This set them apart from other 'Americans' in the West Indian islands. The Jamaican assembly's claims to privileges equal to those of the house of commons, which were as offensive to British opinion as those of any North

[105] To A. Hervey, 3 March 1766, HL, ST 7, vol. 2.

[106] See the discussion in Langford, *First Rockingham Administration*, pp. 172–85.

[107] E. Jenings to R. Beverley, n.d., Virginia Historical Society, Jenings Letter Book, MS J 4105a 1, p. 271.

American colony, had finally been referred to parliament in November 1765. Before that happened, a delegation of those with interests in the island had intervened with the privy council to arrange an acceptable compromise in a way that no North American colony seems either to have been able or willing to imitate.[108] By then the governor of Jamaica had already reported that the Stamp Act had been 'carried into execution'.[109] It was also put into operation in Barbados. In both islands there were vigorous protests, but riot and open resistance only took place in the Leeward Islands of St Kitts and Nevis.[110] The North Americans were unique in the scale and extent of their intransigence.

Not only was the term 'American' becoming synonymous in Britain with North America, but in some British minds it seems that it was also coming to imply a partisan of the northern colonies. The MP James Harris, who supported Grenville, was unimpressed with Franklin when he appeared as a witness before the commons. He seemed to be 'a most complete American, a perfect anti-Briton'.[111] Franklin himself noted a year later that those in Britain who 'showed a disposition to favour us' were 'called by way of reproach *Americans*'.[112] A letter to a newspaper, signed 'No American but a true Englishman', did indeed dismiss the Rockingham government as having been an '*infamous, ridiculous American*' one.[113]

American observers were in no doubt about the extent of popular resentment against the colonies in the winter of 1765–6. Charles Garth wrote on 19 January 1766 that 'people living in the country' took 'great exception' to what they thought of as America's refusal '*to contribute any thing to the expenses of government but to throw and continue the load of their support on the inhabitants of Great Britain*'.[114] A little more than a month later, however, there were reports of popular jubilation in Bristol, Liverpool, Birmingham, and Leeds as well as in London at the passing of repeal of the Stamp Act.[115] There was no doubt a degree both of manipulation and of self-interest behind such effusions. The highly efficient merchants' organizations which had coordinated petitions presumably encouraged appropriate celebrations, while trades people and artisans had been promised that orders would be placed and

[108] Privy Council report, 28 May 1766, PRO, CO 137/34, f. 9.
[109] W. Lyttelton to board of trade, 24 Dec. 1765, ibid. f. 48.
[110] Andrew J. O'Shaughnessy, 'The Stamp Act Crisis in the British Caribbean', *William and Mary Quarterly*, 3rd ser., LI (1994), 203–26.
[111] Diary 13 Feb. 1766, Simmons and Thomas, eds., *Proceedings and Debates*, II. 235.
[112] Cited P. D. G. Thomas, *The Townshend Duties Crisis: The Second Phase of the American Revolution 1767–1773* (Oxford, 1987), p. 2.
[113] *Public Advertiser*, 7 March 1767.
[114] To South Carolina Committee of Correspondence, 9 Feb. 1766, Library of Congress, Force Transcripts, 7E.
[115] Press reports cited in Dora Mae Clark, *British Opinion and the American Revolution* (Cambridge, Mass., 1930) and Thomas, *British Politics and the Stamp Act Crisis*, p. 234.

full employment would return once the Stamp Act had been repealed. Beyond that, it is very difficult to gauge how far the cause of the colonies had at this stage become one with which popular opinion in Britain could identify.

Those in authority were always concerned that subversion might spread across the Atlantic. General Gage was worried about the effect that 'infamous publications', like John Wilkes's *North Briton* no. 45 with its defamatory comments on the king and the peace of 1763, would have in the colonies. He had parliament's proceedings on such publications sent to 'the publick papers', so that Americans could see them 'in their true light'.[116] This was a prescient if futile gesture. In a few years many Americans were indeed to become fervent admirers of Wilkes. Of more immediate concern, however, was the possible spread of American ideas and examples to Britain. A dissentient to the Declaratory Act in the house of lords pointed out that American objections to paying tax could be 'extended to all persons in this island who do not actually vote for members of parliament'.[117] They could indeed be so extended, but there appears to be no evidence that such connections were being overtly made at this time and it was certainly not the intention of the Rockingham administration or of their merchant allies that they should be made. Pressure on parliament was to be strictly apolitical and to concentrate solely on economic not on constitutional grievances. Whether control could have been kept had the movement failed to bring about repeal is another matter. Horace Walpole was expecting 'a general insurrection . . . as the immediate consequence of upholding the bill'.[118]

The most that can perhaps be said is that by 1766 radicals in Britain were beginning to become aware that they and the colonies might potentially have some interests in common. The Grenville government had both taxed America and upheld general warrants and the hounding of John Wilkes. Wilkes himself was initially dubious about American agitation,[119] but in February 1767 one of the toasts of a society of gentlemen who met to commemorate the publication of the *North Briton* no. 45 was 'to the brave Americans'.[120] During the Seven Years War urban radicalism had vociferously supported Pitt's view of the Americans as valiant Protestant Englishmen, whose defence had been neglected by ministers or had been entrusted to autocratic British military men who had oppressed them. Something of this

[116] Gage to Halifax, 6 Feb. 1764, Carter, ed., *Correspondence of General Thomas Gage*, I. 14.
[117] 11 March 1766, Simmons and Thomas, eds., *Proceedings and Debates*, II. 334.
[118] Cited Thomas, *British Politics and the Stamp Act Crisis*, p. 248.
[119] Paul Langford, 'London and the American Revolution' in J. Stevenson, ed., *London in the Age of Reform* (Oxford, 1977), p. 59.
[120] *Public Advertiser*, 18 Feb. 1767.

seems to have survived after the war. Conspicuous in the small minority who had opposed the Stamp Act from the outset was William Beckford, who aspired to lead radical opinion in the City of London. Religious Dissenters on both sides of the Atlantic had long made common cause. Americans concerned about renewed Anglican agitation after 1763 for a colonial bishop sought support in Britain. The Bostonian Jonathan Mayhew's pamphlets denouncing episcopacy were reprinted in London by the free-thinking unitarian and True Whig Thomas Hollis, who also interested himself in the campaign against the Stamp Act. He lobbied Rockingham on the 'the very imminent danger that there is at this time of losing our Northern Colonies'. He was extremely active in plying such parts of the London press as were sympathetic to radical causes with American material.[121] It was at this time that the Wilkes supporter, the publisher John Almon, began his connection with 'American writers [who] constantly sent him their pamphlets and papers to be reprinted in England'.[122]

The support which British radicals gave the Americans has attracted a great deal of historical scholarship, in part because it is relatively well documented and also perhaps because it can be fitted into a long-established narrative of the harnessing of popular involvement in politics behind reforming causes in Britain itself that was to culminate in the making of the English working class in the nineteenth century. Popular resentment at the claims of the colonies is much less easy to document, at least until 1775, when the stark choice was between war and peace. Before then, however, it seems likely that resentment was the dominant if incoherently expressed sentiment, except during the brief euphoria after the repeal of the Stamp Act, even if the chief evidence for it rests on the no doubt highly selective impressions of Americans writing home. Obscurantist and bigoted anti-American feeling may have been, but it merits serious study. The lines forward for popular involvement in politics from the 1760s and 1770s probably lead as much towards the mass loyalism and nationalism of the response to the French Revolution and Napoleon, of which anti-American sentiment can be seen as a precursor, as to the nineteenth-century radical tradition.[123] What was taken to be 'American' assertiveness was falling foul of a rampant Britishness or Englishness, powerfully stimulated by the victories of the Seven Years War. 'When the Americans talk

---

[121] Caroline Robbins, 'The Strenuous Whig, Thomas Hollis of Lincoln's Inn', *William and Mary Quarterly*, 3rd ser., VII (1950), 406–53; Charles W. Akers, *Called Unto Liberty: A Life of Jonathan Mayhew, 1720–1760* (Cambridge, Mass., 1964), pp. 208–12; J. C. D. Clark, *The Language of Liberty 1660–1832: Political Discourse and Social Dynamics in the Anglo-American World* (Cambridge, 1994), pp. 327–8.

[122] *Memoirs of John Almon, Bookseller, of Piccadilly* (1790), p. 32.

[123] This theme is developed in Linda Colley, *Britons: Forging the Nation 1707–1837* (New Haven, 1992).

of resistance', the Quaker John Fothergill wrote, 'the whole mastiff spirit of John Bull is roused' and 'pride and passion would carry him headlong into battle' even against his American 'brother'.[124]

Before the end of the 1766 session the Rockingham administration went some way to redeem the pledges given when they came into office that they would reform the commercial regulations affecting the colonies after an inquiry. The house of commons heard much evidence from merchants and was generally guided by it. Among a number of important reforms, the duty on molasses imported from the foreign West Indian islands was reduced from the 3*d*. a gallon, set in the 1764 Sugar Act, which Americans had regarded as excessive, to 1*d*. At the same time the British West Indies lost their preference in American markets. Their molasses also had to pay 1*d*. The money raised from this and from some other duties was explicitly earmarked 'to be disposed of by parliament', towards defraying 'the necessary expenses of defending, protecting and securing the *British* colonies and plantations in *America*.[125] Americans in London appear to have accepted this without protest. The agent for Rhode Island pointed out to his constituents that 1*d*. per gallon was part of a settlement that removed 'every grievance'.[126]

Rockingham and his ministers received congratulations and thanks from Americans and their supporters. Even James Otis, because of the notoriety of his views probably the last person that any British minister would wish to have gratified, assured them on behalf of Massachusetts of the 'full confidence they repose in the wisdom, justice and equity of the present truly British and patriotic administration'.[127] In retrospect Edmund Burke, who had just started his political career with the Rockinghams, was to portray the ministry as a brief interlude of enlightened statecraft in the gloomy story of the long slide to insurrection and war. It had brought about 'a return of your ancient system, and your ancient tranquillity and concord' in dealings with the colonies.[128]

The Rockinghams certainly deserve much credit for defusing a dangerous crisis, but there could be no return to any 'ancient tranquillity and concord', assuming that such conditions had ever existed. There had not been a full

---

[124] To J. Pemberton, 16 Oct. 1768, HSP, Etting Collection, XXIX, no. 58. The implications for the colonies of 'the stirrings of a heightened sense of British national identity' are stressed by T. H. Breen in 'Ideology and Nationalism on the Eve of the American Revolution: Revisions *Once More* in Need of Revising', *Journal of American History*, LXXXIV (1997), 13–39.

[125] 6 Geo. III, c. 52, sec. 12.

[126] J. Sherwood to Governor, 15 May 1766, *Records of the Colony of Rhode Island*, VI, *1757–1769* (Providence, RI, 1861), p. 491.

[127] To H. Conway, 9 June 1766, PRO, CO 5/755, f. 523.

[128] 'Speech on American Taxation', 19 April 1774, Paul Langford, ed., *The Writings and Speeches of Edmund Burke*, II, *Party, Parliament, and the American Crisis 1766–1774* (Oxford, 1981), p. 449.

retreat from what Bute and Grenville had tried to achieve. The army was still in America, the proclamation line, if constantly being transgressed, was still in existence and the customs officers were still trying to suppress illegal trade with the new powers given to them by Grenville. Under the provisions of the act of 1766, a revenue, if a small one, was actually being collected in America to defray some of the costs of the army. Above all, the doctrine of parliamentary sovereignty, rarely doubted on the British side, had been unequivocally laid down in the Declaratory Act and parliament showed no sign of withdrawing from the active involvement in colonial affairs that had begun under Grenville. In the past apparent acts of disobedience in the ebb and flow of provincial politics, if referred to Britain, were likely to draw no more than ineffective reproofs from the board of trade. Now they would be taken as defiance of the legislative authority of Great Britain that parliament was bound to notice and seek to punish.

Immediately after the repeal of the Stamp Act governors were warning of continuing protest, defiance, and disorder. Even if the Rockinghams had remained in power, conflict would have been hard to avoid. Thomas Penn noted that, much as the colonies were indebted to the ministers, they could not be relied 'upon in any future occasion to be our hearty friends . . . These lords and gentlemen are friends to liberty, but as great enemys to riotous methods of shewing it, as men that have more prerogative notions.'[129] In a conversation with a visitor from Massachusetts Rockingham seemed to be censorious of the governor, Bernard, for having failed to 'make a proper exertion of government' when the riots began.[130] No government would tolerate disobedience in the future.

III

In the summer of 1766 Rockingham ceased to be the king's chief minister, as had been the case with the departure of Grenville, for reasons which had nothing to do with America. He was replaced by William Pitt, shortly to be earl of Chatham, returning to office for the first time since he had resigned in 1761 at the height of his prestige as war minister. Largely on the strength of his speech of 14 January 1766, when he had declared 'internal' taxes like the stamp duties to be unconstitutional and appeared to have justified colonial resistance to them, Pitt was held in very high esteem as a 'friend of America'. Statues of him were commissioned in several colonies. Lord Shelburne, his

---

[129] To W. Allen, 17 March 1766, HSP, Thomas Penn Letter Books, VIII, p. 351.
[130] T. Hutchinson, Jun. to his father, 29 May 1766, MHS, Hutchinson Transcripts, XXV, p. 79.

secretary of state, cultivated visiting Americans who believed him to be another friend to their cause. Even someone with views as extreme as those of Arthur Lee continued to entertain high expectations of Shelburne for a long time to come. Lord Camden, now lord chancellor, was revered in the colonies for his support for Pitt's ideas about the qualified sovereignty of parliament and for his opposition to the procedures used against Wilkes. The chancellor of the exchequer, Charles Townshend, had served on the board of trade, not usually a recommendation in American eyes, but he had held office under Rockingham and had voted for the repeal of the Stamp Act. Some members of the Rockingham administration remained in office. Thus there were high expectations that Pitt's administration would seek to conciliate the colonies.

John Fothergill, however, gave more realistic advice about Pitt to his Pennsylvania friends. 'You are less obliged to him than you think', he wrote.[131] For the leading historian of the American issue in British politics such scepticism was abundantly justified. Pitt, in his view, came into office not to conciliate the colonies but determined to 'assert Britain's authority over America'. Under him, as might well have been the case had Rockingham remained in power, the conciliatory policies of the previous year were abandoned.[132] Pitt's view seems to have been that while Americans had been entitled to object to an unconstitutional tax, they must obey all legal authority without demur. Above all they must submit fully to the Navigation Acts. Within a few months Pitt was to be incapacitated and unable to exercise effective leadership over his government, leaving his ministers largely to their own devices. Shelburne was to propose draconian American measures, Camden was to accept that the colonies might legally be taxed, and Townshend was to sponsor a new attempt to raise a revenue in America.

For all shades of British opinion, America after the repeal of the Stamp Act was very much on probation. Gratitude and future obedience were what were expected. Such expectations were, however, immediately disappointed by New York and Massachusetts, the two colonies that were thought to have been in the forefront of resistance to the Stamp Act.

The elite in New York, a colony which had incurred especial odium in Britain for the threatened attack on the king's fort, were in fact reasserting their authority after the Stamp Act disorders, using British troops in the

---

[131] To J. Pemberton, 30 Oct. 1766, HSP, Etting Collection, XXIX, no. 55.

[132] Thomas, *British Politics and the Stamp Act Crisis*, p. 292. For the Chatham administration, see his *Townshend Duties Crisis*, ch. 2; R. C. Chaffin, 'The Townshend Acts of 1767', *William and Mary Quarterly*, 3rd ser., XXVII (1970), 90–121; Marie Peters, 'The Myth of William Pitt, Earl of Chatham, Great Imperialist Part II: Chatham and Imperial Reorganization 1763–78', *Journal of Imperial and Commonwealth History*, XXII (1994), 397–9.

process to put down protests against their landlords by tenants in some country districts. Thereafter, they were to pursue moderate courses in their relations with Britain for some years; eventually the British government was to have the highest expectations of the colony's loyalty on the eve of the Revolution. Before this became apparent, however, New York succeeded in provoking the Chatham government's ire. In the first place, its assembly was among a number that were failing to vote the full money required for quartering troops under the 1765 Quartering Act. The governor of New York was instructed to enforce the act. Early in 1767 news was received that not only was the New York assembly continuing to prove recalcitrant about the payments under the Quartering Act but that the New York merchants had sent a petition complaining bitterly about the state of trade and asking not only for further modifications in the 1764 Sugar Act but for revision of the commercial reforms embodied in the 1766 act, which was taken by British opinion to have made the greatest concessions possible to the Americans. This petition was widely interpreted as 'praying relief from the chief points in the Act of Navigation'.[133] Chatham took a very dim view of both these developments. He believed that they were so serious as to need to be laid before parliament rather than be dealt with by officials. The apparent resistance to the Quartering Act in particular was 'a matter so weighty and big, with consequences which may strike so deep and spread so wide'.[134] He was, however, unable to offer his colleagues further guidance on what should be done before he felt compelled to give up active business. A number of proposals were discussed, including one from Shelburne that troops might be billeted in private houses, a proposition from which even the Grenville government had backed away. The final outcome was an act suspending the legislature of New York until the payments required for quartering troops had been made. The New York Restraining Act was never to take effect, since the assembly had already voted the money required.

Over New York the Chatham government had succeeded in greatly magnifying a limited and transitory act of disobedience into a major crisis that brought down a severe and contentious exercise of parliamentary power on the head of a colonial legislature. From a British point of view, however, developments in Massachusetts had much more serious implications.

The provincial political elite in Massachusetts, largely consisting of lawyers and merchants, was deeply split. During the war both the governors and the imperial policies that they tried to implement had been strongly supported by a group of whom Thomas Hutchinson, the lieutenant governor, was the best

[133] Germain to J. Irwin, 13 Feb. 1767, WLCL, Germain Sackville MSS, 3, no. 54.
[134] To Grafton, 17 Feb. 1767, W. R. Anson, ed., *Autobiography and Political Correspondence of Augustus Henry, 3rd Duke of Grafton* (1898), p. 119.

known. They had directed a war effort which had cost the colony dear and in the process appeared to their critics to have accumulated rich rewards of office for themselves. The economic dislocation after the war left them vulnerable to their enemies in the 'country' or 'popular' party, who assailed both them and the new imperial policies of closer trade regulation and taxation, which threatened to add materially to the colony's difficulties. The leaders of the country party developed close links with the vibrant popular politics of Boston and the Massachusetts towns, expressed through a lively press, the proliferation of clubs and societies and participation in town meetings. Allegations of plotting by imperial authority, egged on by conspirators in high places in Boston, to impoverish the colony and curtail its liberties had a wide appeal. The Stamp Act seemed to be conclusive proof and provoked a popular explosion over which the leaders of the political opposition temporarily lost control.[135]

Repeal of the Stamp Act did little to improve relations between governor Bernard and the country majority now firmly in control of the Massachusetts assembly. They professed devotion to the king and proclaimed themselves to be 'the most loyal people in the world'. They were, however, still convinced that they were the victims of plots. The governor and his allies were, they believed, systematically misrepresenting them to ministers as driving towards independence, whereas all they sought was to assert the just rights of the assembly.[136] For his part, Bernard believed that the majority were set on 'weakening the power of government and bringing it still nearer and nearer to the levell of the common people'. In this spirit they had got office holders removed from the colony's council.[137] Massachusetts merchants were no more appeased by the commercial reforms of 1766 than were those of New York and made their own protest.[138] The customs administration was being obstructed to the point where it was 'common talk' that no seizures would be made in Boston in future.[139]

Bernard's theme of an unremitting opposition to any effective exercise of imperial authority was reinforced by the gloomy prognostications of his lieutenant governor, Thomas Hutchinson, who had come to believe that the popular leaders were aiming 'to destroy the existing structure of govern-

---

[135] Among recent studies of Massachusetts politics, see Bernard Bailyn, *The Ordeal of Thomas Hutchinson: Loyalism and the Destruction of the First British Empire* (Cambridge, Mass., 1974); William Pencak, *War, Politics and Revolution in Provincial Massachusetts* (Boston, 1981); Richard L. Bushman, *King and People in Provincial Massachusetts* (Chapel Hill, NC, 1985).

[136] S. Dexter to [D. De Berdt], 6 Jan. 1767, MHS, Massachusetts Papers, 1749–1768.

[137] To Board of Trade, 17 July 1766, PRO, CO 5/755, ff. 535–7.

[138] De Berdt's memorial to Shelburne, MHS, Massachusetts Papers, 1749–1768.

[139] Bernard to Board of Trade, 18 Aug. 1766, PRO, CO 5/755, f. 629.

ment and to tear the colonies away from British control'.[140] Bernard bombarded ministers with proposals for charter revision and reconstituting the colony's government, but this was an extremity for which there was as yet no support in Britain. All that the Chatham government would do was to take notice of the way in which the Massachusetts assembly in paying compensation for those who had suffered in the Stamp Act disturbances had usurped the king's prerogative of mercy by granting an indemnity to the rioters at the same time. The privy council disallowed the act and the issue was debated in the house of lords, where it was the pretext for much 'declaiming on the supposed ingratitude of the colonies and that spirit of disregard to the country and the views of independence' attributed to the Americans.[141]

What was by now only nominally Chatham's government also tried to increase the revenue collected in America by act of parliament. On 1 June 1767 Charles Townshend, chancellor of the exchequer, introduced the duties which bear his name. They provoked a new crisis in Anglo-American relations as they set off a fresh round of colonial resistance. Edmund Burke's version, which long held the field, of how by a tragic sequence of accidents the wilful Townshend was able to seize the opportunity offered by Chatham's illness to impose his own ill-considered initiative and thus wreck the amity between Britain and the colonies so carefully restored by Rockingham,[142] now has little support. It is commonly accepted that there was little Anglo-American amity by 1767, that new taxes for America were the policy of the Chatham government as a whole and that this policy was fully endorsed by other political groups, including the Rockinghams. Nor was Townshend acting on the immediate impulse of the moment. He had been in favour of such measures for a long time. The taxes were to take the form of duties on certain items, notably tea, imported into the colonies. It was assumed that these would not be contentious. Americans already paid some duties intended to raise a revenue and they were believed to make a distinction, apparently accepted by Pitt in January 1766, between 'internal' taxes, which were unconstitutional to them, and duties on trade, which were not. The Rockingham government had been contemplating further revenue-raising duties before it left office and out of office members of the party raised no fundamental objections to the duties.[143]

---

[140] Bailyn, *Ordeal of Thomas Hutchinson*, pp. 114–15.
[141] W. S. Johnson to W. Pitkin, 11 April 1767, 'Trumbull Papers, I', *Collections of the Massachusetts Historical Society*, 5th ser., IX (1885), 224.
[142] 'Speech on American Taxation', 19 April 1774, Paul Langford, ed., *The Writings and Speeches of Edmund Burke*, II, *Party, Parliament and the American Crisis 1766–1774* (Oxford, 1981), pp. 451–5.
[143] See ibid. pp. 62–3fn.

Townshend had, however, given revenue-raising a particular twist of his own which made his duties especially contentious. The money derived from them was to be applied not to defence but to providing funds 'for defraying the charges of the administration of justice, and the support of the civil government'.[144] Salaries derived from parliamentary taxes would be paid to judges and governors, who would no longer be dependent on votes of the assemblies. This was a scheme long favoured by the board of trade. Townshend had apparently been interested in it since 1753. The events of the Stamp Act crisis could be interpreted as demonstrating how urgent was the need for executives and judiciaries to be able to act independently in the face of popular pressure. Townshend was making the most ambitious attempt before 1774 to implement the ideals of those reformers who wanted to make colonial constitutions approximate more closely to the English constitution by redressing the balance between the colonial legislatures and the executive and the judiciary. Charles Garth, agent for South Carolina feared that the assemblies would be 'render[ed] . . . rather insignificant in that particular at least', a point that, he reported, was explicitly made during the debate in the commons.[145]

Imperial authority in the colonies was to be strengthened in additional ways. More vigorous direction of the customs administration was to be provided by a board of customs, 'invested with such powers as are now exercised by the commissioners of customs in *England*'.[146] It was to be stationed at Boston. For 'the prevention and punishment of frauds' against the Navigation Acts, four new admiralty appeal courts with royal judges were to be set up in North America.

By the end of the parliamentary session of 1767 Americans in Britain were in no doubt that they had lost any ground which they might have gained in the campaign for the repeal of the Stamp Act. The political landscape was bleak in the extreme. Chatham, in whom they had invested unrealistic hopes, was out of action and was to leave office in October 1768. By then most of his supporters had specifically disavowed his doctrine that internal taxation of the colonies was unconstitutional and had committed themselves to the fullest interpretation of the Declaratory Act. It was reported that 'every member of the administration in both houses have in the strongest terms declared, that they would go as far as any man in maintenance of the king's rights'.[147] The best that Americans with access to Rockingham could relay from him was

---

[144] 7 Geo. III, c. 46, sec. 5.

[145] To South Carolina Committee of Correspondence, 5 July 1767, 'Correspondence of Charles Garth', *South Carolina History and Genealogical Magazine*, XXIX (1928), 299–300.

[146] 7 Geo. III, c. 41.

[147] I. Mauduit to T. Hutchinson, 11 April 1767, MHS, Hutchinson Transcripts, XXV, p. 157.

that he was 'out of all patience' with them; 'that we were determined to leave our friends this side of the water, without the power even of a shadow of an excuse'.[148] Grenville was taking up extreme positions in parliamentary debate and was regarded by Americans as the devil incarnate. Little better in their eyes were his allies, the followers of the duke of Bedford. It was therefore with deep apprehension that Americans saw the government, crippled by the illness of Chatham and the death of Charles Townshend and now led by the duke of Grafton, being reinforced in the winter of 1767 by Bedford's followers rather than by those of Rockingham, who might be supposed to share a more sympathetic attitude to the colonies with what was left of Pitt's appointments. In reality the differences about American policy across the political spectrum were probably not very great at that time.[149] In any case, when a third secretary of state with specific colonial responsibilities was appointed in January 1768 the person chosen was drawn from none of the political groups, but was an old member of the board of trade, lord Hills-borough. One American agent was initially encouraged, finding him to 'profess a greater regard for the interests of America than I really expected'.[150] Within a short time, however, Hillsborough was to add greatly to Americans' gloom about the British political system as they came to detest him.

Americans came to believe that, whatever ministers might intend, they were constrained from doing anything 'in favor of the colonies' by the strength of hostility to them in parliament.[151] An American visitor who attended commons debates noted that extreme sentiments about the colonies were always well received. 'I have been several times in the house of com-mons', he wrote, 'when America has been incidentally mentioned not a friendly speech could be heard, all was attention, all was silent to hear the severest invectives.'[152] Franklin reported that 'we found the general prejudice against the colonies so strong in the house, that any thing in the shape of a favor to them all, was likely to meet with great opposition'.[153]

MPs' hostility to the colonies was thought to reflect the views of a wider public. Americans were prone to generalizations such as that of William Johnson of Connecticut in May 1767 that 'the sentiments of people in general

---

[148] N. Rogers to T. Hutchinson, 2, 3 July 1768, ibid. For an assessment of the Rockinghams in these years, see Paul Langford, 'The Rockingham Whigs and America, 1767–1773' in Anne White-man, J. S. Bromley, P. G. M. Dickson, eds., *Statesmen, Scholars and Merchants: Essays in Eighteenth-Century History Presented to Dame Lucy Sutherland* (Oxford, 1973), pp. 135–52.

[149] Thomas, *Townshend Duties Crisis*, pp. 39–40.

[150] D. De Berdt to T. Cushing, 27 June 1768, 'Letters of Dennys De Berdt, 1757–1770', *Publications of the Colonial Society of Massachusetts*, XIII (1910–11), 332.

[151] W. Johnson to W. Pitkin, 26 Dec. 1767, 'Trumbull Papers, I', 250.

[152] N. Rogers to T. Hutchinson, 17 Feb. 1768, MHS, Hutchinson Transcripts, XXV, p. 246.

[153] To Galloway, 13 June 1767, Labaree et al., eds., *Papers of Benjamin Franklin*, XIV. 182.

are indeed unhappily very unfavorable to the colonies'.[154] Beyond such assertions, agents reporting to their colonies at this time attempted crude social analysis. Two of them, Franklin and Johnson, stressed the enthusiasm of 'the landed men' (Franklin's term) or 'the freeholders' (Johnson's) for forcing the colonies to pay taxes.[155] Perennial concerns about the size of the debt and the level of taxation were especially acute in the early months of 1767. The announcement of an estimate for the cost of the army in America of £405,607 stimulated much indignation against the colonies. After the parliamentary opposition had staged a coup in forcing the government to reduce the level of the land tax, county MPs were congratulated at meetings of their constituents. The electors of Buckinghamshire, Grenville's county, also expressed their repugnance at having had to pay an increase in taxes which ought to have been charged on 'his Majesty's subjects in America'. By 'insurrection and violence' these people had 'refused to contribute any part for their own protection and defence, though required thereto by an act of the British legislature'.[156] An Essex county meeting deplored the burdens that they had to bear from 'duties raised to defray the expences of the late war; expences chiefly incurred for the protection of others, though now left to be paid solely by the mother country'.[157] Both Franklin and Johnson also believed that the alliance between the colonies and British merchants was wearing thin, due, they felt, to the merchants' sense that they had been ill-rewarded for their efforts to get the Stamp Act repealed by continuing American intransigence.[158] The citation for the award of the freedom of the City of London to Charles Townshend on 23 June 1767 commended 'his well tempered zeal in support of the undoubted legislative authority of the king and parliament of Great Britain over all parts of his Majesty's dominions'.[159] When Barlow Trecothick, brought up in Boston and one of the leading advocates for the repeal of the Stamp Act, stood for election as an MP for the City of London he encountered hostility as 'a friend to the colonies, in opposition to the trade of Great Britain'.[160]

[154] W. S. Johnson to W. Pitkin, 16 May 1767, 'Trumbull Papers, I', 235.
[155] Franklin to J. Galloway, 8 Aug. 1767, Labaree et al., eds., *Papers of Benjamin Franklin*, XIV. 229; Johnson to J. Trumbull, 14 March 1767, 'Trumbull Papers, I', 486.
[156] *Public Advertiser*, 5 March 1767.
[157] Ibid. 13 March 1767.
[158] Franklin to J. Galloway, 13 June 1767, Labaree et al., eds., *Papers of Benjamin Franklin*, XIV. 183; Johnson to J. Trumbull, 14 March 1767, 'Trumbull Papers, I', 487.
[159] *London's Roll of Fame* . . . *From the Close of the Reign of George II, AD 1757–1884* (1884), p. 52.
[160] Lewis Namier and John Brooke, eds., *The History of Parliament: The House of Commons 1754–1790*, 3 vols. (1964), III. 559.

10

The Unmaking of Empire, II: North America 1768–1775

Y 1768 informed Americans could have been in little doubt that there was to be no easy way out of the sharp deterioration in relations between the colonies and Britain that, in their view, had been brought about by a series of hostile measures enacted by British administrations since the ending of the war. Hopes that there would be a comprehensive British climb-down had been dashed. The Rockingham administration had indeed repealed the Stamp Act, but they had done so under pressure rather than from any acceptance of the American view of the imperial connection. In any case, the Rockinghams were now out of office. The hero in whom the Americans had invested so many hopes, William Pitt, earl of Chatham, had shown himself to be hostile to most of their pretensions. His government had been responsible for a new measure of taxation and he too was effectively out of office. Power was passing to men whom Americans had no reason to regard as their friends. Nor had they any good reason to regard the mass of MPs or even a wider public as being well disposed to them. On their side, politically articulate Americans were becoming increasingly alienated and despairing of Britain.

Nevertheless, few people on either side of the Atlantic could foresee that colonial–British relations would deteriorate to the point of armed resistance, war and independence. Both sides still profoundly hoped for a lasting accommodation, even if the grounds for one were not easy to envisage, since neither side would make major concessions. The path ahead for the next seven years was not to be a steep descent into catastrophe, but a series of crises succeeded by intervals of relative calm, until the final crisis from which there was no way out.

I

The Townshend duties of 1767 did not initially arouse the same degree of opposition that the Stamp Act had done. In the winter of 1767–8, however,

John Dickinson's *Letters from a Farmer in Pennsylvania* began to formulate a powerful case against them as an act of parliamentary taxation as objectionable as the stamp tax had been. Massachusetts predictably took up this line.[1] The customs commissioners, newly arrived at Boston, added their cries of alarm to those of governor Bernard. They reported that 'the most licentious publications' were 'denying the right of parliament to lay any taxes whatsoever upon the colonies; and some went so far as to assert the most unlimited independency'. Boston was diffusing such principles throughout the colonies.[2] Massachusetts did indeed take formal action to spread its views when its legislature issued a circular letter to the other colonies in February 1768 objecting to the duties as illegal taxes and to the payment of salaries out of them as a threat 'to the happiness and security of the subject'.[3] Boston merchants resolved in March 1768 to cease importing British goods, a strategy that was at first difficult to enforce in Massachusetts let alone elsewhere. At the same time opposition was growing to the customs commissioners, who complained that they were at the mercy of the mob without any protection from those in authority.[4] The long anticipated 'insurrection' against the customs was set off in June 1768 by the seizure of John Hancock's ship the *Liberty*. The customs commissioners were put to flight. The governor believed that plans were being laid for armed rebellion and that 'a short time will determine whether *Boston* is to be subject to Great Britain or not'.[5]

Even more alarming from a British point of view was evidence that the contagion had spread to Virginia. The Virginia council and burgesses petitioned against 'the exercise of anticonstitutional powers' in the Townshend duties and the suspension of the New York legislature.[6] To lord Hillsborough, the new American secretary, this showed that Virginia was in 'a much worse state than even the colony of Massachusetts' Bay'.[7] The king regarded the conduct of Virginia on this occasion as 'so offensive' that no concessions could be offered to them later.[8]

---

[1] House of Representatives to D. De Berdt, 12 Jan. 1768, H. A. Cushing, ed., *The Writings of Samuel Adams*, 4 vols. (New York, 1904–8), I. 137–8.

[2] Commissioners' memorial, 12 Feb. 1768, PRO, CO 5/226, ff. 96–7.

[3] Merrill Jensen, ed., *English Historical Documents*, IX, *American Colonial Documents to 1776* (1969), pp. 714–16.

[4] Memorial, 28 March 1768, PRO, CO 5/226, f. 108.

[5] Bernard to Hillsborough, 19 July 1768, HUHL, Sparks MSS 4/6.

[6] Petitions to king, lords, and commons, 16 April 1768, W. J. Van Schreeven and R. L. Scribner, eds., *Revolutionary Virginia: The Road to Independence*, 3 vols. (Charlottesville, Va., 1973–7), I. 55–63.

[7] T. Bradshaw to Grafton, 22 July 1768, cited P. D. G. Thomas, *The Townshend Duties Crisis: The Second Phase of the American Revolution, 1767–1773* (Oxford, 1987), p. 87.

[8] Memorandum, [Feb. 1769], J. Fortescue, ed., *The Correspondence of King George III, 1760–83*, 6 vols. (1927–8), II. 85.

By 1768 it was clear that a group, if not yet overtly revolutionary then certainly bent on emasculating imperial power, led by lawyers and merchants, was in full control of the Massachusetts assembly. This group had close links with popular activists among the Boston citizenry and was extending its reach into the countryside. Considered realistically, the extent of the disaffection in Massachusetts, a colony that had contributed so much to the imperial cause in two wars, was a very serious blow to the empire. Realistic assessment was, however, often overlaid by British prejudices against a community thought to be contaminated by religious Dissent, by seventeenth-century levelling principles, and by commercial chicanery. Virginia was, however, a society dominated by an old-established Anglican landed gentry who had also contributed notably in the later stages of the war.[9]

The Virginia gentry prided themselves on their conformity to the norms of the English county communities on whom the British state devolved so many responsibilities. They seemed to be natural partners in empire in peace as well as in war. The petitions of 1768 suggested otherwise. In 1769 colonel Washington, who had fought throughout the course of the war, was to write that 'our lordly masters in Great Britain will be satisfied with nothing less than the deprivation of American freedom' and he was considering at what point it might be necessary to resort to arms.[10] British policy had succeeded in alienating a people who, for all their outward similarities with the gentlemen of England, had a sense of their own identity and would only be partners in empire on their own terms, certainly not on those of a parliament in which they did not participate.

Recent writing has shown how a distinctive political culture had evolved within the framework of the common ideals which the Virginia gentry shared with their English counterparts. The Lee brothers of Westmoreland County, for instance, wrote to one another of the need for their children to be educated, as they had been, in England, which Arthur called 'the Eden of the world and the land of liberty and independence'.[11] Yet once established in England, Arthur and William Lee associated with metropolitan radicals, not with country gentlemen. The Lee brothers were scions of a Virginia gentry with a tenacious commitment to personal independence and to local autonomy together with a deep concern for the pervading threat of corruption. Heavy-handed British policies both seemed to threaten the Virginia gentry's independence and to give resistance to these threats the quality of a moral

---

[9] James Titus, *The Old Dominion at War: Society, Politics and Warfare in late Colonial Virginia* (Columbia, SC, 1991).

[10] To G. Mason, 5 April 1769, W. W. Abbot and Dorothy Twohig, eds., *The Papers of George Washington, Colonial Series*, VIII, *June 1767–December 1771* (Charlottesville, Va., 1993), p. 178.

[11] To R. H. Lee, 20 March 1765, Lee Family Papers, University of Virginia microfilm 1714.

crusade for virtue against corruption.[12] The great planter Landon Carter saw British policies as the work of 'ill-designing men' with 'enslaving schemes of tyranny and oppression'. Behind such people he feared was a Britain sunk into a 'universal state of dissipation'.[13]

Ministers were so alarmed at what they were hearing from America by the summer of 1768 that royal regiments were dispatched to Boston from Britain and Nova Scotia. There were, however, to be no rebellions, even in Massachusetts. The troops may or may not have forestalled a stroke against the government, but they could not be used in aid of the civil power in Boston because the civil power would not sanction their use. The colonial elites by themselves maintained a firmer control than they had been able to do in 1765, but in all the colonies the elites were increasingly disaffected with imperial authority. Their disaffection certainly did not extend to an ideal Britain in the abstract, still described by John Dickinson as 'the mother of brave, generous, humane spirits, the chief bulwark of liberty on this globe and the blessed seat of unspotted religion'.[14] Nor were they disaffected with the king to whom they still pledged fervent loyalty. But they were profoundly suspicious of the intentions of Britain's political leadership and increasingly despaired of the society that tolerated that leadership. Theories of conspiracies between governor Bernard, Thomas Hutchinson and their ilk and malign British ministers had long been current in Massachusetts. Recent events strengthened the hold of conspiracy theories in other colonies as well. Not only had there been a new attempt to tax the colonies, but many other fears had been aroused. The provisions for salaried officials raised the spectre of tribes of placemen corrupting colonial political virtue and displacing local notables. The example of the way in which Ireland had been incorporated into the British patronage system was freely cited. Parliamentary salaries that would remove the colonial executives from any check by the assemblies, the act suspending the New York legislature and Hillsborough's instructions to the governors to prorogue or dissolve any assembly that was willing to receive

---

[12] Conspicuous in the abundant recent writing on the Virginia gentry are the essays of Jack P. Greene, ' "Virtus et Libertas": Political Culture, Social Change and the Origins of the American Revolution in Virginia, 1763–76' and 'Character, Persona and Authority: A Study in Alternative Styles of Political Leadership in Revolutionary Virginia' in Greene, *Understanding the American Revolution: Issues and Actors* (Charlottesville, Va., 1995), pp. 164–246, 'Society, Ideology and Politics: An Analysis of the Political Culture of Mid-Eighteenth-Century Virginia' in Greene, *Negotiated Authorities: Essays in Colonial Political and Constitutional History* (Charlottesville, Va., 1994), pp. 259–318; T. H. Breen, *Tobacco Culture: The Mentality of the Great Tidewater Planters on the Eve of the Revolution* (Princeton, 1985); Michal J. Rozbicki, *The Complete Colonial Gentleman: Cultural Legitimacy in Plantation America* (Charlottesville, Va., 1998).

[13] Jack P. Greene, *Landon Carter: An Inquiry into the Personal Values and Social Imperatives of the Eighteenth-Century Virginia Gentry* (Charlottesville, Va., 1967), p. 54.

[14] To A. Lee, 31 March 1770, HUHL, bMS Am. 811 (60).

the Massachusetts letter of protest of February 1768 indicated how precarious the rights of colonial legislatures had become. The movement of troops into Boston graphically illustrated the dangers of a 'standing army' in America. The predatory activities of the supposedly corrupt and rapacious customs commissioners had been given the backing of such unconstitutional powers as writs of assistance and strengthened admiralty courts. Rumours about the appointment of a colonial bishop, however ill-founded, aroused fears not only among the Congregationalists and Presbyterians of New England and the middle colonies, but among the Anglican gentry in the southern colonies, who saw bishops as a threat to the control over the church which they exercised at parish level.

The political leadership in more and more colonies was moving towards a position where they denied that parliament had any legislative authority over America, let alone any right to tax, even though they firmly disavowed any ambitions to independence and were not yet ready to lead their societies into overt resistance to Britain. If they still saw themselves as part of the British empire, it was an empire conceived as a partnership of equals. Attempts to create an empire in America on British terms of subordination to metropolitan authority had no prospect of success in the face of their opposition.

South Carolina was a conspicuous example of growing alienation. As the richest of all the mainland colonies and one which gained greatly from the imperial commercial system, it might be assumed to have been a committed partner in empire. The planters and merchants of South Carolina were both 'nouveaux and exceptionally riche'.[15] Their indigo received imperial bounties and modifications were introduced into the Navigation Acts to facilitate their huge export trade of rice to Europe. Yet Samuel Adams of Boston, while complaining in 1773 of 'the timidity of some colonies and the silence of others', put South Carolina on a par with Virginia for 'active vigilance . . . manly generosity, and . . . steady perseverance'.[16] Although the South Carolina gentry were much less deeply rooted in their own soil than were the gentry of Virginia in theirs, under some pressure from radical craftsmen in Charleston, they proved equally tenacious of their right to lead their community and just as alert to threats from across the Atlantic to their independence and to their political virtue.

Such a threat arose from a long controversy with the British government over the grant made in 1769 by the South Carolina assembly to the London Society of Supporters of the Bill of Rights, a radical group associated with

[15] Robert M. Weir, 'Who Shall Rule at Home: The American Revolution as a Crisis of Legitimacy for the Colonial Elites' in Weir, 'The Last of American Freemen': Studies in the Political Culture of the Colonial and Revolutionary South (Macon, Ga., 1986), p. 85.
[16] To R. H. Lee, 10 April 1773, Cushing, ed., Writings of Samuel Adams, III. 26.

John Wilkes. This was intended as a gesture of solidarity with their equally oppressed 'fellow subjects in Great Britain', who were 'fronting the whole collected fury of ministerial vengeance'.[17] To British ministers not only was this an act of flagrant provocation, but it was constitutionally unacceptable for a colonial assembly to assume the right to issue money for such a purpose on its own exclusive authority. The governor was instructed in April 1770 not to accept any order for payments for other than local services and to ensure that money was only issued with the approval of the whole 'general assembly', that is of the governor and council as well as the commons.[18] The merits of making a gesture in favour of Wilkes quickly ceased to be the issue at stake in a dispute that was to paralyse the working of the South Carolina legislature up to the outbreak of the Revolution. By 1771 Henry Laurens, then in London, thought Wilkes to be 'in a despicable state' and destined for 'a total and eternal downfall', but he still considered that the principle that the commons alone controlled the spending of the people's money was sacred. If the instruction of April 1770 was not withdrawn, South Carolina would lose 'all the right and privileges of a free people'.[19] The commons took this view too and refused to vote taxes until the instruction was withdrawn. For British ministers this was an opportunity 'to restore the constitution' of a colony to British practice, which was that although the commons originated money grants, they required 'the full concurrence of the several branches of the legislature'.[20] Ministers refused to withdraw the instruction until this principle was established in some way.[21] Deadlock meant, as the lieutenant governor reported in 1774, that 'we are now in the course of the sixth year since any provision has been made for the established or contingent charges of government'.[22] Disputes of this sort had long been the staple fare of colonial politics, but in a climate of fear and suspicion of British intentions throughout the colonies they assumed a new importance.

[17] Letter of Committee to R. Morris, 9 Dec. 1769, 'Correspondence of Charles Garth', *South Carolina Historical and Genealogical Magazine*, XXXI (1930), 132.
[18] Additional Instruction, 14 April 1770, L. W. Labaree, ed., *Royal Instructions to British Governors 1660–1776*, 2 vols. (New York, 1935), I. 208–9.
[19] To J. Laurens, 12 Dec. and to T. Franklin, 26 Dec. 1771, P. H. Hamer et al., eds., *The Papers of Henry Laurens* (Columbia, SC, 1986–), VIII. 92–5, 121.
[20] This was Hillsborough's view, C. Garth to Committee of Correspondence, 3 June 1772, 'Garth Correspondence', *South Carolina Magazine*, XXXIII (1932), 239–40.
[21] Jack P. Greene, 'Bridge to Revolution: The Wilkes Fund Controversy in South Carolina, 1769–75' in Greene, *Negotiated Authorities*, pp. 394–428.
[22] W. Bull to Dartmouth, 10 March 1774, K. G. Davies, ed., *Documents of the American Revolution, 1770–1783*, 21 vols. (Shannon, 1972–81), VIII. 64.

II

Once the alarms of the summer of 1768 had subsided, British ministers found themselves back in the position that the Rockingham government had been in 1765–6. They still had no appetite for systematic military repression; the main body of the troops was withdrawn from Boston as soon as it decently could be. They did not wish to provoke a fresh conflict with the colonies by any new measure of taxation and were indeed inclined to get rid of the Townshend duties so long as they did not seem to be yielding to pressure, but the principle of parliamentary sovereignty must be maintained and flagrant American disobedience could not be countenanced. As Thomas Whately put it, 'they will do as they have hitherto done, and keep the affair just where it is, without much exertion or much concession'.[23]

Hillsborough as colonial secretary seems to have been in favour of measures of both exertion and concession. He had no commitment to the Townshend duties and wished to see them go, but action in his view should be taken against Massachusetts, the centre of subversion. He was converted to at least part of the programme of constitutional reform so long advocated by men like Bernard. In particular, the colony's charter must be revised so that the governor was given the support of a nominated council rather than one elected by the assembly under the 1691 charter. He was to put forward proposals to this effect on a number of occasions and legislation was to be drafted, but he could not win the support of a majority of his colleagues, nor on one crucial occasion of the king. No effective action was taken, but in the absence of flagrant acts of defiance, beyond a non-importation agreement that had been slow to get off the ground but was beginning to have some effect, the government felt able to promise that the Townshend duties except for tea would be withdrawn and that no further taxes would be levied. This was enacted by a new administration under lord North on 12 April 1770. North had been in office under Grenville and again under Chatham. His administrative skills and mastery in the house of commons were to keep him as chief minister for the next twelve years. On American questions he seems to have been most influenced by Grenville. The retention of the tea duty is often portrayed as a face-saving device, but tea was in fact the only duty to raise any significant revenue and retaining it represented a reaffirmation of the underlying principle of the Townshend duties, which had been to provide

[23] To Temple, 27 July 1769, 'Bowdoin–Temple Papers, I', *Collections of the Massachusetts Historical Society*, 6th ser., IX (1897), 152.

funds for colonial salaries that would not be under the control of assemblies.[24] Such salaries began to be paid to governors and chief justices in New York and Massachusetts. In as far as lord North had a policy for America, it would seem to have been to avoid conflict as far as was consistent with the strict maintenance of parliamentary sovereignty over the colonies, while building up the power of the colonial executives through salaries paid for by the duty on tea.

Although Hillsborough usually treated those Americans whom he encountered with jovial urbanity, channels of communication between the colonies and the imperial government were silting up. American colonies were increasingly disinclined to make representations to the commons and thereby imply that parliament had authority over them. In any case, it was difficult to find MPs willing to present American petitions. Ministers were coming to regard the colonial agents not as men who were trying to smooth the transaction of business on matters of mutual interest to Britain and the colonies but as opponents of British policy intent on stirring up opposition to it. Dealing with such people was pointless. It was preferable to rely on the letters of the governors for information about the colonies.[25] Holding four agencies himself, Benjamin Franklin was the major figure among the body of agents whose capacity to influence developments was rapidly declining. Ministers became increasingly sceptical of him as having become no more than the mouthpiece of the Massachusetts radicals. By 1772 he recognized that 'I am now thought too much an American . . . to have any interest'. By the 'alienation' of Franklin another natural partner in empire with a long history of cooperation in imperial projects had been cast off.[26]

To Americans in Britain there seemed to be little to expect from any alternative to a ministry that appeared to be increasingly hostile to them. William Johnson doubted whether the colonies could expect significantly different treatment were the opposition, Rockingham or Chatham, let alone Grenville, to gain office. He believed that the colonies only had five or six 'friends . . . upon real principle' in the commons.[27] The merchants and manufacturers who had been the colonies' allies in 1765–6 also appeared to be failing them. Their response to the new non-importation agreements against the Townshend duties was very disappointing. A petition in 1770 from London merchants, prompted by Bristol was the only organized protest,

---

[24] Thomas, *Townshend Duties Crisis*, pp. 137–8.

[25] Michael G. Kammen, *A Rope of Sand: The Colonial Agents, British Politics, and the American Revolution* (Ithaca, NY, 1968), pp. 226–7.

[26] Jack P. Greene, 'The Alienation of Benjamin Franklin, British American' in Greene, *Understanding the American Revolution*, pp. 247–84, quotation on p. 275.

[27] W. Johnson to W. Pitkin, 3 Jan., 18 Sept. 1769, 'Trumbull Papers, I', *Collections of the Massachusetts Historical Society*, 5th ser., IX (1885), 310, 366.

'a veritable mouse compared with the massive petitioning and lobbying movement of 1765–6'.[28] Then petitioning had been actively encouraged by the administration; now government was putting its weight against any such activities. In a phase of buoyant demand in other markets British merchants in any case had less incentive than at the time of the Stamp Act to show sympathy with colonial grievances, which many of them seem to have suspected were aimed not at reversing mistaken government policies but at undermining the whole imperial commercial system. Very few British merchants would support such an objective.[29] The alliance forged in 1765–6 between colonial opinion and sympathetic British politicians powerfully backed by merchants and manufacturers had manifestly failed to be re-enacted in 1769–70.

For most Americans, discouraging as the prospects might be, there seemed to be little alternative to trying to keep lines open to the politicians and hoping that the conditions of 1765–6 might return. The replacement of Hillsborough in 1772 by the apparently more pliant lord Dartmouth, who had served under Rockingham, gave some encouragement. As late as December 1773, Franklin reported that there might be 'a disposition to compose all differences with America before the next general election' under pressure from 'the trading and manufacturing part of the nation'.[30]

Others sought to reach a different audience. They believed that the British political system and the society that it represented were now irredeemably corrupt. Nothing could be expected from any of its leaders. Corruption had spread downwards, as was most conspicuously demonstrated in parliamentary elections, but some goodness perhaps survived among ordinary people. 'The whole remains of public virtue in that country', the Virginian William Lee wrote from London in 1771, 'centers entirely in the middling and lower orders in the state.'[31]

This virtue seemed to have been demonstrated in the agitation triggered off by the Middlesex election of 1769, when John Wilkes had been prevented from taking the seat for which a majority of the freeholders of the county had chosen him. Some Americans derived much encouragement from the apparent politicization of British popular opinion by this episode. In the view of William Lee's brother Arthur, the cause of the American colonies and of the Middlesex freeholders was the same: they were both victims of tyrannical

---

[28] Paul Langford, 'The British Business Community and the Later Nonimportation Movements, 1768–1776' in Walter H. Conser et al., eds., *Resistance, Politics, and the American Struggle for Independence, 1765–1775* (Boulder, Colo., 1986), p. 281.

[29] Ibid. pp. 305–16.

[30] To J. Galloway, 3 Nov. 1773, Leonard. W. Labaree et al., eds., *The Papers of Benjamin Franklin* (New Haven, 1959–), XX. 462.

[31] To R. H. Lee, 19 April 1771, Virginia Historical Society, MSS I. L.51, f. 305.

ministers who were depriving them of their established rights by the exercise of unconstitutional power through a servile parliament. By pointing out these similarities, he had 'not the least doubt' that he could make 'the cause of America popular'.[32]

The cause of Wilkes became extremely popular in America. He was toasted and sent congratulatory addresses on many occasions. A child in Boston was christened 'Wilkes' and Maryland enthusiasts sent their hero forty-five 'curious hams'.[33] The South Carolina commons' vote for the Society of Supporters of the Bill of Rights to sustain 'the just and constitutional liberties of the people of Great Britain and America' was a gesture of support for Wilkes. Boston radicals 'discovered' and lauded an Irish Wilkes in Dr Charles Lucas, who, they believed, upheld virtue 'in the midst of venality and corruption' in a kingdom which now had 'hardly anything more than the name of a free constitution'.[34]

In 1768 Wilkes began to repay American effusions on him in kind. 'Liberty', he told the Boston Sons of Liberty, was 'the birth-right of every subject of the British empire' and all its peoples should unite to 'guard the public liberty if invaded by despotic ministers in the most remote as in the central parts of this vast empire'.[35] How far America was able to win the support of a genuinely popular constituency in Britain is, however, doubtful, at least until 1775 and the outbreak of fighting. Before then, the appeal of America in British popular politics seems to have been largely confined to London.[36] The Lees and one or two others identified themselves closely with Wilkes, becoming active in the Society of Supporters of the Bill of Rights and in London politics. In 1773 two Americans, William Lee and Stephen Sayre, were elected sheriffs of the City of London. The exertions of the Lees ensured that London radicals would keep the cause of the colonies in mind, as they did in their contribution to the great national petitioning movement of 1769. Outside London and Bristol, America was not, however, explicitly raised as a grievance.[37] Edmund Burke was probably correct in

---

[32] To R. H. Lee, 18 Sept. 1769, Lee Family Papers, University of Virginia microfilm 1714.

[33] Pauline Maier, *From Resistance to Revolution: Colonial Radicals and the Development of American Opposition to Britain, 1765–1776* (New York, 1972), pp. 163, 204.

[34] Patrick Griffin, 'America's Changing Image in Ireland's Looking Glass: Provincial Construction of an Eighteenth-Century British Atlantic World', *Journal of Imperial and Commonwealth History*, XXVI (1998), 28–50; S. Adams to Lucas, [12 March] 1771, Cushing, ed., *Writings of Samuel Adams*, II. 163.

[35] To Boston Sons of Liberty, 19 July 1768, HUHL, bMS Am. 1704. 6 (29).

[36] John Sainsbury, *Disaffected Patriots: London Supporters of Revolutionary America, 1769–82* (Kingston and Montreal, 1987); ch. 2 deals with the rise of America as an issue in London radical politics.

[37] Thomas, *Townshend Duties Crisis*, pp. 142–3; Paul Langford, 'London and the American Revolution' in J. Stevenson, ed., *London in the Age of Reform* (Oxford, 1977), p. 63.

pointing out that 'The people were very much and very generally touched' by the abuse of the rights of the Middlesex freeholders, but 'They felt upon this, but upon no other ground.'[38] Lee's expectation that large sections of aggrieved English opinion could be made to see their cause and that of the Americans as one and the same had yet to be realized. Nor did Irish Protestant opinion necessarily accept the analogies that Americans such as Franklin drew for them when he wrote of the 'similarity in our cases'.[39] 'Mere colonies' were not the same thing as 'a kingdom' with its own 'rights and liberties'.[40] More militant Irish Patriots were willing to identify their cause with that of the colonies and of Wilkes, but the bulk of 'The Anglo-Irish community, geographically close to the mother country and dependent upon it for the maintenance of its position in Ireland, could not afford the luxury of supporting the American colonists.'[41] In 1770 the lord lieutenant commended 'the general disposition of his Majesty's subjects' in Ireland in rejecting 'the insinuations of other parts of his Majesty's dominions . . . to make a common cause to distress his government'.[42]

III

Deteriorating Anglo-American relations took place in a context of accelerating economic expansion in the colonies. It was conventionally supposed that the economic relations of empire were set in the mould of the Navigation Acts that required little more than effective enforcement and some fine tuning. Rapid change was, however, creating new problems for British policy-makers. In 1751 Franklin had estimated that the colonial population was doubling every twenty years. A later calculation seemed to confirm that its increase was 'so rapid as to have scarcely any parallel'. In 'the back settlements' the population was thought to double every fifteeen years.[43] Part of this growth was due to increased immigration from Britain, which attracted much anxious attention in the 1770s. More people required more land and the demand for land beyond the colonial boundaries was being stimulated by highly organized speculative interests on both sides of the

[38] To Rockingham, 7, 8 Sept. 1770, L. S. Sutherland, ed., *The Correspondence of Edmund Burke*, II, *July 1768–June 1774* (Cambridge, 1960), p. 155.

[39] To S. Cooper, 14 April 1770, Labaree et al., eds., *Papers of Benjamin Franklin*, XVII. 124.

[40] Jacqueline Hill, *From Patriots to Unionists: Dublin Civic Politics and Irish Protestant Patriotism 1660–1840* (Oxford, 1997), p. 142.

[41] Vincent Morley, *Irish Opinion and the American Revolution 1760–1783* (Cambridge, 2002), pp. 77–8.

[42] Townshend to Weymouth, 25 Sept. 1770, PRO, SP 63/432, f. 20.

[43] Richard Price, 'Observations on the Expectation of Lives, the Increase of Mankind, the Influence of Great Towns on Population', *Philosophical Transactions*, LIX (1769), 121.

Atlantic. Commercial activity in the colonies had been checked in the mid-1760s but overseas trade was resuming at an accelerated pace by the end of the decade and into the 1770s. Living standards in the white population were rising, if probably less rapidly than was commonly assumed.[44]

Metropolitan Britain was of course set to prosper greatly from economic expansion in the colonies, but contemporaries were well aware of what seemed to be the dangers of unregulated expansion: colonial trade might outgrow the framework of the Navigation Acts, colonial manufacturing might become a rival to British manufacturing, emigration might depopulate Britain, drawing off valuable artisans in particular, mass movements of people onto new land in the west would almost certainly plunge Britain into Indian wars, and sooner or later might create settlements beyond effective imperial control. Faced by rapid change, was Britain to allow expansion to take its course or to try to impose controls on it? All the established principles of colonial management were in favour of controls. On the eve of the Revolution aspirations to exercise control were still very strong in British official circles. Whether controls could be effectively enforced was, however, another matter.

New lands in North America had been the most spectacular gain from the Seven Years War. Ever since the enactment of the proclamation of 1763 a variety of interested parties, both in the colonies and in Britain, had been drawing up schemes to breach its prohibition on the settlement of western land. They were given their chance to push for large grants by the Chatham administration's need both to find some alternative to unenforceable parliamentary taxes for funding the huge costs of the army in North America and to contrive a better way of controlling illegal settlement, regulating Indian trade and excluding French and Spanish infiltration from the Gulf of Mexico than the deployment of the army in the west, which was proving to be prohibitively expensive as well as ineffective. New colonies were offered as the answer to all problems. The government would gain a revenue from disposing of land and the new colonies would provide stability, order and strong defensive blocks in the west, as well, of course, as greatly benefiting those who invested in them and who were advocating their cause so persuasively. Would-be land speculators found a sympathetic hearer in lord Shelburne, the southern secretary under Chatham. He embodied their ideas in a minute for the cabinet, probably of June 1767, which, even if it was a statement of the views of interested parties, gave what was to be the most enthusiastic endorsement of unfettered expansion to appear in any official

---

[44] For a recent estimate, see Marc Egnal, *New World Economies: The Growth of the Thirteen Colonies and Early Canada* (New York, 1998), pp. 42–4.

paper.[45] Britain should not 'attempt to set limits to the encrease of our people and the extension of our dominions'. Far from seeking independence or economic self-sufficiency, new colonies must 'long stand in need of the friendly support of Great Britain' and would become a flourishing 'market for British manufactures'. The danger lay rather in restricted coastal colonies where the pressure of over-population would force down labour costs and thus encourage manufacturing. Then 'the colonies finding themselves able to subsist by their interior resources may be induced to shake off all dependency and swerve from their allegiance'.[46] With new colonies providing an outlet to the west, the benefits of empire to Britain would be guaranteed far into the future. A group of merchants was produced who were willing to anticipate great commercial benefits from new colonies.[47]

Nothing was, however, done to turn such suggestions into policy before Shelburne left office and the direction of colonial affairs passed in January 1768 to Hillsborough as the new colonial secretary. Hillsborough was both an apostle of the board of trade's 1763 policy of restricting western settlement to limited orderly transfers of land from Indians and, as a great Ulster landowner, was said to be 'terribly afraid of dispeopling Ireland'.[48] He strongly endorsed a hostile report on Shelburne's proposals from the board of trade of March 1768. This described plans for 'inland colonies' as 'entirely new' and opposed to 'The great object of colonizing upon the continent of North America' which was 'to improve and extend the commerce, navigation and manufactures of this kingdom, upon which its strength and security depend'. This objective was to be attained by improving the coastal settlements. There was more than enough land still to be settled along the coast to encourage 'population and consumption'.[49] Hillsborough stuck tenaciously to his guns over the next few years. 'Remote' colonies, he warned general Gage, could not be kept 'in just subordination to and dependence upon this kingdom'.[50] The land speculators were left to lament the lost opportunity and to lobby against Hillsborough, as Arthur Lee did in the winter of 1768 in 'the small and sociable circle of Bath'.[51]

[45] For assessments of Shelburne, see R. A. Humphreys, 'Lord Shelburne and British Colonial Policy, 1766–1768', *English Historical Review*, L (1935), 257–77; Vincent T. Harlow, *The Founding of the Second British Empire 1763–1793*, 2 vols. (1952–64), I. 183–98; John Norris, *Shelburne and Reform* (1963), ch. 3.

[46] C. W. Alvord and C. E. Carter, eds., 'Trade and Politics, 1767–1769', *Illinois State Historical Library Collections*, XVI (1921), 12–21; see also Shelburne to Board of Trade, 5 Oct. 1767, ibid. 77–81.

[47] e.g. B. Trecothick to Board of Trade, 30 Oct. 1767, PRO, CO 323/24, f. 321.

[48] B. Franklin to W. Franklin, 12 Sept. 1766, Labaree et al., eds., *Papers of Benjamin Franklin*, XIII. 414.

[49] 7 March 1768, Alvord and Carter, eds., 'Trade and Politics', 197–203.

[50] 31 July 1770, C. E. Carter, ed., *The Correspondence of General Thomas Gage with the Secretaries of State and with the War Office and the Treasury*, 2 vols. (New Haven, 1931–3), II. 109.

[51] To R. H. Lee and R. Parker, 23 Dec. 1768, Lee Family Papers, University of Virginia microfilm 1714.

Hillsborough's efforts to block major expansion to the west were to be defeated, not, it would seem, by the triumph of any reasoned case against them but because he could not control events on the frontier and because his political colleagues could not resist the blandishments of the speculators. The Indian superintendent Sir William Johnson was able to induce his charges to part with a large chunk of western land for which the speculators put in their bids. An Anglo-American consortium, the Grand Ohio Company, including many influential figures in British politics, persuaded the government to overrule Hillsborough and make them a huge grant in 1772 to found a new colony to be called Vandalia. Hillsborough resigned rather than implement a policy to which he was strongly opposed, but the grant was never in fact ratified. Instead, on the eve of the Revolution all the western lands to the north, including the putative Vandalia, were put under the colony of Quebec by the Quebec Act of 1774. In theory, the expansion of settlement westwards had been definitively halted. In practice, illegal settlement had been endemic since 1763 and, as the British army abandoned its western posts in the 1770s, ever more settlers moved in. Groups from Pennsylvania and Virginia were in bitter rivalry for concessions. Virginia's governor, lord Dunmore, fought a war against the Shawnees in 1774 that brought land for the Virginians in Kentucky. The transfer of the west to Quebec was never more than a paper transaction terminated by the Revolution and leaving many settlers in actual occupation.

Concern that grants of western land would stimulate emigration from Britain was thought to be a strong motive for lord Hillsborough's opposition to them. Virtually all emigration went, however, to the existing colonies. This still caused concern in Britain. In 1767 the board of trade noted that 'a great number of useful inhabitants of these islands, many of whom there is reason to fear are manufacturers are daily emigrating to the American colonies'.[52] In the early 1770s concern became panic, especially about the outflow from Ulster and Scotland.[53] Physically to prevent people leaving the British Isles was a procedure of doubtful legality and in any case difficult to enforce.[54] The flow could, however, be slowed, or so it was believed, by controlling access to land. In New England or the proprietary colonies, above all in the great magnet of emigrants, Pennsylvania, the crown had no power over the distribution of new land. In the new colonies, Quebec, Nova Scotia, and the Floridas, on the other hand, grants were made in Britain itself on condition

[52] W. L. Grant and J. Munro, eds., *Acts of the Privy Council of England: Colonial Series*, 6 vols. (1908–12), V. 113.

[53] This is the theme of Bernard Bailyn, *Voyagers to the West: A Passage in the Peopling of America on the Eve of the Revolution* (New York, 1986), ch. 2.

[54] Ibid. pp. 52–5.

that the land was intended to be settled by people who were already in America or who were 'foreign Protestants' from continental Europe. In the rest of the colonies, grants were made by the governors on the spot. Here the British government moved late to try to establish control. It had other motives for doing so, apart from limiting emigration. It was a long-standing grievance against governors that they allowed land to be acquired by speculators who held onto them, waiting for the price to rise, rather than settling them immediately. Thus large tracts in the existing colonies remained undeveloped. This practice should be stopped and a proper price together with quit rents should be charged in order to give the crown a revenue. To achieve these ends a prohibition on the alienation of land by governors was enacted in 1773, followed by the issuing of regulations for the conditions under which they would be sold in 1774.[55] These regulations could not take effect before the outbreak of the Revolution.

The commercial relationship between Britain and her colonies had long been assumed to involve a division of labour: Britain manufactured and the colonies provided her with raw materials and foodstuffs. The colonies should neither manufacture extensively for themselves nor import manufactured goods from any other source than from Britain, even if the goods had not been made there. In return they should be given every encouragement to produce more primary products, especially those needed for British manufacturing. Certain specified commodities could only be exported from the colonies to Britain.

Objections to colonial manufacturing on any large scale, as opposed to making things for household or neighbourhood consumption, were axiomatic in British circles. Formal prohibitions were, however, limited to specific items, such as the export of woollen cloth or hats or the setting up of works to produce finished metal goods, and were very difficult to enforce. In disputes with Britain in the 1760s, Americans were fond of threatening that they would accompany non-importation by a programme of self-sufficiency in manufactured goods. The house of commons took this sufficiently seriously to order governors in 1766 to report on the state of manufacturing in their colonies. These reports produced reassuring results. Manufacturing on any commercial scale was still limited.[56] The normally alarmist Bernard confirmed such views. There might be 'some rivalry with Great Britain' from manufactures in Pennsylvania, he wrote, 'but for New England to threaten the mother country with manufactures, is the idlest bully that was ever attempted upon sensible people'.[57] General Gage agreed that the danger was confined to Pennsylvania.

[55] Ibid. pp. 55–7.   [56] Thomas, *Townshend Duties Crisis*, p. 79.
[57] To Shelburne, 21 March 1768, HUHL, Sparks MSS 4/6.

The province was recruiting 'mechanicks and manufacturers' from Britain and Germany as well as from among the British regiments in America. '[I]f they go on as they have hitherto done, they will probably in a few years supply themselves with many necessary articles, which they now import from Great-Britain.'[58] Politicians' responses to colonial manufacturing produced some perhaps surprising reversals of conventional roles. While Pitt insisted that every 'authoritative and forcible restriction' must be used to curb colonial manufacturing,[59] Grenville believed that it would be 'most violent and unjust' to try to prevent all manufacturing.[60] Hillsborough seems to have agreed with him. He was reported to have said that America should not be treated like Ireland in having its manufactures restricted.[61] It was possible for men who were reasonably well informed about conditions in the colonies to disregard the threat of American competition with British manufactures because they were aware, as modern scholarship confirms, that there was as yet little incentive to develop colonial manufacturing beyond the limits of a localized demand.

Colonial imports of manufactured goods from sources other than Britain were thought to be a much more urgent threat. The British customs administration had long believed that illegal importing was rife. Boston merchants' records indeed suggest that the volume of such imports, usually from the Netherlands or via Dutch settlements in the West Indies, was significant.[62] George Grenville, who quoted an estimate that goods worth £500,000 a year that were being imported illegally, was determined to stamp out such practices. His government was responsible for provisions to strengthen the customs administration, which Charles Townshend took further in the creation of a new American customs board. The limited effect of these measures is suggested by a report which has been dated to 1769–70 on 'the ports, districts and towns of America'. Smuggling was said to be rife in all the colonies.[63] In the case of one commodity, tea, the failure to control illegal imports was notorious. About three-quarters of the tea consumed in the colonies was thought to be imported illegally, mostly from Dutch sources via the West Indies.

[58] To Shelburne, 23 Jan. 1768, Carter, ed., *Correspondence of General Thomas Gage*, I. 161.
[59] 4 March 1766, R. C. Simmons and P. D. G. Thomas, eds., *Proceedings and Debates of the British Parliaments respecting North America, 1754–1783*, 6 vols. (Millwood, NY, 1982–6), II. 315.
[60] To W. Knox, 27 June 1768, HL, ST 7, vol. 2.
[61] Franklin to T. Cushing, 13 June 1772, Labaree et al., eds., *Papers of Benjamin Franklin*, XIX. 19.
[62] J. W. Tyler, *Smugglers and Patriots: Boston Merchants and the Advent of the Revolution* (Boston, 1986), pp. 13–17.
[63] BL, Add MS 15484, discussed in Thomas C. Barrow, *Trade and Empire: The British Customs Service in Colonial America 1660–1775* (Cambridge, Mass., 1967), pp. 240–1.

The corollary of discouraging American manufacturing and of trying to prevent imports of manufactures that did not come from Britain was to encourage the consumption in Britain of colonial raw materials. Britain owed it to the colonies, as George Grenville put it, to import as large a quantity of raw materials from them as possible, even though this involved putting duties on cheaper foreign imports and paying out large sums to colonial producers in bounties.[64] Major extensions of the bounty system were made at considerable expense to colonial hemp in 1764, to timber in 1765, intended to enable America eventually 'to supply all the consumption of Great Britain',[65] to raw silk in 1770, and to staves and other materials for casks in 1771.[66] Americans were also given help in gaining outlets for their produce in the foreign West Indian islands by the equalizing in 1766 of the duties on British and foreign molasses. This marked a significant reduction of the privileged position that the British West Indies had enjoyed within the empire. It was not so easy to persuade British manufacturers to subordinate their interests to the common good of empire. British iron masters, for instance, were happy for bounties to be paid for colonial pig and bar iron, but they opposed extra duties on Swedish imports, since the supply from America was too small to meet their needs.[67] A petition to set up machinery, illegal under the Iron Act of 1750, to enable steel to be made in New England met a counter petition from Bristol that this would be 'the ruin of many thousands of industrious persons' in Britain.[68] Franklin's polemic that the interest of any 'small body of British tradesmen or artificers' would always 'outweigh that of all the king's subjects in the colonies' had some substance.[69]

Studies of the working of imperial controls in the last years before the Revolution suggest that where there was a strong enough incentive to do so, the system could be breached. Great combines of speculators did not get grants to found new colonies, but settlers still established themselves across the proclamation line. Controls on access to land in existing colonies and on emigration from Britain could not be applied. Where appropriate raw materials were available and the domestic demand justified it, Americans manufactured extensively for themselves. Illegal trade was still transacted where it was worthwhile. Nevertheless, British productive capacity reinforced by the inclination of colonial consumers to buy British goods kept colonial

[64] To Knox, 27 June 1768, HL, ST 7, vol. 2.
[65] Whately to Temple, 10 May 1765, 'Bowdoin–Temple Papers, I', 53–4.
[66] Oliver M. Dickerson, *The Navigation Acts and the American Revolution* (Philadelphia, 1951), pp. 13–14; George L. Beer, *British Colonial Policy 1754–1765* (New York, 1907), pp. 217–24.
[67] See petitions in 1765, PRO, CO 323/18, ff. 104–7.
[68] I, 23 Feb 1773, Simmons and Thomas, eds., *Proceedings and Debates*, III. 466–7, 473.
[69] 'Causes of American Discontents', 5–7 Jan. 1768, Labaree et al., eds., *Papers of Benjamin Franklin*, XV. 9–12.

markets largely in British hands, while the size of the British market and the efficiency of British merchants as worldwide distributors drew most colonial commodities to Britain. The abundance of British credit further reinforced imperial regulations. In short, the conventional wisdom that the system naturally fitted the needs of both parties was not mistaken, but it had few teeth to enforce compliance where it did not fit needs.

Thus the argument put forward in Chapter 1, that economic expansion could still be contained within the British imperial system and that Americans did not as yet feel compelled to overthrow it as an obstacle to their further progress, still seems to be valid for the early 1770s. On the other hand, the argument that growth was raising the stakes of empire for Britain and increasing apprehensions about the consequences of a loss of control over the colonies seems to be valid too.[70] Fear of economic disaster reinforced determination to maintain due constitutional authority.

The most ambitious and innovative of British merchants may have come to agree with some academic political economists, famously Adam Smith and Josiah Tucker, and to regard controls as an obstacle to commercial expansion.[71] The great bulk of their colleagues seem, however, to have been committed to retaining the system. For mainstream political opinion retaining the Navigation Acts was a matter of the highest priority. If they were not maintained, empire would be dissolved and Britain would be fatally weakened. Were the colonies able to defy the sovereignty of parliament, a train of events would surely follow: they were already refusing to pay taxes as a matter of principle, complete denial of legislative authority would follow and that must include rejection of the Navigation Acts. Characteristic of this line of argument were contributions to debates in the house of lords on 30 November 1774 and 20 January 1775. Lord Lyttelton had asked 'whether that commerce, which had carried us triumphantly through the last war, should be subject to the wise and necessary regulations prescribed by the Act of Navigation . . . or at once laid open at the will of the factious Americans, who were struggling for a free and unlimited trade, independent of their mother country?' Were this to happen, 'America, instead of being subject to Great Britain would, soon give laws to it.'[72] Lord Townshend, formerly lord lieutenant of Ireland, believed that Americans were threatening 'that great Palladium of the British commerce, the act of navigation'. Was that 'great commercial system, on which the strength and prosperity of Great-Britain and the mutual interest of both countries, vitally depended' to be sacrificed 'to

[70] See above, p. 45.
[71] David Hancock, *Citizens of the World: London Merchants and the Integration of British Atlantic Community, 1735–1785* (Cambridge, 1995), pp. 38–9.
[72] Simmons and Thomas, eds., *Proceedings and Debates*, V. 238.

gratify the foolishly ambitious temper of a turbulently ungrateful people?'[73] Ultimate authority must be asserted, even in the face of overwhelming opposition that was to develop in the colonies by the winter of 1774-5.

IV

From 1770 to 1773 Anglo–American relations appeared to be entering into a more tranquil phase. There were relatively few overt acts of defiance in the colonies, apart from the burning of the naval schooner *Gaspée* off Rhode Island in June 1772. Although there were frequent reports, some of them well founded, that measures were being prepared against Massachusetts, the ministry of lord North did not find it necessary to bring a major American question before parliament.

The apparent calm has, however, been dismissed as 'superficial and accidental'.[74] The South Carolina commons were still refusing to vote taxes until their sole right to appropriate money was recognized. Virginia was restive. The Virginia burgesses had set up a committee of correspondence and other colonies were following suit to create a network for inter-colonial cooperation completely outside official channels. Massachusetts was certainly not calm. The government's policy of paying salaries out of parliamentary taxation first to the governor and then to the colony's judges was regarded as a subversion of the constitution defined in the 1691 charter. It provided the pretext for the Boston town meeting to circulate a statement of 'The Rights of the Colonists' on 20 November 1772 denying the 'assumed' authority of parliament to legislate for the colonies 'in all cases whatsoever'.[75] In a controversy with their new governor, Thomas Hutchinson, in January 1773, the Massachusetts assembly defined the colonies as 'distinct states from the mother country'. In their opinion, 'there is more reason to dread the consequences of absolute uncontroled power, whether of a nation or a monarch, than those of a total independence'.[76] In June the assembly sent a petition to the king asking for the dismissal of Hutchinson for opinions that he had expressed in private letters now made public. In October 1773 a Massachusetts committee of correspondence urged the other colonies to consider whether in the event of a war between Britain and a European enemy, the colonies should respond to calls for men and money. They suggested that support must be dependent on a guarantee of 'the rights and liberties which *they ought to enjoy*'.[77] Arthur Lee believed that the next European war would be America's opportunity to

---

[73] Ibid. V. 274.   [74] Thomas, *Townshend Duties Crisis*, p. 221.
[75] Cushing, ed., *Writings of Samuel Adams*, II. 360.   [76] Ibid. II. 424-5.
[77] Ibid. III. 65.

extract what it wanted from Britain.[78] Fears in Britain for the defence of the empire without a proper degree of imperial authority seemed to be abundantly confirmed.

How long ministers were prepared to play a waiting game, ignoring provocations, beyond issuing an emphatic rejection of the Massachusetts assembly's petition against Hutchinson through the privy council in January 1774, is uncertain. They may have hoped that in the long run more and more official salaries would restore the balance of power within the colonies in the governors' favour. The immediate prospect was, however, that imperial authority throughout North America was being reduced to a very low ebb. That was not a situation likely to be tolerated for very long.

In the event the North government was faced with a provocation to which it was deemed impossible not to respond, the dumping of the tea into Boston harbour on 16 December 1773. The 'tea party' was the consequence of new arrangements for supplying the colonies with tea embodied in the Tea Act of April 1773. This was certainly not a deliberate measure of coercion aimed at the colonies, but it had implications for them that were likely to provoke vigorous opposition to it. The scheme was intended to relieve the East India Company from the serious financial crisis that had beset it in 1772.[79] The Company had great stocks of unsold tea and it asked for means to boost its sales in the colonies, where tea smuggled through Dutch sources enjoyed a dominant position. The act granted the Company a concession on the customs duties that were paid in Britain and permitted it to ship tea directly to the colonies through its own agents. There were two highly contentious aspects to this scheme. The Townshend duty that was still being levied on tea was not withdrawn, in spite of the Company's request that it should be, and the Company's direct dealing in tea threatened to damage a great many colonial mercantile interests that dealt with tea, both legally and illegally imported. Ministers were not ignorant of what was at stake. In the commons debate some speakers specifically warned them that Americans would not buy tea, however cheap it was, on which the parliamentary tax was being collected. Lord North, however, declined to make any further concession. He pointed out that the tea duty provided funds for the salaries for colonial officials. Larger sales of tea would provide more funds for a purpose that he had very much at heart. When pressed further, he flatly stated that Americans were 'so little deserving favour from hence'.[80] The agent for Massachusetts

[78] To S. Adams, 11 June 1773, R. H. Lee, *Life of Arthur Lee, LLD.*, 2 vols. (Boston, 1829), I. 230.

[79] See above, pp. 211–12.

[80] Debate of 26 April 1773, Simmons and Thomas, eds., *Proceedings and Debates*, III. 487–92. See discussion of the act in Thomas, *Townshend Duties Crisis*, pp. 246–57; Benjamin W. Labaree, *The Boston Tea Party* (New York, 1964), pp. 70–9.

tried to convince North and Dartmouth that the retention of the tea duty would defeat the purpose of relieving the East India Company. He too was rebuffed and concluded that 'it was thought fit to continue this tax as a badge of sovereignty over you'.[81]

The East India Company chartered seven ships to take tea to four colonial ports. In all four, merchants, particularly those who dealt in smuggled tea, raised strident protests. The Company was depicted as an engine of monopoly and extortion against the colonies in general. John Dickinson feared that the Company, having plundered India, were now casting 'their eyes on America as a new theater whereon to exercise their talents of rapine, oppression and cruelty'.[82] Those to whom the tea was being consigned were subjected to intimidation. At Charleston the tea was stored but never distributed. At New York and Philadelphia it was not even landed. At Boston for complex reasons the three ships could not be extricated from the harbour. The deadlock was ended when a group of Boston activists stormed the ships and put 90,000 lb. of tea into the water.

Outrageous as the resistance to the tea shipments seemed to be to British opinion, ministers still hoped to limit the scope of their response to executive and judicial action, rather than invoking parliament, where resentment was likely to run uncontrollably high. It was agreed that Boston and Massachusetts must be made the target for a response intended to isolate and punish what seemed to be the centre of disaffection. It was hoped that other colonies would be either sympathetic to the curbing of extremism or would at least be sufficiently overawed not to require coercion. More troops were to be sent to Boston under general Gage, who was to be the new governor of Massachusetts. Boston was to be punished by closing its port until restitution was made and by bringing the supposed ringleaders to trial. When it was found that these purposes could not be effected by executive action, ministers turned to parliament with a bill to close the port. Having resorted to parliamentary authority for one measure, the government decided not to stop at the Port Bill but to introduce other reforms to strike at the roots of sedition in Massachusetts. The most important was the bill that became the Massachusetts Government Act. This at last embodied the kind of proposals that would-be reformers had been advocating for so long and that had been taken up by Hillsborough but had never been brought before parliament. The charter was to be revised to strengthen the power of the executive. The chief proposal was to replace the council annually elected by the assembly

---

[81] W. Bollan to Massachusetts Council, 1 Sept. 1773, 'Bowdoin–Temple Papers, I', 310.
[82] Cited in H. V. Bowen, 'Perceptions from the Periphery: Colonial American Views of Britain's Asiatic Empire, 1756–1783' in Christine Daniels and Michael V. Kennedy, eds., *Negotiated Empires: Centers and Peripheries in the Americas, 1500–1820* (New York, 2002), p. 294.

with a council nominated by the crown, as in most other colonies. In addition, the governor was to appoint all judges. Special meetings of the inhabitants of the Massachusetts towns, which had been forums for agitation, were to be regulated; they could only be held with the permission of the governor. Jurors were no longer to be elected but to be nominated by sheriffs. A bill followed which was intended to protect soldiers or customs officials from prosecution in Massachusetts for acts done in the course of their duty. Such cases could be referred by the governor for trial in other colonies or in Britain. Finally, an act was passed to secure quarters for the troops in Boston.

These four coercive acts, quickly dubbed the 'intolerable acts' in the colonies, were a very firm response to what ministers had finally diagnosed as a crisis on whose successful resolution empire in America now hinged. Lord Dartmouth told Gage that what was at stake was not only Britain's 'dignity and reputation, but its power, nay its very existence, depends upon the present moment; for should those ideas of independence . . . once take root that relation between the kingdom and its colonies which is the bond of peace and power will soon cease to exist and destruction must follow disunion'.[83] Lord North told the commons that 'We must decide whether we will govern America or whether we will bid adieu to it, and give it that perfect liberty . . . [U]nless they see you are willing and able to maintain your authority, they will at least in the Massachusetts Bay, totally throw it off.'[84]

The coercive acts had a relatively easy passage through the British parliament. There was very little opposition to the Port Bill. Few seem to have doubted that some punitive measures had to be taken. As had been anticipated, hostility to America seems to have been widely felt by ordinary MPs. Such sentiments were to be a powerful constraint on any inclination that ministers may have had to pursue moderate courses. Burke warned his New York correspondents that 'The popular current, both within and without doors, at present sets strongly against America.'[85] The opposition politicians, the supporters of Chatham or Rockingham, were divided on the bill, some of them opposing it, others speaking in its favour. It passed the commons without a division. The Massachusetts Government Bill was much more contentious. The use of statute to impose revisions of chartered rights without hearing counsel for the colony was regarded by some as a most dubious procedure. It was opposed in both houses, the opposition expressing increasing concern at the coercive powers that the government was assuming. In the lords lord Camden questioned 'how far it may be justifiable by law, to

[83] 3 June 1774, Davies, ed., *Documents*, VIII. 124.

[84] 18 May 1774, cited in P. D. G. Thomas, *Tea Party to Independence: The Third Phase of the American Revolution, 1773–1776* (Oxford, 1991), p. 87.

[85] 6 April 1774, Sutherland, ed., *Correspondence of Edmund Burke*, II. 528.

wrest [and] tear from a people, a charter once solemnly given them. I look upon such a step as tyranical. I think resistance in such a case is lawful.'[86] Government speakers answered such objections by appeals to state necessity.[87] On the main division on the bill in the commons, the government had a majority of 239 to 64.[88]

Members of the parliamentary opposition, such as Burke, together with Americans in Britain generally took a pessimistic view of public feelings about the colonies in 1774. A visitor to Bristol found that 'the Boston Port Bill is generally approved, as a proper punishment for *Rebels;* and little better are the generality of Americans reported to be at present'.[89] Arthur Lee believed that nothing could be done to rally British opinion until 'the popular prejudices begin to abate'.[90] Even London, where American radicals like the Lees had won City offices, did not petition against the coercive acts. Mercantile opinion was generally quiescent. North was complacent that opposition from merchants and manufacturers was not to be expected. He knew, for instance, that 'the people of Manchester had been so used by the colonies, that they chose to have no dealing with them'.[91] American issues are judged to have played very little part in the general election of 1774, outside London, where radical candidates incorporated American grievances into their programmes.[92]

If opposition to the coercive acts against America failed to strike a chord with a wider British public, opposition to another piece of colonial legislation passed in the 1774 session, the Quebec Act, had rather more success. As was explained in Chapter 6, the act to settle the government of a French colony conquered in 1760 could, without too gross a degree of implausibility, be represented as a charter of privileges for Catholics in Quebec and as establishing authoritarian patterns of government within the empire. Probably with little reference to the American crisis but impelled by an urgent need to legalize provisions for the government of Quebec before they were challenged in the courts, the government had pushed through the legislation late in the session.[93] However misleadingly, Americans saw it as a fifth 'intolerable' act and their dislike of it found an echo in the extreme anti-Catholicism of some British radicals. William Lee believed that British opinion was 'very greatly

[86] 11 May 1774, Simmons and Thomas, eds., *Proceedings and Debates*, IV. 421.
[87] See above, p. 172.
[88] For analysis of the debates, see Thomas, *Tea Party to Independence*, chs. 4, 5.
[89] W. Dillwyn to J. Pemberton, HSP, Pemberton Papers, XXVI, p. 120.
[90] To F. Lee 2 April 1774, HUHL, bMS Am. 811. 1(19).
[91] Letter of Hutchinson of 8 July 1774, P. O. Hutchinson, ed., *The Diary and Letters of his Excellency Thomas Hutchinson, Esq.*, 2 vols. (1884–6), I. 182.
[92] Thomas, *Tea Party to Independence*, p. 148.
[93] Peter Marshall, 'British North America, 1760–1815' in P. J. Marshall, ed., *The Oxford History of the British Empire*, II, *The Eighteenth Century* (Oxford, 1998), pp. 378–9.

alarmed at the threatened establishment of Popery by law and raising a formidable Roman Catholic army' of Canadians. He hoped that the act would prove 'fatal' to North.[94] This was wishful thinking of the highest order, but the Quebec Act did at least stimulate a furious press campaign, a petition from London against it, references to its iniquities in some election addresses in 1774, such as those in Newcastle, and the shouting at the king of the slogans 'No Popery! No French laws!' in the London streets.[95]

In spite of the minor furore over the Quebec Act, had the policies which the government launched in 1774 to crush and isolate Massachusetts been successful, there probably would have been very limited public engagement with America beyond endorsement of ministerial policies. It became increasingly clear, however, that the policies of the government had been signally unsuccessful. Massachusetts was far from cowed and much of the rest of the continent was uniting in its support. The scale of the crisis which Britain faced became only too apparent by 1775. Faced with the prospect of full-scale hostilities, a wide public opinion divided sharply.

Gage arrived in Boston on 17 May 1774. With the support of the navy he could enforce the closure of the port of Boston but he was unable to exercise any effective government outside the town, where he had to concentrate his patently inadequate forces and where he and those members of his new nominated council who had not been intimidated into resignation were virtually under siege. Outside Boston the governor's writ emphatically did not run. Authority throughout the province was exercised by town meetings, county meetings and committees of correspondence, and ultimately by the provincial congress of Massachusetts. Boycotts were imposed on British goods and the population seemed to be being prepared for armed resistance. All this was relayed to ministers at the end of August and beginning of September 1774 by Gage, who asked for reinforcements on a very large scale before he could make any attempt to bring the colony into any sort of order. Twenty thousand men was the number that he eventually thought that he would need.

At the same time it was becoming clear that the other colonies were by no means acquiescing in the coercion of Massachusetts by act of parliament. They were rallying to its aid. It has been said of the 'intolerable' acts, taken together with the Quebec Act, that they 'crystallized' all 'American fears and

[94] To R. H. Lee, 10 Sept. 1774, W. C. Ford, ed., *Letters of William Lee*, 3 vols. (New York, 1891), I. 92.
[95] Philip Lawson, *The Imperial Challenge: Quebec and Britain in the Age of the American Revolution* (Montreal and Kingston, 1989), pp. 135, 147–9; Kathleen Wilson, *The Sense of the People: Politics, Culture and Imperialism in England, 1715–1785* (Cambridge, 1985), p. 357; Sainsbury, *Disaffected Patriots*, pp. 59–62.

grievances. They appeared to threaten the Protestant religion, the availability of land in the west, the integrity of the colonial assemblies, the right of taxation, the traditional procedures of jury trial, the civil control of the military, and the sanctity of colonial charters.'[96] These threats were perceived by a colonial leadership who had long since lost all confidence in the good intentions towards them of British parliaments and ministers, and who needed little further proof of what seemed to be malignant plotting in London. If Massachusetts was to be forced to yield to the new regime there could be no doubt to most politically involved Americans that the same fate awaited the other colonies.

At uneven speeds, the colonies moved towards roughly similar objectives: trying to define their rights in relation to Britain, putting pressure on the British government by economic sanctions and creating networks of unofficial committees to organize opposition and to coordinate actions with other colonies. These unofficial bodies were effectively usurping the powers of properly constituted authority in all the colonies. Governors were left impotent and isolated. The desire for coordination found its fullest expression in the calling of the first Continental Congress in September 1774. Colonies whose leaderships in the assembly had generally avoided confrontation with Britain, notably Pennsylvania and New York, were coming under pressure from radical unofficial organizations, a committee of mechanics in New York and a convention in Pennsylvania.

By the time it adjourned on 26 October, the first Continental Congress had called for the repeal of a whole string of objectionable British acts, including of course those passed in 1774. It had formally denied the legislative sovereignty of parliament and asserted in its place 'the free and exclusive power of legislation in their several provincial legislatures' with the proviso that Americans consented to be bound by British acts of parliament that regulated their external trade. It had drawn up an association to enforce a non-importation agreement against British goods to take effect almost immediately with a delayed non-exportation agreement. There was to be a general agreement not to buy imported goods, especially dutied tea. A non-exportation agreement was to come into force a year later. All colonies except New York endorsed the association and a network of committees was set up throughout the colonies, including New York, to enforce the terms of the boycott. Support was pledged for Massachusetts's refusal to obey the coercive acts, while efforts were made to restrain open resistance that might lead to conflict with the soldiers and proposals that the Congress should encourage

---

[96] David L. Ammerman, 'The Continental Association: Economic Resistance and Government by Committee' in Conser et al., eds., *Resistance, Politics and the Struggle for Independence*, p. 265.

military preparations were shelved. Even so, Congress was making demands that no British government could accept and was trying to enforce its demands with economic weapons.

With Massachusetts out of control and with most of the rest of the colonies apparently united in rejecting the sovereignty of parliament and in undermining royal government, ministers seem to have been in the position that their predecessors had found themselves in at intervals since 1765: the only realistic alternatives might seem to have been either full concession or full coercion. Like their predecessors, however, North's government still hoped to avoid that agonizing choice. Retreat beyond the tactical concession that no further taxes would be levied in the foreseeable future, while the sovereign authority of parliament, including the right to lay taxes, must be acknowledged, was unthinkable. Full-scale coercion was still, however, deeply unpalatable and there were serious problems in raising forces to take effective action. Ministers were not yet ready to put the army onto a war footing. The British government therefore sought a middle ground: more force must be applied to Massachusetts but the rest of the colonies might still be made to see the error of their ways by actions that stopped short of military force. In a memorandum the king wrote that although he was in no doubt that 'nothing less than a total independence of the British legislature will satisfy' the colonies, he still believed that were the British to reply to Congress's embargo by enforcing an embargo on any colony that subscribed to its association, the colonial alliance would split apart and 'experience will show them that the interference of the mother country is essentially necessary to prevent their becoming rivals'.[97] Later he was still not in favour of 'new measures' but was 'for supporting those already undertaken'.[98]

Retreat for what was becoming an American leadership expressed through Congress was equally unthinkable: there could be no acknowledgement of the full sovereignty of parliament and the coercive acts must be withdrawn. Even so, outside some circles in Massachusetts and a few extremist groups elsewhere, many Americans too sought a middle way short of armed resistance. They believed that they must stand firm by the embargoes, which would, however long they took, inflict such damage as either to bring the government to see reason or force a change to a more reasonable government. American radicals in London, often unfairly accused of giving naively optimistic assessments of the extent of support for the colonies in Britain, were in no doubt that it would be a long haul. William Lee believed that the colonial cause could not gain ground until the embargoes had time to cripple the

---

[97] Fortescue, ed., *Correspondence of King George III*, III. 48, where is misdated to 1773.
[98] To North, 18 Nov. 1774, ibid. III. 154.

British economy: 'I cannot really think, the contest can be settled in less than two years.'[99]

Both sides were sticking to their principles, while trusting to processes of economic attrition to undermine the will of the other. Americans believed that Britain would become ungovernable under the impact of a trade embargo. British opinion generally assumed that the colonies would not be able to sustain an embargo and that British prohibitions on their trade would bring them to their knees. Such strategies were almost certainly unrealistic, but whatever their merits, violence in Massachusetts was to force the issue long before they had any chance of success.

With the breaking up of the first Continental Congress and the meeting of the first session of the new parliament in the winter of 1774, the initiative was again with the British government. Force was to be applied against Massachusetts; Gage was sent such reinforcements as could be mustered and he was encouraged to be more aggressive. Massachusetts was declared to be in rebellion in February 1775. Force was to be backed by economic sanctions. The New England colonies were prohibited from the fisheries and from trading outside the empire. The threat that similar measures might be applied to other colonies was clear. North thought that Virginia and Maryland would probably be next. Nevertheless, individual colonies were offered incentives to break away from Congress, above all to renounce its embargoes, and to separate themselves from Massachusetts. Colonial legislatures were invited to raise their own contributions to the cost of 'the common defence' and 'the support of the civil government and the administration of justice'. Such proposals would require the approval of parliament, but if that approval was given, parliament would not use its undiminished sovereign power to raise any further taxes on the colony.[100]

Decisions taken in Britain were, however, being overtaken by events in America. News that Gage was being reinforced was countered in Massachusetts by preparations to resist any offensive actions that he might take. Militia units were mustered and put under the command of the provincial congress. Similar measures were taken in other New England colonies and Virginia was being 'put into a posture of defence'. Arms and gunpowder were accumulated by means which included some purloining of royal stocks. It was to frustrate such warlike preparations that Gage eventually sent troops out of Boston to Lexington and Concord, where fighting took place on 19 April 1775. The Massachusetts provincial congress mobilized a provincial army and moved it

[99] To F. Lee, 24 Dec. 1774, Virginia Historical Society, MSS 1. L. 51, ff. 17–19.
[100] *Journals of the House of Commons*, XXXV (1774–6), 161.

towards Boston. Other colonies sent troops to Massachusetts. In June Gage fought a costly battle to dislodge the American troops from Bunker Hill.

On 10 May the second Continental Congress began in Philadelphia. Congress took command of the hostilities outside Boston by appointing Washington to lead what was called 'the American continental army'. On 6 July Congress issued its declaration 'of the causes and necessity of their taking up arms'. 'We are reduced to the alternative of choosing an unconditional submission to the tyranny of irritated ministers, or resistance by force. The latter is our choice.' Even so, Congress still denied any intention 'to dissolve that union' with Britain and petitioned the king to cease warlike measures and to repeal the objectionable statutes against which Americans had so vehemently complained.[101] North's proposals for colonies to tax themselves under the authority of parliament were rejected.

What Congress asked for would not have been conceded at any time, but by the summer of 1775 ministers were finally convinced that rebellion was widespread and that strategies for trying to suppress Massachusetts while hoping for the best elsewhere were no longer adequate. Dartmouth concluded on 1 July that, while Massachusetts was in open rebellion, 'all North America (Quebec, Nova Scotia and the Floridas excepted) is in arms against Great Britain and the people involved in the guilt of levying war against the king, in every sense of the expression.'[102] The king accepted that Gage's request for 20,000 men in America, which had been so unpalatable before, must now be met.[103] The British forces must be supplemented by hiring foreign European troops. A new front was to be opened at New York. The navy was to blockade all the colonies and to launch coastal raids. Lord North sadly concluded that 'the war is now grown to such a height. that it must be treated as a foreign war, and that every expedient which would be used in the latter case should be applied in the former'.[104] On 23 August the colonies were declared to be in 'open and avowed rebellion'. The continuation of empire in most of North America, on terms that the majority of British political opinion would accept, now depended on the outcome of a war which Britain proved unable to win.

V

As British ministers became aware of the scale of the operations that seemed necessary to subdue America they turned for additional manpower to the

[101] Jensen, ed., *English Historical Documents*, IX. 843–50.
[102] To Gage, 1 July 1775., Davies, ed., *Documents*, XI. 25.
[103] Memorandum, 5 Aug. 1775, Fortescue, ed., *Correspondence of King George III*, III. 240.
[104] 26 July 1775, ibid. III. 233.

outlying parts of the British Isles and to imperial possessions apparently uncontaminated by sedition. Military necessity, as it had done during the Seven Years War, again provided a powerful stimulus for the closer integration of the British Isles and of Britain and its empire.

In 1775 the levying of large numbers of recruits in England itself seemed to be impractical, especially as the raising of new regiments was an expedient which the king in particular was reluctant to sanction.[105] '[N]ew raised men', it was said, 'can be had in numbers only in the Highlands and Ireland.'[106]

To many Americans, especially to Virginians, Scotland was the heart of the British counter-revolution. Lords Bute and Mansfield were commonly supposed to be the secret directors of ministerial policy. The Virginian Landon Carter was warned that Scotland was '99 to 1' against America.[107] Ministerial advisers were not always so sanguine. There were fears in 1775 that unemployment in Glasgow would produce 'disorder and mobbing' and that American agents, who were still recruiting emigrants in the Highlands, might be spreading 'American principles' there.[108] Nevertheless, Highland recruits were quickly forthcoming, as were Scottish officers on half-pay to take command of them. The first new regiment raised for America was a Highland one.[109] Ministers also heard encouraging accounts of the disposition of Scots in America, particularly of recent immigrants from the Highlands. They had received an offer from a colonel Allan Maclean to raise an 'association' of Highland Scots from Quebec, Nova Scotia, New York, and North Carolina to be 'assembled in arms on the side of government'.[110] The governor of North Carolina hoped to collect 3,000 fighting men from 'the emigrants from the Highlands of Scotland who are settled here and immovably attached to his Majesty and his government'.[111] The radical news sheet, The Crisis, concluded that the king was dependent on an 'army of Scotch cut throats'.[112]

Towards the end of 1775 a widespread movement began for petitions and addresses to be sent to the crown and to parliament for and against the war in America. Those from Scotland were all in favour of the war and in support of

---

[105] Stephen Conway, The British Isles and the War of American Independence (Oxford, 2000), p. 15; Piers Mackesy, The War for America 1775–1783 (1964), pp. 39–40.

[106] Germain to Suffolk, [16, 17 June 1775], Historical Manuscripts Commission: Stopford Sackville MSS, 2 vols. (1910), II. 3.

[107] From unknown, 25 Sept. 1775, HUHL, Sparks MSS, 5/1, p. 96.

[108] T. Miller to Suffolk, 14 Aug. 1775, PRO, SP 54/46, ff. 443–4.

[109] Andrew Mackillop, 'More Fruitful than the Soil': Army, Empire and the Scottish Highlands 1715–1815 (East Linton, 2001), p. 59.

[110] Dartmouth to Gage, 15 April 1775, Gage to Dartmouth, 24 July 1775, Davies, ed., Documents, IX. 99, XI. 57.

[111] J. Martin to Dartmouth, 30 June 1775, ibid. IX. 213.

[112] Reprinted in Peter Force, ed., American Archives: A Documentary History of the English Colonies in North America, 4th ser., 4 vols. (Washington DC, 1840–3), II. 61.

the government. Even if there are clear indications that Scottish opinion as a whole was by no means unanimously committed to the coercion of America, the American sense that Scotland was strongly against them was not mistaken.[113]

The role of Ireland was crucial in the early stages of the war. Not only was it regarded as a most promising source of recruits, but regular British regiments on the Irish establishment were ready to be sent to America, if the Irish parliament could be persuaded to consent to their release. Moreover, as it became clear that the Americans would try to interdict local supplies to the British army, Ireland must bear most of the burden of feeding the forces in America as well as of supplying the West Indian islands, included in Congress's embargo on exports.

Restrictions on enlisting Irish Catholics into the British army had been formally lifted in 1771. In 1775 they seemed to some observers to be the source of recruits on which the government was placing greatest reliance.[114] Catholic notables offered to raise subscriptions for recruits and presumed to lay 'two millions of loyal, faithful and affectionate hearts and hands' at the king's feet.[115] The regiments on the Irish establishment were trained soldiers rather than raw recruits. Under the terms of the settlement by which the Irish army had been 'augmented' in 1769 a nominal 12,000 men had to be maintained in Ireland, unless the Irish parliament consented to their reduction. Faced with the British government's request that 4,000 men be sent to America, the lord lieutenant decided to make this a test of Ireland's commitment to the empire. He was aware that the British parliamentary opposition was trying to persuade the Irish parliament, as Burke was suggesting, to stand aloof from the conflict, offering to mediate between Britain and America and refusing to pay for troops sent out of Ireland. Thus the ministry would be forced, Burke anticipated, into 'a contest with the whole empire' if they persisted with their policies.[116] Dublin city meetings petitioned for conciliation and for its MPs to oppose grants for the war.[117] The lord lieutenant was also concerned about 'the Presbyterians of the north, who in their hearts are Americans'. Resolutions in the Irish house of commons were proposed by the government, pledging loyalty to the crown and abhorrence of revolution. These were passed by majorities of two to one. Permission for the 4,000 men to go to

[113] See the discussion in Conway, *British Isles*, pp. 132–3.

[114] Germain to J. Irwin, 13 Sept. 1775, WLCL, Germain Sackville MSS, 3, no. 92

[115] Fingal et al. to J. Blacquiere, 30 Sept. 1775, E. W. Harcourt, ed., *The Harcourt Papers*, 14 vols. (Oxford, 1880–1905), IX. 357. For doubts as to whether such effusions of loyalty reflected the views of the mass of Catholics, see Morley, *Irish Opinion*, pp. 106–15.

[116] Burke to Richmond, 26 Sept. 1775, G. H. Guttridge, ed., *Correspondence of Edmund Burke*, III, *July 1774–June 1778* (Cambridge, 1961), pp. 218–19.

[117] Hill, *From Patriots to Unionists*, p. 143.

America later passed by 121 to 76. In 1776 sixteen of the forty-four battalions serving in America had come from the Irish establishment 'augmented to combat strength with Roman Catholics'.[118] In retrospect the lord lieutenant felt that he had united Britain and Ireland as 'connected parts of a great empire'.[119] To the chief secretary, Ireland had made 'an explicit declaration of war against America'.[120] A more realistic assessment is probably that while the majority of 'the Irish political nation' would not openly support the Americans, they had 'considerable misgivings' about the policies being pursued and wished to avoid a conflict if at all possible.[121]

Ministers' anxieties about Ireland at this time were revealed by North's attempts to ensure the supply of Irish provisions going across the Atlantic. To achieve this, it seemed necessary to impose an embargo on other exports, but would this be politic at a time when 'It is so much my constant wish to do what is most acceptable to Ireland and the necessity of being particularly attentive, in the present moment, to please the Irish is so evident'?[122] Such misgivings did not prevent an embargo being imposed. For all their apprehensions, British ministers had been able to carry most of their points in Ireland in 1775. Whether they would continue to do so for long was another matter.

If ready-made soldiers were to be obtained from outside the British Isles, there was no alternative to hiring foreign troops. Approaches were quickly made to a number of sources, but the main supply came from Germany, first from Hanover and then from other German princes. At the same time, British ministers were also determined to mobilize the manpower of the empire. It was always intended that Americans should have a major role in suppressing revolt in America. Indications of loyalism were eagerly sought. Meanwhile, other colonies presumed to be largely uncontaminated by revolt were encouraged to raise troops for their own defence and for offensive action. The highest expectations were held of French Canadians. They were presumed to be a militarized people, thirsting for revenge against their hereditary enemies in British America and now firmly attached to the British crown that had treated them with such enlightened toleration. General Gage believed that 'Canadians' could play a prominent part in his strategy for a

---

[118] Alan J. Guy, 'The Irish Military Establishment 1660–1776' in Thomas Bartlett and Keith Jeffery, eds., *A Military History of Ireland* (Cambridge, 1996), pp. 229–30.

[119] J. Lees, 'Review of Earl Harcourt's Administration in Ireland', 24 Jan. 1777, *Harcourt Papers*, X. 276; see also Harcourt to North, 11 Oct. 1775, ibid. IX. 362–3 and J. Blacquiere to North, 12 Oct. 1775, PRO, SP 63/438, ff. 121–2.

[120] J. Blacquiere to North, 13 Dec. 1775, ibid. f. 144.

[121] Morley, *Irish Opinion*, pp. 78, 81; see also R. B. McDowell, *Ireland in the Age of Imperialism and Revolution 1760–1801* (Oxford, 1979), pp. 239–48.

[122] To Harcourt, 15 Oct. 1775, *Harcourt Papers*, IX. 366.

three-pronged offensive.[123] Such hopes were quickly disappointed. Guy Carleton, the governor of Quebec, had already found that 'the habitants or peasantry' had lost their 'ancient habits of obedience and discipline'.[124] When American troops entered the colony of Quebec, the governor had little success in raising a militia to expel them.[125] There was, however, no question but that Quebec must be preserved for the empire, even if its defence would have to depend on British troops. Nova Scotia with its naval base at Halifax must be preserved too. Indeed its future imperial role was already being mapped out in 1775. It was to be a 'happy asylum' for loyalists who had to flee from New England and it was to be developed as a source of supplies of grain and timber for the West Indies.[126] The governor hoped to be able to raise local troops to aid its defence from Germans, 'neutrals' (that is the remaining French Acadians) and Irish 'without regard to their religion'.[127] The reality was again to be very different. Attempts to enrol Nova Scotia men into a militia or to tax them for the defence of the colony provoked a 'universal ferment' and had to be abandoned.[128]

By calling upon the military services of the French Canadians the British were fulfilling the worst fears of many Americans. They had thrown off the mask: that they intended to impose despotism and Popery on the American continent could no longer be doubted. Yet they were showing themselves capable of even baser turpitude: allying with Indians and slaves. Rumours that the British government would emancipate slaves and incite them to revolt swept through Virginia.[129] The governor of South Carolina reported that 'a Mr Lee in London' (it is not clear whether it was Arthur or William) had sent warnings that the British were arming the Indians and encouraging slave revolts. 'Words . . . cannot express the flame that this occasioned amongst all ranks and degrees' in the colony.[130] The substance behind these rumours was that general Gage certainly believed that 'we must avail ourselves of every resource', including Indians and 'negros'.[131] The governor of Quebec had been told to mobilize the Indians in his colony, although he found that they 'showed as much backwardness as the Canadian

[123] To Dartmouth, 12 June 1775, Davies, ed., *Documents of the American Revolution*, IX. 170.
[124] To Gage, 4 Feb. 1775, ibid. IX. 45.
[125] Carleton to Dartmouth, 7 June 1775, ibid. IX. 158–9.
[126] Dartmouth to F. Legge, 1 July 1775, ibid. XI. 28.
[127] F. Legge to Dartmouth, 31 July 1775, ibid. XI. 61.
[128] M. Arbuthnot to Sandwich, 14 Jan. 1776, G. R. Barnes and J. H. Owen, eds., *The Private Papers of John, Earl of Sandwich, First Lord of the Admiralty 1771–1782*, 4 vols. (1932–8), I. 117.
[129] Woody Holton, *Forced Founders: Indians, Debtors, Slaves and the Making of the American Revolution in Virginia* (Chapel Hill, NC, 1999), pp. 140–1.
[130] Lord W. Campbell to Dartmouth, 31 Aug. 1775, Davies, ed., *Documents*, XI. 94.
[131] To Barrington, 12 June 1775, Carter, ed., *Correspondence of General Thomas Gage*, II. 684.

peasantry'.[132] In July 1775, Guy Johnson, successor to his uncle and father-in-law Sir William as superintendent of the northern Indians, was instructed to urge Britain's traditional allies, the Six Nations, 'to take up the hatchet against his Majesty's rebellious subjects in America'.[133] The southern superintendent, John Stuart, was not given explicit instructions from home, but Gage urged him to activate the Indians in his jurisdiction. He distributed ammunition, although he did not wish to incite 'an indiscriminate attack upon the provinces'.[134] Suspicions about British plots to turn slaves against their masters mostly hinged on the activities of lord Dunmore, the embattled governor of Virginia. He raised the possibility of arming 'Indians, negroes and other persons' and got an encouraging response from London.[135] He later announced that he would arm slaves to protect his person were he to be attacked.[136] Finally, in November 1775 he promised freedom to slaves who deserted their rebel masters and joined him. They were embodied in what he called 'Lord Dunmore's Ethiopian Regiment' and fought skirmishes with the Virginia militia. Although this aroused intense fear and resentment among white Virginians, Dunmore stopped well short of proclaiming a general slave emancipation.[137]

Americans felt themselves isolated and beleaguered by the forces that Britain seemed to be arraying against them during 1775. 'They are arming every hand, Protestant and Catholic, English, Irish, Scotch, Hanoverians, Hessians, Indians, and Canadians against the devoted colonies', wrote an indignant Arthur Lee.[138] Americans could, however, hope for a degree of fellow feeling from the white communities in the West Indies to the southward.

In virtually all the islands, West Indian whites had struggled with their governors and with metropolitan authority for the privileges of their assemblies and for recognition that they were fully entitled to the rights of Englishmen. Yet their role in the disputes over the authority of parliament had been somewhat muted, even though parliamentary taxation was aimed at them as much as it was aimed at the mainland. As the colonial crisis reached its apogee, the attitude of most West Indian whites seems to have been close

---

[132] G. Carleton to Dartmouth, 7 June 1775, Davies, ed., *Documents*, IX. 158.

[133] Dartmouth to G. Johnson, 24 July 1775, ibid. XI. 56.

[134] J. Stuart to [H. Stuart], 24 Oct. 1775, ibid. XI. 163.

[135] To Dartmouth, 1 May 1775 and reply, 12 July 1775, ibid. IX. 110, XI. 45.

[136] To Dartmouth, 25 June 1775, ibid. IX. 204. For the early involvement of Indians in the war, see Colin G. Calloway, *The American Revolution in Indian Country: Crisis and Diversity in Native American Communities* (Cambridge, 1995), ch. 1.

[137] To Dartmouth, 6 Dec. 1775–18 Feb. 1776, Davies, ed., *Documents*, XII. 59; Sylvia Frey, *Water from the Rock: Black Resistance in a Revolutionary Age* (Princeton, 1991); Holton, *Forced Founders*, ch. 5.

[138] To [J. Dickinson?], 4 Sept. 1775, HUHL, bMS Am. 811. 1 (62).

to that of most Irish Protestants. They had little sympathy with British policies and urged conciliation. Conflict was a dire prospect for them. They stood to lose very heavily indeed from the embargoes on trade that both sides were imposing. Yet they could not afford actively to support the colonial cause. They could not conceivably join in the non-exportation movement and, like the Irish, they needed a British garrison in their midst. The Jamaica assembly while petitioning against British policies asked for additional troops to whom it was willing to pay extra allowances. From the point of view of the British government, this was a satisfactory situation. The immensely valuable trade of the West Indies was not going to be lost to Britain as a result of American subversion.[139]

The North government enjoyed some success in rallying Scotland, Ireland (for the time being) and, in a way that prefigured the contours of a future empire without the thirteen colonies, the rest of Britain's Atlantic possessions. Could the government, however, be sure that England itself was united behind the suppression of revolt?

There was opposition to government policies in both the house of commons, the great majority of whose members sat for English constituencies, and the house of lords. After an uncertain response to the Boston Port Bill, the opposition groups led by Rockingham and Chatham, had condemned the coercive measures introduced in 1774. Their opposition to government policy was unequivocal when the new parliament met. Further coercive measures and above all the use of armed force in the colonies were denounced. Chatham moved a resolution for the withdrawal of the army from Boston, supported by Rockingham, who believed that the military conquest of America was not only impractical but, were it to happen, that the outcome would be deeply threatening to British liberty. 'If an arbitrary military force is to govern one part of this empire, I think and fear if it succeeds, it will not be long before the whole of this empire will be brought under a similar thraldom.'[140] Recent attempts to make imperial control more effective should also be abandoned. Chatham was prepared to suspend all the legislation to which congress objected, while the Rockinghams urged the repeal of the coercive acts. Both groups agreed that parliament would not in future try to raise taxes in America.

If they were not prepared to impose imperial control by armed force, the opposition politicians still wished to maintain the kind of imperial connection with the colonies, which, as Chapter 5 tried to show, was common

---

[139] This paragraph draws heavily on Andrew Jackson O'Shaughnessy, *An Empire Divided: The American Revolution and the British Caribbean* (Philadelphia, 2000).

[140] To Manchester, 28 June 1775, cited F. O'Gorman, *The Rise of Party in England: The Rockingham Whigs 1760–1782* (1975), p. 340.

ground for nearly all shades of British political opinion. This was amply demonstrated in the two major statements of opposition policy, Chatham's speech and his draft bill of 1 February 1775[141] and Edmund Burke's great speech on conciliation with America, delivered on 22 March 1775 and subsequently published.[142] For both Chatham and Burke parliamentary sovereignty over all its parts was essential to empire. We 'are as desirous of preserving the superintending and controuling power of this country over her colonies as any the most determined friend of ministry', wrote the duke of Portland, one of the grandees of the Rockingham party.[143] Chatham, however, returned to his position of 1766: sovereignty did not extend to powers of taxing colonies which were not represented in the British house of commons. In all other respects, the colonies must 'recognize and obey . . . the supreme legislative authority and superintending power of the parliament of Great Britain'.[144] As the authors of the Declaratory Act of 1766, the Rockinghams could not as yet admit any formal qualification of parliamentary sovereignty, but Burke insisted that if parliamentary sovereignty was exercised with a proper restraint and only in ways which were beneficial to the colonies as well as to the mother country, Americans would have no objection to it.

The Americans will have no interest contrary to the grandeur and glory of England, when they are not oppressed by the weight of it; and they will rather be inclined to respect the acts of a superintending legislature, when they see them the acts of that power, which is itself the security, not the rival, of their secondary importance.[145]

Commercial regulation most definitely fell within the scope of parliament's sovereignty. It was axiomatic for Chatham that it had 'an indisputable and indispensable right to make and ordain laws for regulating navigation and trade'.[146] Burke was less enthusiastic, but he still thought that the Navigation Acts, 'without idolizing them', were 'in many ways of great use to us' and should be maintained.[147]

Burke's proposals were based on a generally conventional view of the constitutional mechanism for holding together the empire, but his understanding of the nature of that empire was an unusually sophisticated one. He was quick to recognize that the British empire now included a wide diversity

---

[141] Simmons and Thomas, ed., *Proceedings and Debates*, V. 329–37. For the bill, see W. Cobbett, ed., *Parliamentary History of England from the Norman Conquest in 1066 to the year 1803*, 36 vols. (1806–20), XVIII. 198–203.

[142] Warren M. Elofson and John A. Woods, eds., *Writings and Speeches of Edmund Burke*, III, *Party, Parliament, and the American War 1774–1780* (Oxford, 1996), pp. 105–68.

[143] To Burke, 2 Oct. 1775, cited in Guttridge, ed., *Correspondence of Edmund Burke*, III. 226.

[144] Cobbett, ed., *Parliamentary History History*, XVIII. 199.

[145] Elofson and Woods, eds., *Writings and Speeches of Edmund Burke*, III, p. 158.

[146] Cobbett, ed., *Parliamentary History*, XVIII. 199.

[147] Elofson and Woods, eds., *Writings and Speeches of Edmund Burke*, III, p. 138.

of peoples, including French in Canada and Indians in Bengal.[148] In this he was not exceptional, but in his speech on conciliation with America he forcefully urged his listeners to accept that the thirteen colonies were also a special case or a variety of special cases. Suspicion in particular of New England's supposed 'levelling' or 'Oliverian' principles should be replaced by acceptance of what could not be changed. It was futile and unnecessary to try to hold the line in America against subversion at home. Coercion of Massachusetts would be entirely counter-productive. For reasons which Burke tried to explain at length, 'a fierce spirit of liberty' had grown up in the colonies. Their 'governments are popular in an high degree; some are purely popular'. Their religion could be called 'republican'. Disagreeable as all this might be, 'the temper and character which prevail in our colonies are, I am afraid, unalterable by any human art'. Britain must seek accommodation with what it could not change.[149] While the mainstream of British political opinion, as it showed in the raising of forces against rebel America, was coming to accept an empire made up of diverse peoples, Burke was willing also to accept an empire which included diversities of Englishness, even those that mainstream opinion dismissed as profoundly subversive. This showed a breadth of vision unique among Britain's political leadership. In this light, the tendency in current historiography to be dismissive about what Burke had to offer towards resolving the American crisis seems to be misplaced.

What the parliamentary opposition were proposing in 1775 had no chance of being put into effect, since both houses of parliament rejected their proposals by very large majorities. Dissent from government policies in parliament was, however, part of a wider movement of dissent throughout the country during 1775.

Merchant and manufacturing communities had been involved in debates about America since 1766. Their response to the early stages of the crisis in 1774 had been generally sluggish. As it became clear, however, that the Americans were resorting to trade boycotts and that British counter measures were likely, petitions were drafted for the new parliament in attempts to stave off what threatened to be a massive disruption of transatlantic trade. Thirteen petitions asked the government to make concessions.[150] Neither the strength of support for these petitions nor the nature of their demands caused North's ministry much concern, while the parliamentary opposition and the Americans resident in Britain were unimpressed by them. As events moved to war and the threatened trade disruptions became a reality, British merchant and

---

[148] See above, p. 204.

[149] Elofson and Woods, eds., *Writings and Speeches of Edmund Burke*, III, pp. 119–32.

[150] Listed in James E. Bradley, 'The British Public and the American Revolution: Ideology, Interest and Opinion' in H. T. Dickinson, ed., *Britain and the American Revolution* (1998), p. 135n.

manufacturing opinion remained largely quiescent. '[I]f anything', it has been concluded, 'merchants trading to the new world were inclined to encourage the use of force.'[151] Contemporaries speculated more or less plausibly as to why this might be. Economic explanations were offered, such as the buoyancy of non-American markets or the rewards of government contracts as the armed forces were put onto a war footing. Ultimately, however, it seems clear that the great agitation in favour of concession to the colonies in 1766 would never be repeated in the face of discouragement by the government. Merchants were natural supporters of administration and of the maintenance of a colonial system, which most of them saw as essential to the success of their trade. American disaffection now seemed to be threatening this system.[152]

Evidence of wider public involvement in England in American questions in the years after the Seven Years War is scanty. There are, however, indications of a general sense that in return for all that had been done for them during the war, the colonies should be willing to accept reasonable British requirements and, except during the closely orchestrated campaign for repeal of the Stamp Act in 1766, of impatience with their claims. Sympathetic engagement with these claims seems to have been confined to limited circles in London. In the later months of 1775, however, in response to the outbreak of fighting, the situation changed dramatically. Distinguished recent scholarship has revealed widespread expressions of concern for and against the prosecution of the war that found an outlet in 109 petitions and addresses to the crown from English counties, boroughs and a few other corporate bodies.[153] In the autumn of 1775 the figures available for signatures on petitions and addresses amount to nearly 20,000 people signing petitions in favour of conciliation from twenty-one English boroughs and five counties with about 18,500 signing addresses in support of the government from thirty-seven boroughs and nine counties.[154] Certain conclusions seem irrefutable. This was a considerable involvement of a wide public, extending even to shopkeepers and skilled artisans.[155] Expressions of opinion seem for the most part to have represented the views of local communities with relatively little outside manipulation, even though the government of course encouraged addresses of loyalty and some opposition Rockinghamite politicians tried to elicit petitions for conciliation. Above all, there can be no doubt that

---

[151] Ibid. p. 146.
[152] See discussion in Langford, 'Business Community and Nonimportation' in Conser et al., eds., *Resistance, Politics and Independence*, pp. 278–324.
[153] James E. Bradley, *Popular Politics and the American Revolution in England: Petitions, the Crown and Public Opinion* (Macon, Ga., 1986), p. 59n.
[154] Ibid. p. 137.   [155] Ibid. p. 195.

opinion in England was deeply divided: there may have been a slight numerical majority among the signatories for conciliation, but rather more places sent in addresses pledging their loyalty.[156]

The social, economic, religious, and regional influences that might have shaped responses to the crisis of war have been carefully probed. Tentative conclusions seem to be that the north of England generally supported the government, whereas East Anglia petitioned for conciliation. Religious Dissent was largely opposed to the war, as were many Anglicans, but the institutions of the Church of England aligned themselves behind the government. The Rockinghams, who opposed the war, were *par excellence* an aristocratic party and there were other examples of gentry who objected to coercing the colonies. In general, however, it can be argued that support for the war was led from above. 'The supporters of George III and Parliament were gentlemen, merchants, government placemen, loyal officeholders and Anglican clergy'; the petitioners for peace 'were concerned citizens drawn largely from the middle ranks of society who identified their interests with a tradition of liberal thought'.[157] The latter have attracted most attention from historians, who are usually concerned with giving opposition to the American war its place in the genealogy of British radicalism. Popular anti-Americanism remains elusive, although it is conceded that, for instance, London tradesmen might have responded to 'the emotional appeal to loyalty in war time'.[158] Some promising attempts have been made to fit support for the coercion of America into the genealogy of a different kind, that of British nationalism and a popular 'loyalist political culture, animated by a fierce protectiveness toward church and king and fueled by popular consent and desire'.[159]

For the purposes of this book, the addresses and petitions are of great potential interest for what they may reveal of public assumptions about the relationship between Britain and the American colonies and about empire in general. Caution is, however, necessary in using them in this way. The slide into war was of course the occasion for a great outpouring of political rhetoric, but, as all historians who have studied this episode agree, the agendas behind this rhetoric were often as much domestic as imperial. What those who asserted the authority of crown and parliament over America

---

[156] The major contributions to this subject have been those of James E. Bradley in *Popular Politics and the American Revolution*; see also his *Religion, Revolution and English Radicalism: Non-Conformity in Eighteenth-Century Politics and Society* (Cambridge, 1990) and a valuable summary in 'The British Public and the American Revolution' in Dickinson, ed., *Britain and the American Revolution*. Other important works include Sainsbury, *Disaffected Patriots* and Wilson, *Sense of the People*.

[157] Bradley, *Popular Politics*, pp. 201, 213.   [158] Sainsbury, *Disaffected Patriots*, p. 120.

[159] Wilson, *Sense of the People*, p. 279; See also Linda Colley, *Britons: Forging the Nation 1707–1837* (New Haven, 1992), p. 145.

clearly had in mind was the quelling of sedition at home as well as abroad. The sovereignty of parliament had been called in question by Wilkes's supporters as well as by the colonies. Very many loyalist addresses fulminated against a 'discontented faction at home'. Oxford University, for instance, complained about abuses of the freedom of the press, 'licentious' criticism of king and parliament and 'illegal associations' to ferment rebellion in Britain itself.[160] On the other hand, the shorthand of 'pro-American', used by historians to describe petitions against the war, may sometimes be misleading. Some petitioners were primarily attacking a government that they felt was acting oppressively on a whole series of domestic issues as well as in the colonies. 'Many independent [London] tradesmen, habituated to opposition, signed the pro-American petition because, through their jaundiced perception of administration motives, they saw the war as an outcome of corrupt and despotic government policies.'[161]

The petitions and addresses had certain things in common. Nearly all used the concept of 'empire', while placing very different interpretations on it. Even the inflammatory *Crisis* invoked 'this vast and mighty empire, the admiration and envy of the world', that was being ruined by 'corruption and villainy'.[162] Both petitions and addresses agreed on the importance for Britain's wealth and standing in the world of maintaining links with the American colonies. Loyal addressees saw disaffection as threatening the commercial subordination embodied in the Navigation Acts. Trade on 'a true basis' requires 'a proper submission to the government and laws of *Great Britain*'.[163] Conciliatory petitions insisted that Americans accepted the restrictions of the Navigation Acts and that in any case war against them was totally disrupting transatlantic commerce and would ultimately drive them to independence 'against their inclination and interest'.[164]

For the loyal addresses, parliamentary sovereignty was the fundamental basis of empire. It was axiomatic that the legislative power of Britain extends over 'every part of the king's dominions'.[165] Professions of American allegiance to the crown while denying the sovereignty of parliament were denounced in some addresses. Attempts to exalt the royal prerogative over 'the aggregate legislative body' of the kingdom could not be countenanced. They were contrary to the principles of the Glorious Revolution.[166] Most petitions for conciliation also accepted that parliament exercised a rightful

[160] 26 Oct. 1775, Force, ed., *American Archives*, 4th ser., III. 1188.
[161] Sainsbury, *Disaffected Patriots*, p. 119.
[162] Force, ed., *American Archives*, 4th ser., II. 66–7.
[163] Manchester, 6 Sept. 1775, ibid. 4th ser., III. 650.
[164] Southwark, 29 Nov. 1775, Bradley, *Popular Politics*, p. 219.
[165] Newcastle merchants, [11 Nov. 1775], Force, ed., *American Archives*, 4th ser., III. 1519.
[166] Middlesex JPs, [12 Oct. 1775], ibid. 4th ser., III. 1031.

authority over America. The mayor and burgesses of Nottingham wished for 'a due subordination . . . to the authority of the British legislature' to be maintained over the colonies, although this could not be done by force. Attempts by parliament to tax unrepresented colonies were an abuse of sovereignty. Many petitions seem to have accepted the Rockingham group's view that Americans were not questioning the sovereign power of parliament, so long as that power was properly exercised in the common interest. Only the petition of the London livery of 10 April 1775, apparently drafted by Arthur and William Lee, reflected the rejection of parliament's authority by the Continental Congress. '[S]ubordination in commerce . . . is all that this country ought in justice to require.'[167] The interpretation of empire running through most of the petitions for conciliation was that of many Americans in the 1760s: the British empire was an alliance of free peoples enjoying the rights of Englishmen. Americans voluntarily raised men and money in war and traded within the system of regulations made in London. They accepted an ultimate British authority over a 'union of affections, of commerce and of interests'.[168] Such an empire could not be maintained by coercion. Rebellion was not, as the loyal addresses usually asserted, the result of a plot by a few designing fanatics bent on independence; it was 'the general sense of the people' driven to desperation by unwise policies.[169] Conciliation was therefore the only practical policy.

The evidence of the petitions and addresses offers some indications as to how Americans were envisaged. They were universally accepted to be 'fellow subjects' of the crown. Both petitioners and addressers therefore saw the conflict as a civil war. For Edmund Burke and for some of the petitioners the Americans were unequivocally fellow 'Englishmen'. There were protests at a meeting of Middlesex freeholders on 26 September 1775 against sending to America 'armed legions of *Englishmen* . . . to cut the throats of *Englishmen*'.[170] The petitioners often referred to the Americans as their 'brethren', as did some addressers. The pro-government mayor and burgesses of Bristol deeply lamented 'the misfortune our *American* brethren have brought upon themselves'.[171] The conclusion that at the outbreak of the war, most British people still saw Americans 'as part of the same nation' seems well

---

[167] Ibid. 4th ser., I. 1853. For the drafting of the petition, see Sainsbury, *Disaffected Patriots*, pp. 83–4.

[168] Nottingham gentlemen and manufacturers, Force, ed., *American Archives*, 4th ser., III. 1115.

[169] Southwark, 29 Nov. 1775, Bradley, *Popular Politics*, p. 218.

[170] P. J. Marshall, 'Britain and the World in the Eighteenth Century: II, Britons and Americans', *Transactions of the Royal Historical Society*, 6th ser., IX (1999), 13fn.

[171] 28 Sept. 1775, Force, ed., *American Archives*, 4th ser., III. 818.

justified.[172] Nevertheless, the addresses in particular suggest that 'Americans', if not yet seen as aliens, were held in low regard for reasons that had become manifest during and after the Seven Years War. Their 'unnatural' rebellion was an act of gross ingratitude. They had 'uniformly experienced protection, encouragement, and defence, at the expence of millions, and with the repeated effusions of human blood'.[173] They showed 'a want of gratitude to their parent country, and of tenderness to their poorer fellow subjects', who by 'the sweat of their brows had long contributed to the protection and prosperity of America'.[174] They were 'imperiously dictating to the parent state which at the expence of it's blood and treasure, hath raised, nourished and protected them'.[175] Petitioners insisted that Americans were dutiful subjects of the empire, 'loyal, affectionate and grateful'.[176]

Lord North seems to have been disconcerted by the extent of the opposition to the government in England in the later months of 1775. He feared that 'the cause of Great Britain is not yet sufficiently popular' and he had 'reason to fear that the attack upon government during the next session will be very powerful'.[177] He was, however, unduly despondent. His parliamentary position was to remain unassailable for some years. The support that he was getting from uncommitted MPs reinforced the message of the addresses of loyalty to the crown that a strong majority of the 'political nation' of England accepted that Britain had no alternative to trying to assert its sovereignty over the colonies by force and wished to see subversion put down both at home and abroad. A significant majority had openly dissented. They detested both the government and its American policies. They did not, however, reject empire as such; they hoped for a different kind of empire, based on voluntary submission. Hostility to government policy, in spite of rumours to the contrary, does not seem to have been a major obstacle to the mobilization of manpower for the war. Expansion of the army and navy went slowly in the early years of the war because of the government's initial reluctance to resort to emergency measures.[178] From Boston general Burgoyne reported that 'the army is firmly attached in principle to the cause of England. The private men, a very few rascally drafts, and recruits taken out of the Irish jails excepted, have not deserted. On the contrary they appear in

---

[172] Stephen Conway, 'From Fellow-Nationals to Foreigners: British Perceptions of the Americans, *circa* 1739–1783', *William and Mary Quarterly*, 3rd ser., LIX (2002), 85.

[173] Leicester mayor and burgesses, 8 Sept. 1775, *London Gazette*, 12–16 Sept. 1775.

[174] Wiltshire Cloth Towns, ibid. 17–21 Oct. 1775.

[175] Shrewsbury mayor and burgesses, 6 Oct. 1775, ibid. 17–21 Oct. 1775.

[176] Newcastle inhabitants, [27 Oct. 1775], Force, ed., *American Archives*, 4th ser., III. 1201.

[177] To King, 25 Aug., 9 Sept. 1775, Fortescue, ed., *Correspondence of King George III*, III. 249, 255.

[178] Conway, *British Isles*, pp. 13–16.

general exasperated against the enemy.'[179] Britain embarked in relatively good shape on a war that ministers supposed would be brought to an end by a decisive campaign in America before Britain's European enemies had a chance to intervene. These calculations went catastrophically awry.

[179] To Germain, 20 Aug. 1775, WLCL, Germain Sackville MSS, 3.

II

War and its Resolutions 1775–1783

THE War of the American Revolution had some obvious similarities with the Seven Years War. Both were envisaged by Britain as being wars initially undertaken for the defence of its empire and worldwide trades. Both began in North America and spread throughout the world. In the course of both wars, Britain went onto the offensive, attempting to seize colonies from its European rivals. Differences between the two wars were, however, starkly obvious from Britain's point of view. The danger to the empire came at first not from foreign powers, but from a massive revolt of Britain's own subjects in North America. This revolt was never mastered and eventually forced a British capitulation. The king's Irish subjects also extracted major concessions in the later years of the war. France, Britain's main opponent, achieved its principal war aim by its intervention that did much to ensure an American victory. The French and the Spanish also had notable successes in the West Indies. By 1782, the last year of the war, British forces were, however, able to contain and inflict defeats upon the French, the Spanish, and the Dutch in the Caribbean, in Asia, and at Gibraltar. The thirteen colonies apart, Britain had to accept only limited colonial losses at the peace of 1783. Even so, the tone of the addresses to the crown on the peace printed in the *London Gazette* in 1783 were very different from the triumphalist paeans about the 1763 peace. The king was usually congratulated on no more than having extracted his subjects from a damaging war and restored a peace in which it was hoped that commerce would revive.

Whatever its outcome, the American War marked no diminution in Britain's commitment to empire. Even in North America, colonies that had not rebelled, Nova Scotia and Quebec, had been tenaciously defended, although Britain had to part with the Floridas. Elsewhere, the British had clung to whatever they could and had even sought to make new gains. Nevertheless, the loss of the thirteen colonies was by any standards a staggering reversal of fortune. The British had relinquished what they had fought at such cost to protect from 1754 to 1760 and to subdue in the years after 1775. The end of empire in South Asia in 1947 is the only comparable episode in

British history. Yet 1783 no more marked either the end of Britain's imperial ambitions or even a major revolution in imperial strategy than 1947 was to do. In both cases the British had to reconcile themselves to the loss of an immensely significant part of their empire, but not to the loss of empire as a whole or to major changes in the way in which they tried to manage their empire.

I

As with the loss of empire in India in 1947, a degree of disengagement from empire in America had become apparent, at least with hindsight, well before it was formally recognized. The coercive, or intolerable, acts against Massachusetts in 1774 were the last attempt to remodel imperial relations by strengthening metropolitan control. Although arm-chair strategists might suggest that the result of a successful war should be the imposition of a military governor on an America to be divided, instead of the existing colonies, into counties, for whom law would be made in parliament,[1] such draconian solutions had no place in official thinking. There was no doubting the necessity of military coercion, but its limits were always recognized. It was hoped that military force and a naval blockade would disperse armed resistance and cow the refractory, but the systematic conquest of all the colonies could not be contemplated with the resources available, nor would most British opinion have thought it desirable if it had been possible. Lord Dartmouth, former colonial secretary, explained in March 1776 that 'a conquest of America' had never been intended.[2] Even lord George Germain, Dartmouth's much more iron-fisted successor, admitted in the late stages of the war that he had 'never been so sanguine as to believe that we could reduce America to obedience by force of arms'.[3] The peoples of the colonies were not to be forced into an unconditional surrender after which they would have to accept any terms that the British might choose to impose on them. They were to be induced to return to their allegiance on terms acceptable to most of them as well as to Britain. It was a war fought to restore 'union and harmony',[4] not, as became apparent after 1745 in the Scottish Highlands, to remodel a society.

---

[1] D. Raynor and A. Skinner, 'Sir James Steuart: Nine Letters on the American Conflict, 1775–1778', *William and Mary Quarterly*, LI (1994), 768–9.

[2] Cited in P. D. G. Thomas, *Tea Party to Independence: The Third Phase of the American Revolution 1773–1776* (Oxford, 1991), p. 312.

[3] 27 Nov. 1781, W. Cobbett, ed., *The Parliamentary History of England from the earliest period to the year 1803*, 36 vols. (1806–20), XXII. 726.

[4] Piers Mackesy, *The War for America 1775–1783* (1964), pp. 32–3.

The military objectives that the British set themselves were always limited ones: the coercion of Massachusetts in 1775, the destruction of Washington's continental army in the campaigns of 1776 to 1778, and the re-establishment of royal government under military protection in the south, beginning in late 1778 with Georgia and ending in humiliation in Virginia in 1781. Even so, they could never be attained. So the British became more and more dependent on Americans' returning to their allegiance of their own free will and as a consequence the terms became progressively more generous. In 1776 the Howe brothers were authorized to encourage the colonies to submit their grievances to parliament, once they had laid down their arms and dissolved their illegal bodies, including Congress. The terms proposed by the commission under lord Carlisle in 1778 went much further. Congress was to be recognized. Parliament was induced to pass an act renouncing its right to tax the colonies 'for revenue'. The act of 1774 for remodelling the government of Massachusetts was repealed and other acts passed since 1763 to which the Americans objected could be suspended. British influence over the executive in the colonies, weak enough in the past, was effectively to be abandoned. There was to be no binding obligation on the Americans to vote their own taxes for imperial purposes.[5] Had these terms been implemented, the Americans would have enjoyed privileges far greater than those applying to any other part of the empire, as the Irish Patriots noted in pressing their claims.[6] The British government made no more formal offers but waited for the Americans to propose terms. By the last years of the war some continuing 'dependence', involving little more than the theoretical acceptance of the sovereignty of parliament was all that most ministers and even the king himself seem to have expected. North had come to doubt the 'importance of such sovereignty as could now be retained over the colonies' and spoke of 'some federal alliance, or even . . . a less eligible mode'.[7] By then leading sections of the parliamentary opposition, in most cases out of what they took to be an unwelcome necessity for ending the war rather than from conviction, had openly abandoned any claim to assert sovereignty over America. There can be no doubt that the great mass of British political opinion wanted an end to fighting in America after the news of the defeat at Yorktown in 1781. Whether they wished to give up claims to sovereignty over America is much less clear.

[5] Instructions to Carlisle commission, 12 April 1778, *Historical Manuscripts Commission: Carlisle MSS* (1897), pp. 322–33.

[6] Vincent Morley, *Irish Opinion and the American Revolution 1760–1783* (Cambridge, 2002), p. 204.

[7] Stormont to King, 23 Dec. 1781, North to King [21 Jan. 1782], J. Fortescue, ed., *Correspondence of King George III 1760–1783*, 6 vols. (1927–8), V. 325, 337.

As expectations about the substance of empire in the thirteen colonies dwindled, British opinion inevitably began to revise its expectations about Americans and their future place, if any, in the British empire. Although it was official policy, for as long as it was practical to do so, to deny recognition to the United States and to regard the individual colonies as the only legally constituted bodies, tendencies, already established before the war, to envisage the thirteen colonies as a single 'country', that is as 'America', and to treat their inhabitants as a single people, 'the Americans',[8] were greatly reinforced by the war and became the universally accepted usage. Ministers might refuse to recognize that the new America had any legality, but some practical concessions that amounted to *de facto* recognition had to be made. American prisoners captured in arms by the British were effectively treated as prisoners of war, not as rebels or traitors.[9] Eventually even Henry Laurens, the most important American to fall into British hands, at first held as a traitor in the Tower, qualified as a prisoner of war to be exchanged for lord Cornwallis, the most important British person captured by the Americans, also perforce regarded as a prisoner of war.

For some, the increasing separateness of America did not necessarily mean that Americans were ceasing to be British. Americans' Britishness had been insisted upon by those who had petitioned for conciliation and against war in 1775. A few of the bodies that addressed the crown on the peace of 1783 continued to use the same language. The City of London and the Gentlemen, Manufacturers and Traders of Taunton both referred to 'our American brethren'.[10] So did some members of the parliamentary opposition, such as general Conway.[11] In March 1782 Burke was still writing about 'the two branches of the English nation' or of 'the whole British nation on both sides of the Atlantic'.[12] For what was probably the bulk of British opinion, however, a sense that Americans were not only a separate people but an alien one outside the British fold seems to have grown as the full extent of American resistance became apparent.

In the early years of the war it was commonly supposed that opposition to Britain was largely the work of malignant groups, deeply entrenched in New England society as events had shown, but presumed to be a minority

---

[8] See above, pp. 298–9.

[9] Americans held in Britain were finally given the status of prisoners of war by an act of 1782 (22 Geo. III, c. 10). For discussions of prisoners, see Linda Colley, *Captives: Britain, Empire and the World 1600–1850* (2002), pp. 209–27; Eliga H. Gould, *The Persistence of Empire: British Political Culture in the Age of the American Revolution* (Chapel Hill, NC, 2000), pp. 193–5.

[10] *London Gazette*, 25 Feb.–1 March, 13–17 May 1783.

[11] 27 Feb. 1782, Cobbett, ed., *Parliamentary History*, XXII. 1069.

[12] To B. Franklin, 28 Feb. and to H. Laurens, 27 March 1782, J. A. Woods, ed., *The Correspondence of Edmund Burke*, IV, *July 1778–June 1782* (Cambridge, 1963), pp. 419, 428.

elsewhere. The mass of Americans would sooner or later see the error of their ways and come back to the true liberty guaranteed by the connection with Britain and by the British constitution whose spirit their leaders were openly violating. Lord George Germain, who had taken over the direction of the war, hoped that

Boston and Massachusetts Bay will feel the distresses of that war which their detestable principles have occasioned, encouraged and supported. The other colonies are more to be pitied as they have been gradually seduced into rebellion by those independants under the specious pretext of struggling for their liberty.[13]

There could be no question but that New England would require a full-scale military reconquest. It was doubtful whether that would be worth the effort and the cost. New England should be left in isolation, either to languish under blockades and Indian raids until it sought forgiveness or to find a future outside the British empire. If it chose that course, it would be no great loss even in economic terms.[14] Elsewhere, it was supposed that there must be a majority of 'good' Americans waiting to be liberated from republican oppression. A minority of activists were thought to be holding down the rest by intimidation and outright violence. The delusion, commonly held in the 1760s, that at least for reasons of self-interest, the colonial elites, 'gentlemen of weight and influence', would turn back to the empire and 'those principles of freedom which form the basis of the British government' still had a strong following.[15] By 1778 with the entry of France into the war and the diversion of British troops to the West Indies, reliance on Americans to liberate themselves greatly increased. Recruitment of loyalist corps was rapidly expanded. The attempt to recover the south colony by colony depended on loyalist support able to hold territory cleared by British troops. Extravagant assurances given to the house of commons in 1779 by Joseph Galloway about the strength of loyalist sentiment attracted wide publicity. He asserted that four-fifths of the population were potential loyalists. Germain claimed as late as November 1780 that a majority of Americans were well disposed to Britain.[16] The failure of loyalists to assert themselves in either South or North Carolina was, however, becoming manifest by then. Assumptions that the loyalists could take control after British military victories had no reality outside Georgia. The parliamentary opposition had contested government estimates in the past and now claimed in the words of Charles Fox that the

[13] To W. Howe, 18 Oct. 1776, *Historical Manuscripts Commission: Stopford Sackville MSS*, 2 vols. (1904–10), II. 43.
[14] See the opinion of Charles Jenkinson, cited in Mackesy, *War for America*, pp. 158–9.
[15] Undated and anonymous 'Plan for reducing the colonies' in Fortescue, ed., *Correspondence of King George III*, IV. 548.
[16] 6 Nov. 1780, Cobbett, ed., *Parliamentary History*, XXI. 840.

evidence that Americans were 'almost universally attached to the cause of Congress' was irrefutable.[17] Ministers could do little to counter such pessimism.

There were confident expectations that most Americans would not be able to stomach the alliance with Papist and absolutist France that Congress had foisted on them. Such expectations were also disappointed. The apparent solidarity of the French–American alliance did much to turn British opinion against Americans in general. Newspapers proclaimed that the Americans had entered 'into a league with our ancient, inveterate and perfidious foes'. They had ceased to be 'our brethren, and fellow-subjects' and had become 'aliens and enemies'.[18] Germain insisted that America 'should no longer be treated as a British country, but as a part of the dominions belonging to the French crown'.[19] The tone of the great public rejoicings over the major British victories in South Carolina in 1780 by the capture of Charleston and at the battle of Camden show how the Americans had come to be seen as national enemies. In a debate in the commons on a vote of thanks to the victorious British generals this point was explicitly made by MPs who had not been supporters of the war up to then. America was now the confederate of 'the house of Bourbon' and 'the ally of France'.[20] A defeat for the Americans was therefore a defeat for France.

Fears that America would pass irrevocably into the military and economic orbit of France were very widespread. For Germain it was essential to maintain an active British military presence wherever it was practicable in North America, however grim the outlook. Otherwise the Americans would be free to combine with the French to invade Canada again and, the most ominous prospect of all, to attack the British West Indies. The Americans had considerable naval potential, as their privateers had shown. Germain's successor, Welbore Ellis, warned that Britain might see 'French and Americans joined in the West Indies, or perhaps joined in the Channel'.[21] French economic domination of America after the war was to be prevented by any means possible.

Prising America out of the grip of France became the prime objective of British policy. By the end of 1781 few continued to believe that this could be achieved by force. With the obvious failure of the strategy of relying on Americans to liberate themselves and with the surrender of lord Cornwallis's

[17] 6 Nov. 1780, ibid. XXI. 834.
[18] Newspaper reports cited in Stephen Conway, 'From Fellow Nationals to Foreigners: British Perceptions of the Americans, circa 1739–1783', William and Mary Quarterly, 3rd ser., LIX (2002), 98.
[19] 4 Dec. 1778, Cobbett, ed., Parliamentary History, XIX. 1397.
[20] See speeches by Daniel Coke and John Courtenay on 27 Nov. 1780, ibid. XXI. 889, 906.
[21] 12 Dec. 1781, ibid. XXII. 816.

army at Yorktown in October 1781, Britain had few if any military options left. Even North's government decided to abandon offensive operations and not to replace the troops lost at Yorktown. British garrisons were still holding Savannah, Charleston and the army's headquarters at New York, but they gave Britain little leverage over the Americans. Even New York was deemed to be vulnerable to a major assault. The North government remained committed to maintaining the garrisons, but the Rockingham government that succeeded North in March 1782 ordered them to be withdrawn to Halifax. As many troops as possible would then be sent to the West Indies.

The dispatch ordering this redeployment urged the British commanders to accompany it with strenuous efforts to reconcile the Americans, to 'captivate their hearts' and to restore 'affection and confidence'.[22] In short, America could no longer be coerced and must be conciliated. Virtually everyone agreed with that in principle. Even the North government in its very last days launched proposals for a truce and a settlement of differences.

Opinion differed as to how far Britain should go in seeking conciliation. For the king and men like Germain the stakes were very high. There must be some acceptance of sovereignty on the American side. The king believed that American independence would fatally undermine the rest of his empire and that Ireland and the West Indies would follow. Britain would sink into insignificance in the scale of European powers. Germain agreed. He thought that 'this country depended upon its connection with America for its very existence.'[23] Lord Hillsborough restated what had been accepted as axiomatic for so long: 'America lost or abandoned—every thing valuable we possessed as a great trading and maritime nation must shortly follow.'[24] Others were beginning to doubt these eternal verities and to accept that the reincorporation into the empire on any conceivable terms of any significant part of America, not only of New England, was now impossible. Nor might it be desirable. There seems to have been little enough warmth of fellow feeling for Americans before the war. The war had confirmed all prejudices; Americans were alien and likely to prove disruptive within the empire. Even the king came to that opinion: 'knavery seems to be so much the striking feature' of Americans' dispositions, 'that it may not in the end be an evil that they become aliens to this kingdom', he thought.[25]

Some political economists, most notably Adam Smith and Josiah Tucker, had long been questioning the value of an American empire to Britain. Such

---

[22] Shelburne to Carleton, 4 April 1782, K. G. Davies, ed., *Documents of the American Revolution, 1770–1783*, 21 vols. (Shannon, 1972–81), XXI. 54.

[23] 27 Nov. 1781, Cobbett, ed., *Parliamentary History*, XXII. 726.

[24] 27 Nov. 1781, ibid. XXII. 661–2.

[25] To Shelburne, 10 Nov. 1782, Fortescue, ed., *Correspondence of King George III*, VI. 154.

iconoclastic thoughts were beginning to enter into the discourse of politicians as well. By 1782 William Knox, under-secretary to the American department, thought that Georgia and South Carolina were the only part of the thirteen colonies whose commerce made them worth reconquering.[26] A paper copied by the king made a similar point. The tobacco and rice colonies were valuable assets, but the northern colonies had been rivals within the empire to British fishing and shipping.[27] Lord Hawke, son of the great admiral, told the lords that 'the commerce and naval power of Great Britain were not founded on the sands of America', but 'on the solid rock of national situation, national industry and national courage'. He went on to say that in place of the lost empire, it could be expected that an independent America would remain tied to Britain on 'the permanent basis of affection, consanguinity, religion and mutual interest'.[28] Others consoled themselves with expectations that a new and fruitful trading relationship would develop between two separate peoples, cemented by the voluntary commercial agreements that would replace the Navigation Acts.

On 12 June 1781 Charles Fox had urged that 'healing conciliatory and friendly negotiations' should be used to win the Americans away from France.[29] This was to be the objective of the two governments that succeeded North, that of Rockingham from March to July 1782 and that of Shelburne that followed and concluded the preliminary articles of peace in November. Both were prepared to make generous concessions to the Americans, including the recognition of independence, in order to get them out of the war and out of the grip of France and to enable Britain to concentrate its resources against France, Spain and the Netherlands and thus save as much as possible of the rest of the empire all over the world.

Shelburne was the architect of the peace on the British side, once Charles Fox, who had tried to control the negotiations as foreign secretary, had resigned his office in July 1782. The making of the peace was the high point of Shelburne's uneven career. He had been opposed to any surrender of sovereignty over the colonies during the war but was now willing to concede it as part of a comprehensive settlement. He was prepared to be generous to the Americans on specific terms and he was deeply committed to reconciliation with them and to future economic and perhaps even political association between the two countries. '[E]very call under heaven urges you to stand on the footing of brethren' with the Americans, he told the house of

---

[26] *Extra Official State Papers*, 2 vols. (1789), I. 27.
[27] John L. Bullion, 'George III on Empire, 1783', *William and Mary Quarterly*, 3rd ser., LI (1994), 306.
[28] 5 Dec. 1782, Cobbett, ed., *Parliamentary History*, XXIII. 212.
[29] Ibid. XXII. 509.

lords.[30] Historians have long been divided in their assessments of Shelburne's aims in 1782. To Vincent Harlow his conduct of the peace negotiations was driven by free trade doctrines and by a grand vision of 'a young nation in the making' in whose progress Britain had a vital interest as a future trading partner. To aid the growth of the new America, in Harlow's view, Shelburne was willing to make great concessions of the lands in the west that Britain had acquired from France in 1763. Instead of being retained for Canada, which remained in British hands, they would be ceded to the United States, proof, Shelburne is reported to have said, that 'we prefer trade to dominion'. A treaty for freeing trade between Britain and America would, Shelburne hoped, follow the peace. For Harlow this was indicative of a long-term realignment of British policy away from territorial empire to trade without colonies.[31] Other historians have accepted Shelburne's enthusiasm for free trade and his hopes for an Anglo-American alliance and for eventual reunion, but have stressed that he was acting under immediate practical pressures: the need above all to separate America from France and thus to limit any gains that France and Spain might be able to extract from Britain elsewhere. Britain must not be subjected to the kind of dictated peace that she had imposed on her enemies in 1763. Whatever his long-term ends may have been, it is therefore argued, Shelburne had no practical option but to be generous to the Americans and not to haggle about western lands.[32] It can also be added that Shelburne renounced territorial dominion over much of North America in order the better to preserve it elsewhere.

The peace succeeded in its immediate objective of detaching America from France. There seems to have been general recognition in Britain that American independence was the necessary price that had to be paid. Shelburne was, however, vulnerable to accusations that he had given away far too much. He was attacked in both houses of parliament for abandoning the loyalists without guaranteed compensation, for giving up Indians who had allied with the British together with their lands and the fur trade, which was vital to Canada, and for excessive generosity to American fishing access to Newfoundland. Few endorsed Shelburne's appeal, repeated by other ministers, for reconciliation. He was forced to resign by a coalition formed against him.

Further concessions to the Americans in the name of free trade were later rejected. A bill prepared under Shelburne was introduced in March 1783 to prevent American trade being immediately treated as foreign and therefore

---

[30] 17 Feb. 1783, ibid. XXXIII. 409.

[31] Harlow, *Second British Empire*, I. 434–40.

[32] This point is fairly made by C. R. Ritcheson, 'The Earl of Shelburne and Peace with America, 1782–1783: Vision and Reality', *International History Review*, V (1983), 322–45; see also H. M. Scott, *British Foreign Policy in the Age of the American Revolution* (Oxford, 1990), pp. 323–35.

subject to the full restrictions of the Navigation Acts. It was strongly opposed. The most articulate opponent in the commons invoked long-standing fears about the consequences of American independence. It 'must tend to great convulsions in our commerce, the emigration of manufacturers, the loss of seamen, and all the evils incident to a declining country'.[33] Britain could not afford further concessions. In July 1783 an order was issued reserving the huge trade in provisions between America and the British West Indies, before the war almost entirely carried by American ships, to British ships. This was the work of men now restored to government who had been in power under lord North, once again in office after the fall of Shelburne. Their philosophy was that America was now a foreign country by its own choice. Americans were therefore no different from other foreigners. They had renounced the privileges they had enjoyed as members of the empire and Britain's own advantage was now the only criterion that should be applied to dealings with them. In any case, it was likely that Britain would in time recover American markets without any concessions. It was vital for Britain to build up the maritime strength on which her navy depended. So only British ships could be permitted to supply the West Indies.[34] Lord Sheffield, the main publicist for this point of view, saw no need to repine for the loss of the thirteen colonies. The Americans would be the losers; 'We shall regret the money that has been squandered, but it is not probable our commerce will be much hurt . . . Our remaining colonies on the continent and islands and the favourable state of our manufactures may well give us almost exclusively the trade of America.'[35] Within a few years lord Macartney, who was making a career as an imperial proconsul throughout the world, reflected on the British empire without America. America was like a statue that people had taken to be gold, but which was in fact only lead and was anyway 'too heavy for the edifice which it was thought to adorn'. Without it, 'the building not only looks much better but is a great deal stronger'.[36] The bruising experience of a long and unsuccessful war and of an even longer period of colonial recalcitrance and insubordination seems to have produced a widespread public disillusionment with the ex-thirteen colonies and a willingness to regard Americans as aliens rather than brethren.

---

[33] W. Eden, 7 March 1783, Cobbett, ed., *Parliamentary History*, XXIII. 606.
[34] See Harlow, *Second British Empire*, I, ch. 9; C. R. Ritcheson, *Aftermath of Revolution: British Policy toward the United States 1783–1795* (Dallas, 1969).
[35] *Observations on the Commerce of the American States* (1784 edn.), pp. 135, 138.
[36] Commonplace book, 1792–3, Bodleian Library, Eng. Misc., f. 533.

II

Disillusionment with empire in the thirteen colonies cannot be equated with disillusionment with empire in general. There had indeed been a shift in priorities in favour of other parts of the empire in the later years of the war and this emerged clearly in the peace negotiations that ended it.

When France entered the war in 1778, followed by Spain in 1779, the West Indies became Britain's primary concern. In spite of obvious constitutional similarities with the thirteen colonies and being subjected to the same imperial reforms after 1763, including parliamentary taxation, the major part of white opinion in the West Indies had not openly allied itself with the American rebellion in 1775. With British forces heavily deployed in North America, the islands were, however, a tempting target for the French and the Spanish. British policy-makers were well aware of this and indeed intended to get their blows in first. The king was easily converted to the idea that once the French had entered the war operations on land in North America would have to be scaled down to enable forces to be sent to the Caribbean. There they would attack French and Spanish colonies. His view seems to have been that once France had been knocked out of the war, the Americans would have no alternative but to seek peace. He gave a vigorous exposition of conventional views of the supreme importance of the West Indies to Britain.

Our islands must be defended even at the risk of an invasion of this island, if we lose our sugar islands, it will be impossible to raise money to continue the war and then no peace can be obtained but such a one as he that gave one to Europe in 1763 never can subscribe to.[37]

His ministers should not concentrate resources on home defence. 'Troops must be sent sufficient to secure Jamaica and Barbadoes, the capital islands belonging to this island', and he urged consideration of an attack on Saint-Domingue, the main arsenal of French wealth in the West Indies.[38] The opposition shared his sense of priorities. For lord Shelburne, Jamaica was 'first in point of importance to this country, after Ireland, of any of her numerous dependencies'.[39] The cabinet agreed to order 5,000 men to be sent from North America to the Leeward Islands. The primary objective was to be the French island of St Lucia, which was duly captured. Other offensive operations against France and Spain in the Caribbean were canvassed and strong support was eventually given to a somewhat improbable strategy,

[37] To Sandwich, 13 Sept. 1779, Fortescue, ed., *Correspondence of King George III*, IV. 433.
[38] To Sandwich, 13 Sept. 1779, ibid. IV. 434.
[39] 25 Nov. 1779, Cobbett, ed., *Parliamentary History*, XX. 1061–2.

devised by the governor of Jamaica, for an attack on the Spanish empire in central America.

Operations seem to have been planned for the Caribbean in 1778 and 1779 in the spirit of the last phases of the Seven Years War, when British expeditions had seized French and Spanish possessions almost at will. Now the situation was reversed. Britain rarely enjoyed anything approaching naval superiority and French and Spanish forces dismembered the British empire. The French took Dominica in 1778, St Vincent and Grenada in 1779, Tobago in 1781, and St Kitts, Nevis, and Montserrat in 1782. The Spanish drove the British out of West Florida in 1781 and took New Providence in the Bahamas in 1782. Jamaica was the ultimate prize for the allies, but it was to elude them. In the last days of 1781 massive naval reinforcements were sent to the Caribbean from North America and from Britain. Admiral Rodney caught the French invasion fleet and decisively defeated it at the battle of the Saintes in April 1782. This news produced frenzied celebrations throughout Britain on the scale of those in 'the year of victories' of 1759. The ambiguities of fighting the Americans had been replaced by a simple triumph over the French in which every section of British opinion could rejoice.[40]

Having settled with the Americans, saved Jamaica and beaten off the Spanish at Gibraltar, the British were able to recover most of their West Indian losses at the peace negotiations with France and Spain. Very high priority was given to this. Gains might even be made. The king was willing to bargain away Gibraltar in exchange for the Spanish ceding Porto Rico. 'I would wish', he wrote, 'to have as much possession in the West Indies as possible; for it has been my purpose ever since peace has been on the carpet to get rid of ideal advantages for those that by a good administration may prove to be solid ones to this country.'[41] Shelburne agreed. He too was willing to exchange Gibraltar for Caribbean territory.[42] In the event, Britain kept Gibraltar, but was able to recover all its captured West Indian colonies except for Tobago.

Quebec and Nova Scotia were insignificant by comparison with the West Indies in terms of their assumed contribution to Britain's national wealth, but their retention was not in question in the peace negotiations. At the outset Franklin had informally proposed that both be ceded to the new United States, but Shelburne had dismissed such a proposition out of hand and regarded it as too inflammatory to discuss with his colleagues. Extravagant expectations at the beginning of the war about the value of French Canadians

---

[40] Stephen Conway, ' "A Joy Unknown for Years Past": The American War, Britishness and the Celebration of Rodney's Victory at the Saints', *History*, LXXXVI (2001), 180–99.

[41] To Shelburne, 11 Dec. 1782, Fortescue, ed., *Correspondence of King George III*, VI. 183.

[42] Harlow, *Second British Empire*, I. 329.

in subduing the Americans had, in fact, proved groundless. An American offensive against Quebec had been beaten off with difficulty and thereafter its defence became a major drain on the British army. Throughout the war the loyalty of its population was thought to be doubtful. In 1780 the governor believed that a French attack would be 'followed by a revolt of the great part of the province', while, left to themselves, its Anglophone population would join the United States.[43] Nova Scotia was not much better. It too depended on British troops. Its militia was under strength and 'in some parts of it of very doubtful principles towards the king's cause and interests'.[44] Nevertheless, the cession of either colony was unthinkable. The epic of Wolfe's taking of Quebec still cast its shadow in 1783 as it had done in 1763. In addition, the base at Halifax was regarded as indispensable for any British naval presence in the western Atlantic and Nova Scotia in particular offered ministers a partial compensation for what they recognized to be for them the most damaging part of the treaty with America, the failure to secure guarantees for the loyalists. At the close of the war Guy Carleton, the new commander-in-chief in North America, was drawing up plans for 'a reformed and rejuvenated British empire' by the settlement of loyalists in Nova Scotia.[45]

Compensation for the loyalists seems to have been the only reason that might have given Shelburne pause in conceding to the Americans the western lands that had been formally part of Quebec since 1774.[46] The interests of the Native Americans, many of whom had fought tenaciously alongside the British throughout the war, were evidently of no concern to him. 'The Indians in the West were holding their own in 1782. The real disaster of the American Revolution for Indian peoples lay in its outcome.'[47] They were not mentioned in the Anglo American treaty. In the debate in the house of lords Shelburne explained that he had disapproved of involving Indians in the war and in any case it was in their own best interest to be 'remitted to the care of neighbours', who 'knew best how to tame their savage natures'.[48]

---

[43] F. Haldimand to Germain, 25 Oct. 1780, Davies, ed, *Documents*, XVIII. 196–7, 206.

[44] R. Hughes to Germain, 21 Nov. 1779, ibid. XVII. 255–6.

[45] Introduction to ibid. XXI. 19.

[46] To R. Oswald, 21 Oct. 1782, Lord Fitzmaurice, ed., *Life of William, Earl of Shelburne*, 2nd edn., 2 vols. (1912), II. 194.

[47] Colin G. Calloway, *The American Revolution in Indian Country: Crisis and Diversity in Native American Communities* (Cambridge, 1995), p. 272.

[48] 17 Feb. 1783, Cobbett, ed., *Parliamentary History*, XXIII. 410.

III

In extricating themselves from war in India the East India Company had to make treaties with Indian opponents as well as, through the agency of the British government, with the French and the Dutch.

In 1779 the Company was still locked in conflict with the Marathas, following the Bombay presidency's unsuccessful attempts to intervene and to secure a peshwa at Poona who would give it territory yielding enough revenue to supply its needs. The Bombay army had been defeated at Wargaum on its march to Poona in January 1779, but by then Bengal had intervened and a part of its army had crossed India and was operating in Gujarat.[49] Warren Hastings instructed its commander to make war on the peshwa to compel him and his allies to come to terms with the Company. A fresh expedition was sent from Bengal to apply pressure on the most important of those allies, Mahadaji Sindhia. Both the Bengal detachments won successes which were not, however, enough to force peace on the Maratha chieftains, who were becoming parties in a great design for a coalition against the British, to include not only the peshwa and Sindhia, but the raja of Berar, whom Hastings had tried to enlist as an ally against the peshwa, the nizam of Hyderabad, and most ominous of all, Haidar Ali of Mysore. This was a situation of great peril. The British were being left without any significant Indian ally in the face of a most formidable combination of powers.

While fighting continued in western India, the Berar army moved towards Bengal and Haidar Ali broke into the Carnatic with devastating effect. He isolated and destroyed a considerable detachment of the Madras army at Polillur in September 1780, killing some 3,000 European soldiers and sepoys. This was by far the most serious reverse inflicted up to then on British arms in India. It created consternation in Britain and had wide reverberations in India. Not only was Haidar Ali taking control of much of the Carnatic but French warships were already operating in the Indian Ocean and it was presumed to be only a matter of time for a major French expedition to be sent to India. The Dutch had also become Britain's enemies.

The war against Mysore was to last for four years. European reinforcements, including the veteran Eyre Coote who took command, were sent to Madras from Bengal by sea and a force of sepoys marched overland. Cut off from much of its food supplies, Madras was provisioned from Bengal by sea.

---

[49] See above, pp. 240–1.

Bengal also bore the main burden of paying for the Carnatic war: between 1781 and 1784 Madras received nearly £2,500,000 from Bengal.[50]

Coote's force, reinforced by royal regiments from Britain, had neither the numbers nor the mobility comprehensively to defeat Haidar Ali, but it won a series of successes against him. The French eventually came to southern India too late and with inadequate numbers. There was to be no repeat of York-town in India. Ambitious plans had been drawn up by the marquis de Bussy, another veteran of the Seven Years War, for the French to assume a role very similar to that which they were playing with such success in North America. Indian rulers, supported by a French expeditionary force, would be incited, in Bussy's phrase, to bring about 'une revolution dans l'Inde' which would shatter the British ascendancy.[51] For themselves, the French would only take limited accessions of territory around their existing settlements to support their commerce and defray their military costs. Other claims on the French armed forces, however, prevented the dispatch of expeditions until March and November 1781, when Bussy himself set sail. He did not arrive in southern India until March 1783 and then had a force that was well below the numbers that he deemed necessary. He had achieved nothing of sig-nificance before news of the peace signed in Europe reached India. Without successes in India, the French negotiating position at the peace was very weak. They had tried to extract territorial grants from the British, who were obdurately opposed to conceding them. The East India Company was unwilling to yield anything at all. George III was 'perfectly shocked at the [French] demands in the East Indies; it is from thence and the West Indies that we must alone I fear after such a peace as we are likely to make, to expect any chance of putting this country into any flourishing state'.[52] Shelburne was willing to give the French full commercial access to India, but would not permit significant grants of territory.[53]

Mysore continued to fight on until March 1784. By then not only had the French withdrawn from the war, but the other Indian members of the great alliance of 1780 had settled with the British. This was the achievement of Warren Hastings, even if his critics argued that by his domineering diplo-macy and rash interventions he himself had been the chief architect of the coalition against him. Hastings was able to buy off the Berar army by generous payments and then to negotiate peace and an alliance with the raja. His main efforts were, however, concentrated on Mahadaji Sindhia, by

---

[50] Sheila Lambert, ed., *House of Commons Sessional Papers of the Eighteenth Century*, 145 vols. (Wilmington, Del., 1975), LVII. 1009.

[51] Alfred Martineau, *Bussy et l'Inde française 1720–1785* (Paris, 1935), p. 329.

[52] To Shelburne, 14 Sept. 1782, Fortescue, ed., *Correspondence of King George III*, VI. 126.

[53] Harlow, *Second British Empire*, I. 366.

now the dominant Maratha power, and by military pressure and offering the restoration of conquered territory he induced him to make peace too. The peace with Sindhia which ended the long series of conflicts with the Marathas was finally signed in May 1782. In the continuing war against Mysore the British began to threaten its own territory. Neither side made gains from the peace that brought the war to an end.

The Indian wars had been long and extremely costly, leaving much of the Carnatic devastated and the finances of Bengal in dire straits. No new territory was gained, apart from the Dutch settlement at Negapatam in south India and Bombay's long-standing objective of Bassein on the west coast. The French offensive had, however, been contained and no territory had been lost. The British empire in India had survived.

With the acquisition of the Bengal *diwani*, Britain's stake in India was much greater in the American War than it had been in the Seven Years War and the involvement of the forces of the state in what was still essentially the East India Company's war, or rather series of wars, had been on a larger scale. The importance of sustaining empire in India seems never to have been questioned. In any contemporary scale for measuring the relative importance of parts of the empire, India was likely to be placed well below the West Indies, above all below Jamaica, and below the thirteen colonies, so long as their recovery seemed practicable. There are, however, some indications of what historians have come to call a 'swing to the east',[54] at least in terms of anticipating great future benefits from India. The Edinburgh savant, Adam Ferguson, reflecting on Britain's financial difficulties in 1780, believed that

What we gained in the East Indies if it could be ensured, would ballance a hundred millions; but alass riches in that part of the world have wings. And I most earnestly recommend plucking them as fast as is consistent with justice and prudence. For I see no immediate resource as great as that.[55]

John Robinson, the very influential secretary to the treasury under North, wrote in 1781: 'I am enthusiastick ab[ou]t India and look up to it as the salvation, as the wealth, the grandeur, the glory of this country'. Under a good system of government 'riches will flow from it to the whole empire'.[56] Later in the same year lord Hillsborough told the lords that there was not yet enough

---

[54] This term is particularly associated with Vincent Harlow, who defined it as a 'change of outlook on the part of British merchants and politicians [which] effected a diversion of interest and enterprise from the Western World to the potentialities of Asia and Africa' (ibid. I. 62). Few historians accept that such a diversion can be detected before the nineteenth century.

[55] To W. Eden, 2 Jan. 1780, V. Merolle, ed., *The Correspondence of Adam Ferguson*, 2 vols. (1995), I. 230.

[56] To W. Hastings, 19 Feb. 1781, Sophia Weitzman, *Warren Hastings and Philip Francis* (Manchester, 1929), p. 369.

good news from India 'to balance our disasters in the western part of the globe'. Yet what was evidently happening there was 'a circumstance of considerable national importance and good fortune'.[57] In condemning the terms of the peace, lord Stormont argued that 'We might have found in the East Indies a recompence for all our losses in the west'.[58]

Yet in spite of clear evidence that the British had at least succeeded in holding their own in India, there was little triumphalism and much anxiety about British prospects there at the end of the war. In the lords debate on the peace, Shelburne excused insignificant concessions to the French as the consequence of the 'miserable situation' of the East India Company.[59] Young William Pitt was equally pessimistic on behalf of the government in the commons.[60]

From the metropolitan perspective, the Company seemed to be still mired in a crisis very similar to that which had overwhelmed it in 1772 and 1773. The disastrous defeat of the Madras army by Haidar Ali in 1780 had followed the capitulation of the Bombay army to the Marathas in 1779. The costs of the wars were plunging the Company into financial crisis at home, as the directors were forced to meet large sums drawn on them in bills of exchange. The directors again had to appeal to the British treasury for relief.[61] As in the previous crisis, the Company's servants in India were held to be largely responsible for its troubles. Bombay and Bengal had provoked and were apparently prolonging indefinitely an inconclusive and ruinously expensive series of Maratha wars, while the Madras council appeared to have goaded Haidar Ali into attacking them and had then failed lamentably to defend their territory.

The sense of crisis and failure was heightened by the way in which Indian administration, like so much else in the conduct of the American War, had become factionalized and politicized. Controversy raged with especial virulence around the person of Warren Hastings, governor-general since 1773. In his own eyes and those of his supporters, he was the architect of victory. He had saved the Bombay presidency from the consequence of its own folly by dispatching troops from Bengal and eventually bringing the Marathas to peace, while he had saved Madras by sustaining it with troops, supplies and money. Although he had lost their confidence earlier, the North administration came to accept that he must be supported. No one else was likely to be

---

[57] 27 Nov. 1781, Cobbett, ed., *Parliamentary History*, XXII. 662.
[58] 17 Feb. 1783, ibid. XXIII. 401.
[59] 17 Feb. 1783, ibid. XXIII. 417.
[60] 21 Feb. 1783, ibid. XXIII. 545.
[61] L. S. Sutherland, *The East India Company in Eighteenth-Century Politics* (Oxford, 1952), pp. 374-5.

able to steer British India through the dangers that beset it. Hastings had, however, many enemies who publicly blamed the Maratha wars on him and accused him of mal-administration in Bengal. The parliamentary opposition tended to side with these enemies. The case against Hastings was taken up by two parliamentary inquiries, a secret committee that investigated the causes of the wars and a select committee that examined the administration of Bengal. Both condemned Hastings. On behalf of the secret committee, Henry Dundas, who had attached himself to Shelburne, moved for his recall from India, while Edmund Burke, backed by the select committee's reports, denounced him as a criminal worthy of prosecution. For Dundas, he was 'that mad man' who 'had put every thing to the hazard' by his wars.[62] For Burke, he was 'the greatest delinquent that India ever saw'.[63] Hastings was not to be sure of a place in the imperial pantheon as 'the man who had saved India' for some time to come.

By 1783 the British empire in eastern India had indubitably been saved from a formidable challenge, by Hastings, or, as his enemies charged, in spite of him. In either case, Bengal had provided the resources which had enabled Indian and European enemies to be kept at bay. The alliance of mutual convenience between the East India Company and the Bengal elites had held. Yet it required the enacting of a series of reforms in the years after the war, associated in Britain with Pitt and Dundas, and in India with lord Cornwallis, as governor general from 1786 to 1793, for British anxieties about Indian empire to be finally exorcised and for it to become a matter of general pride.

IV

In 1775 the North government could take pride in the way in which Ireland had been integrated into the war effort against the American colonies. The Irish parliament had aligned itself against rebellion, British troops on the Irish establishment had been released for service in America, a big recruiting drive for new soldiers, including Catholics, had been launched and an embargo had been applied that would, it was hoped, guarantee Irish provisions to British forces while denying them to Britain's enemies. Seven years later a British government capitulated to the Irish parliament in a way that was in some respects even more ignominious than the settlement with the Americans. There had been no formal negotiations. The Irish parliament had stated its demands, in crude terms, amounting to the legislative independence of

---

[62] 17 Feb. 1783, Cobbett, ed., *Parliamentary History*, XXIII. 471.
[63] 28 April 1783, P. J. Marshall, ed., *The Writings and Speeches of Edmund Burke*, V. *India: Madras and Bengal 1774–1785* (Oxford, 1981), p. 194.

Ireland, and these had been accepted. Negotiations for a new basis for Anglo Irish relations started after concession and got nowhere.[64]

What was at stake in 1782 for Ireland was, however, from Britain's point of view, much less acute than what was at stake for America. The Irish Patriot movement that was able to coerce Britain was implicitly backed by the threat of force through the Volunteers, and had mobilized Irish opinion to an unprecedented degree, but it was not a mass movement in the sense that the American one had become, and its aims were relatively limited. It strove for the restoration of historic rights, not to establish universal natural rights. The Irish parliament repudiated the authority of the British parliament but it did not contest the authority of the crown. The executive would remain under British control through the lord lieutenant. Ireland would still be part of the British empire and the Patriots generally accepted that trade and defence would be continuing imperial matters. It was unthinkable for all except a tiny minority that they should accept French aid. Indeed, they pledged their loyalty to the crown against any French invasion and celebrated British victories over France. The Irish parliament contributed to the raising of 20,000 extra seamen in 1782.

A majority of Irish Protestant political opinion probably deplored the war, blamed British policies for it and sympathized with American objections to them, short of American claims to independence. As subjects of a kingdom with its own rights and privileges, however, Irish Protestants did not need to be taught by mere colonies what their rights were. Nevertheless, if the Irish were not directly responding to the example of the Americans, the American War still put severe strains on Anglo-Irish relations which provided the incentive and the opportunity for Irish assertiveness. For most of the war, the lords lieutenant were able to maintain their authority and command a parliamentary majority, but the government came under increasing pressure. The embargo on Irish provision exports was much resented. War further disrupted trade and produced an economic recession by 1778 in which public revenue fell sharply. This was the context for a formidable agitation against British economic discrimination against Ireland. The Irish parliamentary opposition was able to organize a movement that brought the mass of the Protestant population into active participation in politics to an

---

[64] Morley, *Irish Opinion and the American Revolution* is a valuable addition to what have long been the standard accounts of Ireland in the American War: Maurice O'Connell, *Irish Politics and Social Conflict in the Age of the American Revolution* (Philadelphia, 1965) and R. B. McDowell, *Ireland in the Age of Imperialism and Revolution 1760–1801* (Oxford, 1979), chs. 4–6. See also Gerard O'Brien, *Anglo-Irish Politics in the Age of Grattan and Pitt* (Dublin, 1987), chs. 1, 2; Jacqueline Hill, *From Patriots to Unionists: Dublin Civic Politics and Irish Protestant Patriotism, 1660–1840* (Oxford, 1997), ch. 5; Martyn J. Powell, *Britain and Ireland in the Eighteenth-Century Crisis of Empire* (2003), chs. 5, 6.

unprecedented degree. The lord lieutenant wrote that 'the attention of the whole nation is fixed upon parliamentary proceedings, and not only the electors but even the mob are instructed that their opinions are to determine the suffrage of the members'.[65] Armed Volunteers under gentry officers with the rank and file drawn predominantly from Protestant farmers and small traders, together with some Catholics, gave this popular participation a menacing aspect. The Volunteers were originally a substitute for a militia which the government could not afford to pay. They were intended to defend Ireland against French or Spanish invasion or Catholic insurgency, but the government became increasingly apprehensive about the uses to which they might be put. This first wave of agitation was bought off when British government conceded most of the 'free trade' demands in December 1779.

For a year or so government was able to reassert its authority, but Patriot agitation began to shift to constitutional issues. Their programme was to free the Irish parliament of all constraints on its independence, chiefly by obtaining the repeal of the 1720 act declaratory of the sovereignty of the British parliament and the amending of the much older Poynings' Law, which in theory gave the British privy council control over Irish legislation. North's government was determined to resist constitutional change, but its authority was destroyed by Yorktown. The Ulster Volunteers endorsed legislative independence at a great rally at Dungannon in February 1782, part of a tidal wave of public enthusiasm, said by the new lord lieutenant to involve

the whole of this country. It is the church, the law, the army, I fear, when I consider how it is composed, the merchant, the tradesman, the manufacturer, the farmer, the labourer, the Catholic, the Dissenter, the Protestant; all sects, all sorts and descriptions of men.[66]

Faced with this solid mass, the new Rockingham government, although its members had no appetite for unconditional surrender, saw no alternative to it. Henry Grattan, the Patriot leader, stated the terms for legislative independence in the Irish parliament on 16 April 1782. The British parliament endorsed them on 17 May. Attempts to define the terms on which Britain and Ireland would continue to cooperate within a single empire were rebuffed by the Irish and such questions were left undecided.

---

[65] Buckinghamshire to Germain, 6 Feb. 1780, cited O'Connell, *Irish Politics*, p. 202.
[66] Portland to Shelburne, 24 April 1782, cited Morley, *Irish Opinion*, p. 294.

V

The first two chapters of this book dealt with worldwide 'expansion', that is with trade, migration and the diffusion of culture and values, and with 'empire', that is with British rule overseas. In the middle of the eighteenth century expansion and empire more or less coincided. Much British long-distance trade certainly went to destinations outside any definition of empire, such as to Spanish America, Brazil, the West African coast and Canton in China, but the bulk of it was transacted within an imperial trading system. The vast majority of British emigrants travelling beyond Europe went to British colonies and the largely British population of these colonies was becoming ever more closely tied to Britain by common tastes and patterns of consumption and by adherence to the same norms of Protestantism and constitutional liberty.

After 1783 expansion and empire were moving on separate trajectories. With the recovery and expansion of British trade with the independent United States, the weakening of the Spanish and Portuguese imperial systems and the great boom in the China tea trade after 1784, the proportion of Britain's overseas commerce transacted within the empire declined markedly. In time, British migration to the foreign United States resumed. Finally, the American Revolution shattered ideals for an empire of equal British communities adhering to an idealized English set of values, extending across the Atlantic: James Otis's empire of equals that was to propagate liberty throughout the world,[67] which Thomas Jefferson later sought to create in America without Britain.[68] Americans were always more strongly committed to such ideals than were those in the mainstream of British politics, but they had provided powerfully emotive slogans for a transatlantic 'British' alliance against the enemies of religious and political liberty in the Seven Years War. Such slogans might serve their purpose in time of war, but they concealed what were already deep differences between British and American interpretations of the British constitution and of the rights and obligations of members of the British empire. Moreover, they were proving increasingly difficult to reconcile with the reluctance of an exclusive English nationalism to embrace transatlantic extensions. Chapter 5 explores these differences, which became more and more manifest as British governments tried to overhaul the machinery of empire after 1763, while Americans elaborated their beliefs in an empire of equals. In place of the alliance of free, Protestant

[67] See above, p. 205.
[68] Peter Onuf, *Jefferson's Empire: The Language of American Nationhood* (Charlottesville, Va., 2000).

British peoples that had fought the Seven Years War, the alliance that the British government was to assemble to curb American resistance in 1775 included Irish Catholics, French Canadians, Native Americans, and to a limited degree Africans,[69] against self-consciously British enemies, who in their turn were to ally with the enemies of religious and political freedom, Bourbon France and Spain, against their fellow Britons. The 'empire of goods', of common tastes and common patterns of consumption could be revived after 1783; the empire of common Britishness had always been a fragile venture and it broke apart on the rock of different interpretations of Britishness.

A considerable part of the empire that survived the loss of the thirteen colonies continued to be British and there were some attempts to reshape that Britishness overseas according to metropolitan norms. There had been pro-American and allegedly 'republican' sympathisers among the whites of the British West Indies, but the dominant groups had adhered to Britain throughout the war, not merely out of crude necessity because of their dependence on British markets and British armed forces, but because of the continuing identification with Britain of a 'predominantly British-educated elite', committed to returning home.[70] In what remained of British North America, Nova Scotia, out of which New Brunswick was carved as a separate colony, and Quebec, there were deliberate attempts to create what were regarded as specifically British conditions. The loyalists, who presumably had chosen to adhere to the empire, provided somewhat more promising material than the often actively disloyal Anglophone merchants and New England immigrants or the cautious *attentisme* of most of the French. Loyalists were deemed to be entitled to the free government that they had enjoyed in the thirteen colonies, but efforts were made to give them a more metropolitan British version of it. The Anglican church was to be actively supported. A bishop was instituted in Nova Scotia in 1787. The commitment to French civil law in Quebec could not be revoked, but the colony was divided into two in 1791 to provide an Anglophone dominated Upper Canada, whose first governor insisted that 'the utmost attention should be paid that British customs, manners and principles in the most trivial as well as serious matters should be promoted and inculcated . . . to assimilate the

---

[69] See above, pp. 338–43.

[70] Andrew Jackson O'Shaughnessy, *An Empire Divided: The American Revolution and the British Caribbean* (Philadelphia, 2000), p. 27. The same point has been made about the Scots in the West Indies, see Douglas Hamilton, 'Patronage and Profit: Scottish Networks in the British West Indies *c*.1763–1807', Aberdeen University Ph.D. thesis, 1999. For a different interpretation of white West Indian attitudes, see Selwyn H. Carrington, *The British West Indies during the American Revolution* (Dordrecht, 1988).

colony with the parent state'.[71] In all the Canadian colonies, efforts were made to contain the 'democracy' of the assemblies, elected as in the thirteen colonies on a wide suffrage, by strengthening the powers of the governors and of the councils, which were intended to be drawn from local aristocracies.

In moving the resolutions for Irish legislative independence, Henry Grattan had spoken of 'the two nations, Great Britain and Ireland'.[72] The Irish Patriots had reclaimed the historic rights of the 'Irish nation' of which they saw themselves as the leaders. Even so, in spite of the constitutional revolution and the ensuing uncertainties, British administrations were generally able to maintain a satisfactory working relationship with the Irish politicians. The lord lieutenant continued to manage the Irish parliament. The important leaders with whom he had to deal were not the Patriot orators of 1782 with their high Whig principles, but what have been called 'a group of Irish "men of business" ',[73] who saw Ireland's future in close relations with Britain and who had a common interest with British governments in maintaining the stability of Ireland, especially in preventing the revolution of 1782 from going any further into such projects as parliamentary reform or undue concessions to Catholics. Although the Catholic elite had been lavish in professions of loyalty during the war, the attitudes of politicized members of the Catholic middle class were less clear and there were indications that many ordinary Catholic people had remained unreconciled Jacobites, hoping for a French or Spanish invasion and even celebrating American success.[74] The Patriots had won a great deal of Catholic support in 1781–2, but many Protestants were deeply apprehensive about the price of such support. For them it was better ultimately to rely on the protection of the British government and its army than to trust themselves to such allies. Irish Protestants were on the way to 'abandoning their experiment with nationalism'[75] and again asserting their Britishness.

The population of large parts of the empire that emerged from the American War were not, however, British at all and in territories where people of British origin exercised political power there were non-British elements which had attracted metropolitan attention after 1763. As Chapter 6 showed, the British government tried to regulate relations with Native

---

[71] J. Simcoe, cited Peter Marshall, 'British North America, 1760–1815' in P. J. Marshall, ed., *The Oxford History of the British Empire, II, The Eighteenth Century* (Oxford, 1998), p. 385.

[72] Cited in W. E. H. Lecky, *A History of Ireland in the Eighteenth Century*, new edn. 5 vols. (1913), II. 301.

[73] David Dickson, *New Foundations: Ireland 1660–1800*, 2nd edn. (Dublin, 2002), p. 175. Continuing executive control over the Irish parliament after 1782 is stressed in James Kelly, *Prelude to Union: Anglo-Irish Politics in the 1780s* (Cork, 1992).

[74] This is a major theme of Morley, *Irish Opinion.*

[75] Thomas Bartlett, ' "This famous island set in a Virginian sea": Ireland in the British Empire' in Marshall, ed., *Oxford History,* II, p. 273.

Americans beyond the frontier of settlement and there was much popular enthusiasm for efforts to propagate Christianity among them. British troops were used to impose a settlement on the Caribs of St Vincent. The condition of African slaves throughout the Caribbean and North America had also attracted concern and debate, both in Britain and in the thirteen colonies. The territorial settlement with the United States in 1783 greatly reduced the number of Native Americans within the British orbit, even though the British kept control for a long time to come of the western forts that they were committed to abandoning. The West Indies remained within the empire, however, even if South Carolina and Virginia with their large black populations had gone. The condition of slaves and trading in them became a huge British public concern with the ending of the war.

Well before the American War few people with any claims to sensibility could be found publicly to defend the practice of slavery. Some plans for reforming slavery in the colonies had been formulated, but actual change had only come in Britain itself through the 1772 judgement on the Somersett case, which, for all its limitations, had made it difficult to hold slaves in Britain. During the war, denunciations of the hypocrisy of slave holding by those who claimed to be resisting British oppression had been part of anti-American propaganda.

After the war, a small group of activists began to focus attention on slavery in Britain's West Indian colonies. There was a movement within the Church of England, led by Beilby Porteus, bishop of Chester, for an improvement in the treatment of slaves as the indispensable pre-condition for effective missionary activity among them. Imposing reform of colonial slave codes sanctioned by local legislatures would, however, be going back onto the dangerous ground of pitting the sovereign power of the imperial parliament against truculent West Indian assemblies defending their internal autonomy. The supply of slaves was, on the other hand, unequivocally within the scope of parliamentary regulation. The idiosyncratic Anglican, Granville Sharp, had already denounced the slave trade as a national crime which implicated Britain as well as her colonies in the same wickedness.[76] The first petition to parliament against the slave trade was drawn up by a group of Quakers in 1783; among their sponsors was no less a person than lord North, who told them that 'the petition's object and tendency, ought to recommend it to every humane breast'.[77] This was a portent that the activists would find support for their attack on the trade from a very wide spectrum of the political elite.

---

[76] *The Law of Retribution or a Serious Warning to Great Britain and her Colonies* (1776).

[77] I owe this quotation as well as much of the argument of this paragraph to Dr Christopher Brown.

The secession of the thirteen colonies, coinciding with the consolidation of empire in India, dramatically shifted the balance between British and non-British peoples within the empire. Although it has been argued in this book that the techniques of imperial management for territories inhabited by predominantly British or by non-British populations, involving negotiation and implied compacts with elites, may not actually have been very different, the rhetoric of empire differed sharply. Older ideals about a free, maritime Protestant empire over equal peoples of British origin were giving way to a new rhetoric based on a hierarchical view of the peoples of the world and what was appropriate for them. For some historians this already involved concepts of race.[78] Government in the new order was likely to be authoritarian. Religious diversity and a plurality of legal systems within the empire were being recognized. Britain was assuming an obligation to 'improve' and to assimilate, above all to christianize, although there were vigorous debates about how far such things might be just or practical in any particular case. Certain peoples needed protection: 'innocent' Hindus, Africans carried away into slavery, or Caribs being victimized by planters. Such debates and campaigns were to be the accompaniment of British imperial rule until far into the twentieth century.

After the war the process of consolidating an Indian empire continued. In India itself, there was a temporary halt to territorial expansion, but the Bengal model of direct Company rule was spreading to the Madras presidency. Muhammad Ali, nawab of Arcot, had lost much of his autonomy during the war as the British took over his revenues. They were returned to him after the war, but his days as an effective ruler were numbered. British officials would soon take control in the Carnatic and the poligars and chieftains who had defied the nawab for so long would lose their forts and their armed followers. Company rule in both Bengal and Madras was being more closely integrated with the rest of the empire. The debacle of the Fox–North government in 1783 when it had tried to eliminate the Company's political role through Fox's India Bill, ensured that rule would still be in the name of the Company. Company rule was, however, put under a much tighter degree of government supervision by the Pitt India Act of 1784. Governors general became effectively agents of the British state, if still formally acting for the Company. In the years before the American War the British state had assumed increasing responsibility for defending India against European powers. After the war, the naval squadron and the royal troops were not withdrawn as had been done after 1763. The external defence of India was

---

[78] Kathleen Wilson, *The Island Race: Englishness, Empire and Gender in the Eighteenth Century* (2003), pp. 11–12; Catherine Hall, *Civilising Subjects: Metropole and Colony in the English Imagination, 1830–1867* (Oxford, 2002), pp. 16–17.

now directed from London, with the East India Company being required after an act of 1788 to pay for whatever forces the government chose to allocate to it. Its own army was increasingly treated as a force available for wider imperial purposes.

India had thus become an integral part of the British empire. The theme of this book is that this process of integration did not mark the launching of a second empire in compensation for the one that had been lost in North America, but that it had moved in tandem with attempts to integrate the thirteen colonies more firmly into the empire too. Impelled by their urgent sense of national danger from European enemies and justified in their own eyes by overweening confidence in the capacity and wisdom of a sovereign parliament, successive British governments had applied much the same pressures to the thirteen colonies and to the East India Company. The outcome had, however, been very different. Closer integration into the empire proved to be feasible for the Company and its Indian possessions; it was rejected in the thirteen colonies. Imperial purposes appeared to be compatible with the interests of significant Indian elites, especially in Bengal, while American elites found them incompatible with their interests as well as ideologically repugnant.

Both the policies that led to the alienation of the thirteen colonies together with the attempt to subdue them by force and the incorporation of Indian provinces into the empire seem to have gained at least the acquiescence of wide sections of British opinion. There were widespread and strongly supported protests against the impending war with America in 1775, but the government was able to weather the storm, buoyed up by powerful expressions of support. In time, the war came to be seen as a patriotic one against Britain's traditional enemies, now joined by the Americans. Popular participation in debates about India was much more limited. There was no equivalent of the mass petitions against war in America in 1775. Among upper-class opinion there were some, if probably a small minority, who desired to have no part in an empire in India and wished that it did not exist. Far more were deeply unhappy about the way in which empire was being conducted and hoped for reform. Edmund Burke was able to give expression to these discontents and to make them of some political consequence in his attacks on Warren Hastings. Burke, who has appeared so often in this book, had a most acute understanding of the transformation of empire that was taking place in his lifetime. For all his foreboding about that transformation, he believed Britain neither could nor should renounce sovereignty over Ireland, America or India, but he did his utmost to moderate the exercise of that sovereignty in ways that he believed would be in the best interest of both Britain and those whom Britain ruled. On India, few shared either his depth of knowledge or his commitment to expose abuses, but most agreed with him in accepting that empire could not be renounced but must be reformed.

With hindsight of gigantic proportions, it is possible to see two destinies beckoning Britain between 1750 and 1783. Were the British to be part of a predominantly Atlantic empire consisting of equal communities of free peoples of largely British origins, in which at best they would be *primus inter pares*, or were they to rule over a polyglot worldwide empire, most of whose members were clearly subject peoples? It seems safe to say that contemporaries could not conceive that they faced a choice in anything like these terms and that if the question had been put to them, they would almost certainly have replied that they did not have to choose: their empire was both one of freedom for people of British origin and of rule over others in ways that were appropriate to them. That is an answer that British people would continue to give for another hundred and fifty years at least, until freedom for all the peoples of the empire came to be adopted as the rationale for British imperialism in the mid-twentieth century. Nevertheless, choices had been made in the later eighteenth century, albeit entirely unconsciously and unwittingly. The American and Patriot Irish version of an Atlantic empire of equals had been ruled out. Britain must have a supremacy, even if it was to be used with the lightest rein. A war in America was ultimately to be fought for that. At the same time, the British had shown few inhibitions about ruling over peoples who were not British.

Concepts of a first and second empire therefore seem to have very little relevance for this period. To expect historians to stop using them, desirable as that might be, is doubtless to expect too much. If they recognize, however, that the making of empire in India and the unmaking of empire in America belong to the same phase of Britain's imperial history, what historians choose to call it is not then a matter of much consequence.

Bibliography

Principal Manuscript Sources Cited

COLLECTIONS IN THE UNITED KINGDOM

Bodleian Library, Oxford University
MS Eng. hist. c. 472 (Laurence Sulivan papers)
MS Eng. misc. f. 533 (Macartney papers)

British Library
Add MS 15484 ('Ports, Districts and Towns of America')
Add MS 15956 (Anson papers)
Add MS 16259 (Impey papers)
Add MS 24266 (Minutes of Managers of Hastings's Trial)
Add MS 29135 (Warren Hastings papers)
Add MSS 32848, 32850, 32851, 32858, 32948, 32950, 32952 (Newcastle papers)
Add MSS 35414, 35422, 35448, 35450, 35637, 35891, 35909 (Hardwicke papers)
Add MS 45440 (Anderson Letter Book)
Add MSS 57817A, 57826 (George Grenville papers)
Egerton MSS 244, 246, 247, 249 (Cavendish reports of Debates)
Egerton MSS 3432, 3488, 3490 (Holdernesse papers)

British Library, India Office and Oriental Collections: Records
A/2/10 (Charters)
B/257 (General Court Minutes)
E/1/41, 43 (Home Correspondence)
E/4/300–03 (Madras Despatches)
E/4/465–66, 468 (Bombay Despatches)
H/84, 93–9, 101–2, 112, 138, 141, 212, 768 (Home Miscellaneous Series)
L/AG/1/1/19–20 (Ledgers)
L/F/10/1–2 (Bengal Establishments)
L/F/10/111–12 (Madras Establishments)
P/1/38, P/2/31 (Bengal Public Proceedings)
P/98/10 (Bengal Committee of New Lands)
P/A/9 (Bengal Select Committee Proceedings)
P/C/48, 51 (Madras Select Committee Proceedings)

European Manuscripts
MS Eur. D. 546 (Walsh papers)
MS Eur. D. 1018 (Evidence to 1767 Commons Committee)
MS Eur. E. 276 (Russell Papers)
MS Eur. F. 149/49, 89 (Malet papers)
MS Eur. G. 4 (Francis papers)
MS Eur. G. 37/35 (Clive papers)
MS OV 28, 36, 64, 293 (Orme papers)

Lambeth Palace Library
MS 1123 (Papers Relating to the American Colonies)

The National Archives, Public Record Office
Adm 1/162 (East Indies)
Adm 1/3912 (East India Company)
CO 5 (North America)
CO 77/18–20, 22 (East Indies)
CO 101/1, 12, 16–17 (Grenada)
CO 137/10, 19, 32, 34, 61, 62, 138/19 (Jamaica)
CO 323/16–19, 24 (Board of Trade)
PRO 30/8/19, 95, 99 (Chatham papers)
SP 54/45–6 (Scotland)
SP 63/416–17, 421, 432, 435, 438 (Ireland)
WO 1/57 (St Vincent)
WO 1/319 (East Indies)
WO 34/77 (Amherst papers)

National Library of Wales
Clive MS 218

COLLECTIONS IN THE UNITED STATES OF AMERICA

Historical Society of Pennsylvania, Philadelphia
Etting Collection, XXIX (Pemberton papers)
Pemberton Papers, XXVI
Richard Peters Papers, IV
Thomas Penn–James Hamilton Correspondence
Thomas Penn Letter Books, III–VI, VIII
Thomas Penn's Official Correspondence, IX
William Smith Papers, II

Houghton Library, Harvard University
bMS Am 811 (Lee papers)
bMS Am 1704 (Palfrey papers)
bMS Sparks 49 (William Johnson papers)
Sparks MSS 4/1, 4/3–4, 4/6, 5/1, 10/2, 38 (Sparks transcripts)

Huntington Library, San Marino
AB 8, 846 (Abercromby papers)
HM 1000 (Pocock papers)
LO (Loudoun papers)
ST 7 (George Grenville Letter Book)
STG boxes 22, 25 (Grenville papers)

Library of Congress, Washington
Force Transcripts, 7E (Garth papers)

Massachusetts Historical Society, Boston
Henry Knox MSS, 50 (Waldo papers)
Hutchinson Transcripts, XXIV–XXVI (Thomas Hutchinson correspondence)
Massachusetts Papers, 1749–1768
Mauduit-Oliver MSS
Miscellaneous Bound Manuscripts
Thomas Penn Letters

Virginia Historical Society, Richmond
MS J 4105a (Edward Jenings Letter Book)
MS 1 L 51 (William Lee Letter Book)

University of Virginia, Charlottesville
Lee Family Papers, microfilm 1714
McGregor MS 2693 (Dinwiddie papers)

William L. Clements Library, University of Michigan, Ann Arbor
Amherst MSS
Charles Garth Letter Books
Germain Sackville MSS
William Henry Lyttelton MSS
Shelburne MSS
Charles Townshend MSS

UNPUBLISHED DISSERTATIONS

G. J. Bryant, 'The East India Company and its Army, 1600–1778', London University Ph.D. thesis, 1975.

R. T. Cornish, 'A Vision of Empire: The Development of British Opinion Regarding the American Colonial Empire, 1730–1770', London University Ph.D. thesis, 1987.

D. Graham, 'British Intervention in Defence of the American Colonies, 1748–56', London University Ph.D. thesis, 1969.

J. D. Gurney, 'The Debts of the Nawab of Arcot, 1763–1776', Oxford University D.Phil. thesis, 1968.

Douglas Hamilton, 'Patronage and Profit: Scottish Networks in the British West Indies c.1763–1807, Aberdeen University Ph.D. thesis, 1999.

B. E. Kennedy, 'Anglo–French Rivalry in India and the Eastern Seas, 1763–1793: A Study of Anglo–French Tensions and their Impact on the Consolidation of British Power in the Region', Australian National University Ph.D. thesis, 1969.

G. K. McGilvary, 'East India Patronage and the Political Management of Scotland, 1720–1774', Open University, Ph.D. thesis, 1989.

J. R. Osborn, 'India, Parliament and the Press under George III: A Study of English Attitudes Towards the East India Company and Empire in the Late Eighteenth and Early Nineteenth Centuries', Oxford University D.Phil. thesis, 1999.

J. P. Thomas, 'The British Empire in the Press, 1763–1774', Oxford University D.Phil thesis, 1982.

R. T. Travers, 'Contested Notions of Sovereignty in Bengal under the British, 1765–1785', Cambridge University Ph.D. thesis, 2001.

Frank Van Aalst, 'The British View of India 1750–1785', University of Pennsylvania Ph.D. thesis, 1970.

Index